W9-ARM-917

Robert W. White is Professor of Clinical Psychology at Harvard University. After undergraduate and graduate training at Harvard, he taught at the University of Maine and at Rutgers University. Dr. White, distinguished for his many contributions to his field, was formerly Director of the Harvard Psychological Clinic.

ROBERT W. WHITE is Professor of Clinical Psychology at Harvard University. After undergraduate and graduate training at Harvard, he taught at the University of Maine and at Rutgers University. Dr. White, distinguished for his many contributions to his field, was formerly Director of the Harvard Psychological Clinic.

THE ABNORMAL PERSONALITY

ROBERT W. WHITE
HARVARD UNIVERSITY

THIRD EDITION

THE RONALD PRESS COMPANY • NEW YORK

6B

Library of Congress Catalog Card Number: 64–11823

PRINTED IN THE UNITED STATES OF AMERICA

Preface

During the years that have gone by since this book was first published there has been great activity in the field of abnormal psychology. Growing recognition of the importance of psychological disorders has brought many new workers to the field and has increased the resources needed for effective research. Much more has been discovered about abnormal psychology than was known when I first sat down to survey its subject-matter. My purpose in this book, however, has not changed: it is still to write about abnormal people in a way that will be valuable and interesting to students new to the subject. A first course in abnormal psychology is not intended to train specialists. Its goal is more general: it should provide the student with the opportunity to whet his interest, expand his horizons, register a certain body of new facts, and relate what he learns to the rest of his knowledge about mankind. The value of a course in abnormal psychology is not, in my opinion, limited to those who plan to become professional workers with abnormal people. I am trying here to present the subject in such a way as to emphasize its usefulness to all students of human nature.

In this third edition I have not thought it necessary to change the general shape and outline of the book, but within this framework there are many changes of detail, and some chapters have required extensive rewriting. I have retained the experiment of two introductions, one historical and the other clinical. This reflects my desire to set the subject-matter in a broad perspective and at the same time to anchor it in concrete fact. Throughout this book the case histories are printed in the same type as the rest of the material. They form an intrinsic part of the exposition and are used recurrently to illustrate various points. The last part of the historical chapter has been altered to do justice to the present wave of interest in somatic aspects of disordered behavior.

Following the two introductions comes a block of five chapters designed to set forth the topics of maladaptation and neurosis. The two chapters on the development and integration of personality are intended to give an account of normal growth while showing at each point how development can go astray. The first of the pair has again been extensively rewritten. I have stated the adaptive process in what I hope to be clearer terms, added new research on dependence and deprivation, changed the account of autonomy to include the idea of efficacy, introduced the concept of ego-identity, and recast my description of parent-child relations to emphasize their interactive character. In the chapter on integration the main change is a separation of social growth into the two strands of group memberships and the more intimate relations of pairs. The ensuing description of neuroses is systematized around the concepts of anxiety and defense. These are first taken up in their simplest forms, then in their more far-reaching effects on personality as a whole, finally in their relation to neurotic symptom formation. Little change has been made in these chapters.

Two sizable chapters are again allotted to psychotherapy. Particularly in the second I have tried to represent the recent activity of research and the restlessness of theory with respect to this vital topic. To suggest the breadth of current interests I have written a new section on psychotherapy as art and as science, describing on the one hand some ideas developed by sensitive seekers after the elusive psychological overtones and undertones of the therapeutic relationship, on the other hand some thoughts inspired by the theory that neuroses and their treatment can be encompassed by simple Pavlovian concepts. It is certainly valuable to analyze treatment in terms of extinction and deconditioning, although as the chapter unfolds it will be seen that I do not discern any ultimate incompatibility between learning and psychodynamic theories. I have also given more explicit consideration to research on the outcome of psychotherapy.

In the account of conduct disorders the main alterations will be found in connection with delinquency, where there are illuminating new studies concerning psychodynamics, parental influences, and treatment. The chapter on psychosomatic disorders holds its place as a bridge to those disorders in which somatic dysfunction, especially in the central nervous system, can be considered the primary factor. The two chapters devoted to these disorders have received some correction of detail, such as adding the newly discovered genetic factor in mongolism; the main change, however, is an extensive rearrangement of the material on injuries and abnormal conditions in the brain, designed to clarify the manifestations of these conditions in behavior.

The description of manic and depressive disorders provides the first opportunity to correct my now outdated emphasis on shock methods of treatment and to take fuller account of the use of drugs. This theme recurs in the chapter on schizophrenia; but here, in what is now by all odds the most prolific field of research in abnormal psychology, extensive rewriting and expansion have been required. I have tried to take account of the now popular distinction between "process" and "reactive" forms of schizophrenia; to include new work on schizophrenic thought processes, childhood forms of the disorder, and the background of parent-child interactions; to indicate new leads in biochemical research; and to sketch the movement toward using the mental hospital as a therapeutic milieu rather than a place of confinement. In my account of the two major psychoses I have made a strenuous attempt not only to set forth fairly both the psychogenic and the somatogenic aspects but also to bring the two hypotheses into an intelligible relation.

In the final chapter the problem of disordered personalities is allowed to expand to its full social dimensions. Treatment, care, and prevention call for social effort and social organization. That I have had to rewrite this chapter extensively is testimony to the changing attitude of society toward mental health and illness. It is a satisfaction to replace pleadings for action with an account of actions already undertaken, and to point out the increasing opportunities that are open for effort both professional and non-professional. Mental health work is still a frontier, but it is no longer one to which the public closes its eyes and ears.

It is a pleasure to acknowledge again the help originally given me by Dr. Silvan S. Tomkins, Dr. Kenneth Diven, Dr. Eugenia Hanfmann, and Dr. Erich Lindemann, and to mention in addition my more recent indebtedness to Dr. John P. Spiegel, Dr. Stanley H. King, Dr. Annette R. Silbert, and Dr. Paul A. M. Gross. My wife, Margaret L. White, to whom this book is dedicated, has performed the important function of telling me whenever she thought that either common sense or intuitive wisdom was being neglected.

ROBERT W. WHITE

Concord, Massachusetts
January, 1964

Contents

THE ABNORMAL PERSONALITY

1

Historical Introduction: Origins of Abnormal Psychology

Sixty years ago abnormal psychology was considered to be a remote province of knowledge, explored only by a few specialists, and it played a distinctly minor part in man's thinking about his own nature. Today it contributes richly to the training of those professional workers, especially psychiatrists, psychologists, social workers, teachers, and ministers, whose duties bring them in frequent contact with troubled people. More than this, it occupies a respected place among general college courses, for it is capable of making a highly significant contribution to all thinking about man's problems and man's quest for a better way of life. Abnormal personalities are not mysteriously set apart from the normal. Their various peculiarities represent exaggerations of what is to be found in every human being. They are therefore well suited to enlarge our understanding of the whole process of personal adjustment. If we know what can go wrong in human development, we are the wiser in making it go right.

When we set outselves to examine the field of abnormal psychology we can proceed in two ways. We can look into the history of the subject and discover how it came to be what it is today. This method offers distinct advantages over an immediate plunge into facts and current problems. Science generally advances in a disorderly fashion. At any given moment the greatest activity occurs at three or four isolated points, the location of which is determined by temporary urgency, by newly discovered techniques, or even by fashion. It is easy to get lost in the details and preoccupations of current research, and the best protection against doing so is to anchor our study firmly in the framework of history. By turning up the facts in the same order in which they confronted past investigators one can better appreciate the really basic difficulties which tend to impede understanding, and one can more readily keep the whole subject in place in the larger context of human affairs. On the other hand we could begin our study in a quite different way: by making a clinical survey of the facts that constitute the subject-matter of abnormal psychology. We could examine a series of cases illustrating the kinds of things we shall be studying in more systematic form throughout the book. The clinical method has the advantage of realistic vividness and of proceeding in the right direction from fact to theory. The advantages of each method are in fact so great that in this book we shall use them both. This chapter contains an *historical introduction* to abnormal psychology; the next one will provide a *clinical introduction.*

THE SUBJECT-MATTER OF ABNORMAL PSYCHOLOGY

At the present time the province of abnormal psychology can be roughly described as the study of *disordered personal reactions* to life and its circumstances. When we say *disordered* we have in mind people whose lives in some way go astray, so that they find themselves frustrated, unhappy, anxious, baffled in their deepest desires, misfits in their society; or, in the most serious instances, people who get so badly out of touch with surrounding life that we call them insane. When we say that the disorder lies in *personal reactions* we intend to limit the field more closely by excluding what may be called the external reasons for frustration and sorrow. Accidents, bereavements, ill health, war and other disasters, unemployment and poverty, lack of opportunities, unfair social barriers, and a hundred other external circumstances may stand in the way of happy and effective living. These obstacles are tremendously important, but it is not the task of psychology to study them in their own right. They are already claimed for other fields of knowledge such as medicine, public health, and especially the various social sciences. To all such circumstances, however, the individual makes a personal reaction. Even to a disease affecting his own body each person reacts in a way that is peculiar to himself. It is at this point, where the personal reaction begins, that we cross into the province of psychology, and we reach the sub-province of abnormal psychology when we concentrate on disorders in the personal reaction.

To illustrate what has just been said let us take the example of unemployment. A man may become unemployed through no fault of his own, purely as a result of economic forces over which he has no control. This external circumstance evokes in him some kind of personal reaction. The professional task of the social scientist is to understand the economic forces which brought about the unemployment; that of the psychologist begins with the personal reaction. Unemployed people react to their misfortune in a variety of ways. Many of these ways it would not occur to us to call disordered or abnormal. Unhappiness and discouragement, indignation and bitterness, seem well justified by the circumstances. Attempts to understand the situation and to change it by organized action seem well adapted to the problem as it stands. Certain people, however, behave in more extreme and peculiar ways. One man may take the blame entirely upon himself, declaring that his misfortune is a well-deserved punishment for his own sin and worthlessness. Another may believe that his former employers formed a conspiracy to throw him out of work and are even now trying to poison his food and take his life. A third may become extremely shy, hiding from his neighbors even when they too are unemployed, convinced that everyone holds him in contempt because he is no longer able to support his family. Still another may decide to shoot the President: this indeed is no fanciful example, for in 1932 a hungry unemployed man fired at the President-elect at a public gathering and killed another public official who was standing near by. These people, we say, are acting in a very peculiar fashion. Their personal reactions are so little warranted by external circumstance, or so poorly designed to achieve desired results, that we cannot avoid considering them disordered. Factors within themselves are contributing disproportionately to their behavior. Abnormal psychology is the study of these disordered and disproportionate personal reactions.

EVOLUTION OF ATTITUDES TOWARD DISORDERED PEOPLE

Only in quite recent years have the milder varieties of maladjustment come under scientific scrutiny. If people were unhappy and irritable, if they were unduly boastful and self-centered, if they did not get along well with their family and friends, if they frittered away their time or took to drink and dissipation, their behavior was censured as a sign of moral inferiority. Their deviations from acceptable behavior were felt to lie within the realm of volition. It was up to them to heed wiser counsels, choose nobler ideals, and mend their ways. This attitude toward the milder forms of disorder has changed so recently, and indeed still prevails so widely, that we have little to learn from searching its earlier history.

Quite the opposite is the case with the severer forms of mental affliction. Here we can observe a distinct evolution of attitudes in Western society from medieval to modern times. Insanity is described in some of the earliest scientific writings. The insane, with their obvious unfitness to take care of themselves and their inconvenience and occasional danger to others, have always managed to establish some kind of claim on public attention. The early history of abnormal psychology is thus the history of attempts to understand insanity.

For the most part this history is a discouraging tale of isolated observations which never grew into a body of tested knowledge. The Greek physician Hippocrates, somewhere around 460 B.C., did his best to bring insanity into the fold of medicine by pronouncing it a disease of the brain and treating it like other diseases. In the writings of the great medical men from Galen in the second century to Weyer in the sixteenth, and of the great observers of human nature such as Vives and Montaigne, one finds many shrewd observations on the nature of insanity, much sympathy for the lot of its victims, and a disposition to seek humane methods to restore tranquillity of mind. Indeed the history of mental disorders reveals many surprising anticipations of what we now like to regard as modern attitudes and modern discoveries. But these prophetic voices of the past cried in the wilderness of an unenlightened, unconcerned public opinion. They were all but powerless to effect the social change upon which any systematic study of the insane was dependent.

One fact overshadows all others: there were no real hospitals for the mentally ill until the very end of the eighteenth century. There were no organized institutions to embody the humane feelings of those few enlightened minds that recognized the nature of mental disorders. This meant that there was no proper opportunity to build up an adequate knowledge of the subject, no chance to accumulate hospital records and compare large numbers of cases. Science could advance but little until suitable institutions were created, and institutions could not be created until public opinion was ready to support them. It was no accident that mental hospitals came simultaneously with the American and French Revolutions. They sprang from the same growing sense of human dignity and social responsibility.

The Insane as Social Outcasts. Before the establishment of hospitals the mentally disordered were treated as outcasts and hardly distinguished from criminals. The community felt responsible for them only to the extent of preventing them from troubling their fellow men. Some of the less troublesome wandered about the countryside, begging and stealing their food and finding shelter in barns and pigsties. Others were thrown into prison where, side by side with criminals, they lived amid revolting filth, often chained, always at the mercy of their keepers. In 1785 a French physician described the situation as follows:

> Thousands of deranged are locked up in prisons without anyone's thinking of administering the slightest remedy; the half-deranged are mixed with the

completely insane, the furious with the quiet; some are in chains, others are free in the prison; finally, unless nature comes to their rescue and cures them, the term of their misery is that of their mortal days, and unfortunately in the meantime the illness but increases instead of diminishing.[1]

Even those rare physicians who interested themselves in lunatics recommended severe and violent treatment. According to one medical authority of the seventeenth century:

> Discipline, threats, fetters, and blows are needed as much as medical treatment. Truly nothing is more necessary and more effective for the recovery of these people than forcing them to respect and fear intimidation. By this method, the mind, held back by restraint, is induced to give up its arrogance and wild ideas and it soon becomes meek and orderly. This is why maniacs often recover much sooner if they are treated with torture and torments in a hovel instead of with medicaments.[2]

Toward the end of the eighteenth century and even during the nineteenth there were many physicians who advocated harsh discipline for excited patients. Even the great American pioneer in psychiatry, Benjamin Rush, who in other respects advanced the cause of humane treatment, described in 1812 "terrifying modes of punishment" for refractory patients, recommending "pouring cold water under the sleeve, so that it may descend into the armpits and down the trunk of the body," or, if this failed, deprivation of food and threats of death.[3]

Hard as was the lot of the insane a century and a half ago, it had nevertheless undoubtedly been worse in earlier times. In the Middle Ages, and indeed in all but the most enlightened periods of human history, it was generally believed that the insane were possessed by evil spirits. Some malignant demon was supposed to be inhabiting the body of the victim or to be directing his lunatic behavior from without. During the fifteenth and sixteenth centuries this general belief reached its extreme development in the institution of witchcraft, borrowed undoubtedly from primitive pagan sources but by this time thoroughly absorbed into Christian theology. What gave to the witchcraft trials their peculiar ferocity was the belief that the accused person had surrendered body and soul to the devil and made a solemn pact to do his evil work. For someone to be possessed was thus not merely a personal misfortune; it put the whole community in great moral danger. Witches, great numbers of whom would now be classed as psychologically disordered persons, were hunted, captured, tried in court, sometimes tortured to obtain con-

[1] J. Colombier, quoted by G. Zilboorg and G. W. Henry, *A History of Medical Psychology* (New York: W. W. Norton & Co., Inc., 1941), p. 316.

[2] T. Willis, *ibid.*, p. 261.

[3] B. Rush, *Medical Inquiries and Observations upon the Diseases of the Mind* (Philadelphia: Kimber & Richardson, 1812), p. 180.

fessions, and if found guilty were publicly burned. Such happenings were not at all uncommon.

Judges were called upon to pass sentence on witches in great numbers. A French judge boasted that he had burned 800 women in 16 years on the bench; 600 were burned during the administration of a bishop in Bamberg. The Inquisition, originally started by the Church of Rome, was carried along by Protestant Churches in Great Britain and Germany. In Protestant Geneva 500 persons were burned in the year 1515. Other countries, where there were Catholic jurists, boasted of as many burnings. In Treves, 7,000 were reported burned during a period of several years.[4]

The Insane as Sick People: Pinel's Reforms. It was thus a step forward when the notion of demon possession gave place to the notion that the lunatic was merely a public nuisance to be kept out of the way. As we have seen, however, the benefits were at first not very great; the mentally disordered were still outcasts and were still subject to brutal inconsideration. This was the situation which toward the close of the eighteenth century at last began to stir the public conscience. As is usually the case, reform was in the air and cannot properly be attributed to a single individual. But the figure of Philippe Pinel (1745–1826) stands out above his contemporaries, and his experiences well illustrate the social movement that was under way. Pinel was a physician and scholar who lived most of his life in Paris, who gradually centered his interest on mental disorders, and who found a golden opportunity to carry out his progressive ideas when in the first years of the Revolution he was made physician-in-chief at the Bicêtre, a hospital chiefly populated by the mentally deranged. His progressive ideas sprang from a rare sympathy for the insane and a persistent, discerning attempt to understand them. "The mentally sick," Pinel declared, "far from being guilty people deserving of punishment, are sick people whose miserable state deserves all the consideration that is due to suffering humanity. One should try with the most simple methods to restore their reason."[5]

Pinel's first step was to remove the chains and fetters with which most of the patients were bound. This required permission from the Commune, and the president came in person to talk with the patients and assure himself that no political enemies were concealed among them. Greeted by shouts and the clanking of chains, his attempts at conversation answered only by curses and execrations, the president is reported to have asked Pinel, "Citizen, are you mad yourself, that you would unchain such beasts?" To this Pinel replied, "It is my conviction that these mentally ill are intractable only because they are deprived of fresh air and

[4] W. Bromberg, *The Mind of Man: The Story of Man's Conquest of Mental Illness* (New York: Harper & Row, 1937), p. 61.

[5] Quoted by Zilboorg and Henry, op. cit., pp. 323–24.

of their liberty."[6] Permission was granted, and Pinel proceeded with his experiment. While in some cases no great benefits resulted, there were numerous instances in which patients hitherto considered dangerous and completely unmanageable became calm and reasonable when released from restraint and treated with kindness. Some who had been incarcerated half a lifetime were shortly discharged from the hospital with their health restored. But above all Pinel showed beyond any doubt that a large mental hospital could be safely and beneficially conducted with a minimum of mechanical restraint.

This was Pinel's most dramatic action, but it was only the beginning of the reforms which laid a foundation for the psychiatry of the future. Soon after the experiments at the Bicêtre he was transferred to the larger Salpêtrière hospital where he applied himself to a huge task of reorganization. He began to train attendants so that they should be something better than guards, and he tried to give the patients the benefit of comfort and a healthful routine. Of enduring importance was his introduction of the psychiatric case history and the systematic keeping of records. This arose from his habit of observing patients closely and taking careful notes. Before his time it often happened that no one remembered when or for what cause a patient had entered the hospital. Obviously it was impossible to build up a sound knowledge of mental disorders until Pinel's custom of making records became an established practice. It was only in a well-regulated hospital, moreover, that methods of treatment could be properly explored, different methods compared, and results followed and verified. Pinel himself completed in 1801 a treatise on the nature and treatment of mental disorders, based largely on his own hospital experience. In the introduction he portrays the new role of the physician as he himself enacted it.

> The habit of living constantly in the midst of the insane, of studying their habits, their different personalities, the objects of their pleasures or their dislikes, the advantage of following the course of their alienation day and night during the various seasons of the year, the art of directing them without effort and sparing them excitement and grumbling, the gift of being able to assume at the right time a tone of kindness or of authority, of being able to subdue them by force if methods of kindness fail, the constant picture of all the phenomena of mental alienation, and finally the functions of supervision itself—the combination of all these must give an intelligent and zealous man an immense number of facts and minute details usually lacking in the narrow-minded physician unless he has taken a special interest during fleeting visits to asylums.[7]

This was indeed the dawn of a new day both for the mentally disordered and for man's whole understanding of his own nature.

[6] R. Semelaigne, *Les grands aliénistes français* (Paris: 1930), Vol. I, p. 41.

[7] P. Pinel, *Traité médico-philosophique sur l'aliénation mentale* (Paris: J. A. Brosson, 1801), p. 15.

The ideas behind Pinel's reforms began to spread slowly through the Western world. At last the public mind was beginning to be ready to receive them. In England William Tuke, a wealthy Quaker merchant, founded in 1796 the York Retreat where amidst quiet country surroundings kind and gentle methods of treatment were put into effect. Yet it was another fifty years before the policy of non-restraint became established in England, and even later in other countries. Naturally it was slow work to secure reforms that entailed greater expense, but it is surprising to realize the force of opposition within the medical profession itself. When Gardiner Hill, around 1840, was fighting to promote the policy of non-restraint and demonstrating in his own Lincoln Asylum that the plan really worked, other British medical men pronounced it the "wild scheme of a philanthropic visionary," indeed "a breaking of the sixth commandment," and asserted that "restraint forms the very basis on which the sound treatment of lunatics is founded."[8] Not until 1857 could it be reported that non-restraint was generally accepted in British hospitals.

The Insane as Public Charges: State Hospitals. To provide a sufficient number of hospitals for the mentally disordered was itself a major crusade. Here the contribution of the United States was particularly noteworthy. Several hospitals were opened early in the nineteenth century to embody the new humane principles: the Friends' Asylum at Philadelphia in 1817, McLean Hospital in Massachusetts in 1818, Bloomingdale in New York in 1822, and the Hartford Retreat in 1824. By 1840 there were fourteen mental hospitals in the United States capable of accommodating altogether something like 2,500 patients. But the census of the same year showed over 17,000 insane, of whom scarcely more than 5,000 were supported as public charges.[9] The great mass of the mentally ill were still without benefit of treatment, public support, or proper accommodations. The correction of this state of affairs was one of the many reform movements which spread through the country toward the middle of the last century. It was set in motion largely by Dorothea L. Dix, a Massachusetts schoolteacher who on her own initiative began to investigate the almshouses, jails, and private homes where the pauper insane were kept. In 1843 she presented to the Massachusetts legislature a memorial describing in detail what she had seen: insane persons "confined in cages, closets, cellars, stalls, pens . . . chained, naked, beaten with rods, and lashed into obedience."[10] The success of her petition marked the beginning of a long, remarkably effective career. Miss Dix personally investi-

[8] Bromberg, *op. cit.*, p. 105.

[9] A. Deutsch, *The Mentally Ill in America* (Garden City, N. Y.: Doubleday & Co., Inc., 1937), p. 232.

[10] D. L. Dix, *Memorial in Behalf of the Pauper Insane and Idiots in Jails and Poorhouses Throughout the Commonwealth* (Boston: Monroe & Francis, 1843), p. 4.

gated conditions throughout the United States, presenting reports and arguing with state legislators, until she had become the chief moving force in the founding or enlarging of more than thirty state hospitals. She afterwards extended her activities to Scotland and England, and her tours of inspection in most of the countries of Europe carried her influence still farther afield. Few people today remember how much the modern system of state hospitals owes to this indomitable worker. Her influence was in no small measure responsible for the trend revealed in the following figures. In 1840 the mental hospitals of the United States housed 2,561 patients, this being 14 per cent of the estimated number of insane in the country. Half a century later, in 1890, the mental hospitals housed 74,028 patients, this being 69 per cent of the insane in the country.[11] The neglected lunatic of previous centuries at last stood a good chance of finding proper shelter, food, and medical attention.

The Mental Hygiene Movement. By 1900 the care of mental patients had greatly improved, but there was still much to be accomplished. A vivid picture of conditions in that year can be found in the autobiography of Clifford W. Beers, who later inaugurated the mental hygiene movement. As a young man of twenty-four, recently graduated from college, Beers became depressed, attempted suicide, and for the next two years saw the inside of three different mental hospitals from the point of view of a patient. After returning to health he wrote the story of his illness in *A Mind That Found Itself* (1908), a book destined to achieve a tremendous influence toward the understanding of mental disorders. Beers admitted that he was a difficult patient. During the latter part of his illness he was elated, arrogant, dictatorial, doubtless exceedingly irritating to those in charge, and inclined at times to create rather violent scenes. Considering this, and comparing his treatment with what was meted out in earlier centuries, his care was a model of patience and forbearance, yet he was choked and thrown to the floor, kicked and spat upon, kept lightly clad in a cold cell, bound painfully tight in a strait jacket, and treated with childish displays of temper by the attendants, as when his holiday dinner was snatched away because he dallied over it. It is perhaps not surprising that the attendants displayed shortcomings; the first training school for mental nurses in this country was then not quite twenty years old, and the practice of hiring untrained guards was still widespread. On the doctors' part, what we miss is not so much a lack of humanity as a lack of insight and of that attitude which makes it possible not to be irritated by the patient's refractory behavior. In small and useless ways Beers was thwarted and thereby infuriated. His clothes were withheld, he was denied pencil and paper, and once he was

[11] Deutsch, *op. cit.*, p. 232.

even forbidden to collect some harmless corncobs that happened to strike his fancy. Moreover, there was practically no attempt to study his mental processes or to understand how the illness came about. "It was upon the gradual but sure improvement in my physical condition," Beers wrote, "that the doctors were relying for my eventual return to normality."[12]

Beers and his book became the agents of another forward stride in reform. In 1909 Beers established the National Committee for Mental Hygiene, later expanded to international dimensions, having in view three main purposes. (1) One of the chief aims was to alter the widespread popular belief that mental disorders were incurable and that they carried a stigma of disgrace. Much progress has been made in changing public opinion on this score, although it is still true that many people, willing enough to admit a bodily ailment, vigorously deny that any peculiarity in themselves or their relatives could be of mental origin. There still lies ahead a large task of public enlightenment on this subject. (2) Another aim of the mental hygiene movement was to encourage the early recognition and prevention of mental disorders. Around 1922 this purpose became embodied in *child guidance clinics* designed to study and treat problems of behavior before they grew to more serious proportions. Here again much has been accomplished, but a vast amount remains to be done before this essential health service becomes available to all children. (3) The third goal of mental hygiene was to improve those conditions in mental hospitals which Beers' own experiences brought so clearly into the open. While it is probably true that many hospitals today function only a little better than those in which Beers was confined, nevertheless the best mental institutions can claim a decisive advance over those of 1900. Improvement of resources is noteworthy, whether they be medical techniques, psychological examinations, or the chance for diversions and interesting occupations. Equally important are the greater patience and skill of the thoroughly trained attendants who know how to avoid petty squabbles and who treat the patients with real consideration. Most promising of all, however, is the changing attitude of the doctors: they make a serious attempt to understand each patient as an individual and to treat him as such.

The care and treatment of the insane is a task for highly trained specialists: psychiatrists and psychiatrically trained nurses and attendants. The conduct of child guidance and mental hygiene clinics is an equally specialized task shared by the professions of medicine, psychology, and social work. At first glance it might appear, particularly when we confine ourselves to the severer mental afflictions, that the whole business of mental health belongs in the hands of specialists and is of no concern to

[12] C. W. Beers, *A Mind That Found Itself* (Garden City, N. Y.: Doubleday & Co., Inc., 1931), p. 73.

the ordinary citizen. Quite the opposite is the case; it is by no means too emphatic to say that "from the standpoint of prevalence, as well as economic loss, the problem of mental disease is without question one of the major issues facing medical science and political organization as well as all modern society."[13] None of the goals of the mental hygiene movement can be achieved without active support by the ordinary citizen. He alone can sustain a climate of public opinion that is favorable to the proper treatment of disordered people. If disorders are to be promptly recognized as psychological problems, rather than forms of moral disgrace, it will be because the ordinary citizens in the community are acting as the bearers of this enlightenment. If maladjusted children are to find help at guidance clinics, it will be because the citizens are supporting such institutions. If mentally disturbed patients are to be cared for in up-to-date hospitals with opportunities for abundant individual attention, it will be because the voters have favored appropriations far larger than those now made for state mental institutions. Today in the United States we have more than six hundred mental hospitals, a state of affairs that would doubtless have seemed to Pinel, Tuke, and Miss Dix like a dream come true. Yet there is scarcely a hospital that does not justly complain of overcrowding and understaffing. We have not yet fully solved the economic and social problem of making these hospitals function at the high level necessary to make an effective application of our present scientific knowledge. There is work here for the citizen as well as the specialist.

MENTAL DISORDERS CONCEIVED AS DISEASES OF THE BRAIN

In the early stages of scientific study progress consists largely in ordering and classifying the facts. Not until this preliminary step has been accomplished is it possible to develop hypotheses and put them to any kind of crucial test. Because of the absence of hospitals, records, and facilities for observation, the study of mental disorders lingered long in the first stage. During the twenty-three centuries from Hippocrates to Pinel there were thousands of attempts to make a satisfactory classification. But Pinel himself, when writing his treatise in 1801, felt that the time was not yet ripe for sharp distinctions and clearly defined categories. He preserved only the little that was common to the earlier attempts and contented himself with distinguishing four large groups: mania, melancholia, dementia, and idiocy.

Difficulties in Classifying Mental Disorders. With the establishment of hospitals and the taking of systematic records, a wealth of facts began to accumulate. Examples of insanity became available in large numbers.

[13] C. Landis and J. D. Page, *Modern Society and Mental Disease* (New York: Farrar & Rinehart, 1938), p. 26.

To understand this rich experience, to arrange and organize the facts in some intelligible fashion, became for the curious scientist an increasingly urgent problem. But the difficulties proved at once to be enormous. "Mental disease," Pinel remarked, "appears greatly to tax the attention of good observers because it presents itself to us as a mixture of incoherence and confusion."[14] By their very nature the phenomena seemed to defy understanding. Moreover, the really good observer was likely to be baffled by the wide range of individual differences. "When one has seen many insane people," wrote one of Pinel's contemporaries, "one can recognize that there are as many differences among them as there are personalities among individuals whose minds are healthy. It is therefore really difficult to make up classes of diseases which would not prove fictitious."[15]

These were real difficulties, but by all odds the greatest problem arose out of the nature of symptoms. As we view them today, symptoms such as delusions and hallucinations, failure of memory, depressed or excited moods, are merely the surface phenomena of disordered behavior. They can be, and they have been, classified in various ways. Some of the most barren pages in the literature of science are those devoted to the classification of symptoms arranged according to the mental functions supposedly affected or by some similar purely logical scheme. Because symptoms are surface phenomena their logical classification corresponds scarcely at all to the logic of the underlying disorders. It is a good deal like classifying books according to the material and color of their bindings rather than by what is discussed inside. It is necessary in every case to go behind the symptoms if we are to understand the nature of a patient's trouble. In addition, symptoms do not fit together, even on the surface, in such a way as to provide an intelligible classification. Delusions and hallucinations, for example, appear under the most widely different circumstances and in the greatest variety of combinations with other symptoms: in connection with excitement, with depression, and with dementia; accompanied by paralysis or without it; following extreme alcoholic intoxication; in the delirious states resulting from high fever or acute infection; and sometimes virtually alone. Clearly it is necessary to penetrate beneath superficial phenomena if we are to arrive at the underlying and essential factors responsible for abnormal behavior.

The Somatogenic Hypothesis. About the middle of the nineteenth century there was a strong revival of Hippocrates' original belief that mental disorders were diseases of the brain. Underlying and essential factors were to be looked for in conditions affecting the central nervous system. This way of looking at the problem was strictly in accord with the general

[14] Pinel, *op. cit.*, p. 1.

[15] Fodéré, *Traité du Délire* (Paris: 1817), quoted by Zilboorg and Henry, *op. cit.*, p. 392.

outlook of medical science which constantly sought to establish the bodily conditions and tissue changes responsible for illness. Because it looks for the *genesis* of the trouble in the body or *soma,* this theory is commonly called the *somatogenic hypothesis.* Representative of the trend toward somatogenesis was the German psychiatrist Griesinger (1817–1868) who recognized no distinction between neurology and psychology and who considered a diagnosis valid only when it specified a physiological cause. In France the same tendency was illustrated by Magnan (1835–1916) who gave his most careful attention to disorders associated with very obvious bodily conditions such as alcoholic intoxication, paralysis, and the changes accompanying childbirth. In 1857 a major treatise was published by the French psychiatrist Morel (1809–1873) whose thinking was organized around the theory of degeneration: briefly stated, that mental disease was the result of hereditary neural weakness. These workers and many others who accepted their premises believed that when the brain and the human constitution revealed their secrets the riddles of mental disorder would be solved.

But to make the brain and the human constitution reveal their secrets soon proved to be a long campaign. Only the gross anatomical divisions of the nervous system—cerebral hemispheres, cerebellum, medulla oblongata, spinal cord, and peripheral nerves—were known in the first half of the nineteenth century. More precise localization of functions began only in 1861 with Broca's discovery of a center controlling speech. The mapping of cortical areas was accomplished between 1870 and 1900, but is still a matter of some dispute. Of similarly recent date is our knowledge of microscopic structure. Not until 1889 did improved microscopy disclose the existence of the synapse, thereby showing that each nerve cell and its fibers formed an anatomically separate unit. Thus before 1900 only the very grossest abnormalities of brain structure could have been perceived. Griesinger, Magnan, Morel, and their followers had little sound knowledge at their disposal. The confidence in somatogenesis was based more on faith than on facts, and was reasoned out by analogy with the rest of medical practice.

Notwithstanding these difficulties, the somatogenic hypothesis was a great advance in the understanding of mental disorders. It demanded a search for essential causes rather than a preoccupation with surface phenomena. It called upon methods long used with success in the study of bodily ailments. There was a long-standing tradition, recognized even by Hippocrates, that each separate disease had a characteristic *beginning,* a typical *course,* and a typical *outcome.* Each disease, furthermore, was represented not by a single symptom but by a typical pattern of symptoms or *symptom-complex,* which might vary in detail from one case to another yet still signify a common underlying disorder. If one could show that certain symptoms frequently occurred together, that they made their first appearance in some fairly regular way, that they ran a typical course which led to a typical outcome, then one was probably well on the way toward isolating a specific disease produced by a specific condition of the brain. Let us examine this method in action, choosing what is probably its greatest triumph in the field of behavior disorders.

The Discovery of General Paresis. One of the most creditable chapters in the modern history of medicine was the discovery of general paresis. This disorder, alternatively called *dementia paralytica* or *general paralysis,* was first clearly described in 1798 by Haslam, who noticed among patients at the Bethlehem Hospital a frequent association of delusions of grandeur, dementia, and progressive paralysis. Haslam was unable to carry his observations further than this; he simply recognized a common association of symptoms, a *symptom-complex,* and thus set apart certain patients from the undifferentiated mass of the insane. He characterized these patients as follows:

> Speech is defective, the corners of the mouth are drawn down, the arms and legs are more or less deprived of their voluntary movements, and in the majority of patients memory is materially weakened. These patients as a rule fail to recognize their condition. So weak that they can hardly keep on their legs, they still maintain they are extremely strong and capable of the greatest deeds.[16]

A few years later, in 1805, a French physician, Esquirol, who later succeeded Pinel at the Salpêtrière, observed that patients having this symptom-complex never recovered; deterioration and paralysis progressed fairly rapidly to a fatal outcome. Esquirol thus called attention to a typical *course* and a typical *outcome.* It is worth noting that such observations, necessarily extending over a period of time, could scarcely have been made except under the conditions of hospital care and record keeping that Pinel had but lately established in Paris.

As experience increased, so that reliance could be placed upon statistics, it became clear that general paresis occurred in men about three times as often as in women. The *time of onset* was found to be rarely earlier than the age of thirty or later than fifty. The *mode of onset* proved particularly baffling. Attempts to reconstruct the patient's history generally showed an insidious beginning marked at first by barely perceptible abnormalities of behavior. Only after a period of time did this behavior come to be sharply at variance with the patient's previous mode of living.

The identification of the organic disorder proceeded slowly at first, handicapped by the prevailing ignorance of brain structure and brain function. In the first half of the century post-mortem examination of

[16] J. Haslam, *Observations on Insanity* (London: F. & C. Rivington, 1798), p. 259.

paretic brains showed something to be wrong with the tissue. Various writers spoke of irritation, inflammation, and degeneration, these being hardly more than guesses. Around 1860 improved microscopy revealed an excessive growth of connective tissue in the cortical substance together with a widespread destruction of nervous tissue. The cause of these changes still eluded observation, and the next forward step came with the help not of the microscope but of the case history. In 1894 Fournier showed from various statistical studies that a history of syphilis was obtained in 65 per cent of paretics, as compared with 10 per cent in other mental illnesses. He offered the hypothesis that general paresis had its origin in syphilitic infection which, even though apparently cured, had in some way invaded the tissues of the brain.

At first it seemed a weakness in this theory that histories of syphilis were not obtained in all cases of general paresis. In answer to this objection it was pointed out that correct histories of previous syphilis are by no means easily obtained; patients have strong motives for concealing the indiscreet sexual adventures that led to infection. A bold experiment by Kraft-Ebing in 1897 greatly strengthened the theory of syphilitic origin. Nine paretic patients who denied previous infection were inoculated with the syphilitic virus. None of them developed syphilis. This surprising immunity constituted proof that the patients, despite their denials, had once been infected and had subsequently recovered. Further evidence accumulated during the next fifteen years as a result of newly discovered laboratory methods for recognizing syphilis. The blood and the cerebrospinal fluid of syphilitics can be made to show highly characteristic chemical reactions, and these reactions were now demonstrated with great regularity in paretic patients.

The final step, sufficient to dispel any lingering doubts about the origin of the disorder, came with the discovery of the syphilitic infectious agent in the brain tissue of paretic patients. This infectious agent, a minute organism known as *Treponema pallidum,* was not identified as the cause of syphilis itself until 1905, but the search for it in nervous tissue proceeded thereafter without delay. In 1913 Noguchi and Moore found *Treponema pallidum* in the nerve-cell layers of the paretic cortex, thus at last accounting for the tissue destruction recognized but not explained nearly a century earlier. The essential cause of general paresis now stood fully revealed, and the way was opened for preventive measures and for research on methods of treatment.

This is the kind of story of which medical science is rightly proud. Careful observation, patient research to which hundreds of workers contributed, the constant development of more refined techniques which carried the investigation forward in unexpected ways, led at last to the discovery of underlying causes and thus to the possibility of prevention and treatment. Zilboorg weighs the accomplishment in the following words:

> It proved a blessing for hundreds of thousands of unfortunates suffering from a syphilitic infection which had not been properly cured and which had become invisible for a period of years, only to reappear in the form of a devastating disease of the brain and spinal cord—a disease which was destructive to the whole personality of the individual and was invariably fatal. Studies in serology and empirical therapeutic efforts, stimulated and made possible by the discovery of the nature of general paralysis and its cause, had finally reduced substantially the number of fatal outcomes, increased the number of recoveries, and, what is most important, led to rational preventive measures which at least in some countries (Scandinavia) almost entirely eliminated general paralysis as a disease.[17]

Similar stories could be told for other varieties of disorder, notably those connected with senile changes and those dependent upon metabolic deficiencies. But since it is our purpose here to sample the main trends and grasp the persistent problems, rather than to set forth an exhaustive history, we can be satisfied with the example of general paresis, postponing until Chapter 12 a systematic consideration of the somatogenic disorders.

Kraepelin's Outlook on Mental Disorder. The culmination of the idea that mental disorders are physical diseases, analogous in every respect to ailments that have no mental symptoms, occurred in the work of Emil Kraepelin (1855–1926), the German psychiatrist whose great textbook, passing through eight editions from 1883 to 1913, stamped its impression deeply on subsequent psychiatric thinking. Building on the observations of predecessors as well as his own, he tried to accomplish for all mental disorders what was being done so brilliantly with general paresis. He tried to achieve a sifting, sorting, and grouping of mentally disordered patients in order to bring out the typical symptom-complexes and the typical patterns of onset, course, and outcome which distinguished one disease from another. If patients could be properly classified according to certain regularities in the symptoms and course of their illness, if one could thus correctly name and distinguish the different disease entities, then the energies of research could be bent toward finding the specific bodily condition responsible for each disease.

Kraepelin brought to this task a genius for combination and classification. His work was carried out in large hospitals, with large numbers of patients, and with extensive hospital records—a proper culmination of Pinel's reforms. He was in tune with the objective scientific trend of his times. The work of Pasteur and Lister had prepared the way for the understanding and mastery of infectious diseases. Remarkable triumphs

[17] Zilboorg and Henry, *op. cit.*, p. 399.

in clinical medicine were occurring all around him; within a short space of time a great many varieties of bodily disease had been isolated and clearly defined. The growing resources of the physiological laboratory were constantly at his disposal and he followed with keen interest all developments along this line. As a result his conception of the possible bodily aspects of mental disorder was far richer than the original notion of a defect or injury in the brain. In addition to gross destruction of nervous tissue, such as occurred in general paresis, he was aware of the possible effects of metabolic changes, improper bodily economy, and disorders of the endocrine glands.

Thus oriented and equipped, Kraepelin studied large quantities of case histories. He examined not only the story of each illness and its course while the patient was in the hospital but also the history of the patient's previous life, and he followed the histories of patients who were discharged from the hospital. In this way he was able to establish regularities concerning the symptoms and course of disease. Discounting individual variations, he sorted out what was common to numerous cases and arrived at classifications. Working along these lines, he came to the conclusion that in addition to the entities already recognized there were two major mental diseases: *manic-depressive psychosis* and *dementia praecox* (now generally called *schizophrenia*). In forming the first of these two disease entities he drew together the excited, elated conditions (mania) and the melancholy, depressed states (depression), showing that in many cases these moods succeeded each other in the same patient. As had been done with paresis, he here isolated a symptom-complex having a typical beginning, course, and outcome. The symptom-complex was centered around abrupt changes of mood and did not include signs of deterioration such as defects in gait, speech, and memory. The onset was sudden rather than gradual; the course was periodic rather than steadily progressive; the outcome was spontaneous recovery though with a strong likelihood of future recurrence. Each of these points emphasized the fundamental difference between manic-depressive psychosis and general paresis. Dementia praecox represented an even larger synthesis of previously recognized disorders. Kraepelin felt justified in making this combination because all the subvarieties, outwardly rather different, had two central features in common: they all showed an early onset and they all progressed in the direction of incurable dementia. Here was a disease that had its onset earlier than either paresis or manic-depressive psychosis. Its course was progressive rather than periodic, and its outcome was complete dementia, not including, however, paralysis and early death.

Progress in understanding these two mental disorders was urgently needed. Together they included nearly two thirds of the patients in mental hospitals, claiming nearly two thirds of the doctors' effort and time. Kraepelin postulated that manic-depressive psychosis was caused by an irregularity in metabolic function. Because the disorder seemed to run in families he assumed that the metabolic irregularity was based on some kind of hereditary defect. In the case of dementia praecox he proposed the hypothesis that the sex glands were at fault, producing an unfavorable chemical state which affected the nervous system. He justified this guess by pointing out frequent associations between the onset of the disease and changes in sexual function: the changes of puberty, menstrual irregularities, childbirth, and the involution period. He thus applied the type of reasoning that prevailed in general medicine and searched for the causes of disorder where any physician would look for them: in tissue changes, endocrine disturbances, hereditary peculiarities; in short, in some specific derangement of the bodily economy.

Kraepelin has often been criticized for a one-sided commitment to the somatogenic point of view. He gave little heed to those personal strivings and frustrations which have since been recognized as often important for the full comprehension of disordered conditions. It must be remembered, however, that his field of observation was the hospitalized insane, where the somatogenic hypothesis is most likely to be appropriate. Subsequent research has advanced far beyond his speculations, but it has not discredited the general idea that manic-depressive and schizophrenic psychoses have many of the attributes of bodily disease. Certainly the main advances in treating these disorders have come through physical rather than psychological methods. Historically, the psychogenic hypothesis emerged from observations made outside the walls of hospitals. As we shall now see, it was the study of neurotic patients, whose condition almost never requires hospitalization, that led to new advances in psychological understanding.

BEGINNINGS OF PSYCHOPATHOLOGY: THE STUDY OF HYSTERIA

The Psychogenic Hypothesis. In contrast to the somatogenic hypothesis, which holds that disordered personal reactions have their genesis in somatic or bodily disturbances, the psychogenic hypothesis attributes causative significance to psychological processes. We can give it a crude first statement, to be much refined in later sections of the book, by saying that disordered personal reactions occur because the patient's thoughts, feelings, and strivings are disturbed. His somatic processes, even his brain and central nervous system, may be working in an entirely normal fashion; it is the content of what he feels and imagines that throws his personal reactions into disorder. We can begin to speak of *psychopathology* at the point where ideas or some other psychological processes are held responsible for disordered behavior. Pathology means the science of disease processes; psychopathology deals with those disorders which have their origin in psychological processes rather than tissue or chemical dysfunction.

The psychogenic hypothesis won its way into modern medicine through the study of hysteria. In its early stages this study was much assisted by the use of hypnotism, which itself offered an interesting trial ground for the psychogenic point of view. Hypnotism first became widely known through the activities of an Austrian physician, Mesmer, who set up a flourishing practice in Paris shortly before the French Revolution. Hundreds of patients were cured of diverse ailments by attending Mesmer's magnetic sessions, as they were called. Mesmer's methods were highly theatrical, but they inspired serious investigation. His followers very quickly discovered all the main phenomena of hypnotism as we know them today. They showed that a hypnotized person was highly responsive to whatever was suggested. For instance, he could apparently be made to see things which were not there (positive hallucinations) or not to see things which were there (negative hallucinations). Parts of his body could be temporarily paralyzed and made insensitive to touch and pain. He could move about, answer questions, talk and think clearly, but upon awakening have no recollection of what had transpired. Some of these curious phenomena were valuable in effecting cures. If a patient complained of aches and pains, for instance, these might be made to disappear by suggestion in the hypnotic state, so that the patient would wake up magically cured, remembering nothing of the process.

By what mechanism were these striking changes produced? Mesmer explained them by supposing that an invisible fluid passed between himself and the patient, influencing the patient's body in a distinctive fashion. By analogy with the action of magnets he christened this influence *animal magnetism*, and his writings on the subject show that he considered it a strictly physical process. A commission appointed to investigate his activities made a number of careful experiments which contradicted his theory. The commissioners showed that the phenomena supposed to be produced by magnetism occurred only if the patient knew he was being magnetized, and they drew the conclusion that the demonstrable effects were obtained through "the excitement of the imagination." At that time this conclusion had the effect of discrediting Mesmer, but it was actually an alternative hypothesis for explaining the observed facts of hypnotism. One of Mesmer's pupils aptly put the question: "If Mesmer had no other secret than that he was able to make the imagination exert an effective influence upon health, would he not still be a wonder worker?"[18] A later follower, Bertrand, reasoned that hypnotism

[18] Quoted by P. Janet, *Psychological Healing, a Historical and Clinical Study*, trans. E. and C. Paul (London: Allen & Unwin, 1925), Vol. I, p. 161.

"served merely to render conspicuous and to amplify phenomena dependent upon the working of the general laws of imagination, expectant attention, and desire."[19] This was a fully psychogenic hypothesis, seeking to explain hypnotic behavior by appeal to psychological processes.

Charcot's Investigation of Hysterical Symptoms. In 1878 a new line of investigation opened at the Salpêtrière in Paris, the hospital which many years before had been the scene of Pinel's momentous reforms. The patients who became the objects of this study were classified under *hysteria*. This disorder, recognized even by the ancients, is characterized by an amazing variety of bodily symptoms: total or partial blindness, total or partial deafness, paralysis or anaesthesia in certain areas of the body, occasionally convulsive attacks ("hysterical fits"), and not infrequently gaps and peculiarities in memory. Apart from these symptoms the patient's mind is perfectly clear; only the most severely incapacitated cases came to the attention of J. M. Charcot who began to investigate them in detail.

Charcot was a distinguished neurologist who served as visiting physician at the Salpêtrière. He was a remarkably keen observer of visible behavior. Current methods for examining reflexes in search of damage to the nervous system owe a great deal to Charcot's genius. By training and long experience he favored the somatogenic hypothesis. For a long time it did not occur to him that hysteria, despite its manifold symptoms, differed from any other disease of the nervous system. Hysterical symptoms lent themselves to examination by Charcot's established methods because, apart from the fits, they mostly took the form of specific bodily ailments.

Charcot himself had never practised hypnotism, but some of his assistants at the hospital became interested in the subject and experimented with the patients. One day they showed their chief some remarkable facts. Before his eyes they demonstrated that by means of hypnotism it was possible to produce artificially all the typical bodily symptoms of hysteria, and afterwards to remove them again. By hypnotic suggestion a patient's perfectly healthy arm could be rendered paralyzed and anaesthetic; Charcot himself, examining the patient, could not tell the difference between this and a natural hysterical paralysis with anesthesia, except that it disappeared upon further suggestion. The whole array of hysterical symptoms could be brought into and put out of existence at whatever speed and in whatever form one chose. How could the nervous system do it?

Challenged by this discovery, Charcot set to work to investigate hysterical symptoms. Clearly they were not caused by local injury to the

[19] *Ibid.*, p. 157.

nervous system. He tried to discover how the symptoms started, and found that the circumstances were often peculiar. One patient, for instance, was in a street accident during which, so he thought, a carriage ran over his legs. At the hospital both legs remained paralyzed for months, but as a matter of fact the carriage had not even touched the patient. A young girl stepped lightly out of bed one morning only to find her left leg paralyzed in a rigid clubfoot position. Charcot examined many such cases: the initial circumstances were never sufficient to account for the symptom. The disappearance of symptoms also occurred in a strange fashion. Sometimes a paralysis would end abruptly during a moment of emotional excitement. Sometimes it could be removed by hypnotic suggestion. Charcot discovered that Mesmer's claims were partly justified: the young girl with the clubfoot paralysis was cured after a strenuous series of hypnotic sessions.[20] Again it appeared that symptoms were capable of migration. Paralysis might shift spontaneously from one side of the body to the other. One of the most startling discoveries was that the hysterical symptom might cease to operate when the patient was inattentive or asleep. Janet, a student at the Salpêtrière whose work we shall presently consider, tells of a man paralyzed in both legs who was addicted to walking in his sleep. He often climbed out on the roof and had to be rescued by the attendants with extreme care because his legs became totally paralyzed the moment he was awakened.[21]

Probably the most significant of Charcot's discoveries was that hysterical symptoms often made what we might call anatomical nonsense. Sometimes a patient would have a paralyzed hand with anaesthesia which stopped at the wrist, thus including roughly the area that would be covered by a glove. Such an anaesthesia is anatomically impossible in the sense that no conceivable nerve injury could produce it. The arm is supplied by three main nerve trunks extending down into the hand. Injury to any one would involve only part of the hand and would affect part of the arm as well. Injury to the center in which the three paths join would produce an anaesthesia including the whole arm and shoulder. The glove anaesthesia therefore is a perfect example of anatomical nonsense which strikes the final blow at a somatogenic hypothesis for hysteria.

How, then, does a glove anaesthesia come into existence? We can see that there is an oddly mental character to this seemingly physical symptom. The area of anaesthesia corresponds to the idea one has of the hand as an anatomical unit. The first patient's paralysis likewise corresponds to an idea he had that a carriage ran over his legs. But we must

[20] J. M. Charcot, *Œuvres Complètes* (Paris: Lecrosnier & Babé, 1890), Vol. IX, pp. 462–78.

[21] P. Janet, *The Major Symptoms of Hysteria* (2d ed.; New York: The Macmillan Co., 1920), p. 28.

beware of jumping to the conclusion that these patients are simply putting on a conscious act. Mental origins do not necessarily mean conscious or voluntary origins. That patients often had no conscious idea about their symptoms was testified in many ways. Sometimes examinations revealed an area of anaesthesia, or perhaps even a blindness of one eye, of which up to that moment the patient had been totally unaware. The most telling fact, however, which absolved hysterical patients from conscious deception, was that sometimes the symptoms made perfect anatomical sense. There were cases, for example, clearly hysterical and curable by suggestion, in which paralysis of the entire right side was accompanied by disturbances of speech. One certainly could not suppose that in 1880 clinical patients of slight education had an idea about the location of the speech centers in the left cerebral hemisphere and the control by this hemisphere of the right side of the body.

Charcot left the problem at this point. Hysteria, the medical mystery, was far from solved. The symptoms were mental, yet not wholly mental; they were psychological, yet mixed up in a puzzling way with bodily processes. This was truly bewildering, but out of the bewilderment there came at last a highly significant illumination.

Janet's Study of the Mental State in Hysteria. The next step in the process of enlightenment was taken by Charcot's student, Pierre Janet, who during the 1890's began to publish his acute observations of the mental state of hysterical patients. Janet's work illustrates the progress that sometimes comes by looking at old and familiar facts from an entirely new point of view. Before his work, the fits and the bodily symptoms had been taken as the central and characteristic phenomena of hysteria. Janet shifted the emphasis to the mental state. He listened to the patients and tried to find out what was characteristic and peculiar about their mental processes. In this way he gradually came to center his thinking around *somnambulism,* which appeared to him to be at bottom an abnormality of memory.

He began with pure cases of somnambulism, those in which a system of ideas and actions takes possession of the patient for a short period of time but afterwards appears to be forgotten. His classic example was the case of Irène, a young woman whose memory was normal except that she seemed to have forgotten the recent tragic death of her mother. Every so often she would fall into a somnambulistic state during which, oblivious to everything around her, she would act out with extraordinary vividness the harrowing scene at her mother's deathbed and her own subsequent frantic expressions of grief. No sooner was the drama finished than she would return to her normal state and go on calmly with whatever she had been doing. Janet interpreted these facts as follows.

During the crisis itself, two opposite characteristics manifest themselves; first, a huge unfolding of all the phenomena connected with a certain delirium; second, the absence of every sensation and every memory that is not connected with that delirium. After the crisis, during the state that appears as normal, two other characteristics appear, opposite, to all appearance; the return of consciousness of sensations and normal memory, and the entire forgetfulness of all that is connected with the somnambulism. Let us remember all these notions that here seem very simple, and we shall afterwards see them unfolded in every hysterical phenomenon.

Things happen as if an idea, a partial system of thoughts, emancipated itself, became independent, and developed itself on its own account. The result is, on the one hand, that it develops far too much, and, on the other hand, that consciousness appears no longer to control it.[22]

The same processes can be observed in those cases technically called *hysterical fugues,* generally referred to in newspapers as cases of amnesia. Janet described several such cases, of which the following is typical. A youth of seventeen who had chosen the placid occupation of grocer's boy used to visit a public house frequented by old sailors who fired his imagination with tales of adventure at sea and in foreign lands. At home or at work he rarely thought about travel, but occasionally, after a visit to the public house, he would set forth on a journey determined to reach the sea. During these trips there was but one idea in his head: to get to the sea and sail for the enchanted lands he had heard described. Family and job were completely forgotten. One of the fugues lasted three months, during which he moved slowly toward the south of France working on canal boats. When a chance remark reminded him of his parents he suddenly "awoke," so to speak, oblivious to the last three months and supposing himself to be still in Paris.[23]

The Concept of Dissociation. In this case, as in the previous one, a system of emancipated ideas temporarily seizes control of behavior and begets amnesia for the patient's normal existence. The emancipated system is organized in a slightly different way: with Irène it was the memories of a particularly painful experience that were set apart, whereas with the grocer's boy the desire for novelty, adventure, and manliness gave shape to the ideas underlying the fugues. But in any event the same peculiarities of memory prevail. A healthy person cannot split up his memories in this way, no matter how strong the inducement. Janet believed that this phenomenon was the central fact in hysteria, and he gave it the name of *dissociation.* The concept of dissociation was designed to account for the pathological separation or insulation between systems of ideas which normally would interpenetrate and influence each other. The special mark of this insulation was amnesia, the patient's failure in

[22] *Ibid.,* pp. 36, 42.
[23] *Ibid.,* p. 53.

his well states to remember the sick ones or in his sick ones to remember the well. The effect of this insulation was the overdevelopment of those systems which no longer enjoyed communication with the integrated conscious self. In hysteria, Janet conceived, the personality lost some of its normal organization. Certain systems fell out of the hierarchy, so to speak, and escaped from the restraining influences of the ego. The emancipated systems provoked behavior not unlike that of a hypnotized person.

Janet believed that the classical bodily symptoms could be understood as dissociations of neuro-muscular systems. If a patient was unable to walk it was because the organized system of images and sensations which functioned during walking had become dissociated from the rest of the personality. Charcot's patient who believed himself run over by a carriage had a dissociated idea that his legs were paralyzed, and this idea, simply because it was dissociated, became overdeveloped—like Irène's drama of grief—and actually controlled the motility of his legs. Here Janet was dealing not so much with systems of ideas as with natural subsystems of the neural mechanism. In this way the concept of dissociation could be made to cover all the phenomena of hysteria.

Dissociation was a purely descriptive concept. As such it was of great value in the history of abnormal psychology. Janet drew attention to a very far-reaching characteristic of hysteria: the breaking of behavior into insulated subsystems and the failure of the ego to control what was going on. His work strengthened the conviction that hysteria and the other neuroses belonged in the sphere of psychology and had to be conceived as disorders of the personality as a whole. Dissociation was not an explanatory concept. It was not designed to tell *why* personality disintegrated in the fashion described. In his *explanation* of hysteria Janet hovered between psychogenic and somatogenic theories. He believed that these patients suffered from an hereditary weakness in their capacity to organize their experience. On the other hand he described the conditions that had worn the patient down, frustrated and discouraged him, thrown him into a state of exhaustion, piled up upon him until he could no longer function properly. Janet was a sensitive observer of the struggles and problems that occupied his patients' lives, but he paused on the brink of psychogenic explanations. It was left for others to discern in these very struggles and problems the effective causes of the illness.

Breuer and Freud's Discovery of Abreaction. The most unsatisfactory feature of Janet's theory was that it failed to explain individual symptoms. How does the hysterical symptom get selected and placed? Sometimes we feel that the symptom bears a sensible relation to strivings which we can readily understand. Irène, for instance, forgets her mother's death—that and nothing else—because the memory is extremely painful to her. More often, and especially when the symptoms take a crude bodily form, there is no apparent logic in the locality chosen. The clubfoot paralysis of Charcot's patient, starting when she stepped out of bed, seems almost like a chance phenomenon, and this impression is even stronger when a patient has a rapidly changing succession of bodily symptoms or a great many at one time. To make sense out of such a jargon of symptoms seems as hopeless as making sense out of the ravings of a lunatic. But both things can be done. The man who opened the door upon hysterical symptom formation was a Viennese physician, Joseph Breuer, who shortly enlisted the collaboration of a younger colleague, Sigmund Freud (1856–1939).

Between 1880 and 1882 Breuer had under treatment a curious and difficult case of hysteria. The patient, a girl in her early twenties, was bedridden for several months with a long array of symptoms. Both legs and the right arm were paralyzed, sight and hearing were greatly impaired, the neck muscles were uncomfortably contracted, and there was a persistent nervous cough, occasional nausea, and periodic difficulty with speech. One could scarcely imagine a more senseless jargon of symptoms. Besides all these afflictions of the body there were frequent alterations of mental state: confusions and a dreamy condition which Breuer called "absence." It was the sympathetic observation of these mental states that gave Breuer his first clues concerning the symptoms and his first success in alleviating them. During her periods of "absence" the girl often mumbled to herself as if her thoughts were busy. Breuer took note of her words and later, after inducing an hypnotic state, repeatedly gave them back to her. In this way she was led to reveal the fantasies that occupied her in her dreamy states. When she had unburdened herself of these fantasies she felt relieved, and awakened from the hypnosis temporarily much improved.

Almost by accident Breuer had hit upon a means of temporary cure, but the effects lasted only for a few hours. Presently he discovered that under certain rather special circumstances a symptom might be permanently removed. If during hypnosis the patient could remember the situation in which the symptom began, and if the accompanying emotion was freely and fully expressed, the symptom would disappear for good. Breuer discovered that the patient's eye trouble had its origin during a long and painful period of her life when she was helping to nurse her father through his protracted last illness. One evening she was sitting near his bed, worried and tearful, when he awoke from a nap and asked her what time it was. Her tears kept her from quickly seeing the clock, but she exerted her eye muscles desperately to clear her vision so that she could reply without revealing her distressed condition. When the patient not only recalled this forgotten incident but also experienced again fully the emotion she had so forcibly suppressed, her visual symptoms permanently disappeared.[24] A similar origin and cure was found for all her symptoms. The paralysis of her right arm, for instance, had its roots in an occasion when she herself dozed off at her father's bedside and had a nightmare; a huge black snake was attacking her father and she tried in vain to fend it off with her right arm. She awoke terrified, freed her arm which was over the back of the chair and perhaps "asleep," and hastily suppressed her feelings lest her father perceive her fear. The removal of this, like the other symptoms, was not a matter of a single hypnotic recall. The incident had been elaborated in many fantasies, and Breuer had to work steadily back along this chain before the patient recalled the original nightmare and gave full vent to her original terror.

In the course of time this patient was completely cured. The process was always the same: recovery during hypnosis of some drastic incident in which emotion had been suppressed, full and dramatic expression of the emotion, permanent disappearance of the symptom that had been laid down on that occasion. The release of suppressed emotion—of "strangulated affect"—was the core of Breuer's discovery, and received the name of *abreaction.* Reviewing this case some years later, Freud set forth the theory in the following words.

> It is especially to be noted that Breuer's patient in almost all pathogenic situations had to suppress a strong excitement, instead of giving vent to it by appropriate words or deeds. While she was seated by her father's sick bed, she was careful to betray nothing of her anxiety and her painful depression to the patient. When later she reproduced the same scene before the physician, the emotion which she had suppressed on the occurrence of the scene burst out with especial strength, as though it had been pent up all along. We are forced to the conclusion that the patient fell ill because the emotion developed in the pathogenic situation was prevented from escaping normally, and that the essence of the sickness lies in the fact that these imprisoned emotions undergo a series of abnormal changes. In part they are preserved as a lasting charge and as a source of constant disturbance in psychical life; in part they undergo a change into unusual bodily innervations and inhibitions which present themselves as the physical symptoms of the case.
>
> You see that we are in a fair way to arrive at a purely psychological theory of hysteria, in which we assign the first rank to the affective processes.[25]

It was in thus assigning first rank to the affective processes that Breuer and Freud made their noteworthy departure from the position reached by the French psychiatrists. Instead of emphasizing a very generalized

[24] J. Breuer and S. Freud, *Studies in Hysteria,* trans. A. A. Brill (New York: Nervous & Mental Disease Publishing Co., 1936), pp. 26, 27.

[25] S. Freud, "The Origin and Development of Psychoanalysis," in *An Outline of Psychoanalysis,* ed. J. Van Teslaar (New York: Modern Library, Inc., 1924), pp. 30, 31.

state of weakness which allowed ideas, memories, and neuromuscular systems to fall out of synthesis, they worked out a specific dynamic explanation for each symptom and related it to the individual strivings of the patient. Even today hysterical symptom formation is not fully understood, but Breuer and Freud were moving in the right direction. They showed that hysterical symptoms were intelligible when one thought of them as expressions, however distorted, of the patient's struggle with conflicting impulses.

FREUD'S BASIC DISCOVERIES

After his study of the Breuer case it seemed clear to Freud that hysteria could be cured by the release of pent-up emotion. The therapeutic problem was to secure abreaction so that the energy of strangulated feelings might come to normal expression instead of "spilling over" into bodily symptoms. Abreaction, however, could not take place without recall of the original pathogenic situations, and these seemed often to be completely forgotten. In the Breuer case it was necessary to enlist the aid of hypnosis in order to bring forward the crucial memories. It looked as if hypnotism would become the chief tool of the newly discovered treatment.

Freud began to put these ideas into practice with his neurotic patients. Almost at once he ran into serious practical difficulties. Many patients proved insusceptible to hypnosis. Even though apparently eager to do so, they could not enter an hypnotic state of sufficient depth to increase their recall of pathogenic experiences. Furthermore, with those patients who responded well to hypnotism the treatment did not always progress smoothly. Success depended upon an unbroken friendly relation between doctor and patient, the most brilliant results being obliterated whenever this relation was even slightly beclouded. That Freud noticed this problem so early in his work with hypnotism shows us the nature and direction of his peculiar genius. Almost the opposite of Charcot, whose gift was the minute observation of visible behavior, he was attuned with rare sensitivity to catch the emotional and personal meaning behind the patient's utterances, to follow, so to speak, the *emotional logic* within the thoughts and actions described to him in the consulting room. Hypnotism had been practiced for a century with only the most superficial attention to its character as a personal relationship. Realizing the importance of this feature, Freud felt that hypnotic methods were likely to be uncertain and fragile, so he looked elsewhere for a technique of abreaction.

The Method of Free Association. Baffled in his attempts to capture significant memories by active means, Freud turned to a method in which both patient and physician adopted a passive attitude. Instead of requiring the patient to talk about some particular subject, Freud asked him "to abandon himself to a process of *free association*, i.e., to say whatever came into his head, while ceasing to give any conscious direction to his thoughts."[26] He was told that he must report all that occurred to him, resisting any temptation to choose among his thoughts. His only obligation was to communicate everything in the order of its occurrence and to make no attempt to supervise the course of his associations in the interests of logic, decency, or conventionality. In order to make this relaxed attitude easier, Freud carried over the practice, derived from his hypnotic methods, of having the patient lie on a couch, he himself sitting out of range of the patient's vision.

This is the method of free association. Freud's simple discovery proved to be one of the really momentous events in the history of abnormal psychology. He had discovered a way in which people could gradually reveal their real feelings, even the feelings which at first were concealed from themselves. In the end free association proved to be far more than a technique for releasing imprisoned emotions. It gave an entirely new insight into the nature of neurosis and it made a significant contribution to our whole conception of human nature and human strivings. When we first hear about free association it is hard to believe that a device so simple could be the means of such important contributions to knowledge. Nothing could seem easier than to abandon oneself to the spontaneous drift of one's thoughts, but how is this going to cure neurosis or illuminate human nature?

In order to understand free association we must bear in mind that two conditions are present which do not ordinarily prevail when we abandon ourselves to revery. (1) In the first place, all the associations have to be communicated to a listener. The reveries have to be made public, which at once brings into play all of one's desires to make sense, to be logical, and to put up a good front. Under these circumstances it is by no means an easy matter to tell everything that drifts through one's head. Patients may require weeks and even months of practice before they can really abandon themselves to free association. (2) In the second place, the patient is suffering from a neurosis and has come to the physician in order to be cured. This circumstance dominates the whole situation and exerts an influence upon the course of the associations even when the patient makes no conscious attempt to control them. Freud probably put the matter too strongly when he claimed that nothing will occur to the patient that is not somehow related to his neurosis. But the therapeutic purpose is always present and constitutes the most consistent factor influencing the train of thought. It was perhaps unfortunate to

[26] S. Freud, *The Problem of Lay-Analyses* (New York: Brentano's, 1927), p. 25.

call this process "*free* association." It is free from many conventional restraints, but it is not free in the sense of being an idle wandering of fancy. Freud himself declared that "free association is not really free." It is dominated by the therapeutic situation, and its course is further determined by those forces in the patient which contributed to making him neurotic. Thus it offers a hitherto unsuspected opportunity to observe those forces in action.

Resistance and Repression. The adoption of free association led to Freud's next discovery. His patients found it impossible to obey the fundamental rule of telling everything.

> The patient tries in every way to escape its requirements. First he will declare that he cannot think of anything, then that so much comes to his mind that it is impossible to seize on anything definite. Then we discover with no slight displeasure that he has yielded to this or that critical objection, for he betrays himself by the long pauses which he allows to occur in his speaking. He then confesses that he really cannot bring himself to this, that he is ashamed to; he prefers to let this motive get the upper hand over his promise. He may say that he did think of something but that it concerns someone else and is for that reason exempt. Or he says that what he just thought of is really too trivial, too stupid, and too foolish. I surely could not have meant that he should take such thoughts into account. Thus it goes, with untold variations, in the face of which we continually reiterate that "telling everything" really means telling everything.[27]

If driven from these simpler tactics the patients found more complicated ways of resisting the fundamental rule. They might embark upon elaborate arguments about the theory and soundness of the procedure. They might show an eager curiosity to be instructed in such a way that they might practice it alone in the privacy of their own rooms. They might even begin to act out toward the physician various anxious and hostile feelings set off by the task of associating. In countless ways Freud's patients showed a strong resistance against telling everything. The task is by no means as easy as it sounds.

Resistance does not go on forever. In the course of time a patient, perhaps after hours of circling around the topic, becomes able to bring forth some of the memories and feelings which underlie his illness. This material may have reached his own consciousness some time before he could bring himself to tell it to the physician. More commonly he is himself ignorant of the crucial matters and is even more astonished than the doctor when they at last return to his mind. The situation is indeed a curious one: it seems as if the patient actively resisted his own cure.

27 S. Freud, *A General Introduction to Psychoanalysis* (New York: Liveright Publishing Corp., 1920), pp. 249, 250.

It was on this observed fact of resistance that Freud based his theory of repression. Strong forces evidently prevented the patient from remembering certain emotionally charged experiences. Freud reasoned that these same forces, which now opposed the entry of the forgotten ideas into consciousness, must have been responsible for their original banishment. He called this original process *repression,* and considered it to be attested by the observed facts of resistance.

Freud next asked himself why such a process should occur. He came to the conclusion that repression was a device whereby the personality is protected from unbearable pain. In all his cases it appeared, after the forgotten material had been recovered, that in the original situation a wish had been aroused which conflicted sharply with the person's other desires, especially with his "ethical, aesthetic, and personal pretensions." The appearance of such a wish in consciousness created sharp and painful conflict which was solved by repression. The ideas which were the bearers of the wish were ejected from consciousness, for practical purposes forgotten, although such forgetting was very different from the ordinary fading of neutral memories. Painful conflict was avoided, but at a cost. The wish itself could never be wiped out in this way; blocked from direct expression, it discharged itself instead into the various symptoms of hysteria. When the physician tried to call up the repressed memories in order to withdraw the energy of the wish from symptom formation he was met by the full force of the ethical, aesthetic, and personal pretensions which originally found the wish intolerable.

Repression is not an observed fact. Like Janet's dissociation it is a hypothetical concept designed to explain the observed facts. No one is ever present to witness the original act of repression. The evidence comes at first from the patient's resistance against admitting repugnant thoughts when they begin to emerge during free association; only later is the hypothesis of repression confirmed by the actual recall of some shocking fantasy. All of Freud's discoveries were based on facts observed while his patients gave free associations: resistance, followed by the emergence of memories and thoughts of which the patient had been unaware. Repression was a hypothesis designed to explain the temporary inaccessibility of these memories.

The Importance of Sexual Strivings. What are the wishes that conflict so violently with ethical, aesthetic, and personal pretensions that they fall under the ban of repression? What kind of strivings are so repugnant to the personality that they must be denied recognition, yet so strong that they take their revenge by precipitating a neurosis? Freud asked himself these questions, and as he listened to his patients he felt that he was discovering the answers.

Freud's practice was not confined to cases of hysteria. He saw all kinds of "nervous invalids," including those who suffered from obsessions and compulsions, those who complained of anxiety attacks and morbid fears, and those whose trouble was a constant feeling of fatigue and exhaustion. It was from some of the latter patients rather than from the hysterics that he obtained his first clues about the troublesome wishes. Particularly in those cases where fatigue was the chief complaint—the variety of neurosis called *neurasthenia*—he found grave disturbances in the patient's current sexual life. In his own words: "The more I enquired into such disturbances (bearing in mind that all men conceal the truth in these matters) and the more adept I became at persisting in my interrogations in spite of denials at the beginning, the more regularly did pathogenic factors from sexual life disclose themselves, until there seemed to me little to prevent the assumption of their general occurrence."[28] This much he obtained from direct inquiry, but the use of hypnosis and later of free association presently led to discoveries far more startling. In patients with all varieties of neurosis, including hysteria and the obsessive-compulsive states, the same thing happened again and again: the associations led back into the patient's past until "experiences were finally reached which belonged to his infancy and concerned his sexual life; and this was so even when an ordinary emotion, not of a sexual kind, had led to the outbreak of the disease. Without taking into account these sexual traumas of childhood it was impossible to explain the symptoms, comprehend their determination, or prevent their return. After this, the unique significance of sexual experiences in the aetiology of the psychoneuroses seemed incontestably established."[29]

The words just quoted were written in 1905, the same year in which Freud produced his monograph, *Three Contributions to the Theory of Sex*. In 1905 the ideas advanced in this monograph were considered extremely radical and were quite generally met by shocked repugnance. During the nineteenth century there had grown up a peculiarly secretive and rejective attitude toward the sexual need. People acted as if the sexual need first came into existence at puberty, at which time it suddenly prompted boys to fall in love with girls and girls to fall in love with boys. The function of morality was to suppress this development until age and circumstances were suitable for marriage. This strange delusion about human nature began to crumble rapidly during the third decade of the present century, and it seems likely that Freud's work had no small share in loosening its foundations and precipitating its downfall. The claims to which Freud was led by the free associations and recollec-

[28] S. Freud, *Collected Papers*, trans. J. Rivière (London: International Psychoanalytic Press, 1924), Vol. I, p. 273.

[29] *Ibid.*, p. 275.

tions of his patients can be summarized in the following statements. (1) The sexual need is active in infancy and to a lesser extent throughout childhood. (2) It is more diffuse in its nature than the adult need, consisting of a variety of "partial impulses" not strongly dominated by genital excitation, showing itself in such actions as thumbsucking, display of the naked body, inquisitiveness about the bodies of others, masturbation, pleasures connected with anal excretion or retention, and anything else that yielded pleasurable stimulation of sensitive or erogenous zones of the body. (3) The sexual need is not innately attached to any particular objects, the choice being accomplished by learning; in childhood, therefore, members of the family and playmates of either sex may become its objects. (4) It is subject to an active campaign of adult disapproval which tends to encourage repression. (5) The childhood history of sexual experiences, fantasies, and repressions exerts a powerful effect on sexual behavior following the strengthening of the urge at puberty. Both the methods of satisfaction and the object choices must be revised if the person is going to advance to a normal adult sexual life.

After reaching these conclusions Freud was prepared to revise the theory developed in his work with Breuer. Neurosis, he now asserted, arose specifically from a strangulation of the sex need, not from the mere fact that emotion was suppressed. When a neurosis broke out in an adult the sequence of events seemed to be somewhat as follows. The precipitating factor was failure to obtain expression for the sexual need and its attendant emotions. This failure might result from external obstacles, but Freud was more impressed by the action of internal obstacles. Internal obstacles existed when there had been such a wholesale repression of childhood sexual impulses that the individual, even after growing up, could not tolerate any part of his sexual nature. The sexual urge, however, is too strong to be permanently obstructed in this fashion. Denied its adult form of expression, it tended to provoke a continuing animation in fantasy and desire of those forms of sexual behavior that had yielded gratification in childhood. For the adult this could obviously be no solution. The persisting of infantile "partial impulses," which by all adult standards could only be regarded as perverse, evoked strenuous repression on the part of the patient's ethical, aesthetic, and personal pretensions—of his *ego-instincts,* as Freud now decided to call them. Out of this conflict between the ego-instincts and the renewed elements of infantile sexuality neurosis with its symptoms was born.

Transference. If neurosis occurs because a conflict between the ego-instincts and the sexual needs has been solved by repression of the latter, the goal of treatment may be described as the lifting of the repression. Freud said that the usefulness of his new method, which he called from the start *psychoanalysis*, lay in "replacing the unconscious by the conscious." When this could be accomplished, he added, "we do away with suppressions, we remove conditions of symptom formation and transform a pathogenic into a normal conflict which can be decided in some way or other."[30] Obviously it was impossible to abolish repression by merely telling the patient that he was repressing something and guessing as to what it might be. Treatment by psychoanalysis consisted rather in long, slow, persevering sessions of free association in the course of which resistances manifested themselves and could be pointed out to the patient. In applying this method Freud soon found himself confronted by another unexpected fact: the patient, instead of attending strictly to his own conflicts, began to manifest a variety of personal feelings toward the physician. Usually the earliest signs would be an interest in the doctor's affairs, but before long the character of the feeling would betray itself more clearly in cordiality, expressions of gratitude, enthusiasm for the treatment, and an eagerness to accept every interpretation. Freud described as follows the manifestations of this attitude outside the treatment:

> At home the patient never tires of praising the physician, of prizing advantages which he constantly discovers. "He adores you, he trusts you blindly, everything you say is a revelation to him," the relatives say. Here and there one of the chorus observes more keenly and remarks. "It is a positive bore to hear him talk, he speaks only of you; you are his only subject of conversation."[31]

This behavior could only be understood as the expression of an intense affection for the doctor. In the early days of psychoanalysis, when the discoveries concerning sex were still very shocking to many people, Freud was often charged with making his patients fall in love with him. As a matter of fact Freud was at first much disturbed by these manifestations which seemed likely to interfere seriously with the business of therapy. Fortunately he did not discontinue his observations and he was soon rewarded by a more penetrating insight into the patients' strange behavior. He found, in the first place, that the affectionate relation developed in every case, that it did so without encouragement on his part, and that it occurred even under the most grotesque circumstances, as when the patient was an elderly woman. In the second place he quickly observed that affection was not the only feeling which cropped up spontaneously in the course of treatment. Sooner or later there would be feelings of an opposite character, hostile and angry, displaying themselves in a multitude of criticisms and in a stubborn intensification of all resistances. Convinced that all these feelings had little or nothing to do

[30] Freud, *General Introduction, op. cit.*, p. 375.
[31] *Ibid.*, p. 380.

with the actual situation or with the behavior and personality of the doctor, Freud christened the newly discovered phenomenon *transference*, distinguishing the affectionate from the hostile variety by designating them *positive* and *negative transference*.

If we limit ourselves to the barest facts, transference refers to the emotional attitudes displayed toward the physician during the course of psychoanalytic treatment. Freud was adding an element of interpretation when he said that these attitudes were transferred from the past. But there was a good deal of justification for his belief that they could not be explained by the current situation in the consulting room. There was sharp disparity between the patient's often stormy passions and the self-effacing, professional attitude of the analyst. Furthermore, the patient's attitudes quickly revealed their childhood origins in such tell-tale signs as the whining voice of a demanding child or the terrified guilt of a child that has offended and angered its parents. Thus Freud assumed that he was being made the object of feelings repeated or carried over (transferred) from earlier relationships.

Perhaps Freud's discovery of transference was less remarkable than his discovery that instead of interfering with treatment it could be made an instrument of progress. He was the first to utilize it consciously and purposefully to increase the patient's insight and to extend the patient's mastery over his own impulses and feelings. The patient could be shown that the emotional attitudes which he experienced during treatment were transferred from past relationships; the very vividness of the current experiences made it easier to recall their origins in childhood. Thus the transference proved to be of distinct service as a means of lifting repressions and restoring memories centered around infantile sexuality.

The Influence of Unconscious Motives. As we have seen, Freud's understanding of human behavior centered around motivation. He was acutely sensitive to the subtle action of strivings and wishes in the things his patients told him, and he learned to look for motives, especially a conflict of motives, behind even the most casual bits of behavior. But the most radical feature of Freud's thinking was not merely his insistence upon motivation. It was his claim that people are often *not aware* of their motivation; that a great deal of behavior is motivated *unconsciously*. This followed directly from his concept of repression: it was always *unacceptable strivings* that succumbed to repression and that painfully re-entered consciousness when resistances were overcome during psychoanalytic treatment. Freud collected a great deal of evidence to show that repressed wishes, banished from conscious recognition, exert a significant influence upon behavior. Probably his ideas would have met with opposition on this point even if he had never said a word about sex. We like to think of ourselves as being fully aware of our own motives; it is unsettling to learn that we may be pushed around, so to speak, by motives which are not known to us.

Freud certainly did not discover unconscious motivation. It has been known to wise people in all times. But Freud greatly enlarged our understanding of the way unconscious motives come to expression and influence the course of behavior. He showed that they could express themselves in neurotic symptoms, and he devoted some of his most detailed studies to the analysis of unconscious motivation in dreams. These studies will concern us later, but for illustration we shall glance at another phase of his work. Freud devoted considerable attention to analyzing various kinds of mistakes, not only in his patients but in himself and his friends as well. Often he was able to show that what looked like a chance error, scarcely worthy of notice, made perfectly good sense as the intrusion of an unconscious motive. He came to believe that mistakes in reading and writing, slips of the tongue, inadvertent actions, and forgetting of names and intentions very often occurred as expressions of unconscious motivation. These matters seemed so unimportant that no one had bothered to study them before; they were rather casually set down to minor slips in the machinery of behavior. But poets and other sensitive observers had long been aware of some such possibility as Freud now pointed out. In *The Merchant of Venice,* for instance, when Portia has completely lost her heart to Bassanio but is under the strictest obligation to conceal this fact, Shakespeare makes her tongue slip as follows:

> One half of me is yours, the other half yours,
> Mine own, I would say.

Many similar examples could be combed from literature, but most of us, if we stop to think of it, are already convinced that certain errors contain a measure of unconscious motivation. When a boy has to explain why he missed a date, his girl listens with little patience to stories of empty gas tanks or late buses. She adheres firmly to the theory of unconscious motivation, and Freud certainly would have agreed with her. He noticed that when his patients were in a phase of positive transference they tended to arrive on time, if not early, for their appointments. During periods of negative transference they came late and even "forgot" their appointments.

In this section of our historical survey we have been dealing mainly with Freud's discoveries, not with his theories. We have been concerned with *facts of observation,* almost all of which came to light during the process of free association: resistance, the gradual emergence of forgotten memories and wishes, the prominence of sexual wishes dating even to early childhood, the intrusion of feelings and attitudes directed toward the physician. We have dealt also with various *concepts* designed to make these facts intelligible: repression, the conflict of ego-instincts and sexual instincts, infantile sexuality, transference, the sexual theory of neurosis, and the concept of unconscious motivation used to explain such diverse observed phenomena as symptom formation, errors, and dreams. The core of his contribution was the giving of a central place to motivation. In contrast to Kraepelin, who looked for what was common to large numbers of patients in order to discover the general characteristics of their disease, he gave his attention to personal problems in all their individuality. Unlike Janet, who perceived frustrations merely as the last straws that broke down a weak nervous constitution, he traced in detail the conflict of motives and worked out the internal drama of opposing forces. Listening quietly to free associations for hours on end, he perceived his patients not as examples of brain diseases, not as victims of hereditary nervous weakness, but as troubled human beings whose strivings, hopes, fears, daydreams, and intimate feelings were mixing them up and destroying their health and happiness. The vicissitudes of motivation, and especially unconscious motivation, gave the clue to understanding the neuroses. This was the central insight needed to establish the *psychogenic hypothesis* on a sound basis.

EXPANSION OF PSYCHODYNAMICS

In Freud's time motivation was conceptualized in terms of energy and force. Instinctual energies were presumed to have their origins in bodily processes, but psychoanalysis learned about them through their mental representations. The branch of physical science that dealt with forces was called *dynamics,* and it soon became customary to refer to theories growing out of Freud's work as *psychodynamics.* The main developments in psychopathology during the first thirty or thirty-five years of the present century represent a combination of criticism and expansion of Freud's basic discoveries. In some of these developments Freud himself participated, for he continued in active work right up to his death in 1939, from time to time revising his earlier thinking. Considerable progress was also made by workers who accepted his most fundamental contentions and used the psychoanalytic method of treatment but who somehow observed things differently so that they arrived at divergent ideas, especially concerning the character of the motives and conflicts responsible for neurosis. One of the earliest and most important workers to diverge in this way from Freud was Alfred Adler, whose contribution we shall briefly examine.

Adler's Study of the Striving for Superiority. Alfred Adler (1870–1937) belonged originally to Freud's group and used Freud's methods in the treatment of neurotic patients. But as he listened to free associations his attention began to be caught by a different theme. Instead of sexual fantasies and derivatives of the sexual life of childhood, he noticed everywhere the subtle workings of a striving to dominate, degrade, and triumph over others. He found the ruling motive in neurosis to be the striving for superiority.

Obviously it is not true that neurotic patients are more domineering and assertive than other people. On the whole the opposite is nearer the truth. The neurotic striving for superiority worked by indirect and subtle means. Instead of asserting what they wanted, Adler's patients had developed neurotic symptoms which excused them from struggling directly with the world but allowed them through illness to dominate the immediate household. Through symptom formation they acquired the privileges accorded to invalids and forced other people to serve them. A patient, for example, might develop a morbid fear of going alone on the streets, thus forcing some member of the household to go with him whenever he went out. A similar motive could be read in the headaches, fatigues, even in the hysterical paralyses which put the patient to bed and obliged everyone to wait upon him. Why did these patients resort to such devious means for asserting their wills? Adler became convinced that at heart they felt inferior, weak, and inadequate: they suffered from deep *feelings of inferiority* and their illness was an attempt at *compensation.*

In looking for the source of inferiority feelings, Adler, like Freud, turned his attention to childhood. In the recollections of his patients he found an infantile striving for power just as Freud had found an infantile sexuality. If a child was made to feel inferior on account of his looks, for instance, or his capacities or his achievements, he would attempt to compensate for the felt shortcomings by proving himself in one way or another superior. He might strive for superiority along the very lines in which he felt inferior: for example, becoming an athlete after early failures in games. He might deflect the aim a little, substituting strength in school politics, for instance, for an unattainable physical strength. He might abandon altogether the activities in which he was inferior but struggle for distinction along some other line, like the frail child who, kicked around on the playground, throws his energy into getting the highest school marks. Such compensations may be entirely successful, but there are many times when they necessarily fail. The average person who harbors an inferiority complex and who struggles for compensation will find himself continually frustrated. The schoolboy is miserable unless he gets the highest marks, but try as he may he perhaps always comes out somewhere in the middle of the class. At first he over-compensates, tries so hard that he gets nervous and exhausted and cannot even do his best work. The next solution is neurosis: he falls ill, develops symptoms, stays at home, dominates his parents, and becomes the center of attention in the household. In such a fashion Adler explained the neuroses.

> Every neurosis can be understood as an attempt to free oneself from a feeling of inferiority in order to gain a feeling of superiority. The path of neurosis does not lead in the direction of social functioning, nor does it aim at solving given life-problems, but finds an outlet for itself in a small family circle, thus achieving the isolation of the patient. The exemptions and privileges of illness and suffering give the patient a substitute for his original hazardous goal of superiority.[32]

On the surface it seems as if Freud and Adler had observed selectively and concentrated their attention on quite different strivings. Actually the difference is not so much in what was observed; it was rather in the immediate inferences drawn from the observations. If we stay close to the facts and speak only of manifest strivings we shall have to agree that there are many kinds of motives. But this does not settle the problem; assumptions and concepts must be introduced in order to make a patient's behavior fully intelligible. Freud and Adler diverged at this point. Freud had shown that neurotic behavior became intelligible when one worked out the full history, from earliest childhood, of the patient's sexual strivings and assumed the persistent action of unconscious sexual motives. Adler now showed that a similar intelligibility could be reached by seizing the element of inferiority and compensation in each act of the patient and assuming the persistent working of an unconscious, or at least unnoticed, striving for superiority. When in a later chapter we study motivation systematically we shall find it possible to utilize the better elements in both conceptions. Adler made an enduring contribution to our understanding of motivation.

Neurosis in the First World War. We have traced in some detail the development of psychopathology from Charcot to Freud and Adler. In 1914 this work was barely known to the medical profession at large. Psychiatrists were schooled in the tradition of Kraepelin, trained mostly in mental hospitals, and thus knew relatively little about the neuroses and about the theories growing up around them. When the First World War broke out, the medical services of all countries were forced to recognize the widespread occurrence of neurotic breakdown under the stress of combat. Neuroses were found to be very common among military personnel. At first it was natural to look for organic causes. The word "shell-shock" came into common use, expressing the hypothesis that

[32] A. Adler, *The Practice and Theory of Individual Psychology* (New York: Harcourt, Brace & World, Inc., 1929), p. 23.

breakdown occurred because of subtle injury to the central nervous system caused by the concussion effects of violent explosions. Very soon this hypothesis was realized to be practically worthless: the majority of breakdowns occurred with no history of near-by explosion, often long before the man had reached the front lines, sometimes while he was still in training in safe locations. Out of sheer necessity the medical services were forced to take account of neurosis and of psychogenic factors behind breakdown.

In reports of war neuroses it is possible to find the counterpart of nearly every symptom or symptom-complex described in earlier writings on neurosis. All the symptoms of hysteria as described by Charcot and Janet reappeared among soldiers. Earlier we considered Janet's *monoideic somnambulism,* represented in the dramatic case of Irène. Identical symptoms occurred many times in soldiers who had passed through harrowing battle scenes and subsequently, except for brief periods of reliving, forgotten all about them. There were instances of *hysterical fugue,* comparable to Janet's case of the grocer's boy, in which men under the stress of battle or threat of danger wandered off sometimes on long journeys with a complete loss of personal identity. *Hysterical deafness, blindness, tremor,* and *paralysis* happened often, taking forms identical with civilian hysteria. Charcot, it will be recalled, had a patient whose left leg was paralyzed in a rigid clubfoot position as a consequence of stepping out of bed. Charcot cured this patient after many weeks of strenuous hypnotic suggestion, but he never found out what lay back of the illness and could think of no better explanation than a constitutional weakness of the nervous system. A French soldier in 1915 had an identical clubfoot paralysis, but under different and rather more transparent conditions. His foot was injured during training so that he was laid up for a month. As the injury healed there was no corresponding return of flexibility and mobility to the foot and leg. Complete paralysis persisted for six months until at last the patient fell into the hands of a medical officer who suspected its hysterical character. In one sitting the paralysis was removed by strong suggestions coupled with the passing of mild electrical currents through the leg.[33] Charcot's assumption of constitutional inferiority was entirely superfluous in such a case. It was merely necessary to discern the unconscious motivation—the wish to be excused from duty and danger because of illness—in order to understand this instance of hysterical paralysis.

The parallel between war neuroses and those of civilian life was by no means confined to hysteria. *Compulsive* and *obsessive states,* though somewhat less common, were not unknown under war conditions. *Anxiety*

[33] G. Roussy and J. Thermitte, *Shell Shock: Or the Psychoneuroses of War* (London: University of London Press, 1918), p. 21.

states, phobias, fatigued states, and various ailments affecting the circulatory and digestive systems were very common. Equally important was the finding that no new forms of neurosis and no wholly new patterns of symptoms made their appearance under the stress of war. It was clear that *war neuroses did not differ fundamentally from the neuroses of civil life.* Because of their relatively rapid development and simpler character they greatly hastened the understanding of neurosis in general.

The neuroses of war still further enlarged and greatly clarified what was known about motivation. Repeatedly it was discovered that even in cases where some violent incident precipitated the illness there was a long preceding history of conflict and anxiety. Collapse under battle stress occurred typically in men for whom this stress came as a "last straw" or climax to mounting irritability and anxiety. Such cases could be well described by applying Freud's concepts of conflict, repression, and the reappearance of the repressed strivings in the form of symptoms. The repressing motives correspond closely to his notion of ego-instincts, in this case the man's sense of duty and self-respect. But certainly nothing was gained by trying to reason that the repressed motives were in every case of an infantile sexual character. Adler's concepts could also be employed, especially the idea of the patient's attempting to escape through illness his hazardous responsibilities. But nothing was gained by claiming that in every case his motive was to achieve the superiority as an invalid that he could not win as a fighting man. The neuroses of war depended on a different problem of motivation. The conflict in most cases was between sense of duty and fear of death.

Anxiety as the Central Problem of Neurosis. It was natural that theories of motivation and conflict should thus branch out indiscriminately in various directions. Once the step had been taken of recognizing that personal strivings could produce results as important and troublesome as neurosis, the whole vast field of human motivation suddenly stood open for scientific study. Each investigator set forth in his own direction, and most of them turned up valuable new facts concerning the devious and complex action of human strivings.

For a while the fascination of untangling unconscious motives absorbed every worker's attention. But presently, and especially after the First World War, it became clear that something was missing in the problem of neurosis. Conflicts of motives occur in most people's lives. The psychoanalysts made a strong case that unconscious motives and unconscious conflicts act even in the lives of healthy, efficient individuals. It was necessary to find a specific point of difference between normal conflicts satisfactorily solved and neurotic conflicts solved only in the uneconomical and painful fashion of crippling symptom formation. In order to deal with this problem, attention was turned more and more to those forces in personality which Freud had called ego-instincts and which now began to be called simply the *ego*. With this shift of emphasis, interest became centered on the *defensive activities* performed by the ego in order to protect itself from pain or harm. Freud had originally conceived of repression as a means of avoiding pain. In 1926 he published an important work, *Inhibition, Symptom and Anxiety*,[34] in which he further developed this point of view. Repression, he concluded, is but one of several *defense mechanisms* directed against the emergence of unbearable impulses. What is it that makes impulses unbearable? They are unbearable when their emergence is felt as a threat and gives rise to *anxiety*. Freud arrived in this way at a much-needed simplification. Neurosis is not merely an attempt to solve conflicts among motives, conscious or unconscious. It is the outcome of *an attempt to avoid anxiety*, accomplished by the application of various rather desperate and unsuitable defense mechanisms such as repression.

Freud was led to this conclusion chiefly by a reconsideration of his civilian patients, but in thus giving the central place to anxiety and defense he brought his thinking into line with the inescapable conclusions which others had drawn from the war neuroses. The avoidance of danger was obviously a major motive in war. Involuntary defense mechanisms and the involuntary production of symptoms showed themselves with convincing simplicity. The anxiety theory could be applied with equal propriety to the sort of patient described by Adler. If feelings of inferiority were so severe and painful that they created unbearable anxiety, then the patient was driven into overcompensation—into excessive and irrational strivings for superiority—as a means of defense against anxiety. The new emphasis on anxiety thus gave unity to the divergent trends that had developed in considering the problem of neurosis.

Extension to Other Varieties of Disorder. The psychogenic hypothesis was developed and tested in work with neurotic patients, but it was clearly destined for a larger career. Before long the new insights were being extended to an increasingly wide range of human problems. The psychogenic element was sought in delinquency, criminal behavior, chronic alcoholism, drug addiction, sexual deviations, and many other serious social problems. It was sought in the more severe mental illnesses, especially the manic-depressive and schizophrenic disorders. In addition, a large number of personal *maladjustments*, not severe enough to be called neuroses, came under scrutiny as problems of psychodynamics.

One of the boldest forays made under the psychogenic banner was

[34] Translated by H. A. Bunker with the title *The Problem of Anxiety* (New York: W. W. Norton & Co., Inc., 1936).

the development known as *psychosomatic medicine.* Under the leadership of Flanders Dunbar and Franz Alexander a series of attempts was made to demonstrate a psychogenic element in bodily disorders such as ulcers, high blood pressure, asthma, skin diseases, arthritis, and migraine headaches. In these cases there is no question about the existence of a physical disorder. The symptoms do not make the anatomical nonsense that impressed Charcot in his studies of hysteria; they are real, and they must be treated by appropriate physical measures. The psychogenic element lies a little further back. Chronic personal problems throw the patient into frequent states of emotional tension, and this means that the bodily reactions that accompany emotion are severely overworked. Eventually some organ system, unequal to the perpetual stress, breaks down into a state of disease. Physical treatment may produce recovery, but relapse is to be expected unless the psychological irritants, so to speak, can be removed. In his first major report in 1934 Alexander described cases in which chronic ulcers, for instance, permanently cleared up only when psychotherapy resolved the patient's personal difficulties and thus put a stop to his enduring tension.[35] It was obvious, of course, that the psychogenic hypothesis would not explain all forms of bodily disease. Organ systems are subject to many ailments besides those that can be traced to emotional tension. Nevertheless, the psychosomatic idea today occupies an important place in the general practice of medicine, and it has staked out a large new territory for the field of abnormal psychology.

As an instance of the extension of psychodynamic concepts to milder problems, we may take the example of difficulties in school work. School failure had always been attributed to inadequate mental equipment, faulty methods of study, or a lamentable lack of the will to work. These causes are not to be lightly dismissed, but sometimes it comes out that the student's effort has been blocked by disordered personal reactions arising out of his relation to family, friends, and teachers. Perhaps he wastes hours brooding over social failures, sex, or the unjust actions of teachers and parents, or perhaps he dashes from one thing to another in an attempt to forget these problems. Even when failure is restricted to one subject, such as reading or arithmetic, the disability can occasionally be traced to a clustering of anxiety-laden associations around a particular mental operation. Failure sometimes occurs, in short, either because school work has an unconscious personal meaning that invests it with anxiety or because anxieties elsewhere in the pupil's life drain his energies away from study.[36]

[35] F. Alexander, "The Influence of Psychological Factors upon Gastro-Intestinal Disturbances," *Psychoanalytic Quarterly* (1934), pp. 501–39.

[36] See especially G. H. J. Pearson, *Psychoanalysis and the Education of the Child* (New York: W. W. Norton & Co., Inc., 1954).

Extensions of this kind eventually brought psychological thinking into direct contact with social science. The personal meaning of school work has been shown to vary with social class and with parent's interest in upward social mobility.[37] Sociologists, too, have shed new light on school failure; the *psychogenic* story cannot be complete unless the *sociogenic* story is also told. Nowhere is this more apparent than in the extension of the psychogenic hypothesis to such traditionally social problems as alcoholism and delinquency. Chronic alcoholism can be conceived as a disordered personal reaction in which alcohol is used to relieve frustration and anxiety. Yet the availability of alcohol and the social sanctions surrounding its use—things which vary a great deal in different parts of our society—clearly influence the choice of this particular method for relieving frustration and anxiety, and treatment will not proceed far if it ignores the social situation. In like fashion, cases of delinquency can often be illuminated by psychological study, but the social environment must be carefully considered both in explaining the delinquent behavior and in trying to correct it. The student of abnormal psychology can scarcely avoid becoming to some extent a student of society.

RENEWAL OF INTEREST IN SOMATIC BASES

Pinel and his enlightened contemporaries undertook to care for disordered people by measures both physical and psychological. The subsequent history of abnormal psychology has been presented here in the form of two successive major campaigns of scientific discovery. The somatic exploration started first and dominated the scene for more than half a century. The psychological search came later and reached the peak of its popularity in fairly recent years. It would be a distortion of history, however, if we failed to recognize the advance since Kraepelin of research animated by the somatogenic hypothesis. If this advance was unspectacular, producing no miracles in understanding or treating the major mental disorders, it was because so much still had to be learned about biochemistry and the physiology of the nervous system. The recent flourishing of these sciences has produced a renewed interest in the somatic bases of disordered behavior and a hopeful feeling that significant discoveries are not far away. A strong impetus has been provided by two developments in treatment.

Discovery of Treatment Through Shock. In 1929 Manfred Sakel hit upon the idea of using insulin shock as a means of treating schizophrenia. He had been working with morphine addicts, using insulin routinely to effect a mild lowering of the blood-sugar level. In certain cases a standard

[37] See especially A. B. Hollingshead, *Elmtown's Youth* (New York: John Wiley & Sons, Inc., 1949).

dose occasionally had a stronger effect, throwing the patient into shock or coma. Sakel noticed that this experience sometimes created an apparent improvement in the confused mental state of his addicts, so he tried the same experiments with confused schizophrenics. The results were startlingly good. Even after the first treatment, and more durably after several treatments, many of the patients reached altogether new levels of lucidity, so that for the first time they began to respond to psychotherapy. Sakel was insistent that the temporary gains achieved by insulin shock needed to be consolidated by appropriate psychotherapy. In this he was not always followed by later workers, some of whom convinced themselves that shock treatments alone were sufficient. Sakel's discovery, made incidentally in the course of other work, illustrates both the stumbling nature of scientific advance and the crucial importance of imagination on the part of the scientist. Insulin shock treatment was not derived from a well-developed thesis about somatic events. Quite the opposite: even after thirty-five years there is no generally accepted theory of how it works.

Overdosing with insulin is not the only way to produce shock, and other methods, less time consuming and less disagreeable for the patients, were shortly brought under investigation. Most widely used today is *electroshock*, a procedure introduced in 1938 by Cerletti and Bini in Italy. The technique consists of attaching electrodes to the head and passing controllable electrical currents through the brain. The resulting shock differs considerably from the coma produced by insulin, and the method has proved most successful with manic and depressed conditions rather than schizophrenia. In contrast to an insulin treatment, which requires several hours under constant nursing care, electroshock takes but a short time. Current is applied for only a few seconds; the patient immediately loses consciousness and there is a brief but violent convulsive reaction of his whole body. As he awakens, his mind is apt to be cloudy and his memory disturbed, but within an hour these impairments have largely passed. So brief are the confusing after-effects that electroshock is now sometimes used in office practice with patients who are not hospitalized.

To give a person a severe shock would hardly seem on the face of it a sensible way to go about curing a mental disorder. At first the roughness of the method awakened misgivings and no little opposition, but the early results were so hopeful that the technique spread rapidly from hospital to hospital and from land to land. New hopes were raised also in the minds of research workers whose interests lay in physiology and biochemistry. It seemed unlikely that shock acted wholly in a psychological way; the benefit could be more readily attributed to somatic changes which somehow counteracted an existing bodily disorder. Kraepelin's beliefs about schizophrenia and manic-depressive psychosis took a new lease of life, and there was heightened activity in the search for somatic happenings that might explain the curative properties of the new treatments.

Treatment by Means of Drugs. On the heels of treatment through shock came the discovery that mental disorders responded favorably to tranquilizing drugs. Chlorpromazine and reserpine seemed to have a beneficial effect especially upon patients who were agitated, anxious, and confused. As their feelings became more calm, their thinking became less peculiar and their relation to other people more intelligible, sometimes to the point that psychotherapy could be undertaken for the first time. Treatment with drugs is by no means perfect. Any preparation strong enough to produce a real tranquilizing effect is likely to have other effects, some of which may not be desirable. The control of these side effects is a major research problem as different drugs are compounded and tested. In spite of these difficulties, drug therapy is currently in widespread use. To some extent it has supplanted treatment through shock, although the two methods can sometimes be used in conjunction.

There is no reason to suppose that drugs, any more than shock methods, touch the fundamental causes of disorder or fortify the patient against relapse. Admitting that these particular physical methods are palliative rather than fundamental, we must nevertheless assign them a significant place in history. They have built new hope in the minds of workers whose interests lie in physiology and biochemistry. They have also given a tremendous boost to the morale of workers in mental hospitals. At last something can be done besides keeping patients comfortable and waiting for nature to take its upward or downward course. The use of drugs seems at last to have stemmed the tide of constantly growing hospital populations. It has recently been pointed out that the patient population of mental hospitals in New York State, which for some time had been increasing by 2,000 or more every year, dropped by 500 through increased discharges during the first year in which chlorpromazine and reserpine were in general use. Within the hospitals still further consequences could be observed.

> One of the most outstanding values of the use of tranquilizing drugs in mental institutions is reflected in the data on restraint and seclusion. In two years' time these figures were reduced by 75 per cent. This is only a mathematical expression of what has been a revolution in the care and treatment of mental patients.[38]

[38] H. Brill and R. E. Patton, "Analysis of 1955–56 Population Fall in New York State Mental Hospitals in First Year of Large-Scale Use of Tranquilizing Drugs," *American Journal of Psychiatry,* CXIV (1957), p. 516.

It is interesting to reflect that Pinel's mission in striking the chains from the insane has only now come close to complete fulfillment.

The revival of interest in somatogenesis reminds us that abnormal psychology has always had one foot on either side of the psychic-somatic divide. In some respects psychological understanding is today more advanced than knowledge of the body. Psychotherapy is better understood than somatic methods of treatment. Blocking of emotional development by anxiety and defense is more clearly discerned than upset of biochemical regulation by happenings in the nervous and endocrine systems. The forward march of somatic research may presently close the gap, but this will only sharpen the confrontation between psychological and physiological findings and increase the need to reconcile them in common or related concepts. Specialization in science and differences in aptitude and interest tend to create rivalry between psychogenic and somatogenic experts, each side hoping that its specialty will explain away the other. In the nature of the case, no one-sided solution is to be expected. The student should make it his goal, recognizing that abnormal psychology is inevitably a psychosomatic, biosocial discipline, to take a lively interest in problems both somatic and emotional and to develop his insight as fully as he can into both spheres.

SUGGESTIONS FOR FURTHER READING

The history of psychiatry and abnormal psychology is surveyed in detail by G. Zilboorg & G. W. Henry, *A History of Medical Psychology* (New York, W. W. Norton & Co., Inc., 1941). This thorough history begins with the earliest known ideas about medical psychology; the topics covered in the foregoing chapter are discussed in Chs. 8–11, 13, 14. A less scholarly but informative and entertaining account is given by W. Bromberg, *The Mind of Man: The Story of Man's Conquest of Mental Illness* (New York, Harper & Row, 1937), especially Chs. 6–14. Students who wish to examine the care and treatment of mentally disordered persons as an aspect of American social history, and to see the intimate relation between general social progress and progress within a single scientific specialty, will find profit in A. Deutsch, *The Mentally Ill in America* (Garden City, N. Y., Doubleday & Co., Inc., 1937). Clifford Beers' autobiography, *A Mind That Found Itself* (Longmans, Green & Co., 1908; now published by Doubleday & Co., Inc.), still retains its value and fascination not only as the fountainhead of the mental hygiene movement but also as a description of the mental state of a temporarily insane person.

The work of Mesmer, Janet, Freud, and Adler is briefly set forth by Clifford Allen, *Modern Discoveries in Medical Psychology* (2d ed., London, Macmillan & Co., Ltd., 1949), Chs. 1, 2, 4–6. No one has ever equaled Janet in the art of clinical description: *The Major Symptoms of Hysteria* (2d ed., New York, The Macmillan Co., 1920), while in several respects out of date, conjures up the excitement that originally surrounded the study of this neurosis when it was an outstanding medical mystery and leaves the reader's mind full of memorable cases. Anyone interested in tracing the progress of the theory of neurosis will want to examine Breuer & Freud's *Studies in Hysteria* (New York, Nervous & Mental Disease Publishing Co., 1936), which contains the "Breuer case," along with several others, and which sets forth the theory of abreaction.

Freud's own introduction to his work is still the most satisfactory: *A General Introduction to Psychoanalysis* (New York, Boni & Liveright, 1920; now published by Garden City Publishing Co.). It is essential to read in conjunction with this book its continuation, *New Introductory Lectures in Psychoanalysis* (New York, W. W. Norton & Co., Inc., 1933), at least Chs. 1, 3, and 4, bearing in mind that these later lectures change in several respects what is set forth in the earlier, especially Chs. 24 and 25. Many of Freud's works, including these two, have now been published as paperbacks. The scientific status of Freud's methods and findings is discussed in a symposium, *Psychoanalysis, Scientific Method, and Philosophy,* edited by Sidney Hook (New York University Press, Inc., 1959); the first three chapters, by Heinz Hartmann, Ernest Nagel, and Lawrence S. Kubie, are particularly relevant.

Adler's most systematic work was *The Neurotic Constitution* (New York, Dodd, Mead & Co., Inc., 1926), but the gist of his contribution and samples of his shrewd insight into human motives can be gathered from his numerous lesser works, such as *Understanding Human Nature* (Philadelphia, Chitton Co., 1927). A systematic presentation of his whole work, mainly in selections from his writing, is to be found in Heinz L. and Rowena R. Ansbacher's *The Individual Psychology of Alfred Adler* (New York, Basic Books, Inc., 1956). The most convenient introduction to the experience with neuroses in World War I is the work of a group of British writers edited by E. Miller: *The Neuroses in War* (New York, The Macmillan Co., 1940). The active part played by psychiatry in World War II is shown by J. R. Rees in *The Shaping of Psychiatry by War* (New York, W. W. Norton & Co., Inc., 1945).

2

Clinical Introduction: Examples of Disordered Personalities

INTRODUCTION TO THE CASES

In the first chapter the field of abnormal psychology was described as the study of disordered personal reactions to life and its circumstances. We shall now pursue this study by examining some representative examples of disorder. What does it mean to be psychologically disordered? How does it feel, and how does it express itself in behavior? What are the symptoms? What sense can be made out of a disorder, and how can its causes be untangled? The answers to these questions are complicated, the more so because here, as in every matter pertaining to personality, it is necessary to allow for a very wide range of individual differences. But for this very reason we shall get a fairer impression of the problems if we start with case histories rather than with lists of symptoms or theoretical formulations. Disordered reactions occur in people. It is important to look at them first in their natural habitat. Case histories, moreover, are the chief element in the foundation of fact upon which abnormal psychology is built.

The reader should be forewarned that the five cases described here will be frequently referred to in later chapters of the book. They display to advantage many of the problems and principles that will occupy us when we undertake to build up a systematic account of abnormal psychology. It will be assumed that the cases given in this chapter are well remembered, and with this in mind the reader should not only go through them but study and compare them rather carefully.

Main Varieties of Disorder. To gather up the matters discussed at the end of the last chapter, and to provide a framework for everything that follows, we shall begin by giving a rough classification of the main varieties of disorder.

1. Psychoses. The distinguishing mark of psychosis is a substantial loss of contact with the surrounding world. This loss of contact is often referred to as a break or withdrawal from reality. Behavior is peculiar, speech is irrational, and the patient seems to make little effort at conformity with the world and people around him. *Psychosis* is roughly equivalent to *insanity*. The psychotic person gives scarcely any evidence of realizing that he is sick. However strange his world appears to others, it is reality to him. Naturally, psychotic patients cannot manage their lives in a way satisfactory to others, and they constitute the great majority of the inmates of mental hospitals.

It was once customary to subdivide the psychoses into *organic* and *functional*. Organic psychoses were those having a known physical or organic basis; functional psychoses were those in which the disorder appeared to be the culmination of severe conflict or of lifelong poor habits of adjustment. The distinction is a useful one, but it should not be considered absolute. Some psychoses have prominent *somatogenic* elements which are probably sufficient to account for the disorder. Other cases seem to lend themselves more readily to explanation by the *psychogenic* hypothesis. More commonly it is necessary to weigh the contributions made from both sources, and nothing is gained by throwing the disorder arbitrarily into one or the other category.

2. Neuroses. In the neurotic individual there is no break with reality. The patient lives in the same world as the rest of us, but he lives there uneasily and unhappily. He is the victim of inner conflicts which show themselves in anxiety, unjustified fears, obsessions and compulsions, and hysterical symptoms such as were discussed in the last chapter. He is aware that something is wrong with him, but he does not have insight into the real basis of his problems and is thus powerless to solve them. On the whole, he conforms to social demands. His inner emotional strife is taken out upon himself in the form of symptoms and a generally self-defeating way of life.

3. Psychosomatic Disorders. The third category contains those disorders in which the patient suffers from a genuine bodily ailment of some kind but in which the ailment was originally provoked, in part, at least, by chronic conflict or emotional disturbance. The patient lives with sufficient emotional stress so that his bodily economy becomes deranged and breaks down at some point. Chronic digestive disorders, ulcers, certain kinds of high blood pressure, asthma, arthritis, and skin diseases seem to have at times a substantial psychogenic component. The conflicts and anxieties are usually, as in neurosis, concealed from the patient's awareness; typically, he feels that he would be all right if the doctor could fix up his ailing body.

4. Delinquent and Psychopathic Personalities. In contrast to the neurotic group, there are certain psychologically disordered persons who take out their troubles on the world either by actively violating its codes and conventions or by passively leading a disorganized, irresponsible, and useless life. Habitual criminals, ne'er-do-wells, chronic alcoholics, certain varieties of sexually abnormal people, can be included in this group. These individuals are not psychotic; their contact with reality is in no sense injured. Their underlying conflicts and emotional disturbances are, as we shall see later, somewhat similar to those of neurotics, but the outcome in behavior is sufficiently different to warrant putting them in a separate category.

5. Lesser Maladjustments. There are many forms of maladjustment that are less serious and less far-reaching than the four varieties of disorder just described. In order to have a place for these milder disorders, the study of which is just as profitable as that of the more serious varieties, we introduce a fifth category rather indefinitely called *lesser maladjustments.* When we speak of disorders as less serious we imply both that their effects are less crippling and that recovery is less difficult. Mild maladjustment may be a chronic condition: sometimes unsolved problems are carried along throughout life. More commonly it is a temporary state rather closely related to difficult situations, and it is often resolved by the person's own effort and insight with little or no help from outside. In general we shall reserve the expression *lesser maladjustments* for those unhappy, uneasy, poorly adapted states which yet do not involve loss of contact with reality, an array of neurotic or psychosomatic symptoms, or an habitually delinquent or disorganized way of living.

The five cases selected for study in this chapter can be regarded as roughly representative of the range of disorders. We begin with an example of adolescent maladjustment with spontaneous recovery. There are so many varieties of maladjustment that no one case can be considered typical, but the example to be described here is representative in this respect: the subject is unhappy and bewildered, at odds with himself, unable to use his capacities fully, but not so hopelessly stuck as to prevent further growth. Of our five cases, this one is the least seriously disordered. In the next two examples, a fairly severe neurosis and a case of persistent delinquency, the disorder is considerably more profound so that outside help proves necessary to change it for the better. Only in the last two cases, however, do we enter the realm of psychosis, where the patient's behavior is so peculiar and his talk so bizarre that we think of him as insane or out of his head. Roughly speaking, the five examples are arranged in order of severity. The last case, with irreparable damage to the nervous system, cannot possibly be cured.

The Student's Attitude Toward Abnormality. Many students feel a certain uneasiness when they first take up the study of abnormal psychology. Sometimes they have been told that the subject is upsetting. Perhaps they anticipate that descriptions of mental disorders and emotional conflicts will disturb and even alarm them. This uneasiness is not really justified, but the reader who feels it need offer no apology. Throughout history the behavior disorders, especially the various forms of insanity, have been viewed with suspicion and dread. This attitude lies deeply embedded in our cultural tradition, and few are wholly exempt from its subtle impress.

If seen in the proper perspective, abnormal psychology is not in the least upsetting. But it is important to keep the proper perspective. The best way to do this is to have clearly in mind, at the outset, *two important facts,* easily overlooked if one plunges heedlessly into the midst of the subject-matter: (1) that abnormal psychology deals rather largely with phenomena which are simply exaggerations of normal processes, familiar to everyone in everyday life; and (2) that it puts a one-sided emphasis on breakdown and disorder in personality.

It is naturally disconcerting to read a case history, to recognize in it many experiences that are exactly like one's own, and then to remember suddenly that one is reading about an insane person. Yet strangely enough, it is exactly this sort of experience that the student ought to have if he is to understand the nature of disordered personal reactions. These can be understood because they are made up of the common stuff of human nature; they represent the outcome, under peculiar and trying conditions, of the person's struggle to live and satisfy his deepest needs. It is to be expected, therefore, that readers whose psychological health is flawless will find much in case histories that is familiar in their own experience. Like the patients, they are struggling to live and satisfy their deepest needs. The difference is in the outcome.

There is an experience reported so often by medical students that we might facetiously refer to it as "medical students' disease." This consists of feeling vividly in themselves all the symptoms they are studying in their textbooks: distinct palpitations when they are studying disorders of the heart, ticklings of the throat and labored breathing when they read about respiratory diseases, curious pains in the abdomen when they examine pictures of gastro-intestinal ailments. The student of abnormal psychology should not be alarmed if he, too, has numerous attacks of "medical students' disease" while reading about disordered behavior. Every type of disorder has much about it that can be duplicated in the experience of perfectly healthy people, though it occurs in healthy people with less prominence and disproportion. As a matter of fact, it is most unsatisfactory to be immune to "medical students' disease." A touch of the ailment is a sign that the reader is really opening himself to his subject, trying to grasp it and feel it rather than just reading about it.

It should never be forgotten that abnormal psychology deals with inferior and unsuccessful forms of adjustment. Because of this fact, it draws a picture which tends to exaggerate failure and helplessness at the expense of successful self-direction. People are described who seem helpless in the grip of powerful forces. They appear to be at the mercy of anxieties, conflicting drives, unconscious attitudes, or subtle damage to their nervous tissue. Their behavior seems to be compelled by forces external to their better selves, so that they cannot direct their lives toward their own most cherished goals. This helplessness is not unknown to even the most healthy people. We do not live continuously at the level of our best moments, and even the most enterprising efforts slacken here and there along the way. It is important to remember, however, that most people are not helpless. Constructive activities are possible for them so that they overcome the main difficulties in their path. A course in abnormal psychology may encourage a person to start assessing his liabilities. Reading about symptoms, anxieties, defenses, moods, and other psychological liabilities, he will find plenty of them in himself. He should always remember that abnormal psychology does not offer a parallel opportunity for assessing his assets. There is no classification of the chief varieties of heroism, fortitude, and persistence in the face of obstacles; there are few careful case histories of magnificent behavior in shipwrecks and fires, on dangerous military missions, or under circumstances of prolonged severe stress. It is our purpose in this book to compare the abnormal with the healthy, wherever possible, but the material upon which we draw is necessarily weighted on the side of breakdown and failure.

1. AN ADOLESCENT MALADJUSTMENT: JOSEPH KIDD

Our first example is a young man bearing the fictitious name of Joseph Kidd.[1] During his high-school and college years he became progressively more and more maladjusted. Most of the time he was extremely unhappy and more or less incapacitated for serious effort. He did not, however, directly seek professional advice. He was a volunteer subject for a series of personality studies being conducted at a university psychological

[1] R. W. White, *Lives in Progress: A Study of the Natural Growth of Personality* (New York: Holt, Rinehart & Winston, Inc., 1952), chap. v.

clinic. It is likely that he volunteered for this work in the hope of increasing his self-understanding, thus mastering his own troubles, but he never entered the status of a patient nor received treatment beyond occasional friendly advice. The following description draws heavily upon his own account of his life, partly as he wrote it and partly as he gave it in interviews.

Present Difficulties. At his lowest point, during his junior year at college, Joseph Kidd suffered from acute distress in all relations with people. He was bothered by severe self-consciousness, feeling always a painful uncertainty as to his standing in the opinion of others, and with this went an irresistible submissiveness designed to avoid conflict with people and win their favor. He could neither control this submissiveness nor accept it. If anyone showed him friendliness he immediately, as he put it, "began acting like his son or kid brother," but he was ashamed of this afterwards and wished that he could behave like a man. "I can't make a decision on my own and back it up," he wrote at one point; "it's always guided by some factor outside my own intellect." With his girl he was equally troubled. He was completely dependent on her affection and very jealous if she so much as danced with somebody else. Realizing that he acted toward her "too much like a spoiled child, crying for my own way," he yet could not bring himself to take a more manly and independent attitude. In consequence it became increasingly clear that the girl was bored with him and did not really respect him.

Why did he not take a different attitude? He wanted to, and there was every inducement to do so, but in this respect he was not free. The pattern of his personality was such as to resist this particular change. He expected people to give him a great deal of easy appreciation; when they did not do so, he was worried and hungrily asked for it. Kidd felt that he had no personality of his own, and he tried the following rather desperate expedient:

> I began trying to fit a personality to my make-up. I began acting out personalities, and tried observing people and copying them. But these personalities were all short-lived because they pleased some and not others and because they didn't produce that underlying purpose of making people like me; and every time, unconsciously, I would resort to my childish attitude to make myself noticeable. Examples of these personalities are independence (but I couldn't keep it up); arrogance (but people were arrogant back at me); hatefulness (people paid no attention to me); extreme niceness (people took advantage of it, kidded me about it); humorous nature (but I was only being childish, silly); quiet and studious (but people were only passing me by and I kept feeling I was missing something). I became a daydreamer so intensively that now I find I'm daydreaming almost all the time. I became conscious of a person's approach and would become flustered, would try to make a friend of him no matter who he was, but I overdid it.

Clearly Kidd's problem was not an unusual one. It is a universal problem to develop adult independent attitudes. Everyone learns from experience how to adapt successfully to the people around him; everyone finds out gradually what roles are congenial to himself and others. It is also a universal problem to develop a stable conception of oneself, an enduring sense of personal identity. Kidd's case is peculiar not in kind but in degree. It will be noticed that he was satisfied with a "personality" only if it pleased everybody; he was unwilling that anyone should fail to notice and like him. From his own description we can see that he was making a frantic search for affectionate esteem. His overwhelming motive was to make people like him, and his well-practiced method, when all else failed, was to make himself noticeable. Failure cast him into despondency and alarm. At times he lapsed into passive daydreaming, but at other times he struggled to learn new and more appropriate attitudes. Eventually, as we shall see, his struggle met with success.

Personal History. Whenever it appears that a disorder lies in the sphere of motives and the acquired methods for satisfying them, we must look for enlightenment in the past history. Joseph Kidd was the second son of hard-working, socially ambitious parents. He was a very pretty child with blue eyes and long golden curls, far more attractive than his older and younger brothers. His delighted parents showered him with notice and praise. His early memories were crowded with scenes in which he was patted on the head, dressed up, shown off, placed in the center of attention; once the teacher stood him on her desk so that all the pupils might see his new velvet suit with lace collar. He basked happily in this warm light of admiration. The effect on his subsequent development was not so happy. For one thing, his constant exposure to the eyes and praises of other people laid the foundation for that intense self-consciousness which later harassed him. For another thing, he was receiving praise for gratuitous qualities—for good looks and fine clothes, or at best for slight accomplishments—so that he felt little incentive to work for what he got. He formed an habitual expectation of high esteem income received at no greater cost than making himself noticeable.

In school Kidd progressed well, and through the machinations of his ambitious mother he was given a double promotion from the fourth to the sixth grade. This put him in the same class as his older brother and automatically made him the youngest and smallest of his immediate group. To keep up his popularity he fell into the role of what he called "a clown and a stooge"; he made the other boys laugh and did errands for them. Entering high school in a distant neighborhood, he found these roles no longer productive of esteem. His income in this respect was sharply lowered when he realized that his new companions were contemptuous of his childish ways. Filled with resentment at this turn of events, he began to feel that everyone was against him, so he withdrew from sports and social activities and spent his time at home listening to the radio. He experienced great shame over masturbation, which further increased his feeling of inferiority and unwillingness to mingle with others. Even his interest in studies dwindled, so that he barely passed his examinations for college.

At college he found nothing in the curriculum that awakened enduring interest. His failure to make friends soon cost him the esteem of his parents, who looked upon college as a means of social advancement and compared him unfavorably with his sociable brothers; in addition, he seriously offended his parents by espousing the theory of evolution which they considered at variance with their religious faith. As we have seen, his girl began to withhold her esteem. He sought consolation in promiscuous sexual episodes, which gave him at least a momentary feeling that he was acceptable as a man and could get what he wanted. But when he regaled his fellow students with these proofs of his enterprise and manhood, he got much less admiration than he expected. He who had been rich was now indeed destitute of esteem.

Spontaneous Recovery. Under these circumstances it is not surprising that his mediocre academic record went completely to pieces and that he was presently looking for a job. It was at this point that his suffering was most acute and that he fully realized the failure of the various "personalities" he had been trying to assume. After a while, however, things began to go more favorably. He took the step of leaving home to escape the now irksome parental supervision, and he parted with his girl. He found a small business position, acquitted himself well, and enjoyed the company of other young people in the office, most of whom were college graduates. It was a white-collar job which met his parents' social expectations, so that he was somewhat restored in their favor. He resumed his interest in sports and began to read instead of daydreaming. Another girl came upon the scene. Starting the relation on a better footing, he was soon the happy recipient of a fair esteem income from her. His life was again moving forward, and he began to be mildly satisfied with himself.

Having made a good work record for a year, he was permitted to return to college. Ultimately he graduated, but at the cost of a setback in his personal development. Many of the old problems reappeared, particularly his distaste for study and his hunger for the good opinion of his fellow students. When he entered military service it was with a decided sense of relief: at last he could put school behind him and silence his parents' clamor for further professional training. As a private in a health survey unit he was not exposed to the dangers of combat, and he found great satisfaction in the comradeship of the other men in the unit. He resumed the social growth that had been brought to a standstill by his double promotion at school and subsequent estrangement from other boys. He became more assertive, but not to the point of welcoming the role of officer, in which he did so badly that he was at one point demoted. "I like to be *with* other fellows," he said, "not *over* them." Some years later he looked back to his period in the Army as the happiest time in his life.

Returning to the family home, he was at first immersed in some of the old conflicts, but the changes in his personality proved to be enduring. He was no longer at the mercy of parental desires, nor was he enslaved by his hunger for esteem. When an opportunity arose to reorganize his father's dwindling business he took charge of the project and carried it to a successful conclusion. This accomplishment substantially increased his self-respect as well as his income of esteem from others; it also permitted him to feel that he had repaid his parents for their earlier sacrifices on his behalf. Throughout these developments his environment was fairly kind to him, but he displayed initiative and took an active part in overcoming his difficulties. Under moderately favorable circumstances he proved capable of developing new channels for satisfying his needs and promoting his growth. It is this that distinguishes Kidd's maladjustment from the more severe psychological disorders shortly to be described.

What do we learn from this case? How did it happen that Joseph Kidd became a maladjusted, unhappy young man during his college years? How did it transpire that he worked his way back to a reasonable state of adjustment and happiness? In a rough sort of way we might say that we know already, just from reading the history up to this point. But the processes involved are of such central importance in the whole theory of adjustment and maladjustment that we cannot afford to leave our understanding of them in too rough a stage. Two points need further consideration: the part played by Kidd's *range of abilities* in determining his difficulties, and the *problem of motivation and learning* involved both in his maladjustment and in his recovery from it.

Contribution of the Range of Abilities. The range and pattern of abilities play an important though often silent part in steering the growth of personality. Assessment of abilities is rapidly becoming an essential feature of the clinical study of disordered people. There is evidence that Kidd's natural endowment contributed significantly to his maladjustment. We can best grasp this contribution by considering, in addition to the things he did, the things he did not do. There were always various possibilities besides the ones he chose. Some youngsters, for instance, would have refused to take the role of "clown and stooge," preferring to hurl themselves actively into sports, even at a disadvantage in size, and become known as "scrappy little fellows." This would require exceptional physical endowment, and Kidd's physique, while vigorous and equal to most sports, was a trifle too sluggish for so energetic a solution. Others, in withdrawing from social participation, might have turned to craftsmanship, artistic pursuits, or mechanical interests, such as learning to build radio sets, thereby developing new interests which might ultimately return them to a position of esteem. Kidd seemed to possess no natural inclination in any of these directions; when at home he sat in a chair and merely listened to the radio. Some people who meet frustration in social life throw their energies strongly into intellectual pursuits, finding new sources of interest and new ways of displaying excellence. Why did not Kidd become interested in his college studies? Again, why did he not progressively transform the role of clown into the role of wit, so that he could have retained an acceptable position as one who contributes to laughter and merriment? These last two questions find a partial answer in his mental endowments which were not such as to encourage either solution. In various intelligence tests he revealed little of the quick flexibility of mind that is necessary for wit. The limit of his possible success along this line was reached in the "raising cain and acting silly" that he described in high school. The tests also showed distinct limitations in reasoning, associative thinking, and power of organization, although his over-all scores were not much below the average for college students. This particular pattern of intellectual endowments does not preclude going through college, but it rarely leads to the development of lasting intellectual interests. General ideas and theoretical reasoning are grasped too laboriously—one might say too uncomfortably—to yield an enduring satisfaction.

When we consider the range of Kidd's abilities and temperamental peculiarities it appears that he was meant, so to speak, for social life, affectionate relations, and perhaps a modest business career. These were the lines of his natural excellence. His resources did not invite him to grow in other directions.

A Problem in Motivation and Learning. However important the contribution of natural endowments, we may consider them secondary to Kidd's central problem, his progressive failure to find satisfaction for a compelling and all-pervasive need for affectionate esteem. It is necessary to consider how this need became so strong, how it became associated with certain action patterns or habits, why these habits eventually failed to yield satisfaction, and why it was so difficult—for a time almost impossible—to acquire new habits and establish new channels which would provide the much needed esteem. The critical point is the adolescent period when new learning for a time failed and finally succeeded. Dependent as we are on current observation and the young man's own narrative, we cannot be absolutely certain of what happened, but the following seems a likely reconstruction of the history.

During his early years Kidd enjoyed very high gratification in the form of affectionate esteem. As the center of admiring attention he became accustomed to expect a large income of appreciation from those around him and to stand out as a quite special person. His desire was thus strengthened by repeated reward. Because the praise came so easily he was not obliged to learn difficult action patterns: it was sufficient to call attention to himself and cry or whine for what he wanted. When he was promoted in school and became the youngest of his group his income of esteem was sharply threatened, but he developed two new esteem-seeking patterns, playing the "clown" and being the "stooge," and was again able to feel himself well liked. But this success was only temporary. On entering high school with its new demands he was again in the position of either having to accept a greatly diminished esteem income or finding new ways of behaving that would win his companions' liking.

To live without esteem was impossible. The esteem of others is apt to be a strong and central motive in anyone's life, and in Kidd's case the desire had been strengthened by excessive reward. When frustrated it acted like a hunger; in fact, there is a close analogy between Kidd's desperate trying out and discarding of different "personalities" and the behavior of a hungry animal in a puzzle box trying out one random action after another and quickly discarding each unrewarded response. Kidd's responses were unrewarding partly because of the impossibly high level of reward to which he had become accustomed. As a small child he had been, to borrow a phrase from the movies, the "great smash hit" of his family and neighborhood. When his school companions and his parents themselves began to treat him as if he were merely an average boy he felt as if nobody valued him or cared for him at all. But we must bear in mind also that his attempted "personalities" probably received little actual reward because they were carried out without practiced skills and in some cases without the help of natural abilities. He was a blundering amateur at expressing arrogance and hatefulness, and he was poorly equipped to play the humorous or the quiet and studious roles. The conditions for new learning were not favorable.

A further complication in the learning process was the presence of a conflicting motive in the form of hostility. In his reports, and especially in tests of fantasy, he gave evidence of considerable anger toward people who did not esteem him. When you want people to like you and when at the same time you are angry with them, the situation is peculiarly frustrating. Efforts to win esteem are disturbed by the conflicting motive of wanting to pay off or hurt the person who is so niggardly with his appreciation. It was apparently this conflict from which Kidd at times retreated into solitude and daydreaming. Fortunately the hostility was not so strong as to prevent fairly frequent attempts at new social growth. It is also likely that his distaste for college studies sprang in part from resentment against his parents, who insisted that he climb the hard ladder to success but showed no appreciation of what this might be costing him. Here his salvation lay in resisting parental ambitions and finding his own way of life.

Kidd's improvement came when he again began to experience reward. New and more appreciative girl friends, social growth during military service, success in business ventures, gradual restoration to parental favor, all rescued him from the famine of his college years and provided him with rewards sufficient to bring about the learning of more appropriately mature patterns of behavior. The process of recovery, like the process of maladjustment, thus appears in the light of a problem in motivation and learning. We can understand the case of Joseph Kidd when, making due allowance for the range of his abilities, we unravel the history of those learnings that served his need for affectionate esteem and when we work out the conditions under which new learning had to be undertaken.

2. A NEUROSIS PRECIPITATED BY COMBAT STRESS: PEARSON BRACK

Our second example is a young man whom we shall call Pearson Brack, a member of the United States Army Air Forces.[2] At the time when his difficulties began he was serving as a B-25 bombardier in the Tunisian theater of operations in World War II. He was referred to his Flight Surgeon because on his tenth and eleventh bombing missions he was found to have fainted when the airplane reached an altitude of 10,000 feet. That something was wrong with him became evident to other members of the airplane crew who tried in vain to communicate with him over the interphone. Brack himself was aware only of having felt cold and sleepy and then waking up to find himself leaning on the bomb sight.

Narrow Escape from Death. The two missions on which Brack had fainted were his first after a period of four weeks in the hospital. During his ninth mission he had sustained an injury when the airplane narrowly escaped disaster. The mission was an important one in support of ground forces which were engaged in very hard fighting. On the way to the target

[2] This case is taken from R. R. Grinker and J. P. Spiegel, *Men Under Stress* (Philadelphia: The Blakiston Co., 1945), pp. 197–206. To make the cases in this chapter easier to recall, fictitious names are assigned to all of them.

considerable flak and fighter opposition were encountered, but the bombers passed through without damage. Several planes flying in formation were approaching their target when without any warning Brack's plane jolted and rolled over, then began to fall. The dive seemed to go on forever. Fortunately the pilot regained control just in time to avoid crashing on the ground and was able to bring the ship back into formation and resume the mission. During the plane's fall Brack was thrown violently against the bomb sight, receiving such a heavy blow on the left side of his chest that he at once began to cough up blood. In spite of this he was able to release his bombs on the target and the mission was successfully completed.

On return to the home field Brack was sent to the hospital on account of his injury. At the end of four weeks his symptoms had disappeared and he was returned to full duty. It was on the next two missions that the fainting occurred.

Signs of Repressed Anxiety. Because of the recent history the Flight Surgeon assumed that Brack might be suffering from some residual organic defect which caused his fainting at higher altitudes. This seemed highly improbable to the medical board which reviewed the case, and the question arose whether or not the fainting might be connected with anxiety. Fainting is the result of anoxia—insufficient supply of oxygen through the blood stream to the brain—and this in turn may occur as one of the normal bodily accompaniments of fear. The psychiatrist accordingly undertook to discover whether Brack was suffering from anxiety when flying. In view of what had occurred on the ninth mission it seemed not unlikely that his confidence had been shattered. When interviewed, however, Brack denied that he felt anxious during flights. He laughed at the idea and said that he had never been afraid of anything. He was proud of his skill as a bombardier and impressed with the importance of his work. His attitude was carefree and jocular, confident and aggressive; he wanted to return to combat flying and asked only that he be assigned to a unit that would not fly above 9,000 feet. Even when shown that such an assignment was quite impracticable he continued to demand it with rather childlike insistence.

Although the interview failed to elicit a direct admission of anxiety, certain features of Brack's behavior suggested latent uneasiness. There were two such signs: his stubborn insistence on an impractical assignment, and a somewhat theatrical, overplayed impression created by his attitude of jocular confidence. It was determined to try another means of testing him, a pentothal interview. This technique consists of placing the patient in a quiet semidarkened room and injecting sodium pentothal, a narcotic which produces a sleepy, dream-like but talkative state. In this state the patient can be reminded of previous incidents in his life which he then sometimes recalls with all the vividness of dreams, in fact of present realities. If emotion was involved in the incident, this emotion now breaks forth in all its original strength, the whole experience being lived over again with great dramatic intensity. With Brack, however, the pentothal interview produced no outburst of anxiety. He described the ninth mission in great detail, talking with various members of the crew as if he were actually there again, but he remained completely calm and unemotional. The only hint of buried fear was a sort of aside in which he urged the crew to keep on going even though he himself would surely die if they did so. From this remark one could infer a deep conviction that he would die on a mission, but after awakening from the drug Brack had not the slightest idea what his words could have meant.

Still unconvinced, the psychiatrist tried a third experiment. He accompanied Brack on a practice flight to observe his reactions while in the air. On the way to the field and during the early stages of the flight the bombardier was exceedingly talkative and full of jokes, showing a forced cheerfulness that sounded very much like whistling in the dark. His confidence lasted only until the airplane reached an altitude of 10,000 feet. Then he began to tremble all over, his face appeared pale and drawn, and his breathing became faster and faster. He denied fear but said that he felt sleepy and shut his eyes for long moments. He was ordered to breathe slowly and deeply, by which means fainting was prevented during the fifteen minutes that the altitude was maintained. When the plane came down to 8,500 feet he became alert again, his tremor ceased, and his cheerful confidence reappeared.

It now seemed more than ever certain that Bombardier Brack was suffering from anxiety rather than organic injury. But the patient was still completely resistant to any such interpretation. The doctor might think what he pleased; he himself knew that the after effects of his injury made him faint. Under these circumstances—strong resistance and conviction of organic illness—psychological methods of treatment are clearly out of the question. The patient is not ready or able to cooperate and there is no way to force him to do so. Defending himself against the recognition of his own anxiety, he does not feel the need for help in overcoming it. The psychiatrist accordingly recommended a trial return to duty. Brack completed another mission, performing his duties efficiently over a rough target, but he returned covered with perspiration and so completely exhausted that his Flight Surgeon referred him again to the hospital. Another doctor made the diagnosis of possible heart damage. Brack was told that he should not fly again for six months, but that with proper rest his heart condition would surely clear up within that time. He was well pleased with this news. The previous forced bravado gave place to a calm cheerfulness. This time the medical board returned him to the United States for further observation and treatment.

Change of Symptoms After Return Home. Pearson Brack left the theater of war in good spirits, but as soon as he reached home his mood began to change. Although he enjoyed his leave with his wife and child, as time went on he felt increasingly nervous and increasingly depressed. He was troubled by nightmares of falling in an airplane. He was also troubled by self-reproach because he had not been able to complete his tour of duty overseas, and it was this thought that made him feel most depressed. As his symptoms seemed to be increasing he was admitted, pale, tense, and unhappy, to a convalescent hospital where he found himself confronting the same psychiatrist, transferred in the meantime to the United States. He admitted at once that the doctor had been right about his nervousness overseas although he himself had not then recognized it.

The situation was now completely changed: no longer cheerful and confident, the patient felt the need for help and begged the doctor to make him feel the way he did before he ever went overseas. But as he could not attach any content to his anxiety it was decided to try another pentothal interview. When thoroughly sleepy he was told that he was on a bombing mission, and he began to talk as follows:

> Going up to North Italy . . . have to take evasive action—flak and fighters around—plenty of evasive action—got to have it. Well, the plane suddenly shook, pulled up back of three other ships, rolled over on its back . . . falling down . . . down . . . down . . . down . . . down we fell, falling down . . . falling down, fast, faster . . . faster . . . faster. I didn't expect it. We came out of it, but I was hurt—my chest hurt bad—my head was hurting—I was scared. Me scared! I didn't think I'd ever be scared—didn't think any man could scare me. I felt our cause was much bigger. Pilot wanted to go back, but I wouldn't let him. We had a job to do. Boys . . . our boys were having trouble on the ground—our boys, our infantry—we had to go. Every bomb had to count. If we turned back they wouldn't count. We dropped them——hit the target—smackeroo! Banzai!! Chest was hurting, spitting blood—didn't like the sight of blood.

It was now abundantly clear that Brack's fainting was the outcome of a struggle with mounting anxiety generated by his panic on the ninth mission. Brack did not realize this simply as a result of one pentothal experience. It was only after several interviews, one more of which included the use of pentothal, that he finally admitted being very scared of flying. "I know it now, but I didn't know it before," he said. "I know I'm scared of falling in an airplane. I am really worried about a lot of things and I don't like to admit it." As soon as he realized the full force of his terror it was possible for him to work toward recovery. He could be shown that his fear was a very natural reaction to the danger to which he had been exposed. He could realize that he need not feel disgraced by his failure to complete a tour of duty, that what had happened was involuntary, and that he would get over his difficulties. As he gradually grasped the full import of these things his depression disappeared and his nervousness subsided. He hoped that he would be sent back to flying so that he might finally conquer his fear.

In actual fact it was decided to assign the patient to ground duty rather than returning him to the air. The basis for this decision lay in an estimate of his ultimate strength, not so much a constitutional stability as the strength he had developed in the course of his life experience. We must admit that Brack had strength, even though we describe his reaction as neurotic. Not everyone could have dropped bombs accurately on a target a few minutes after staring straight into the face of death and while spitting blood from a painful injury. Not everyone could have forced himself to enter a plane for another mission. If he had not been exposed to combat he might have gone through life without ever breaking down. But Brack's reaction was still not adequate, and the question of whether or not he could endure combat stress in the near future hinged on the nature of those habits of reaction acquired earlier in life which formed his present personality. The central problem in his case was his inability to admit weakness, to others or to himself. If he had become afraid of flying, why could he not simply say so instead of starting an internal, unconscious conflict that ended in fainting and depression? American airmen are thoroughly instructed about anxiety so that most of them are prepared both to feel and admit it. Why was Brack unable to avail himself of this enlightened attitude?

Brack's case displays to advantage certain of the mechanisms that are common in neurosis, notably repression and symptom formation. It also displays the embeddedness of the neurotic reaction in the personality as a whole. To understand why he could not admit weakness we have to look into his personal history much as we did in the case of Joseph Kidd.

Repression and Symptom Formation. Brack was terrified when the plane fell on his ninth mission. The whole basis of his confidence was shaken by the unexpected danger. But he could not admit this shortcoming in himself; something inside him required that he should take measures of defense against the weakness that had suddenly appeared. This something inside him we shall call his ego-ideal, the image of himself as a courageous, responsible man whom nobody could scare. The defensive process consisted of denying that he was afraid and strengthening his outward attitude of jocular confidence which, however, showed the effects of this extra strain by its forced and theatrical character.

His denial was not simply a conscious concealment from others; the anxiety was actually repressed out of his own awareness. His behavior during treatment displayed precisely the sequence of events that led Freud to his original formulation of the concept of repression: prolonged resistance against admitting the presence of an inferior motive, final emergence of that motive into consciousness, feelings of painful humiliation at such a blow to his "ethical, aesthetic, and personal pretensions," in short, to his ego-ideal.

Brack's system of defense worked successfully so long as the anxiety did not become too acute, but when he went into the air and when the plane rose to a higher altitude the reminders of dangers became too forceful and something had to break. When the physical symptoms of anxiety—trembling, palpitation, rapid breathing—became urgent, and when panic threatened to invade consciousness, there was no solution except to faint. The symptom of fainting served a definite purpose: it allowed him to preserve his ego-ideal by not recognizing his terror. Brack emerged from his faints feeling confident, assured that some organic ailment had temporarily knocked him out. Actually he was knocking himself out by suppressing his anxiety until anoxia occurred. On the practice flight the symptom of fainting was blocked by the psychiatrist's commands to breathe slowly. That the symptom was produced in this way, that it served an immediate purpose, and that it afterwards served to get him out of combat, should not lead us to accuse the bombardier of voluntary deception. Like most neurotic symptoms his fainting was wrought in panic; it was a completely involuntary protective device. He did not have to faint in order to be grounded. Airmen were constantly grounded because overt anxiety rendered them unfit to perform their duties. The special achievement of this symptom was to prevent him from recognizing that he, Pearson Brack, who did not think anything could scare him, had been on the brink of panic.

We are thus dealing with a man who simply could not admit to himself that he was too scared to carry out his tour of fifty missions and that he could not meet the responsibilities imposed on him by the war. To learn how his ego-ideal assumed so uncompromising a form we need to reconstruct its history.

History of the Ego-Ideal. The most natural starting point for a boy's ego-ideal is identification with his father. Pearson Brack's father was a drunkard. In the face of any difficulty or family problem he took refuge in alcohol. But there was a grandfather, a distinguished physician, who set a contrasting example of stable responsible living. As Pearson grew up he felt the need for his father's companionship and support; he described himself as lonesome for a father. But this need was not satisfied, and during adolescence he became more and more a "spoiled brat" who tried to get everything the easiest way without accepting responsibility. One day his grandfather took him aside and gave him a serious talk, saying that if he did not learn to work hard and take responsibility he would grow up to be just like his father. After this talk Pearson made an abrupt change in his way of life. Though busy with high school studies he followed his grandfather's suggestion of obtaining an evening job and began to support himself. He rejected his father's example and modeled an ego-ideal after his grandfather; this entailed, besides supporting himself, an attempt to play the part of a good father toward his younger brother.

These facts were given in interviews. To understand their importance we must resort to hypothesis. For Pearson, we can assume, the statement that he would be like his father was anything but an idle threat. He had undoubtedly lived through a series of exasperating situations in which the father earned universal contempt by passing into a drunken stupor instead of helping meet the crisis. When the grandfather plainly showed him the likeness between this contemptible picture and his own "spoiled brat" adolescent behavior Pearson was suddenly and strenuously motivated to do something different. He began at once to live according to an ideal of self-sufficiency and responsibility. Apparently he was successful, and when he entered military service he expanded the ideal to include the carefree, fearless airman who completes his assignments and thus discharges his responsibility to his country. We can make the guess that failure possessed for him a peculiarly disagreeable meaning. If he could not complete his tour of duty, he was not only letting down his country and showing himself inferior to his comrades; he was also proving that he was no better than his father and would never amount to anything in any sphere of life. Failure to meet his ego-ideal meant total and final personal failure.

The uncompromising nature of Brack's ego-ideal can thus be related to the peculiar part it had played in his personal history. We may note further that the conditions under which his ego-ideal was built were not such as to give it mature strength. It was adopted suddenly, much as an actor adopts a part, but then, because the grandfather could not be around to reward him with approval, it became a burdensome duty which did not satisfy or displace those more dependent tendencies suggested by his previous disorganized behavior and by his statement that he was lonesome for a father. Under these circumstances an ego-ideal tends to produce an imitation of responsible behavior rather than becoming a firm, well-integrated structure. Even when he entered the service Brack's carefree and aggressive attitude was only an imitation of what some airmen truly feel. We can use the metaphor that his courage was brittle rather than tough; it was shattered rather than merely injured by his harrowing experience. These considerations influenced the psychiatrist in deciding to keep Brack on ground duty even after his nervousness and depression had cleared.

The change in his symptoms after his return to the United States can probably be understood in the following way. The immediate pressure of danger was lifted, but he had to consider an ultimate return to combat. Apparently the removal of the fundamental conflict into the future relaxed the whole system of defense just enough to let anxiety creep into his dreams and into his waking behavior in the form of nervousness. This necessarily brought about depression, a feeling of self-reproach because he had not been able to perform his whole duty, and back of this a deep humiliation because, like his father, he had failed in responsible behavior. This loosening of the conflict between anxiety and his ego-ideal gave just the needed opportunity for the psychiatrist to assist his insight and give him the encouragement necessary to restore his confidence and self-respect.

3. A PERSISTENT BUT UNSUCCESSFUL CRIMINAL CAREER: BERT WHIPLEY

The young man who will next occupy our attention differs in many respects from the two foregoing examples. The most important difference lies in his attitude toward society. Unlike Joseph Kidd and Pearson Brack, who struggled painfully to adapt themselves to society as they found it, this youth rebelled against social obligations and for a dozen years has conducted a losing battle with the forces of law and order. Economic circumstances played a part in shaping his criminal career, but as we look into his history we find many instances of misguided, self-defeating behavior which point to an underlying psychological disorder.

Example of a Bungled Crime. Our subject, whom we shall call Bert Whipley, comes to professional attention because of a remarkable series of events that occurred one week end during the summer when he was twenty-three. Early one Saturday morning, having completed his sentence on several charges involving larceny of cars and burglary, he was given his release from the State Reformatory. His sister was waiting to take him home. On the way they stopped to call on a young married woman with whom they were both well acquainted. Before his imprisonment Bert and this young woman had spent considerable time together, with a rather one-sided result: she fell in love with him, but his emotions remained somewhat confused. During his stay at the Reformatory she expressed her devotion by visits and frequent letters. On this particular Saturday she declared herself eager to leave her husband and suggested that she and Bert go together to a distant part of the country where they might both find jobs and start a new life. Bert's replies were evasive and noncommittal. After the call he and his sister drove home to join their parents and several brothers and sisters, the Whipleys being a very large family. The rest of the day was spent contentedly enough, but by evening Bert felt restless and tired of talk, so he made a solitary round of several bars. Next day, a hot summer Sunday, the whole family went to a lake to swim and did not return until late afternoon. Toward dusk Bert wandered off by himself, found a car parked with the keys in it, and drove away on a main road leading out of the city.

He had gone about seven miles when he became aware of a car overtaking him and heard the challenging sound of its horn. Terrified, he put on all possible speed and swung out to pass the car ahead. He was approaching a curve around which another car suddenly burst into view. To avoid a collision Bert swerved off the road, coming to a jolting stop in a potato field. The pursuing car turned in after him and he immediately gave himself up to the men who stepped out. Almost at once he discovered that these men were not police officers, as he had supposed; they were the owners of the potato field returning to their farmhouse. But it was too late to escape. In the first breath he had admitted stealing the car, and he was turned over to the police.

This time Bert Whipley was sentenced to State Prison, but while awaiting transfer he managed to escape from the county jail, located downtown in his home city. To avoid detection before darkness fell, he slipped into a near-by moving picture theatre where he sat trembling and shaking every time someone came down the aisle. Driven out by his own restlessness before dark, he made his way along the main street of the city hoping to reach a safe place where he could telephone to a friend to bring him a different suit of clothes. Caution demanded that he go by side streets and back alleys, but he wandered for half a mile along the central thoroughfare until he was picked up by the police. He received an addition to his sentence and landed in State Prison with four to six years staring him in the face.

What is the explanation of this curiously self-defeating behavior? When we consider all the circumstances it is not surprising that he turned again to crime. There was very little to induce him to "go straight." His previous experience with job hunting consisted mainly of having doors slammed in his face, and now, stigmatized as a convict, his chances were even poorer. His home was crowded and noisy; we can already judge from his behavior on that first evening that he found it disagreeable and irritating. It was much easier, skilled as he was in burglary, to fill his pockets quickly and go far away with his devoted girl friend. Burglary was his purpose when he stole the car and began the ill-fated drive that ended in a potato field.

That he preferred such a course to the miserable prospect of job hunting is easily understood, but what are we to make of his failure to carry out his criminal program? Judging from the criminal's point of view he could hardly have made a worse mess of it. Quite without justification he assumed that a car behind him on the road was in pursuit; he lost his nerve, wrecked the stolen car, and surrendered himself to civilians who had not the slightest intention of punishing him. Later he escaped from jail but concealed his whereabouts so poorly that it was an easy matter for the police to find him. He wants to be a criminal but he virtually brings about his own punishment, an inconsistency that points to severe internal conflict.

Examination of the Patient in Prison. Suppose we visit the prison and look first at the prisoner's record. He made his first appearance in court at the age of seven, charged with "malicious mischief"—breaking windows in a school building. At fourteen he was arrested on various charges of stealing and was sentenced to the State Reform School. When he left reform school he went to another state where he was soon in its reformatory on charges of burglary and larceny. After serving his sentence there he returned to his native state, resumed burglary and larceny, and earned himself a long sentence in the State Reformatory. During nine years, up to the age of twenty-three, he was at liberty in the community for only twenty-two months. No self-respecting criminal would have any patience with such a record. Bert Whipley must have bungled many an enterprise before the episode with which we are familiar.

When we turn to the prisoner himself we find a mild-mannered young man of rather slight build and a somewhat anxious but intelligent expression. His general intelligence, as measured by various tests, is equal to that of the average college student. Serious literary interests appear in his conversation: besides good current literature he is reading Montaigne's *Essays,* and he tells us that his favorite book is Dostoievsky's *Crime and Punishment.* We discover that he has served as librarian at the Reformatory and that he is remarkably skilled in certain lines of craftsmanship. At any sign of interest in his work, however, he becomes self-critical and pronounces his efforts entirely worthless. This attitude of self-contempt proves to be pervasive. If we ask him about himself he quotes the opinions of the prison authorities to the effect that he is lazy, stubborn, disinclined to take courses and improve himself, unwilling even to learn a trade; and he does not seem to entertain any different opinion of his own. He tells somewhat guardedly about his various crimes, admitting that he has often been careless, thus contributing to his own capture. When he plans a burglary it never occurs to him that he might fail, but he becomes tremendously excited when carrying out his carelessly laid plans and is not unlikely to leave some tell-tale clue. Further study of Bert Whipley shows that in spite of his criminal behavior he has an unusual familiarity with feelings of guilt. In tests of imagination he produces two odd but pertinent stories. In one of these the principal character, having just completely a long prison sentence, gazes contentedly from a window which has no bars, but then in some inexplicable manner falls out the window to his death. In the other story the hero cheats on a school examination, but suffers untold torment and agony until he confesses to the authorities. When we compare these themes with Dostoievsky's *Crime and Punishment,* which describes a guilty conscience with such extraordinary detail and which culminates in a similar voluntary confession, we can hardly doubt that our subject is no stranger to the experience of guilt.

The Pattern of Contributing Causes. How are we to understand the personality and the self-defeating existence of this young man potentially so gifted? Like anyone else he has been exposed to cultural pressures designed to encourage stable, persistent, socially acceptable behavior. He possesses good abilities, better in some respects than Joseph Kidd's or Pearson Brack's. In spite of this he has become an habitual criminal with a propensity for getting caught. Our inquiry resolves itself into two questions: (1) how did the criminal tendencies, the persistent stealing, become fixated at the expense of stable socialized living; and (2) why does he fail in his criminal enterprises, losing his cunning at the critical moment so that he practically exposes himself to capture and punishment?

As might be expected, the answers are not simple. Several factors make their contribution. Some part is played by chronic environmental stress: poverty, unemployment, poor neighborhood influences, tempestuous scenes in the home. But the crucial influences are those attributable to modes of personal adjustment acquired during childhood and adolescence. In order to understand our subject's contemptuous attitude toward society, and his equally contemptuous attitude toward himself, we have to examine the history of the learning process whereby these attitudes were established.

The Whipley family circle contains many examples of psychological disorder. Bert's father has recently been committed to the State Hospital on account of chronic alcoholism and some suspicion of mental disease. His uncle has been in mental hospitals several times, being finally committed for life to an institution for the criminally insane. An older brother has a record of delinquency and drunkenness. Two sisters have had severe breakdowns, requiring psychiatric treatment. A generation ago this loading of the family history with psychological disorders would have been accepted as sufficient evidence for hereditary instability. Constitutional weakness of the nervous system would have been invoked to explain Bert's delinquency. Perhaps it is true that he carries an hereditary load which makes adjustment difficult, but we are never justified in assuming such a thing merely because the family history is weighted with disorders. The presence of even one disordered person in the household creates an unusual environmental pressure for the other members. While it is possible that Bert's alcoholic father transmitted some weakness through the channels of heredity, it is certain, as we shall see, that he influenced his offspring directly and powerfully through the avenues of learning. In Bert's case the history of the learning process is largely open to observation. When we examine the atmosphere in which he grew up, and when we notice the rewards and punishments he received, the assumption of innate weakness to explain his delinquency becomes superfluous.

1. *Attitudes Encouraged by the Parents.* In our two previous cases we noticed the importance of the child's relation to its parents. The influence of Bert's parents was, if anything, even more decisive. His father was in a respected line of skilled work, not only practising but teaching his skill. Rather suddenly the demand for this type of work ceased. Thwarted and angry, the father was at home a great deal, used alcohol excessively, and literally terrified the household by his outbursts of furious rage. He tried to teach Bert, but lost his temper on the spot if there was any hitch in the learning. Gradually Bert became his scapegoat, receiving torrents of sarcasm, criticism, and abuse. Everything the son tried to do was made a subject of ridicule by the father. The mother, an easygoing housewife, tried to soften the quarrels, but her influence was small. She was indulgent to Bert when his father was not around. If he balked at household chores, she did them herself rather than make her son's lot harder. Sometimes when the parents had noisy and violent scenes, the neighbors would advise Mrs. Whipley to separate from her husband, but when he returned sober, tearfully apologizing, she always took him back. Bert grew up with a rankling sense of injustice. In front of callers, Mr. Whipley posed as the ideal loving parent, but the door would hardly be closed before he turned on his family to heap them with abuse. He posed as a religious man but slandered the church in private. He was brutal to his wife but was always taken back. So far as his father was concerned, Bert could see no justice in the family world.

Throughout his childhood and early adolescence, therefore, Bert's self-respect was steadily battered down by his father's ridicule and criticism.

Neither parent offered real encouragement to stable and responsible behavior. Bert was in a state of chronic suppressed anger, nursing a sense of injustice, filled with contempt for law, order and good behavior, as hypocritically preached by his father. His parents unwittingly trained him into a pattern of domestic behavior that consisted of criticizing his father whenever possible, dodging the father's anger, and coming around for a hand-out from his mother.

2. *Attitudes Encouraged by Neighborhood Companions.* Meanwhile poverty brought the family into a neighborhood where Bert found many of his companions occupied with petty larceny. There were "good" boys and "bad" boys in the neighborhood, but it was among the latter that Bert began to find life most rewarding. Among these new friends he discovered a way of proving himself a "big guy" and commanding respect. He assisted two older fellows in stealing a car, in return for which he was allowed to go on a joyride which included pursuit by a police car and successful escape. He soon became an expert, organizing his own joyrides. The experience held a peculiar fascination for him because he found esteem and a sense of triumph, while at the same time hurling defiance and contempt at the symbols of law and order. He became a great fellow in a delinquent gang and his criminal career was fast established. In reform schools and jails he later met many unrepentant criminals who taught him that people who work for a living are "suckers," and who instructed him in the techniques of an easier way to get along. At the same time he began to find a curious satisfaction with prison life. When released, he experienced distinct uneasiness and anxiety.

The factors thus far discussed explain the strength of Bert Whipley's criminal tendencies. To put the whole matter in a nutshell: he was exposed to a system of rewards and punishments which discouraged every attempt at stable, socialized behavior and which generated an unusually strong satisfaction in criminal enterprises. What is not yet explained is the failure of Bert's crimes, his frequent capture and long imprisonments, together with the self-contempt and feelings of guilt which we found prominent in his personality. If it were merely a question of frequent capture, we might suppose that, being not very stable, he went to pieces under stress and lost his cunning because of excitement. This explanation, however, would ignore his guilt feelings, his careless planning, and the almost gratuitous exposure of himself to arrest. It appears that crime and punishment have a highly personal meaning to Bert Whipley, the understanding of which takes us again into his history.

3. *Castrophic Event in Early Childhood: Death of Baby Brother.* Sometimes events in early childhood play a tremendous part in shaping

personality. When Bert was four years old he was jealous of his baby brother. This situation is a peculiarly difficult one for a small child to handle. He feels anger toward his new rival and resentment against his faithless parents, but if he shows any of this hostility he only makes matters worse by antagonizing his parents. At all events Bert was sick with a contagious disease, and his parents warned him to keep away from the smaller child. While his parents were out he lured the baby into his room and played with him for some time. Soon the brother was sick, and Bert's position deteriorated: the parents paid more attention than ever to the baby. His resentment rising, Bert's next act was unequivocally hostile. When no one was looking he slipped into the baby's room and set fire to the curtains so that the room filled with smoke and the baby began to cough. Fortunately the flames did not spread, but a few days later the baby's condition grew worse and he died. Bert received no punishment for his hostile action, but he was well aware of his parents' grief. Believing that he had killed the brother, he was left with a heavy load of guilt. For months afterwards he was haunted by a voice which seemed to ring in his ears saying, "Put it out, put it out," and he would run to his mother screaming with terror. Ten years later he still sometimes heard the voice and experienced the rising panic. Nineteen years later he related the unforgotten incident with distinct signs of distress.

This incident in early childhood appears to have left an indelible mark on Bert Whipley. It left him liable to feelings of intense worthlessness, an overwhelming sense that he ought to be punished, and these feelings tended to creep up on him precisely at those moments when his criminal tendencies were most active. However strong his present motives toward crime, each criminal act was destined to *feel* like that original act of hostility toward his brother; and, *feeling like that,* to call up the aftermath of frightful guilt. Successful crime had once caused him untold misery and terror, the terror that comes to a child who believes that his parents can never love him again. All future crimes were stamped with this personal meaning. He felt that he deserved to be punished; he almost wanted to be punished. His criminal accomplishments were regularly undermined by his feelings of guilt.

Single events in childhood do not usually have such a drastic effect. It is only when the meaning of the event is particularly catastrophic, as in this case, that it can be supposed to leave a permanent imprint. In Bert's case, moreover, the whole conflict was kept alive because of his stormy family life, the constant battering of his self-respect, and the wonderful satisfaction which he presently discovered in delinquent behavior.

Classification of the Resulting Disorder. Whipley's behavior belongs under the heading of *delinquency*, and the official diagnosis at the prison was *psychopathic personality*. The latter label is generally applied when the following characteristics are present: habitual delinquent behavior, a marked lack of moral scruples, insensitivity to the rights of others, and a generally erratic and purposeless way of living. This state of affairs differs from *neurosis* in that the underlying difficulties, whatever they may be, display themselves in overt behavior directed against society. Instead of being felt as internal, in the form of unhappiness and symptoms of various kinds, the troublesome tendencies are turned into overt action of a delinquent or criminal sort. Whipley corresponds in several respects to the typical *psychopathic personality*, but on one point the prison diagnosis must be considered wrong. It is highly characteristic of the psychopath that he feels no guilt or remorse. In respect to the rights of others—the victims of his stealing, for example—Whipley is quite free from self-reproach, but as we have seen he is heavily weighted with a much less appropriate feeling of guilt which originated in his early childhood. In this one respect, then, his condition resembles *neurosis* rather than *psychopathic personality*. It seems proper to say that he started with an early childhood neurosis and that his later experiences then turned him forcibly toward delinquency without entirely obliterating the effects of the earlier condition.

The reader may find this confusing, but he must be prepared for just such confusion throughout his study of abnormal personalities. We try to classify the various disorders and distinguish them so that they do not overlap. In reality, however, this proves to be impossible; there are very few pure cases which fit neatly into a single category. Several kinds of disorder can coexist in the same person, and it is always more important to understand the person than to classify the disorder. The case of Bert Whipley, with certain features of psychopathic personality and others of neurosis existing side by side, is more truly representative than any pure case. If we follow his career a little further we discover that his disorder became even more complex. After serving three years of his sentence he was released from State Prison on parole. Serious attempts were made to help him, and jobs had become readily obtainable, but in spite of this he broke down after two difficult and unhappy months and was sent to a mental hospital with symptoms of *psychosis* resembling in certain respects those of the example next to be described. At this point in our study we would stray from our purpose if we continued his history and described the attempts made to cure him. Suffice it to say that his disorder is much more serious than those of our first two examples, and that changing him into a healthy, adapted person, if possible at all, would be a long and arduous task.

4. A PSYCHOSIS WITH LONG-STANDING DELUSIONS: L. PERCY KING

The next example is a somewhat older man, L. Percy King, who has been a patient in a State Hospital for twenty-eight years. To his own way of thinking he has arrived at discoveries of revolutionary importance which he does not hesitate to call "the greatest psychological phenomena extant." The doctors in charge of the hospital do not put such a high estimate on his ideas and refuse to return him to circulation in the community. Infuriated by this persecution, which he considers "a state calamity and a national disgrace," King occasionally addresses to someone in the outside world a long letter detailing his experiences, outlining his system of ideas, and demanding justice and recognition. Like the hospital staff, readers of these letters find his ideas somewhat curious, but in another sense the letters are of exceptional value, for they give us in detail and with feeling the inside story of a severe psychosis.

Example of a Fully Developed Delusional System. We shall begin by examining L. Percy King's present beliefs—his great discoveries—arrived at after years of reflection and a long sifting of his experience. He believes that all his misfortunes, including his long imprisonment at the hospital, are brought about by the activities of a group of pursuers who have been after him ever since he left his home state, thirty years ago, and took a job in New York City. These pursuers are equipped with very unusual but entirely explicable powers, which he describes as follows:

> Among these pursuers, I was later to gradually discover by deduction, were evidently some brothers and sisters who inherited from one of their parents some astounding, unheard of, utterly unbelievable occult powers. Believe it or not, some of them, besides being able to tell a person's thoughts, are also able to project their magnetic voices—commonly called "radio voices" around here —a distance of a few miles without talking loud and without apparent effort, their voices sounding from that distance as though heard through a radio head set, this being done without electrical apparatus. This unique occult power of projecting their "radio voices" for such long distances apparently seems to be due to their natural bodily electricity, of which they have a supernormal amount. The vibration of their vocal cords evidently generates wireless waves, and these vocal radio waves are caught by human ears without rectification. Thus, in connection with their mind-reading ability, they are able to carry on a conversation with a person over a mile away and out of sight, by ascertaining the person's unspoken thoughts, and then by means of their so-called "radio voices," answer these thoughts aloud audibly to the person. An uninitiated person would probably be very much startled over such phenomena. For example, what would you think if you were on a level, desolate tract of land

without any vegetation or places of concealment upon it, and without a human being within miles, when you heard a mysterious, seemingly unearthly voice answer a question you were just thinking about?

Not only can the pursuers read one's thoughts and speak in answer to them, but they can also create bodily sensations in their victims. Thus it is possible for one of them to take a whiff of perfume and the victim, far away from any perfume, receives the same sensation. If some irritation causes a pursuer's skin to tickle, then the victim's skin tickles in the same place, and when the victim scratches the spot, the feeling of relief is conveyed to the pursuer. King explains this by likening the nerves of the skin to tiny radio antennae capable of both sending and receiving sensations if one of the persons possesses unusual bodily electricity. In this two-way transmission of sensations lies the pursuers' chief means of working their malicious intentions.

He often makes a practice of keeping persons awake nights tickling their erogenous zones. There must be a stop put to this. He must be made to refrain from tickling married women's teats and from tickling them between their legs. Parents don't want their sons and daughters tickled in such places to cause them to form bad habits. This pursuer persists in the tickling for such long times, and the tickling feels so unbelievably strong that it is enough to drive a person frantic.

It feels good to certain mind-reading pursuers to have patients masturbate. This is how certain pursuers go about it to get patients to masturbate. They lie to patients, telling them sad stories, saying their property has been disposed of, that they can never go home again, that their wives are keeping fast company, that their loved ones are sick, suffering, or dead, or some other sad stories to make them cry if possible. Then certain bitches of the pursuer party make love to them, offering to sleep with them, have illicit intercourse with them, and talk it over with them about the nasty things they will do together, about unnatural sex acts, and sometimes pretend they are having coitus with male pursuers, or pretend they are being raped or other such sex story. Then, if all this fails to bring results, certain pursuers, from the distance without corporeal contact, tickle the patients between their legs and in their erogenous zones or coax them to masturbate. This sort of thing has been going on for over twenty years.

Would you like to have the "radio voices" tell all your financial, social, marital, medical, physical, and sex secrets to thousands of persons a day? These mind-reading pursuers can ruin or disgrace anyone. I do not believe anyone's life is safe with some of them around! They are able to coerce anyone into doing almost anything.

One begins to wonder on what basis the pursuers select their victims. Why are they so bent on annoying hospital patients, particularly L. Percy King? In his logical fashion King, too, has pondered this question, and has arrived at the following answer, which constitutes the most startling and original feature of his great discoveries.

With these pursuers are some helpless young women, who are either the writer's sisters, or illegitimate daughters, or both. These sisters were born at the same time he was. At birth their souls evidently became attached to his body, as well as to their own bodies, so that some of them sense with his organs of sense instead of entirely with their own organs of sense. He never moves in any way unless one or more of them move or will him to. His breathing and heart action is synchronous at all times with that of one of them. They think with his brain as well as with their own brains. He has their emotions and personalities. If their souls were withdrawn from his body, he would be dead. Marvellously, this is actually being written by one of them. When she moves her hand to write with it, his hand moves the same way at the same time. This phenomenon is unique and unprecedented! !

The ugly motives of the pursuers now spring into a clear light. They wanted to keep the helpless young women under their control for immoral purposes, but they could not take them far away from L. Percy King lest the soul connection be broken and the helpless women languish and die. In order to enter profitable business in the city where the hospital is located, the pursuers conspired to drag King with them from New York by forcing him to act in an insane fashion. This malicious plot explains most of his troubles, but it fails to account for certain features of his subsequent persecution. An additional hypothesis proves necessary.

There is also a large unconscious male person who is suspended upright by straps, framework, etc., and who is also "tied up" to the writer by the same strange "soul connections." Whatever sensation this male person is caused to feel, the writer himself feels just as strongly. By causing the closed fingers of the said male person's hand to spread apart, the writer's fingers are also thereby made to spread apart against the writer's will. By manipulating his magnetic hands near the genitals of the said male person, a pursuer is able to give both the male person and the writer involuntary erections of the penis. This has been of frequent occurrence. Such business must be stopped.

Projection and Reality Testing. These are the ravings of a sick man. One may be tempted to dismiss them as utter nonsense, but to do so would be to throw away the evidence which upon closer scrutiny allows us to understand what is wrong with L. Percy King. The outcome of his reasoning may be completely absurd, but he is obviously attempting to reason and to make some kind of sense out of his experience. His queer ideas are not random productions as if the machinery of thought had suddenly disintegrated. If we look closely we find consistent themes and a consistent process of distortion. The patient has experienced *hallucinations*—false perceptions—such as hearing voices actually speaking to him or feeling peculiar bodily sensations. From these he has worked out *delusions*—false beliefs—such as the machinations of the pursuers and the existence of the unconscious male person strapped in his frame. Both of these symptoms, which are common in many varieties of psychosis, show a failure in the patient's contact with reality. He does not engage in sufficient *reality testing*. He does not weigh the possibility that he might have imagined the sound of voices or that sexual desires might arise within his own body. To a remarkable extent he seems bent on assigning all initiative and all motives, all action of any kind, to forces outside himself, so that even his letter is being written by one of the helpless women, even his emotions originate in them. Here we see the consistent distortion that enters his interpretations. He uses the device of *projection* to assign to outside forces nearly everything that takes place in his mind. Unless we believe his theory about radio voices, we must assume that, when his thoughts are answered, it is by further thoughts of his own. But the patient, for some reason, cannot accept this, and his reality testing breaks down, falsifying the outside world, before the alternative of assuming responsibility for those further thoughts. Going on like this for years, he almost loses the feeling of himself as an active agent; he becomes virtually depersonalized.

Reality testing is such a fundamental process that its disturbance can only indicate some very unusual condition. Healthy people stubbornly persist in testing reality even when real events are going pretty much against them. We can best understand the nature and strength of the forces involved in King's psychosis if we go back to the time in his life, twenty-eight years ago, when reality testing first began to fail. His letter includes a vivid description of this period.

Onset and Early Stages. One day King was taking a walk in an unfamiliar part of New York City. "Being a stranger," he writes, "I was surprised to hear someone exclaim twice: 'Shoot him!' evidently meaning me." Thinking that gangsters might have mistaken him for someone else he rushed from the spot, trying to disappear in the crowd and reach the subway. But the gangsters pursued him: "I knew they were pursuing me because I still heard their voices as close as ever, no matter how fast I walked." Back at his lodgings he told no one about his adventure "for fear they would be incredulous."

So far as we know, this was the first time that King was hallucinated. Reality testing was by no means abandoned: he himself found the experience so strange that he did not expect anyone to believe it. His whole reaction, however, was peculiar. He instantly assumed that some overheard talk was directed menacingly at him, and he fled in such panic that there was no opportunity to test this particular bit of reality. His behavior at this point shows *exaggerated self-reference*. Shortly afterwards the same thing happened again. Among the threatening phrases he distinctly heard a woman's voice say, "You can't get away from us; we'll lay for you and get you after a while." Then he noticed that one of the unseen pursuers, "repeated my thoughts aloud, verbatim." This was the beginning of that process of projection whereby he ultimately disowned most of his own thoughts and sensations. At this stage the pursuers merely repeated his thoughts; soon they would begin to answer them and then initiate them.

King's life gradually turned into a nightmare. He noticed that whenever he entered a room someone would cough twice, then someone else, until everyone in the room had coughed twice. "I would go to the movies where one patron after another would cough twice until dozens had coughed." Reality testing was still attempted: "I would have thought everyone had colds had not each one coughed twice, and in summertime with no colds going around." How could he interpret the coughing? "Was there really an organized movement afoot against me?" Coughing and other persecutions at the office where he worked finally convinced him that this was the case, and he resigned from his job.

Now he was completely miserable. Pursuers left him no peace of mind. As he sat in his lodgings, murmurings in the street below told him all too plainly that his murderers were assembling. Voices on the stairs revealed that a lynching party was creeping toward his room, so that in panic he called upon a neighbor to protect him. At last he could stand it no longer and tried to kill himself. His self-inflicted wounds proved not to be fatal, but they led to the summoning of his mother, his return home, and his commitment to the State Hospital. During the psychiatric examination he was depressed and indifferent, speaking as little as possible. Later he realized that pursuers had forced this behavior upon him so that he would be judged insane. At the time he was badly confused and much upset about one of the "radio voices."

> An effeminate, male voice called down to me from some place overhead, saying, "I am God!" I had heard this voice in New York, all the way home on the train, and now, after having traveled hundreds of miles, I still heard his voice. If he were not God, why did I hear him everywhere? If he had followed me, why?

King's break with reality reached its extreme point during this episode and during his first few months at the hospital. We have noticed that reality testing was lost only after a struggle. It gave way before a steadily mounting conviction that the world was filled with hostile forces bent on his destruction. That this conviction could overthrow a process as fundamental as reality testing means that it was backed by tremendous forces in King's personality. It must have been unwittingly chosen as an alternative to something completely unbearable. The belief that unseen pursuers are trying to persecute and kill you seems hardly a comfortable solution to inner conflict. We must regard it rather as a desperate expedient preferable only to some solution still more devastating. Why must he use such drastic devices? What are the things inside himself that he cannot bear to admit? The answer can be inferred from his letters, partly by examining his state of mind before the hallucinations began, partly by inspecting the content of his current system of delusions.

Basic Conflict Underlying the Psychosis. For some time before his first hallucination King had felt that he was an object of criticism and contempt in the eyes of those around him. He began to notice that remarks made in his presence often had more than a casual meaning. He lists seventeen such remarks of which the following are representative.

"I'll tell the world!" This remark insinuates that I had been in the habit of telling the world what to do, or telling the world defiantly where to go to. This remark insinuates that in my supreme arrogance I had been telling the world some of my opinions held by me to be of more importance and consequence than the opinions of all the rest of humanity put together.

"Ambition." This word used to be my nickname. Instead of being called by my real name, I was called "Ambition." This slur applies to my striving to make something of myself in spite of attempts to make me weaken and give up trying to progress intellectually.

"How do you get that way?" I used to have that question thrown up to me nearly every day. The inference is that I am odd and queer, so the question arises as to what makes me so eccentric. As though there was something wrong with me.

"He needs a woman." This is self-explanatory. It infers I am a masturbator, and that I need a woman to straighten out my sex life, but that I cannot get one.

"All he does is follow them around." This insinuates that I follow the handsome young women around, but that I am so shy, bashful, sedate, and reserved that I am afraid to approach such young ladies to make dates for petting and necking parties.

"Making a man out of him." The word "him," in this quotation, refers to me. The remark insinuates I was not a man, but someone was trying to do things to me in order to transform me into a man so that I would not "need a woman."

"Outside of that he's all right." Which means outside of some awful sin, fault, crime, I am all right.

These quotations make it clear that a tendency toward exaggerated self-reference prevailed in King's personality before he became psychotic. Perhaps he was really criticized a good deal, but from the account given it is plain that he reacted in oversensitive fashion, finding criticism even where none was intended. Such exaggerated self-reference implies that the person is unwittingly engaged in criticizing himself. There are aspects of himself for which he would feel strong contempt if he allowed himself to recognize their internal location. By projection he protects his self-esteem from an unbearable blow. He turns what is very likely a well-merited self-contempt into a senseless persecution from outside, and he feels only indignation against his persecutors. From the remarks detailed in King's letter we discover what it is that he finds so unbearably contemptible in himself: his masturbation, his lack of manliness, his failure to prove his sexual adequacy. These are painful realizations for one whose personality has been organized on the basis of high pretensions, self-forwarding ambition, and a contemptuous attitude toward others. In King's case the threat to his inflated self-esteem was intolerable. All the contempt he was accustomed to direct upon others threatened to come showering back on him if he really possessed such a grave flaw in his manhood. It was easier to believe that the world persecuted him out of sheer malice than to admit his own vulnerability.

The basic underlying conflict in King's psychosis is between his self-confidence, arrogance, and ambition on the one hand, and his effeminacy and sexual timidity on the other. It is curious to observe how the whole conflict is condensed and symbolized in the hallucination that followed him from New York to the State Hospital: an effeminate male voice kept saying, "I am God."

Function of the Delusional System. The theme of effeminacy is considerably elaborated in the system of delusions that King worked out during his years at the hospital. Once he adopted his central hypothesis about pursuers, he found it possible to admit the presence of masturbatory and even homosexual desires. Strictly speaking, these desires were not his own; they were implanted in his person by the electrical activities of the pursuers. Likewise, he could admit all his symptoms and eccentricities: these, too, were devices of the pursuers to insure that he would be judged insane and kept near their place of business. The pursuer theory can be looked upon as a systematic hypothesis designed to account for all his experiences, and at the same time shield his self-esteem. It involves, of course, a liberal use of projection and a slipshot testing of reality so that it never succeeds in convincing the doctors. But it achieves with some success its more personal purpose for L. Percy King. He is now far less disordered and far less distressed than he was when he entered the hospital indifferent and hopelessly confused.

In the beginning he was unable to admit his effeminacy. Now he can admit it completely, though accepting no personal responsibility. In his delusional system he becomes completely united and identified with the helpless women, having their emotions and thinking their thoughts. The unconscious male person was perhaps conceived as a symbolic expression of his own not fully awakened masculinity. These constructions permit him to indulge in many fantasies of a passive sexual nature: the pursuers satisfy their lust upon the helpless women, whose sensations are promptly transmitted to King's own body, and the pursuers use the unconscious male person as the object of homosexual attentions. But all of this, through the mechanism of projection, no longer touches the fortress of

King's self-esteem. Quite the contrary, it positively enhances his self-esteem, for are not the discoveries concerning his union with the helpless women "the greatest psychological phenomena extant"? What would happen if the hospital staff stopped persecuting him and concealing his discoveries?

When the public finds out that some of these helpless women make the writer talk, etc., and that the phenomena are without precedent, that the writer in that respect is the most wonderful person alive, that no one has ever lived like him, his photo and write-up will be published in every important newspaper and magazine on earth. These helpless women and he will receive so many tons of fan mail that the post office will have to employ extra mail trucks to handle it. Throngs of people will crowd here on the grounds to get a peek at him, so that special police will have to be employed to keep them off the grounds. He and these helpless women will receive visits from world-famous scientists from everywhere and will receive offers to go on the air, into the movies, on the vaudeville stage, will be offered large sums to appear before psychic investigators. These helpless women will be showered with so many presents from all over the world that the presents will have to be stored in a special building. He and they would be invited to appear before the State Assembly, in special session, and will be invited to the State House. He will be pensioned for life by the State and will go home in a special train and be met at the station by a band.

From what has been said it becomes clear that L. Percy King's delusions serve a purpose and make a certain sense. This sick man is not wholly different from others. Like the healthiest person, he tries to reason and explain the things that happen to him. Like Joseph Kidd, he struggles with the problem of esteem and with his feelings of personal unworthiness. Like Pearson Brack, he cannot accept the full realization of his inferiority. Unlike all these, however, the course upon which he embarks takes him out of contact with reality and leads to psychosis. His method of defense, projection, when carried to extremes has a far more destructive effect on personality than the devices used by Kidd or Brack. King's psychiatric diagnosis is *schizophrenia, paranoid type.* There is little reason to suppose that he will ever recover sufficiently to leave the hospital.

To complete our understanding of the case it would be necessary to know how he came to develop the high pretensions, the ambition, and the arrogance that made him so vulnerable to anything that threatened to lower self-esteem. We would need to know whether any features of his history, or of his constitution, tended to arrest the development of masculine feelings and strengthen his passive sexual tendencies. It is a common experience for boys in early adolescence to feel that masturbation conflicts with their better selves and to wonder about their untried sexual adequacy. In King's case these problems were lifted to extraordinary intensity so that at last his sanity was shattered. The reasons for this intensity lie somewhere in the history of his personal development. But we have learned enough for our present purposes if we understand the dynamics of his psychosis in its developed form.

5. A PROGRESSIVE BRAIN DISEASE: MARTHA OTTENBY

For our fifth example, we take up the case of a woman, fifty-six years old, who suffers from a degenerative disease of the brain.[3] Martha Ottenby led a contented though rather uneventful life up to the age of fifty-four. At that point her husband and friends began to notice peculiar changes in her behavior, changes which steadily increased until it became necessary to send her to a mental hospital. She was found to have a rare brain disease for which no cure is at present known, and which is almost certain to bring about her death within a few years. In the meantime, however, she lives pleasantly enough in the hospital, unaware that her mind is disordered and that her recovery is impossible. To the student of abnormal psychology such cases offer an unusual opportunity to learn about the functions of the brain. By examining the evolution of symptoms, and by noticing the results of mental tests, we can construct a picture of the functions performed by those areas of the brain that have been injured by disease.

Nature of the Organic Disorder. It will be easier to understand this case if we first consider the nature of the patient's brain disorder. Martha Ottenby is diagnosed as having *Pick's disease,* a quite rare degenerative disorder which has nevertheless been of especial interest to neurologists because it acts selectively on the frontal lobes of the cortex and spreads only later to other areas. The cause of this condition is as yet unknown. There is some evidence that it runs in families, but in many cases, including the present one, a search of the family history reveals no other victims. Evidence for an infectious origin is altogether lacking. The time of onset is almost always in later middle life, suggesting that Pick's disease may be connected with aging and may be conceived as a premature aging of certain parts of the cerebral cortex. At all events, when a post-mortem examination of the brain is made, there is found to be a marked atrophy of the cortex, especially of the frontal lobes. In the affected areas the gray and white matter appears shrunken and of an abnormal color. Microscopic examination reveals that many nerve cells have disappeared, while those that remain show characteristic alterations of a degenerative type. The cortex seems to be undergoing a process of decay.

[3] This case is taken from K. Goldstein and S. Katz, "The Psychopathology of Pick's Disease," *Archives of Neurology and Psychiatry,* XXXVIII (1937), pp. 473–90.

While it is doubtless proper to conceive of Pick's disease in this way, we must remember that the decay goes well beyond what is normal, even in very old people. We must also remember its highly localized character, confined to the cerebral cortex and in most cases still further limited, at least in the earlier stages, to the frontal lobes. Except for her brain disorder, Martha Ottenby is anything but decayed; she is not even old for her years. Her hair is gray, but she is a plump, ruddy woman with a strong healthy pulse, satisfactory blood pressure, normal reflexes, and every indication of sound physical health. Only one physical examination gives conclusive evidence of abnormality. This is a procedure, recently developed, known as the air encephalogram. It is performed by introducing air under slight pressure into the brain cavity, then taking X-ray pictures to show how the air has distributed itself among the tissues. Martha Ottenby's air encephalogram revealed a great deal of air congregated over the frontal lobes, especially at the frontal poles, indicating that the cortical tissue was considerably shrunken in these areas. This is as decisive evidence for Pick's disease as can be obtained prior to post-mortem examination.

It is like telling a story backwards to give the final diagnosis before relating the history of the case. In the present instance, we are justified by the extra profit to be derived from studying the history and the earliest symptoms when we know the nature of the underlying brain disorder. We shall now return to chronological order and see what can be gleaned from the patient's past life.

Personal History. Martha Ottenby was born in Sweden, where she grew up a jolly, sociable, active child of average intelligence. So far as could be ascertained, none of her grandparents, neither of her parents, and none of her five brothers and sisters, ever showed signs of mental disorder. Martha became a dressmaker at the age of twenty, and soon earned the reputation of a skillful worker. When thirty-two she came to the United States; at the late age of forty she married. This last event was not entirely happy, inasmuch as the husband shortly lost his money and ran into debt; moreover, in his discouragement he occasionally resorted to alcohol and came home badly intoxicated. To keep the household going, Martha continued her work as a dressmaker. It was hard to earn enough in this way, so that she was constantly worried about the precarious financial situation. But in spite of these difficulties Martha's life was not without its satisfactions. Except when marred by alcoholic episodes the marriage was happy and the atmosphere of the home pleasant. Martha was a neat housekeeper. She enjoyed her home and this made her able to be patient with her husband's difficulties and her own.

Earliest Symptoms. The earliest symptoms of Martha's disorder was an apparently trifling matter: on several occasions she allowed food to burn on the stove. Her husband, having been married to her for fourteen years, was astonished at these lapses from her usual domestic efficiency. It seemed as if she were growing a little forgetful, so that when she momentarily turned away from her cooking it slipped out of her mind. Before long it became apparent that in several other ways her behavior was changing. She felt tired a good deal of the time, and had to lie down often during the day. Sometimes she was bothered by mild headache. Her interest in dressmaking began to diminish; she sat at home and spent most of her time reading weekly magazines. Presently her husband noticed another curious sign of forgetfulness: Martha read the same stories over and over without any loss of interest, apparently not realizing that she had read them several times before. Her standards of physical appearance declined; the neat, trimly dressed Martha began to look "sloppy" and untidy. If her attention was called to some carelessness in her personal appearance, she would become very angry. On the whole her mood was a little sad, in noticeable contrast to her previous cheerful disposition.

At about this point in her illness her brother died. Her reaction to this loss revealed clearly that her mind was becoming disordered. She kept imagining that she saw her brother outside and would run into the street to talk with him, sometimes forgetting that she was not fully dressed. If questioned, she knew that her brother was dead, but a short time later she would again be convinced that she saw him. She told of long conversations with the brother during his last illness, all of which the husband knew could not have occurred. At times she even launched into an actual conversation just as if her brother were making a call.

Her mental confusion became increasingly obvious and difficult. She herself began to feel "all mixed up," and she was confused about the identity of people around her, though continuing to recognize her husband, her sister, and her dog. Bizarre thoughts came to her mind. Faulty perceptions occurred: she saw a strange cat across the street with legs all over its body, and she imagined that it would progress by rolling rather than by walking. At this point it was decided to take her to the hospital.

Behavior at the Hospital. Upon arrival at the hospital, Martha's sadness increased to a point of real distress. She fancied that a cat had come along with her, had died, and now lay behind her bed. Her brother was still much on her mind. She believed that he had been in the ward and had made a disturbance there; at other times she saw him in the street and cried because he was being sent away hungry. These unhappy imaginings soon gave place to a more cheerful mood. She occupied herself with reading and without the least trace of self-consciousness would sing loudly as she read.

In the course of time she settled down to a cheerful, quiet, orderly way of life. She was generally to be found sitting on a bench, arms folded, a smiling expression on her face, attentive to what was going on around her. Visitors were greeted with smiles and friendly gestures, but no further conversation would follow unless it were prompted by the other person. She was cordial to the doctors and nurses, although unable to remember their names. When engaged in conversation she showed animated interest. The form and structure of her speech was not in the least impaired, the only difficulty being a tendency to slip into Swedish, her mother-tongue, and it seemed impossible to make her understand that the hospital staff was not familiar with this language. She spent a good deal of time knitting in the workroom, performing her work with interest and skill.

When called upon for an interview, or when given tests, Martha became uneasy. She gave quick, brief answers, waiting anxiously to see whether they met the requirements. Suitable questioning revealed various defects in her mental processes. She continued to report strange ideas, hallucinations, and delusions, chiefly centered around her brother. She was badly mixed up about her age, her recent history, when she was married, when she came to the United States, how long she had been at the hospital. She could not give her home address correctly, and stated that she lived with her children whose names she gave; these proved, however, to be the names of her brothers and sisters, for Martha had no children of her own. Along with these striking defects of memory there could be observed a marked lack of initiative. Though friendly, Martha started no conversations. She never asked for things nor began enterprises on her own account. It did not occur to her to wash herself, although she did so willingly enough if the nurse took her to the washroom. When she grew sleepy in the evening, she lay down fully dressed unless told to undress herself.

At first glance it is hard to make sense out of these mental changes. At one moment we seem to see a person hopelessly confused about the most elementary matters: her age, her address, her brother's recent death. The next moment we observe someone behaving in alert, friendly fashion, helping in the ward, knitting in the workroom, able to perform simple arithmetic problems. Just what is wrong in such a case? Is it possible to describe the mental changes in such a way as to make them intelligible?

Comparison with the Previous Case. We can begin our attempt to do so by contrasting Martha Ottenby with our previous example, L. Percy King. This will bring into prominence the difference between *psychogenic* and *somatogenic* factors in psychosis. If there is something wrong with King's brain, it is certainly not such a gross injury as is represented in Pick's disease. King has lived with his disorder for twenty-eight years. Strange as his ideas may be, he is perfectly clear about his age, his identity, and the fact that he lives in a hospital; he reads the papers intelligently and is well informed about current world events. One might have a fairly sane and sensible conversation with him if one could keep off the topic of his pursuers. In contrast, Martha Ottenby seems hopelessly confused. It is not just that she has crazy ideas: the whole structure and machinery of her thinking seems to have disintegrated.

We arrived at an understanding of L. Percy King's delusions by working out the purposes they served in his personality. We found that his delusional system served as a defense against the recognition of unbearable inferiorities, at the same time affording him an opportunity to gratify in fantasy certain of the strivings which he otherwise condemned in himself. Thus we saw the origin of his illness in a sharp conflict of basic motives, a conflict which he was able to solve only at the cost of a break with reality. In Martha Ottenby's case, likewise, we can observe the presence of unsatisfied needs and other personal problems. In the delusion that she lived with her children there is probably the fulfillment of a wish denied in her actual life. The centering of her disordered thoughts around her dead brother points to an unusual dependence upon this brother and need for his supporting presence. Personal problems creep into her thoughts, just the way they sometimes influence a healthy person's thinking. But although these problems are discernible, we do not get the least impression that the patient became ill on their account or that her illness represents the outcome of a sort of strategy designed to solve them. In Martha's case, the illness does not seem to constitute an adjustment of any kind. It does not have much personal meaning, and it serves no personal purpose. The disorder began in the brain tissues, not in the strategy of adjustment which the brain learns to carry out.

These two examples of psychosis serve to point up the distinction made in the first chapter between somatogenic and psychogenic explanaations. The somatogenic hypothesis, as it might have been employed by Kraepelin, applies well to the case of Martha Ottenby, whose condition is the result of a disease. The examination of behavior and the analysis of mental changes has in her case the purpose of guiding the investigator to a correct diagnosis of conditions in her brain tissues. If a method of curing or preventing Pick's disease is found, it will undoubtedly have to do with chemical or metabolic conditions in the brain. The investigator can afford to overlook Martha's problems about children and about her brother except in so far as the expression of these problems displays mental deterioration. Quite the opposite is the case with L. Percy King, whose condition remains inexplicable unless one plunges into the very heart of his personal problems. Still more clearly, in Pearson Brack's case, one can observe that the possibility of cure depended entirely on a correct understanding of the conflict between duty and fear and the conditions that made his sense of duty so uncompromising. The somatogenic hypothesis applied in the wrong place leads to blunders such as the diagnosis of Brack as having damage to the wall of the heart. The effect of this diagnosis, had it remained unchallenged, would have been to prevent the patient from receiving the psychological treatment he needed. Equal folly results from misplaced application of the psychogenic hypothesis. The investigator hunts relentlessly for personal conflicts and fails to see the evidence for a brain condition or other bodily ailment that could be arrested or cured. The really good psychiatrist must be equally alert to the signs of bodily disorder and the indications of emotional disorder, no matter how obscure and elusive these signs may be.

Reduction of Behavior to the Immediate and Concrete. In Martha's case, we want to make intelligible the behavior and mental changes brought about by her illness. What has the destruction of frontal lobe tissue done to her? As a first attempt at analyzing the changes one is apt to inspect the record and find out what mental functions seem to be impaired. Language is undisturbed, but grave weakness is found in the sphere of memory. Loss of interest and initiative played a prominent part in the description, and there were also changes of mood with evidence of a lowered capacity to control emotional expression. Such an analysis forms a natural starting point, but we must be very careful not to treat these various mental functions as if they were separate faculties of the mind. Are we right in saying that memory, as a whole, is weakened, and that interest and initiative have declined? Let us look again at the patient's behavior, this time with a careful eye for those small details which best serve to clarify a case.

One day the patient was asked to lead the way to the workroom, situated on an upper floor of the hospital. She went directly to the door of the ward and turned to the nurse to unlock it. Given the key she opened the door, locked it behind her, returned the key to the nurse, rang for the elevator and entered it upon its arrival. When let out at the proper floor she went straight to the workroom and sat down at her usual place, asking the supervisor for her knitting. Thus far she behaved without hesitation, even with vivacity. When asked almost at once to put away her work and accompany the doctor, she became bewildered and obeyed only after much urging. At this point an experiment was made. The patient was stopped a short distance from the elevator and led a little way along a corridor. The ground plan of the various floors being identical, this corridor corresponded to the one the patient would take on her own floor to reach her sleeping room. She now walked straight along the corridor and turned into the room corresponding to her sleeping room. Naturally she was perplexed to find herself in a strange room, but the most curious outcome of the experiment was that even after being told she was on the wrong floor she could not understand how the mistake had come about and was quite unable to find her way to the proper floor.

This sample of behavior deserves our most careful attention. It is not correct to say that the patient has lost the use of her memory. She remembers the way to the workroom, remembers that the ward door is locked and that it must be locked again behind her, remembers her place in the workroom and the knitting on which she was engaged. Memory images arise appropriately when they are necessary to carry out a definite task. Similarly, once a specific task has been instituted she shows no impairment of interest and initiative. Yet the patient would never have started for the workroom of her own accord, and when interrupted in the course of her return she become completely disoriented as to the different floors. In practice she could follow the complicated route perfectly well, but when asked to describe it—to think of it in the abstract—she became altogether confused. She seems to fail when it is necessary to deal with experience abstractly, in her mind, without immediate perceptual promptings.

The hint that we get by examining this piece of behavior can be strengthened by looking at some other samples. Martha is asked about the season of the year, but she cannot tell what season it is. When the form of inquiry is changed to whether it is warm or cold, she answers that it is warm, referring, however, to the temperature of the room. Only when she looks out the window and sees snow does she decide that it is a cold season and agrees that it must be winter. She is given a test performed in the following manner: the experimenter makes a little design by laying small sticks on the table, then breaks it up and asks her to reproduce the design. Martha succeeds or fails in this test, not according to the complexity of the pattern or the number of sticks used, but according to the possibility of perceiving the design as a concrete and familiar object. Thus she succeeds in reproducing designs that remind her of a flag, a roof, a window, and even a letter of the alphabet, but she fails with quite simple designs when they do not resemble an object.

When we consider the various peculiarities of Martha Ottenby's behavior, it appears that she performs with relative success in concrete situations or when dealing with immediate impressions. Her trouble seems to come in dealing with any kind of abstraction. She is unable to stand apart from the immediate properties of the situation or to resist the behavior which it invites. She reproduces designs when they remind her of concrete objects, but not when they seem like abstract figures. She reacts correctly to the temperature of the room and to the sight of snow outside, but has a struggle to relate these facts to the relatively abstract idea of winter. She finds her way successfully, but cannot tell anyone how she did it and is hopelessly lost if the sequence of her actions is interrupted. What strikes us most about Martha's behavior is *immediacy* and *specificity.* It is governed by concrete impressions and present circumstances, by sight of corridor and snow, by the impression that somebody walking on the street is her brother. These immediate impressions exert such a powerful force on the patient that she cannot resist them or detach herself from their influence. It can be shown, by questioning, that she knows her brother is dead: she has not forgotten this fact. Yet when she sees someone who resembles him she surrenders so fully to this impression that for the moment she does forget not only that he is dead but that she herself is not properly dressed to run out on the street. This is what is meant by saying that her behavior is reduced to an immediate and concrete level. She has not lost memory, interest, initiative, or imagination as such; she has lost the power to use these processes in other than wholly concrete situations.

We thus learn a great deal from Martha Ottenby, even though it is impossible to cure her. As students of the brain we learn that there is probably an intimate relation between the frontal lobes and the capacity to transcend the immediate and the concrete. As students of mental processes, we obtain an enriched picture of what is meant by such transcendence. Even in commonplace acts it is necessary to detach oneself from immediate experiences, whether they arise from outside or from one's own thoughts. When we see a person who reminds us vividly of a former friend, we detach ourselves from the immediate force of this impression long enough to remember whether the friend is alive or dead, where we were accustomed to see him, whether it is at all likely that he might now be here. It is also often necessary to give an account of one's actions "in the abstract," that is, while not actually performing them. We can tell someone how to get from one place to another, without ourselves actually traversing the route. We can return to an interrupted task, picture it as a whole, and continue from where we left off, without having to go back to the beginning. These accomplishments seem commonplace enough, but Martha Ottenby's plight serves to remind us of their importance. Transcendence of the immediate and concrete seems to depend upon an intact cerebral cortex.

RETROSPECT ON THE EXAMPLES

In this clinical survey we have examined five representative examples of disordered behavior. We have seen five very different personalities, and we have looked at a wide range both of symptoms and of underlying difficulties. The examples represent most of the main varieties of disorder. Joseph Kidd, who suffered from a shy self-consciousness that injured all social relationships, is an instance of *lesser maladjustment* capable of spontaneous recovery. Pearson Brack tended to faint on military duty and later experienced considerable anxiety and depressed feelings, a pattern of symptoms which places him in the category of *neurosis*. Bert Whipley, given to criminal behavior with a compulsion to get punished, is probably best classified as a *delinquent personality*, although there were features of neurosis in his case. The other two cases exemplify *psychosis*. Psychogenic elements are prominent in L. Percy King, who has organized for himself a fantastic system of delusions and hallucinations, but whose mental processes in other respects seem not very badly impaired. Somatogenic psychosis is illustrated by Martha Ottenby, the victim of a degenerative disease of the brain tissues which leads to a marked reduction in her capacity to behave in other than concrete and immediate ways.

The diversity of symptoms, considered by themselves, could hardly be more striking. Symptoms, however, are surface phenomena, the outward manifestations of some underlying condition of disorder. The diversity of symptoms teaches us merely that underlying disorders can find their way to expression through almost any channel: bodily processes, such as fainting; moods, such as depression; social attitudes, such as shyness or brash self-confidence; cognitive processes, such as recognition of people or orientation in time and space; intellectual processes, as in the evolution of a delusional system.

The diversity is scarcely less great when we turn from symptoms to underlying difficulties. Our fifth case depended on deterioration of tissues in the brain. In the first example we were able to trace the contributing influence of the presumably innate range of abilities. We gave a greater share of attention to difficulties having their origin in conflict, anxiety, and defense—to psychogenic disorders. Joseph Kidd could be understood by untangling the history of his need for esteem and noticing the drastic progressive reduction of his esteem-income with its fatal effect on the learning process. To understand Pearson Brack we were obliged to study the quite different problem of the ego-ideal and the conditions under which it functions with an excessive rigidity that invites breakdown. Both Bert Whipley and L. Percy King reminded us again of the importance of esteem, but neither the source nor the outcome of their struggles followed Kidd's pattern. The case of Whipley introduced the theme of guilt, and demonstrated the pervasive effects of chronic bad conscience. King, in contrast, arrived at a serenely clear conscience and a splendid self-esteem, but only at the cost of a fatal break with reality.

Is there any order in this diversity? Can we do more than explain single cases? Can we find out how the difficulties of life make one person maladjusted, another neurotic, another delinquent, another psychotic, while another passes through comparable vicissitudes without impairment to his psychological health? That is the task of abnormal psychology: to bring order, system, and understanding into facts as diverse as those described in this chapter. Obviously, the possibility of curing disorders, still more of preventing them, depends upon our being able to perceive them as expressions of general lawful processes. This requires that they be seen in relation to normal development, which forms the essential background for any systematic study of disordered behavior.

SUGGESTIONS FOR FURTHER READING

Two collections of case studies illustrating all the main varieties of disordered behavior have been published by A. Burton and R. E. Harris, *Case Histories in Clinical and Abnormal Psychology* (New York, Harper & Row, 1947) and *Clinical Studies of Personality* (New York, Harper & Row, 1955). Another two-volume work is *Case Studies in Childhood Emotional Disabilities,* edited by George E. Gardner (New York, American Orthopsychiatric Association, Vol. I, 1953, Vol. II, 1956). A case study that has become a classic is that of a delinquent by C. R. Shaw, *The Jack Roller* (Chicago, University of Chicago Press, 1930).

Of special value to the student who wants to try his own hand at interpreting case materials is a book by H. Weinberg and A. W. Hire, *A Case Book in Abnormal Psychology* (New York, Alfred A. Knopf, Inc., 1956), which consists of detailed clinical case reports with practically no interpretative comments.

Case studies of people more or less normal or but slightly maladjusted are to be found in R. W. White's *Lives in Progress* (New York, Holt, Rinehart & Winston, Inc., 1952) which includes a ten-year follow-up study of Joseph Kidd; in H. E. Jones's *Development in Adolescence* (New York, Appleton-Century-Crofts, Inc., 1943); and in Lois B. Murphy's *Personality in Young Children* (New York, Basic Books, Inc., 1956), Vol. II.

3

The Development of Personality

The study of single cases is likely to leave a confused impression. In the last chapter we examined five cases representing five very different varieties of disordered behavior. To some extent it proved possible to understand each case in itself, even though we could not always be sure that our inferences were correct. But the concepts that were found helpful in understanding one case often had little bearing on the next example; it was as if we had to draw upon a different series of ideas, sometimes almost a different province of knowledge, in order to understand each new instance of disordered personal reactions.

We shall now undertake to look for general lawfulness within the diverse phenomena of abnormal psychology. We need to have a relatively systematic knowledge in at least two spheres: *psychological development,* in order to understand the psychogenic aspects of disordered behavior as exemplified in cases like Joseph Kidd and Bert Whipley, and *physiological processes,* in order to understand the somatogenic aspects; for instance, disorders of the nervous system like Martha Ottenby's, or disorders in which metabolic and glandular derangements play an important part. Closely related as the psychological and bodily aspects of disorder may be, we shall have to study them separately, and our starting point will be the psychological events that constitute the development of personality.

In order to understand any kind of abnormality it is necessary to have a clear conception of the normal. Just as the normal structure and functions of the nervous system stand as the basis for studying neurological disorders, so the normal development of personality forms a necessary point of departure for studying psychogenic disorders. In this chapter and the next we shall be concerned with the *normal course of psychological development.* As we proceed we shall indicate how maladjustments arise out of each stage or process of growth. Thus the description of maladjustments will run alongside the account of normal development. These two chapters will provide a foundation for understanding not only the lesser maladjustments but also the neuroses (Chapters 5-7), delinquent and psychopathic personalities (Chapter 10), psychosomatic disorders (Chapter 11), and the possible psychogenic elements in some of the psychoses, particularly manic-depressive disorders and schizophrenia (Chapters 14 and 15).

THE ADAPTIVE PROCESS

Disordered and disproportionate personal reactions represent failures to behave adaptively. The person has not succeeded in bringing about an endurable state of affairs between himself and the realities, physical and social, amidst which he lives. On the one hand, he has not adapted himself to the demands and limitations imposed by reality; on the other hand, he has not found ways to deal with these realities so that they become more satisfactory. The concept of adaptation implies a constant interaction between the person and his environment, each making demands on the other. Sometimes adjustment is accomplished when the person yields and accepts conditions which are beyond his power to change. Sometimes it is achieved when the environment yields to the person's constructive activities. In most cases adaptation is a compromise between these two extremes and maladjustment is a failure to achieve a satisfactory compromise.

The concept of adaptation is indispensable for understanding human development. Unfortunately it is often surrounded by unwarranted implications. All too commonly it is conceived as a one-way process instead of an interaction between a person and his environment. It is then made to imply that all change must take place within the person so that he will conform to the expectations of others and to the prevailing demands of the social order. This view ignores the historic part played by individuals in changing their social as well as their material surroundings so as to make the environment more hospitable to human needs. Sometimes this misunderstanding of adaptation is innocent, but it easily lends itself to political perversion by those who want to force conformity upon others.

Another common misunderstanding is that of defining adaptation not as a process but as an end-state such as happiness, contentment, or peace of mind. The well-adjusted person, according to this view, is a happy, confident, buoyant person unburdened by problems. Unwittingly this notion ignores the tragic aspects of human experience and implies that all problems can be happily solved. There is nothing in the concept of adaptation that warrants blithe illusions about reality. In some circumstances the best possible adjustment may still entail discouragement, sorrow, and enduring frustration.

Adaptation refers to a process, a struggle of the person to come to terms with his environment. Sometimes he will have to accept poor terms which largely frustrate his own interests. Sometimes he exacts such exorbitant terms that the environment suffers and problems are created for others. At other times a mutually satisfactory bargain can be struck. Maladjustment occurs when the bargain is less satisfactory than the circumstances permit. It is then that we can most clearly discern the hampering part played by disordered personal reactions, which are the main concern of this book.

The Conditions Imposed by Reality. When we consider the demands of reality we are likely to think first of the demand for change. Adaptation is never finished: it must go on from day to day and from period to period in a person's life. The child must adjust to changes such as weaning, feeding himself, meeting the larger world that results from locomotion. He must learn to get along with people of different ages—his parents and brothers and sisters—and then with people who are the same age and size as himself. As he goes from one school to another, and perhaps moves from one neighborhood to another, he must establish a working relationship with new and different groups. In childhood the boy is expected to be tough and strong; in adolescence he must break out in a new line and acquire the gentle arts of social charm and courtship. Presently the young man must become a good provider and a success in comparison to his fellow workers. The young married woman must turn into a good housekeeper, a friendly neighbor, and a patient practitioner of the art of bringing up children.[1] Every step calls for something new. Old ways of adaptation can never be transferred without substantial change. This is true even in a quiet and uneventful life. Neighbors come and go, friends and relatives die, changes occur in the community, and the person himself is not the same as he grows older. Under conditions of war and social catastrophe the demand for changed adjustment will be enormously multiplied.

It is important to realize, however, that reality also imposes the opposite kind of demand and limitation: it forbids change that would be most welcome to the person. Take the case of an accountant who has

[1] G. Murphy, L. B. Murphy, and T. Newcomb, *Experimental Social Psychology* (New York: Harper & Row, 1937), pp. 325–27, give a more detailed account of the sequence of adjustments expected of young people in our culture.

never been able to imperil the security offered by his first job: for forty-five years he goes to the same office by the same route at the same time and does the same work, returning at night to the same house with the same feelings of fatigue and left-over irritations of the day. Consider the farm wife who sets out three hearty meals a day for a family of ten, washes all the dishes in a dishpan, handles the whole family laundry including successive generations of diapers, and helps with the farm chores in her spare time. Even the fortunately situated scientist or artist, whose work is new and exciting, has to persist through weary and frustrating hours in order to reach worthwhile accomplishments. Months and years of patient investigation and grubby toil lie behind the triumphs of scientific discovery. Protracted rehearsals and endless practice lead up to the triumphs of stage and concert hall. Reality demands constant change, but it also imposes a constant demand for persistive endurance.

We can understand these two opposite kinds of restriction if we bear in mind certain well-known facts about our own natures. As children, and only somewhat less as adults, we tend to be alert, responsive, but a little distractible and impulsive. Our attention wanders over the scene around us, we like to follow inclinations as they arise, and we can comfortably stick to one thing only when it ministers to strong needs or profound interests. Children find the requirement of persistence a hard one, as we can see when it is withdrawn during recess periods or after school. We cope with this quality in our natures by learning habitual patterns of behavior, especially in connection with the satisfaction of recurrent needs. Through the process of learning, we gear ourselves, so to speak, to act in regular ways that lead to reliable satisfactions. Here is where the requirement of change may upset us. The virtue of habituated behavior is its automatic, almost effortless character; and it cannot always be readily unseated under altered conditions. Thus in some ways we tend to be too flighty, in other ways too regular and repetitive, to deal effectively with the environment.

This way of putting it should not obscure the larger fact that both of these tendencies have great adaptive value. Together they are the source of our strength. An alert, eager, vigilant responsiveness to surroundings serves the cause of adaptation in many circumstances of animal and human life; habituated ways of arriving at vital need satisfactions serve the same cause under other circumstances. We should remember, moreover, not to picture the environment as a source only of restrictions. It contains also the means of finding new and better satisfactions at each stage of life.

Adaptation requires a range of behavior as wide as the conditions imposed by reality. It calls for a happy combination of change and persistence. Various metaphorical expressions have been used to describe the capacity to adjust. The best of these metaphors would seem to be *flexible strength*. We are apt to call those people *rigid* who lack the element of flexibility and cannot easily change. For those who cannot endure monotonous tasks or persist through hardships, we are apt to use the epithets *weak* and *flighty*. Adjustment is possible when the person is able to act with either flexibility or strength, depending on the circumstances.

Analysis of the Adaptive Process. Our understanding can be increased by making a closer analysis of what is involved in the process of adaptation. To this end we shall select two familiar problems which are often met successfully but which are sometimes the occasion for disordered personal reactions. The adjustments that must take place when a person meets a new situation, or when he begins to find an old one unendurable, are by no means simple. Change in a living system can rarely be confined to one spot; it spreads to other parts of the system and creates a broad pattern of related effects.

1. *Transition from School to College*. The problems of the first year at college will serve us as a first example. When a freshman arrives on the campus he is in many ways prepared by past experience to fit comfortably into his new life, but he will rarely be able to make the transition without distinct efforts toward adjustment. In several respects he qualifies as maladjusted until he can accomplish certain new steps in growth. For one thing he is quite likely to be a stranger in the material environment. He has to learn a new local geography so that he can find his way around. He must also learn new routines and schedules, and it is often true that he must take suddenly increased responsibility for managing his life. Perhaps for the first time he must do his own shopping, handle his own money, watch over his own health, and plan his work to meet deadlines a week or even a month ahead. Many study problems turn out to be difficulties in reaching this higher level of self-management. Similarly the freshman must learn to interact with new people whose backgrounds may differ widely from his own, whose histories he has not shared, whose interests he must discover. Often there are feelings of loneliness and isolation until progress can be made in the new social field. The strength of such feelings is attested by the joy that is experienced upon finding someone who comes from one's own county or who shares a favorite hobby. Part of a freshman's problems, then, can be summarized by saying that he has lost his habituated interactions with the familiar objects and people of his home environment, and that he must try out new behavior in order to establish comfortable interactions with the college environment.

There is a second aspect of the freshman's problem. Not only must he learn new ways of behaving; he must also arrive at what we may call a new economy of happiness. In his previous life he has probably worked out some kind of balance between joys and sorrows, satisfactions and frustrations; a balance sufficiently favorable so that his life has seemed worth while and valuable. To some extent he will have found his lines of excellence, maintained a basis of security, made some kind of rewarding place in his society. This balance is now temporarily upset, and it can be restored only in the course of time. Freshmen often experience a sharp and painful drop in prestige. As seniors in high school they may have attained local eminence as athletes, debaters, editors, actors, and officers of organizations. At college they are jolted down again to the youngest level of society. It may be that a freshman will learn to interact smoothly enough with his new environment but will nevertheless feel discontented, unable to find a living wage of happiness in a life so lacking in personal distinction. Sometimes a visit to his old school—a return to the scene of his former triumphs—will give his spirits a sudden boost, but he can reach a permanent new equilibrium only by finding sources of satisfaction, prestigeful or of other kinds, appropriate to his life of the present and future. Many students eventually find college life far more satisfying than anything they have known before, but they can mostly report that it took them time to make this discovery, to "find themselves." Building an economy of happiness is a new situation takes energy and patience.

A third feature of the adaptive process comes to light when we examine its emotional accompaniments. Many freshmen are assailed by sadness at being separated from home and familiar surroundings. They may feel a little like crying and they may suffer at times from acute homesickness. Another not uncommon feeling is a certain anxiety over one's prospects of making the grade in the new enterprise. This anxiety may be experienced as a diffuse but lasting discomfort or it may become focalized upon social activity or upon scholastic exercises, particularly examinations. To the extent that sadness and anxiety obtrude themselves disruptively they are likely to have a further poor effect: these are feelings which one has been taught to suppress as much as possible, and their reappearance seems like a childish weakness. The emotions thus add insult to injury. But perhaps the most troublesome emotion is that of anger, usually experienced in the more subdued form of an indiscriminate dislike for the new surroundings and the new people. It is the college community that is making one feel frustrated; what more natural than to feel resentment toward the source of frustration? Yet this feeling, too, is not wholly acceptable. Presumably it conflicts with a desire to like the place and do well there; certainly it creates an obstacle, as we saw in the case of Joseph Kidd, to wholehearted attempts at adjustment. The mobilizing of strong emotions that are difficult to manage may interfere seriously with the adaptive process.

Finally we must take note of a tendency that is aroused in everyone when conditions are difficult. This is a tendency toward regression; that is, a tendency to fall back on forms of behavior that were satisfying earlier in life but have since been outgrown. A high school debating hero, for example, may come to college realizing that his new companions will not want to hear about his former triumphs, but if he meets hard sledding in his attempts to find common grounds of new interest he may discover, to his own consternation, that he is proudly telling about the three-state cup won by his debating team, that he is talking in his platform voice, or that he has reverted to a sophomoric self-confidence in pronouncing judgments. His awareness of what is needed may not prevent him from slipping back a few steps to earlier modes of adjustment. Sometimes regression reaches further into the past. Bewilderment in the new scene may reinstate a dependent attitude in a person lately quite competent; he expects someone to take care of everything for him, or he asks for guidance in matters he could clearly work out for himself. Loss of one's most recent adjustive habits tends to throw one back on earlier ways of behaving just at the moment when new behavior is most needed. There is competition between the new and the old, and sometimes the old displays a disconcerting tenacity.

Our analysis of this process of adaptation thus shows that there are at least four important aspects of the problem. Confronted by a new situation, the person experiences a loss of habituated interactions with his surroundings, material and social; he experiences also an upset in his established economy of happiness; emotions tend to well up in him that are disruptive and hard to manage; and regressions to earlier forms of behavior compete with his attempts to initiate something new. Adaptation to new circumstances is not a simple process. Even when the difficulties are easily surmounted it must be conceived as an over-all operation, a concerted effort on the part of the person to come to terms with all aspects of the new challenge in his life.

2. *Staying in College: the Sophomore Slump.* Our second example will illustrate the problem of adaptation when the main requirement is not for change but for persisting endurance. Let us suppose that our hypothetical freshman makes a successful transition to college, so that everyone who cares about him is pleased with his progress. There may come a time when the excitement of novelty wears off, when studying is felt as an increasingly wearisome grind, when efficiency breaks down and time seems to be more wasted than used. The student is beset by bore-

dom and restlessness, perhaps also by feelings of anxiety and guilt when he realizes how badly he is using his opportunity for a college education. Some students find college, with its many paths of interest, so much to their liking that they never pass through a period of real misgiving. Others are but mildly troubled and put themselves back in tune with the college world by a change of major, a reconsidering of vocational choice, or an alteration in extracurricular life. But for some students, things come to a real crisis: habits of work collapse; social life loses its savor; feelings of worthlessness and self-reproach become disturbing; and the situation may end by flunking out, leaving school, or (in extreme but not frequent instances) by a real mental breakdown.

Troubles of this kind may happen at any time, but they occur often enough during the second year to be nicknamed "sophomore slump." At the start the problem does not turn on a loss of habituated interactions with the environment, although something of this sort may occur later; on the contrary, there may be a strong feeling that habitual interactions have become stale, and part of the difficulty may seem to lie in a craving for novelty and excitement. But the other features of the adaptive process show themselves quite directly: the economy of happiness has gone wrong, disruptive and unmanageable emotions are intruding themselves, and behavior is tending to regress to earlier forms.

Although it is always necessary to allow for wide ranges of individual difference, we can perhaps recognize a common central theme in the loss of happiness. The glow of early success loses its warming power. The student has proved to himself that he is equal to college studies and that he can keep afloat in college life. He has proved to his parents and his teachers back at school that he can fulfill their expectations for him. But these motives are not enough to sustain him in those repeated acts of initiative, planning, and self-discipline that are necessary for success at the college level. Schoolboy motives of pleasing parents and teachers and of proving that you can get high marks have to be superseded by something that is more in accord with the mature adulthood upon which the student feels himself to be entering. His education must become meaningful for his own life. This may come about easily if he finds college studies intrinsically interesting and knows that he will always want to have some part in intellectual activities. It may come about naturally if his studies have a clear relevance to a vocation he knows he wants to enter. When actions are subordinated to strong personal needs and cherished personal goals, we are able to resist distractions and endure frustrations in order to perform them. Sometimes a student goes through college groaning all the way over his academic chores, then enters a business which he perceives as his career and manages painlessly a thousand routine details far less interesting in themselves than college studies.

In severe cases of sophomore slump, there is difficulty in connecting college work with more mature motives. The student is no longer able to drive himself in order to fulfill other people's expectations or to run a race with his classmates, but he may not yet know what he wants to do with his life and may not feel that studies have much bearing on his future. For him the economy of happiness breaks down. He finds small emotional rewards in what seems like a pointless struggle.

We must be careful at this point to avoid assuming that everyone ought to adjust to college. The student in sophomore slump, wasting his time and seemingly going to pieces, may be trying to carry out a sort of rebellion against a kind of life that is not at the moment valuable for his personal growth. It may be more important for him to take a job or to try something highly adventurous, proving his worth and finding his interests in action rather than in studies. Students are sometimes well advised to drop out of college for a while, deciding later whether or not they want to return. The majority, however, want to find their way out of sophomore slump without interrupting their academic education.

Upset in the economy of happiness may be regarded as the starting point, but disruptive emotions may then be mobilized which hinder a clear perception of the problem. Frustration over studies can easily beget anger at the college authorities who set the tasks, at parents who expect fine performance, at friends who are having a more fortunate time. There may be guilt feelings over the failure to meet expectations, and there may be painful feelings of inferiority over failure to make the grade. Anxiety may be experienced over the failure to control and organize one's own behavior. These emotions make it harder to work one's way toward a solution of the problem.

Regressive patterns become increasingly prominent as behavior loses its organization. There are many similarities to the actions of a child resisting unwelcome demands: dawdling, loafing, filibustering, doing senseless naughty things, running away. The appearance of these patterns compounds the difficulty of making the self-discoveries that might lead the student to find a mature relation between himself and his studies.

Occasionally the compounding of all these difficulties leads to an outright breakdown. When this occurs, the symptoms can often be seen as derivatives of the processes we have been describing. Perhaps the predominant manifestation will be a depressed state with hopelessness and feelings of unworthiness. Perhaps the disorder will take the form of confusion with a regression to early dependent patterns. Perhaps resentment will dominate the picture, spoiling friendships and generating a derogatory view of the world. Anxiety may take the lead, with its associated symptoms of tension and sleeplessness. Disruptive emotions, if long continued, may lead to psychosomatic disorders of various kinds, especially in the realm of digestive processes. It is important to notice that none of the reactions are inappropriate in themselves: *their inappropriateness lies in their excess.* The difference is one of degree rather than kind, of quantity rather than quality. Disordered reaction consists of a marked exaggeration and persistence of one or more of the many responses that anyone must make to stress.

Two problems deserve attention at this point. (1) How can we explain the *excess* in the reaction? Such reactions appear to be of no help to the person; they are rigid and indiscriminate, hindering the course of adaptation, and they are often a cause of suffering in their own right. Why should a person be prey to such self-defeating behavior? (2) How can we explain the *choice* of the reaction that becomes excessive? Why does one person develop a digestive disorder while another person bcomes mentally confused without digestive upset? Why does one feel personally inferior and worthless while another treats the world with angry contempt? We must suppose that there is lawfulness behind both the self-defeating behavior and the selection of its particular channels.

These two problems are not peculiar to adaptation in college. They are perhaps the most central problems in the whole field of abnormal psychology. We shall meet them repeatedly in the further course of this book.

GROWTH PROBLEMS OF EARLY LIFE

Up to this point we have considered the adaptive process in quite specific situations. We must now turn our attention to a much larger question: what are the main problems that put strain on the adaptive process in early life, and how do the child's struggles with these problems affect the course of his development? Most of the major issues of growth and of human relationship are encountered quite early in life. The young child must attempt some solution to these problems, and his first patterns of reaction establish precedents, so to speak, which leave him a little less free to use other solutions on later occasions.

In shifting attention from specific adjustive problems to the major crises of early life it is necessary to enlarge the scope of our thinking. As will soon become apparent, the main problems endure for long periods; they are also somewhat subtle and pervasive in their impact. We must therefore not base our thinking on the analogy of simple learning situations or of problem solving when all the elements are clearly in view. The child learns slowly, by successive attempts, to deal with his major problems. He learns unwittingly, with but little sense of the true nature and scope of the problems. He learns also with the limited understanding and experience that is appropriate to his age, which means that he may sense the problem in a way that differs greatly from an adult view of the matter. We often speak metaphorically of the child's "first collisions" with the major problems of growth, but we must remember that his early patterns of reaction are wrought over weeks and months, not produced once and for all in well-defined critical situations.

In the following sections we shall consider four main growth problems of early life. The importance of these problems has been established partly through the study of disordered behavior, to which they frequently make a significant contribution, but it seems likely that they are central in the development of any personality, even the most healthy. These problems are (1) dependence and deprivation, (2) autonomy and discipline, (3) sexual development, and (4) aggression and its management. Obviously this list does not exhaust the problems of growth in childhood, but it includes what we can reasonably suppose to be the outstanding emotional problems, those that most tax the adaptive process to mediate between vital urges in the person and the social patterns in which he must learn to live. Theories of development are best reserved until the problems have been more fully described. At this point it is enough to indicate that although these problems extend pretty much throughout the course of development they reach their peaks at somewhat different times. Dependence and deprivation have first place on the calendar, constituting the outstanding problem of the first year of life, the "oral stage" in the scheme introduced by Freud. The child's struggle with discipline, his attempt to reach a balance between his own autonomy and the requirements of the domestic social order, comes to prominence in the second and third years, the period called the "anal stage" by Freud who believed that bowel training was the leading issue. Sexual development has two distinct times of crisis in our society: the fourth and fifth years, when it appears to reach its childhood peak, and puberty, when maturing reproductive capacity brings a strengthening of the sexual urge. Only in the case of aggression is it difficult to discern natural points of climax. Management of aggression often forms part of the other problems, and it occurs in its own right when frustrations of any kind reach serious proportions.

Response to the major problems of development in childhood may be highly successful, but it may fall short of success in various ways. The solutions achieved in the early years, good or bad, exert an influence over the subsequent course of development. According to some workers they determine basic traits of character which stay with us throughout life. For our present purpose a more limited claim is sufficient: when poorly adjustive solutions are reached in childhood there will be difficulty in meeting similar situations in later years. It is worth noticing, furthermore, that the concept of regression implies a reanimation of earlier ways of behaving. When later obstacles bring out regression, the importance of childhood patterns of behavior is likely to be much increased. These points will become clearer as we examine the main growth problems in detail.

DEPENDENCE AND DEPRIVATION

Childhood Dependence. The child begins life in a state of virtually complete helplessness. Discomforts are removed and gratifications provided almost entirely through the actions of those who are taking care of him. Outside of restless activity and the very important act of crying there is not very much that the small baby can do about his troubles. For the first six months or more it is fair to say that his world revolves around hunger and its satisfaction. In a healthy baby hunger is the outstanding pain and its relief the outstanding satisfaction. The lips, mouth, and tongue are among the most sensitive regions of his body. Around the act of feeding cluster a great many secondary sources of pleasure: stimulation of the mouth; the pleasurable act of sucking and swallowing; being picked up and rocked and cuddled.

The child's earliest experiences of want and of gratification thus take place in connection with feeding. They also take place in connection with the mother, or whoever is regularly taking care of the child. The mother becomes the first important human object in the baby's world. Her behavior toward him has a lot to do with establishing a feeling of security. Depending on her attitude, the baby's world can become a place where you get what you need within a comfortingly short time and in good measure, or at the other extreme a place where you have to cry yourself black in the face for niggardly rewards.

Different cultures vary greatly in their attitudes toward the infant and his needs. In some parts of the world there is great leniency and indulgence at this stage; in others it is believed that early deprivations harden the infant for the difficulties that lie ahead. Our own society has undergone a decided change of attitude during the last fifty years. In 1914 the United States Children's Bureau first published a bulletin called *Infant Care.* Since then there have been frequent revised editions which tell a remarkable story of changing fashion in expert opinion.[2] As regards the first year of life the trend is clearly in the direction of greater indulgence. In the earlier editions the baby was to be efficiently fed according to a regular schedule, regardless of his own indications of hunger, and weaning was to be accomplished with firmness and decision. Today it is

[2] Martha Wolfenstein, "Trends in Infant Care," *American Journal of Orthopsychiatry,* XXIII (1953), pp. 120–30.

recommended that babies be fed when they cry ("self-demand schedule"), that they be held and cuddled and played with, and that they be weaned gradually so that the feeling of deprivation will never become unbearable. Behind this recommendation lies the idea that dependence, ultimately a liability to be outgrown, is at first a thing to be encouraged and strengthened. Helplessness is the natural condition of the infant; he should be made happy in it and given gratification.

Naturally one wonders whether or not this attitude toward infancy is just another turn of the wheel of fashion. Probably not; the present outlook is based upon considerably better observation than has ever before been available. In a long series of studies at a children's hospital Ribble has collected evidence that infants prosper better when they are given plentiful "mothering"; that is, when they are held, cuddled, patted, rocked, and given a surplus of loving attention beyond the strict necessities of daily care. "Mothering" has a favorable effect even on physical development: it promotes stronger respiration, firmer sucking and swallowing, better digestion. One might almost suppose that the infant's nervous system needed the extra priming that comes from the stimulation involved in "mothering." However this may be, Ribble's observations include cases of severe disorder, physical and emotional, when "mothering" was for some reason interrupted without provision of a substitute who could act and feel much like the real mother.[3] These observations have been sustained by other workers, particularly by Spitz, who made a comparative study of children reared in a foundling home and children reared in the nursery of a penal institution. At the foundling home one adult took care of each group of seven or more children, obviously with little time to spare. The nursery children, in contrast, were in the care of their own mothers, who, being inmates of the institution, had plenty of time to spare. The differences between the less "mothered" and the more "mothered" children were striking. Rate of mortality and susceptibility to illness were much higher in the foundling home; motor and language development were much retarded: signs of distress, such as screaming and odd repetitive behavior, were much more common. Spitz gives the name "hospitalism" to the pattern of defects observed so frequently among the foundling children, and he points out the many ways in which close interchange between mother and child fosters the growth of security and confidence.[4] In another study Spitz has shown that children of six months or so who are abruptly separated from their mothers

[3] Margaret A. Ribble, *The Rights of Infants* (New York: Columbia University Press, 1943); "Disorganizing Factors of Infant Personality," *American Journal of Psychiatry*, XCVIII (1941), pp. 459–63.

[4] R. A. Spitz, "Hospitalism: An Inquiry into the Genesis of Psychiatric Conditions in Early Childhood," *Psychoanalytic Study of the Child*, I (1945), pp. 53–74.

sometimes develop a depressed and lethargic condition that is difficult to cure.[5]

Experimental Studies of Deprivation. At first these findings were greeted with a certain amount of skepticism. Critics thought they detected a note of unscientific sentimentality in the emphasis on mothering. Yet it is a matter of common knowledge that cats mother their kittens and dogs their puppies with ministrations such as licking that go far beyond the mere provision of nourishment. Experiments were begun with various species of animals to test the consequences of particularly early deprivations. Puppies were reared in an artificial environment that restricted both sensory input and motor activity.[6] Chickens were separated from the flock and raised in social isolation.[7] Chimpanzees were deprived of visual experience by being kept in darkness for the first three months of life.[8] These and many other experiments, summaries of which are now available,[9] showed that an insufficient exercise of natural capacities at the beginning of life would often injure the later use of these capacities. In some cases it was even shown that portions of the nervous system did not develop properly when no demands were made upon them in the form of stimulation.[10]

Particularly pertinent are the experiments made by Harlow in which baby monkeys were provided with mechanical mother surrogates.[11] The artificial mothers, made of cloth or of wire, provided abundant milk through a conveniently placed nipple, emitted bodily warmth, and were set in positions suitable for clinging; in all these respects, they were designed to be good mothers. Harlow was able to show, in the first place, that clinging and contact are of great importance for satisfaction and security. To a baby monkey a cloth mother is far more acceptable than one made of wire. In the second place, observing the animals' development into adulthood, he showed that the mechanically reared

[5] R. A. Spitz, "Anaclitic Depression," *Psychoanalytic Study of the Child,* II (1946), pp. 313–42.

[6] W. R. Thompson and W. Heron, "The Effect of Early Restriction on Activity in Dogs," *Journal of Comparative and Physiological Psychology,* XLVII (1954), pp. 77–82.

[7] A. Baron, G. B. Kish, and J. J. Antonitis, "Effects of Early and Late Social Isolation on Aggregative Behavior in the Domestic Chicken," *Journal of Genetic Psychology,* C (1962), pp. 355–60.

[8] A. H. Riesen, "Arrested Vision," *Scientific American,* CLXXXIII (1960), pp. 16–19.

[9] D. W. Fiske and S. R. Maddi, *The Functions of Varied Experience* (Homewood, Ill.: The Dorsey Press, Inc., 1961), chaps. 3, 4.

[10] A. H. Riesen, "Effects of Stimulus Deprivation on the Development and Atrophy of the Visual Sensory System," *American Journal of Orthopsychiatry,* XXX (1960), pp. 23–36.

[11] H. F. Harlow, "The Nature of Love," *American Psychologist,* XIII (1958), pp. 673–85.

monkeys remained almost completely unresponsive to other monkeys, so much so that very few of the females produced offspring and only one was observed to try to nurse her young. The central deprivation to which they had been exposed, that of interaction with a living member of the species, resulted in a permanent incapacity for social response.[12]

The effects of deprivation have been closely analyzed in an experiment with kittens by Schneirla and Rosenblatt.[13] A technique of temporary isolation was used in which one kitten was removed from the litter for a period of time and provided with an artificial mother something like Harlow's cloth model. When the isolated kitten was returned to the litter, it was noticed that nursing did not begin at once; there was considerable delay and awkwardness in resuming the original relation to the mother. In a common phrase we might say that the kitten had gotten out of the habit, but the situation is really a little more complex. The normal nursing process is an interaction between cat and kittens that undergoes a constant development. At first, for example, the mother cat initiates the proceedings; but progressively the kittens take a more active part. The isolated kitten does not keep up with this development and is therefore no longer quite at home with either the mother or the other kittens when returned to the litter. This experiment helps us to understand what is involved in human cases in which there is deprivation of mothering. The crucial thing is the absence of opportunity to engage in those continuous gratifying interactions with the mother that make her a familiar and agreeable object and that provide training for later interactions with other people.

Adaptive and Maladaptive Possibilities. The importance of the first year of life for later growth becomes clearer when we take a broad view of what the infant is learning. Specific acts such as sucking and swallowing do not tell the full story of his accomplishment. Through his contact with the mother he forms an initial estimate of the goodness or badness of the social environment, and through his experiences of need and gratification, pain and relief, he makes an appraisal of the general goodness of the conditions of life. Freud offered the suggestion that a gratified oral stage would make for lasting optimism; conversely, frequent deprivations would produce a sour pessimist. This idea has been elaborated by Erikson, who chooses "trust" and "mistrust" as the words best suited to express what the infant is learning.

[12] H. F. Harlow and M. K. Harlow, "A Study of Animal Affection," *Journal of the American Museum of Natural History*, LXX (1961), No. 10.

[13] T. C. Schneirla and J. S. Rosenblatt, "Behavioral Organization and Genesis of the Social Bond in Insects and Mammals," *American Journal of Orthopsychiatry*, XXXI (1961), pp. 223–53.

For the first component of a healthy personality I nominate a sense of *basic trust,* which I think is an attitude toward oneself and the world derived from the experience of the first year of life. By "trust" I mean what is commonly implied in reasonable trustfulness as far as others are concerned and a simple sense of trustworthiness as far as oneself is concerned. . . . The firm establishment of enduring patterns for the balance of basic trust over basic mistrust is the first task of the budding personality and therefore first of all a task for maternal care.[14]

Development of a sense of trust is an adaptive outcome which will stand the infant in good stead all his life. When the outcome is mistrust, children are apt to be left with a strong lingering hunger for the provision of their wants by others, even though they have little hope of obtaining such gratification. They remain sharply sensitive to deprivation, which makes it difficult for them to place trust in others and to maintain friendly relationships. If traits of independence and self-reliance are developed they are apt to be accompanied by feelings of bitterness and isolation from others. This outcome was illustrated in the case of Bert Whipley, who could organize delinquent joy rides and execute solitary feats of burglary but who felt himself an outcast and secretly yearned for the provided life of a prison inmate. Deprivation and rejection do not produce a solid and reliable independence founded upon basic trust. Such independence as they stimulate is likely to have the brittle character of a reaction-formation, a point already exemplified in the case of the bombardier, Pearson Brack. As we saw, Brack attempted to suppress his dependent and irresponsible tendencies by adopting a strenuous ideal of self-sufficiency, extending it in military service to include the carefree, aggressive airman. Under pressure, however, his reaction-formation cracked open and his dependent yearnings came to light.

The animal experiments and the observations of Ribble and Spitz have to do with deprivations very early in life. Children remain dependent in many respects much longer, and a lack of affectionate support presumably has cumulative effects. That the effects can be detected in later years is shown in a study by Goldfarb.[15] Fifteen children brought up in institutions to the age of 3 were carefully matched with fifteen whose early years had been spent in the more favorable climate of foster homes. The children were examined and tested at about 12 years of age, by which time it might be supposed that the consequences of their early upbringing would be obliterated. The two groups proved to be signifi-

[14] E. H. Erikson, "Identity and the Life Cycle," *Psychological Issues,* I (1959), No. 1, pp. 55–56.

[15] W. Goldfarb, "Emotional and Intellectual Consequences of Psychologic Deprivation in Infancy: A Revaluation," in P. H. Hoch and J. Zubin, *Psychopathology of Childhood* (New York: Grune & Stratton, Inc., 1955), pp. 105–19.

cantly different in several respects: the institutional children were behind on various tests of intellectual ability, their speech was less well developed, they were rated much lower on friendly contact with the examining adults, and in an experimental game they much more often broke the rules without signs of guilt. These findings support the idea of an enduring lack of trust in the human environment, and they suggest that such mistrust tends to retard the development of abilities in general.

The problem can be approached more directly—though still, of course, somewhat indirectly—by clinical studies of the parents of severely disturbed young children. One type of such children, called *autistic,* shows progressively in the second and third years a striking lack of responsiveness to human beings. The autistic child does not interact with his caretakers, does not gaze at them or smile, cannot be inveigled into interactive play such as pat-a-cake, and is retarded in the use of speech which depends so much on imitation. With inanimate objects the child seems more at home and may give evidence of an approximately normal development.[16] The cases studied do not come from situations of poverty, neglect, or insufficient physical care. The parents are found, however, to be cool, detached, preoccupied with their own concerns, and inclined to treat the child's care as a problem in efficient management following regular schedules.[17] One is reminded of Harlow's wire mothers who offer small monkeys everything that is needful for physical care but nothing in the way of a living, comforting interaction. Apparently the results tend to be of similar long duration. Follow-up studies of autistic children show a poor record of adjustment in later years.[18]

There is thus a good deal of evidence in support of the idea that infants should be encouraged in their dependence and given gratification of their needs. The value of mothering, conceived as the simultaneous provision of general stimulation and the specific comforts of holding and cuddling, has a good deal more than a sentimental basis. In our minds, of course, there is always the idea that sometime the child has got to grow up. We would not want to spoil him by making life too easy. Will he not become fixated in dependent passivity and grow up to be an adult who thinks the world owes him a living? The question here is one of timing, and we can understand it only when we examine the forces in the child that make for independence.

[16] L. Kanner, "Autistic Disturbances of Affective Contact," *The Nervous Child,* II (1943), pp. 217–50.

[17] L. Eisenberg, "The Fathers of Autistic Children," *American Journal of Orthopsychiatry,* XXVII (1957), pp. 715–24.

[18] L. Eisenberg, "The Course of Childhood Schizophrenia," *A. M. A. Archives of Neurology and Psychiatry,* LXXVIII (1957), pp. 69–83.

AUTONOMY AND DISCIPLINE

Careful observation shows that even from the beginning there is another side to the infant besides passive dependence. Very early there are signs of spontaneous activity, taking forms such as following and fixating with the eyes or exploring and experimenting with the hands. The nature of this activity becomes clearer toward the middle of the first year, when manipulation becomes an absorbing occupation. By the time he is a year old, the child may be spending as much as five or six hours of his waking day in exploratory play which is not related to the hungers, pains, and anxieties that still require the mother's ministrations. He develops his repertory of actions by manipulating all objects within reach; he tests in playful babbling his power to make various kinds of sounds; and he learns about the properties of his own body by successive attempts to sit up, crawl, and take steps in an upright position. This kind of activity appears to be self-rewarding, and its biological function seems to lie in learning about the properties of things and what can be done with them—in other words, in becoming competent to deal with the environment.[19]

The zest for active exploration presently invades the sphere of the mother's ministrations. It is discovered that water can be dribbled from the wet washcloth on to the floor, that milk will spread in an interesting way over a flat surface, that utensils produce a gratifying series of sounds when banged or thrown from the high chair. David Levy selects what he calls "the battle of the spoon" to illustrate the nature of such actions and their relation to being mothered.[20] One day the child seizes the spoon and undertakes to load it and steer it into his mouth. As the spoon is likely at first to miss its target and to reach some other part of the face upside down, the maneuver is far from resulting in a more efficient intake of food; but the child may continue it insistently, resisting his mother's attempts to recapture her maternal role. Levy points out that the behavior cannot be classed as aggressive; it is not done to annoy the mother, however surely it may produce this result when she thinks about cleaning up. It is part of an urge to do things autonomously, to control the environment as much as possible through one's own initiative.

It is important to notice that this movement on the child's part toward competent independence will often conflict with his mother's desire to minister to his wants. The most important reward for the child lies in

[19] R. W. White, "Motivation Reconsidered: The Concept of Competence," *Psychological Review,* LXVI (1959), pp. 297–333.

[20] D. M. Levy, "Oppositional Syndromes and Oppositional Behavior," in Hoch and Zubin, *op. cit.,* pp. 204–26.

the feeling of efficacy that comes from producing an intended result through his own expended effort. This is not something the mother can bestow. The point is made clear in an intensive observational study of mothers and their babies.[21] Certain mothers were happiest during the infant's first six or eight months, when his helplessness called forth and deeply gratified their desires to provide. The emergence of autonomous activity frustrated them and irritated them, as in the following example.

> It was both reported by Mrs. A. and observed that Billy was more difficult to dress. He did not "co-operate" in this as he had before and it looked as if his mother's usual ways of restraining him by distraction or touch could no longer control his drive to activity. . . . When his mother tried to hold him on her lap, he tried to get down. He was reaching out and scratching at her neck or face in a provocative way and she was scolding him with a new sharpness in her tone. . . . He also was making persistent grabs for the spoon during feeding and she found this annoying.

In contrast, other mothers felt themselves somewhat imprisoned during the early months and joyfully welcomed the signs of autonomy, seeing in them both proof of the child's normality and a harbinger of greater freedom for themselves.

During the second and third years of life the child emerges rapidly from his early condition of helplessness. One of the major advances is learning to walk. This makes it possible to explore the house and yard, to venture into the street, and sometimes to escape from parental supervision. Particularly important is the increased mastery of speech, permitting the child to name objects, form concepts, issue commands, grasp more fully the things that are said to him. In due course he discovers the powerful properties of the word "no" and begins to test the extent to which he can resist and control the human part of his environment. These experiments on his part usher in a time that has often been called the period of two-year-old negativism. When the child begins to issue or resist commands, there is a direct confrontation of wills, a clear-cut problem of who is going to prevail. The child, as Stern expressed it, now "realizes himself as a living entity, a one complete center of power; he wishes to affirm himself, his existence, his importance, and to increase it."[22] The parents, too, have something to affirm, partly in the child's interest, partly in the service of their own pride. Autonomy is in full collision with authority and discipline.

The foremost place now comes to be occupied by learning to deal with parental rules and regulations. The child discovers that there are many

[21] R. W. Coleman, E. Kris, and S. Provence, "The Study of Variations of Early Parental Attitudes," *Psychoanalytic Study of the Child,* VIII (1953), pp. 20–47.

[22] W. Stern *Psychology of Early Childhood* (New York: Holt, Rinehart & Winston, Inc., 1930), p. 492.

restrictions upon his freedom. He must not order his parents around or be rude to visitors. There are also things that he is supposed to do, such as sharing his toys with other children, finishing up the food on his plate, putting away the playthings that a busy day has scattered all over the house and yard. The world proves to be full of strange moral hazards, and one must learn how to accommodate one's desires to the often mysterious requirements of the social order.

One of the fields of battle is toilet training. The parents demand a change in what must seem like the eminently satisfactory plan of relieving the bowels whenever one feels so inclined. Dollard and Miller, analyzing the requisite learning in stimulus-response terms, point out the inherent difficulty in the problem that is set for the child. The naturally strong connection between pressure in the bowel and the response of evacuation must be weakened so that a whole series of new responses can be inserted: at first, calling parents; later, going to the bathroom, unbuttoning, sitting on the toilet. This learning must be accomplished, moreover, at a time when the child is still far from adept at the use of verbal cues and can have little understanding of the purpose of the training.[23] The parents, trained in their own childhoods to feel disgust toward evacuation and its products, often find it hard to conduct the educative program with patient tolerance. It is not surprising, therefore, that strong emotions are often aroused on both sides and that the adjustive solution reached upon this issue sets a strong precedent for later responses to discipline and authority.

The problem of discipline and autonomy should not be conceived simply as a struggle between the child's desires and the parents' restrictions. What the parents require is not a complete suppression of the child's impulses; they ask rather that he guide his impulses into socially acceptable channels. As Murray has pointed out, cultural and parental prescriptions can usually be described as "time-place-mode-object formulas which are allowed or insisted upon for the expression of individual needs."

> A child is allowed to play during the day but not at night (time). He may defecate in the toilet but not on the floor (place). He may push other children but not hit them with a mallet (mode). He may ask his father but not a stranger in the street for money (object). No need has to be inhibited permanently. If an individual is of the right age and chooses the permitted time, the permitted place, the permitted mode and the permitted object, he can objectify any one of his needs.[24]

[23] J. Dollard and N. E. Miller, *Personality and Psychotherapy* (New York: McGraw-Hill Book Co., Inc., 1950), pp. 136–38.

[24] H. A. Murray, *Explorations in Personality* (Fair Lawn, N. J.: Oxford University Press, 1938), p. 136.

The child is being asked to pattern his behavior in ways which may seem at first quite difficult and frustrating, but the culture does not require the complete surrender of fundamental desires. In the end it is no hardship to use the toilet if one is available or to give up playing in the street if there are other places to play.

These considerations are necessary in order to grasp the true nature of the growth problem when discipline and autonomy are the major issues. There is almost always something for the child to do if he can become able and willing to do it. The crucial point here is his willingness: can he learn to pattern his behavior without damage to his growing sense of autonomy? For his early collisions with discipline come at a time when, as Erikson puts it, he is beginning to "attach enormous value to his autonomous will," when he "delineates his world as 'I' and 'you,' 'me' and 'mine,' " when he is particularly eager to feel in control of his behavior and particularly anxious when this control appears to be threatened. "From a sense of self-control without loss of self-esteem comes a lasting sense of autonomy and pride."[25] But such an outcome is not easy when the child is a mere toddler and the source of constraint is the very adults upon whom his security depends. At first, the two most available responses are helpless yielding or angry resistance. Neither of these responses leads to feelings of autonomy and pride. Anxious surrender to discipline means the simultaneous sacrifice of one's desires and one's self-direction. Impassioned resistance salvages pride only for a moment and cannot long be maintained against the force of parental disapproval. Autonomy can here be built only upon willing acceptance of what is required.

Adaptive and Maladaptive Possibilities. To the problem of achieving the desirable outcome described by Erikson—"a lasting sense of autonomy and pride"—the child brings definite assets. He may seem resistant to constraint, but on the whole he would like to grow up. There can be very substantial rewards in becoming able to meet adult requirements. Self-esteem is increased when obedience to regulations carries with it a feeling of achievement. Becoming socialized entails sacrifices, but it is not entirely a bad bargain. Parents can make the bargain more favorable in two ways: by permitting the child's initiative to have a part in the learning, and by greeting his achievements with expressions of true respect. The first point is partly a question of timing. It is obviously foolish to expect successful bowel training before the neuromuscular system is sufficiently mature to control the sphincters, or to expect the child to be quiet before he is capable of sustained inhibition. The timely moment for a piece of training is one at which the child himself initiates

[25] Erikson, *op. cit.*, pp. 198–99.

appropriate acts. In a recent study of child development, made in a situation where many of the parents believed in a maximum of permissiveness, it was observed that the children often insisted upon feeding themselves, dressing themselves, and using the toilet in adult fashion before the parents had taken steps toward training.[26] The second point is a question of the parents' attitude. It goes without saying that they do better when they are patient and allow for relapses and slowness in the learning process. But the crucial feature would seem to be respect: the possibility of taking generous pleasure in the child's accomplishments and giving expression to affectionate esteem.

Maladjustive solutions occur when the learning process deviates too widely from the course just described. Departures can occur in two directions. There can be spoiling, in this case generally called *indulgence,* when the parents make too few serious demands—when they do not have the firmness to require that the child pick up his toys or inhibit his aggressiveness, for example. Permissiveness can be carried to the point at which adult friends hate to call at the house, knowing that the atmosphere will be too child-centered for serious conversation. There are even instances in which a family has found it difficult to rent living quarters, so disastrous has been the effect of childhood self-expression on real estate previously occupied. The effect of this laxity is to delay the growth of autonomy: the child is given too little incentive to master and control his impulses, and remains longer their victim. The problem of meeting discipline is thus postponed, leaving it to teachers and playmates who can hardly be expected to deal with it patiently. Probably the more serious maladjustments spring from the opposite course, which here takes the form of *coercion.* When discipline is brought about by coercive methods the results are not apt to be satisfactory. Whether the child is tricked into obedience by clever parental devices, ridiculed and made to feel shame, or threatened with painful and terrifying punishments, he will have a sense of being forced and there will be little willingness in his response. He is left with no middle ground between a hopeless fight and unconditional surrender.

The effects of coercive discipline can be conveniently grouped into two patterns. One solution can best be described as *anxious conformity.* Desires and resentments are suppressed, and the person becomes a model of cleanliness, goodness, sharing, and all-around propriety. If these traits persist into later life they may create an outwardly good adjustment to society and its requirements, but behavior will lack spontaneity and confidence, and the person will be ill prepared when the environment begins

[26] S. Chess, A. Thomas, and H. Birch, "Characteristics of the Individual Child's Behavioral Responses to the Environment," *American Journal of Orthopsychiatry,* XXIX (1959), pp. 791–802.

to make conflicting demands upon him. The other solution is an enduring *resentment against demands,* an essentially negative attitude even when overt resistance is impossible. In extreme cases the person might become a professional noncomformist, doing everything in a way that obviously differs from social expectations. More commonly he might conform in outward behavior but not with any sense of willingness or warmth; his latent rebellion is then apt to leak out in irritating ways like missing appointments or keeping everyone waiting. Major problems of adjustment will obviously confront him when he enters the responsibilities of adult life as worker, parent, and member of the community.

SEXUAL DEVELOPMENT

Early Childhood Sexuality. One of Freud's most important contributions was the discovery that sexual needs are active throughout childhood. As we saw in the first chapter, Freud called attention to many aspects of child behavior that should clearly be called sexual, even when allowance is made for the fact that genital maturity and power of procreation have not been reached. The most indisputable example is masturbation, which is universally practiced by children of both sexes, generally with increasing interest during the fourth and fifth years. Growing directly out of this is curiosity about the sexual organs and the anatomical differences between the sexes. This may lead to experimentation with other children and a quest for information from adults. Sexual excitation is undoubtedly much less differentiated from other forms of pleasant bodily stimulation than it will be after puberty when the special excitability of the genital organs reaches full development. Nevertheless we would overlook crucial problems of development if we tried to deny the presence of sexual elements in childhood behavior.

For the child to bring his sexual activities into line with adult demands is an early and difficult problem of adjustment. In spite of changes for the better, our culture is still fairly hostile toward childhood sexuality. Many parents are still misinformed about the effects of masturbation, whether it be in childhood or later. It is widely believed to produce nervousness, injury to the genitals or to reproductive capacity, physical weakening, feeble-mindedness, and insanity, although there is not a scrap of evidence for any of these contentions.[27] Many parents therefore try to stamp out masturbation and do not hesitate to use coercion and direful threats.[28] The child's requests for sexual enlightenment are condemned as dirty and disgusting. Even parents who consider themselves unusually

[27] E. H. Jaques, "Misconceptions of Parents Concerning Child Health and Behavior," *American Journal of Orthopsychiatry,* XII (1942), pp. 202–13.

[28] M. Huschka, "The Incidence and Character of Masturbation Threats in a Group of Problem Children," *Psychoanalytic Quarterly,* VII (1938), pp. 338–55.

tolerant are apt to quail at the prospect of their young reeling off the facts of anatomy and childbirth in front of their neighbors. The United States Children's Bureau bulletin *Infant Care* reflects a radical change in expert opinion between 1914 and 1951. In the 1914 edition childhood masturbation figured as an "injurious practice" that "easily grows beyond control. . . . Children are sometimes wrecked for life." Later editions state that it will "pass away unless it is emphasized by unwise treatment on the part of adults. . . . A wise mother will not be concerned about this."[29] The earlier attitude is still deeply embedded in the culture, and rapid change cannot be expected on a topic so charged with emotion. In large segments of our society the young child, and later the adolescent, is asked to constrain sexual impulses within a quite rigid formula of time, place, mode, and object. The sexual impulse often does not take kindly to the expected constraints, and its control can become a source of severe conflict.

The Family Circle. Childhood sexual feelings are probably at first associated only with the parts of the body from which they are derived. Their attachment to outside objects results from learning. From his study of the free associations and memories of neurotic patients, Freud came to the conclusion that the child's sexual feelings become attached first to members of his own family. Freud brought the matter under more direct observation when in 1909 he published the detailed case of a five-year-old boy named Hans.[30] This boy not only played with his own penis but on occasion invited his mother to do so and frequently asked to be taken into her bed and cuddled. At the same time he was afraid of his father, and when the many suppressions and disguises of this fear were untangled it proved to be directly related to the anger he supposed his father was feeling on account of his cuddling with his mother. Since then it has become a commonplace to notice that children around four and five take what looks like an erotic interest in their mothers, fathers, and siblings. The display often includes demands for an exclusive relation, with jealousy and hostility toward those who claim to share it. Freud was particularly interested in the little boy's erotic attachment to his mother. He called this the Oedipus situation, naming it from the tragedy by Sophocles in which Oedipus unwittingly kills his father and marries his mother. Freud also described the little girl's interest in her father and jealousy of her mother, which has sometimes been called the Electra complex.

The importance of these erotic attachments has been vigorously debated. It can be pointed out that love and sex are not the same, that the

29 Wolfenstein, *op. cit.*, p. 122.

30 S. Freud, "Analysis of a Phobia in a 5-Year-Old Child," *Collected Papers* (International Psycho-analytic Press, 1925), Vol. III, pp. 149–289.

child's love for his mother is deeply grounded in the satisfaction of his dependent needs, that the Oedipus complex reflects "the possessive attachment to a person upon whom the child depends for his gratifications and security, with jealousy and hostility against competitors."[31] Sometimes fear of rejection seems to be an important element: "hanging on to a person out of sheer anxiety is easily confounded with love, and in the child's own mind seems like love."[32] Again, the Oedipus situation can be viewed as one in which the child, now increasingly aware of himself as a person and wanting to be treated like an adult, finds the desired esteem imperiled by his parents' interest in each other and in his siblings: "what hurts anyone, whether boy or girl, is to be pushed aside in favor of another—jealous dogs show the same mechanisms as children."[33] Seen from a sociological angle, the Oedipus situation can be treated as a problem of group structure. For the first time the child, hitherto secure in a two-person (diadic) relationship with his mother, confronts a three-cornered (triadic) relationship. The human triangle is essentially unstable, tending to become a pair with the third person "relegated to an inferior rank; in other words, the triadic pattern has a tendency to exclude one of the three participants through pair combination."[34] It is not surprising that in his first brush with the "eternal triangle" the child should experience important adjustive difficulties.

Most problems of development can properly be viewed from several angles. It should be noticed that none of the views just described challenges the importance of affectionate relationships and jealousies within the family circle. On this point Freud is sustained; the challenge is directed rather at interpreting the main motives as sexual ones. For our present purpose we need claim only that erotic motives are likely to be included in the pattern. Sexual feeling is a natural accompaniment of affectionate relations, especially when they include caresses and other bodily contacts. The important point is that members of the family are the earliest available objects to which sexual feelings can become attached. However strong or weak it may be, the child's erotic interest rests at first within the family circle. This initial learning must all be unlearned at a later date when the sexual urge reaches maturity and the force of the culture's incest barrier is more clearly apprehended.

[31] F. Alexander, "Educative Influence of Personality Factors in the Environment," in C. Kluckhohn, H. A. Murray, and D. M. Schneider, *Personality in Nature, Society, and Culture* (2d ed.; New York: Alfred A. Knopf, Inc., 1953), pp. 421–35.

[32] Karen Horney, *New Ways in Psychoanalysis* (New York: W. W. Norton & Co., Inc., 1939), p. 83.

[33] G. Murphy, *Personality: A Biosocial Approach to Origins and Structure* (New York: Harper & Row, 1947), p. 533.

[34] J. H. S. Bossard, *Parent and Child* (Philadelphia: University of Pennsylvania Press, 1953), p. 40.

Sexual Tendencies in Later Childhood. It was one of Freud's contentions that sexual excitability reaches a peak during the fourth and fifth years, then declines and rests latent until the changes of puberty. The so-called latency period now appears to be a phenomenon produced entirely by cultural pressures. It has no discoverable physiological basis, and it does not appear among primitive peoples, lower-class children in our society, or upper-class children in the permissive environment of a progressive school.[35] It is the result of ordinary upper-class and middle-class attitudes, and consists of a driving underground of sexual interests and behavior. During later childhood there is a culturally determined segregation of the sexes. Boys play with boys and girls play with girls, each group viewing the other with hostility and contempt. This arrangement collapses rather suddenly at puberty, but it has one important consequence for later sexual adjustment. Especially as the sex urge increases in the year or two before puberty, the available objects of erotic interest are almost exclusively members of the same sex. Learnings may get under way which will have to be unlearned again when the sex urge emerges more clearly into the open and the cultural ban on homosexuality is fully understood.

The Relearning Required at Puberty. Puberty is marked by a fairly rapid series of physiological changes. Secretion of sex hormones is sharply increased, the sensitivity of the genitals is heightened, and the sex urge assumes its adult form as a powerful drive that demands periodic relief of some kind. This change in itself, coupled with the appearance of the secondary sex characteristics of the body and the attainment of adult stature, represents a formidable problem of adjustment. The management of a strengthened and unruly impulse precipitates new conflicts and calls for new learning. But this is not the whole difficulty. As we have seen, sexuality already has a history, and this history has provided a highly unsuitable training for the adjustment that society now demands. Sexuality has been chiefly experienced in the form of masturbation. Insofar as it has connected itself with other people, they are people who now constitute forbidden objects: parents, siblings, friends of the same sex. On top of this, the young person is very apt to be carrying a heavy load of obstacles to new learning. If he has learned to feel that sex is a dirty, disgusting, dangerous urge, he will certainly be in conflict over its sudden strength in himself, and his new learning will take place under great disadvantage.

Fortunately there are strong forces on the side of growth. One of these is the sex urge itself, which activates fantasy and inquiry even when

[35] G. H. Seward, *Sex and the Social Order* (New York: McGraw-Hill Book Co., Inc., 1946), pp. 158–62.

behavior is blocked. Another is the changed attitude of society, which brings a certain pressure toward heterosexual interests. As the young person matures, remarks are made about the dates that will soon begin, and even the old convention of the chaperone contains the clear if implicit suggestion that if left alone for a moment the young people would promptly be overcome by passion. Among his age-equals the adolescent finds strong support in channeling his sexual urge toward young members of the opposite sex. From adults the encouragement is likely to be qualified and less enthusiastic. It may amount to positive discouragement when the parents are overconcerned about financial and social status, wanting economic success to precede a socially suitable marriage. On the whole, however, it is misleading to represent that the adolescent battles his way to sexual adjustment through a solid phalanx of cultural prohibitions. The adjustment is inherently difficult, and cultural pressures may be out of step with bodily development, but there are considerable forces working on the side of relearning.

Maladaptive Possibilities. Sexual maladjustments can arise at any point in development. Disordered behavior in young children sometimes has its roots in misunderstandings about sex and in anxieties created by injudicious threats and punishments. Psychiatric work with young patients almost always includes explanation of the "facts of life," which enables the child not only to get the facts straight but also to realize that they can be talked about without shame. Childhood troubles in the sphere of sex can readily extend their influence by blocking the relearning that is required at puberty. Difficulties in adult life can be conceived as failures to accomplish this relearning. When sex has been treated with respect rather than disgust or fear, when it has been gently restrained without creating alarm, then its inappropriate childhood history can be readily outgrown during adolescence and the foundation laid for good adult adjustment. When stages of the childhood history become fixated, or when the relearning after puberty is directly blocked by hostile cultural attitudes, maladjustment is likely to ensue.

For the sake of a symmetrical theory we might list indulgence as one of the causes of fixation. Such evidence as we have, however, does not make a strong case for harmful consequences of indulgence. As we have seen, it is no longer supposed by the students of the subject that childhood masturbation either injures the child at the time or makes for difficulty in achieving later sexual adjustment. So effective is the incest taboo that parents rarely indulge the child to the point of permitting a riotous growth of erotic interests within the family circle. What happens with neighbor children behind bushes or in cellars is more apt to satisfy curiosity than to produce erotic overindulgence, and we might find in it at least the merit of taking sex interest out of the family. The Kinsey reports show that homosexual contacts of one kind or another are fairly common experiences in childhood and early adolescence[36]; it cannot be supposed that their mere occurrence creates a fatal obstacle to the growth of heterosexual interest. It is possible, of course, that unrestrained erotic indulgences before puberty may increase the difficulty of later relearning, but the frequency of sexual incidents in the candid story of almost anybody's childhood suggests that indulgence is not a weighty cause of maladjustment.

The outstanding cause of fixation and blocking of development is therefore the association of sex with feelings of inferiority, guilt, disgust, and especially fear. When sexual feeling is suppressed and denied because it implies something shameful and dirty, or when it is even more completely repressed because it awakens anxiety, the chances of its participating in new learning at puberty are sharply reduced. The consequence may be a general inhibition of sexual interest and behavior. In extreme cases the person never dares to venture into an erotic relationship and is thereby barred from marriage. More commonly the interference is less complete, but sex can be experienced only as something shameful and demeaning; its power to deepen love and happiness and to strengthen the marriage relationship is thus thrown away. Sometimes the inhibitions upon sex are opposed by a reaction-formation, much energy being thrown into demonstrations of sexual freedom, but the need to furnish constant proofs of liberty, potency, and seductive capacity usually interferes with the attainment of satisfying mutual relationships. Fully developed shared sexuality implies a freedom from anxieties, inferiority feelings, compensatory motives of conquest; and it is just these intruders that constantly spoil it when sexual development has taken place in an atmosphere of prudish intolerance.

The following excerpt from a case history illustrates some of these points. A college freshman found himself waking up in the night with terrible attacks of anxiety, the only content of which seemed to be the fear of going insane. It appeared that when he was 4 or 5 his mother tried to stop him from masturbating by telling him that he would go insane. This threat did not suffice, but it was sharply reinforced when the family happened to drive by a state hospital. The boy saw patients behind barred windows making frightening noises, while his mother explained that those people were insane, a condition worse than death. This was a real threat, being locked up and separated from your parents, and it precipitated a reaction-formation. Throughout childhood and even

[36] A. C. Kinsey *et al., Sexual Behavior in the Human Male* (Philadelphia: W. B. Saunders Co., 1948), pp. 168–71, 623–31; *Sexual Behavior in the Human Female* (Saunders, 1953), pp. 113–14.

throughout his high-school years the boy renounced sex in all its forms. He had many activities and many friends. A group of congenial boys and girls "tore around" together, but he was careful to emphasize the "wholesome cleanness" of their relations. Arriving at college he was shocked by dormitory conversation, still more shocked to notice that his eyes tended to linger on magazine pictures of pretty girls before he hastily turned the page. He did not permit himself to masturbate, and his sole sexual outlet consisted of wet dreams from which he awakened in acute anxiety. At 5 he had been so scared that at 17, confronted by the rising strength of the sex need, he could only repeat the desperate defense of complete suppression, a defense which he could maintain during the day but not at night. He was unable to avail himself of the encouragement toward heterosexual interest offered by his classmates or even to accept the permissive attitude of a college counselor whom he consulted. During his college years he fell in love several times, but he broke off each affair with the decision that full devotion to his lifework required celibacy. His fear of sexual feelings made it almost impossible to achieve the relearning required at puberty.

THEORIES OF DEVELOPMENT

The developmental problems described thus far in this chapter were first brought into prominence by Freud and one of his earliest collaborators, Karl Abraham. As we saw in connection with the Oedipus complex, Freud's theories have not passed unchallenged; indeed, there is lively controversy today upon almost every aspect of his ideas concerning emotional development. Few will deny that Freud and Abraham opened a vitally important territory, but many workers question the theoretical formulation that followed. We have reached a convenient place to examine different theories of early development and to compare their ordering of the known facts.

The Libido Theory. It is often said of Freud that he reduced all motivation to sex. This is not an accurate statement, but it is true that he enlarged the conception of sex and perceived erotic elements in behavior that no one had previously thought to be sexual. Freud's expanded conception of sex is embodied in the libido theory, which is still a cornerstone in the psychoanalytic theory of development. As Fenichel pointed out in a searching treatise, Freudians do not deny the independent existence of vital urges such as breathing, hunger, thirst, defecation, urination, but they regard these as so fixed in their aims and so little capable of variation that they play only a minor part in psychological development. Sexual urges, on the other hand, "if they cannot find gratification in their original form, have the capacity to change, to alter their objects or aims, or to submit to repression by the ego and then to make themselves apparent again in various ways and in different disguises."[37] They therefore play a significant and complex part in the shaping of personality.

According to the libido theory, all pleasurable stimulation of sensitive regions of the body is to be classed as erotic. Pleasurable excitation of the lips by thumbsucking, pleasurable excitation of the anal zone by passing or withholding feces, pleasurable excitation of the genitals by masturbation are all expressions of a single basic energy, the libido. It is assumed that all these manifestations have "a common chemistry as their basis," hence the conclusion that "there is but one libido which may be displaced from one erogenous zone to another."[38] Psychological development is believed to depend so centrally upon libidinal urges that it can be adequately conceptualized as a succession of *stages of libidinal organization*. The first year is the oral stage, when the mouth is the most excitable area. The second and third years form the anal stage, when libido is more readily excited in the mucous membranes of the anal region. The fourth and fifth years constitute the phallic stage, the final genital stage being reached at puberty. Many traits and tendencies in later life are looked upon as derivatives of the infantile stages of libidinal organization. Thus a dependent adult is referred to as an oral character; it is conceived that he became fixated in the oral stage and did not properly advance through the later stages of libidinal organization, or perhaps that he has regressed to the oral stage as a consequence of frustrations. Similarly, adult stubbornness and stinginess are described as anal retentive traits derived from the child's refusal to sacrifice the pleasure of retaining his stool when asked to move his bowels on schedule.

Stages of libidinal organization thus constitute the main theme of growth, the motivational center of all that is happening. For Freud and Abraham the child's experiences with oral, anal, and genital gratification determined the whole course of development. Interests in other spheres could be understood as derivatives of interest in these zones; curiosity about objects and how they work, for example, would draw its energy from curiosity about the genital organs and the act of copulation. Anxieties and conflicts surrounding zonal gratifications were the causes of all other anxieties and conflicts. In his later thinking Freud introduced aggression (the "death instinct") as an equal partner with libido. "In biological functions," he wrote in his last substantial essay, "the two basic instincts work against each other or combine with each other. . . .

[37] O. Fenichel, *The Psychoanalytic Theory of Neurosis* (New York: W. W. Norton & Co., Inc., 1945), pp. 55–57.
[38] *Ibid.*, pp. 56, 74.

This interaction of the two basic instincts with or against each other gives rise to the whole variegation of the phenomena of life."[39] Libidinal energy, however, was still responsible for the different stages of growth and maintained its position as the central reservoir of life energies.

Revisions of Freudian Theory: The Neo-Freudians. Many workers during the past thirty years have dissented from Freud's formulation and attempted to revise his conception of development. The focus of their displeasure is the idea of libido. The libido theory is, after all, a very large generalization about human motives, one which subordinates all strivings except aggression to the urge for pleasurable stimulation of oral, anal, and genital zones. It is argued by neo-Freudians such as Karen Horney,[40] Erich Fromm,[41] and Harry Stack Sullivan[42] that the course of development does not turn on happenings in the realm of instinctual energies; the critical thing is the evolution of human relations, especially those between child and parents. The part played by motivation can best be understood by considering how motives of various kinds—erotic, aggressive, and the need for security—become clustered around the important human beings in the child's life. Sullivan, for example, attached great importance to the child's need to enjoy the approval and esteem of the significant people in his environment and to avoid the anxiety engendered by disapproval. When the child's conduct brings approval, he experiences happiness and zest; when he meets disapproval, he falls into a state of discomfort, anxiety, and constriction. The course of development thus becomes directed toward obtaining a favorable balance of approval, and this is clearly a problem in human interaction.

In practice the shift from libido to human relations produced a smaller change than might have been anticipated. Two facts justify us in calling this movement neo-Freudian rather than something wholly new. In the first place, most of the workers used the psychoanalytic method of therapy or something very like it. They kept seeing some of the things that Freud had seen, particularly the evidence for the child's pleasure and interest in the body and its functions. In the second place, they did not (with the exception of Sullivan) discard the typical situations upon which development turned in Freud's theory: the infant at the breast, the small child on the toilet, the slightly older child concerned about genital impulses toward family members. These prototypes were not

[39] S. Freud, *An Outline of Psychoanalysis* (1938), trans. James Strachey (New York: W. W. Norton & Co., Inc., 1949), p. 21.

[40] Karen Horney, *The Neurotic Personality of Our Time* (New York: W. W. Norton & Co., Inc., 1937).

[41] E. Fromm, *Man for Himself* (New York: Holt, Rinehart & Winston, Inc., 1947).

[42] H. S. Sullivan, *The Interpersonal Theory of Psychiatry* (New York: W. W. Norton & Co., Inc., 1953).

rejected; they were simply reinterpreted, as in the following statement by Silverberg:

What Freud described as universal phases of development was, I believe, the *areas of experience* and their order of succession as they are usually presented to the children of western civilization by parents performing the task of acculturating their offspring. . . . Each of these experiential areas of early life presents its characteristic issues and problems to the growing child; problems of deprivation in the oral area; problems of obedience, conformity, and rebelliousness in the disciplinary one; problems of genital gratification and of comparison and competition in the phallic area.[43]

It is of interest to notice here that Dollard and Miller, in a systematic use of learning theory (reinforcement theory) for analyzing the problems of childhood, follow a similar course designed to preserve Freud's important observations without taking over his theoretical formulation.[44] Discussing the early learning of conflicts, they select four "critical training situations": the feeding situation, cleanliness training, sex training, and the training of anger responses. "The culture has a design" for each of these situations; out of the child's collisions with this parents' version of the design can come "acute emotional conflicts" as well as "long-lasting effects on character and habits."[45] Dollard and Miller's analysis of the many things a child may be learning in the critical training situations is a valuable contribution to our understanding of development.

Erikson's Theory of Ego Development. The most detailed revision of Freud's ideas is the one worked out by Erik H. Erikson.[46] Based on extensive psychoanalytic work with children, it does full justice to Freud's insights regarding infantile sexuality, while at the same time recognizing other aspects of children's growth and emphasizing the formative importance of human interactions. Neither instinctual urges alone nor human relations alone can provide a sufficient basis for describing the course of growth. Erikson therefore gives his account in the form of *stages in the development of the ego*. In psychoanalytic theory the ego is that part of personality which is responsible for organizing behavior in relation to the realities of the environment. Erikson's stages of ego development thus emphasize the inherently interactive nature of behavior.

[43] W. V. Silverberg, *Childhood Experience and Personal Destiny* (New York: Springer Publishing Co., Inc., 1952), pp. 41, 45.

[44] J. Dollard and N. E. Miller, *Personality and Psychotherapy* (New York: McGraw-Hill Book Co., Inc., 1950), chap. x.

[45] *Ibid.*, p. 132.

[46] E. H. Erikson, *Childhood and Society* (New York: W. W. Norton & Co., Inc., 1950), especially chaps. ii and vii. See also "Identity and the Life Cycle," *Psychological Issues,* I (1959), No. 1, pp. 50–100, for a more detailed account.

Erikson sees early development as a process of mutual regulation between child and parents. The idea that the parents regulate the child is familiar, but there is a real sense in which the child also regulates the parents. The infant's helplessness is necessary to call forth and gratify the mother's nurturing tendencies, just as the mother is necessary to gratify the infant's needs. The child's changing capacities and the parents' changing demands lead to a series of decisive encounters, the outcomes of which are fateful for future growth. We have already referred to Erikson with respect to the first two decisive encounters, that of the first year when the basic issue is between trust and mistrust, and that of the second and third years when the child is finding out whether autonomy or shame and doubt will prevail. These two stages of ego development are reminiscent of the oral and anal stages in Freud's scheme. The third stage, characterized by the conflict of initiative and guilt, concurs chronologically with the "phallic" period (3 to 5 years); and the fourth, which may issue favorably in a sense of industry or unfavorably in feelings of inferiority, occupies approximately the time up to puberty which Freud designated the "latency period." It will be noted, however, that Erikson's terms do not refer to erotic events springing from instinctual energies. They signify decisive encounters between the child's urges and capacities and the urges and demands of adults.

We shall refer later to further stages in Erikson's scheme, especially to his concept of ego-identity. It is a virtue of his account that it does not stop, like Freud's, with the attainment of adult sexuality but extends over the whole span of life. This enables it to transcend the family circle and encompass the individual's place in society. In this chapter we are concerned with the early stages, and it is important to notice here an additional feature of the theory. To provide a broader biological base than the one furnished by Freud's theory of instinctual drives, Erikson includes in his thinking the whole sphere of sensorimotor development. The state of the child's capacities, whether for understanding or for performance, affects very directly his interactions with the important people and things of his environment. Erikson points out, for instance, the significance of grasping, manipulating, and letting go at the onset of the stage of autonomy, and of growths in locomotion, language, and imagination for the crises over initiative and guilt. He relates sensorimotor development to ego stages by means of the concept of *mode*. The first stage is dominated by the incorporative mode, which means that everything the infant does, even his visual and tactile exploration, has the character of a taking in of experience. The second stage is dominated by retentive and eliminative modes, which show themselves alike in bowel functions and in the familiar manipulative sequence characterized by grasping and a little later by letting go and throwing away. The third stage brings to full flower the intrusive mode, which includes "the intrusion into other bodies by physical attack; the intrusion into other people's ears and minds by aggressive talking; the intrusion into space by vigorous locomotion; the intrusion into the unknown by consuming curiosity."[47] These sensorimotor modes, it will be noticed, are congruent with the libidinal prototypes: the passive receptiveness of the nursing infant, the retention and elimination shown by the child on the toilet, the erotic assertiveness of the child during the Oedipal period.

Efficacy and Competence. It is one of the strengths of Erikson's account that it includes this specific recognition of sensorimotor development and the level of the child's capacities. The possibility should be considered, however, that modes deserve greater independence than Erikson has given them. Sensorimotor development, as we mentioned in our discussion of autonomy, takes place in large part through free exploratory play, its biological significance being the growth of competence in dealing with the environment. The division of this continuous process into modes characterized by incorporative, retentive, eliminative, and intrusive trends is not entirely in accord with the facts; and it does not call attention to what is most important about the facts. When the child around his first birthday undertakes to feed himself, the action is only partly incorporative. It is intrusive into the mother's functions; and the spoon, if successfully guided, is intrusive into the mouth. Similarly, in manipulating a toy the child shifts rapidly from picking it up to putting it down to holding it firmly to pushing it against something else—the modes are completely scrambled.

The most significant thing about sensorimotor growth is not these directional trends. It is the growth of competence in dealing with the environment, achieved by finding out what effects it is possible to have on what objects. To the extent that the child exerts an influence upon things, his exploratory play is rewarded by feelings of efficacy. Such feelings eventually build up in him a *sense of competence* that contributes to self-esteem and that makes him less vulnerable to anxiety. In a recent paper Freud's psychosexual stages have been reinterpreted with the help of the concept of competence.[48] This treatment makes it possible to construct a consistent account of the growth of independence and to emphasize continuities from stage to stage in the building up or tearing down of confidence and self-esteem.

[47] Erikson, *Childhood and Society, op. cit.*, p. 83.

[48] R. W. White, "Competence and the Psychosexual Stages of Development," in M. R. Jones, *Nebraska Symposium on Motivation* (Lincoln, Neb.: University of Nebraska Press, 1960), pp. 97–141.

AGGRESSION AND ITS MANAGEMENT

In this book we shall use the word *aggression* with a limited meaning. It will be restricted to tendencies that aim at injury and destruction. Such tendencies are accompanied, when fully conscious, by feelings of anger and hate. In everyday speech and even in the psychological literature one frequently finds aggression confused with self-assertive behavior such as competition or dominance. While it is true that aggression can easily become fused with assertive tendencies, we shall stick closer to facts if we distinguish the two and reserve aggression specifically for man's angry, destructive, and hateful inclinations.

Nature of Aggression. In the infant's earliest responses to discomforts such as hunger, sleepiness, and unpleasant external stimulation, it is impossible to distinguish between rage and anxiety. The pattern of rage presently emerges as a general struggling and vigorous flailing of the arms and legs. The situations that most clearly evoke this response involve interference with activities and a restriction of movement, as in dressing or changing the diapers; and the child's movements, although not yet directed at an object, are of some service in getting rid of the restriction. In the second half of the first year, the child's manipulative activities, in themselves exploratory rather than aggressive, may lead at times to frustration and pain. An animal too roughly explored, for instance, may act in self-defense; and the child, perhaps after being consoled, may try rather insistently to repeat the rough treatment. During the second year of life, there is clear emergence of acts with an aggressive intent. Striking and kicking may be "carried out with a mischievous facial expression and with clear signs of enjoyment. . . . Finally the child clearly realizes that what he does *hurts*. The child has experienced pain and discomfort from aggression directed toward him, and he now connects his inner experience with his own overt activity. This usually takes place during the third year of life."[49] It is now possible to speak of truly aggressive, hostile behavior.

It is valuable to compare these facts, found by direct observation of young children, with what has been learned through psychoanalysis about the conscious and unconscious workings of hostility later in life. Here it appears that aggression has some of the characteristics of a drive like sex, although it is not based on a somatic state that urges toward periodic satisfaction. The same words apply to aggression that Fenichel applied to sex: aggressive urges, "if they cannot find gratification in their

[49] B. Mittelmann, "Motility in Infants, Children, and Adults," *Psychoanalytic Study of the Child,* IX (1954), pp. 161–62.

original form, have the capacity to change, to alter their objects or aims, or to submit to repression by the ego and then to make themselves apparent again in various ways and in different disguises." Suppose that a man's ire is aroused at work when his boss unjustly criticizes him. He says nothing, but when he gets home he kicks open the front door, yells at the dog, criticizes his wife's cooking, remembers to pay his union dues, decides to attend a political rally which is aiming to throw the incumbent party out of power, goes to bed and dreams that he knocked a heavier opponent out of the ring. The postponements and ramifications of aggression, like those of sex, are many and subtle. Nursery school teachers now the sight of angry and distressed children throwing things around, breaking toys, hitting other children, not because of anything that happened in school but because of chronic frustration at home. Adults sometimes harbor resentments and grudges for years, finally taking them out through channels far removed from the original circumstances. Aggression can wait and can transform itself in innumerable ways.

The facts about aggression have led to two rather different conceptualizations. According to one view, aggression is always a response to frustration.[50] It is instigated by outside events: events which prevent the attainment of some needed gratification, which restrict or interfere with free activity, or which constitute a painful injury either to the body or to the self-esteem. Without frustration there would be no aggression. The other conceptualization, advanced by Freud, sees aggression as the product of a pool of instinctual energy, the "death instinct," which is bound to overflow even without unusual frustrating provocation.[51] Freud's idea fits in with the age-old conviction that there is an evil streak in human nature; but his equating of this with instinctual drive energy has evoked much criticism, particularly from those who do research on the physiology of instinctual processes. But the frustration hypothesis should not be conceived as leading to a blithe disregard of the destructive elements in behavior. Frustration is an inevitable consequence of the socialization process and of the objective conditions under which life takes place. If we take into account the nature of our mental processes, our capacity to remember, to imagine, and thus to brood upon unfairness or insults to our pride—and even to do so unconsciously—there is no real incompatibility between the frustration hypothesis and the simmering rages and lasting resentments that suggest pools of aggressive energy.

[50] J. Dollard, L. W. Doob, N. E. Miller, O. H. Mowrer, and R. R. Sears, *Frustration and Aggression* (New Haven: Yale University Press, 1939); and see the account by B. R. Sappenfield, *Personality Dynamics* (New York: Alfred A. Knopf, Inc., 1954), chap. v.

[51] S. Freud, *Beyond the Pleasure Principle* (London: Hogarth Press, Ltd., 1922).

Problem of Channeling Aggression. In childhood, aggression manifests itself in relatively crude forms such as angry outbursts and temper tantrums. The tantrum is a forceful method of securing what one wants, but it meets with decreasing success as the months go by and the child grows more capable. The restrictive force comes from the mother, who discovers that if she does not curb tantrums in her child she will have to curb them in herself. This illustrates the difficulty of the educative process, but children are entitled to help in controlling their explosive outbursts. No child enjoys being in a temper. The violent force of the urge may even arouse his anxiety. What he wants is not to be angry but to remove the cause of frustration. In the course of time he will be able to learn that frustrations can be better removed if anger is controlled sufficiently to permit coherent and perceptive action. One learns, for instance, that losing one's temper in an argument makes one both ridiculous and ineffective. The young child is ready enough to express his aggression, but he is also soon able to realize that he gets better results by controlling it. On this his parents and teachers can build.

It soon happens, however, that aggression is caught up in more complex patterns, and these create far greater adjustive difficulties. The child's daily social experiences, taking place mostly within the family circle, occur with people upon whom he is dependent, whom he loves, but who make demands on him which arouse aggressive feelings. His parents meet his needs and give him affection but also move him along the road toward socialization. One of the things that complicates human relationships even in the earliest years is the alternation of love and hate that we call *ambivalence*. The objects of love and aggression are the same; at times they call out these conflicting feelings practically at the same moment. The child soon discovers that there can be no easy solution to this problem. If anger, complaints, and criticism are expressed too freely they are likely to invite return expressions of hostility and to imperil future harmony. Frustration begets aggression but aggression may bring about a disastrous loss of security and esteem. Thus aggression is always potentially present in the family circle as an added complication to the other problems of emotional growth.

In a most general sense there are three possible types of reaction to any problem involving frustration and aroused aggression. Following the scheme originally proposed by Rosenzweig, these can be named the *extrapunitive, intropunitive,* and *impunitive* types of reaction.[52] The extrapunitive reaction implies that hostility is directed outward: objects or people other than oneself are indignantly perceived as to blame for the experienced frustration. The intropunitive reaction represents a di-

[52] S. Rosenzweig, "Types of Reaction to Frustration," *Journal of Abnormal and Social Psychology,* XXIX (1934), pp. 298–300.

recting of blame and anger against oneself: it is my fault that I did not act more wisely or that I provoked anger in others. The impunitive reaction seeks to minimize or condone the aggressive elements in whatever has transpired: the episode should be forgotten or not taken seriously. Each of these general ways of dealing with aggressive impulses is appropriate and realistic under certain circumstances. The child, however, is hardly in a good position to know what is appropriate and realistic, especially when he is dealing with obscurely perceived ambivalences in himself and in those around him. Under these circumstances it is easier for him to take his cue from the general attitudes of his parents, a matter in which families greatly differ. Recent studies with young adult subjects indicate that some people are quite consistently extrapunitive, others consistently intropunitive, in their response to frustrations both in daily life and in laboratory tests. There is evidence to suggest that these preferences are established in childhood and are influenced by the attitudes prevailing in the family circle.[53]

It is in relationships already inherently ambivalent that the child must find out about sharing love. Perhaps abruptly, through the birth of a sibling or the father's return from war, perhaps gradually as he apprehends that his father and older siblings have claims on his mother equal to or greater than his own, he must learn that love has to be shared with others and cannot be an absolute monopoly. He must contend with feelings of jealousy and find out that these must be controlled if one is to retain even one's share of affection. He must learn to make peace with the rivals with whom he is obliged to live and to discover the positive satisfactions that may be gained by associating with them.

The problem of adjusting loves and hates within the family circle is well illustrated in the example of sibling rivalry. With the birth of a new sibling, the older child has to accept a reduction in parental attention. He witnesses the baby enjoying privileges of dependence that he himself is in the process of outgrowing. Inevitably he feels jealousy and expresses hostility, but this does not remove the frustration nor win back the parents' love. Levy has shown that jealousy of a younger sibling can lead to all kinds of problems: night terrors, negativism, loss of acquired bowel and bladder controls, self-injuries such as head-banging, and even speech disorders. These symptoms can be relieved by allowing and encouraging the child to express his jealous anger in destructive play with dolls representing the baby and the mother.[54] The success of this method

[53] D. H. Funkenstein, S. H. King, and M. E. Drolette, *Mastery of Stress* (Cambridge: Harvard University Press, 1957).

[54] D. M. Levy, "Hostility Patterns in Sibling Rivalry Experiments," *American Journal of Orthopsychiatry*, VI (1936), pp. 183–257; and "Release Therapy," *ibid.*, IX (1939), 713–36.

of treatment indicates that for these cases the original difficulty lay in excessive suppression. The child was made to feel so guilty and fearful that he could not allow himself to express his anger, perhaps even to feel it, in direct form. As a result it overflowed in disguised and indirect ways. Sibling rivalry can be overcome if the child is made to feel that the parents still love him just as much, even though they have to fuss over the baby, and if he is given extra approval in the role of a bigger child who perhaps helps with the baby's care. In the course of time playing with the baby will prove to be fun. But these new learnings cannot take place when the child behaves outwardly as if all were well, so that the parents see no need to help him, and when he boils with an inward anger that conflicts with every impulse toward friendliness. Levy's method of play therapy awakens in many people the fear that after smashing the mother doll and baby doll the child will go home and smash the real baby and mother. This fear is based on a defective theory of learning. The smashing of the dolls, with the permission and even encouragement of the therapist, discharges the pent-up resentment and frees it from the suppressive burden of shame. Conditions favoring new learning are thus re-established. The child goes home ready to feel his aggression without shame, but also ready to respond to parental affection, accept restrictions, work out an adjustment to the new situation.

In an ideally mature person aggression is managed by a flexible system of controls and outlets. Such a person may lose his temper over irritating trifles, allowing himself a brief verbal outburst when the door sticks or the car will not start, but his anger readily subsides when he sees the frustration in its true proportions. He is able to control such outbursts when necessary without building up a feeling of resentment. With greater annoyances, such as unmerited criticism or infringements on his rights, his anger will be channeled into defending himself coherently and reaching an understanding. Against major and chronic frustrations his aggression will be still further channeled into constructive action, very likely in association with others, designed to lessen and remove the cause of frustration. Many people count it a great experience when they discover an effective way to combat evils instead of merely resenting them. Aggression alone is apt to be an explosive, irrational thing. Aggression channeled with other tendencies can become an important asset for civilization, as in the work of those who have been angry at man's inhumanity or at the unnecessary ravages of disease.

Maladaptive Possibilities. A flexible system of controls and outlets is most easily attained when the child begins his development in an atmosphere that is tolerant but firm on the subject of aggression. Maladjustive possibilities lie in too wide a divergence in either direction:

when little attempt is made to curb aggression, or when the attempt is so strenuous that no outlets are left for reducing the tension.

The first may appear on the surface to be the lesser of the two evils. Adults who, when angry, smash the furniture or punch somebody in the face are scarcely conducive to socialized living, but their behavior does not necessarily imply enduring malice or calculated hate. There are, however, more complex patterns of childhood influence in which the inadequate curbing of aggressive tendencies leads to very serious consequences. One can take as an example the case of Johnny Rocco, recently published by Evans.[55] A boy is brought up in a large family in desperate financial straits. He is given rough treatment by older siblings, receives scant affection from his harassed mother, is early turned out into the streets of a badly disorganized neighborhood. The family has a bad reputation with the police, and he is treated roughly in that quarter. He thus grows up in an environment where aggression is curbed only by other aggressions, where the obvious avenue to security lies in being more toughly aggressive than the other fellow, where at the same time serious frustrations constantly mobilize his hostility to a maximum. In situations of this kind, which appear frequently in the history of delinquents and criminals, poor control of aggression is by no means the only problem. It is true, nevertheless, that when other frustrations are severe the failure of family and neighborhood control over aggression leaves wide open an outlet that can have serious maladjustive consequences for both the individual and society.

When aggressive impulses are met with too strenuous a campaign of suppression, several possible consequences may follow. The most obvious pattern is that of a person who can never openly express aggression nor even become aware of hostile feelings in himself. Such people show serious blocks in asserting themselves even in the most legitimate fashion. They must avoid aggression by such a wide margin, so to speak, that they cannot express any desires with which it might be remotely connected. We can scarcely assume that hostility is dead in these people; we must therefore suppose that it is aroused but somehow spends itself internally. Perhaps the intropunitive reaction brings about a kind of self-hate and feeling of unworthiness, or perhaps the anger is bottled up with no outlet except a chronic raising of the blood pressure or some other somatic effect. Neither consequence is compatible with good adjustment or good health. Horney describes the "vicious circle" that is likely to operate when aggression is too heavily suppressed.[56] A child who has to stifle his hostility finds himself placed all too often in a weak

[55] Jean Evans, *Three Men: An Experiment in the Biography of Emotion* (New York: Alfred A. Knopf, Inc., 1954), pp. 3–87.

[56] Horney, *The Neurotic Personality of Our Time, op. cit.*, chap. iv.

position. He cannot defend himself or demand justice. An unfair punishment has to be accepted, favoritism toward a sibling has to be overlooked or even taken as a true sign of one's inferiority and worthlessness. Thus the child must simply put up with it when others encroach upon his rights and wishes, and this allows them to do so more and more. Furthermore, in order to maintain the repression of his own hostility, he can hardly prevent the adjustive mechanism of projection from coming into play. He perceives his own hostility as an attribute of other people, but this only makes him feel still weaker, a helpless person in a hostile world.

In many cases the suppression of hostility is less complete. Sometimes the rejected aggression creeps back in the form of a general ambivalence: the person has difficulty liking what he wants to like or loving the people he wants to love. There is always something a little wrong with everything, a little deserving of criticism. In other cases aggression displays itself only in particular channels, generally with somewhat remote objects, but displays itself here with peculiar force and irrationality. To take one example, Frenkel-Brunswick and Sanford have found that anti-Semitic sentiments are strongest in individuals whose outward behavior conforms closely to the standards of middle-class propriety. The outstanding feature of a group of strongly anti-Semitic American college women studied by them was a "restricted, narrow personality" with a strict conventional upbringing "to which there is complete surrender. Basic impulses, which are conceived as low, destructive, and dangerous, have to be kept repressed and can find only devious expressions, as for instance in projections and 'moral indignation.'"[57] When aggression is too forcibly driven underground it either wrecks individual adjustment or comes back again in dangerous and irrational ways. An adjustive pattern of controls and outlets must be compatible with both individual health and social welfare.

THE INTERACTION OF PARENTS AND CHILDREN

Throughout our study of the problems that offer special adaptive difficulties, we have had before us the picture of young children in interaction with their parents. In the earliest learnings, in fact throughout childhood, the behavior of the parents is a highly significant feature of the child's environment. As we sketched the normal course of development, we kept thinking of the parental attitudes likely to encourage it. This led us to conceive that maladjustment results in part from one of two extreme deviations in parental attitude: either an *excessive indulgence* of childhood tendencies with a minimum of emphasis on growing up, or an

[57] E. Frenkel-Brunswik and R. N. Sanford, "Some Personality Factors in Anti-Semitism," *Journal of Psychology*, XX (1945), pp. 271–91. The complete description of this research is to be found in T. W. Adorno *et al., The Authoritarian Personality* (New York: Harper & Row, 1950).

excessive suppression of these tendencies with an expectation that the child can grow up all at once rather than through the slow learnings that result in channeling and renunciation. Parental attitudes are not the only determinants of psychological development, nor are the experiences of childhood the only ones that shape personality. But the effect of parental attitudes is sufficiently important so that we should examine some recent research on the topic.

We have just passed through a period in the history of abnormal psychology during which the problems of parent-child relations were seriously oversimplified. The relation between mother and child, for instance, was not described interactively but was seen as a one-way sequence of cause and effect: the mother's behavior and feelings were the cause; the child's behavior and feelings were the effect. Perhaps we should excuse this as a legitimate attempt to simplify a difficult scientific problem, and it certainly led to some valuable research; but unfortunately it also led to making the mother the scapegoat for whatever was wrong with the child. The mother was pictured as the whole cause of the child's illness, and the therapist perceived his task as the hard one of undoing her evil influence. Clinical descriptions of twentieth-century mothers were at times more than faintly reminiscent of seventeenth-century accounts of witches.

We have seen, and we shall continue to see, that maternal attitudes are of great importance in the child's life. But we must get beyond the idea that they are causes in a simple cause-effect relation. Thinking interactively, we must allow that the child brings something to the relation. He is more than formless clay; each child is born with a certain individuality which from the very start exercises an influence upon the mother. We must also allow that before very long the other members of the family begin to have some importance for the young child, who becomes a member of a domestic social system with ramifying interactions. The attitudes of father and siblings begin to be felt, and one can interpret their effects only in the light of the positions and interactions of each member of the family constellation. These two changes in the image or model of what we are studying do not make the problem of parent-child relations simpler, but they keep us more faithful to the facts.

We begin with some studies done largely under the older outlook, after which we shall consider individual differences in young children and the family as a social system.

Studies of Parental Attitudes. 1. *Acceptance-Rejection.* Acceptance implies that the child is loved and receives kind and thoughtful treatment. Rejection means that the child is in some sense unwanted, so that love, care, and consideration are lacking in his life. The importance of the acceptance-rejection variable is widely recognized. Horney made rejection her central theme in explaining neurotic anxiety.

> A child can stand a great deal of what is often regarded as traumatic—such as sudden weaning, occasional beating, sex experiences—as long as inwardly he feels wanted and loved. Needless to say, a child feels keenly whether love is genuine, and cannot be fooled by any faked demonstrations. . . . More frequently than not, in my experience, the essential lack of warmth is camouflaged, and the parents claim to have in mind the child's best interest. Educational theories, oversolicitude, or the self-sacrificing attitude of an "ideal" mother are the basic factors contributing to an atmosphere that more than anything else lays the cornerstone for future feelings of immense insecurity.[58]

Baldwin and his collaborators reach the conclusion that "acceptance-rejection is the fundamental dynamic; it is the amount of acceptance which determines and delimits the other aspects of parental behavior."[59] This team of investigators observed a population which included among others a group of farm families and a group of college teachers and professional people whose status and background were equivalent to those of an upper middle class urban group. As a group, the latter parents showed a fairly high degree of acceptance and a slight tendency toward indulgence. In contrast, the farm parents tended toward an attitude described as "casual." "Children on a farm," these investigators comment, "are, as a rule, neither warmly and affectionately accepted nor coldly rejected and resented. Instead they are accepted in a matter of fact way, given sufficient attention to take care of their needs, but left on their own a good deal of the time."[60] This study brings out the close relation between parental attitudes and cultural background. In the small urban family of today, which has lost most of its economic and educational functions, the meaning of home to the child becomes virtually equivalent to his emotional relations with his parents. Acceptance or rejection, in particular, becomes the overwhelmingly important feature of home life. When acceptance reigns the child may be provided with an unusually favorable atmosphere. When rejection prevails—a "lack of genuine warmth and affection," as with Horney's group of urban patients—the results may be serious enough to precipitate neurosis.

There have been quite a number of studies on the effects of acceptance and rejection. Accepted children are found to be more confident, stable, and friendly. They may be calm and deliberate or lively and enthusiastic, but in either case their interest in their surroundings tends to be alert and unimpeded. In contrast, rejected children are more apt to be unstable and confused, either restless and rebellious or apathetic and indiffer-

58 Horney, *The Neurotic Personality of Our Time*, *op. cit.*, p. 80.

59 A. L. Baldwin, J. Kalhorn, and F. H. Breese, "Patterns of Parent Behavior," *Psychological Monographs*, LVIII (1945), No. 3, p. 53.

60 *Ibid.*, p. 58.

ent, and in any case poorer in application to school work. Bert Whipley, the chronic delinquent described in the last chapter, was a severely rejected child, at least on his father's part, and in one way or another he exemplifies every one of these characteristics.

2. *Dominance-Indulgence.* When children are strongly dominated, the effects are likely to show in their attitude toward authority and their power of initiative. Much depends, of course, on whether the domination is fused with acceptance or with rejection—on whether discipline is kindly or cold. As Baldwin points out, socialization requires a certain amount of control and restriction, but if the pressure is too strong the child's conformity is secured "at the expense of personal freedom in areas which are not intended to be restricted. Conformity to cultural demands is not easily obtained without robbing the child of that personal integrity which gives him a mind of his own and which supports him in his attempts to satisfy his curiosity and to carry out his ideas and phantasies in dealing with the real world."[61] Studies of strongly dominated children bear out this contention. Such children are apt to be obedient, well-behaved, and in good control of quarrelsome and other disruptive tendencies, but the control seems to spread to unintended areas such as affection, curiosity, and fanciful invention; as a consequence the children feel shy, perhaps inferior, and they are easily bewildered in dealing with other children or with new school work. Parental indulgence, at least when not extreme, seems favorable to resourcefulness and independence, but along with these go tendencies toward rebelliousness and overconfident conceit. With respect to this particular dimension it appears that when parental attitudes deviate either toward excessive suppression or excessive indulgence the children are likely to run into adjustive difficulties.

3. *Maternal Overprotection.* Some of the relationships discussed in this section emerge with striking clearness in a study of maternal overprotection by Levy.[62] This investigator studied in great detail twenty cases of extreme maternal overprotection. The mother's behavior was characterized by (1) excessive contact (mother being the child's sole and constant companion even up to ages such as 12 and 16), (2) infantilization (dressing child of 8 and accompanying him to school, shining shoes for boy of 15), (3) prevention of independent behavior (helping with homework, excusing from chores, preventing the formation of friendships). Levy points out that such a situation almost constitutes a controlled experiment in parent-child relationships: the effect of maternal

[61] A. L. Baldwin, "Socialization and the Parent-Child Relationship," *Child Development*, XIX (1948), pp. 127–36.

[62] D. M. Levy, *Maternal Overprotection* (New York: Columbia University Press, 1943).

overprotection is to minimize other influences acting upon the child, even the influence of his father. The twenty cases were selected in such a way that they all represent a marked degree of *acceptance*. But the cases break down into two sharply differentiated groups on the dimension *dominance-indulgence*. Part of the mothers were very much bent on trimming the child to a desired shape. Their offspring were docile, clean, neat, obedient, polite, diligent in school work, but so timid and submissive on the playground that their companions called them sissies and fools and their teachers considered them problems in social adjustment. In the rest of the cases the maternal attitude was so indulgent as to give what Levy calls "a luxuriant growth to infantile tendencies" with no barriers to the expression of aggression. At home these children would often break loose with slapping, kicking, throwing food on the floor, impudence, and a general high-handed tyranny. With other children they were cocky and bossy, inclined to show off, very poor at friendship and cooperation.

The twenty children were all patients at a guidance clinic, and Levy reports that efforts at therapy were rather ineffective, inasmuch as neither mother nor child really desired to change. Nevertheless in a follow-up study several years later it was found that only four were seriously maladjusted and several were doing very well. In spite of their early handicap of either excessive domination or excessive indulgence, they had at least enjoyed the advantage of being accepted—the assurance that they were loved and esteemed by the most important person in their world.

Individual Differences in Children. We turn now to the child as an active participant in family interactions. As Erikson puts it, "a baby's presence exerts a consistent and persistent domination over the outer and inner lives of every member of a household. It is as true to say that babies control and bring up their families as it is to say the converse."[63] If such be the case we must certainly begin to consider the *effects of the child's attitudes on the parents*. Do overprotective mothers choose dominative or indulgent roles out of their own preference, or does the child's docility or activity force these roles upon them? Do infants show from the start persistent differences in level of activity and in responsiveness to the mother's ministrations?

On the question of activity level, the extensive observations of Margaret Fries are of great interest.[64] During the first ten days of life, infants

[63] E. H. Erikson, "Growth and Crises of the 'Healthy Personality,'" in C. Kluckhohn, H. A. Murray, and D. M. Schneider, *Personality in Nature, Society, and Culture* (2d ed.; New York: Alfred A. Knopf, Inc., 1953), p. 189.

[64] Margaret E. Fries, "Psychosomatic Relationships Between Mother and Infant," *Psychosomatic Medicine*, VI (1944), pp. 159–62; Fries and P. J. Woolf, "Some Hypotheses on the Role of the Congenital Activity Type in Personality Development," *Psychoanalytic Study of the Child*, VIII (1953), pp. 48–62.

can be readily classified as quiet, moderately active, or active. The differences are stable and can still be observed five years later. Everything the child does is influenced by his activity level. Extreme passivity, showing itself in a small amount of curiosity and exploratory play, delays the growth of reality testing and competence in dealing with the environment. Extreme activity may result in an impulsiveness so great that the child achieves little stable mastery of his surroundings. From the very start activity level affects the character of interactions with the mother. A quiet baby sucks less avidly and may even fall asleep during nursing, causing the mother to feel rejected. Active babies, on the other hand, sleep less well and cry more often; later, their adventurous zeal may put the mother's patience under great strain and cause her to feel excessively dominated. In another study starting at the time of birth, Washburn showed that individual babies remain consistently jolly, serious, or more or less expressionless throughout the first year of life.[65] Anyone whose smile at a baby has been answered by a solemn stare, or whose troubles have been dispelled by a baby's sudden laughter, will realize the important effects such consistent differences might have on the attitudes of a mother. Case studies have been published which show the widespread influence of activity level on interactions within the family and on the general growth of personality.[66]

Without doubt there are other important dimensions to the individuality that shows itself so early in the child's behavior. Recent reports from a growth study of normal children suggest possible value in a scheme of no less than nine variables, though some of these may prove to overlap.[67] The authors of these studies use distractibility as a variable separate from activity level; they speak also of positive and negative mood, high vs. low response thresholds, intense vs. mild reactions, approaching vs. withdrawing, and the degree of regularity in behavior. The studies seem to indicate that quite a variety of child-rearing regimes can lead to excellent results, especially with children who do not have extreme scores on these variables. The research thus lends support to the common belief that healthy average babies take most things in their stride and flourish in spite of inexpert upbringing. They sail smoothly through weaning, toilet training, the mother's return to work, the Oedipus

[65] Ruth W. Washburn, "A Study of the Smiling and Laughing of Infants in the First Year of Life," *Genetic Psychology Monographs,* VI (1929), pp. 397–537.

[66] A. Alpert, P. B. Neubauer, and A. P. Weil, "Unusual Variations in Drive Endowment," *Psychoanalytic Study of the Child,* XI (1956), pp. 125–63.

[67] S. Chess, A. Thomas, and H. Birch, "Characteristics of the Individual Child's Behavioral Responses to the Environment," *American Journal of Orthopsychiatry,* XXIX (1959), pp. 791–802; A. Thomas, H. Birch, S. Chess, and L. G. Robbins, "Individuality in Responses of Children to Similar Environmental Situations," *American Journal of Psychiatry,* CXVII (1961), pp. 798–803.

situation, and other critical encounters; and they thrive under widely different degrees of acceptance, dominance, and maternal protection. The drastic bad effects of certain parental attitudes perhaps occur only (1) when the attitude is fairly extreme and (2) when the child is fairly vulnerable because he tends, for example, toward low response threshold, intense reaction, and negative mood. The child's response immediately influences the behavior of the parents, who may thus be pushed to more rejective or more protective attitudes than they had in the beginning. If we think in these interactive terms, it is much easier to understand the fact that in most families with an emotionally maladjusted child there are other children who fare much better. Parental attitudes are not complete fixtures; they develop in interaction with each particular child.

The Family as a Social System. Remembering that each person in a family interacts with every other person, we can understand that in the end each family must be interpreted as a social system. As Henry and Warson point out, "We must attempt to understand child development in terms of household—or even broader—configurations."[68] Increasingly the eyes of research are being focused on the *family constellation.* Henry and Warson describe such a constellation in the case of a certain little girl by saying that she lives in five families: one including her grandmother and her sister, one including her parents and her sister, and so forth. These five families represent somewhat different systems of interactions among the actual people present in the household. To speak of five families is somewhat metaphorical, but it conveys a vivid impression of the range of significant influences in family life.

The case of Bert Whipley has already provided an example of the way a child's interaction with two parents is affected by their interaction with each other. The father, frustrated in his occupation, vented his anger on both wife and son. The son became critical and resentful of the father, rejecting his authority. From the kindly mother he received some consolation; but because of her submissive, indulgent relation to the father, she could give him no sense of support and security. If in fancy we leave unchanged the attitudes of the two parents toward Bert but alter their relation to each other, conferring on the mother the strength to control her husband and thus to protect and fortify her son, it is easy to see that the atmosphere of the household would have been entirely different. The pattern of interaction that actually prevailed among these three members of the Whipley family was recognized some time ago by Aichhorn, in his studies of delinquency, as peculiarly fatal

[68] J. Henry and S. Warson, "Family Structure and Psychic Development," *American Journal of Orthopsychiatry,* XXI (1951), pp. 59–73.

for socialized development.[69] Support for this contention has recently been provided by Bandura and Walters in a controlled investigation of aggressive adolescent boys.[70]

The study of the family as a social system requires in the first place concepts to express interactions between pairs of people. This side of the problem has been developed by Ehrenwald, who describes mutual interactions in terms such as "domineering-submissive" or "domineering-rebellious."[71] Ehrenwald uses these concepts in working out the idea that neurotic reactions may spread within the family constellation in a manner analogous to contagion. He takes as an example a family of fourteen members, extending over four generations, in which a strongly compulsive, rigid, and domineering type of personality was transmitted from one generation to the next, and was augmented from outside, so to speak, through selection of marriage partners who fitted into the pattern. This kind of analysis needs to be augmented by concepts that capture more general aspects of the family constellation, as in Ackerman's attempt to identify over-all types of family adaptation.[72] The understanding that can be gained from detailed analysis of a family is shown in a paper on the use of an emotionally disturbed child as a family scapegoat.[73] When the relation between the parents is full of unresolved conflicts which threaten to disrupt it, tension may be relieved by deflecting hostility and blame to one of the children. The victim is unconsciously selected because he most readily symbolizes the parents' conflict. When the mother, let us say, is fiercely ambitious and the father lazily unsuccessful, the conflict is most easily visited on the child who makes a poor start in school. Becoming a bone of contention, the child is exposed to the confusing cross fire of maternal nagging criticism and paternal defense with implicit support of failure. The family stays together but at the cost of a hard time for one of its younger members.

In this chapter we have dealt chiefly, though not exclusively, with the early childhood aspects of development. We considered the general nature of the adaptive process, then examined in some detail certain problems of growth that are likely to offer difficulties: dependence and

[69] A. Aichhorn, *Wayward Youth* (New York: The Viking Press, Inc., 1935), chap. iv.

[70] A. Bandura and R. H. Walters, *Adolescent Aggression* (New York: The Ronald Press Co., 1959), p. 312.

[71] J. Ehrenwald, "Neurosis in the Family: A Study of Psychiatric Epidemiology," *Archives of General Psychiatry*, III (1960), pp. 232–42.

[72] N. W. Ackerman, *The Psychodynamics of Family Life: Diagnosis and Treatment of Family Relationships* (New York: Basic Books, Inc., 1958).

[73] E. F. Vogel and N. W. Bell, "The Emotionally Disturbed Child as a Family Scapegoat," *Psychoanalysis and the Psychoanalytic Review*, XLVII (1960), pp. 21–42.

deprivation, autonomy and discipline, sexual development, and the management of aggression. In each case we indicated both successful and maladaptive ways of meeting these problems. With these facts in mind we have now looked into the effects of the family circle on the child's development. The treatment thus far has done scant justice to growth in later childhood and adolescence, and it has neglected the integrative aspects of personality. In the next chapter these questions will be our chief concern.

SUGGESTIONS FOR FURTHER READING

For a more extended description of the developmental problems of childhood the reader is referred to O. S. English & G. H. J. Pearson, *Emotional Problems of Living: Avoiding the Neurotic Pattern* (New York, W. W. Norton & Co., Inc., 1945). Although development is divided into oral, anal, phallic, latent, and adolescent periods, the book is not rigidly committed to the original libido theory; it is a realistic and practical account of psychological development. The student who wants a rapid but extraordinarily just and lucid introduction to Freud's system will find it in Calvin S. Hall's *A Primer of Freudian Psychology* (Cleveland, The World Publishing Co., 1954). Clear exposition of a complicated subject also marks Clara Thompson's *Psychoanalysis: Evolution and Development* (New York, Hermitage House, 1950), which sketches the history of Freud's thinking and adds the contributions of the several workers who have made important revisions in psychoanalytic theory. G. S. Blum's covering of the same general ground is organized systematically rather than chronologically and provides guidance to the relevant experimental literature (*Psychoanalytic Theories of Personality,* New York, McGraw-Hill Book Co., Inc., 1953).

The general problems of development are painted on a wide canvas by Erik H. Erikson (*Childhood and Society,* New York, W. W. Norton & Co., Inc., 1950). Based more on "representative description rather than theoretical argument," this book draws on case histories, anthropological field studies, folk literature, and biography to set individual development in the full perspective of social organization. More technical in purpose is J. Dollard & N. E. Miller's *Personality and Psychotherapy: An Analysis in Term of Learning, Thinking, and Culture* (New York, McGraw-Hill Book Co., Inc., 1950), which analyses the processes of development, neurosis, and therapy in the concepts of a particular learning theory—reinforcement theory. For the student who wishes to pursue Freudian theory in detail there is Otto Fenichel's complete and scholarly work, *The Psychoanalytic Theory of Neurosis* (New York, W. W. Norton & Co., Inc., 1945), of which the first six chapters present the developmental psychology. A great deal of material relative to sexual tendencies is brought together in G. H. Seward's *Sex and the Social Order* (New York, McGraw-Hill Book Co., Inc., 1946). The survey includes sexual behavior of animals, sexual development in man, and changing sex roles in western culture. An important book on aggression is *Frustration and Aggression* by J. Dollard, L. W. Doob, N. E. Miller, O. H. Mowrer & R. R. Sears (New Haven, Yale University Press, 1939). The same topic is discussed in the light of extensive experimental work by A. H. Buss, *The Psychology of Aggression* (New York: John Wiley & Sons, Inc., 1961).

In *The Changing American Parent* by D. R. Miller and G. E. Swanson (New York, John Wiley & Sons, Inc., 1958) will be found a valuable review of American child training as well as a new research study of families in and around Detroit. A good descriptive as well as systematic account of the effects of various child training practices is contained in *Patterns of Child Rearing* by R. R. Sears, E. E. Maccoby, and H. Levin (New York, Harper & Row, 1957). D. M. Levy's *Maternal Overprotection* (New York, Columbia University Press, 1943), primarily a report of a specific research, is one of those rare monographs that conveys a rich experience of interest and insight. A fine exposition of parental attitudes and their effects on development is given by A. L. Baldwin, *Behavior and Development in Childhood* (New York, The Dryden Press, 1955), Chs. 20, 21.

4

The Integration of Personality

In a living organism a great many processes go on at the same time. These processes affect each other and work according to some kind of pattern. It is almost impossible to talk about this pattern of happenings without taking it to pieces and considering one process at a time. In the last chapter we dealt with several important problems of adaptation, but we did not undertake to work out the effect of one problem upon another, nor did we consider the overall styles of adaptation that might result from the total experience of childhood. When we took up the effects of parental attitudes on development we were inevitably propelled toward more integrative concepts; we found it necessary to treat the family as a social constellation in which the child has an active and complex part. However important it may be to consider things one at a time, we must not lose sight of the fact that living systems operate as wholes. Separate tendencies become joined in larger patterns; learned behavior builds up in hierarchies. When solving a problem in college mathematics we are served by a hierarchy of habits which has been gradually developing ever since the first number work in primary school. When solving the larger problems of living we are similarly served by hierarchies of acquired attitudes built up over the whole course of growth. Some of these developed systems are so firmly organized and so enduring in their influence that it is appropriate to call them *establishments* in personality. The main motives of adult life, often combining a variety of needs and satisfactions, can properly be called establishments. The same can be said of those complex abilities—for example, administrative ability—that are built up through long experience, and of such things as enduring interests, opinions on public affairs, and the system of guiding ideas known as conscience. Of all establishments the most comprehensive is that of the self, which we shall take as the starting point for this chapter.

THE CONCEPT OF THE SELF

Taking a short historical perspective, it can be said that the self or ego has recently emerged and risen to prominence in psychology. Taking a longer perspective, the self has experienced a brief absence from the center of the psychological stage and has now returned to play the indispensable role allotted to it by serious thinkers throughout the ages. The self was placed in obscurity only for that brief period—perhaps from 1880 to 1930—when psychology, fascinated by the methods and models of the physical sciences, devoted itself to experiments on elementary processes and postponed the attempt to understand the person as we know him in everyday life. From abnormal psychology, which of necessity continued to take people as its subject-matter, this concept was never really absent. The self or ego is one of the most difficult concepts in the whole realm of thought. It would simplify things if we could do without it. But no one can write sensibly about people without using this concept or its equivalent. As Allport puts it, "the existence of one's own self is the one fact of which every mortal person—every psychologist included—is perfectly convinced."[1]

The necessity of using the concept of the self does not confer the privilege of misusing it. As we use concepts in our thinking, they tend to get firmer and harder. Thought about fluid events tends to curdle and form solid clots. Before long we begin to think of the self as if it were a lump in the personality. It becomes an entity so sharply bounded that arguments begin as to whether a certain piece of behavior belongs in the self or out of it, proceeds across an ego boundary, or involves a collision between the ego and something else. In the end the self is standing like a solid boulder of granite in the midst of personality, and one's thinking about it is as flexible as granite. Yet perhaps a more serious danger lies in animating the boulder again in order to invest it with magic powers. "What is unnecessary and inadmissable," says Allport, "is a self that is said to perform acts, to solve problems, to steer conduct, in a trans-psychological manner, inaccessible to psychological analysis."[2] If the self is reinstated as a little man in the head who directs behavior, one's thinking about it becomes as realistic as a children's television program or a cartoon comedy.

Need for a Unifying Concept. In spite of its dangers we need the concept of the self. Without it we have no point of anchorage for the personal pattern of tendencies that is characteristic of each individual.

[1] G. W. Allport, "The Ego in Contemporary Psychology," *Psychological Review*, L (1943), pp. 451–78.

[2] G. W. Allport, *Becoming: Basic Considerations for a Psychology of Personality* (New Haven: Yale University Press, 1955), p. 55.

When we speak of a personal pattern our phrase carries several implications. It means, first, that the individual's tendencies form an *arrangement of related strivings*, rather than a list or chance conglomeration. It means, in the second place, that this pattern has no standard form, but *differs from one person to another* according to his nature and history. It must have still a third implication if we are going to talk about living people rather than inanimate systems. It must mean that the tendencies are patterned in order to accomplish the maintenance and expansion of a living unit. They function within an organism, and they are *patterned to make that organism live and grow*. That is the principle that governs the patterning and makes it intelligible.

The concept of the self helps us to bear in mind the basic fact of the unity of the organism. If we forget this basic fact, we are apt to talk about urges and differentiated tendencies as if they were tenants in a boarding house, each leading an independent life and submitting to a pattern of rules and regulations only because the other tenants interfere so badly. In practice none of us regards either himself or anyone else as a boarding house full of independent tendencies. If I lose my temper and make a childish scene, I do not blame one of my tenants, the aggressive urge; I blame myself for letting this tenant get out of hand. If my neighbor starts an unpromising venture and makes a success of it, I do not congratulate his need for achievement; I congratulate the man. We think of ourselves and others not as conglomerations, not even just as patterns, but as units. Some writers maintain that it is a mistake to talk in the first place about separate tendencies, urges, or drives. Goldstein, for instance, believes that "the facts which are taken as foundations for the assumption of different drives are more or less abstractions from the natural behavior of the organism." He prefers to speak of "only one drive, the drive of self-actualization," manifesting itself in different ways under different circumstances.[3] The concept of self-actualization has commended itself to a number of workers who dislike the artificiality of traditional drive theories and who want to emphasize the unitary character of human motivation.[4]

Most of us show our loyalty to the concept of a unitary self by our surprise when it is questioned. Stevenson's *Dr. Jekyll and Mr. Hyde* strikes us as a profoundly true yet extremely fantastic tale. Profound truth lies in its description of conflict between different tendencies within the person. But it seems like wild fantasy to suppose that such a conflict could divide the personality into two separate selves with separate iden-

[3] K. Goldstein, *Human Nature in the Light of Psychopathology* (Cambridge: Harvard University Press, 1940), pp. 144–45.

[4] A. H. Maslow, *Motivation and Personality* (New York: Harper & Row, 1954), pp. 91–93 and chap xii.

tities and an imperfect awareness of each other. Stevenson himself, even with all the freedom of fiction at his disposal, felt it necessary to introduce a magic drug to accomplish the transformation. There are, of course, real cases of multiple personality in which two or more selves function within the same individual.[5] That they are so rare, and that they strike us with such wonderment, testifies to the stubborn tendency of personality to become organized into a unitary self.

A unifying concept becomes particularly valuable when we want to take account of man's constructive and long-range behavior. The setting of distant goals, the discharging of obligations, the making and keeping of promises, the taking of initiative and persisting against obstacles, the struggle to live up to ideals, the whole forward movement whereby a person becomes an independent, effective and at the same time reliable human being—all of this activity implies a very high degree of organization. It implies a hierarchy of tendencies so ordered that the ones affirmed to be of most importance are given right of way over the less important. To say that this hierarchy takes shape in the interests of the *self,* and that things are more important or less important to a *self,* seems at present the most satisfactory way to conceptualize the whole difficult subject. But in order to keep the self from solidifying into a block of granite in our thoughts, we must consider its history and perceive it as a growing and changing system.

Formation of the Self. There can be no doubt that the self, like everything else in an organism, develops and changes a great deal in the course of life. Its nucleus appears to be what is experienced as "I" and "me," as distinguished from everything else that is "not me." This distinction, whatever its primitive basis, is amplified and strengthened by learning: children find out by investigation that the foot is part of "me" and the favorite toy is not.[6] As time goes on, "myself" assumes a fuller and richer meaning. It is compounded of bodily sensations, feelings, the image of one's body, the sound of one's name, the continuity of one's memories, all leading to the experience of oneself as a unique and separate person having a continuous existence. Particularly important is the feeling of activity and initiative. One's self is experienced not only as an object but as an agent. This feeling of activity, whatever its nature, is a highly characteristic feature of the ego system. In experiments using hypnotism it is possible to divest behavior temporarily of the feeling of active participation. It is then experienced as occurring of its own accord, and the experience is indeed a curious one.

[5] See below, pages 269–71.

[6] Observations and experiments on the development of the ego in childhood have been reviewed by M. Sherif and H. Cantril, *The Psychology of Ego-Involvements* (New York: John Wiley & Sons, Inc., 1947), pp. 158–78.

Around this enduring nucleus are presently gathered many accretions. Awareness of oneself and knowledge about oneself are heavily influenced by social interaction. A child builds up his sense of self out of the responses made to him by other people; through their acts and attitudes he learns how they perceive him and is influenced to perceive himself in the same way.[7] This process can be observed in bald form when parents apply adjectives to children and children begin to apply them to each other. The child's knowledge that he is strong, naughty, smart, or silly becomes formulated to a considerable extent through the labels applied by others. Gardner Murphy describes the situation as follows:

> Children are forever classifying one another by the use of good and bad names, applying to one another the nouns and adjectives which they have heard used in such a tone as to make them appropriate for praising or damning. . . . Most of the trait names that are used represent general action tendencies; and as soon as they are applied to oneself, or as soon as one finds himself applying them to others, they stimulate a trait psychology in their user. . . . Generalities are evoked by means of labels; the child lives up to the terms employed. . . . The child forms general ideas about himself. *In short, the self becomes less and less a pure perceptual object, and more and more a conceptual trait system.*[8]

These accretions to the enduring nucleus of the self are subject to continuous change. The pattern is formed and reformed many times in the course of life. You may remember but little of what you were like as a child, though you do remember it as *your* childhood continuous with your life today. You may remember more clearly yourself as a high-school sophomore, though only with a pleasant sense that you are not like that any more. A less sympathetic observer might point out more continuities than you would care to admit, but certainly you are not just the same from year to year. A particularly large reworking occurs at adolescence, when family membership weakens and social acceptability becomes a more vital attribute of self. In the course of time the pattern of selfhood becomes more stable. In this it is assisted by social pressure. "With age and greater responsibility, the individual organism is persuaded more and more to act like a unit, to phrase the multiplicity and incongruity of its wants in terms of the multiple expressions of a fixed self."[9] It is easier to live with others when they function as unified selves, and we encourage them to do so. The self is thus shaped into a unity from both

[7] The influential views of C. H. Cooley and G. H. Mead, who made social interaction the central concept in the *origin* of the self, are well summarized by Kimball Young, *Personality and Problems of Adjustment* (2d ed.; New York: Appleton-Century-Crofts, Inc., 1952), chap. vii.

[8] G. Murphy, *Personality: A Biosocial Approach to Origins and Structure* (New York: Harper & Row, 1947), pp. 505–6.

[9] *Ibid.*, p. 489.

directions at once. On the one hand it is attached to the enduring nucleus represented by one's sense of personal identity. On the other hand its various accretions are pressed toward unity by the requirements of social living.

Ego-Identity. This shaping toward unity from both directions is captured by Erikson in the concept of *ego-identity*. This expression signifies a sense of being a distinct individual in one's own right within a social framework. It includes one's self as a continuous, active personal being; and it also includes one's self as a meaningful part of the surrounding human group. As Erikson puts it:

> It is this identity of something in the individual's core with an essential aspect of a group's inner coherence which is under consideration here: for the young individual must learn to be most like himself where he means most to others—those others, to be sure, who have come to mean most to him. The term identity expresses such a mutual relation in that it connotes both a persistent sameness within oneself (selfsameness) and a persistent sharing of some kind of essential character with others.[10]

The sense of identity is strengthened by the progressive mastery of useful actions such as walking, talking, reading, or carpentry. These are experienced as achievements by the child himself, and their value is further affirmed by consistent recognition on the part of adults. But their value for ego-identity depends upon their being relevant to adult reality; they open the way to a feeling of partnership in a larger world—to the feeling that one has a place and function in the world.

The process of *identification* plays an important part in this growth. "Ego identity," says Erikson, "develops out of a gradual integration of all identifications," patterned "in order to make a unique and a reasonably coherent whole." Identification refers to copying or imitating the behavior of others when this is done out of a feeling of wanting to be in some respect like the other person. Children are not obliged to discover for themselves the whole repertory of behavior that is needful for growing up. They are surrounded by models providing patterns that, for better or for worse, can be copied. Beginning with the models available in the family circle, the child imitates selected aspects of other people's behavior all along the way, strengthening those patterns that seem to suit him and dropping out the ones that prove unworkable. Joseph Kidd, in his belated and rather breathless acting out of different "personalities" in late adolescence, gives us a dramatic image of what is usually a more extended and less conscious process of growth. He stands also as an

[10] For the exposition of this concept, see E. H. Erikson, *Childhood and Society* (New York: W. W. Norton & Co., Inc., 1950), especially pp. 207–18, 237–43; also "The Problem of Ego Identity," *Psychological Issues*, I (1959), No. 1, pp. 101–64.

example of a young man in whom the sense of ego-identity is confused and unstable. Erikson regards adolescence as the decisive crisis for ego-identity, when there is the greatest danger of identity diffusion and when the time is first ripe for establishing a firm sense of identity in adult perspective.

In this chapter we describe the normal development of the self and its establishments, indicating some of the ways in which maladaptation may occur. The account is broken down in such a way as to focus on important, though not necessarily all-inclusive, developmental processes. First we consider the growth of the self under the heading of "Sense of Competence and Self-Esteem." The qualities of the person himself, his physique, temperamental traits, mental abilities, and special aptitudes exert a marked influence over his behavior. They affect both his evaluation by others and his evaluation of himself. This self-evaluation may range from a supreme and arrogant self-confidence through all the degrees of normal self-esteem to miserable feelings of inferiority. Our next heading, "Social Development," calls attention to the part played by others in the development of the self. Here we shall particularly emphasize the growth that takes place outside the family circle through interaction with friends, schoolmates, and playmates. The account is divided into "Relations with Groups" and "Intimate Relations," the effects of these two kinds of social experience being quite different. We next round out our integrative picture by examining "Conscience and Ideals." Finally we shall direct our attention to the place of "Fantasy" in the growth and integration of personality. Daydreams, revery, and night dreams, however idle they may seem to be, perform important services of a balancing and prospective sort.

SENSE OF COMPETENCE AND SELF-ESTEEM

In discussing the young child's exploratory play and his movement toward autonomy, we introduced the ideas of feeling of efficacy and sense of competence. Acts such as reaching and grasping, pulling and crawling, standing up and walking without support are done intentionally and, to the extent that they are successful, they yield a feeling of efficacy. The baby trying to pick up a ball finds himself either competent or incompetent to do so. The child trying to walk a few feet from one support to another knows whether he succeeds or fails. In his attempts to walk the child is apt to have an appreciative audience which gives him a large social reward, but he does not require approval in order to know that he has succeeded. Mind and muscles have been pitted against an unknown but unmistakable force that tries to pull him to the floor, and they have proved competent to triumph over this force.

The Experience of Efficacy. In the course of a day's fishing it will often happen that some fish are landed while others get away. These outcomes produce sharply contrasting experiences in the fisherman. Let us assume, contrary to legend, that the fisherman is an entirely candid person; he will then probably recognize differences in his own performance that have a bearing on his success or failure. He will realize that he was too quick and impatient in playing one of the fish that escaped, and he will glow with pleasure as he remembers how perfectly he handled another that now lies in his creel. Similarly contrasting experiences visit the woodsman who fells one tree exactly where he intended it to fall but lands another so that it crushes neighboring growth and cannot easily be sawed. These examples of everyday acts introduce an important concept for understanding the nature of self-esteem. When the fish lands in the net, when the tree falls on the intended line, the person not only achieves a goal but senses himself as having been able or *competent* to achieve it. He has pitted his mind and muscles against natural obstacles and resistant forces, and he has been able to bring about the change that he intended. This is what we mean by the experience of efficacy.

There can be no doubt that self-esteem is tremendously affected by the income of esteem that is received from others, a point that was amply evident in the case of Joseph Kidd. There can also be no doubt that a good many kinds of excellence have to be socially defined before the child can have any way of judging success or failure. It is a mistake, nevertheless, to suppose that self-esteem is wholly a matter of esteem income—that no coin can ever be minted within. The esteem we feel for another person is not whimsically bestowed; it is related to what he has actually done. He, too, can often judge what he has actually done. In addition, he can appreciate the full discrepancy, if such there be, between what he did and what he intended to do. The experience of efficacy, based on the effectiveness of one's own activity in dealing with the environment, is a vital root of self-esteem. Silverberg puts the matter strongly:

> Throughout life self-esteem has these two sources: an inner source, the degree of effectiveness of one's own activity; and an external source, the opinions of others about oneself. Both are important, but the former is the steadier and more dependable one. Unhappy and insecure is the man who, lacking an adequate inner source for self-esteem, must depend for this almost wholly upon external sources. It is the condition seen by the psychotherapist almost universally among his patients.[11]

[11] W. V. Silverberg, *Childhood Experience and Personal Destiny* (New York: Springer Publishing Co., Inc., 1952), p. 29. "Activity" has been substituted for the author's word "aggression," a procedure which he sanctions (p. 18, footnote).

The contribution of competence to self-esteem can be seen most clearly when mind and muscles are pitted directly against inanimate obstacles. The issue is unmistakable in such problems as whether one can climb a cliff, drive a tractor so as to plough a field, fix up an ancient jalopy so that it will again speed over the road. It is equally proper, however, to speak of *social competence*, even though the many purposes and subtle nature of human interactions tend to obscure one's discernment of effective activity. Our intentions as regards other people are not always clearly conscious, and the approval or disapproval we encounter often seems to supply the only criterion of success. It is true, nevertheless, that there are tremendous individual differences in social competence, ranging from the person who feels unable to influence others at all to the person in whom a habit of command has become second nature. Feelings of social competence are presumably built up out of experiences in which one has found it possible to produce intended effects in other people: to make them respond to you, help you, serve you, love you, accept your love, learn from you. Competence has the same meaning, if not the same ease of observation, in social interaction as it has in dealing with natural forces.[12]

Competence During the School Years. A child's sense of competence and self-esteem is strongly affected by his experience in the family circle. Occasionally it is so blasted by criticism and ridicule that the child can no longer trust his own experience of competence. We have already examined one such instance, the case of Bert Whipley, whose father's impatience and sarcasm completely undermined his feeling that he was good for anything. As an adult, Bert apologized for everything he did, and he often threw away perfectly acceptable work because he was sure it could not measure up to standard. Usually the balance between encouragement and discouragement is more favorable to self-esteem so that the child is better able to utilize his own sense of competence. In any event an important chapter in establishing self-esteem has already been written before the child leaves the bosom of the family.

Nevertheless it is fair to say that a whole new arena opens when the child ventures outside, particularly when he goes to school. In the worlds of school and playground he finds an opportunity for a new deal as regards the estimation of competence. In the schoolroom there are new tasks, new challenges to competence, and he soon comes to realize that these tasks have ultimate significance in the grown-up world, which gives him, as Erikson expresses it, "a token sense of participation in the world

[12] For comparative case studies of people strong and weak in social competence, see R. W. White (ed.), *The Study of Lives* (New York: Atherton Press, 1963, chap. iii.

of adults."[13] Perhaps this participation can be sensed most easily in learning to master tools and produce useful objects, but the "three R's," if at first a little abstract, can soon be appreciated as part of the equipment needed to take part in adult affairs. At its best the school serves to develop and maintain in the child what Erikson calls "*a sense of industry* and a positive identification with those who *know* things and know how to *do* things."[14] This opens a prospect upon new kinds of excellence which put pressure especially on mental competence or intelligence. Being good at school work, finding oneself comfortably effective in the operations required by one's lessons, becomes a bastion of self-esteem for part of the pupils, while for others the wearisome daily grind produces a general sense of inadequacy in this sphere.

There is also the playground, where the experience of competence depends upon a different repertory of effective actions. Strength, agility, and good coordination are important foundations of self-esteem in this sphere, with qualities more socially colored, such as assertiveness and humor, coming in as important adjuncts. In direct comparison with others of the same age, the child must prove himself worthy of respect because he handles himself well in the games and banter of the group. It is a sharp strain for many children when they pass from the atmosphere of a child-centered home into the competitive realities of even a friendly play group. They must now show what they have in the way of physical prowess, courage, manipulative skill, outgoing friendliness, all in direct comparison with other children of their age. The penalties for failure are humiliation, ridicule, rejection from the group. Even the last is probably a less basic threat than rejection from parental love, but it is none the less an acute threat.

As the child grows he meets an increasing array of situations which put his competence to the test. His experiences of competence and incompetence become differentiated with respect to different spheres of activity. A boy proves particularly competent, let us say, in walking and running, not as good in building with blocks or handling small objects, decidedly poor in drawing, writing, and other fine coordinations. The ratio of success and failure is different in each sphere, and if the experiences of competence continue in a fairly consistent fashion there will eventually be differences in the confidence with which each sphere is approached. The boy of our illustration, entering a new school, will run buoyantly to the playground, confident that he can deal with whatever he may encounter, but he will enter the crafts room somewhat dubiously

[13] E. H. Erikson, "Growth and Crises of the 'Healthy Personality,'" in C. Kluckhohn, H. A. Murray, and D. M. Schneider, *Personality in Nature, Society, and Culture* (2d ed.; New York: Alfred A. Knopf, Inc., 1953), p. 212.

[14] *Ibid.*, p. 214.

and will take up penmanship with a weary feeling that he is never any good at this kind of stuff. Children show decided differences in over-all level of confidence, but they also typically differentiate their competence in different spheres, and this tendency increases with age. In the normal course of growth self-esteem is nourished more and more from one's better spheres of competence, injured less and less by one's poorer spheres.

Individual Differences in Physique. Physique plays a dual part in the development of personality. It is related to one's competence along lines of physical prowess and vitality. It is also the basis for social judgments having to do with beauty and personal attractiveness. Individual differences of physique have been studied for many centuries, but the crude knowledge thus acquired reached the level of exact measurement only in modern studies, especially those of Sheldon.[15] This writer developed a technique for measuring the important dimensions of the body from photographs taken at a fixed distance. Measurement of a series of 4,000 young men of college age allowed the conclusion that physique has three chief components which Sheldon named *endomorphy, mesomorphy,* and *ectomorphy.* Any individual physique is a combination of the three components, but the proportions may differ greatly. When endomorphy predominates, the digestive viscera are massive relative to other structures, and the body form is characterized by soft roundness, though not necessarily fat. In predominant mesomorphy, the somatic structures—bone, muscle, and connective tissue—have the first place, the body being hard, firm, strong, somewhat rectangular in outline. When ectomorphy predominates, the body is fragile, linear, and delicate in structure, the arms and hands, for instance, being slender and poorly muscled and the chest rather flat. There is considerable though not yet conclusive evidence that the individual physique or *somatotype* does not change in the course of life.[16] There are minor changes in hardness of muscle depending on physical fitness, and major changes in appearance due to fat deposits, but neither of these change the basic structural properties of the body.

The importance of these bodily differences is very great, especially for boys. Weakness in the mesomorphic component makes athletic success virtually impossible. Considerable endomorphy can be utilized in sports where weight is an advantage, and considerable ectomorphy can be valuable in the quick and agile games like tennis and fencing, but a substantial amount of mesomorphy is necessary in either case to supply

[15] W. H. Sheldon, S. S. Stevens, and W. B. Tucker, *The Varieties of Human Physique* (New York: Harper and Row, 1940). A condensed account is given by Sheldon in J. McV. Hunt (ed.), *Personality and the Behavior Disorders* (New York: The Ronald Press Co., 1944), Vol. I, chap. xvii.

[16] Sheldon *et al., op. cit.,* pp. 221–26.

the requisite sturdiness. High athletic ability may go far to counteract developmental handicaps. An actual case is a young man severely rejected at home, solitary and socially awkward, who entered high school in a strange community and after a short period of lonely confusion became a popular and admired student because of what his magnificent mesomorphic body could do on the athletic field. The mesomorphic component also favors acceptance by girls, who are likely to prefer the athletic type to the soft endomorphs and skinny ectomorphs.

The body, including both its competence and its attractiveness, takes a significant place in the development of self-esteem, especially between the ages of 5 and 20. Any marked deviations from the norm, unless they are on the side of athletic ability in boys and beauty in girls, are likely to create sharp feelings of inferiority. As Zachry has shown in a research on high-school pupils, these problems rise to a climax at puberty when changes draw attention to the body and make it peculiarly "symbolic of the self."[17] The fashion department of the magazine *Seventeen* receives pleas like the following:[18]

> How about showing some clothes for the short, chubby teen-ager? We all want to look like the rest of the crowd—but you know how some of us look in sweaters and skirts.
>
> You put too much emphasis on the petite junior miss and leave her skyscraper cousin out in the cold!

The importance of defects and blemishes is well displayed in the detailed case report of 15-year-old Betty, by Blos.[19] Betty had a mole on her cheek, and this fact dominated her self-consciousness and held down her self-esteem for several years.

One of the problems that affects both girls and boys, though in different ways, is deviations in the time of sexual maturation. It has been found that early maturing girls, big for their age, and late maturing boys, small for their age, are quite likely to be temporarily maladjusted.[20] Joseph Kidd got into this trap on account of skipping a grade in school. His difficult adjustment to a strange high school was complicated by his being the only pre-pubescent boy in his group. The problem was considerably greater in the case of John Sanders, reported by Jones.[21] John's predominantly ectomorphic physique at no time contributed much

[17] C. B. Zachry, *Emotion and Conduct in Adolescence* (New York: Appleton-Century-Crofts, Inc., 1940).

[18] Quoted by Sherif and Cantril, *op. cit.*, p. 227.

[19] P. Blos, *The Adolescent Personality* (New York: Appleton-Century-Crofts, Inc., 1941), pp. 29–109.

[20] N. Bayley and R. Tuddenham, "Adolescent Changes in Body Build," *43rd Yearbook, National Society for the Study of Education* (1944), pp. 33–55.

[21] H. E. Jones, *Development in Adolescence* (New York: Appleton-Century-Crofts, Inc., 1943), especially chaps. v and x.

to his self-esteem, but when in addition his adolescent growth spurt and secondary sexual characteristics were delayed, so that for a year or more he was still a little boy among adolescent boys and girls who practically ceased to be aware of his existence, his whole precarious adjustment and even his school work rapidly deteriorated. This case shows with remarkable clearness the importance of physique, its competence, and its social acceptance.

Individual Differences in Abilities. No human ability has been more widely studied in the last fifty years than *general intelligence.* It is defined in different ways, but nearly all definitions bring it into relation with our present theme by emphasizing the central position of adaptation. Intelligence has to do with learning, problem-solving, judgment, and thinking. It can be called the cognitive side of one's capacity for adaptation, in rough contrast to the motivational aspects of the adjustive process. There is growing evidence that general intelligence is really a cluster of more or less independent abilities. But the concept of the I.Q. is so firmly entrenched that most studies of deviations in mental ability treat intelligence as though it were in fact general. There is also growing evidence that intelligence is not the utterly fixed, innate endowment it was once supposed to be; motivation and environment have some influence upon it.[22]

It is obvious that high intelligence favors adaptation and that low intelligence obstructs it. When the I.Q. falls short of 50, the individual is unable to achieve adjustment to the world around him except under the simplified conditions of a custodial institution or its equivalent. Problems of adjustment are more acute with the so-called "high-grade subnormals," often subdivided (in ascending order) into moron, borderline, and dull normal groups, and lying in the I.Q. range between 50 and 90. Superficially, these individuals do not appear handicapped and may easily be expected to perform in ways that are beyond their competence. In a study of high-grade subnormal adolescent girls by Abel and Kinder,[23] it is shown that the retardation may remain essentially undetected until the child has gone some distance in school.

When a child's intellectual limitations become unmistakably apparent, she is generally placed in one of two situations, depending on the type of the school system to which she belongs. If no special classes are available for the mentally retarded, the girl remains in the regular classes, usually repeating grades and acquiring a reputation of being both dull and the perennial despair of teachers. If the school system provides for special classes, the subnormal girl

[22] J. McV. Hunt, *Intelligence and Experience* (New York: The Ronald Press Co., 1961).

[23] T. M. Abel and E. F. Kinder, *The Subnormal Adolescent Girl* (New York: Columbia University Press, 1942).

may find the work she is expected to do much easier and more in keeping with her interests. But she still has to combat the disapprobation of more intelligent girls, who remain in the regular classes and make her feel inferior in some way. Either course lessens her possibilities for later adjustment by emphasizing her feeling of inferiority.[24]

Feelings of inferiority may well have begun at home, especially if siblings and parents are of better ability. When they are reinforced at school it becomes virtually impossible to develop a satisfactory level of self-esteem. As a result many high-grade subnormals, who under favorable conditions might make a perfectly good adjustment at fairly routine work, either fall into delinquent ways or isolate themselves in pleasant fantasies. Both forms of behavior constitute a "revolt against an intolerable situation."[25]

Superior intelligence is in general an aid to adjustment. It does not, of course, preclude maladjustment. Intelligence, alone and by itself, does not even guarantee scholastic success, which depends on a favorable pattern of motives as well as mental ability. But the weight of evidence still favors the conclusions reached by Terman, who reported in 1925 that gifted children (I.Q. above 140) are superior to the general average in health, physique, breadth of interests, social adjustment, and emotional stability and that they maintain these advantages as they grow older.[26] The popular stereotype of the highly intelligent child as a puny, awkward, narrow eccentric has its basis in the unusual case and does not apply to the majority of gifted children.

Special problems arise, however, when the mental superiority is so great that it throws the person out of contact with those around him. Leta Hollingworth made an intensive study of children with I.Q.'s of 180 or better. In the course of twenty-three years of professional work in the New York area, she discovered 12 such children.[27] The mental competence of these children is so far ahead of their contemporaries that they simply cannot maintain mutual interests and common understanding. They are almost certain to be advanced in school, and therefore to be at a physical and social disadvantage. Friendships are difficult, because it is so hard to find someone who functions at approximately the same mental level. Out of his social isolation and feelings of social inferiority, the highly gifted child is sorely tempted to build a compensation

[24] *Ibid.*, pp. 51-52.

[25] *Ibid.*, p. 135.

[26] Terman *et al.*, *Genetic Studies of Genius*, Vol. I: *Mental and Physical Traits of a Thousand Gifted Children* (Stanford: Stanford University Press, 1925). A condensed account brought up to date appears as chap. xvii in R. G. Barker, J. S. Kounin, and H. F. Wright (eds.), *Child Behavior and Development* (New York: McGraw-Hill Book Co., Inc., 1943).

[27] L. S. Hollingworth, *Children Above 180 I.Q.* (New York: Harcourt, Brace & World, Inc., 1942).

which takes the form of contempt for all the fools in the world, including teachers and others in authority. This leads neither to happiness nor to the ultimate full utilization of his rare gifts for the benefit of society. Hollingworth was led by her studies to the concept of an "optimum intelligence" for total adjustment.

There is a certain restricted portion of the total range of intelligence which is most favorable to the development of successful and well-rounded personality in the world as it now exists. This limited range appears to be somewhere between 125 and 155 I.Q. Children and adolescents in this area are enough more intelligent than the average to win the confidence of large numbers of their fellows, which brings about leadership, and to manage their own lives with superior efficiency. Moreover, there are enough of them to afford mutual esteem and understanding. But those of 170 I.Q. and beyond are too intelligent to be understood by the general run of people with whom they make contact. They are too infrequent to find many congenial companions. They have to contend with loneliness and with personal isolation from their contemporaries throughout the period of immaturity.[28]

The question of individual differences in *special abilities,* apart from general intelligence, has great practical importance, especially in vocational adjustments. Often a person is unhappy and frustrated in his work even when all the surrounding conditions, such as pay, status, and congenial companions, are entirely satisfactory. For example, a man rises rapidly in an engineering company because of his craftsmanship and inventiveness in designing machines. As he is promoted to higher and better-paid positions, he gradually gets out of engineering itself and has more to do with business policy, sales, and personnel. He becomes progressively miserable, yearning to go back to designing, yet unable to resist the social pressure to move onward and upward. There is a strong presumption in such a case that the design of machines was backed by high aptitude, executive work by a much lower aptitude, so that the better-paid work is experienced as disagreeable, laborious, and frustrating. Unfortunately we know all too little about such special abilities. They are so apt to be entangled with problems of motivation that it is almost impossible to devise tests that will measure them in isolation. But this does not diminish the probability that they are important in mediating both good and bad adjustments.

Ability and Adaptation. High ability of any kind is potentially a strong asset in adaptation. Whether it be in sports, in craftsmanship, in school work, in music, in art, in managing others, it can serve as a point of integration for the personal pattern of tendencies. Actions that are performed well are performed with a feeling of satisfaction, quite apart from any social reward that may be added. When the child Handel

[28] *Ibid.*, pp. 264–65.

sneaked into the garret at night to play his harpsichord in spite of his father's threats of punishment, he was seeking the reward that results from exercising a strong talent. Behavior that is backed by talent should be looked upon as to a certain extent self-rewarding. It is affected by social rewards: good abilities can be suppressed by ridicule and mediocre ones inflated by praise. But the exercise of high competence brings satisfaction in its own right. It may even be so engrossing that little attention is paid to the immediately surrounding world. When engaged on an important work, Handel locked himself in his room and went without food and sleep for many days at a time, composing with extraordinary concentration and speed. The life of Handel cannot be explained as the result of parental encouragements, reaction formations, social rewards, economic need, and the expectations of the culture, although it probably cannot be fully explained without them. The central theme and ruling determinant was his possession of an extremely high special ability and special sensitivity. The line between ability and motivation in such a case is hard to draw. The competence is self-rewarding and needs to be exercised.

The integrative action of competence can be conceived as follows. High ability offers a fairly reliable line along which the person can function with growing ease and mastery. In the sphere of his excellence he repeatedly enjoys the experience of competence and thus provides his self-esteem with a strong inner source. It may be that no one in his environment will admire his particular kind of talent, in which case it is not likely to become a central pillar in his self-esteem. More commonly his ability will bring social as well as intrinsic rewards, and his development will then be guided by an efficient selective principle. Confident of esteem in one area, he can begin to discard the skills and roles that offer less promise. His tendencies thus assume an hierarchical pattern. Moreover, he can begin to select the groups and the companions whose esteem he will seek and value. He no longer has to care about the esteem of every "bunch" in his high school; he needs only the esteem of the "bunch" that is keen on science, for example, and more particularly, the few radio experts in the school. If he goes to college he will probably know what subjects he most wants to study, and he will shortly discover a group of like-minded companions among whom he will achieve his social adjustment. Very likely he will never know problems of vocational adjustment so long as there are opportunities in the line dictated by his central cluster of competence and interest.

The Inferiority Complex. Our examination of competence and its relation to adjustment will help us to understand how feelings of inferiority arise and how they can be overcome. The inferiority complex, as it is usually called, is the most common deviation from the healthful growth of competence and self-esteem. For the sake of a rounded picture we should include the opposite deviation, the development of a boundless overconfidence and conceit, which presumably might result from a combination of high natural abilities, opportunities, and exceptional social rewards. Possibly some such people are successfully absorbed in occupations that make a virtue of overconfidence, but more commonly they cannot escape being trimmed down both by circumstances and by other people, often with a painful loss of zest and with real suffering to themselves. Extreme conceit persisting in adult life is usually to be regarded not as a simple overconfidence but as a compensatory tendency or reaction formation against dangerous feelings of worthlessness.

As we saw in the first chapter, the concept of the *inferiority complex* was introduced by Alfred Adler, who made it central in his theory of neurosis if not in development as a whole. Adler's concept is so valuable that we should not ruin it, as some of his followers have done, by indiscriminate use. Everyone is inferior in a great many ways. Most people do not mind this in the least. Their self-esteem is dependent on only a small range of excellencies. Failure in many areas may mean little if it is compensated by success in just one area. As Allport observes, "Only in terms of ego-psychology can we account for such fluid compensation. Mental health and happiness . . . depends upon the *person* finding *some* area of success *somewhere*. The *ego* must be satisfied."[29] Much the same point was made by William James with memorable illustrations.

> I, who for the time have staked my all on being a psychologist, am mortified if others know much more psychology than I. But I am content to wallow in the grossest ignorance of Greek. My deficiencies there give me no sense of personal humiliation at all. Had I "pretensions" to be a linguist, it would have been just the reverse. So we have the paradox of a man shamed to death because he is only the second pugilist or the second oarsman in the world. That he is able to beat the whole population of the globe minus one is nothing; he has "pitted" himself to beat that one; and as long as he doesn't do that nothing else counts. He is to his own regard as if he were not, indeed he *is* not.
>
> Yonder puny fellow, however, whom everyone can beat, suffers no chagrin about it, for he has long ago abandoned the attempt to "carry that line," as the merchants say, of self at all. With no attempt, there can be no failure; with no failure, no humiliation. So our self-feeling in this world depends entirely on what we *back* ourselves to be and do.[30]

In a relatively integrated personality, which enjoys reasonable esteem somewhere, feelings of inferiority will be absent or transient and of

[29] G. W. Allport, "The Ego in Contemporary Psychology," *Psychological Review*, L (1943), pp. 451–78.

[30] W. James, *The Principles of Psychology* (New York: Holt, Rinehart & Winston, Inc., 1890), Vol. I, p. 310.

small importance. It is justifiable to speak of an inferiority *complex* only when the person continually makes unfavorable comparisons between himself and others, covering far more lines of excellence than any one individual could hope to carry. If such a person hears someone tell a story well, he wishes he might possess this excellence and laments his inferiority as a storyteller. The next moment someone else entertains with a song, and he feels miserable that he cannot do likewise. Then card playing starts, and he has a chance to deplore his mediocrity at cards. A single evening will provide him with an opportunity to feel inferior in a dozen ways. But it is not these dozen inferiorities that trouble him. It is rather the over-all fact that he does not have sufficient competence anywhere to form a nucleus of self-esteem and satisfy the self as a whole. If he could find some real excellence of his own, he would be willing to forego distinction in story-telling, singing, and cards.

The inferiority complex is apt to occur when obstacles, either internal or external, prevent the development of some personal pattern of excellence capable of supporting self-esteem. Obstacles may lie very much outside the individual, as when, for instance, his best competences are not valued in his society or there is an oversupply of his particular skills. Internally the greatest obstacle is a real lack of ability; we saw that people of subnormal intelligence were particularly exposed to severe feelings of inferiority. Apart from these very general obstacles, it is possible for situations to occur in which the development of a feeling of competence and self-esteem is blocked, even though excellent potentialities are present. A typical example, familiar to child guidance workers, is the situation in which two siblings near together in age constantly compete for the same excellencies, the ones most valued by their parents and by their group. The weaker competitor is constantly falling short, but it is hard for him to shift to other lines of excellence because these do not command an equal amount of esteem. The stronger competitor stands astride the prescribed avenue to esteem and the weaker cannot pass him.

It follows from what has been said that any measures designed to encourage the development of some area of excellence will help to reduce if not prevent an inferiority complex. Recognized competence is the thing that counteracts inferiority. Experiments by Jack and Page have shown that children who were very submissive in competition could be made more ascendant by giving them practice in advance in the games to be played.[31] Educators currently advise teachers to be at great pains to

[31] L. M. Jack, "An Experimental Study of Ascendant Behavior in Preschool Children," *University of Iowa Studies in Child Welfare,* IX (1934), No. 3; M. L. Page, "The Modification of Ascendant Behavior in Preschool Children," *ibid.,* XII (1936), No. 3.

develop for each child some area of success and social approval. Parents who are willing to recognize different kinds of excellence, even encourage them, provide more favorable circumstances than those who love only one pattern. In one family of five sturdy boys, each youngster was encouraged to specialize in a different sport. The result was five local champions and no inferiority complexes.

SOCIAL DEVELOPMENT: RELATIONS WITH GROUPS

The development of personality is influenced from the very beginning by social interaction and its consequences. Even the smallest infant leads his life in a social environment, depending upon others to respond to his cries and minister to his major needs. It has long been recognized that man is a social animal, but only in recent years have reflection and research shown the full extent to which he is shaped by the culture, by society, and by the people immediately around him. Interactions with other people, we now know, play a large and highly significant part in forming personality.

In studying this aspect of growth it is useful to distinguish two themes: *interactions with others singly*, particularly when the relationship is a close and intimate one, and *interactions with others in groups.* Each kind of interaction makes its distinctive contribution to the full growth of personality. We shall take up first the developmental consequences of memberships in groups.

Effects of Membership on the Individual. When an individual becomes a member of a group, his life is in many respects enriched and expanded. His strength is increased: the group can accomplish many things and resist many pressures where he alone would be helpless. His courage is increased by the sense of shared responsibility and group support. His purposes become solidified and his feelings of personal worth becomes established in the framework of group purposes and group values. He receives an income of friendliness, approval, recognition, and he gladly expends these things upon other members of the group. In time of stress he has the double satisfaction of helping others and receiving help from them.

On the other hand, membership in a group entails certain restrictions. The individual can no longer do just what he pleases. His initiative may be submerged because the group decides to do something some other way. He may want to play third base, but the group puts him in right field. The group defines for him a number of possible *roles* and helps him to select those he is best fitted to play. It provides him with a set of *norms,* indicating by approval or disapproval the kinds of behavior considered within that group to be right or wrong, good or bad, loyal or disloyal. These roles and norms constitute a social structure or framework within which he finds his place as a member of the group. If membership yields him sufficient satisfaction and enrichment, he willingly accepts the restrictions of the social framework.

A person may be said to occupy a position or status in society as a whole, but it is through membership in much smaller groups, starting even with the family, that he actually discovers his status. The play group, the bunch, the gang, the clique, the unit at the shop, the crowd at the office, the folks in the neighborhood constitute the groups that directly affect him and determine his social position. His conception of his place in society as a whole is to a considerable extent learned from the place of these groups in society, the relations of in-group and out-group, rival group, superior and inferior groups, and so forth. Through identifications with groups a person becomes able to identify himself as a member of society.

The action of groups and their effect on the individual can best be observed under relatively simple conditions. Sherif and Cantril select urban street-corner delinquent gangs as ideal exhibits of group psychology.[32] Drawing on the important studies of gangs by Thrasher, Zorbaugh, Clifford Shaw, and W. F. Whyte,[33] they point out that such gangs form spontaneously and build up their own internal organization with little influence from historical tradition or from the norms of the existing social order. In spite of their informal origins and lack of legal and conventional sanction, these gangs exert a tremendous effect on their individual members. Within his gang, the boy, often from a distressing home in a disorganized neighborhood, finds himself accepted, esteemed, taken seriously. In company with gang members he can perform deeds of recklessness and bravado that would be impossible alone. When sick or in trouble, he receives sympathy and assistance. The gang becomes a point of anchorage in the social ocean. He feels strong and happy with his group, lonely and depressed if he is separated from it. As Thrasher expresses it:

> Any standing in the group is better than none, and there is always the possibility of improving one's status. Participation in gang activities means everything to the boy. It not only defines for him his position in the only society he is greatly concerned with, but it becomes the basis of his conception of himself.[34]

[32] Sherif and Cantril, *op. cit.*, chap. x.

[33] F. M. Thrasher, *The Gang* (1927); H. W. Zorbaugh, *The Gold Coast and the Slum* (1929); C. R. Shaw, *The Jack-Roller* (1930); *The Natural History of a Delinquent Career* (1931), *Brothers in Crime* (1938); W. F. Whyte, *Street Corner Society* (1943). All published by the University of Chicago Press, Chicago.

[34] Thrasher, *ibid.*, p. 332.

Within these gangs there is a definite hierarchical structure. There are leaders and followers, and there are all kinds of specialized roles based on particular talents. Social pressure in the form of applause and preferment, ridicule, scorn, and ostracism keeps the individual members in their places and enforces the norms of the gang. In delinquent gangs the most serious offense is "squealing," which sometimes receives even the death penalty. If a gang member is caught, he is expected to "take the rap" no matter how hard it may be. Living in a precarious relation to the police, the gang must always act as a loyal unit. There can be no fraternizing with outsiders or members of rival gangs. The individual member comes to occupy a clearly defined place both within the group and in relation to the rest of the social order.

The effects of group membership cannot be listed wholly on the side of developmental assets. As we saw in the last chapter, the family circle, itself a group, sometimes has a destructive effect on an individual member, especially when this member is rejected, intimidated, or given stifling discipline. Groups outside the home are fully as likely to have an injurious effect on some of their members. Groups at school, well run by an adult supervisor, may sometimes achieve an atmosphere that is highly favorable to growth, but spontaneous groups of children or adolescents, dedicated not at all to developmental goals, may work in quite the opposite fashion. They can be cruel in rejecting a member who is slow, clumsy, or not "on the ball" in group activities. They can seize upon handicaps, peculiarities of appearance, class status, religious and ethnic differences, and use them as grounds for psychological ostracism if not outright expulsion. They can intimidate those who object to the way things are done, buying conformity with the threat of ridicule or physical violence. When a few "strong men" are in control of a group they can stifle initiative with as much force as an authoritarian parent. It would doubtless be possible to spell out the good and bad effects of groups on development just as in the last chapter we weighed the consequences of various parental attitudes. Neither group memberships nor family memberships invariably favor healthy growth.

Formative Influence of Memberships at Different Ages. It is during the early school years that group activity begins to assume an important place in children's lives. The period that extends roughly from six to twelve has been called the *juvenile era* by Sullivan, who saw *competition* and *compromise* as its chief problems in social learning.[35] Sullivan pointed out that "juvenile society itself encourages competitive efforts of

[35] H. S. Sullivan, *The Interpersonal Theory of Psychiatry* (New York: W. W. Norton & Co., Inc., 1953), chap. xv.

all kinds," and that "in addition, the authority figures encourage competition—that is, they do in any culture that values competition."[36] Compromise likewise is valued and enforced by juvenile society and favored by the school authorities. It is apparent that this stage of group life will be of great importance in developing a child's experience of social competence. What amount of influence will he have over others, in the sense of winning competitions, leading and persuading others, making suggestions, or at least being included in activities? In a study of cabin groups at a boys' summer camp each boy was questioned as to "who is able to get the others to do as he wants them to do." Within each cabin of eight boys there was substantial agreement, even quite early in the season, as to the degree of social influence exerted by each member; a clear hierarchy had already been established.[37] Groups during the juvenile era provide schooling in the give and take of social living in its less personal and intimate aspects. According to Sullivan, "the school years are a time when a degree of crudeness in interpersonal relations, very rarely paralleled in later life, is the rule. But, in spite of this, the opportunity which is laid before the young juvenile for catching on to how other people are looked upon by authority figures and by each other is an exceedingly important part of the educative process.[38] For some children this may be a hard chapter in social growth, but for others the juvenile era is a season of flowering in which certain unfortunate consequences of life in the family circle can be remedied.

During adolescence the functions of age-mate groups become more complex. The society of one's peers begins to take over the supporting role that has hitherto been maintained by the family. Blos points out that "belongingness to the group" to some extent "replaces family ties"; this is the secret of the adolescent's tremendous dependence on the esteem and approval of his peers.

> The group of contemporaries is uncompromising in its demands that the adolescent conform to its standards of behavior and belief. It offers him in return a security in group belongingness and in collective responsibility at a time when he is abandoning childhood relationships and reorienting himself in terms of mature goals. In response to the pressures of peer culture, his family patterns of relationship, identification, and feeling life are gradually modified in the direction of group norms. . . . The great dependence on group support and belongingness is naturally at its height at a time when the adolescent leaves the family, its protection and support, and has not yet the capacity to function independently on a mature level.[39]

36 *Ibid.*, p. 231.
37 R. Lippitt, N. Polansky, and S. Rosen, "The Dynamics of Power," *Human Relations*, V (1952), pp. 37–64.
38 *Ibid.*, p. 230.
39 Blos, *op. cit.*, pp. 250–54.

The height of dependence on the group comes at fourteen and fifteen years. Thereafter the young person becomes increasingly able to choose the groups with which he will become identified and to influence the roles he will assume. During adolescence, group memberships mediate the transition from family-member and child roles to roles as an independent maturing adult.

In adulthood, group memberships play a significant part in the individual's conception of the value and meaning of his life. He becomes identified with his occupation: he is a doctor, banker, teacher, skilled worker, farmer, etc. Within the broad category of occupation he becomes identified with smaller subgroups. As a doctor he is more specifically a psychiatrist, with a feeling that the rest of medicine is an out-group—a feeling, however, that will evaporate if medicine as a whole is attacked by a still-more-out group. Within psychiatry he is even more specifically a psychoanalyst with a psychogenic point of view, feeling rivalry with hospital psychiatrists whose outlook is somatogenic. He may belong to a local society of psychoanalysts, and within that society may associate himself with the subgroup that favors public lectures as opposed to a conservative subgroup that thinks lectures would do more harm than good. Outside of his occupation he is a member of this or that group that tries to effect changes in the community. His membership in clubs and informal social groups will influence his feeling of position in the community. On a larger scale he may feel himself identified with a political party and with groups working for far-reaching causes, such as world peace. Examples could be multiplied endlessly. The point is that each person is a member of many groups, and of subgroups within groups. However active he may be in choosing his memberships, these groups react upon him, shape him in the direction of their norms and expectations, and strongly affect his conception of what he *is* and what he is *doing* in the world.

Maladaptive Possibilities. In a rough way we can distinguish two general maladaptive possibilities in the realm of group relations: (1) *social isolation,* in which the person does not sufficiently receive the educative benefits of membership in groups; and (2) *social enslavement,* in which the person has learned to respond so automatically to the expectations of everyone around him that he develops no stable sense of self, no real ego-identity of his own.

1. *Social Isolation.* Many forces may conspire to prevent a child from entering readily into groups. Fragile physique or unusual sensitiveness may handicap him from the start, predisposing him to shy, tense withdrawal from the normal bruisings of child society. Geographical isolation may get the child off to a poor start as regards social experience. A

serious obstacle is offered by parental overprotection. Perhaps the parents apprehensively interfere with the child's social contacts or try to bind him by creating a too perfect environment at home. If he is accustomed to whine for his own way or to demand it aggressively, he will react badly to the give and take of the group and probably suffer rejection. On the other side of the picture, the difficulty may lie less with the individual than with the groups he is in a position to join. The first available group may be dominated by children with bullying tendencies who enjoy making the newcomer miserable. Or it may be that after an auspicious beginning the child discovers himself rejected because he belongs to a different class, race, nationality, or religion from the majority in the neighborhood. If he moves a great deal, he will experience a certain feeling of rejection merely because he is a newcomer who must be assimilated to already existing groups.

When circumstances pile up to hinder satisfying membership in the more available groups, it sometimes happens that the difficulty is solved by searching out or even bringing together a small and special group with congenial interests. In such cases the child is not isolated from other human beings, though he may feel ill at ease in large and boisterous groups.

In the event that this avenue is not open, maladaptation tends to develop along one of two lines, sometimes along both at once. The person may remain shy, retiring, homebound, limited in his interests to things that can be done by himself. He does not learn the give and take of group relations, remains a stranger to convivial good fellowship, and lacks the sustaining experience that it is possible to communicate deeply with another person in an intimate relationship. He may compensate in fantasy for the lack of expanded selfhood that comes from human interactions at their best, but he will never feel quite certain of his actual position in the social organism. Certain developments will be harder for him, especially those which depend on separation from parental support. Without the compensating support of his age-mates at adolescence, he will feel less confidence in separating himself from parental supervision and opinions and in carrying out a mature sexual adjustment. Unless he is in the meantime developing exceptional talents that bring him back into relation with others, he is likely to feel progressively isolated and insignificant.

The other line of maladjustment has the character of a reaction-formation. Rather than realize that his social inclinations are frustrated and that he himself is rejected, the person develops the role of contemptuous independence. He rejects the very idea of membership in stupid, commonplace groups with their plebeian interests and petty politics. He tends to inflate himself into an important personage who can achieve great things if not hampered by the mob or by the interference of friends. He tries to pump up in himself the feeling of strength and importance that actually comes most readily through social memberships. With exceptional talent such a person may accomplish something, but his usual fate is essential isolation, ineffectiveness, and bitter resentment.

2. *Social Enslavement.* Another path along which social development can go astray is excessive conformity to the expectations of others. The person who travels too far in this direction comes to guide his behavior entirely by what other people want of him or expect of him. He finds it impossible to make suggestions or express wishes of his own unless these are sure to please the people immediately around him. Depending heavily on group affiliation, he may make himself unusually skillful at playing the right role in the right place. People oriented in this way become expert in meeting the expectations of each company they happen to be in, and they never err by telling the sex joke, the Scotch joke, the joke on the President, the joke on the party out of power, to the wrong audience. This sensitivity to what will please others has the effect of pleasing others and is therefore judged by them to be evidence of remarkable social adjustment. Never troublesome to others, such a person may be regarded as something of a mouse, but he is not in danger of criticism or rejection. And these seem to be the dangers his behavior is intended to avoid.

Social enslavement is favored by various circumstances. To some extent it can be absorbed directly from parents: discrepancies between parents' well-mannered behavior toward other adults and the things they say about them in private must often strike the child as meaning that his parents are afraid of other people. When children are forced prematurely into group activities, when their social careers are pushed by their parents rather than by their own motives, interaction may become a chore best dealt with by falling in with what the other children want. If entrance into groups proves difficult, the child may undertake to buy his way by deference and docility. If the child's social hunger is particularly acute, as is sometimes the case when he has experienced rejection in the family circle and needs a new source of security, it will be difficult for him to run the slightest risk of not being accepted.

The maladjustment that underlies excessive conformity comes to light most clearly when the person is faced by conflicting expectations. This is particularly likely to happen in times like the present, when social standards and values are changing. There is inherent contradiction among some of our long-cherished values: for example, between brotherly love and competitive success. With such conflicting norms in the background, it is all the more likely that the groups available to any one person will uphold contradictory values. When a socially enslaved person is forced to decide which of two group values he will espouse as his own, he is likely to feel confused and bewildered. No stable inner pattern, no integrated self, can serve him as a point of reference. He must announce his true colors, but he is a chameleon. The core of his maladjustment lies in the fact that he has leaned on social judgments and has not brought his own desires, peculiarities, and sense of competence into his conception of himself. The self-picture is diffused and fails in its integrative function.

One form of social enslavement has been described by Erich Fromm under the title of *marketing orientation.*[40] Economic success is increasingly dependent upon getting along with other people in a large concern and commending oneself to the purchasing public; this invites the young person of today to consider himself and his personality in the light of a marketable commodity. To receive promotions or new jobs one must be saleable and in fashion, fitting the current pattern of a personable young businessman or businesswoman. Self-esteem here depends upon conditions more or less beyond one's control, and there thus tends to develop a constant fear of setbacks, a relentless striving for success, and a ceaseless need for confirmation by others. Success is so heavily defined as being what others want you to be, rather than as doing certain things with effective skill, that the opinions of others become almost the sole source of self-feeling and self-esteem. "The marketing personality," in Fromm's view, "must be free of all individuality."[41]

The problem of overadjustment to social expectations has been examined with particular care by the Swiss psychiatrist, C. G. Jung.[42] It is seen most clearly in cases having the following pattern: the patient is a person in middle life who has been well adjusted and successful, but who feels an intolerable discontent, uneasiness, frustration, and sense that his life has become meaningless. To understand such cases Jung introduces the concept of the *persona.*

> The word "persona" is really a very suitable expression for it, since *persona* originally meant the mask worn by an actor to signify his role. . . . It is a compromise between the individual and society as to the kind of semblance to adopt, what a man should "appear to be." He takes a name, earns a title, represents an office, and belongs to this or that. . . . Society expects, and indeed must expect, that every individual should play the role assigned to him as completely as possible. Accordingly, a man who is also a pastor, must not only carry out his professional functions objectively but at all times and seasons he

[40] E. Fromm, *Man for Himself* (New York: Holt, Rinehart & Winston, Inc., 1947), pp. 67–82.

[41] *Ibid.*, p. 78.

[42] C. G. Jung, *Two Essays on Analytical Psychology,* trans. H. G. and C. F. Baynes (New York: Dodd, Mead & Co., Inc., 1928), especially pp. 163–71 and 202–32.

must play the role of pastor in a flawless manner. Society demands this as a kind of security. . . . It is therefore not surprising that everyone who wants to be successful has to take these expectations into account.

The construction of a collectively suitable persona means a very great concession to the outer world. It is a real self-sacrifice which directly forces the ego into an identification with the persona, so that there are people who actually believe themselves to be what they present to the public view. . . . These identifications with the social role are a very fruitful source of neuroses. A man cannot get rid of himself in favor of an artificial personality without punishment. The mere attempt to do so releases, in all the ordinary cases, unconscious reactions in the form of moods, affects, fears, compulsive ideas, feelings, vices, etc.[43]

When a person has made the mistake of identifying himself too completely with his social roles—with his persona—and is paying the price in irritability and discontent, he can restore his well-being only by striking a new bargain with the demands of society. He must remove the "false wrappings of the persona," as Jung put it, and regain contact with those aspects of himself that have been suppressed in the process of social adjustment. In his new bargain with society there will be room for the fulfillment of what is more or less peculiar to himself. Instead of a persona he will become, in today's popular phrase, a "real person."

SOCIAL DEVELOPMENT: INTIMATE RELATIONS

Interacting with others in groups is an important educative experience, but it does not offer a complete curriculum in social development. One of the attributes of maturity is to be capable of sustaining and enjoying intimate relations with one's spouse and closest friends. Behavior in groups, which is relatively public behavior, does not provide the conditions that are essential for the growth of intimacy. These conditions can be met only in what we may call a private relationship between two people, one in which confidences can be exchanged and secret aspirations shared. In later childhood most children seek a closer, more personal relationship with someone who can be considered a special friend or chum. Important new developments in social interaction get under way.

Because these developments are apt to appear at a time when puberty is not far away, and because later an intimate relationship is often also a sexual one, it is sometimes supposed that the friendships of the years from ten to thirteen can be attributed to the burgeoning sexual need. The full significance of these relationships is overlooked, however, if we think of them as solely erotic, especially if, because they typically start between children of the same sex, we regard them simply as a disturb-

[43] *Ibid.*, pp. 164–65, 209–10.

ance on the way to heterosexual adjustment. Close friendships between children play a highly constructive part in the growth and integration of personality. They strengthen the understanding of oneself and others, and they lay important foundations for appreciative, loving relationships in later life.

In their early stages close friendships may engage but a small part of the child's feelings. Helene Deutsch points out that girls between 10 and 12, as part of the process of breaking away from dependence upon parents, develop a strong need for secrecy. To surround her person with secrecy, the girl needs a partner, and she is apt to find one in another girl like herself in age and interests, "with whom she giggles and titters, with whom she locks herself up in her room, to whom she confides her secrets."[44] Some of these secrets may have to do with the sexual facts of life, but Deutsch's studies indicate that "expression of intense tenderness between girls is not found at this time, and mutual masturbation almost never occurs under normal circumstances."[45] The close relationship serves the purpose of ego development rather than erotic satisfaction. Guilt is lessened by sharing supposedly guilty secrets; support is obtained in the process of emancipation from adult control; above all, "identification with a similar being can strengthen the young girl's consciousness that she is an independent ego." "The positive aspects of such friendships are paramount," Deutsch concludes, "and lack of them is a serious loss in this period of life."[46]

A unique part is played by close friendships in discovering and defining the self. From the competitions and compromises that occupy juvenile groups one may emerge with a fairly clear sense of one's social competence and reputation for prowess, but the more private aspects of experience can be defined and corrected only in an intimate relationship. Here it is possible to speak of things that one would not disclose to the world at large, to consider new dimensions of personal worth besides those that receive group approval. Here it is possible, for example, to speak of the fears one has endured and combatted in order to meet a group standard; great relief and strengthening may follow the discovery that the other person, too, has been fearful in situations where externally he performed well. Here also it is possible to mention one's hopes and aspirations for the future and thus to secure some social reflection on what has hitherto been private—but perhaps not wildly fantastic. When in adolescence the desire for intimacy shifts to a member of the opposite sex, the goal of self-definition still plays a prominent

[44] Helene Deutsch, *The Psychology of Women: A Psychoanalytic Interpretation* (New York: Grune & Stratton, Inc., 1944), Vol. I, p. 13.

[45] *Ibid.*, p. 15.

[46] *Ibid.*, pp. 27–28.

part. In Erikson's words, "to a considerable extent adolescent love is an attempt to arrive at a definition of one's identity by projecting one's diffused ego images on one another and by seeing them thus reflected and gradually clarified. This is why many a youth would rather converse, and settle matters of mutual identification, than embrace."[47]

In the course of time, very often before the shift of interest to a person of the opposite sex, youthful friendships become charged with strong emotional meanings, and it is through this that they perform their most important service for development. This topic has been most fully expounded by Sullivan, who attributed to the close friendships of preadolescence the power to correct various faults in the child's previous social growth.[48] The friend takes on a new meaning: his interests and his happiness assume an importance equal to one's own. With his chum the child "begins to develop a real sensitivity to what matters to another person; and this is not in the sense of 'what should I do to get what I want,' but instead 'what should I do to contribute to the happiness or to support the prestige and feeling of worthwhileness of my chum.' "[49] This interest in the other person can properly be called love, even when no overt sexual element is discernible. It involves wanting to understand the other person, wanting to encourage and help him, wanting to share interests with him, all of which maximizes the chances that true mutuality will emerge. Fortunate experiences of this kind pave the way for the mutual affectionate relationships of adult life.

Maladaptive Possibilities. It is as true of friendships as it is of groups that their effect on development is not always constructive. Sometimes one of the partners dominates or exploits the other. Sometimes the overtures from one side are not answered by real interest or understanding. Perhaps the need for intimacy in one partner evokes only a need for erotic experience from the other. Rebuffs in forming intimate relationships may produce wariness, reserve, and a tendency to shut in one's private concerns. Sometimes, on the other hand, a friendship will prosper so warmly that jealousy is aroused when either of the partners takes an interest in someone else. The consequences may be painful and may discourage future attempts at closeness; in such cases, however, the person may well have experienced developmental benefits before the relation came to grief.

Even though the going is not always smooth, it is a mistake to keep children out of a major pathway toward maturity. Sometimes teachers and group workers make a policy of breaking up pairs of children so that they will mingle more widely in the group. Presumably in some

[47] Erikson, *Childhood and Society*, *op. cit.*, p. 228.

[48] Sullivan, *op. cit.*, chap. xvi.

[49] *Ibid.*, p. 245.

cases the children continue their friendship in secret, thus learning the valuable lesson that adult ineptitude need not spoil your growth. Otherwise they can only assume that there is something wicked about intimacy, which will certainly hinder their progress toward emotional maturity. It is a common complaint among young people that they have lots of acquaintances but no real friends. On this account they feel lonely, but they also feel a little like strangers to themselves, for they have not had enough chances to find out, through intimate interaction, what they are really like.

CONSCIENCE AND IDEALS

Some of the most noteworthy human actions occur in the service of conscience and ideals. Considerations of immediate reward, of self-interest, even of harmony with fellow group members, may be laid aside in favor of principles that are felt to be in the interests of broader human welfare. In extreme situations a person may have to choose between his life and his ideals, and he may choose his ideals. People who have died for their country, gone to the stake for their religious faith, endured poverty for their art, gone to jail or into exile for their political beliefs, all show the extent to which ideals can govern behavior. Many of the most admired human achievements demand concepts such as conscience and ideals.

In recent years, however, such concepts have been under a cloud. Talk about ideals is sometimes only a sham, a piece of window-dressing whereby a person seeks to give commonplace or dishonest motives a noble appearance. The patent insincerity of advertisers, politicians, dictators, and other self-interested people has gone a long way to sour our respect for the kind of ideals they proclaim. Conscience has had an even harder time. Freud unmasked it as one of the causes of neurosis and of many shortcomings in personal development. Going further, Chisholm makes conscience responsible for all the blindness, guilt, fear, and frustration that make men unable to prevent war. "The necessity to fight wars," he says, is an "irrational behavior pattern resulting from unsuccessful development and failure to reach emotional maturity." The human race seems perpetually liable to this form of irrational behavior. The one psychological force capable of producing such recurrent folly, says Chisholm, is "morality, the concept of right and wrong." Only when men escape from the conviction of sin and the equally damaging conviction of moral superiority can they achieve "the qualities of adaptability and compromise" which would put an end to war.[50]

[50] G. B. Chisholm, "The Reestablishment of Peacetime Society," *Psychiatry*, IX (1946), pp. 3–11.

It is confusing to think of conscience as the cause of neurosis, war, and highly integrated noble deeds. But it does no harm to start from this confusion if it makes us attentive to the different meanings attached to conscience. Conscience and ideals have a history in the individual. Like everything else, their development can go astray so that they enter into the composition of neurosis, war-mongering, dictatorship, cruel self-righteousness, and many other forms of individual and social maladjustment. They can also develop in ways that make men dedicate their efforts to human betterment. Most of the trouble comes from the fact that conscience begins in childhood before the child can understand what it is about.

Freud's Concept of the Super-Ego. Freud developed the concept of the super-ego in order to explain the irrational guilt feelings and self-punishments observed in the free associations of neurotic patients. He felt justified in considering it a separate entity because it seemed to act with remarkable independence, forcing its norms upon the patient even when the patient did not want to accept them. Irrational guilt feelings often occur in normal people. An old lady, nearing eighty, feels a little guilty when she knits on Sunday, even though she is making socks for soldiers, because in her childhood her parents forbade work on the Sabbath. A young man of very strict training decides he will adopt the standards of his college companions, but when he smokes or allows his lips to touch alcohol he still feels as if he had committed a crime. Such things are more far-reaching and crippling in neurotic patients. The moral compulsions and scruples seem completely autonomous or *ego-alien:* "the individual seems to have no say in the matter of the self-imposed rules; whether he likes them, whether he believes in their value, enters as little into the picture as his capacity to apply them with discrimination."[51]

The reason for the power and irrationality of the super-ego lies in the circumstances of its origin. It goes back to infancy; Freud said to the fourth and fifth years, but later workers with children trace it to the earliest parental restrictions. Conscience, Freud observed, is not present from the very beginning.

> Small children are notoriously amoral. They have no internal inhibitions against their pleasure-seeking impulses. The role which the superego undertakes later in life is at first played by an external power, by parental authority. The influence of the parents dominates the child by granting proofs of affection and by threats of punishment which to the child mean loss of love and which must also be feared on their own account. . . . It is only later that the secondary situation arises, which we are far too ready to regard as the normal state of affairs; the external restrictions are introjected, so that the superego takes the

[51] Karen Horney, *New Ways in Psychoanalysis* (New York: W. W. Norton & Co., Inc., 1939), p. 208.

place of the parental function, and thenceforward observes, guides, and threatens the ego in just the same way as the parents acted to the child before.[52]

The concept of *introjection* has been considerably elaborated in psychoanalytic writings. The introjection of parental restrictions has sometimes been likened to a very simple learning process: the child acts on some impulse, the behavior is punished (or punishment threatened), and this linkage with punishment causes the action to be internally inhibited thereafter. The super-ego, however, is conceived to include not only prohibitions but also positive ideals such as cleanliness, self-reliance, perfection. All the attitudes and valuations that are taken over wholesale from the parents during the earlier years of childhood are included in its composition. It is the childhood version of conscience, and Freud offered evidence that it functioned as an independent establishment in personality quite early in the child's career.

Shortly after Freud directed attention to these matters, it became apparent that the super-ego was not always a faithful copy of parental attitudes. Delinquent children showed practically no introjection of parental restraints, even when these were strongly applied. It could be assumed in such cases that the child had not been offered a good bargain: there was too little love to make it worth his while to inhibit things he wanted to do. More puzzling was the situation in which mild and amiable discipline reappeared in the child as a severe and violently punishing super-ego. How could conscience grow so far beyond its source? The answer seemed to be that the child's own feelings of aggression got mixed up in the process. Angry because of his frustration, he projected this feeling into the parents and assumed that they, too, were angry. Thus he introjected a badly falsified image of the parental code.

The child's misapprehension of norms goes much further than this. We have to ask how a child understands rules and ideals quite apart from emotional involvement with them. How does an immature mind grasp the difficult notion of morality?

Piaget's Study of Child Morality. As part of his investigation of children's thinking, Jean Piaget, at Geneva, has studied the growth of moral judgments in children from five to adolescence.[53] He used the technique of the provoked value judgment; that is, he initiated conversations or played games with children in the course of which he could ask them about the rules for playing marbles or how they felt about such faults as clumsiness, stealing, and lying. Piaget found that for all the younger

[52] S. Freud, *New Introductory Lectures in Psychoanalysis* (New York: W. W. Norton & Co., Inc., 1933), p. 89.

[53] J. Piaget, *The Moral Judgment of the Child* (New York: Harcourt, Brace & World, Inc., 1932).

children, a rule has an absolute status, like a thing that exists, an outlook which he christened *moral realism.* The younger ones assumed that the rules for marbles had always existed, and that it would be impossible to change them even if everyone agreed to do so. To offenses they attributed an equally unchanging status; circumstances and actual effects played no part in the moral judgment. In contrast to this, the older children were able to take a point of view which Piaget called *moral relativism.* They could see that the rules for marbles were matters of mutual agreement for mutual benefit and could be changed by agreement. Moral relativism means judging the quality of an act by its actual effects on others.

In view of this analysis, it becomes plain that the super-ego, originating as it does in the earlier part of childhood, will embody the outlook of moral realism. Even our everyday illustrations showed this: it is wrong to work on the Sabbath, even if you are assisting the war effort, and it is sinful to touch tobacco and alcohol, even if your mature self can perceive no harmful consequences. The super-ego can thus be considered the irrational, and, indeed, often unconscious conscience that is left over from childhood. Like any childhood function, it should develop and keep pace with a maturing outlook. Freud showed that in many cases this development did not take place, with the result that the super-ego persisted with force and with ego-alien independence.

Development of Moral Insight. The outgrowing of moral realism depends to a large extent on being able to see things from another person's point of view. Young children can be utterly confused by questions that involve putting themselves in somebody else's place: for instance, "How many brothers has your brother?" In an attempt to study perspectives, Lerner told children a story about an offense which, from an adult point of view, would be judged very differently by the different characters included in the story. The younger children did not grasp the different perspectives, and made each character give exactly the same judgment of the offense, even those who had benefited by it.[54]

The development of perspective enabling the child to see that events affect different people differently—that what gives pleasure to him and his friend, for instance, may be disadvantageous or painful to a third child—is partly a matter of mental maturation, but it is partly the result of particular kinds of experience. L. B. Murphy has shown that nursery-school children display very real sympathy for each other's distress, and that this sympathy is stronger when the child himself has been in a

[54] E. Lerner, "The Problem of Perspective in Moral Reasoning," *American Journal of Sociology,* XLIII (1937), pp. 249–69.

similar plight.[55] Isaacs gives instances, also from nursery school, of children discontinuing behavior that annoys others because they grasp, with a little help, the image of how they would feel if they were the victims.[56] Especially important for understanding morality are situations in which others violate the rules to the child's disadvantage. The functions of a promise dawn on him with crystal clearness when his parents forget that they were going to take him to the circus. The reason for the rules of a game strikes him when another child violates them and starts to pocket his marbles. To be sinned against is one of the crucial experiences giving insight into the nature of sin.

Many writers do not distinguish between super-ego and mature conscience. Freud did not do so, but he made a rather similar distinction when he pointed out that children, as they grow older, copy the norms and ideals of other people besides their parents. These identifications, he said, "regularly provide important contributions to the formation of character; but these only affect the ego; they have no influence on the super-ego, which has been determined by the earliest parental imagos."[57] It is probably true that even the most mature, independently worked out conscience contains traces of the super-ego as it existed in early childhood. Nevertheless we miss an important aspect of development if we attempt no theoretical distinction. We shall regard the super-ego as a childhood conscience, built upon moral realism, irrational in character, borrowed straight from parental sanctions *without reflection or the use of his own experience on the part of the child.* Mature conscience begins when the child's sympathy and insight get to work so that he sees a purpose—other than pleasing his parents—behind restraints and ideals. It continues when he discriminates the effects of his actions on everyone who is affected by them, judging his acts accordingly and freeing himself from blind literal obedience to a code. Murray describes this process as the integration of the super-ego into the ego, the integration being accomplished by cognitive activity and independent judgment.[58] To the extent that this integration is accomplished, the super-ego ceases to exist as an ego-alien force in the personality.

Fixation of the Super-Ego. When the super-ego is not outgrown in the manner just described—and we must admit that much of our moral train-

[55] L. B. Murphy, *Social Behavior and Child Personality* (New York: Columbia University Press, 1937).

[56] S. Isaacs, *Social Development in Young Children* (New York: Harcourt, Brace & World, Inc., 1937), pp. 275–78, 369–75.

[57] Freud, *op. cit.*, p. 92.

[58] H. A. Murray, *Explorations in Personality* (Fair Lawn, N. J.: Oxford University Press, 1938), pp. 136, 190.

ing seems designed to prevent it from being outgrown—it remains an autonomous and often rather disturbing force in personality. The person may be subjected to an unbearable burden of guilt and fear as his super-ego passes its archaic moral judgments on his behavior. He may try to rebel and act the part of a libertine, but he cannot do it with peace of mind. He may surrender to the force he is unable to integrate and become a literal embodiment of all the virtues. This sacrifice is likely to make him envious of anyone who dares violate a single rule, so he attacks such people with the cruel venom of the self-righteous. It is these manifestations of a fixated super-ego that justify writers such as Chisholm, quoted above, who see so much evil in conscience and the concept of right and wrong. A mature conscience is another matter.

In general, the super-ego becomes fixated when the child feels that he is loved, yet when there is also a certain anxiety about retaining this love. Recent research has shown that disciplinary methods which involve a denial of love produce the strongest evidences of guilt and the most strenuous introjection of parental standards.[59] Of course the child must have something to lose by disobedience; if he does not feel loved in the first place he will not be much affected by the idea that his parents cannot love him when he is naughty. There must be love, but there must also be a sense of danger that love can be lost. Under these circumstances the child does not dare to question parental norms or to behave in any way that may imperil the tenuous relation. He is scared. This blocks the growth of sympathy and insight, the outflow of feeling toward other children who might help him gain new perspectives. It prevents the use of his own experience and judgment. So much is at stake in being perfect as the parents mean it that he cannot give up or modify those patterns of behavior. Fixation of the super-ego is encouraged by society's timidity in allowing the individual to think for himself, especially on moral matters. The image of moral chaos, doubtless greatly exaggerated, makes men hesitate to encourage individual moral maturity. It is easier and safer to keep people in line. Under these circumstances the outgrowing of an initial fixation is doubly difficult.

The Ego-Ideal. Ego-ideal means simply the self that one wants to become. It may take the form of an ideal of personal conduct: to be an upright man, a charming woman, an altruistic person, a topnotch gangster. It may be identified with desired accomplishments: the person wants his life to mean clean city government, freedom for artistic expression, a world without alcohol, a world-wide fascist revolution. Our examples are chosen to suggest that the concept of ego-ideal is im-

[59] R. R. Sears, E. E. Maccoby, and H. Levin, *Patterns of Child Rearing* (New York: Harper & Row, 1957).

portant, regardless of the wisdom and ethical character of the self one wants to become. Like the ego itself, the broader concept with which we started this chapter, the ego-ideal is an integrative concept. People may have what others consider to be conflicting aims. But they rarely think of the "selves" they would like to become. Their ideals are linked to one organism, one ego, one personal identity, integrated somehow into a single ego-ideal.

When we think of idle and drifting lives, or of lives so bound by circumstances that they seem to run themselves out as a matter of routine, the concept of an ego-ideal may appear superfluous. It is needed, however, perhaps even to understand these lives, and certainly to understand those contrasting lives that achieve things of importance and change the world. It is not necessary to conceive that an effective ego-ideal must be conscious and communicable in words. Sometimes an outside observer can say more clearly than you yourself what you seem to be living for, even though he does not have the advantage of introspection. An ego-ideal can be functionally effective without being consciously formulated. In fact, when a person can formulate his ego-ideal too readily, we may suspect that the verbal statement is drifting loose from the functionally effective guides of his behavior and is being used to impress, if not to deceive, himself and others.

Ego-identity refers to the self we feel ourselves to be. Ego-ideal is the self we would like to be. In the forming of these two establishments, a similar part is played by identification. To the actual people the child may be moved to imitate, the culture adds a large variety of ideal models. From the time when the little boy is urged to act like a big boy to the time when, let us say, he enters a religious order that patterns its activities on St. Francis of Assisi or a political group that espouses the philosophy and program of Lenin, he is proffered an array of more or less ready-made ego-ideals. He may reject most of them, but the accepted ones may have an important influence upon him. Images of living or once-living people quicken his imagination and enlist his energies more strongly than would otherwise be possible. The concept of ego-ideal emphasizes the forward movement that is characteristic of human behavior. We are rarely satisfied with ourselves as we are, always trying to make things a little better.

FANTASY

"Fantasy is popularly thought of," writes Symonds, "as the fairyland, the unreal part of the mind. Actually, it is very real and in a way tough—a part of the mind that cannot be so easily dispensed with. Even though fantasy is intangible and fleeting, it still has an actual existence and is influential in shaping personality and guiding behavior."[60]

Freud's discovery of free association, which we described in the first chapter as an important landmark in the study of human nature, drew scientific attention to the less logical, less controlled, more spontaneous and dreamy thought processes. In a first attempt to study these processes, Bleuler, in 1912, introduced the distinction between *realistic* and *autistic* thinking.[61] Realistic thinking is oriented toward correctly understanding the world around us and toward communicating with others. It implies vigilance, an intention not to be deceived or misunderstood, and it therefore has a toilsome quality that leads to fatigue. Autistic thinking is experienced as free from effort. It goes forward spontaneously, unhampered by realistic and logical constraints, and appears to be guided by feelings and wishes. Bleuler's distinction is convenient and useful, but it is probably more correct to conceive of the whole thing as a continuum rather than as two distinct ways of thinking. There are all degrees of freedom from realistic constraints. Starting with cold hard problem-solving, we can run down the line through imaginative speculation, shared playful fantasy, free association, and private daydreams until we reach the elaborate fantasies that occur under the influence of drugs and the bizarre experiences that constitute our night dreams.

Everyone engages in revery a good deal of the time. Most of it is quickly forgotten, but anyone can attest its frequency by noticing his thoughts for a few hours. Sometimes our reveries awaken considerable feeling and even influence our bodily reactions. We may feel hot with embarrassment as we recollect some blunder, and our pulse may rise as we angrily rectify, in fantasy, some insult or unjust criticism. The fact that these daydreams do not actually engage with real life and change the real situation makes us a little apologetic about them. Much of their content, moreover, strikes us as a little humiliating. They are full of hurt feelings, petty pride, spiteful retaliations, or absurdly glorious roles we would like to play. They abound with repartee that did not occur to us in time, and with imaginary conversations in which we display sparkling wit or heavenly eloquence. Pride invites us to overlook these vanities in ourselves, but the psychologist cannot neglect this "very real and in a way tough" realm that shapes and sustains the personality.

Most people will readily admit, though perhaps only to themselves, that their daydreams and fantasies reflect personal tendencies and reveal things of importance concerning their private worlds. That the same

60 P. M. Symonds, *The Dynamics of Human Adjustment* (New York: Appleton-Century-Crofts, Inc., 1946), p. 487.

61 Cf. E. Bleuler, *Textbook of Psychiatry* (New York: The Macmillan Co., 1942), pp. 45–47; here Bleuler substituted *dereistic* (away from reality) for the term *autistic*.

should be true of night dreams is apt to be conceded with more hesitation. Sometimes a dream shows excellent plot and organization, but generally it is a piece of sheer nonsense. How can we find personal significance in the weird actions and incongruous situations that make up a dream? Many scientists reject the whole idea and dismiss dreams as only the chance "rumblings of brain molecules." But there is a certain similarity between dreams and spontaneous revery. In drowsy states it is possible to witness a transition between the two. If we find significance in fantasy, we are justified in seeking it behind the scrambled language of the dream.

Balancing and Prospective Aspects of Fantasy. Adjustment always takes place at a cost: that is, it entails the giving up of certain tendencies and privileges in order to enjoy the fuller satisfaction of other tendencies. The constraints of circumstance, time, and social requirements set limits to the expression of inclination and interest. Even when a good psychological bargain can be struck, a great many aspects of oneself are neglected and sacrificed in order to live a mature and useful life. It is in the realm of fantasy that we can observe the balancing operations that help maintain the integration of personality in spite of these necessary limitations. It is also in the realm of fantasy that we find constant preparation for the future, the incubation of images and ideas on their way to become conscious plans. In a very real sense fantasy is the staging area for future operations.

The cost of adjustment is well illustrated in the case of a college undergraduate named Helmler.[62] By the time he reached high school it was clear that tendencies toward friendly sociability and tendencies toward dominating others were both strong in his make-up. Only in one situation, however, up to the time of graduation from college, did he find it possible to satisfy both tendencies without conflict. He was chosen for a summer camp designed to give training in leadership. He rose in the hierarchy, "was given a good deal of authority as one of the camp leaders," and at the same time "made about fifteen close friends." These circumstances conspired to make his camp experience the outstanding satisfaction of his life. In high school he became a prominent politician, which satisfied his love for dominance but cost him his close friendships. To his regret, he found himself considered "a rather serious stuffed shirt, out for all I could get." At college the situation was reversed. His friendliness flourished, but he achieved no prominence. He was adjusted, but with a gnawing sense of discontent. Compared to its high-school glory,

[62] R. W. White, S. S. Tomkins, and T. G. Alper, "The Realistic Synthesis: A Personality Study," *Journal of Abnormal and Social Psychology,* XL (1945), pp. 228–48.

his life seemed unimportant and trivial. He had daydreams in which he assumed important roles in government, business, or military service. One evening, during some horseplay at the dormitory, he suggested, all in a spirit of fun, that his companions gather around and call him God.

For the most part daydreaming is prompted by unrelieved tensions of one kind or another. Its themes are the minor frustrations of the day and the major frustrations of the person's life as a whole. In so far as the daydream merely wishes things around into a more pleasing shape, it might be regarded as a cheap substitute for actual achievement. Even though cheap, however, it is a substitute. It helps us to get used to the frustrations that exist, while at the same time presenting images of a more hopeful state of affairs for the future. Thus daydreaming can be seen as a kind of balancing activity in which existing frustrations are made less painful and burdensome.

Imagined actions have an element of practice or rehearsal about them, and this practice may affect actual behavior on some future occasion. Children can often be observed trying out roles in play and then putting them into practice in reality. A little boy is scared by the banging and squeal of a hay fork and refuses to go near the barn. With parental help he presently builds a barn out of blocks, rigs up a hay fork with string, brings a toy truck and trailer to the scene, and for some time makes the truck lift the imaginary hay out of the trailer. He then announces that he is going to the barn where he pulls on the ropes and moves the hay fork by his own effort—an action which apparently could not be managed without the intermediate step of rehearsal in fantasy. Daydreaming, similarly, is not necessarily idle. It may contain, along with its too-easy satisfactions, an important element of imaginative practice for the future.

Modern psychopathology has probably increased the disrepute in which fantasy is held. Schizophrenia, the most common of the psychoses, first became intelligible when its manifestations were perceived as analogous to dreams and daydreams. Generalizing too hastily from this discovery, people began to deplore daydreaming on the ground that it would lead to schizophrenia. In our case material in the second chapter, there were two examples of excessive daydreaming. Joseph Kidd, when discouraged with the failure of his various attempted "personalities," found himself daydreaming most of the time. But when he found an appreciative girl and a satisfactory job, the daydreaming ceased to be a subject for complaint. His daydreaming was a symptom of maladjustment, not a cause, and there is no reason to suppose that his frequent reveries slowed the process of readjustment. In L. Percy King's case, daydreaming reached far more serious proportions, so that large blocks of fantasy became for him indistinguishable from reality. But it is meaningless to say that he became schizophrenic because he daydreamed too much. We saw that his illness arose from intolerable conflict, a conflict that was merely reflected in fantasy. Even in his case the prospective, rehearsing aspect of fantasy can be observed. In his thoughts he tried to explain things more coherently and to shape his behavior more realistically, and he actually improved his adjustment. That the attempt was not successful enough to restore his full sanity should not lead us to overlook its readaptive direction.

In view of the current fashion which considers fantasy merely as a maladjustive process it is important to call attention to what happens when fantasy is constricted and suppressed. A person in whom this has occurred wants everything to be realistic, concrete, and clearly structured. He shies from whatever is vague or poorly outlined, from anything that cannot be pinned down in unequivocal terms. He is apt to settle for a humdrum, routine way of life and appears to others to miss much of the experience that should be within his reach. Here again the attitude toward fantasy is symptom rather than cause: conflicts and anxieties lie behind the wariness of imagination. Such a personality, however, is the kind that is often referred to as impoverished, which fits the conception that the cut-off realm of fantasy is in many respects a source of riches.

Understanding Personality Through Fantasy. Close study of a person's fantasy life would tell us a great deal about his personality. If we could open a door and observe the free streaming of his revery, we would be rewarded by many insights that could never be obtained through conversation or by observing his behavior from the outside. We would see his private world and learn the personal meaning of events in his life. For this very reason most people are unwilling to disclose what goes on in their reveries. They prefer that the private world should stay private. The spontaneous daydream cannot often be the object of scientific study.

Better suited to investigation is the kind of imaginative process a person can be induced to use in responding to a psychological test. Shortly after 1900 Jung devised the *word association test,* in which the experimenter calls out a list of words and the subject replies with the first association that comes to his mind. In 1921 Herman Rorschach published his work with *ink blots,* showing that a person's choices as to what he saw in relatively meaningless figures could reflect significant aspects of personality. In 1935 Morgan and Murray introduced the *thematic apperception test,* in which the subject is given a series of pictures, mostly of somewhat indefinite content, and asked to make up a story about each picture. Since then there has been a wave of interest in man's playful and imaginative behavior, and many tests have been devised to stimulate spontaneous associative processes. Tests of this kind are generally called *projective tests,* on the theory that the subject unwittingly "projects" certain aspects of himself into his performance.[63]

Many kinds of information can be derived from projective tests. Here a single illustration must suffice: the status of aggressive impulses in Joseph Kidd, as deduced from his stories in the thematic apperception test. From Kidd's history it could be assumed that he would harbor resentment against his parents who had first favored him but later withdrawn their esteem; in interviews, however, he expressed only mild aggression toward them. In his stories the situation was different. The "heroes" or principal characters were often driven by hostile and destructive tendencies which proceeded unchecked to gory results followed by torments of remorse. In one tale, for instance, a young man degraded by poverty was driving a stolen car and "chose to run down an elderly woman, mother of seven children, rather than risk smashing up." When caught and "faced in the morgue by the mangled body, he could not bear it and screeched for mercy before collapsing." Sometimes, in contrast, the "hero" learned to control aggressive impulses and became a reformed man. Kidd's handling of this theme displayed certain unwitting assumptions that provided valuable clues to his own problems of control. The indispensable condition for reform, as shown in the three plots in which it occurred, proved to be the kindly intervention and sympathetic interest of an older man. Thus in one plot a young surgeon, callous and impatient for success, performed unnecessary operations rather than seeking safer but slower methods of treatment; he mended his ways when a kind old physician took him in hand and showed him what operations mean to the patients. Kidd's plots thus imply that control of aggression requires the reward of a father's affectionate interest. When this is lacking there is a danger that aggression may break forth and lead to a nightmare of remorse.

Even *dreams,* for all their incoherence, can be used as an avenue to understanding personality. Freud's monumental work on this subject discusses in great detail the transformations that presumably go on in the construction of a dream, and French in a recent book emphasizes the balancing and prospective functions as shown in a long series of dreams collected from a patient during the course of psychoanalytic treatment.[64] Many tendencies can find expression through the medium of the dream. Of greatest interest for the student of abnormal psychology are those

[63] For an early overview of this work, see R. W. White, "Interpretation of Imaginative Productions," in J. McV. Hunt, *Personality and the Behavior Disorders* (New York: The Ronald Press Co., 1944), Vol. I, chap. vi. A detailed survey is edited by H. H. and G. L. Anderson, *An Introduction to Projective Techniques* (Englewood Cliffs, N. J.: Prentice-Hall, Inc., 1951).

[64] S. Freud, *The Interpretation of Dreams,* trans. A. A. Brill (New York: The Macmillan Co., 1933). T. W. French, *The Interpretation of Behavior,* Vol. II: *The Integrative Process in Dreams* (Chicago: The University of Chicago Press, 1953).

dreams that appear to be activated by *repressed tendencies.* Sometimes the careful study of a dream shows that it is pieced together out of thoughts and experiences of the previous day that passed virtually unnoticed at the time. These thoughts have the common property that they tend to activate tendencies which the person does not want to recognize in himself. He is able to avoid recognizing them during the day, but at night the activated tendency disturbs sleep and gives rise to dream formation.

The process can be clarified by an illustration. Hendrick reports the dream of a patient which consisted simply of this scene: Two Negro boys were wrestling.[65] When the patient had given exhaustive free associations to each element of the dream, and in so doing had recaptured several fleeting memories from the previous weeks and from childhood, it turned out that the latent wish behind his dream was the desire to express his much inhibited sexual need. He recalled that he saw a Negro couple the day before and noticed the woman's attractive figure. A week earlier he had seen a Negro woman with a white man; his companions had made ribald comments. This led him to recall tales of erotic adventure recounted by his friends. The idea of wrestling called up an incident of early childhood when he had been given one punishment for two misdemeanors: wrestling with a boy and erotic mischief with a little girl. He remembered also having once thought that certain wrestlers' holds were like those of amorous couples. All of these thoughts and incidents had been pretty well suppressed at the time they occurred. But in one way or another they all bore a relation to his chronic problem, the desire to satisfy his sexual need like other men of his age. This problem was stimulated by seeing the Negro couple, and it proceeded to activate a dream which utilized a mass of past associations to produce the highly condensed and still disguised image of two Negro boys wrestling. This dream represented the young man's sexual wish as fulfilled, but it disguised the fulfillment sufficiently so that he was not awakened by anxiety.

Our study of daydreams, fantasy productions, and night dreams has shown the importance of the less rational levels of experience. All these forms of expression lie open to whatever bothers us in the way of unsolved personal problems and emotional tensions. If the person can find no peace unless, like Joseph Kidd, he wins back the esteem of parents and girl friends, or unless, like the young man who dreamed of Negro boys wrestling, he breaks down the obstacles to mature sexual expression; in other words, if some vital problem is pressing for solution, it constantly invades the less rational forms of behavior even when it must do so in disguise. It will keep appearing in revery, it will influence

[65] I. Hendrick, *Facts and Theories of Psychoanalysis* (New York: Alfred A. Knopf, Inc., 1939), pp. 21–22.

selective perception, and it will activate dreams. It is likely to crop up when the person is shown the Rorschach ink-blots, and it will probably exert an influence on his stories if he is given the thematic apperception test. None of these expressions solves the problem or even necessarily causes it to be understood by the subject. Yet they serve as a kind of practice toward new and better solutions of emotional problems, and they throw light on the ceaseless struggle to overcome difficulties. We cannot have a well-rounded conception of human behavior, normal or abnormal, unless we realize how much of it takes place at a level that corresponds to revery and imagination rather than to thinking and volition.

SUGGESTIONS FOR FURTHER READING

The best account of the growth of the sense of self is G. W. Allport's chapter on the subject in *Pattern and Growth in Personality* (New York, Holt, Rinehart & Winston, Inc., 1961), Chap. 6. The concept of the self and the pitfalls in its use receive judicious treatment in the same author's *Becoming: Basic Considerations for a Psychology of Personality* (New Haven, Yale University Press, 1955), Chs. 10–13. Long a champion of the ego in psychology, Allport nevertheless fears that the concept may become hopelessly solidified; in its place he favors calling "all the regions of our life that we regard as peculiarly ours" the *proprium,* then attempting to build up an adequate description of the various propriate functions. Erik H. Erikson in *Childhood and Society* (New York, W. W. Norton & Co., Inc., 1950) develops the important idea of *ego-identity,* which serves to relate the concept of self to the individual's place and function in society; see especially pp. 161–234. Erikson's conception of the self, like the one presented in this chapter, places emphasis on the experience of competence as well as the social responses evoked by one's behavior. See also his detailed discussion, "The Problem of Ego Identity," in *Psychological Issues,* Monograph No. 1, pp. 101–64 (New York, International Universities Press, Inc., 1959).

Many of the topics taken up in this chapter are discussed in Gardner Murphy's *Personality: A Biosocial Approach to Origins and Structure* (New York, Harper & Row, 1947). In Chs. 3, 4, and 7, Murphy considers the question of constitutional differences; in Chs. 20–22 the origins, evolution, and enhancement of the self; in Chs. 32 and 34 and in Part Six as a whole the problems of group membership, social roles, and cultural determinism. Murphy's treatment is reflective and theoretical, not easy but eminently worth while. Valuable especially for its many concrete illustrations is M. Sherif's and H. Cantril's *The Psychology of Ego-Involvements* (New York, John Wiley & Sons, Inc., 1947), especially Chs. 7–9 on the genetic formation and re-formation of the ego, and Chs. 10–11 on the effects of group memberships and identifications.

Noteworthy contributions to the theory of social development were made by Harry Stack Sullivan, whose recorded lectures are available in book form (*The Interpersonal Theory of Psychiatry* [New York, W. W. Norton & Co., Inc., 1953], especially Chs. 12–18). The manner in which individual behavior is shaped by memberships in groups is the subject of an informative chapter in T. M. Newcomb's *Social Psychology* (New York, The Dryden Press, 1950), Ch. 14.

Freud's large book, *The Interpretation of Dreams* (New York, The Macmillan Co., 3d ed., 1933) is a remarkable and thought-provoking work, but his contribution can be grasped in a shorter time by reading Chs. 5–15 of *A General Introduction to Psychoanalysis* (New York, Liveright Publishing Corp., 1920), together with Ch. 1 of *New Introductory Lectures on Psychoanalysis* (New York, W. W. Norton & Co., Inc., 1933).

The subject of conscience is treated in broad terms by Erich Fromm in *Man for Himself* (New York, Holt, Rinehart & Winston, Inc., 1947), pp. 141–72. Fromm's distinction between authoritarian conscience and humanistic conscience corresponds roughly to the one described above between super-ego and mature conscience.

5

Anxiety and Defense

The next three chapters will be devoted to the study of neurosis. Before we begin this undertaking it will be well to look backward for a moment and summarize what we have thus far accomplished. To understand disordered personal reactions it is necessary to have in mind the normal course of development from which they deviate. Just as knowledge of sound vision should precede the attempt to understand eye troubles, just as knowledge of the normal intact nervous system should precede the study of neurological disorders, so knowledge of the normal growth of personality should stand as the basis for comprehending the psychogenic aspects of disordered behavior. In the last two chapters we have tried to lay this essential foundation. We have studied adaptation in order to establish points of reference for maladaptation. At each point we described not only the normal course of events but also the maladjustive possibilities peculiar to that particular developmental process.

It is impossible to have a simple theory that would cover all kinds of *maladaptation.* There are a hundred ways in which a person can become maladjusted. Even in our condensed account we have seen very diverse possibilities. Failure to outgrow the dependent tendencies of childhood, failure to achieve a working compromise between disciplinary requirements and autonomy, difficulty in guiding one's sexual and aggressive tendencies into socially workable channels, warping by the effects of the family constellation, unusual patterns of ability, troubles in establishing self-esteem based on competence and its recognition by others, insufficient or unfortunate social experiences both with groups and with close friends, conflicts among socially expected roles, an unabsorbed super-ego, unfortunate options in the way of identification figures, weakness of ego-identity, failure to internalize an effective hierarchy of strivings and a guiding ego-ideal—each of these maladjustive possibilities exists and plays a significant part in one life or another. In the nature of the case there can be no one theory of maladaptation. The best we can do is to work out the normal course of development and see all the ways in which it can go astray.

In contrast, there is a real possibility of having a unified theory of *neurosis*. We saw at the end of our historical survey (Chapter 1) that many students of psychogenic disorder had begun to organize their thinking around the central concepts of anxiety and defense. Motivation —especially unconscious motivation—and conflict—especially conflict among unconscious strivings—proved indispensable in understanding neurotic patients, but it was impossible to build up a satisfactory theory without considering the peculiar importance of anxiety and of the defensive measures used to hold anxiety in check. When Freud characterized anxiety as "the fundamental phenomenon and the central problem of neurosis," he summarized the impressions of many workers besides himself and the members of his psychoanalytic school. Neurosis can be considered a kind of maladjustment in the common meaning of the word, but it can be distinguished from lesser maladjustments by qualities that owe their being to a fundamental struggle with anxiety.

A THEORY OF NEUROSIS

The Nuclear Neurotic Process. An anxiety theory of neurosis takes its start from the general notion that neurosis is an outcome of the individual's struggle for safety and security. Its root is in self-preservation. It is of course not the only outcome of that universal struggle, and it is certainly a warped outcome, but it can be considered as the only possible outcome when certain combinations of circumstances prevail in the person's life. His troubles have their origin in being scared, and represent the only way he can feel safe. Perhaps he is scared by a few terrifying experiences, more often by chronic situations that threaten to undermine his security. He unwittingly applies defensive measures to prevent a recurrence of threat, and these cripple in certain respects the further development of his personality. If further difficulties accumulate, his anxieties and his defenses may both be intensified to a point of breakdown and symptom formation, or to a point of unpleasantness that he can no longer tolerate. This in rough outline is the conception of neurosis that we shall set forth in the next three chapters.

There is a catch in the statement that we can have a unified theory of neurosis based on anxiety and defense. No matter how simply we describe the nucleus of the neurotic process, neurosis occurs in a *person* and its effects may ramify widely throughout the personality. Thus a complete theory of neurosis necessarily includes all those processes of development that we have attempted to describe in the preceding chapters. Neurotic personalities, like normal ones, exhibit very great diversity. In the chapter following this one we shall give explicit recognition to this aspect of the problem by studying the far-reaching effects of chronic neurotic conflict on the personality as a whole. It is still legitimate, however, to speak of a unified theory of neurosis. The claim to unity lies in this contention: all the forms of neurosis are the outgrowth of a fairly uniform nuclear process involving anxiety and defense.

With this in mind we shall attempt to study the nuclear process in the simplest possible cases. We need to examine the effects of frightening experiences and the way in which these effects are overcome. Frightening experiences entail learning; to overcome anxiety requires new learning, and this new learning takes place, as we shall see, under somewhat difficult conditions. The core of a neurosis lies at the point where anxiety has blocked or distorted the learning process so that new adaptive learning cannot take place.

Frustration and Conflict. It should be noted that other concepts have a certain claim to the central position we are here assigning to anxiety and defense. Some students of neurosis prefer to make *frustration* their basic concept; others believe that *conflict* is the indispensable element. This divergence of opinion has less to do with the facts than with the best way to conceptualize the facts. It is hard to imagine a neurotic process that does not entail frustration and conflict as well as anxiety and defensive operations. Argument centers on what is to be chosen as the truly peculiar and nuclear element—the pathogenic factor—in neurosis.

The work of Pavlov, who first demonstrated the possibility of producing an *experimental neurosis* in dogs, led to the hope that this question might be settled by crucial experiments with animals. Pavlov produced breakdowns by establishing conditioned responses to two signals, one always reinforced and the other never reinforced by food. The two signals were then gradually made so similar that the animals could no longer discriminate between them, with the result that ordered behavior broke down.[1] Research along similar lines has been carried forward by several workers in this country: Gantt with dogs, Maier with rats, Liddell with sheep, pigs, and goats, Masserman and Dworkin with cats, Hebb with chimpanzees.[2] Artificial breakdown in animals is of course only

[1] I. P. Pavlov, *Lectures on Conditioned Reflexes* (New York: International Publishers Co., 1928), chap. xxxvi.

[2] For a summary of earlier researches, see H. S. Liddell, "Conditioned Reflex Method and Experimental Neurosis," and F. W. Finger, "Experimental Behavior Disorders in the Rat," these being chaps. xii and xiii in J. McV. Hunt (ed.), *Personality and the Behavior Disorders* (New York: The Ronald Press Co., 1944), Vol. I.

roughly analogous to neurosis in human beings. In the case of rats the disturbed behavior seems almost closer to epileptic seizures. *Experimental neurosis* is thus a presumptuous and somewhat misleading term, but it remains in widespread use. When an animal's disturbed behavior outwardly resembles a human anxiety state, it is fair enough to examine it for clues to the neurotic process.

Unfortunately there is still no answer from this source to the basic question we are here considering. It is impossible to create a breakdown situation in which frustration, conflict, and fear can be isolated. Take the situation used by Masserman: when the hungry cat is about to feed it is subjected to a sudden blast of air—an event that is apparently shattering to feline equilibrium as indeed it might be to human. The hunger drive is *frustrated,* there is *conflict* between the urge to eat and the urge to escape, and the resulting reactions (crouching, trembling, dilated pupils, rapid breathing, etc.) "obviously parallel those that accompany the subjective experience of normal and neurotic *anxiety* in the human."[3] Pavlov and his early followers described the conditioning procedure as if it were an impersonal learning situation involving conflict between two conditioned responses. Liddell, in contrast, considers it a traumatizing procedure leading to fright. Viewing the animal's situation a little more broadly, so that we include the long hours of monotonous and unsatisfying repetition that go with training, the restraint in the apparatus, and the dependent relation that is built up by the animal toward the experimenter, we can hardly avoid regarding even the Pavlov procedure as a severe shock.[4] The situation would be roughly analogous if a kindly school teacher in the middle of the second semester suddenly set an impossible problem and gave the children electric shocks when they failed to solve it.

In the absence of decisive evidence, the choice of concepts becomes determined by success in putting the known facts into an intelligible order. It is maintained here that the linked concepts of anxiety and defense perform this service with greater consistency than either frustration or conflict. In the following chapters we shall try to show that the origins of neurosis, the formation of symptoms, the varieties of developed neurotic personality, and the process of psychotherapy all lend themselves to understanding in accordance with a theory based on anxiety and defense. We therefore turn our attention to the study of fear in human beings.

[3] J. H. Masserman, *Principles of Dynamic Psychiatry* (Philadelphia: W. B. Saunders Co., 1946), p. 127.

[4] Liddell, *op. cit.*, pp. 391–97.

ANXIETY AND THE BREAKDOWN OF ORDERED BEHAVIOR

Nothing is gained at this point by making a systematic distinction between *anxiety* and *fear*. Many distinctions have been proposed.[5] Roughly speaking, it is customary to use *fear* when the object of danger is clearly perceived, *anxiety* when the object is unknown or vaguely discerned. Such distinctions are more linguistic than psychological. Whatever the status of the arousing object, the basic emotional reaction is the same. In the literature on neurosis, *anxiety* is the term most often encountered, but it is used in a sense that includes all degrees of the fear reaction.

Course of the Fear Reaction. We begin our detailed study of anxiety by tracing the course of the fear reaction from an initial state of calm through mild anxiety to severe panic. The early stages of this progression are well known in everyday life, but severe anxiety and panic can best be observed under conditions in which an individual is exposed to unusual and lasting danger. Such a state of affairs is repeatedly encountered in modern warfare, and the best current descriptions have been given by military psychiatrists. One of these, Emilio Mira, who was chief psychiatrist for the Spanish Republican Army, differentiates several stages in the evolution of fear and regards them as corresponding to "different phases of functional disintegration of the higher brain centers."[6] A similar conception is utilized by Grinker and Spiegel, who describe the increasing anxiety reaction as a progressive weakening of the ego with loss of its organizing and controlling functions.[7] These characterizations are highly suitable for the more advanced degrees of anxiety, but the early stages do not present a picture of disorganization. Like other emotions, fear serves the useful purpose of "arousing, sustaining, and directing activity;"[8] more specifically, it forms part of a behavior pattern in which there is increased vigilance, greater alertness to outside events, and preparation of bodily resources for strenuous activity.[9] Disorganization sets in only when the danger cannot be dispelled. The anxiety reaction

[5] K. Goldstein, *The Organism* (New York: American Book Co., 1939), pp. 291–307; P. M. Symonds, *The Dynamics of Human Adjustment* (New York: Appleton-Century-Crofts, Inc., 1946), pp. 136–38.

[6] E. Mira, *Psychiatry in War* (New York: W. W. Norton & Co., Inc., 1943), pp. 31–35.

[7] R. R. Grinker and J. P. Spiegel, *War Neuroses* (Philadelphia: The Blakiston Co., 1945), pp. 123–27.

[8] R. W. Leeper, "A Motivational Theory of Emotion to Replace 'Emotion as Disorganized Response,'" *Psychological Review*, LV (1948), pp. 5–21.

[9] W. B. Cannon, *Bodily Changes in Pain, Hunger, Fear and Rage* (2d ed.; New York: Appleton-Century-Crofts, Inc., 1929), especially chaps. ii and xii; H. S. Liddell, "The Role of Vigilance in the Development of Animal Neurosis," in P. H. Hoch and J. Zubin (eds.), *Anxiety* (New York: Grune & Stratton, Inc., 1950).

is then driven beyond its point of efficiency and produces widespread internal chaos.

The earliest premonitions of danger may be barely conscious and seemingly free from feelings of anxiety. A small amount of risk, such as entering an argument or speaking to an audience, is often experienced as a stimulus and challenge that causes a person to extend himself. People who have been caught in sudden emergencies sometimes recall with amazement how promptly they thought of things to do and how energetically they behaved. Such examples illustrate the constructive effects of fear. If the danger is somewhat greater, or perhaps merely less definite in location, activity will begin to be limited and possible danger situations given a wide margin. One can picture the change by thinking of the slower steps and more attentive observation displayed by a person on foot who finds the ground suddenly marshy, or the cautious driving of a motorist who discovers the road to be slippery. With continuing threat the struggle to maintain control will prove increasingly costly. It will demand extreme concentration and meticulousness, or perhaps it will show itself in a suspiciously exaggerated display of confidence. This last reaction was characteristic of the bombardier Pearson Brack (Chapter 2) when taken on a practice flight after his narrow escape from death.

Thus far the control of anxiety dominates the picture. It is important to notice that the presence of danger tends to restrict behavior. Attention is concentrated upon possible sources of threat; spontaneity is lost; certain features of behavior are exaggerated in order to maintain control. The effects of anxiety are for a while uniformly in the direction of lessened flexibility.

As danger mounts, control becomes increasingly difficult. The person's mind begins to be occupied incessantly with the danger. He can no longer inhibit the bodily signs of anxiety: perspiration, tremor, restlessness, fast-beating heart, quickened breathing force themselves upon him. Thought and judgment deteriorate, actions are erratic and poorly controlled, new acts are started before old ones are completed. As he finds it impossible to pull himself together, the person "experiences an extremely unpleasant sensation of losing his mental balance" (Mira). Danger seems to be everywhere. When panic begins to reign, the conscious state resembles a nightmare, "consisting of a peculiar, irregular stream of delirious, distorted mental images, most of which are forgotten when the subject returns to normal." Scarcely aware of what he is doing, the panic-stricken person may rush wildly about, laughing, shouting, crying in rapid succession. These reactions sometimes lasted many days in soldiers exposed to prolonged fire. In some cases a stuporous and comatose state follows the peak of panic.

It is clear that the fully developed fear reaction has no value for continuing existence. It represents the collapse of everything that might serve to extricate a person from danger. The trembling musculature and clouded memory are of little service; above all, the mental confusion, the failure to observe and to test reality correctly, is a fatal handicap to further adaptive efforts. The experience of intense fear thus seems to accompany a more or less complete breakdown in the ordering of behavior.

The Experience of Panic. Everyone knows what fear feels like when experienced in slight or moderate intensities. Few people, however, can remember the full force of their childhood panics, and fewer still, even of those who have been in great danger, can report the contents of acute anxiety in adult life. If we are to appreciate the dynamic role of anxiety in neurosis, we must realize the overwhelming nature of the experience of panic. The following excerpts describe a severe attack in a 36-year-old writer and teacher, William Ellery Leonard. In contrast to Mira's description, in which battle dangers precipitated the fear, there was in this case absolutely no immediate danger. Leonard was standing on a bluff looking out over a quiet lake, having left his walking companion in the woods behind. Painful recent events, the suicide of his wife for which most of the community held him to blame, had been causing mounting apprehension and waves of anxiety. As a small child he had narrowly escaped being run down by a locomotive, and it was this that gave special significance to a train which passed along the opposite shore of the lake and brought the panic to its climax.[10]

I stand looking out over the silent and vacant water, in the blue midday. I feel a sinking loneliness, an uneasy, a weird isolation. I take off my hat; I mop my head; I fan my face. Sinking . . . isolation . . . diffused premonitions of horror. "Charlie" . . . no answer. The minutes pass. "Charlie, Charlie" . . . louder . . . and no answer. I am alone, alone, in the universe. Oh, to be home . . . home. "Charlie." Then on the tracks from behind Eagle Heights and the woods across the lake comes a freight-train, blowing its whistle. Instantaneously diffused premonitions become acute panic. The cabin of that locomotive *feels* right over my head, as if about to engulf me. I am obsessed with a *feeling* as of a big circle, hogshead, cistern-hole, or what not, in air just in front of me. The train *feels* as if it were about to rush over me. In reality it chugs on. I race back and forth on the embankment. I say to myself (and aloud): "It is half a mile across the lake—it can't touch you, it can't; it can't run you down—half a mile across the lake."—And I keep looking to *make sure,* so intensely in contradiction to what the eye sees is the testimony of the *feeling* of that cabin over my head, of that strange huge circle hovering at me. . . .

Meanwhile the freight chugs on toward Middleton. I rush back and forth on the bluffs. "My God, won't that train go; my God, won't that train go

[10] W. E. Leonard, *The Locomotive-God* (New York: Appleton-Century-Crofts, Inc., 1927), pp. 304–7.

away!" I smash a wooden box to pieces, board by board, against my knee to occupy myself against panic. I am intermittently still shrieking, "Charlie, Charlie." I am all the while mad with the terror and despair of being so far from home and parents. I am running around and around in a circle shrieking, when Charlie emerges from the woods.

It should be added that this experience of panic was so intense and unbearable that it was almost immediately forgotten. Leonard remembered only that he had had some sort of attack on the bluff. The full memory was gradually recovered more than ten years later during states of relaxation induced to promote recall.

Experimental Studies of Disorganization. In the interests of more precise knowledge, it is desirable to supplement field observations of this kind with experiments carried out under controlled conditions. Experimentation with anxiety in human beings is obviously a precarious business. The subject's welfare requires that anxiety should not be too strongly aroused, but one must also avoid the fault of awakening so weak a replica of fear that his behavior has nothing in common with reactions to genuine threat. We shall examine some experiments that avoid both pitfalls, but first we shall glance at the animal experiments where such problems are less acute.

Disorganization in Animals. Except in the case of rats, the signs of *experimental neurosis* in animals are, according to Liddell, "reducible to a fairly simple common plan. Experimentally neurotic behavior is stereotyped and varies from somnolence, inertness, and immobility to hypersensitivity and overactivity, carried in some instances to the point of manic excitement."[11] Gantt has described in detail the symptoms in a dog called Nick whose neurosis lasted for more than nine years.[12] Nick's troubles are typical enough to serve as a general pattern for the hypersensitive and overactive type of reaction. Possibly Nick was constitutionally predisposed: of three dogs treated in the same way, he was the only one to break down. After being subjected for a while to the difficult discrimination, he resisted being brought into the laboratory and whimpered and howled when there. He was restless, active, and one might say confused; sometimes he barked at food instead of eating it, and he forgot all he had learned about the signals used in the experiments. Disturbance at the autonomic level was shown by inhibited salivation, irregular elevation of heart and respiratory rates, a peculiar raucous breathing, frequent urination, erections without any reference to the presence of sexual

[11] Liddell, in Hunt, *op. cit.*, p. 404.

[12] W. H. Gantt, "The Origin and Development of Nervous Disturbances Experimentally Produced," *American Journal of Psychiatry*, XCVIII (1942), pp. 475–81. Reprinted in S. S. Tomkins (ed.), *Contemporary Psychopathology* (Cambridge: Harvard University Press, 1943), chap. xxxii.

stimuli. Social responsiveness was upset. The activity of a normal dog runs parallel to that of dogs in neighboring cages. Nick's ups and downs of activity no longer bore any relation to his neighbors. Sometimes the presence of the experimenter quieted him, but at other times he paid no attention to the experimenter's friendly advances and instead made up to strangers—an attitude with which many readers will sympathize. Gantt points out in conclusion that "once the disturbance is thoroughly established, therapy is difficult. Improvement has been seen with a complete change of environment—removal to farm life for eighteen months. Rest in the environment of conflict was unavailing."[13]

Autonomic Disorganization. As we saw both in canine and human cases, the disorganization of behavior under stress affects those functions that are controlled by the autonomic nervous system. To borrow a picturesque phrase from Mira: "The anarchy present at the conscious level spreads to the internal organs as well."

Before amplifying these statements we must notice that they do not agree with Cannon's now classical emergency theory. Cannon offered the theory that strong emotions—he specifically named pain, rage, and fear—were accompanied by a consistent set of internal reactions which served to prepare the body for violent exertion such as fighting or flight.[14] He sharply distinguished the functions of the *sympathetic* and *parasympathetic* divisions of the autonomic nervous system. To the sympathetic he assigned the function of energizing for fight or flight, to the parasympathetic the stimulation of vegetative processes such as digestion; one might call them respectively a war ministry and a peace ministry. Under warlike conditions—that is, situations calling forth fear, rage, or pain—the sympathetic division discharged in such a way as to prepare the body for crisis, the parasympathetic being relatively inhibited and vegetative functions suspended.

When this theory is applied to the acute fear reaction, however, it is plainly inconsistent with both the behavioral and the introspective facts. Instead of being highly energized and prepared for violent action, the terrified person is tremulous, confused, weak to the point of falling, perhaps even paralyzed by fright. Far from being prepared to deal with the emergency, he is in the worst possible condition to meet it. Moreover, Arnold has assembled evidence which casts substantial doubt on the notion that sympathetic activity by itself has an energizing function.[15] That adrenalin serves such a purpose, as Cannon maintained, is now also

[13] *Ibid.*, p. 481.
[14] Cannon, *op. cit.*
[15] M. B. Arnold, "Physiological Differentiation of Emotional States," *Psychological Review*, LII (1945), pp. 35–48.

in grave doubt.[16] A theory begins to take shape that the sympathetic overactivity postulated by Cannon might result in a visceral storm rather than a well-adapted energizing of the body.

The nature of this visceral storm becomes clearer in work more recent than Cannon's, especially that of Gellhorn and his associates.[17] From this work it appears that Cannon exaggerated, at least in his reasoning, the antagonism between the sympathetic and parasympathetic divisions of the autonomic nervous system. Gellhorn has shown that the two divisions act with much more intimate cooperation. During strong emotion, or in animals following direct stimulation of the hypothalamus, there is extensive discharge over both divisions. The sympathetic predominates in this reaction, but the parasympathetic is also activated beyond its normal level. This arrangement still serves the purpose of energizing the body for crisis; in fact, it serves it better than the pattern proposed by Cannon. To take one example: the sympathetic, as Cannon showed, is responsible for the release of glycogen, thus heightening the concentration of sugar in the blood and making available to the muscles an increased source of energy. The blood sugar, however, cannot be fully utilized unless there is increased output of insulin, and this reaction is controlled by the parasympathetic division. The best preparation for violent muscular exertion is thus a burst of sympathetic activity closely followed by parasympathetic discharge.[18] Balance between the two systems is essential for an efficient emergency reaction.

Recent work on the adrenal glands tends to emphasize still more strongly the necessity for balance. One part of the gland, known as the *medulla*, mediates the quick mobilization described by Cannon, but the reaction is brief and wasteful of resources. The heart, for instance, is stimulated to a level which helps muscular action for a few moments but cannot be maintained without extensive additional changes in the bodily economy. These further changes are produced by the more slowly aroused adrenal *cortex*, the functions of which have only lately been discovered.[19] Indeed, the autonomic and biochemical responses to danger are proving to be so complex that it can now be considered "unprofitable to view adaptive and protective reactions as stemming primarily from the opera-

[16] J. M. Rogoff, "A Critique on the Theory of the Emergency Function of the Adrenal Glands: Implications for Psychology," *Journal of General Psychology*, XXXII (1945), pp. 249–68.

[17] E. Gellhorn, *Autonomic Regulations: Their Significance for Physiology, Psychology, and Neuropsychiatry* (New York: Interscience Publishers, Inc., 1943), especially chaps. xiv and xv.

[18] Gellhorn, *op. cit.*, p. 221.

[19] S. Cobb, *Foundations of Neuropsychiatry* (5th ed.; Baltimore: The Williams & Wilkins Co., 1952), pp. 27–31.

tion of one part or system."[20] Effective balance among many related systems seems to be the essential thing for normal functioning in emergencies. The bodily reactions accompanying acute and lasting fear represent a disastrous loss of balance. The stressful situation vigorously activates the immediate emergency responses and keeps them at such a level that the compensatory reactions cannot overtake them. When not sufficiently compensated, the emergency responses become not only useless but harmful, and behavior approximates the picture of helpless fright.

Motor and Associative Disorganization. A Russian investigator, Alexander Luria, devised an ingenious technique for showing the disorganization of motor and associative behavior.[21] As a base-line from which to measure the effects of anxiety, he developed a standard situation calling for a controlled and organized response. Subjects were seated in an armchair with the fingers of each hand resting on a plunger. They were given a form of the word association test with instruction to respond to each word by saying the first word that came to mind and simultaneously pushing down the plunger with the right hand; the left hand was to remain motionless throughout the experiment. Simple as it sounds, this action calls for good coordination and good timing: the subject must produce an associated word, depress and then release the plunger as he utters the word, and at the same time prevent his left hand from moving. The response thus easily qualifies as a piece of organized behavior. It is also readily measurable, the two plungers being so arranged as to make tracings on smoked paper.

Under normal circumstances it is not hard to perform this organized act with smoothness and regularity. Of course, some word in the list may touch an emotional complex and momentarily upset the subject. We are concerned here, however, with the general effect of anxiety on organized behavior. For this purpose Luria's most valuable experiment is one in which subjects were tested while awaiting an extremely important oral examination. With these subjects there could be no question of too shallow emotional involvement. They were plucked from a line where they stood awaiting an ordeal which was to decide whether or not they should continue their higher education. Most of them were in a state of at least moderate anxiety throughout Luria's test. They fidgeted in the chair, talked and laughed excitedly, and showed many other signs of agitation.

The disorganization of behavior associated with anxiety could be observed in the character of the word associations, in the motor processes,

[20] H. G. Wolff, *Stress and Disease* (Springfield, Illinois: Charles C Thomas, 1953), p. 125.

[21] A. R. Luria, *The Nature of Human Conflicts* (New York: Liveright Publishing Corp., 1932), chaps i and ii.

and in the coordination between verbal and manual responses. Normally the average reaction time in a word association experiment is about 1.5 seconds; for the anxiety-laden subjects it became 2.3 seconds. The variability of reaction times increased greatly, with some responses coming only after 8 or 10 seconds. Examination of the response words showed an unusually large number of disturbances in the associative process. Frequently the subject gave senseless associations, named objects around the room, repeated the stimulus word, or fell into the habit of giving the same response to every stimulus. "The affect," Luria stated, "provokes a functional lowering of the associative possibilities."[22] The anxious subjects were both distractible and stereotyped; they found it difficult to keep at the imposed but not very relevant task of giving meaningful word associations.

Disorganization of the motor process was shown by great irregularities in the smoked-paper tracings. By calm subjects the plunger was depressed and released in a single firm movement. In the anxious subjects, this movement was often badly shattered. The plunger was held down too long or let up slowly with signs of muscular tremor. Sometimes these irregularities were accompanied by disturbances in the left hand which increased its tremor or made some downward pressures of its own.

Particularly important was the disturbance of timing. On several occasions the motor response preceded the verbal response and remained in a disrupted state until the association was given, sometimes even longer. In other cases the plunger was correctly pressed and released, but there followed a whole series of extra pressures, irregular and somewhat tremulous, filling the space until the next stimulus word was called.

All of these disturbances reveal a breakdown in the regulating control that characterizes normal behavior. Luria explained his results by the hypothesis that during anxiety there is an excessive mobilization of excitatory processes which break through the more delicate inhibitory barriers and which cannot be sufficiently discharged by those small actions permitted in the experiment. The uneasy subject overreacts to all stimuli, just as a panic-stricken person overreacts to all sounds and sudden movements, however innocent, that take place around him. The uneasy subject fidgets in his chair, cannot stop talking, laughs too loudly, and then, when the experiment begins, cannot hold back his pressure on the plunger while he hunts for a word association. All of these instances show a loss of regulatory control: motor impulses rush to expression in a senseless way. One is reminded of Nick running about and barking at his food, and of Leonard breaking a box and rushing back and forth on the bluff. If the subject does succeed in restraining his motor impulse long enough to make his verbal response, then the piled-up excitation

[22] *Ibid.*, p. 51.

breaks out belatedly in a series of extra pressures or in unintentional activity of the supposedly resting left hand.

The disruptive effects of anxiety on orderly mental processes have been the subject of many experiments. It is known that strong anxiety decreases the span of attention, interferes with recall, lowers the efficiency of reasoning. Most college students have experienced at one time or another the injurious effects of anxiety on their performance in important examinations. Routine tests for which one feels well prepared may go smoothly enough, but crucial examinations may set off an uneasiness that is anything but conducive to clear recall and fluent thinking. The difference is dramatized in some experiments by Mandler and Sarason, who selected two groups of subjects differing widely in their habitual level of anxiety when taking tests.[23] In the course of a series of experimental tests the subjects were put under pressure by being told, for instance, that they had thus far done very poorly or that they had done very well and must keep it up. For the high anxiety subjects this pressure produced a falling off of performance on the next test; their anxiety level was raised enough to interfere with intellectual efficiency. The low anxiety subjects, in contrast, improved their performance when under pressure. If their level of anxiety was raised, it was only to the point of improved vigilance and concentration, not to the point of disruption.

Incubation and Generalization. Two further features of the fear reaction were first demonstrated in an experimental study by Diven.[24] Fear sometimes increases with the passage of time, even though the person is not continuously exposed to the danger. This phenomenon, known as *incubation,* is well known in everyday life. It is to prevent incubation that we urge a motorist to drive again, or a pilot to fly, as soon as possible after an accident. Another consequence of fright is *generalization;* instead of remaining closely attached to the original threat, apprehension spreads to all kinds of related objects. These two phenomena were shown under controlled conditions in Diven's experiment.

In order to create stress, the experimental situation was made as awesome as possible. Without much explanation the subject was strapped into a formidable apparatus, one hand in the liquid electrodes used to measure the galvanic skin response, one foot in electrodes wired to what looked like a standard electric socket in the baseboard. He was told that the experiment had to do with muscular coordinations which could be measured only by placing his body in an electrical circuit with the apparatus. Practically all subjects confessed afterwards that these preliminaries made them distinctly uneasy.

23 G. Mandler and S. B. Sarason, "A Study of Anxiety and Learning," *Journal of Abnormal and Social Psychology,* XLVII (1952), pp. 166–73.

24 K. Diven, "Certain Determinants in the Conditioning of Anxiety Reactions," *Journal of Psychology,* III (1937), pp. 291–308.

The experiment proceeded with a form of word association test. The subject was instructed to give a series of associations to each word in the list, continuing until asked to stop. The stop signal was called at twelve seconds. In the word list there was a repeating element: six times the word *red* occurred, followed by the word *barn.* When the subject had associated to *barn* for twelve seconds, he was given a startling and somewhat painful electric shock through the electrodes on his ankle. Upon completion of the word list, a time interval was introduced, after which the whole procedure was repeated except that no electric shocks were given. For part of the subjects this time interval was only five minutes; for others, the second session was delayed twenty-four or forty-eight hours, allowing an opportunity for possible incubation.

Results concerning *incubation* came out of a comparison between the immediate second sessions and the delayed second sessions. The galvanic skin responses (*GSR*'s) provided the necessary quantitative index. The total amount of *GSR* activity throughout the session, regardless of conditioning to particular words, can probably be accepted as an index of the subject's general upsetness. In subjects who received the second (no shock) session immediately after the first, this index was smaller for the second session. In subjects who were forced to wait a day or two, the index was larger for the second session. General upsetness or apprehension was thus distinctly increased when a time interval elapsed before the subject returned to the dangerous situation.

The results bearing on *generalization* constitute one of the most striking results of Diven's experiment. Toward the end of the first session and throughout the second, the largest *GSR*'s occurred on the word *barn*—the actual signal for the shock—but significantly above-average responses accompanied three other classes of words. These were (1) the word *red* which always preceded *barn,* (2) the word, whatever it might be, that followed *barn,* and (3) all words in the list having a distinctly rural association, such as "hay," "plow," "pasture," "sheep," in contrast to urban words like "pavement," "subway," "streetcar." The anxiety reaction was thus generalized to other signals related to the original signal either by *contiguity in time* (preceding or following it), or by *meaning* (belonging in the same area of experience, in this case the country). One subject, a foreigner, showed attachment of *GSR*'s to the preceding and following words but none to the rural words. It was found afterwards that because of his imperfect knowledge of English he had failed to catch the meaning of the word *barn.* In the great majority of the other subjects the meaningful associations of this word were utilized as channels of generalization.

Even more surprising than this result was the finding that the same generalization occurred when the subjects failed to realize consciously that *barn* was the actual signal. Of the fifty-two subjects who took part in the experiment, twenty-one were unable to say what word preceded the shock. This seems less remarkable when we remember that the shock was separated from *barn* by twelve seconds during which the subject gave a chain of word associations. It appeared, however, that failure to recognize *barn* consciously did not in any way prevent the attachment of anxiety to the rural words. This feature of the experiment illustrates *unconscious perception:* the signal character of *barn* is somehow apprehended, but the subject is not aware of this fact and cannot report it. If the generalization of anxiety can start from dangers unconsciously perceived, the possibilities for meaningful but unwitting elaboration of neurotic symptoms become virtually unlimited. In a later repetition of Diven's experiment, it appeared that generalization spread more widely, on the average, when the connection between signal word and shock was perceived only unconsciously.[25]

This phenomenon of generalization appears in clinical descriptions and has even been reported in some of the animal experiments. Liddell's sheep first displayed their anxiety only in the experimental room, but gradually their fear extended to other rooms and even to the living quarters, although no electric shocks were given in these locations.[26] In clinical practice it is noticed that phobias sometimes expand with the passage of time. One day the patient is afraid to go in the subway; the next day he is also unable to take the surface vehicle and feels anxious when he walks under an arched gate. Perhaps the condition described by Grinker and Spiegel in men who had endured prolonged exposure to danger can be taken as the limiting case of generalization where threat is felt practically everywhere. "The patient is actually intolerant of any but the most gentle stimuli from his environment. Even when absolute quiet reigns, he may be seized with a spasm of momentary trembling, as if shaken by some unseen danger."[27] Any sharp or sudden noise, even so small as the striking of a match, or any unexpected motion, makes the patient jump and tremble violently.[28] He acts as if any kind of stimulation must be accepted as a portent of danger.

[25] J. R. Lacey, R. L. Smith, and A. Green, "Use of Conditioned Autonomic Responses in the Study of Anxiety," *Psychosomatic Medicine*, XVII (1955), pp. 208–27. Reprinted in C. F. Reed, I. E. Alexander, and S. S. Tomkins, *Psychopathology: A Source Book* (Cambridge: Harvard University Press, 1958), chap. xix.

[26] Liddell, in Hunt, *op. cit.*, p. 410.

[27] Grinker and Spiegel, *op. cit.*, p. 5.

[28] A systematic analysis of generalization and displacement is undertaken by N. E. Miller, "Theory and Experiment Relating Psychoanalytic Displacement to Stimulus Response Generalization," *Journal of Abnormal and Social Psychology*, XLIII (1948), pp. 155–78. A summary of this work and its application to disordered personal behavior will be found in J. Dollard and N. E. Miller, *Personality and Psychotherapy* (New York: McGraw-Hill Book Co., Inc., 1950), especially pp. 172–77.

RECOVERY FROM FRIGHTENING EXPERIENCES

In the last section we examined the course of the fear reaction from the point at which danger is first perceived to the point at which behavior becomes totally disorganized. We studied the disorganization as it shows itself in animals subjected to experimental neurosis. We saw that effective autonomic patterns were disrupted in acute anxiety and that motor and associative behavior was thrown out of gear. The phenomena of generalization and incubation still further emphasized the far-reaching consequences of fright. Acute fear means collapse of the whole organization of behavior. The experience of panic is uniquely horrible. Neurosis occurs in order to avoid this kind of thing.

To continue our account of the dynamics of neurosis, we need now to consider this avoidance. The nuclear process involves both anxiety and *defense*. It is possible, probably typical, for a neurosis to be built up without actual moments of acute panic. It is constructed, one might say, straight out of the defenses used to prevent the occurrence of panic. How this works will be considered in more detail in the next chapter. For the present we shall continue to confine our discussion to the simplest cases, those in which catastrophic situations actually occur. But our attention will turn to the recovery from fearsome experiences—to the way a frightened organism comes to terms with what has happened.

Relearning After Fright. Following a fright, the overwhelming impulse is simply to avoid the whole frightening situation. Perhaps the danger is so great that no other response is possible. Very often, however, the danger was only momentary (like a motor accident) or is such that, given a second chance, the person could really cope with it perfectly well. Furthermore, many dangers are incurred in the pursuit of vital interests which the person cannot sacrifice. The pilot whose plane crashes cannot afford to give up his livelihood. The active child does not want to surrender his explorations and adventures because on one occasion he has been frightened. Pride may be involved: the person is ashamed to continue being afraid. Then there are incubation and generalization to consider. If no action is taken, the anxiety may be experienced as getting worse and as spreading to so many related stimuli that the whole world seems to be unsafe. One has to come to terms with the circumstance of having been frightened. This means acting in direct opposition to the impulse to avoid. It means *renewed contact* with the threat, a *new appraisal* of its threatening character, and *new actions* to cope with it. It means, in short, new learning in the face of a strong motive to avoid new learning.

Obviously this is a precarious learning situation. It can easily happen that the dictates of safety will prevail, in which case avoidance will continue and the appraisal of danger will not be altered. We noticed in the case of the dog Nick that the anxiety reaction, once it had become fully established, continued in full force until the dog was removed far from the neighborhood of the laboratory. Several investigators of animal behavior have reported great difficulty in extinguishing responses that were first made to avoid shock or some other fearsome stimulus. In one experiment, for example, rats badly frustrated and punished in a discrimination problem continued indefinitely to make a fixed response, thus never discovering that punishment could be avoided by a more varied repertory.[29] In another study, dogs learned in a few trials how to avoid a severely painful electric shock, then continued to make the avoidance response through as many as 650 trials unreinforced by further shocks.[30] These observations give the impression that avoidance responses have been built into the animals' behavior with a firmness that defies the usual modification by new experience. Precisely the same impression is conveyed by human neurotic behavior. William Ellery Leonard, frightened as a child by a locomotive, years later experiences an overwhelming urge to flee from a locomotive that is half a mile away across a lake, and becomes panic-stricken when he cannot do so. Bert Whipley as an adult continues to punish himself for the fancied childhood crime of killing his baby brother. Behavior learned in the service of avoiding anxiety seems endowed with peculiar and often quite damaging persistence. Mowrer refers to this as the *neurotic paradox*, "the paradox of behavior which is at one and the same time self-perpetuating and self-defeating."

> Common sense holds that a normal, sensible man, or even a beast to the limits of his intelligence, will weigh and balance the consequences of his acts: if the net effect is favorable, the action producing it will be perpetuated; and if the net effect is unfavorable, the action producing it will be inhibited, abandoned. In neurosis, however, one sees actions which have predominantly unfavorable consequences; yet they persist over a period of months, years, or a lifetime. Small wonder, then, that common sense has abjured responsibility in such matters and has assigned them to the realm of the miraculous . . .[31]

The persistence of neurotic behavior seems less miraculous when we consider the unfavorable learning situation created by fright. Safety is involved: it is nip and tuck whether there will be new learning or a renewed attack of anxiety which will make future new learning all the more difficult. The whole problem is beautifully illustrated in Masser-

[29] N. R. F. Maier, *Frustration: The Study of Behavior Without a Goal* (New York: McGraw-Hill Book Co., Inc., 1949).

[30] R. L. Solomon and L. C. Wynne, "Traumatic Avoidance Learning: The Principles of Anxiety Conservation and Partial Irreversability," *Psychological Review*, LXI (1954), pp. 353–85.

[31] O. H. Mowrer, *Learning Theory and Personality Dynamics* (New York: The Ronald Press Co., 1950), p. 487.

man's studies of experimental neurosis in cats, studies that include the process of recovery. We give a few examples.[32]

Masserman's cats were trained to depress a switch that first set off a bell or light signal and then dropped a pellet of food into a food box. When this habit was well learned, the cat was subjected to a sudden air blast at the moment of feeding, this being repeated on several occasions until neurotic behavior (as described earlier in this chapter) became well established. Various procedures were then adopted to study the process of recovery. Three of these are of particular interest here.

1. Solution of the conflict between fear and hunger was *forced* by placing the hungry cat in the cage and slowly pushing it toward the food box by means of a movable partition. All animals reached a state bordering on panic as they approached the scene of former air blasts. Some, upon seeing the food in the box, dove at it desperately and managed to eat; this put them on the way to recovery. Others became wildly panic-stricken, ate nothing, and left the situation in a state far worse than before.

2. Another method, called *retraining,* consisted of petting, stroking, and feeding the cat by hand when it was replaced in the experimental cage. Under this treatment the cat gradually calmed down and by slow degrees recovered the possibility of feeding from the box and depressing the switch. It even learned to tolerate the air blast and eat in spite of it. But if the process were rushed and the signals and air blast reintroduced too soon, the cat was thrown back into its neurotic condition and further efforts at retraining were far less effective.

3. The third method, *spontaneous working-through,* called for putting the hungry cat in the cage and leaving it entirely to its own devices. This procedure illustrates particularly well the fine balance between fear and the hunger-driven urge to overcome fear. At first the animal ignored the switch, even refusing to eat a pellet of food placed upon it. As hours went by, however, the cat became increasingly restive and would approach the switch, touching it very gently. The first time the switch was depressed sufficiently to set off the bell or light signal, the cat would hastily retreat and make no effort to secure the pellet in the food box. After a while, growing bolder, it would depress the switch freely and feed without signs of alarm. Reintroduction of the air blast somewhat renewed the neurotic behavior, but in time the animal could learn that even this was harmless.

Defensive Obstacles to Relearning. The cats just described practiced defenses against a renewal of anxiety, but they did not continue their

[32] J. H. Masserman, *Principles of Dynamic Psychiatry* (Philadelphia: W. B. Saunders Co., 1946), pp. 135–42.

defenses long enough to prevent relearning. Let us suppose that one of these defenses had become rigidified so that its abandonment was impossible. Suppose the cats had continued to ignore the switch, resolutely "denying" its existence; or suppose they had continued to retreat hastily when the bell rang, never eating the food that fell in the box. Under these circumstances relearning would have been impossible. Recovery from the experimental neurosis could not have taken place.

This freezing of defenses is highly characteristic of the neurotic process in human beings. We shall examine an unusually clear example, the *case of Patrick,* reported by Anna Freud and Dorothy Burlingham from their work in children's nurseries during the Second World War.[33]

Patrick was an English boy, just over three years old, living with his parents in London when the heavy air raids began during the summer of 1940. He was evacuated to the country, but was sent back after a few days because he fretted so much for his mother. Then he came down with measles and was put in the hospital—a second separation. When he recovered he was taken to the Hampstead Nursery, the doctor having directed that after illness he should not go to the subway station where his parents were regularly sleeping. His mother, as she left him at the nursery, urged him not to cry and promised to visit him.

Patrick put on a brave front but kept telling everyone that his mother would come for him. She would put on his coat, and take him home. If contradicted, he broke into violent grief which none of the staff could assuage. In the course of two or three days his self-reassuring behavior became increasingly rigid: compulsive nodding of the head as he stated that his mother would come, and a growing list of garments that she would put on him. "She will put on my overcoat and my leggings, she will zip up the zipper, she will put on my pixie hat," he said over and over again. When asked if he could stop this monotonous talk, he became silent, but his moving lips showed that he was repeating the reassuring sentences to himself and his gesturing hands enacted the putting on of the clothing. He would not play with the other children, but stood in a corner moving his head, hands, and lips, a tragic expression on his face. He refused almost all food except milk.

Patrick's mother meanwhile had come down with influenza and could not visit him for more than a week. When she arrived, his stereotyped behavior stopped, but he clung to her tenaciously and followed closely at her heels. She alone was allowed to wash him and put him to bed, and for several nights she slept next to him in the air-raid shelter. In a few days his anxiety was reduced so that he could play with the other children and tolerate short absences of his mother. The length of these

[33] A. Freud and D. T. Burlingham, *War and Children* (New York: Medical War Books, 1943), pp. 99–104, 122–23.

absences could then be gradually increased up to the point where the mother resumed her usual life. Some months later she was again obliged to go to the hospital. This time Patrick endured the separation with scarcely a sign of anxiety.

One of the points illustrated by this case is the *incubation* of anxiety. Within a short space of time Patrick experienced three separations from his mother. Only on the third occasion did his behavior take the ominous form we have described. Of more central concern for our present discussion is the fact that Patrick's *defenses* against the anxiety of separation actually *prevented him from overcoming that anxiety*. If he had been able to take his food, begin play with other children, trust himself however tentatively to the mothering ministrations of the staff, he would have found that he was in no danger and that life contained rewarding possibilities. Freud and Burlingham point out that when children have lived several months at a nursery they sometimes come to regard their parents' visits as an unwelcome interruption to their play with the group.[34] Patrick was at first kept from this relearning by the intensity of his anxiety and the compelling force of his defenses. The nodding head, repeated words, and stereotyped gestures of dressing—his symptoms—arose directly from his attempts to reassure himself that he was not deserted and that his mother would return. They constituted an assertion that she would return and a denial of her continuing absence. Naturally they did not change the actual situation nor do away with his anxiety. Yet they kept him just short of panic and made him feel just enough better so that he could not stop repeating them. Thus his attention and energies could not be freed to reappraise the situation and take new action of any kind.

We are now in a position to clarify our general theory of neurosis. The nuclear neurotic process takes its start when serious threat is present and when conditions are just right to freeze some of the defenses. Because they are staving off unbearable anxiety these defenses cannot be relaxed, but they prevent reappraisal of the threat and new action in regard to it. The conditions that are just right to freeze defenses probably bear a close relation to the severity of threat and the intensity or anticipated intensity of anxiety. Patrick's sense of threat reached the requisite level only upon his third separation from his mother. It is also probable that all of the more primitive defenses such as are called forth by these desperate circumstances have the character of obstructing relearning. In order to serve as defenses when rational appraisal fails they have to deny, conceal, or in some way distort the true import of the situation. Patrick's defense was a simple *denial* that his mother was not reappearing

[34] *Ibid.*, p. 124.

before his eyes. Pearson Brack *repressed* and thereby concealed and denied the fact of his own anxiety, thus making it impossible to change the sequence of events that ended in his fainting. L. Percy King *projected* the bitter conflict between sex and pride, thereby denying the presence of such tendencies in himself and making it impossible to rectify his peculiar judgments about reality. In each case the defense stood squarely in the way of renewed contact with the true situation and thus effectively blocked relearning.

NEUROSES PRECIPITATED BY ACUTE FRIGHT

We are now in a position to apply what we have learned about anxiety and defense to the problem of *traumatic neuroses.* A more suitable designation for these breakdowns would be *neuroses of traumatic onset;* they are in any event neuroses precipitated by acute fright. It seems fair to say at the outset that these neuroses do not differ in their fundamental character from the more chronic neuroses that may build up quite slowly in the course of an outwardly uneventful life. Both are based on nuclear processes of anxiety and defense. Very often the symptoms are of a quite similar character. Neuroses of traumatic onset do not constitute, therefore, a separate class of neuroses, except in respect to the suddenness of onset. It is this very suddenness, and the transparency of the surrounding conditions, that gives them special value in the study of the neurotic process.

The immediate response to a traumatic event—a plane crash, a prolonged bombardment, a disaster of some kind—consists of varying degrees of the fear reaction. Soldiers brought to the hospital after severe fighting may be in a condition of wild panic and delirious excitement or they may be comatose and paralyzed. As these acute reactions disappear, some of the victims move slowly but steadily back to a normal condition. With others events take a different course. During a period that may be a week or that may extend over several months the acute reactions give place to a stabilized and consolidated neurosis. The patient is better than he was at first, but his recovery is only partial and his life continues to be badly crippled. Why do these patients fail to recover from their acute fright?

Kardiner's Description of Traumatic Neuroses. Several hundred patients of this kind, veterans of World War I, were studied by Kardiner between the years 1922 and 1925. By that time their neurotic condition was thoroughly stabilized, and treatment of any kind was not at all easy. In describing the cases, Kardiner draws an important distinction between the presenting *pattern of symptoms* and certain *secondary character changes.* The symptom syndromes appear in the greatest possible variety, but the secondary character changes are more or less uniform for all cases.[35]

Among the symptoms are all varieties of hysterical phenomena: anaesthesias affecting parts of sensory systems, paralyses affecting parts of the motor system. There are also many disorders in functions controlled by the autonomic nervous system, the psychosomatic disorders that we shall study in a later chapter. Particularly interesting because they are sometimes so readily traceable to the original fright are two classes of symptoms called by Kardiner *defensive rituals* and *syncope* (periodic attacks of unconsciousness). One patient, for example, was unable to go to sleep at night even five years after the trauma unless he carried out a ceremonial which consisted of lying flat on his stomach, nose in the pillow, hands at each side of his face, holding his breath as long as possible. If he did not lie in this position, he experienced dreamlike images that threw him into violent anxiety. This ritual proved to be a literal repetition of his frantic attempts to protect himself and adjust his gas mask during the night gas attack that precipitated his breakdown.[36] Another patient experienced the following sequence of events whenever rain fell upon him: itching in the face, breathlessness, fainting, waking with his face swollen and scratched. This sequence repeated the events of a long rapid advance in heavy rain when the patient was felled by a superficial wound, lay unconscious, and awoke with his face burned by mustard gas which had leaked through his defective mask.[37] In each case the patient acts on certain occasions as if the original danger still existed unchanged. This last statement is more than a manner of speaking. The patient has applied such rigid defenses against even recalling the trauma that he has never been able to reappraise the original situation. While he knows that he is now at a veterans' clinic in time of peace, some defensively warded off and unassimilated part of him still behaves as if threat were present.

When we turn to the secondary character changes, more or less common to all patients, one of the outstanding facts is the presence of terrible nightmares which either faithfully reproduce the original traumatic event or develop new situations in which the patient is deserted and utterly helpless. These nightmares, sometimes called "battle dreams," again display the failure to reappraise the original danger. Occurring as they do in sleep, when defenses are relaxed, and throwing the patient into

[35] A. Kardiner, *The Traumatic Neuroses of War* (New York: Paul B. Hoeber, Inc., 1941). An excellent summary of this difficult monograph is given by Kardiner under the title "The Neuroses of War," reprinted from *War Medicine*, I (1941), pp. 219–26, in S. S. Tomkins (ed.), *Contemporary Psychopathology* (Cambridge: Harvard University Press, 1943), chap. xii.

[36] Kardiner, *The Traumatic Neuroses of War, ibid.*, pp. 15–20.

[37] *Ibid.*, pp. 46–48.

renewed anxiety, they accomplish nothing in the way of new learning. The other secondary character changes can all be understood as evidences of lowered efficiency and shattered self-confidence. Decreased control is shown in the patient's irritability, his oversensitiveness to sound, his difficulty in preventing outbursts of rage or of tearfulness. Lowered competence expresses itself in the inability to perform sustained work and in the general impoverishment of interest. The patient's energies are badly divided. He is still carrying on a struggle to feel safe, and he does not have enough energy left to conduct a normal life.

Defensive Inhibition. The key to understanding neuroses of traumatic onset is the concept of defensive inhibition. The basic principle is extremely simple: as Kardiner says, "an activity which fails or causes pain tends to become inhibited."[38] Under circumstances of acute danger, inhibition operates on a vast scale and in indiscriminate fashion. It may attack functions indispensable for further adaptation: for example, paralyzing the legs because the patient was running at the time of the trauma. On the mental side, the inhibition rests on remembering the traumatic situation. If the scene is remembered, it will cause another panic—as indeed it does when during the night the defenses weaken enough to permit a battle dream. An indiscriminate area of the patient's experience and adaptive equipment becomes defensively inhibited, warded off from further participation in his ongoing life processes. If this defensive reaction becomes frozen and consolidated, a new adaptation has to be effected with whatever remains of the uninhibited personality. What remains is inadequate, weak, subject to occasional terrifying eruptions from the warded-off memory traces of the catastrophe. The patient does not dare renew his contact with the memory traces. As a result, the situation is never reappraised.

Undoing the Defense. These ideas about defensive inhibition sound a little metaphorical. But they seem justified by what has been learned during two wars concerning the treatment of such cases. They are difficult to treat if the whole neurotic structure has had time to harden, especially if, in addition, the patient has established a parasitic relation to government funds. Even when successful, the process is slow and laborious, and sometimes the whole effort is a failure. Kardiner reports success with one case in which over a period of fifteen months he slowly aided the patient to see the connection between his symptom and the traumatic experience, to appreciate the protective devices he was using, to realize that all his defensive actions had miscarried, to grasp that he perceived the world not as "a free and familiar place in which he operated with confidence" but as "a realm filled with all varieties of hazards

[38] "The Neuroses of War," in Tomkins, *op. cit.*, p. 197.

and dangers against which he felt helpless." The patient suffered as these insights developed, but eventually achieved recovery. Kardiner adds, however, that "the success of treatment in this case was the exception and not the rule."[39]

The results are quite different if therapy is applied early, before the neurotic pattern is consolidated. The most advantageous time to cure a traumatic neurosis is within a few days of the terrifying experience, although cure is possible a good deal later. The principle involved is a simple one: to make the person resume contact with the traumatic experience, now represented by memory traces, so that he can reappraise the danger that is now actually past and relax his defensive inhibitions against it. The therapist, according to Grinker and Spiegel, "introduces the ego to its recent past." This can be done by direct encouragement or by inducing vivid recall in hypnosis, but it is best accomplished by what is called *narcosynthesis,* based on the use of sodium pentothal, a technique we have already described in the case of Pearson Brack (Chapter 2). This drug may possibly dampen the force of the anxiety reaction, but in any event it favors extremely vivid recall and reliving of past experiences. The drug alone is of little avail unless the therapist takes an active part in the proceedings. "He must make contact between the partially restored ego and the anxiety situation. Left to itself, the ego would never establish contact with this past experience; the resistance remains too strong."[40] On the one hand the therapist prods the patient to remember, even helping to describe the scene and participating as a character in the drama. On the other hand, if anxiety develops too intensely, he can give comfort and support and remind the patient of the present safe situation. In this way the past experience is not only recalled, but recalled at a pace and with an encouragement that allows the associated anxiety to be tolerated. Thus the person can gradually win in his new struggle to come to terms with fright, and the freezing of a defensive system with its toll on his energies becomes unnecessary.

Two historically honorable concepts, *dissociation* and *abreaction,* described in the first chapter of this book, receive a certain justification in this account of traumatic neuroses. Janet's dissociation was intended to describe just such a separation between the personality and part of its memories as occurs in respect to the traumatic event. Breuer and Freud's abreaction, with its emphasis on releasing the pent-up affect connected with some past event, applies descriptively to the cures that occur in narcosynthesis. Both concepts, however, receive new meaning and make better sense when brought into relation to the nuclear process of anxiety and defense. The reason for dissociation, the force that pro-

[39] Cf. Tomkins, *op. cit.,* pp. 200–201.
[40] Grinker and Spiegel, *op. cit.,* pp. 136–37.

duces separation, is defense against danger. Dissociation is thus to be conceived as a sign of defensive inhibition. Similarly, abreaction is of therapeutic value because it occurs under circumstances that permit a relaxation of defense. Abreaction is to be conceived as a sign that defensive inhibition is breaking down.

DEFENSE MECHANISMS

The concept of defense was introduced by Freud in some of his earliest writings. Before long he substituted repression, which became for a while one of the keystones of his thinking. Later he reversed his position to the extent of reinstating defense as the general concept, with repression standing as one of the defense mechanisms alongside of projection, reaction formation, regression, turning against the self, and some four or five others. Anna Freud, in her book on defense mechanisms, takes the same general position, but recognizes that repression is entitled to a somewhat special status. She points out, for instance, that other defenses are very often combined with repression, and she entertains the possibility that "other methods have only to complete what repression has left undone." More specifically, she puts the problem as follows:

> Theoretically, repression may be subsumed under the general concept of defence and placed side by side with the other specific methods. Nevertheless, from the point of view of efficacy, it occupies a unique position in comparison with the rest. In terms of quantity it accomplishes more than they, that is to say, it is capable of mastering powerful instinctual impulses in face of which the other defensive measures are quite ineffective . . . It is also the most dangerous mechanism. The dissociation from the ego entailed by the withdrawal of consciousness from whole tracts of instinctual and affective life may destroy the integrity of the personality for good and all . . . The consequences of the other defensive methods are not less serious, but even when they assume an acute form they remain more within the limits of the normal.[41]

Clearly, there is something about repression that differentiates it from the other defense mechanisms. It is more fundamental, more drastic, more primitive than the rest. That this should be the case becomes intelligible from our description of neuroses precipitated by acute fright. The defensive inhibition that results from acute fear corresponds in many respects to repression. It can properly be said that the terrified soldier represses all memories connected with the traumatic event, and that during the pentothal interview the repression is lifted. Repression, therefore, is to be conceived as a direct manifestation of what we have discerned to be the basic protective device: defensive inhibition. For this reason we shall classify repression, along with denial, as a *primary* defen-

[41] A. Freud, *The Ego and the Mechanisms of Defence* (London: Hogarth Press, Ltd., 1937), pp. 52–55.

sive process. Other defense mechanisms will take their place as secondary processes serving to fortify the primary defense and adjust the person to its consequences.

The Primary Defensive Process. The primary defensive process is inhibition. Inhibition is, of course, a constant and indispensable feature of all ordinary activity in the nervous system. Even such relatively simple acts as walking cannot be performed without synchronized inhibitions of certain muscle groups. Defensive inhibition is no different in principle from what goes on all the time; it is simply an *intense, indiscriminate* inhibitory response called forth by serious threat. We have seen that under conditions of mounting anxiety a person's behavior progressively loses its inhibitory controls, becoming disorganized and indiscriminate. The panic-stricken person performs senseless acts, like breaking up boxes, and is unable to localize the source of danger which seems to be everywhere. As the threat passes and inhibitory action becomes possible, it takes the same senseless and indiscriminate form. Perhaps the hands that were breaking up the box become paralyzed, perhaps the whole situation is forgotten. Defensive inhibition is not a discriminating response to danger; it is a desperate and primitive response.

Denial. In considering the case of Patrick, we suggested the possibility that all primitive defenses achieve their purpose simply by a denial of the existing threat. If the person cannot escape or attack the threat, the only bearable alternative is to deny it. Thus a small baby carried into a room full of strangers may simply gaze at the door until he musters courage to peek at some of the unknown faces. Anna Freud devotes a section of her book to what she called the "preliminary stages of defence" —the ways in which a small child avoids outside dangers.[42] She describes two varieties of denial, one using fantasy, the other using words and acts. Denial in fantasy is well illustrated in the case of a timid child, who imagined that he owned a tame lion which he could easily control but which terrified everyone else. This fantasy was of great importance to the child; it was carried through endless variations and became his constant companion and support. Denial in word and act was well shown in Patrick's stereotyped words and gestures asserting that his mother was about to return. These simple mechanisms of denial remain available to a child only so long as he can tolerate the side-by-side existence of a play or pretend world and a real world. As his power of reality-testing grows, he can no longer deny real facts in the interests of everyday defense. But in acute emergencies, when reality-testing breaks down his defenses, he may regress to the basic unadorned process of denial. Everything is inhibited which might tell him of the presence of threat.

[42] *Ibid.*, especially chaps. vi and vii.

Repression. The concept of repression is ordinarily reserved for a particular kind of denial: the forgetting, or ejection from consciousness, of memories of threat, and especially the ejection from awareness of impulses in oneself that might have objectionable consequences. Repression thus refers to the denial of that in oneself—memories or impulses—which, if not held in check, would create some kind of threat. When denial is applied directly to external dangers, as in the case of Patrick, the word "repression" is not customarily used. But the similarity of all these denials is obvious. Equally obvious is their basic character as defensive inhibitions.

Under certain circumstances it has proved possible to demonstrate repression in laboratory experiments. Obviously the investigators could not evoke acute anxiety, but there is no objection to supposing that milder stress will call out mild defensive inhibition. In Diven's experiment, cited earlier in this chapter, repression was shown in regard to the words the subjects could remember. If asked to recall the word list when they came back on the second day to what they feared might be another session of electric shocks, the subjects recalled a predominance of "neutral" words having no connection with the signal of shock. If asked to recall again when the session was over and the experiment announced to be at an end—when they were safe—the subjects recalled a predominance of "traumatic" words related in some way to *barn,* the signal for shock. When the "traumatic" words were reminders of an unavoidable impending threat, they were harder to remember; when threat was withdrawn, the difficulty in remembering them disappeared.[43] Other workers have investigated subjects' recall of a series of tasks on part of which they failed. The tasks were presented on some occasions as a casual matter of helping the experimenter to select some tests; on other occasions as part of an important competition likely to be challenging to self-esteem. Under the latter circumstances the uncompleted tasks—the failures—were distinctly less well recalled than they were when the work was first done in a casual atmosphere.[44]

Secondary Defensive Adjustments. Close inspection of the other defense mechanisms shows that they quite regularly presuppose an element of denial or repression. In other words, they consist of defensive inhibition

[43] K. Diven, "Certain Determinants in the Conditioning of Anxiety Reactions," *Journal of Psychology,* III (1937), pp. 291–308.

[44] S. Rosenzweig, "The Experimental Study of Repression," in H. A. Murray, *Explorations in Personality* (Fair Lawn, N. J.: Oxford University Press, 1938), pp. 472–90; T. G. Alper, "Memory for Completed and Incompleted Tasks as a Function of Personality: An Analysis of Group Data," *Journal of Abnormal and Social Psychology,* XLI (1946), pp. 403–20; A. F. Glixman, "Recall of Completed and Incompleted Activities under Varying Degrees of Stress," *Journal of Experimental Psychology,* XXXIX (1949), pp. 281–95.

followed by secondary adjustments that serve to strengthen the inhibition and bring the person to terms with it. These secondary adjustments are part of the repertory of normal behavior. They become defense mechanisms only through their linkage with defensive inhibition which causes them to have the characteristics of excess and rigidity.

Projection. The deluded schizophrenic patient, L. Percy King, provides us with a classic example of projection. His security was founded on the idea of being a highly superior person. This security was threatened by any shortcomings in himself—his sexual timidities and peculiarities, his arrogance, his contempt for others—that might cause him to be ridiculed by his acquaintances. He therefore became defensively blind to these qualities in himself. This defense proved insufficient. He felt himself superior and worthy of admiration, but he was confronted by the cold fact that others seemed completely indifferent to his excellencies. This residual problem, or problem consequent on the initial defense, was met by the secondary adjustive device of projection. He seized and magnified every sign of indifference or hostility until he built up the elaborate system of persecutory delusions which we studied in the second chapter. So successful was this secondary adjustment that it eased the burden placed upon repression. He could become aware of all kinds of sexual impulses, once he had assured himself that they arose from the electrical activities of his pursuers.

Projection is usually defined in some such way as the attribution of one's own thoughts, feelings, and impulses to other persons or objects in the outside world. Its basis lies in the fact that our own feelings tend to influence our perception of the world. Murray performed an experiment in which children were given two opportunities to judge the emotions being expressed in a series of photographs. Between the first and second judging, the children played a scary game of "murder," with the result that they found the faces markedly more malicious when seen the second time.[45] Sears used a method in which subjects rated themselves and each other on various personality traits. When subjects lacked insight into their own traits, they tended to give unduly high ratings on these traits to their acquaintances.[46] It is out of such raw materials—such motivationally colored perceptions—that the projective process is constructed. It becomes a defense when the recognition of one's own feeling entails anxiety and evokes protective inhibition. Projection then has so

[45] H. A. Murray, "The Effect of Fear upon Estimates of the Maliciousness of Other Personalities," *Journal of Social Psychology,* IV (1933), pp. 310–29.

[46] R. R. Sears, "Experimental Studies of Projection; I. Attribution of Traits," *Journal of Social Psychology,* VII (1936), pp. 151–63. This and Murray's study are reprinted in S. S. Tomkins (ed.), *Contemporary Psychopathology* (Cambridge: Harvard University Press, 1943), chaps. xli and xlii.

much work to do in maintaining the defense that it may reach the pathological proportions of a loss of reality testing.

Other Mechanisms. Projection can serve as a model for all the secondary defensive adjustments. We shall briefly mention some of the more important ones. At several points in our discussion of maladjustments, we referred to the mechanism of *reaction formation.* This means the development of tendencies or traits that are the very opposite of tendencies we do not like in ourselves. To take a simple example, suppose a man comes to realize that he is very dependent and, feeling a bit ashamed of this discovery, resolves to be scrupulously self-sufficient in all respects. He may carry his independence somewhat to a fault, but it does not reach the proportions of desperate defense. Normal development often proceeds in just this way. Suppose, however, that his reaction formation is preceded by defensive inhibition: dependence means for him utter degradation, awakens anxiety, and is repressed from his awareness. Now the reaction formation serves the purpose of a daily denial of threat. He has to be self-sufficient in order to avoid fear, and his reaction formation will probably become extremely rigid. He will be one of those people who cannot even ask for a match.

Two further defensive processes are shown in the case of a young woman briefly described by Anna Freud.[47] The central problem was a jealous hatred of her mother, which, however, she dared not express lest she lose her mother's love. The first protective maneuver was a *displacement* of the negative feelings onto another woman. "Her mother continued to be a love-object, but from that time on there was always in the girl's life a second important person whom she hated violently." This hatred entailed less anxiety than hating her mother, but it still caused her suffering. Next she *turned inward* the aggression that was felt toward others. "The child tortured herself with self-accusations and feelings of inferiority, and did everything she could to put herself at a disadvantage and injure her interests, always surrendering her own wishes to the demands made on her by others." That this could be a solution shows the force of her anxiety lest her mother desert her, but after a while it too became unbearable. To relieve herself of such a burden of guilt, she resorted to projection and began to imagine herself the innocent victim of hate and persecution by others.

One further group of secondary defensive adjustments deserves mention because of its central importance in obsessional neurosis. To the group as a whole we can give the name *intellectualization,* referring to the tendency to take emotional conflicts into the sphere of intellect, divest them of affective and personal meanings, and work on them as

[47] A. Freud, *The Ego and the Mechanisms of Defence, op. cit.,* pp. 47–50.

problems in metaphysics, religion, political theory, etc. The word *rationalization* has been applied to this type of defense, though usually not in its original meaning of "making rational" but in the debased sense of "making excuses." Special forms of intellectualization have been called *isolation* and *undoing*. The details of these processes can best be left to the later chapter in which we study obsessional neurosis. At this point it is sufficient to notice again that we are dealing with a normal adjustive process which becomes a rigid mechanism only by association with a primary defensive inhibition. The whole attempt to understand the world means capturing it in the realm of intellect and making allowance for possible distortions that spring from emotions and personal meanings. Only when intellectualization is preceded by the defensive inhibition of threatening personal tendencies and is prostituted in the service of concealing such tendencies can we call it a pathological mechanism.

SUGGESTIONS FOR FURTHER READING

The problem of anxiety is not at all the exclusive concern of abnormal psychology. It has been placed in its proper perspective as a general problem of the twentieth century by Rollo May in *The Meaning of Anxiety* (New York, The Ronald Press Co., 1950), who examines the contributions of "psychologists, philosophers, social historians, and other students of humanity," and who attempts to formulate their ideas so as to find "common ground for further inquiry." The first six chapters of this book provide an illuminating excursion through modern thought on this significant problem.

The classic work on anxiety in relation to neurotic illness is Freud's little book, *The Problem of Anxiety,* written in 1926 (New York, W. W. Norton & Co., Inc., 1936). A thorough attempt to work out a general theory of neurosis will be found in Otto Fenichel's *The Psychoanalytic Theory of Neurosis* (New York, W. W. Norton & Co., Inc., 1945), especially Chs. 7–10. Fenichel's exposition is detailed and complex, but it gives the central place to anxiety and defense. A shorter account is given by I. Hendrick, *Facts and Theories of Psychoanalysis* (New York, Alfred A. Knopf, Inc., 1939), Ch. 7.

Most of the work on experimental neuroses in animals is to be found in monographs and journal articles. A good impression of it can be gained from J. McV. Hunt's *Personality and the Behavior Disorders* (New York, The Ronald Press Co., 1944), Vol. I, Chs. 12–14. To be recommended also is J. H. Masserman's survey and report of new experiments, *Behavior and Neurosis* (Chicago, University of Chicago Press, 1943), and his weaving together of animal experiments and clinical concepts in *Principles of Dynamic Psychiatry* (Philadelphia, W. B. Saunders Co., 1946), especially Chs. 8–12. For experiments with human beings under conditions of stress (often called "experimental psychopathology") see S. S. Tomkins, *Contemporary Psychopathology* (Cambridge, Harvard University Press, 1943), Chs. 40–42. In this category also belong the experiments on semi-starvation made for military purposes during World War II; see the paper by B. C. Schiele and J. Brozek in the journal, *Psychosomatic Medicine,* 1948, Vol. 10, pp. 31–50.

The student who wishes to plunge into the intriguing problem of anxiety in relation to learning theory can get a first orientation from May's book, pp.

96–112. The next steps might include O. H. Mowrer's *Learning Theory and Personality Dynamics* (New York, The Ronald Press Co., 1950), especially Chs. 1, 3, 5, 18, and 19; and J. Dollard and N. E. Miller's *Personality and Psychotherapy* (New York, McGraw-Hill Book Co., Inc., 1950), especially Ch. 5. From there the trail leads into recent issues of the psychological journals.

For the neuroses of traumatic onset the reader is referred again to the fascinating book by R. R. Grinker & J. P. Spiegel, *Men Under Stress* (Philadelphia, The Blakiston Co., 1945) and to their earlier publication, *War Neuroses* (Blakiston, 1945). A. Kardiner's monograph, *The Traumatic Neuroses of War* (New York, Paul B. Hoeber, Inc., 1941) is difficult but rewarding reading; it is best preceded by Ch. 12 in Tomkins, which will serve as a lucid introduction.

The best book on defense mechanisms is Anna Freud's *The Ego and the Mechanisms of Defence* (London, Hogarth Press, Ltd., 1937).

6

Neurotic Conflict and Its Effect on Personality

Let us suppose that a man in his middle thirties goes to consult a psychiatrist in order to obtain relief from attacks of anxiety. Let us suppose, further, that his country has not been at war during his adult years so that he has never been in military service nor exposed to the dangers of combat. He is satisfied with his occupation which yields a good income. He is happily married and enjoys his children. Of what is he afraid?

Our example may not be typical, but there are certainly many cases of neurosis in which the outward circumstances of life are just as placid and just as fortunate as in this one. It is cases of this kind that account for the contempt that is sometimes felt toward neurotics. The patient's neighbor, who lives in a much smaller house and cannot afford a car, who has been lame since childhood, whose job situation is always precarious, whose wife is in poor health and whose children are having difficulties in school, will be pretty scornful when he hears about those anxiety attacks. He will probably wish that the patient had some real problems, like his own, to worry about. That the patient is privileged to worry about nothing will fill him with profound envy.

No one who has seen a neurotic patient in the grip of anxiety will feel envious. If the neighbor could change places with the patient for a few days, he would probably be glad to go back to his outwardly harassed life. Even when the patient does not experience attacks of anxiety, his fatigues and bad moods and the discouraging sense of constant inner frustration are anything but enviable. But we may well press the question: Of what is he afraid? Against what dangers is he defending himself? According to the theory of neurosis developed in the preceding chapter, this man is struggling with a vital threat, is experiencing eruptions of panic, and is using defenses that tie up his energies and prevent him from continuing his normal life. Where lies the vital threat?

CHILDHOOD ORIGINS OF NEUROTIC TENDENCIES

The first step of the answer is that the threat occurred in childhood. The patient is afraid, let us say, that his mother is going to desert him. But this raises the further question: why is he afraid of this thirty-year-old threat which is no longer in the least dangerous? In reply we can say that when the threat became so serious in childhood as to create real panic, it was subjected to defensive measures that violently denied it and that warded it off from any further learning. The radical defenses applied in infancy prevented the patient from learning that separation from the mother was not a threat to life but rather something that in the course of time he could learn to tolerate. He grew up with the blocked-off idea that desertion by the mother was a vital threat. In this his behavior is analogous to that of the untreated victims of traumatic neurosis described in the last chapter. These men acted as if battle danger still existed. The danger of being gassed was present every night to the veteran who could not fall asleep until he had performed the ritual gestures of burying his face, holding his breath, and adjusting his mask. To our hypothetical patient, the danger of desertion remains actively present, though warded off from consciousness.

Just as the veteran does not go through the streets dodging bombs at every corner, the patient does not have to conduct an hourly defense against the threat of desertion. He learns to substitute a bond of love for the physical presence of the mother, and to displace his dependence onto other symbols of security, such as his wife, his friends, his bank account. But his life must be built up in such a way as to minimize the possibility of being directly and forcibly reminded of the threat of desertion. This limits the freedom and spontaneity of his whole development. His growth is pervaded by the necessity of avoiding situations that resemble desertion. Outwardly he may do very well, making a good adjustment to his exaggerated fear. But he is always vulnerable to a primitive desertion stimulus, just as the combat veteran remains vulnerable to sudden loud sounds. Perhaps the impending death of his aged mother serves as a sufficiently primitive stimulus. Perhaps something happens to one of his displaced security symbols: his wife is chosen president of the women's club and has less time for him, or his bank account is slightly pruned by a business recession. Threats to symbols may be trifling in themselves, but they touch the blocked-off infantile terror and the patient arrives at the psychiatrist's office feeling like a child who is about to be deserted by his mother.

The Nuclear Neurotic Process in Childhood. In the last chapter it was stated that the original nucleus of a neurosis lies at the point where anxiety has blocked or distorted the learning process so that new learning essential to adjustment cannot take place. The blocking or distortion comes about because of the application of a primary defensive process which prevents new contact with the threat. The nature of the nuclear neurotic process has been discussed by Kubie, who approaches the problem not through animal studies nor the traumatic neuroses but through psychoanalytic treatment of more or less chronic neurotic patients.[1] In all behavior, Kubie points out, there is a tendency toward repetition, but this is usually balanced by a certain amount of variation and novelty. In the play of young children, for example, actions may be repeated a good many times, but eventually variations begin to appear or the whole game may be abandoned in favor of something else. One of the earliest phenomena to appear in childhood that might be called neurotic is a stereotyped, rigid repetition of certain acts in play. These acts do not yield the relaxed pleasure that usually accompanies playful behavior; instead, they display "the earnest, rigid intensity which characterizes neurotic phenomena." Such symptoms in play lie very close to the nuclear neurotic process and exhibit its repetitive character, but even the long course of psychoanalysis of an adult neurotic patient leads ultimately to a similar repetitive core. However elaborate the superstructure, the underlying pathology is always a kind of behavior that displays "automatic repetition irrespective of the situation, the utility, or the consequences of the act." Fenichel characterized the essence of neurotic behavior in similar terms: "the patients, instead of reacting vividly to actual stimuli according to their specific nature, react repeatedly with rigid patterns."[2] And in the following words Alexander and French describe what they deem to be the essential element in the origin of neurosis:[3]

> In normal development, patterns from the past undergo progressive modification. One learns from experience by correcting earlier patterns in the light of later events. When a problem becomes too disturbing to face, however, this learning process is interrupted and subsequent attempts to solve this problem

[1] L. S. Kubie, "The Repetitive Core of Neurosis," *Psychoanalytic Quarterly,* X (1941), pp. 23–43; "The Fundamental Nature of the Distinction Between Normality and Neurosis," *Psychoanalytic Quarterly,* XXIII (1954), pp. 167–204.

[2] O. Fenichel, *The Psychoanalytic Theory of Neurosis* (New York: W. W. Norton & Co., Inc., 1945), p. 542.

[3] F. Alexander and T. M. French *et al., Psychoanalytic Therapy* (New York: The Ronald Press Co., 1946), p. 74.

must, therefore, assume the character of stereotyped repetitions of previous unsuccessful attempts to solve it. A neurosis may be defined as a series of such stereotyped reactions to problems that the patient has never solved in the past and is still unable to solve in the present. In other words, a neurosis is the result of an interrupted learning process.

For simplicity's sake one may be tempted to take as a model some situation in which the learning process is interrupted once and for all by overwhelming panic. Undoubtedly it is true that some adult neuroses have their origin in violently frightening childhood events. The nuclear neurotic process in such cases is no different from what we described in connection with neuroses of traumatic onset. The theory has long since been abandoned, however, that all neuroses, or even a majority of neuroses, take their start from traumatic events. The nucleus can be formed more gradually. It can develop out of a chronic situation that exists between the child and his parents rather than out of dramatic moments of crisis. Threat of desertion or violent punishment never quite materializes, but if the child senses these things as real possibilities he will take defensive measures which gradually become strong enough to interrupt the learning process.

How this works was well described by Karen Horney, using the example of the child's struggle with his own aggression.[4] Many parents, especially those who have strong rejective tendencies, cannot stand hostile behavior from their children and react to it with an irritation and subsequent coldness that may be quite frightening. At first the child may not understand just what it is that alienates his parents' affections, but gradually he reaches the generalization that his own aggressive impulses and hostile expressions are the cause of this recurrent danger. It thus becomes a matter of vast importance—a life-saving measure—not to express hostile feelings. Increasingly they raise the spectre of desertion, begetting an anxiety that requires their repression. There is now a kind of impulse that can no longer be expressed, a range of behavior that is no longer open to the child. He cannot experiment with indirect or modulated forms of aggression, which in fact might prove to be less offensive. He cannot find out whether or not people other than his parents would be tolerant toward his aggression and perhaps even yield to it. The danger cannot be given a new appraisal; feelings of hostility in himself continue to signify desertion and utter helplessness. Yet since it is impossible for such feelings never to be stirred, the problem cannot be permanently set aside. Whenever he is frustrated the child will respond automatically with outwardly placating behavior and an inner constriction of his feelings. To the problem of frustration and aggression

[4] K. Horney, *The Neurotic Personality of Our Time* (New York: W. W. Norton & Co., Inc., 1937), chap. iv.

he now gives a repetitive, stereotyped reaction that precludes new learning and the discovery of a better solution.

Danger Situations of Childhood. It is easier to appreciate the force of the nuclear neurotic process if we examine what constitutes danger for a small child. A good deal has been written about birth as the earliest traumatic event and as the first occasion of profound anxiety. Conceivably, a severe birth experience might lower the threshold of the fear reaction, thus predisposing the person to later anxieties, but there is really no satisfactory evidence for such a contention. A better point of departure for one's reasoning is the actual helplessness of the infant. He cannot supply his own most basic needs, and if he were left alone, his continued existence would be threatened within a very few hours at the most. Freud pointed out that "the situation which the infant appraises as 'danger,' and against which it desires reassurance, is therefore one of not being gratified, of an *increase of tension arising from non-gratification of its needs*—a situation against which it is powerless."[5] We are so used to thinking of danger as external that we tend to forget the close association in infancy between danger and the non-gratification of internal needs.

The infant experiences need satisfaction chiefly from his mother or from whoever feeds him and regularly attends to his wants. The presence of the mother or nurse is soon learned to be the best guarantee of security. Separation from the mother can thus easily become a serious danger signal. At the outbreak of the Second World War, with the threat of large-scale bombing of cities, much fear was felt concerning the shattering effects of air raids on children's feelings of security. Experience showed that for small children, at any rate, the danger of separation from the family circle had a far more devastating effect than the bombings. Most children up to the ages of six or seven took the raids quite calmly so long as their mothers were with them, whereas many emotional difficulties resulted from the attempt to place them in safe areas away from their parents.[6]

It is because of this firm linkage between security and parental support that events in the family circle have so vital a bearing on the child's sense of security. Freud and his followers repeatedly emphasize weaning, toilet training, punishment for sexual activity, sibling rivalry, and the jealousies contained in the Oedipus and Electra situations as

[5] S. Freud, *The Problem of Anxiety* (New York: W. W. Norton & Co., Inc., 1936), p. 100.

[6] A. Freud and D. Burlingham, *War and Children* (New York: Medical War Books, 1943), p. 37; R. Pritchard and S. Rosenzweig, "The Effect of War Stress upon Childhood and Youth," *Journal of Abnormal and Social Psychology*, XXXVII (1942), pp. 329–44.

outstanding sources of threat in childhood. It is plain that these situations can easily arouse anxiety because they threaten in one way or another the central point of the child's security, his relation to his parents. It must be recognized, furthermore, that just as the infant is helpless to provide for his own wants, the child is relatively helpless in regard to parental relationships. If he feels that his parents are being unfair in favoring a sibling, for example, there is very little that he can do about it. He is especially helpless in the face of parental quarrels and the sort of events that lead up to divorce. Whenever he feels helpless in the face of a threat, he is at the mercy of fear and may be able to ward it off only by defensive processes that interfere with further development.

The child's perception of dangers is dependent upon his cognitive capacity. In one sense the immaturity of his understanding spares him a great deal of worry. Even such dangers as storms and air raids may awaken no more than curiosity if he feels safe in parental protection. On the other hand his limited experience often leads him to exaggerate the danger of things which happen within the family circle. Parental grumpiness on the morning after a late party, or a spirited argument on some issue of local politics, may be perceived as signs of an alarming emotional tempest. Furthermore, it is often difficult for a young child, not yet proficient in labeling things with words and forming precise concepts, to grasp correctly what is involved in punishments and other forms of frustration. Anxiety becomes associated with much more than what the parents intended to punish. They were irritated, perhaps, by loud shouting and running about, but the child cannot discriminate these specific actions from the impulses and feelings that accompanied him, so he learns that there is something wrong about high spirits in general. In the illustration used on a previous page we imagined a child in whom all hostility is repressed because of the danger of losing parental affection. Such global repressions, involving whole clusters of impulse and feeling, occur most readily in earlier stages of cognitive development. If we fancy a similar threat occurring for the first time at the age of eight or nine it will be clear that the child would make better discriminations. He would be able to pin down the kinds of acts that caused trouble, and he would have more realization that other people in his environment might not share the attitude of his parents.

Several of the foregoing points are illustrated in the following incident. A mother was giving a large costume party, and her plan called for a little tableau in which her four-year-old son should appear as Cupid, coming down the stairs carrying a bow and arrow and otherwise clad in the traditional costume of Cupid. The child violently objected, feeling genuine anxiety at going down among so many costumed strangers. The mother was unable to sacrifice her tableau, so she applied arguments such as doing it for her sake and not disappointing the guests. At this point the child realized that his interests and his terror were of no importance; he was simply being used for his mother's enjoyment. Fury arose, but anxiety stamped it down. He was suddenly overwhelmed by the need to keep anything he could of his mother's affection. That purpose could not be served by standing up for his rights. It could be served only by surrendering and going downstairs into the nightmare. This incident was one of a series that played a part in what became a fairly severe adult neurosis.

Our discussion thus far has allowed us to expand somewhat our conception of the nuclear neurotic process. In the last chapter it was presented as an outcome of the defenses applied in acutely frightening situations. Now we can see that a similar nucleus can be established more gradually. It can originate from the defenses applied to the chronic threat that the parents will withdraw their interest and support. Returning to the question raised at the beginning—"Of what is the adult neurotic patient afraid?"—we must now add that he may be afraid of his own impulses, especially his aggression, but also his sexual and other tendencies. He is afraid of them because in childhood they imperiled a precarious parental relationship, and he has never been able to learn that they no longer do so. The problem is still one of anxiety and defense. But we see it now as embedded in the vitally important parent-child relationship, and as further complicated by the child's own impulses becoming signals of danger.

It is impossible, however, to answer fully the question of neurotic anxiety until we study what happens after the establishment of a neurotic nucleus in childhood. The development of personality does not stop, but it goes forward in such a way as to create a protective organization against the recurrence of vital threat.

NEUROTIC PROTECTIVE ORGANIZATION

In order to understand neurotic protective organization, we shall begin with an analogous but much clearer problem. Suppose that a child is afflicted with infantile paralysis and recovers with substantial loss of locomotion. His whole development must now take place in such a way as to allow for his limitation. In building up competence and seeking the esteem of others, he will be unable to use athletic achievement. Social adjustment must be accomplished without his being able to dance or to drive a car. Some interests will be closed to him because they demand prolonged standing. This particular defect does not preclude a well-rounded and even distinguished career, but it nevertheless illustrates with simple clarity the effect of a limitation on the process of development.

When a neurotic nucleus is established in childhood, further development must proceed so as to take account of this limitation. The defense of warding off all memories of childhood danger situations, and all impulses that might recreate those dangers, may serve well enough at the time, but it leaves the person in a vulnerable position. New situations may forcibly remind him of the danger. His aggressive, sexual, or other tendencies are bound to be aroused. Repression is not a permanent solution, and he has to build up his life in such a way as to forestall the arousal of what is repressed. Taking as an example a child who senses real danger of losing parental affection, we can say that this child has got to develop in such a way that he will never, so far as possible, offend his parents. The surest way to do this is to subordinate his own wishes to those of his parents. As his world expands outside the family circle, his fear of rejection may be so generalized that he becomes vulnerable to additional threats. Rejection by his teachers, by his playmates and friends, later by his wife and employers and business associates, has the power to call up severe anxiety. He has to please them all. Any coolness, inconsideration, or belittlement becomes a thing to be avoided at all costs. His whole pattern of traits and tendencies is colored by this necessity. It sounds like a bad pun, but we might truly say that an infantile paralysis grips any tendencies in himself that might get him into a situation strongly reminiscent of the danger experienced in childhood. One can see the far-reaching limitation that affects his human relationships. He must never offend others, and they must always treat him well. The many traits and tendencies that he develops in order to bring about this result constitute his protective organization.

It is convenient to distinguish two kinds of constituent that make up the neurotic protective organization. In the first place there is usually evidence of *overdriven strivings:* certain goals in life and certain types of relationship with other people are pursued with a relentless intensity that betrays underlying anxiety. In the second place there are evidences of *protective traits* which serve to prevent the person from being stimulated in ways that would arouse his particular anxieties. If we conceive that both of these constituents have the purpose of making the neurotic person feel safe, the overdriven strivings accomplish this goal by an active seeking of symbols of security, whereas the protective traits achieve it by resistive exclusion of symbols of threat. The distinction does not imply, of course, that the two methods are mutually exclusive. We would expect to find them both at work in any well-developed protective organization.

Overdriven Strivings. An overdriven striving should not be conceived as wholly different in character from a normal or healthy striving. It is rather an exaggeration and rigidifying of an ordinary way of behaving. Nowhere is it more important than here to bear in mind the continuity between healthy and neurotic behavior, and nowhere in our study is one more likely to have attacks of the "medical students' disease" described in an earlier chapter.[7] Overdriven strivings are exaggerations of certain tendencies that are well-nigh universal in human behavior. They become exaggerated in the service of defense against anxiety.

These points can be made clearer by examining Horney's broad classification of overdriven strivings, which she called "neurotic trends."[8] Believing that the more important anxieties have to do with relationships with people, she proposed that overdriven strivings should be grouped under the three headings: moving toward people, moving against people, and moving away from people. Moving toward people, also called a compliant trend, implies that the person feels a certain helplessness and tries to win the affection and esteem of others so that he can lean on them for support. Moving against people, also called an aggressive trend, means that the individual strives to surpass and defeat others, making himself strong enough to disregard their possible hostility. Moving away from people, detaching oneself from others and building up a more or less independent existence, has the effect of avoiding whatever threats may be contained in human relationships. Clearly these purposes are not in themselves neurotic. There are times when each one of the three is fully appropriate and highly desirable. Overdriven strivings are thus not brand new ways of behaving toward other people. They are exaggerated and rigidified versions of strivings that appear in everyone.

Normal people differ a great deal in the balance they establish among moving toward, moving against, and moving away from others. Our study of normal development would lead us to expect this on several grounds. We would expect different patterns to result from different kinds of parental encouragement and from the social opportunities afforded by the neighborhood and the available groups. We would expect differences of temperament and ability to be influential. A considerable overemphasis on one or another trend is not inconsistent with good adjustment. We cannot call one of these strivings overdriven, then, unless in addition to having been favored by temperamental and environmental influences it is being seriously overworked in the interests of defense.

Criteria for Judging a Striving To Be Overdriven. There are three criteria by which defensive overworking can be recognized. (1) The first is indiscriminateness: a given attitude is assumed not only when appropriate but even in the most unsuitable circumstances. A person

[7] See page 53.

[8] K. Horney, *Our Inner Conflicts: A Constructive Theory of Neurosis* (New York: W. W. Norton & Co., Inc., 1945), chaps. ii–v.

who craves affection and approval, for instance, must have it from everyone, even from bus drivers and store clerks who are of no real importance in his life. He may even require it from his children and pet animals. The trend has a compulsive intensity that does not permit it to be adapted to circumstances. (2) Another attribute of overdriven strivings is their insatiable character. The person seems never satisfied; he does not reach repose, but always needs a little more of the same kind of satisfaction. The man who moves toward people wishes that even a very congenial evening had been a little more congenial. The man who seeks triumphs wishes that even a signal success had been a little more glorious. The man who manages to separate himself from all close ties wishes that he could also be free from minor personal contacts. (3) The blocking of overdriven strivings creates disproportionate frustration, probably with signs of anxiety. If aggressive competitiveness, for instance, is serving a neurotic purpose, to be beaten in some competitive enterprise will throw the person into a state of desperation. For him the defeat means vital threat.

Neurotic Conflict. Even if a person's life history loads him with overdriven strivings, he will try his best to achieve some kind of workable integration. He is under the same influences that prompt a healthy person to function as a unified and harmonious individual. His task, however, is much harder. Because of their compulsive intensity, overdriven strivings tend to block and exclude other tendencies. As Horney pointed out in her discussion of moving toward, against, and away from people, neurotic trends are incompatible with good social adjustment. If any one of these three attitudes is lifted to neurotic intensity, it more or less wrecks the chances of using the other two. Yet because the other two represent more or less universal human needs, it is not really possible to subordinate them completely. A person whose anxiety in human relationships can only be held in check by an overdriven striving for seclusive withdrawal does not thereby obliterate his wishes for affection, esteem, and glory. These wishes needle him from time to time; he cannot feel satisfied with the limitations imposed by his chief defense. If a second trend is also reinforced in the interests of defense, the situation is still more difficult. He feels anxious if he cannot have seclusion and he feels anxious if he cannot have competitive success. The very intensity and indiscriminateness of overdriven strivings make it almost impossible to harmonize them with each other and with the rest of the person's tendencies. The result is chronic conflict: *neurotic conflict,* because one at least of the conflicting tendencies is an insatiable neurotic trend.

Protective Traits. In the course of growth a person builds up an array of traits which facilitate his adjustment to the world around him. He develops characteristic and relatively fixed ways of doing things. Gestures, for example, may be typically bold and sweeping in one person, small and hesitant in another; speech may be loud or soft, fast or slow; desks may be kept tidy or messy; work habits may be regular and persistent or spasmodic but intense. Such traits, like strivings, can be lured into the service of defense against anxiety. In addition to their convenience in general adjustment they can participate in a protective action against possible arousals of nuclear neurotic threats. A well-developed series of protective traits can serve as a police patrol against the outbreak of neurotic anxiety.

The adjustive function of traits can be illustrated from a study of speech styles by F. H. Sanford.[9] Samples of recorded speech were analyzed in great detail with reference to length of sentences, number of clauses, frequency of different parts of speech, and many other measurable variables, not including, however, general impressions of the speech or qualities of voice. From the speech structure alone it was possible to assemble a character sketch of the speaker, or, more accurately, to predict the purposes that would presumably be served by the speaker's characteristic way of structuring his speech. Sanford describes as follows the contrasting speech styles of two subjects, Chatwell and Merritt, who were subjects also in extensive studies of personality.

> In his verbal behavior Chatwell is *colorful, varied, emphatic, direct, active, progressing always in a forward direction.* His responses are *well coordinated, closely interconnected,* more *evaluative* than *definitive,* and somewhat *enumerative.* He covers *extensive* areas, verbally, and is *disinclined to consider details* or *precision of reference.* His speech is *confident, definite, independent.* In general he appears to use speech not so much to describe the external world and its relations as to *express his own individuality and to impress the auditor.*
>
> Merritt's speech is *complex, perseverative, thorough, uncoordinated, cautious, static, highly definitive,* and *stimulus-bound.* If we go one step further toward synthesis and generalization, we might conceive of his whole style as *defensive* and *deferent.* Most of his verbal behavior seems to reflect a *desire to avoid blame or disapproval.* He is cautious and indirect, rarely making a simple or bald statement. Once he makes a judgment he explains it and presents all aspects of it, leaving little to the auditor's imagination and little for the auditor to question. His concern for the adequacy of every response results in a re-examination of the response and this, in turn, brings about roughnesses in his discourse. His disinclination to venture out "on his own" makes him feel more comfortable in the stimulus-bound situations.

That these characterizations truly fitted the two men was attested by the independent personality studies.[10]

[9] F. H. Sanford, "Speech and Personality: A Comparative Case Study," *Character and Personality,* X (1942), pp. 169–98.

[10] The two cases are described more fully in R. W. White (ed.), *The Study of Lives* (New York: Atherton Press, 1963), chap. iii.

Chatwell's speech has little protective purpose, being mainly in the service of other needs. In Merritt's case, however, there can be no mistaking the signs of anxiety and the desire to avoid being challenged on unguarded, downright statements. In actuality Merritt would not be classed as neurotic, but he is a very cautious man who feels his way uneasily into human situations and prefers to keep most of his relationships on a somewhat formal basis. The traits of his speech are protective, but certainly not to a point of crippling inflexibility.

Quite otherwise were the speech and surface traits of a neurotic patient described by Reich, who introduced the striking expression *character armor* to describe behavior of this kind.[11] When first seen, the patient created an immediate impression of refined arrogance. His facial expression was haughty, his speech quiet and measured, his gait slow and restrained. He lay down on the couch in a composed fashion, his legs neatly crossed. Even when discussing painful recollections he maintained his evenness and dignity; in fact, these traits became more conspicuous when he approached topics presumably of high emotional importance. "One day tears came and his voice began to choke; nevertheless, the manner in which he put the handkerchief to his eyes was composed and dignified."[12] This patient was suffering from severe neurotic difficulties, and he knew that his cure depended upon a free expression of his feelings during his hours with the psychoanalyst; yet he was so strongly armored with habitual protective traits that for many weeks it was impossible for him to do anything but resist his own cure.

The services performed by protective traits become clearer when, as in the course of psychoanalytic treatment, they can be slowly broken down. When this occurred in Reich's patient, a second layer of character armor came to light. Beneath the courtly surface his attitude toward other people, including the physician, was highly critical, hostile, and derisive. He took delight in the misfortunes of others and was constantly on the alert for their shortcomings. Yet this, too, was in the nature of a defense, for it concealed very sharp and painful feelings of inferiority. A person who carries a burden of inferiority feelings can ease his load somewhat by discovering equal or greater weaknesses in others, but to express such disparagement openly would invite dangerous reprisals and countercriticisms. By his dignified protective traits the patient managed to look politely contemptuous while at the same time preventing any real arousal of his own disturbing feelings of hostility and inferiority.

Protecting the Self-Picture. Traits do not usually stand as separate items in a person's repertory of behavior. They form an organized pat-

[11] W. Reich, *Character-Analysis*, trans. T. P. Wolfe (3d ed., New York: Orgone Institute Press, 1949), especially chaps. iv and ix.

[12] *Ibid.*, p. 181.

tern, and to some extent they participate in the image or picture that each person has of himself. Most people are inclined to cherish and defend a favorable self-picture. To do so is by no means a neurotic phenomenon. Gardner Murphy describes as follows the human tendency to paint the self-picture in the best possible colors.[13]

> Both perception and valuation of the self are complicated processes that take a long time to crystallize. But the result of all these developments is that, like the childhood rag doll, the self, scarred and tattered as it is, becomes a deeply treasured possession; for most of humanity, at least in competitive cultures, it is probably the central value of existence. However poor, confused, and inconsistent it is, it is central, and it must be defended not only against outer attacks but against a clear perception of its unloveliness.

When there is a heavy burden of neurotic anxiety, the self-picture becomes involved in the protective organization. Its defense becomes an acute issue. The patient cannot tolerate any blemish on this outermost layer of his armor, even in matters that seem remote from his central anxieties. Like other processes captured for defensive ends, the self-picture becomes rigid and cannot be modified in the light of new experiences. It also becomes, as Horney has shown, much more a creation of fantasy designed to put overdriven strivings and protective traits in a noble and glorious light.[14] The self-picture is apt to be most highly embellished in psychotic patients such as L. Percy King, but in neurotics it can also be quite rigid and exaggerated, though usually less clearly conscious. Reich's patient provides a perfect illustration. One day the analyst, commenting on his aristocratic surface, called his behavior "lordly," and this led to the discovery that he cherished a very real image of himself as an English lord. This fantasy was based on a mere rumor that his grandmother had had an affair with an English lord and that his mother was half English; it included the notion that he was not the true son of his father, a small Jewish merchant in the German town where they lived. These fantasies had been elaborated consciously during the patient's childhood, and at puberty he had been able to translate them into actual protective behavior by imitating a very lordly and immaculate school teacher. The necessity of defense against neurotic anxieties caused the patient to preserve and act upon this juvenile self-picture well into adult life.

It is only when we take into account the whole protective organization that we can properly return to our initial question: Of what is the adult neurotic individual afraid? At any given moment it is usually right to say that he is afraid his protective organization is going to be broken

[13] G. Murphy, *Personality: A Biosocial Approach to Origins and Structure* (New York: Harper & Row, 1947), pp. 529–30.

[14] Horney, *Our Inner Conflicts, op. cit.*, chap. vi.

in some way. He is afraid that his established techniques for making himself feel safe are going to be challenged. This is the *immediate* threat, but it is a serious threat only because he is still *basically* afraid of the danger situations of his childhood. He has done no relearning in regard to these dangers, and he is still vulnerable to the fear, for example, that his parents will be angry and leave him destitute of all support. It is to prevent the recurrence of such dangers that the whole protective structure has been put together in the course of development.

EXAMPLES OF NEUROTIC PATTERNS

In the last section we were concerned to round out the description of the dynamics of neurosis, including the development of protective organization and the conflicts occurring within it. We were therefore niggardly in our description of larger patterns of neurotic behavior. Such patterns are full of individuality, and they can take a variety of forms barely suggested by the notions of moving toward, against, and away from people. Any listing of neurotic tendencies is bound to be unsatisfactory and incomplete. In order to understand how such things work, it will be more useful to describe a few samples, without making any pretense at completeness.

Need for Affection. That a striving to obtain affection could serve as a neurotic trend was early recognized by Freud and his followers. The neurotic need for affection has been best described by Horney.[15] To have affection is certainly a good thing in itself. Such a striving, therefore, qualifies as neurotic only when it meets the three criteria previously described: it is indiscriminately compulsive, it is insatiable, and when frustrated it gives rise to disproportionate despair if not outright anxiety. This intensity, this overdriven character, comes from the fact that the striving for affection is also serving as a striving for security. The person must have affection not only because it is good in itself but also in order to feel safe.

Horney points out that the neurotic individual who seeks his security in this particular trend keeps working himself unwittingly into situations of conflict. He is in great need of love from others, but he is more or less incapable of giving anything in return. The original neurotic nucleus contained a repression of hostility in the interest of retaining parental affection. Lurking within him, but kept very firmly out of his awareness, is a resentful distrust of other people. Emergence of this hostility into consciousness would constitute a basic threat, calling up the original danger situations in which anger had to be repressed lest it offend the parents. But in every relationship from which he seeks to gain

[15] Horney, *The Neurotic Personality of Our Time*, *op. cit.*, chaps. vi–viii.

affection, this dangerous hostility is stimulated. He needs too much affection; he cannot tolerate the other person's being interested in some third person, and he cannot bear to be the object of any demands or criticisms. In other words, he expects a degree of blind devotion that he is highly unlikely to obtain from anyone, and he is therefore continually frustrated. He continues, however, to think of himself as loving the other person. Unable to become aware of the mixture of hostility in his feelings, he can never allow for them, outgrow them, perceive his deficiencies as a giver of love, and achieve in his relationships a reasonable balance of give and take. "In short," says Horney, "for a person who is driven by his basic anxiety and consequently, as a means of protection, reaches out for affection, the chances of getting this so-much-desired affection are anything but favorable. The very situation that creates the need interferes with its gratification."[16]

Because rejection was originally a danger signal, the neurotic person is highly sensitized to it. As a result he overacts in indiscriminate fashion to anything that may be considered a rebuff. If an appointment has to be changed, or if he is kept waiting a few minutes, his equilibrium will be badly upset. Going further, he may anticipate rejection wherever there is the least possibility of receiving it. "A person may, for example, ask a question angrily, because in his mind he has already anticipated a refusal."[17] It will be hard for him to take the initiative in seeking affection because he is so acutely sensitive to the possibility of being rejected. This is typical of the self-defeating conflicts that arise out of neurotic trends. He must have affection, but at the same time he hardly dares seek it. If he is lucky enough to find an affectionate relationship, he will almost inevitably wreck it by his sensitiveness, demandingness, and failure to give anything in return. Under these circumstances it is obvious that the whole development of personality will be badly impoverished. The vital problems of friendship and love can never be made to come out right.[18]

Invalidism. In the historical introduction we mentioned the work of Alfred Adler, who first showed the importance of feelings of inferiority and the compensatory striving for superiority. If we assume that feelings of inferiority are associated with anxiety, Adler's notions fit perfectly into our present account of neuroses. The striving for superiority can then be considered a typical neurotic trend developed for the sake of feeling secure.

16 *Ibid.*, p. 114.

17 *Ibid.*, p. 136.

18 The subtle ramifications of a neurotic overdriven striving can be fully appreciated only by reading a detailed individual case. In her book, *Self-Analysis* (New York: W. W. Norton & Co., Inc., 1942), Horney gives such a case, centering around a young woman's "morbid dependency" on a man. See pp. 47–52, 75–88, 190–246.

Adler was most adept at tracing the roundabout workings of this striving. Reading his work today, one is apt to be troubled by his lack of systematic thinking; almost every neurotic mechanism and neurotic trend is lumped together under the striving for superiority. But this should not obscure the shrewdness of his clinical insights. We select for description a neurotic trend (or character trait, as he called it), which can be described as invalidism.[19]

The goal of this neurotic trend is to establish a favored position at home. The person settles for attention, sympathy, and service rather than more glorious goals, compensating himself by the opportunity afforded to dominate the household and prevail over its other members.

Adler illustrated neurotic invalidism by the following case. The youngest of several sisters, always in delicate health as a child, was accustomed to much pampering attention. As she grew older, this attention decreased, but she noticed that her mother, when occasionally sick, was able to dominate the household very completely. Before long the daughter began to find it not unpleasant to feel badly from time to time. As Adler expressed it: "Soon she acquired so much training in being sick that she could easily be ill whenever she desired it, and especially when her heart was set on attaining some special object." She developed many subsidiary techniques for remaining the center of attention. If her mother did not have the breakfast tray at her bed on time, she would awaken her husband to find out what was the matter with her mother. If the husband was delayed in returning from work, he would find his wife suffering an attack of violent anxiety. Everyone soon learned that it was easier to be punctual. If she went out to a social gathering or to the theater, she would soon feel ill and have to be taken home. Finally, she could leave the house only if some member of the family escorted her. Thus she managed for a while to satisfy the overdriven striving that required the constant presence of solicitous people sacrificing themselves to her welfare.

It is hardly necessary to comment on the impoverishment of personality that results from so forceful a neurotic trend, nor to point out that the situation can hardly be maintained throughout the patient's life. An interesting question arises, however, concerning the production of the various illnesses—the anxieties, headaches, faint feelings, etc., that seemed always available when the patient needed them. We can understand this phenomenon if we bear two points in mind. (1) We must assume—differing here from Adler—that there was a basis of real anxiety. To be neglected and unnoticed was a childhood danger signal embedded in the nuclear neurotic process and thus never unlearned. The anxiety

[19] A. Adler, *Understanding Human Nature* (Philadelphia: Chilton Co., 1927), pp. 200–207.

reaction, with its manifold bodily accompaniments, was thus easily arousable. Most people try their best to suppress the anxiety reaction, but for this patient there was a definite advantage in letting it develop at least to the point where palpitations, sweating, trembling, changes in blood pressure, slowing of digestive functions, etc. would make their appearance and serve as a means of worrying the household. Portions of the anxiety reaction were thus used to simulate heart attacks and other disorders. (2) In the experimental study of hypnotism it has been shown that the vivid imagining of situations while in the hypnotic state can produce bodily reactions not usually under volitional control, such as sweating in a suggested hot climate and shivering in a cold one. When sickness serves a neurotic protective purpose, it is much to the patient's interest to imagine ailments, and strongly motivated imagination can produce surprising results even without hypnotic technique. The combined forces of vivid imagination and the bodily accompaniments of anxiety could easily produce bodily upsets sufficient to suggest apoplexy or heart attacks and terrify both patient and household. They could do so, moreover, without the patient's being in the least aware that his motives were involved.

Need for Power. Both Adler and Horney were shrewd observers of overdriven strivings for power in neurotic patients. In a culture which places a high value upon competitive success the goals of power and prestige are attractive to many people. Striving for these goals might be described as already culturally overdriven in many sectors of American society. This makes it easy for power and prestige to become symbols of security and to be chosen as the objects of neurotically overdriven strivings on the part of people whose basic anxieties have to do with inferiority and humiliation. When the need for power is overdriven by childhood anxieties it soon exhibits the familiar qualities of indiscriminateness and insatiability. There is a constant search for new worlds to conquer. The patient is an autocrat in his office, takes a commanding part in business conferences, tells his wife and children how things are to be done at home, tries to raise the biggest dahlias of anyone in town, dominates the discussions at the parent-teacher association, and can be heard as the loudest and most frequent speaker even in casual gatherings. At the same time he is tremendously vulnerable to any obstruction of his need for power and prestige. It is then that anxiety creeps up on him, perhaps even to the extent that he looks for psychiatric rescue.

Implicit in the neurotic striving for power is the belief that everyone is hostile. Life is a competitive struggle, and the only way to avoid going under is to be on top. Along with the desire to have control over others there is usually an interest in recognition, in having one's power affirmed and acclaimed by others as an additional guarantee that they will not dare to be openly hostile. The intense concentration on the relationship of power, and the distrust of others which it both implies and engenders, crowds out other relationships and thus impoverishes the patient's life in other dimensions. It will be hard for him, for instance, to think of his wife in any other way than as a person to be dominated to satisfy his own needs or as a person who will enhance his social position and economic prospects.

Horney described a young man of this kind who in daily life was "domineering, inclined to exploit, driven by a devouring ambition." He kept himself aloof from close relationships except for adventures along sexual lines. "There was present, however, a distinct tendency to comply, together with a need for approval that interfered with his craving for power." The patient needed to feel not only powerful but also in the right. These necessities were neatly embodied and reconciled in a glamorous self-picture to which he clung with great tenacity:

> In his idealized image he was the knight in shining armor, the crusader with wide and unfailing vision, ever pursuing the right. As becomes a wise leader, he was not personally attached to anyone but dispensed a stern though just discipline. He was honest without being hypocritical. Women loved him and he could be a great lover but was not tied to any woman.[20]

Inhibition of Feeling. In view of the prominent part played by protective inhibition in the nuclear neurotic process, it is not surprising that the same sort of defense should sometimes be extended widely throughout the personality. In contrast to trends like the neurotic need for affection or neurotic vanity, where a positive tendency is taken up and intensified because of its service in overcoming childhood anxiety, the inhibitory pattern represents a direct extension of the defensive process. This occurs most readily when the patient's own impulses have repeatedly gotten him into situations of threat from his parents. The child learns to consider all impulse and all strong feeling as dangerous. He extends the defense as he grows older and as new stimuli threaten to arouse his impulses. Anna Freud points out that during puberty, when the strengthening of the sex need makes the whole problem of managing impulses suddenly more difficult, one sometimes sees a generalized defense taking the form of asceticism.[21] All bodily pleasure may be renounced: intake of food is cut down to a bare subsistence level, only the lightest clothes are worn in cold weather. The renunciation may include anything that stirs feeling, such as music, dancing, or the theater. As a phenomenon of

[20] Horney, *Our Inner Conflicts, op. cit.*, p. 108.

[21] A. Freud, *The Ego and the Mechanisms of Defence* (London: Hogarth Press, Ltd., 1937), pp. 167–72.

puberty, this defense generally breaks down after a while, in some cases even swinging to its opposite of libertine gratification. But occasionally the attitude remains as a more or less enduring and extending neurotic trend.

In persons who show the inhibitory pattern, impulse and deep feeling are experienced as danger signals, more or less regardless of their particular character. The person must always be very well controlled. He does not like emotional storms in others, in the movies, or even in books and music. Fenichel illustrates this protective trend with the extreme case of a man who hated almost everything in life—his work, friends, family, amusements—and felt happily at ease only with his hobby of mathematics, a field in which no emotions were involved.[22] In less extreme form, the defense may be carried on by the technique of not perceiving the feeling element in life. The patient criticizes the vocal technique when a sad song is sung, or tries to figure out how the camera was placed to take a scene that forms the emotional climax of a movie. Generalized inhibition of this kind tends to limit very greatly the range of experiences the person can allow himself to have. It is particularly disastrous to intimate human relationships, where feeling is always important and where impulsive outbursts cannot always be avoided. Like other neurotic protections, it imposes so many restrictions that a well-balanced and rewarding life becomes impossible.

GENERAL CONSEQUENCES OF NEUROTIC PROTECTIVE ORGANIZATION

Our sampling of neurotic patterns shows that they can take a variety of forms. Underneath this diversity, however, the neurotic nucleus has a fairly simple pattern. Because he has not been able to outgrow the danger situations of childhood, the person develops in a world that offers unusual threat to his security. A disproportionate part of his energies must be devoted to security, and a disproportionate part of his choices must be dictated by defense. This is the cause of the impoverishment that we have mentioned in connection with each neurotic pattern. The maintenance of a protective organization occurs at constant cost. When we see the problem in this way it becomes legitimate to speak of certain general consequences of neurotic protective organization.

We have already met this problem in our study of neuroses of traumatic onset.[23] We noticed that in addition to the diverse symptoms there were certain constant features called *secondary character changes.* In practically every case there were nightmares, representing the breaking

[22] Fenichel, *op. cit.,* p. 477.
[23] See above, pages 208–10.

through of the repressed memories of danger. There were also diffuse signs of lowered efficiency and lowered competence which could be understood as resulting from the division of the patient's energies. We envisaged the patient as having a great deal of energy tied up in the struggle to feel safe; as a consequence, all the rest of his life had to be conducted with seriously diminished resources.

The neurotic whose troubles date from childhood is in much the same situation as regards energy resources. Disproportionate energy is put into neurotic trends and into the task of integrating a workable protective pattern. The general consequences of neurotic conflict can be discussed under three headings: fatigue, disturbing tensions, and chronic dissatisfaction.

Fatigue. It is not true that all neurotic individuals go around in a drooping, exhausted condition. Some are highly energetic and appear most of the time to be more active than the average. Nevertheless, fatigue in some form is one of the universal problems of the neurotic personality. Fatigue is an unpleasant and inefficient state. It interferes with concentration, initiative, the making of decisions, and it lowers the whole level of interest in things. Neurotic conflict, with its drain on energy resources, tends to increase all these manifestations. Fatigue may be present in chronic form, so that the person feels tired even in the morning and gets little refreshment out of vacations or periods of rest. In other cases the general level of activity is unimpaired, but the person has spells of fatigue that are extremely unpleasant. This can be characterized as episodic fatigue in contrast to the chronic form.

Neurotic fatigue can entail a good deal of suffering. The difficulty in concentrating and persisting in tasks has the effect of making the ordinary affairs of life laborious. Instead of running themselves off with comfortable efficiency, they seem to require a distinct and unpleasant expenditure of effort. The impairment of interest may be particularly discouraging, especially if the person is in a line of work where interest and zest are important.

Disturbing Tensions. Even the most successful protective organization cannot be uniformly effective. The things that are being held in check intrude themselves from time to time in a fashion that can be very disturbing. Many neurotic individuals complain of a feeling of restless tension even at times when they also experience fatigue. This is perhaps the most generalized form in which the tendencies thwarted by protective organization make themselves felt. Another characteristic neurotic phenomenon is to have spells of irritation and frustration that do not seem sensibly related to existing circumstances. Fears also may contribute their part to making the neurotic's life disagreeable. Without really reaching panic, he may find himself bothered by fears of accident, fears of death, fears of going insane. The fear of going insane is particularly common. It bears no relation to any real likelihood of going insane, but rather expresses in a symbolic way the person's dread of the confusion and anxiety that would overwhelm him if the protective organization broke down.

Tension manifests itself most clearly in disturbances of sleep. To sleep well requires genuine relaxation. The neurotic individual has difficulty in relaxing, not because of external or physical stimulation but because of his conflicts and underlying anxiety. The disturbers of sleep are rarely so clear as in the battle dreams of soldiers which literally revive the scene of overwhelming danger. Nevertheless the dreams of neurotics are full of trouble and often of anxiety. Neurotics sleep badly and dream frequently because their unsolvable problems will not let them alone. Although there are occasional exceptions, disturbance of sleep is one of the most universal burdens of the neurotic personality.

Chronic Dissatisfaction. Neurotic conflict tends to wax and wane, depending on the extent to which it is stimulated by external circumstances. Neuroses have their good and bad periods. But running through all these ups and downs there is a thread of chronic dissatisfaction and hopelessness. Such a result comes inevitably from the nature of overdriven strivings. They tend to be insatiable. Even when circumstances permit them a large amount of gratification, they do not lead to enjoyment and repose. They are serving in the cause of defense as well as enjoyment. The childhood danger still exists for the patient, and no amount of defensive action can fully silence its threat. Furthermore, it is likely that a number of natural desires, possibly even some imperious bodily cravings, become blocked by neurotic trends. The neurotic nucleus might have nothing to do with sex, for example, but adequate sexual satisfaction would be blocked if a neurotic trend toward seclusive withdrawal became dominant in the patient's life.

The eternally unsatisfied need for security and the other needs that become blocked in the protective organization tend to create a constant feeling that life is not rewarding or fully satisfactory. As time goes on and the situation does not improve, the person becomes increasingly discouraged. He may change his job, move to another place, get married or divorced, but these alterations do not relieve him of the burdensome consequences of neurotic conflict. If he begins to realize that the obstacles to happiness are within himself, he still cannot see any way to change or remove those obstacles. His feelings of discouragement and futility are apt to trouble him more and more.

Comparison with Healthy Organization. Before leaving this topic it is well to remind ourselves once more of the continuity between normal and neurotic behavior. Fatigue, tensions, and dissatisfaction are part of the normal human lot; no one can get through life without considerable visitations by these unpleasant states. Obviously one cannot always be contented, buoyant, and optimistic, especially in a time like the present which is beset by grave and formidable problems. It is hard to draw the line between those fatigues, disturbing tensions, and chronic dissatisfactions that may be entirely suitable responses to a real situation and those that result from the exactions of a neurotic protective organization. In theory, the neurotic protective organization exists as a means of defense against the dangers of childhood, dangers which are no longer real in the environment of the adult. It is activated by subjective dangers rather than real ones, and its tax on the person will be most exorbitant when subjective, not real, dangers are most pressing. Therefore the fatigues, tensions, and dissatisfaction that spring from neurotic sources should be experienced as more irrational, more senselessly persistent, less linked to real happenings than those which arise in response to the actual vicissitudes of life. Sometimes neurotic patients are clearly aware that their bad experiences make no sense. The conditions of life are satisfactory enough, but their own emotions prevent them from living happily. Such insight, however, is by no means always present. Some forms of protective organization require the patient to believe that his behavior is correct and his feelings appropriate to what is going on around him. In such cases the judgment of neurotic origins can be made only by an outside observer, often only by one with considerable experience in clinical diagnosis.

PRECIPITATING FACTORS IN NEUROTIC BREAKDOWN

Before proceeding further, we must stop to clear up the confusion that exists with respect to the words *neurosis* and *neurotic*. This confusion in terminology is rooted in history. So long as the somatogenic theory was the accepted pattern, it was conceived that a person could "have" a neurosis in just the same way that he could "have" pneumonia. He was either sick or well; he either "had" it or he didn't. Whether he was an eccentric and unhappy person before he "had" it was completely irrelevant. It is still customary to say that a person has a neurosis only when he has hysterical symptoms, compulsions and obsessions, phobias and anxiety attacks, or some other highly focalized, crippling outcome of the whole neurotic process.

The psychogenic theory changes this all around. The acute neurosis with its symptoms is now seen as the end result of a long process of development. The trouble starts with what we have called the neurotic nucleus, a process by which anxiety, typically in childhood, is subjected to such radical defense that a new evaluation of the danger cannot be made. The trouble continues with the formation of overdriven strivings, tendencies that are exaggerated in the effort to maintain security. Overdriven strivings are likely to conflict with each other and with other tendencies in the personality, a situation that we have called neurotic conflict. Integrative efforts continue, however, and the person steadily builds for himself a protective organization, becoming a full-fledged neurotic personality. At any point along the way the situation may get out of hand: anxiety may increase, and the defenses may become more desperate. The person feels much worse, and it is usually at such a point that symptom formation occurs. We shall refer to this as *neurotic breakdown.* In the older terminology it is at this point that the person starts to be sick and to "have" a neurosis. In our present understanding, the neurotic breakdown is a sort of climax that occurs when the protective structure is seriously threatened and can no longer be maintained intact. Neurotic breakdown occurs only on the basis of an already existing neurotic personality.[24]

In many cases, of course, a neurotic breakdown never occurs. People with considerable neurotic burdens often work out a way of life that meets reasonably well their special needs for security and still makes room for usefulness and a living wage of happiness. Others seek professional help because the general consequences of neurotic conflict, especially the chronic dissatisfaction and discouragement, wear them down as they get older. Such cases as these can be properly conceived as neurotic personalities who stop short of neurotic breakdown and acute symptoms.

Failure of an Established Equilibrium. What causes a character disorder to eventuate in neurotic breakdown? Under what circumstances does the protective organization collapse? These questions can be answered, following Fenichel, by the general statement that circumstances have brought about the failure of an established equilibrium.[25] Such failure can be produced by alterations in the strength of any of the important forces that serve to maintain the existing equilibrium. The possibilities can be schematically covered as follows.

24 A possible exception to this rule is breakdown and symptom formation under acute prolonged combat stress. While the majority of persons having neuroses of traumatic onset show a history of neurotic trends, like the case of Pearson Brack in Chapter 2, there may be some cases in which no such history exists.

25 Fenichel, *op. cit.*, pp. 454–57. Fenichel acknowledges indebtedness to earlier papers by Freud and by James Strachey on the same subject.

1. *There is an intensification of the reminders of childhood dangers.* Fenichel says: "Most precipitating factors are experiences that are (objectively or subjectively) somehow similar to the childhood events that gave rise to the decisive conflicts.[26] (a) It may be that newly arising dangers literally resemble the childhood ones. For example, the individual finds himself working for a boss who threatens to fire him, much as his father used to threaten punishment. (b) More commonly, the intensification affects certain strivings in the person which created childhood threat for him. We considered such a case in an earlier chapter: a young man who had received frightening threats for sexual play in childhood, and had renounced all interest in sex throughout his boyhood, began to have anxiety attacks when puberty brought an irrepressible strengthening of the sex need and its associated interest.[27] Similarly, a person might get into a line of work that was full of irritating frustrations, offering constant stimulation to the aggressive impulses that once made him dread parental rejection.

2. *There is a weakening of defensive processes.* (a) Prolonged overwork, exhaustion, sickness and anything else that depletes the person's energies may have the effect of weakening his defenses. Breakdown under the stress of war was often preceded and presumably facilitated by long periods of exhausting strain. When depleted in this fashion, the person becomes less able to deal with any difficult problems, including that of maintaining a protective organization. (b) Defense can also be weakened when circumstances block the working out of an important overdriven striving. Suppose that security is being sought through extreme dependence on a partner: the departure or death of this partner then constitutes a sudden withdrawal of the means whereby anxiety was prevented from developing. Similarly catastrophic will be the effect of a business failure on someone who has built personal security on a neurotic striving toward competitive success.

3. *There is an intensification of defensive processes.* The very opposite change, the strengthening of defenses, can also have the effect of destroying a precarious neurotic equilibrium. Heightened threat is successfully controlled by increasing the defenses, but the burden of carrying so much protective organization proves to be itself intolerable. One might draw the parallel of a nation increasing its armaments, lest an enemy nation disrupt its internal economy, only to have that economy disrupted anyway by the burden of such expensive armaments. The heightening of overdriven strivings increases the conflicts among them, decreases the satisfaction of other needs on which they encroach, and increases the

[26] *Ibid.*, p. 457.
[27] See above, page 121.

general consequences of protective organization: fatigue, disturbing tension, chronic dissatisfaction.

An Example of Neurotic Breakdown. A single example cannot illustrate all of these possibilities, but it can give us a more vivid idea of how neurotic breakdown comes about. The following case is taken from Malamud.[28]

A married man of twenty-eight was in a motor accident. He sustained minor scratches and was otherwise apparently unhurt, but he emerged from the accident completely blind. The absence of any injury that could be responsible for loss of vision led to a diagnosis of hysteria. It was discovered that the accident occurred while he was driving to the maternity hospital to see his wife and first-born child. His first remark to the psychiatrist was that he could not tie his wife down to a blind man and would now divorce her.

This strange sequence of events becomes intelligible if we work out the patient's history and discover the personal meaning of the situation that so startlingly made him blind. First we discover a clearly *overdriven striving* in the patient's previous behavior, an exaggerated trend toward independent self-sufficiency. He early separated from his parents and established an independent life for himself, resolving at the same time that he would never marry. He was attracted to women, but kept all relationships at a purely sexual level and discontinued them at the first hint of deeper feeling and especially at the faintest threat of marriage. His history showed that the purpose of this overdriven striving was to hold in check all feelings of dependence on women. The mother had been extremely domineering and the father weakly submissive. While we cannot precisely recover the *neurotic nucleus* in this case, it evidently had something to do with the parental relationship. Dependent longings entailed unwilling submission to the mother's iron rule, a thing to be hated and feared because it made one resemble the weak and helpless father. Therefore dependent longings constituted a danger, and the neurotic trend toward self-sufficiency served to hold them in check.

The patient's overdriven striving was not allowed to prevent the satisfaction of his sexual needs; it functioned merely to prevent his relationships from satisfying anything besides sex. His safety lay in his freedom to walk out of any relationship. An equilibrium was established which worked well enough for several years. *Disturbance of the established equilibrium* began when his sexual adventures brought him in contact with a woman who in certain respects reminded him of his mother and stimulated his dependent longings. This was so satisfactory that he

[28] W. Malamud, "The Psychoneuroses," in J. McV. Hunt (ed.), *Personality and the Behavior Disorders* (New York: The Ronald Press Co., 1944), Vol. II, chap. xxviii.

permitted the relation to develop. He sought her advice and allowed her to make decisions. He grew increasingly uncomfortable—anxiety was evidently stirring—but he finally consented to marriage on the condition that they would never have children.

One can say at this point that he had suspended his overdriven striving in order to gratify dependent longings, but he kept the guarantee that he could escape at any time if this new equilibrium proved unbearable. His tension and discomfort show that it was only just bearable. Then suddenly his avenue of escape was blocked: his wife became pregnant. He demanded an abortion, but she refused. Throughout the pregnancy he was increasingly uneasy. He did not know why he felt this way, but in the course of later analytic treatment he recovered memories that showed how earnestly he had hoped the pregnancy would not mature and how tenaciously he clung to the notion that escape from the marriage would still be possible. When his wife went to the hospital his anxiety came into the open, taking the twisted form of terror lest something happen to the mother or child. Finally he learned that both were well, and that he could see them. He jumped into the car and drove toward the hospital. Then the accident happened, and he was unable to see them.

Knowing about the patient's past and his chief neurotic striving, we can understand that the successful birth of the child pushed him to the point of panic. His protective organization collapsed; he prevented acute panic only by the completely primitive defense of denial. Protective inhibition fell on the function of vision, throwing it wholly out of action. A neurotic personality passed into *neurotic breakdown* with the production of a typically hysterical *symptom syndrome.*

In the next chapter we shall study the symptom syndromes of neurosis, trying to understand how symptoms come into existence. This case can serve as one of our illustrations. Why was blindness the symptom? The patient certainly believed that blindness gave an excuse for divorcing his wife, even though she had a child to support. If this idea was in his mind before the motor accident, it might have influenced the direction taken by defensive inhibition. Then there is the question of seeing or not seeing the child: perhaps he had hoped that he would never live to see this day, to see the proof of his now permanent bondage. Such thoughts might have the effect of focalizing the danger on seeing, so that going blind became the only way to prevent contact with the threat. This is sheer speculation, of course, but when we think of Diven's experiments[29] in which the anxiety reaction was displaced along lines of meaningful, associative connection, it does not seem impossible that defensive inhibition should follow similar channels. The motor accident itself raises

[29] See above, pages 200–202.

interesting questions. Was his anxiety so acute that he did not know what he was doing? Was his vision already beginning to fail? Were his guilt feelings so strong that part of him wanted an accident to happen by way of punishment? Did he unwittingly try to kill himself rather than endure further anxiety? Again we can only speculate and suggest possibilities. The lawful processes that produce neurotic symptoms are difficult to unscramble. But in the next chapter we shall look for whatever lawfulness can be found.

SUGGESTIONS FOR FURTHER READING

The outstanding indebtedness of this chapter is to the writings of Karen Horney, who more than any other worker tried to trace the complex ramifications of neurotic defense throughout the personality. The most relevant books at this point are *The Neurotic Personality of Our Time* (New York, W. W. Norton & Co., Inc., 1937) and *Our Inner Conflicts: A Constructive Theory of Neurosis* (New York, W. W. Norton & Co., Inc., 1945). There is considerable similarity between Horney and Alfred Adler, who described the equivalent of neurotic trends under the heading of "character traits" and whose concept of a "style of life" is close to that of protective organization. Adler's *Understanding Human Nature* (Philadelphia, Chilton Co., 1927) satisfactorily describes his outlook.

Much of the material discussed in this chapter is treated by Freudian writers under the heading "character disorders." Fenichel's compendium, *The Psychoanalytic Theory of Neurosis* (New York, W. W. Norton & Co., Inc., 1945), brings together in well-organized though highly concentrated form the extensive material on this topic; see Ch. 20.

Erich Fromm in *Escape From Freedom* (New York, Farrar & Rinehart, 1941) makes a significant application of ideas concerning neurotic defense to political and social problems. See especially Ch. 5 on mechanisms of escape.

7

The Symptom Syndromes of Neurosis

Symptoms are the surface phenomena of neurosis. They are the focalized outcome of a long series of events. For this reason they cannot be understood by themselves; there are perhaps no phenomena in nature that make so little sense as neurotic symptoms when these are studied without reference to their underlying determinants. It is on this account that we have postponed them to the present chapter. The neurotic nucleus, defense mechanisms, conflict, protective organization, and neurotic breakdown must all be understood before it is possible to perceive lawfulness in symptom formation.

THEORY OF SYMPTOM FORMATION

A person who has managed to synthesize a workable protective organization may live his life at a relatively mature level. But when circumstance destroy his established equilibrium, he is thrown back to a more primitive level of defense. The intensified anxiety is childlike, and the defenses become similarly childlike. Neurotic breakdown occurs when the patient is driven out of his protective organization and forced back upon the neurotic nucleus. In this sense it is proper to say that the patient *regresses* toward childhood. His attempts to regain equilibrium will occur at a regressed level. The processes back of symptom formation are therefore of a distinctly primitive character.

Sources of Neurotic Symptoms. The symptoms of neurosis are derived from various elements of the nuclear neurotic process. They can be conceived as reflecting either (1) the anxiety reaction itself, or (2) the defensive processes, or (3) the impulses in the patient that create anxiety.

Naturally it is not uncommon to find that two or even all three sources have been utilized in the production of symptoms.

1. The most important elements of the *anxiety reaction* are its various involuntary bodily processes, such as trembling, sweating, speeded pulse, rapid breathing, slowing of digestive processes. In studying the case of Pearson Brack, we noticed that his symptom of fainting was a direct product of the anxiety reaction. Similarly, when we considered neurotic invalidism in the last chapter, we saw that portions of the anxiety reaction formed the chief material out of which the patient magnified his more or less imaginary ailments. One authority, T. A. Ross, gives the central place to the anxiety reaction as the source of neurotic symptoms.[1]

2. The second source of symptoms is the *defensive processes* used to ward off anxiety. These may consist of direct inhibitions, as in the case of the man described in the last chapter who was struck blind while driving to the maternity hospital. Most hysterical symptoms contain a large element of direct inhibition. The defensive processes may take the slightly more elaborate form of phobias or of stereotyped ritualistic acts. The case of the child, Patrick, (Chapter 5) demonstrated the rigid repetion of acts which constituted a denial of the existing threat. In obsessional neurosis the symptoms consist largely of defensive processes displaced into the sphere of thinking. Obsessional symptoms often become highly complex, but their derivation from defensive processes is not thereby obscured.

3. Symptoms are sometimes colored by the impulse which is the source of danger: the *anxiety-linked* impulse. It can be observed that while the symptom is mainly defensive in character, it also permits some indirect gratification of the prohibited need. This sort of compromise is represented in the following phobia: a woman patient could go on the street only when accompanied by a relative; otherwise she was terrified that she would faint. It turned out that the street had the personal meaning of sexual temptation, being a place where she might be picked up by a man. Her phobia constituted a defense against this danger, but if she went out accompanied by a relative she could safely enjoy erotic fantasies whenever an attractive man passed by.[2]

This analysis of the sources or materials out of which neurotic symptoms are made constitutes a first step in the search for lawfulness. The process of symptom formation is tremendously complicated by individual associations and personal meanings. It is necessary to know that for one patient the act of seeing is directly connected with the existing

[1] T. A. Ross, *The Common Neuroses* (2d ed.; Baltimore: Wm. Wood & Co., 1937), especially chaps. iv–vi.

[2] This case is reported by F. Alexander in *Psychoanalysis of the Total Personality* (New York: Nervous & Mental Disease Publishing Co., 1930), pp. 60 ff.

threat, and that for another the sexual fantasies have become channeled into the idea of being picked up on the street. But behind all this personal coloring it is usually possible to discern that the symptoms are offshoots of the nuclear neurotic process: portions of the anxiety reaction, portions of the defense, or expressions of the anxiety-linked impulses.

Primary Gain and Secondary Gain. Although they are made of these primitive materials and primarily serve the purpose of carrying on the struggle to control anxiety, neurotic symptoms sometimes seem designed to achieve certain effects on the environment. One of the most common results of symptom production is that the patient enters the status of a sick person rather than a nervous or foolish or irritating or selfish one. He may now be excused from work and receive sympathy and service from the household. If on dangerous military duty, he may be sent back to a position of safety or even honorably discharged. Adler was particularly fond of pointing out these gains from illness, as we saw when discussing neurotic invalidism. Perhaps a need to dominate is served by the symptom: fear of going on the street forces some member of the household to accompany the patient at the latter's pleasure. Perhaps aggressive tendencies are satisfied: failure to perform the sexual act satisfactorily serves to disappoint and frustrate the partner. Thus in various ways the symptoms seem to have a certain strategic value, bettering the patient's external situation and providing scope for the satisfaction of thwarted needs.

It is by no means true that neurotic symptoms always serve a strategic purpose of this kind. They are quite as likely to cause the patient nothing but suffering, and to put him at a disadvantage in his adjustment to the world. Symptoms that bring no external advantages remind us that the primary forces involved in symptom formation are internal. The struggle with heightened anxiety is the focus; effects on the environment have a secondary character. To make this distinction explicit, Freud introduced the notion of *secondary gain.* The primary process in symptom formation is simply the nuclear neurotic process, sharply intensified by the breakdown of protective organization or by sudden external danger. The symptoms appear—one might say that they are pushed into existence—as part of the struggle between anxiety and the regressed or primitive defensive processes. The *primary gain* derived from them is the increased control of anxiety. In contrast, *secondary gain* consists of whatever advantages are found to accrue from the fact of having symptoms: gains from illness and other effects on the patient's environment.

Logically the distinction between primary gain and secondary gain can be drawn sharply. Secondary gain has no part in producing the symptoms in the first place. The patient does not develop symptoms in order to enjoy these advantages, any more than a maimed war veteran, to borrow Freud's illustration, "has his leg shot away only that he may thereafter live in indolence on his pension."[3] It is undoubtedly an aid to clear thinking to draw this sharp logical distinction, but we must immediately follow Freud in admitting that the line becomes badly blurred when we study actual cases. Anticipations of the effect a symptom will have on the environment sometimes enter into the primary process whereby the symptom is formed. This is particularly true of hysterical symptoms. We suspected it to be true in the case of the man who became blind on his way to see his wife and newborn child. Logically speaking, the primary process in his case would be the direct inhibition of vision, preventing him from seeing the child who signified his permanent imprisonment in marriage. Secondary gain would come from the fact that, as a blind man, he could honorably seek divorce rather than being a burden on his wife. Can we say that anticipations of this secondary gain played no part in producing the symptom? Much the same doubts arise in connection with war neuroses. Hysterical symptoms that began under combat stress were sometimes preceded by a half-conscious wish to sustain some injury that would result in withdrawal from danger. In actual practice, then, the logical distinction between primary gain and secondary gain cannot be sharply maintained.

It is hard to talk about symptoms, especially when we are thinking about secondary gain, without making their formation sound like a conscious and volitional process. The production of a neurotic symptom is in no sense to be conceived as consciously planned strategy. Symptoms are manufactured to avert impending panic. If a certain foresight of secondary gain creeps into the process, it is involuntary, unconscious, and never half as sensible as a rational plan would be. The man who became blind and hoped to use this as an excuse for dissolving his marriage could certainly have thought of some better way to deal with his problems if he had been sufficiently free from anxiety to engage in rational planning. When symptoms and ailments are consciously feigned, we do not speak of neurosis but of *malingering*. It is not very difficult in practice to differentiate between the two.

Classification of Symptom Syndromes. Observers have always been impressed by certain natural groupings among the symptoms of neurosis. There appear to be three nodal points: *anxiety states, obsessional neurosis,* and *hysteria.* Almost every attempt at classification acknowledges these three very general categories. Mixed forms sometimes occur: in particular, anxiety states at one period may give place to obsessional

[3] S. Freud, *The Problem of Anxiety* (New York: W. W. Norton & Co., Inc., 1936), p. 33.

conditions or hysterical symptoms at another. In the majority of cases, however, the symptoms cluster within one of the three main categories. It almost never happens that a hysteria turns into an obsessional neurosis or vice versa, and some patients persistently have anxiety attacks without any further elaboration of symptoms.

Apart from these three nodal points, the classification of neurotic symptoms is a matter of endless dispute. A good example of the confusion is afforded by *phobias.* Janet began the practice of classifying them with obsessions. He found them associated with obsessions more often than with hysteria. This led him to the hypothesis of an underlying nervous weakness, *psychasthenia,* which was the root cause of both phobias and obsessions. The Freudian school took an entirely different tack with regard to phobias. Freud believed them akin to hysteria because of an assumed underlying similarity in the basic conflict and the point in libidinal development to which the patient regressed. He gave phobias semi-independent status, however, with the designation *anxiety hysteria.* Both Janet's concept of psychasthenia and Freud's concept of anxiety hysteria are still widely used. The disagreement between them lies in the realm of theory and interpretation rather than bare clinical fact. Phobias occur in patients with obsessions, as Janet observed, but they are not unknown in hysteria and in patients who otherwise have only anxiety attacks. In such a situation it is wiser to give up the attempt at classification and simply try to understand phobias in their own right. The important thing is to study the crucial processes of anxiety and defense.

The divisions used in the rest of this chapter recognize the three nodal points already mentioned: anxiety states, obsessional neurosis, hysteria. They acknowledge the difficulty of classifying phobias by simply leaving them with their own heading. For convenient exposition we shall separate from the main body of hysteria those symptoms that take a more "mental" form—amnesias, fugues, and multiple personalities—in contrast to the "bodily" symptoms such as paralyses and anaesthesias. These *dissociated conditions* repay a study that is out of proportion to their frequency because they often reveal the process of symptom formation with transparent simplicity. They are not sufficiently different from the rest of hysteria to warrant separation on any other ground.

ANXIETY STATES

On first thought, it might seem that anxiety states constitute a refutation of the whole anxiety theory of neurosis. If a neurosis, with all its elaboration and all its cost to the personality, comes into existence to prevent anxiety, how can one of its symptoms be the very anxiety it is supposed to prevent? This apparent dilemma vanishes if we realize that neurotic protective organization is not necessarily invulnerable. A neurosis can be unsuccessful, with the result that anxiety breaks through all defenses and appears in its undisguised form as fear bordering on panic.

Partial Failure of Defenses. Anxiety attacks can be considered to represent a partial failure of adequate defenses. Even in the face of highly disquieting fear, the patient does not produce defenses sufficient to bind and suppress his fear. The situation is not, however, equivalent to a total collapse with regression to the condition of a terrified child. Such collapse and regression were sometimes seen in men who were exposed to prolonged severe combat stress.[4] They bear little resemblance to the anxiety states that occur in civilian neuroses. These take a less sweeping form: the patient is panic-stricken but not disintegrated; from time to time he is flooded by terror, but he struggles with it, brings it somehow under control, resumes his daily life until another attack breaks through, gets himself to a doctor's office if the attacks continue. The anxiety attacks are temporary eruptions of panic. Defenses are insufficient to prevent the eruptions, but the person fights them and stamps them down.

It is characteristic that the patient is not aware of any reason for his terror. He may feel that he is going insane, that he is trapped amidst dangerous forces, or that something dreadful but unnameable is going to happen. The diffuseness and indefiniteness of the danger are the most trying features of the attack. The cartoonist Steig represents this by drawing a little gesticulating demon on the end of a stick attached to the back of a person's head—whichever way the victim turns, the demon is out there behind him, never in sight.[5] This circumstance indicates that part of the defense is being maintained. Repression still effectively prevents the patient from remembering the childhood danger situations or from becoming aware of the danger-linked impulses in himself. It is, then, only the anxiety that escapes from control and breaks through the defenses. Even at their worst, anxiety attacks represent only a partial failure of defenses. Neither the primitive defenses of childhood nor the adult protective organization give way completely.

An Illustrative Case. In order to make our description concrete we shall summarize a case reported by H. V. Dicks.[6] A man of forty came for treatment on account of severe anxiety attacks characterized especially by fear of enclosed places, difficulty in breathing (especially at night),

[4] For examples see W. McDougall, *Outline of Abnormal Psychology* (New York: Chas. Scribner's Sons, 1926), pp. 285–92, and R. R. Grinker and J. P. Spiegel, *War Neuroses* (Philadelphia: The Blakiston Co., 1945), pp. 4–14.

[5] W. Steig, *About People* (New York: Random House, Inc., 1939), drawing entitled "Anxiety," p. 105.

[6] H. V. Dicks, *Clinical Studies in Psychopathology* (Baltimore: Wm. Wood & Co., 1939), pp. 27–28.

and a most unpleasant sense of impending disaster. He had always been contemptuous of psychology and sought the aid of a psychiatrist only as a desperate last resort. He had just resigned after a distinguished career in the Government service. Considering the Government's policy too liberal, he made his resignation a matter of principle. He was living at home and considering starting out as a novice in a new profession when the anxiety attacks began to overwhelm him.

Working back through his career it was discovered that he had had some earlier bouts with anxiety. The most recent occasion was at the time of demobilization following World War I, in which he served as battalion commander and was decorated at a very early age. This circumstance well illustrates the lack of relation between neurotic anxiety and real danger: it was when demobilized and safe that the patient had attacks of anxiety. Previous to these attacks he had had another round of trouble when he entered college as a freshman. For a while he could not sit in lectures; if he went at all he took a seat next to the door so that he could leave at any time. Before this there was one attack at the age of seven when he had to sit through a church service under dimly lighted Gothic arches. Various anxieties connected with the Oedipus situation were uncovered, but they showed few links with the contents of his anxiety attacks. Finally the chain of incidents was completed by the patient's recalling a scene that took place in infancy when he had an attack of bronchial pneumonia. He was lying in a cot, coughing and nearly suffocating, in acute panic but at the same time furiously angry with his mother, who stood by unable to relieve his distress. The images included a tent over his cot and various other details. From outside sources it was possible to verify that he had had bronchial pneumonia at the age of eighteen months, and that a tent over the bed was one of the measures used for treatment.

The form of the patient's anxiety attacks—the breathing difficulty and fear of enclosures—was apparently set by this nuclear panic. His attack in church would seem to have been stimulated by the heavy arches (reminding him of the tent) and the necessity to sit still (helpless restraint). But we can understand his later attacks, especially the ones that sent him for treatment, only if we know something about the development of his personality. The patient was the eldest son and also the eldest of his circle of cousins. His parents encouraged him strongly to take the role of a big boy. He successfully assumed this role, becoming proud and markedly independent. Identifying himself with authority and the moral code, he emerged as the leader and disciplinarian of his younger relatives. This pattern was continued in school, won again in college, given much scope when he served as an army officer, and carried on while he was in the Government service. He became an energetic and successful man with a strong need for superiority. One can discern, however, that his career had something of the overdriven quality that characterizes a neurotic protective organization. It was when activity, success, and superiority were blocked that he gave way to anxiety attacks: when he lost his school distinction and became a "nobody" at college; when he lost his military distinction and became a "nobody" at demobilization; when he lost his distinction as a Government official and became a "nobody" without a vocation.

This case illustrates the early establishment of a neurotic nucleus as the result of one tremendously frightening experience. We may presume that this incident was reinforced by other frights, but its determinative significance is shown by the way it colored the symptom picture nearly forty years later. The incident involved not only terror but the frustration of dependence on the mother and anger at this frustration. As the patient's personality developed, it was encouraged to take a form that happened to serve admirably as a means of counteracting his neurotic liability. His pattern emphasized independence (rejecting the useless dependent longings), activity (preventing a passive state of helplessness), and power (the opposite of being unable to influence his mother). These strivings were effective, yielded gratification, and led to a constructive life. There was only one flaw: when they were all blocked, so that he was reduced to the status of a "nobody," he developed not just the frustration that anyone might feel under such circumstances, but more than that—acute anxiety attacks. The flaw was a small one. If circumstances had permitted him to advance steadily as a Government official, having his own way and directing others until he became at last a respected elder statesman, his attacks at demobilization might have been the last and he would have been counted a well-adjusted man.

Problem of the Choice of Symptoms. When it is possible to work out the history of a case with the fullness and coherence of the one just studied, one feels as if one had reached an explanation of the patient's neurosis. The patient's own sense of certainty often strengthens such a feeling, and a successful therapeutic result still further fortifies one's confidence in the historical reconstruction. But the phenomenon has been explained only in a very limited sense. Even granting that the reconstruction is flawless, which may be far from true, the patient's neurosis has been explained only in the sense that one event has been related to another in an intelligible sequence and that the whole thing has been envisaged as a compromise between the growing personality and its need for security. What have not been explained are the things that did not happen. Why did the patient develop no phobias to keep him from getting into the crucial situation of being a "nobody"? Why did he develop no delusions of grandeur to help him through such situations? One can easily think of various neurotic devices that seem to fit the circumstances well enough. These ways of dealing with his problems were not chosen by the patient. Phobias and delusions seem not to have been available to him. In order to have a full explanation of the case, we would need to be able to state why certain alternative solutions were not available.

The problem thus raised is generally referred to as the problem of the choice of neurosis. Let us admit from the start that expressions such as "choice of neurosis" and "choice of symptoms" are singularly unhappy, suggesting as they do a conscious and volitional process of choice. The production of neurotic symptoms is of course not in the least a conscious act. The central question still exists, however, and can be phrased as follows: how does it come about that the patient develops just this kind of neurotic symptoms rather than some other kind? Why hysteria rather than obsessional neurosis? Why anxiety attacks rather than hysteria? Then, pressing the question into a narrower focus, why hysteria in the form of blindness rather than in the form of deafness? A general discussion of this problem is more appropriate at the end of the chapter when our description of the common symptom syndromes is complete. The question is raised at this point simply to call attention to something that is easily overlooked in attempting to understand the lawfulness of neurotic symptom formation.

PHOBIAS

A phobia can be defined as a morbid dread of an object, act, or situation. The word "morbid" differentiates it from a normal fear, and is inserted to indicate that we speak of phobia only when the thing that is feared offers no actual danger. When a patient shows great fear of something that is in fact perfectly harmless, we have to assume that the real threat lies somewhere else. The phobic object is serving as a symbol or a distant reminder of some danger that is extremely real to the patient, even though its origin may have been in childhood.

Phobias cannot readily be classified. They have sometimes been named according to the object or situation that is feared. At one time medical writers favored attaching Greek prefixes to indicate every possible object of morbid dread. A few of these fancy names, such as claustrophobia (morbid dread of closed or constricted spaces), have become harmlessly lodged in the scientific vocabulary. In older medical literature there were literally hundreds of them: for instance, melissophobia (morbid dread of bees), gephyrophobia (morbid dread of crossing water), parthenophobia (morbid dread of virgins), homilophobia (morbid dread of sermons). The list becomes endless because there is really nothing that cannot be an object of morbid dread. Lest the reader become a victim of onomatophobia (morbid dread of names), he should be assured that this pretentious vocabulary is now largely obsolete.

Phobia as a Defense. If a phobic patient comes in contact with the object of his fear, he is thrown into a severe anxiety attack. To this extent phobias resemble anxiety states; there is at times a break-through of panic. The phobia, however, offers one great advantage over diffuse anxiety. The patient can arrange to avoid contact with his phobic object. It is impossible to escape from danger when it is felt to be everywhere around you. The focusing of danger upon a single external object or situation immediately restores the possibility of constructive action, even if this consists of no more than keeping away from the threat.

The dynamics of phobia are neatly illustrated in the following incident.[7] A boy of ten, who suffered from various neurotic difficulties, was brought for treatment to a child guidance clinic. Mother and child sat close together in the waiting room until the boy was asked to go into the psychiatrist's office while the mother went elsewhere to talk to the social worker. After a visible attempt at self-control, the boy began to cry, saying, "I'm just scared and I don't know what it is." Plainly he was experiencing diffuse anxiety at separation from his mother and at being in a strange room with an as yet strange man. After a while the child spied a brief case and said, suspiciously, "What's in that—what's behind it?" It was suggested that he go and investigate, which he did while muttering, "Maybe there is a gun." Discovery that the brief case held no threatening contents made it possible for the young patient to smile and relax for the first time. It is quite clear that localizing the fear on a definite object constituted a step in overcoming his anxiety. It restored his mobility; instead of remaining frozen to his chair, he became free to avoid the brief case or to investigate it. His choice of the second alternative completed the overcoming of his fear.

Channels of Displacement. The mechanism at work in the formation of phobias is displacement. Anxiety is displaced in order to find a less terrifying and more avoidable object. It makes one feel less helpless to be afraid of a brief case than to be just plain afraid. Displacement is particularly serviceable when the source of danger is an impulse or need that has been linked with anxiety in childhood history. There is no escape from an internal impulse or need, but if the fear can be localized on an outside object the chances of avoidance seem much better. Displacement must be presumed to occur along associative channels. We

[7] F. H. Allen, *Psychotherapy with Children* (New York: W. W. Norton & Co., Inc., 1942), pp. 169–71.

examined the general operation of this process when studying Diven's experiment.[8] Associative connections served as effective guides for generalization, even when the subject was unaware of the whole process. Going back to an example used earlier in this chapter—the woman who was afraid to go alone on the street lest she faint—it is easy to see that sexual desires and the idea of finding a partner on the street might have been linked together in half-conscious revery or in dreams forgotten upon awakening. Links of this kind are constantly recovered during psychoanalytic treatment. Associative channels are thus prepared which serve as avenues for displacement when sexual pressure increases and its associated anxiety and guilt threaten to overwhelm the patient. So far as the patient's awareness is concerned, she knows only that she feels suddenly faint on the street. It is most frightening, so she does not run the risk of going on the street again.

Phobias are only partially explained, however, by pointing out the general fact of channeling along associative lines. They are not fully explained even when we allow for very personal meanings and even symbolisms that are peculiar to the individual patient. Just as in normal thinking we call up ideas that are relevant and appropriate to our present need, so the phobic patient fastens upon associations that neatly substitute for his real source of threat. If a phobic patient had been terrified by something that happened in a barn, he would not, in a fashion analogous to Diven's normal subjects, become vaguely uneasy about everything rural. He would come down hard on a single item, such as hay. Panic would seize him at the sight or smell of hay. This would keep him out of barns and out of the country without constantly making him think of barns. The whole trouble would be safely concentrated on hay.

A remarkable example of the process of displacement is to be found in Freud's case of the five-year-old boy, Hans.[9] This case was an important milestone, not only for its demonstration of childhood sexual interests, but also for its untangling of the roundabout lines of association that made a path from nuclear fear to phobic symptom. The child was in the midst of the Oedipus conflict, and his nuclear fear was of the angry punishment he anticipated from his father because of his possessive feelings and actions toward his mother. His fear did not present itself in this form, but rather in the form of a phobia of horses on the street. This was an avoidable threat, whereas the father could not be avoided. The connecting lines passed through all kinds of childhood scenes, fantasies, and ruminations. Hans played with his father, who pretended to be a horse; he saw a horse with a black muzzle that reminded him of his

[8] See above, pages 200–202.

[9] S. Freud, "Analysis of a Phobia in a Five-Year-Old Boy" (1909), reprinted in *Collected Papers* (New York: Basic Books, Inc., 1959), Vol. III, pp. 149–289.

father's mustache; he played with other children, pretending that he was a horse, and fell down in the course of the play; he saw a horse fall down and struggle with its feet. All these and many other elements entered the associative tissue, until at last he was in panic at seeing horses on the street and hearing the sound of their feet. With the achievement of this symptom he was no longer afraid of his father.

Expansion of the Phobic System. From what has been said it might seem that the formation of a phobia was an ideal solution to all problems of neurotic anxiety. It would indeed be a perfect scheme if the phobia could only be prevented from expanding. Internal dangers, especially those linked with strong recurrent needs, will not let the patient off so easily. The danger continues to be present. The patient avoids the phobic situation but cannot thus achieve full peace of mind. Before long some other situation is felt to be dangerous, and the patient has two phobias. In the end he has had to keep employing his phobic mechanism so extensively that he is back in the state of being more or less afraid of everything.

Not all phobias expand indefinitely. Sometimes a phobic system becomes stabilized and serves fairly well as an enduring defense. The tendency to expand, however, is a very natural consequence of the displaced or substitutive character of the phobic symptom. Avoiding the phobic object does not usually mean taking any effective action against the real threat. The fundamental problem remains unsolved and the phobic mechanism does not really bind the anxiety.

Ross describes a case in which a man became phobic for the number 13.[10] The real fear proved to be that he would recall some juvenile sexual escapades with a superstitious maid who believed in the bad luck associated with 13. This chapter in his history had been repressed as his personality developed along lines of superiority and morality. The case illustrates particularly well the expansion of a phobia. The patient began by staying in bed on the thirteenth day of the month so that he would not come in contact with calendars and newspaper dates. Soon he discovered that "twenty-seventh" contained thirteen letters, and he was condemned to bed two days each month. He next began going to work by a roundabout route to avoid the thirteen-letter sign, "Peter Robinson," that hung prominently on the direct route. Presently he experienced uneasiness when people said, "Oh, good morning," or when they said, "Good afternoon" without the "Oh" that would have given the greeting a safe fifteen letters. He began hopping over the thirteenth step in a flight, counting his own footsteps, counting the streets he passed,

[10] Ross, *op. cit.*, pp. 219–23.

until finally he had time for nothing but avoiding the number thirteen. One laughs over the case, but the patient was not fencing with will-o'-the-wisps. His phobic defenses later broke down. He remembered the sexual adventures and became exposed to deep sources of anxiety. As a result he was for some weeks deeply depressed and dangerously suicidal. His recovery from this still worse state occurred at the cost of reinstating a good part of the phobia.

School Phobia. Recently there has been a good deal of interest in a problem known as school phobia. This is a disorder that develops out of the anxiety often felt by children when they start to go to school. That going to school awakens anxiety is easy to understand; the child must endure separation from his mother and immersion in an unfamiliar world where he is but one of many who claim the teacher's attention. This common anxiety can be said to have evolved into a phobia when, instead of wearing off in the course of time, it increases to the point of panic. The child becomes unable to remain at school without the mother's constant presence, or he wakes up in the morning with pain and nausea that expresses his dread of going at all. Often the parents and the school authorities, fearing the consequences of panic, agree to postpone school attendance for the time being; but things may go no better when the attempt is resumed.

It is technically correct to call this a phobia because it involves a displacement of anxiety to an outside object. Fear may become attached to "the teacher, the other children, the janitor, eating in the lunchroom, or almost any detail of school life. . . . When we trace the anxiety to its source, it is invariably found to originate in the child's fear of being separated from his mother."[11] This fear is transparently present when the child will go only if the mother accompanies him and stays in sight throughout the school day. We are led at once to the expectation that school phobia will occur when the child is already highly dependent on the mother and has built up little faith in his own competence. Clinical investigation shows that this is the case; but it shows also, in accord with an interactive interpretation of parent-child relations, that the dependence is not wholly on the child's side. On the basis of a strong affection coupled with a good deal of doubt about her maternal competence, the mother identifies with her offspring, tends to be overprotective, and makes herself unnecessarily subservient to the child's needs and whims. The child comes to have a certain power over the mother, but his "parasitic clinging is resented by the mother as it impinges on her

[11] S. Waldfogel, J. C. Coolidge, and P. B. Hahn, "The Development, Meaning and Management of School Phobia," *American Journal of Orthopsychiatry*, XXVII (1957), pp. 754–80.

own freedom of movement. . . . The child responds as well to the rejection he can sense as to the indulgence in which he luxuriates."[12]

In this entangling relationship, separation is felt to be dangerous by the mother as well as the child. The situation is complicated by the mother's unwitting communication of her anxiety. Her verbal reassurances may be given in a quavering voice, accompanied by tremulous gestures. The child may readily pick up these cues and, just as unwittingly, exploit the mother's dread to escape from his own. School phobia thus represents the historic French conception of *folie à deux,* a disorder that is created out of the interaction between two people.

OBSESSIONAL NEUROSIS

There are two names for the symptom syndrome to which we now turn our attention. Some workers prefer the designation *obsessional neurosis,* others prefer *compulsion neurosis.* Sometimes it is proposed to subdivide the syndrome into conditions dominated by obsessional thoughts and conditions in which compulsive actions predominate. The underlying processes are probably too similar to justify the separation.

Characteristics of the Symptoms. An obsession is an idea or desire which forces itself persistently into the patient's mind in what he experiences as an irrational fashion. A compulsion is an act actually carried out, which similarly forces itself upon the patient. Obsessive ideas and compulsive acts are often closely linked: for instance, the obsession that there may be dangerous germs on one's hands leads to the compulsion of handwashing. Minor obsessions and compulsions are familiar in everyone's experience. We keep wondering whether we turned off the gas burner, or we knock on wood after mentioning our good fortune. These everyday phenomena resemble neurotic obsessions and compulsions to the extent that they are sensed as irrational. We know they are foolish, but they seem to have a little push of their own and it is easier to let them have their way. In neurotic obsessions and compulsions, this quality is greatly magnified. The ideas and acts are like foreign bodies, forcing themselves upon the patient yet experienced as no part of the self. Moreover, they often betray that they are working in the service of defense. If the patient tries to stop his obsessive ruminations or his compulsive rituals, he is plunged into an attack of anxiety.

Obsessional symptoms occur in great variety. The patient's mind may be full of thoughts about infection and disease, making it necessary for him to wash his hands a hundred times a day and to take precautions that would put a modern hospital to shame. He may have rituals in

[12] L. Eisenberg, "School Phobia: A Study in the Communication of Anxiety," *American Journal of Psychiatry,* CXIV (1958), pp. 712–18.

regard to dressing or going to bed which make these actions laborious and time-consuming. He may be troubled by intrusive blasphemous thoughts when he is trying to concentrate on his prayers. Orderliness may become the demon in his life, committing him to an endless task of straightening, arranging, recording, and filing. Particularly trying are obsessions concerning harmful and violent acts: the patient is invaded by ideas of burning the house down, cutting his wife's throat, strangling his children, throwing himself in front of a truck. The danger that such acts will be carried out is small to the vanishing point, but the patient has no feeling of control over them and constantly fears that he will turn them into realities. The lives of obsessional patients are easily reduced to ineffectiveness and misery. Their energies are tied up in symptoms, and they are filled with doubt, vacillation, uneasiness, and helplessness. Occasionally an attack of anxiety breaks through.

Close scrutiny of the contents of obsessive symptoms shows that they can be classified under two headings: (1) Part of the symptoms give expression to aggressive and sexual impulses. Murderous hostility, destructiveness, dirtiness, and sexual urges in a crude and violent form reveal themselves in the content of obsessional thoughts. It is as if the suppressed *antisocial impulses* returned in this guise to plague the patient. (2) The rest of the symptoms give expression to *self-corrective tendencies.* Orderliness, rituals, cleanliness, propitiatory acts, self-imposed duties, and punishments all testify to the patient's need to counteract and set right his antisocial tendencies. Guilt feelings are his almost constant companions. Perhaps he reads in the paper about a murder that was committed many miles away. So strong is his guilt that he becomes obsessed with the idea that he committed the murder and deserves terrible punishment. The division of the symptoms into these two classes, *antisocial impulses* and *self-corrective tendencies,* gives an immediate insight into the nature of the underlying conflict. Nowhere is the Freudian concept of the super-ego more applicable. The childish conception of evil joins battle with the childish conception of righteousness and punishment.

Obsessional symptoms sometimes have a sudden onset, but very often they make their appearance gradually. In this neurosis it is not easy to draw the line between focal symptoms and a gradually developed protective organization. When the symptoms develop gradually, it is almost always the self-corrective ones that make the first appearance. The symptom picture is first occupied by derivatives of the defensive process. Only later do signs of the anxiety-linked impulses creep into the scene.

Distinctive Features of Obsessional Neurosis. Although the obsessional syndrome frequently overlaps with others, especially with phobias, it has a number of characteristics which roughly differentiate it from the other patterns.

1. The elements of the underlying conflict are more fully represented in consciousness than is the case in any other neurotic syndrome. The antisocial tendencies and the self-punitive tendencies can be read in the patient's obsessions and compulsions. The representation in consciousness is of course somewhat peculiar, falling far short of a frank recognition of one's tendencies. There is much symbolizing and disguising, and in any event the patient does not experience the tendencies as a part of his ego. They have a peculiar status. The patient knows that his obsessions and compulsions are inside him; he does not use projection and attribute them to external forces. Yet they feel to him like foreign bodies, not part of the tissue of the self. They intrude themselves from unknown parts of his mind. Apparently the mechanism of repression plays a less drastic part in obsessional neurosis. Its place is taken by this semi-detachment of the impulses from the self.

2. Secondary defenses are very highly developed. The struggle between anxiety-linked impulses and defensive processes is carried on in the realm of intellect. In this realm it is possible to make an extensive use of displacement. The patient finds himself ruminating on the philosophical implications of the dichotomy between love and hate rather than perceiving that he has certain hateful impulses toward someone he loves. The treatment of obsessional patients is often badly delayed by this tendency. The patient raises theoretical objections to the physician's way of conducting the treatment and tries to get into a long argument on basic assumptions.

3. Overt anxiety is moderately well avoided. There is an undercurrent of uneasiness, but acute anxiety attacks are infrequent. Obsessional neurosis is not as successful as hysteria, however, in doing away with anxiety.

4. It seems generally agreed that aggressive impulses occupy an unusually large place in the obsessional patient's basic conflicts. Sexuality is by no means excluded, but hostility is so predominant that it may be considered the central issue.

5. Certain character traits appear to be particularly common among obsessional patients. These patients seem to favor a certain pattern of protections. Generally they show a great interest in orderliness and cleanliness, which they carry to extremes. They are also conscientious and idealistic; they want to be never angry, always kind and considerate of others. All of these traits are socially desirable if not carried to extreme lengths, but their force in the patients suggests a strong reaction formation against aggressive, destructive, messy tendencies. Two other traits often appear in the pattern: stubbornness and stinginess. For all

their idealistic outlook the patients do not want to be hurried or directed, and they hate to have others make demands on them. The whole pattern of traits suggests that the crucial childhood difficulties had to do with autonomy and discipline—with the problem of submitting to adult demands and coping with the anger that resulted from parental interference. In the Freudian scheme this pattern is taken to indicate fixation at the anal stage of libidinal development.

Example of the Mechanisms of Isolation and Undoing. It is hard to convey the degree to which the obsessive patient's actions and thought processes become clogged unless we use an actual illustration.[13] A boy of seventeen had severe conflict over masturbation. His pastor gave a talk denouncing the practice, and advised that one should never associate with a boy who masturbated. The patient knew a boy who masturbated, and he now found it difficult to keep away from him. But when he passed him on the street he felt distinctly uneasy. The first symptom was a little ritual consisting of turning around and spitting whenever he passed the wicked boy. This is a perfect example of *undoing:* the patient cleansed himself and expressed rejection immediately after permitting the danger of contact. The symptom was insufficient, however, to deal with the anxiety generated by these threatened contacts, and the next defensive strategy was a phobia. The patient had a morbid dread of meeting the bad boy, avoiding the possibility as much as possible. The phobic system soon began to expand until it included the whole section of the city in which the other boy lived. The patient made a compulsive stipulation that no member of his own family should enter that section.

From this point the symptoms invaded his thinking more and more fully. A severe obsessional neurosis took the place of the phobias. The patient found himself thinking about the forbidden section of the city. Even this contact in thought had to be prevented. He developed an elaborate technique of *isolation:* he would stand still and fix upon an image of the forbidden region until the image was bereft of all meaningful connections and stood all alone in his mind. To effect one of these isolations took quite a while, often as much as an hour. Before long he was dividing the whole world into good and bad, which increased the scope of his isolations. Even language fell into the two categories, so that he had to choose carefully lest a good and bad word make contact by being in the same sentence. The whole thing became so laborious that he deliberately thought about the forbidden things in order to strengthen the images and make their isolation easier. Thus the anxiety-linked impulses crept stealthily back into the symptoms.

[13] O. Fenichel, *Outline of Clinical Psychoanalysis* (New York: W. W. Norton & Co., Inc., 1934), pp. 160–64.

This excerpt from a case history has been given only to illustrate the mechanisms of undoing and isolation and the general blocking of normal thought processes that occur in obsessive patients. The reason for his extreme anxiety on the subject of masturbation must be assumed to lie somewhere in the boy's childhood history. We shall now examine a longer excerpt from another history in order to show the neurotic process in relation to the whole development of personality and to specific crises occurring in the course of life.

An Illustrative Case: Peter Oberman. Peter Oberman had the misfortune to lose his faith in both of his parents at about the same time. While small he enjoyed his mother's affectionate and watchful care and the week-end visits of his father, who was a traveling salesman. Growing independence soon taught him to regard his mother as an object of contempt. She was an extremely timid woman who felt the world to be a dangerous place in which one must be constantly on guard against sickness, injury, accidents, and kidnappers. She constantly restrained him with images of danger, and as he became an active boy of eleven he resented the resulting overprotection. With a boy across the street he began to study electricity and radio. His mother, who greatly feared electricity, expressed her apprehension, and this was the last straw for Peter. He saw the full absurdity of her timid ways and began to treat her as a fool.

At this juncture his father changed jobs and was at home a great deal. He interested himself in his son's affairs with which he seriously interfered. Very close with his money, he would occasionally buy expensive presents for which he would expect the deepest gratitude, but they were never the right presents. When Peter wanted a photography set, his father got him a pool table; when he wanted a bicycle, he was given a moving-picture outfit. His father deplored his taste in radio programs and forbade him to listen. If Peter came home a minute later than the expected time, he had to brace himself for a veritable tirade. He was terrified, and he could see that his mother also was terrified by his father's insistence and anger. Furious at the domestic dictatorship, he never quite dared to resist it. At length things came to a more severe crisis. He frequently saw his mother in tears, comforted by his grandfather. The father had fallen in love with another woman and was spending nights away from home. Peter's emotions were deeply involved in the tangle; he swore at his father and used obscene language about the other woman. The father, now harboring some guilt feelings of his own, would stalk away in silence.

Both of Peter's identification figures thus crumbled into the dust of his contempt. From neither could he expect esteem or really considerate love. He turned to his grandfather, lately a widower, who occupied the apartment upstairs. The lonely old man responded warmly, and soon there was an active sharing of interests. The grandfather, a scholarly man, was an ardent admirer of Marx and the doctrine of economic determinism. He and Peter followed with intense interest the progress of the war in Spain. The grandfather bestowed much affection and praise, and at the same time inspired the eleven-year-old boy with ideas about science and the social order which must have been somewhat beyond his understanding.

Since he had rejected his mother and his father, since the atmosphere at home was completely intolerable, it became for Peter Oberman an overwhelmingly important matter not to lose his grandfather. The old man had suddenly become his only source of reliable affection. The idea of losing him aroused a desperate anxiety. But he was old; like the grandmother, he might die. Peter began to be visited by anxious thoughts which seemed to force themselves into his mind. He had images of the house catching fire; he was afraid it would be struck by lightning or shattered in a high wind. He thought of various ways in which harm might come to his grandfather, and then he began to develop symptoms which had the character of magical acts designed to prevent this catastrophe. If the thought crossed his mind that the house might burn, he felt compelled to touch something in order to avert the danger. If he had such a thought while stepping on a crack, he had to step on the crack again to cancel the thought. Soon he needed to perform extra touchings for good measure, and sometimes he would spend nearly an hour going through one of these operations. When people began to notice his peculiar behavior, he developed a technique for discharging all the unlucky thoughts of the day in the privacy of his bedroom at night. If he pointed four times (a lucky number) to the southwest (a lucky direction), he could counteract the danger. But he never felt satisfied. He had to point $4 \times 4 \times 4 \times 4$ times, 256 times, and this took half an hour. He invented short cuts like stamping his foot to stand for groups of numbers, but in the end no time was saved. If the ritual could not be completed, he felt absolutely miserable. He was at the mercy of *obsessive thoughts* and *compulsive actions,* all of which had the significance of *undoing* the harm contained in a destructive thought.

It may seem paradoxical that Peter should entertain destructive thoughts that included his grandfather, the very source of his remaining security. It becomes less strange when we consider the circumstances from the point of view of an eleven-year-old boy whose faith in his father and mother has lately been shattered. He well knew that his father could show loving affection, yet quickly withdraw it and let him down. He well knew that his grandfather represented in a sense a false security, because he was old and would presently die. The trouble was that he needed love so badly that he could not resist the grandfather's affectionate interest, yet it was a restraint, an unwelcome restraint, for an eleven-year-old boy to spend so much time with an old man and hear him talk endlessly about barely comprehensible subjects. Though for the most part he could not stand the thought of his grandfather's dying, there were times when part of him secretly desired this event.

When Peter was twelve his grandfather did die. The fatal ailment was attributed by relatives to distress over the father's love affair—a further proof of the father's power to destroy Peter's happiness. Peter's grief was uncontrollable. His tearfulness lasted for several months, and his digestion was badly upset. He wanted to preserve his grandfather's apartment just as it was, and when this proved impossible he photographed every room from every angle, not even omitting the toilet, keeping the negatives locked up where no harm could befall them. He began a diary in which was recorded every incident that in any way reminded him of his lost protector. But his feeling of weakness and helplessness was now so great that he required more far-reaching reassurance. His maturing intellectual powers seized upon ideas received from his grandfather and developed the notion of a universal determinism, the understanding of which would give him complete control over everything. He dedicated his life to the laws of the electron and the atom, which he conceived as universal laws applicable to society and man as well as nature; his grandfather had already schooled him in economic determinism. Then he began to draw up life plans for himself, listing his liabilities and assets, taking hours to get every detail in perfect order. At fourteen he read Einstein, believing that if he could understand this great man he could understand anything.

This turn of events represents the launching of an overdriven striving. To restore some measure of confidence in himself, he developed a compensatory striving for superiority in the special form of omniscience. Through understanding, through familiarity with the basic laws of nature, he was going to control everything, including his father and his own tempestuous emotions. That a boy with superior intellectual gifts should become interested in philosophy between twelve and fourteen and should be attracted by sweeping generalizations is not in itself extraordinary. In Peter's case, however, curiosity was a secondary motive; he was using philosophy to compensate himself for a feeling of weakness, to make himself feel masterful and omnipotent. His preoccupation with ideas and future plans was more than a natural unfolding of real powers; it was a desperate measure designed to avert anxiety. As a result he overdid it, set his goals too high, and spent fruitless hours struggling to work out an unchallengeable system of truth. It is this excess, this rigidity, that distinguished his overdriven striving from a straightforward expression of healthy impulses.

When Oberman reached college, his condition had considerably improved. At high school he had done well, achieved some social participation, and contrived to overcome his compulsive rituals. His overdriven striving gave sufficient security without wrecking his social adjustment. The new environment, however, revived several of his problems, and the threat of compulsory military service touched off many of his early childhood fears. His first course in philosophy challenged the naturalistic system he had worked out for himself. He spent so much time trying to revise his thinking and free it from contradictions that he neglected his regular studies, lost appetite, and, as he himself put it, "walked around in a daze all summer." When in the company of his classmates he found himself showing off, giving a "big line," trying to impress with his superior knowledge, even telling lies in his struggle to put himself foremost. Any little failure brought on protracted daydreams of omnipotence. One day he bungled a recitation in elementary German: for hours he daydreamed about a future invitation from the university to give a series of lectures in German. The overdriven striving was speeded up and stiffened to a point where it was again indistinguishable from obsessive symptoms.

Impending military service awakened a host of fears. He was afraid of being kicked around at training camp, of being torpedoed on the transport, above all of physical injury. His relations with his father had not prepared him to react well to authority. Anxiety mounted steadily, so that after two months in training he arrived at complete neurotic breakdown. Separated from the service, he sought professional help for a thorough treatment of his neurosis.

DISSOCIATED CONDITIONS

We turn now to a group of disorders generally classed with hysteria, but characterized by peculiarities especially in the realm of memory. Whether we are dealing with a brief amnesia, a more extended fugue, or a fully developed double or multiple personality, the central feature of the disorder is a loss of personal identity. The patient forgets who he is and where he lives. He loses the symbols of his identity and also the memories of his previous life that support a continuing sense of selfhood. The phenomenon is familiar through newspaper reports of cases of amnesia. Perhaps the patient is so confused by the loss of memory that he approaches a police officer to ask for help. In other cases—these are the ones technically called *fugues*—he may go on for quite a while functioning as an adequate new person, perhaps with a new name. There are reports of cases in which a patient has remained in a fugue state for months and even years. Conceivably, such a change might be permanent, but we would have no access to such cases.

It is a little unfortunate that the term *amnesia* has been captured by the press for just this particular type of memory disorder. Literally, *amnesia* means any kind of pathological forgetting, whether caused by drugs, brain injuries, old age, or psychogenic factors. The cases we are considering here represent a particular type of amnesia, the forgetting of personal identity. This particular pattern seems to be wholly psychogenic in character. The forgetting is somehow connected with neurotic conflict and represents an attempt to do something about that conflict.

Amnesia for Personal Identity. We begin with an example reported by McDougall, remarkable for its transparency.[14] A British color-sergeant in World War I was carrying a message, riding his motorcycle through a dangerous section of the front. All at once it was several hours later, and he was pushing his motorcycle along the streets of a coastal town nearly a hundred miles away. In utter bewilderment he gave himself up to the military police, but he could tell absolutely nothing of his long trip. The amnesia was ultimately broken by the use of hypnosis. The man then remembered that he was thrown down by a shell explosion, that he picked up himself and his machine, that he started straight for the coastal town, that he studied signs and asked for directions in order to reach this destination.

It is clear, in this case, that the amnesia entailed no loss of competence. The patient's actions were purposive, rational, and intelligent. The amnesia rested only on his sense of personal identity. The conflict was between fear, suddenly intensified by his narrow escape, and his duty to complete the dangerous mission. The forgetting of personal identity made it possible to give way to his impulse toward flight, now irresistible, without exposing himself to the almost equally unbearable anxiety associated with being a coward, failing his mission, and undergoing arrest as a deserter. When he achieved physical safety the two sides of the conflict resumed their normal proportions and his sense of personal identity suddenly returned.

In wartime there are many cases of amnesia and fugue which, like the preceding one, originate under traumatic conditions. In civilian life the same phenomenon occurs under less violent circumstances, but generally in connection with what amounts to an emotional crisis in the patient's life. Abeles and Schilder in a study of sixty-three cases found that "some unpleasant social conflict, either financial or familial, was significant in the immediate cause of the amnesia," although behind

[14] McDougall, *op. cit.*, p. 258.

these immediate conflicts "deeper motives are found."[15] A more detailed report of five cases from the Menninger Clinic has the special advantage that the precipitating events and the content of the amnesic period were carefully recovered in all their personal meaning to the patient.[16] From this report we select the following illustration.

A man of twenty-nine had developed a high ideal of independence and manliness. He had been induced, however, to take work in his father-in-law's business, where he found himself dissatisfied and poorly paid. He was sometimes unable to meet family expenses, and was greatly humiliated to be extricated by his father-in-law on these occasions. One day, again in difficulties, he drove with his family to the town where his father-in-law lived, but could not bring himself to ask for the needed loan and turned the car homeward. He became so preoccupied with the thought of finding a new job and making money, that by the time he reached home he no longer knew who he was nor recognized his wife and children in the car. Taken to the hospital, he spoke only of his new job. He falsified reality to the extent of interpreting everything in the hospital as though it were the operation of a business firm. Two days later he emerged spontaneously into his normal state, not remembering the amnesic episode. Shortly afterward he recalled the episode, including the suicidal despair that had filled him at the thought of asking his father-in-law for more help.

The patient's amnesic state shows certain similarities to dreams and sleepwalking. "Sleepwalking is not sharply differentiated from fugue states, and there is a striking similarity in the psychological make-up of persons who develop fugues and of sleepwalkers."[17] In dreams, suppressed wishes come to expression in hallucinatory form, but the person does not have to accept responsibility for the foolish things he dreams. In amnesic states and fugues, suppressed wishes come to expression in the form of real actions, but on condition that the person lose his identity and hence his responsibility for them. The businessman desperately wanted to get a better job and regain his sense of manliness and independence. Hemmed in as he was by family debts and responsibilities, such a plan was completely impracticable. When the fantasy grew too strong for him, he could tolerate it only by forgetting his identity, thus forgetting the wife and children whose presence made the fantasy so impracticable.

In summary it can be stated that the psychogenic loss of personal identity, such as occurs in amnesias and fugues, represents another way

[15] M. Abeles and P. Schilder, "Psychogenic Loss of Personal Identity," *Archives of Neurology and Psychiatry,* XXXIV (1935), pp. 587–604.

[16] E. R. Geleerd, F. J. Hacker, and D. Rapaport, "Contribution to the Study of Amnesia and Allied Conditions," *Psychoanalytic Quarterly,* XIV (1945), pp. 199–220.

[17] *Ibid.,* p. 213.

of coping with neurotic conflict. The loss of identity is a defense against intolerable conflict when some powerful need or wish becomes uncontrollable. As is so often true, the wish is ordinarily suppressed because the patient is what he is, occupying a certain social position and having certain responsibilities and obligations. When the wish is so strengthened, usually by some external crisis, that he can no longer keep it suppressed, his personal identity has to be ejected from consciousness.

Multiple Personalities. A psychiatrist may live out a long and active professional career without encountering a single case of multiple personality. Such cases are not at all common. Taylor and Martin combed most of the literature up to 1944, and found only seventy-six reported cases.[18] Nevertheless multiple personalities are worthy of attention because of the important problems they raise.

Multiple personalities can be considered as more extreme forms of what we saw in amnesias and fugues. In well-developed cases there is a loss of personal identity, but instead of the amnesic period being dominated by one imperious wish, it becomes an arena in which a whole new personality develops. The patient feels like a different person, and he gradually builds up the memory system of a different person. A second independent personality does not spring into existence all at once. The second sense of personal identity can be created only out of accumulated memories. But once the second system has begun to round itself into a separate self, the person may begin to function as two individuals. Today he is Mr. X, who has no memory of anything Mr. Y has ever done. Tomorrow he may be Mr. Y, who has no recollection of anything Mr. X has ever done. One can imagine the hopeless confusion this creates not merely for Mr. X and Mr. Y but for everyone with whom Mr. XY comes in contact.

The study of multiple personalities in a way recapitulates the history of abnormal psychology. At first they were looked upon as queer nervous weaknesses. Later the emphasis was placed on dissociation. Cures were attempted by using hypnosis to reassociate the dissociated fragments. When Morton Prince wrote *The Dissociation of a Personality* in 1905, describing the celebrated Miss Beauchamp who had three main personalities, he emphasized the dramatic changes from self to self, the ensuing complications, and the problem of synthesizing the different selves by making them aware of each other's memory systems.[19] Fifteen years later he carefully reconsidered the case in the light of the newly developing

[18] W. S. Taylor and M. F. Martin, "Multiple Personality," *Journal of Abnormal and Social Psychology*, XXXIX (1944), pp. 281–300.

[19] M. Prince, *The Dissociation of a Personality* (London: Longmans, Green & Co., Ltd., 1905).

dynamic psychology.[20] He showed that one of the personalities had "existed" for a long time as the rebellious and playful fantasy life of an otherwise very prim and proper child. This meant that when, in early adult life, the patient reached a severe neurotic breakdown, there already existed in her a long-standing semi-independent series of memories that served as the nucleus for one of her new selves. He also showed that each of Miss Beauchamp's three personalities could be conceived as representing a group of strivings, with their associated attitudes and values, such as would offer a certain inherent contradiction even in the most healthy person. One personality embodied a series of saintly virtues, another a strong independent ambition, another an impish and playful quality. In short, Prince conceived that Miss Beauchamp developed separate personalities where a healthy person would simply have conflict of motives. Twenty years later the case was again reconsidered by McCurdy, who viewed the several personalities in the light of reactions to the physician.[21] Dr. Prince was the center of the patient's world during several years of treatment. In her saintly personality she was submissive and respectful toward him. Her impish self was slangy, saucy, teasingly affectionate. The ambitious and independent side of her represented rebellion against his dominance and made its first clear appearance at a time when there was conflict between patient and doctor. McCurdy suggests that these more contemporary motives lay behind the different personalities, and that the apparent separateness of the selves was encouraged by the constant use of hypnotism for treatment.

It is well to be skeptical about multiple personalities, especially when the opportunity has existed for them to be dramatized in hypnotic states. Undoubtedly a case of multiple personality can be played up or played down according to the physician's predilection. It is nevertheless probable that they are perfectly genuine phenomena which sometimes occur quite apart from the attitude of the doctor. One of Prince's cases, the case called B. C. A., was already a dual personality when she first came for treatment.[22] The gradual, spontaneous evolution of the split between a narrow constricted self and a gay and expansive one could be traced back many years. B. C. A. illustrates Murphy's generalization that "the main dynamics in most cases of double and multiple personality seems to be an exaggeration of a conflict situation which is present in nearly all of us,

[20] M. Prince, "Miss Beauchamp: The Psychogenesis of Multiple Personality," *Journal of Abnormal Psychology,* XVI (1920), No. 1. Reprinted in Prince's *Clinical and Experimental Studies in Personality,* ed. A. A. Roback (Cambridge: Sci-Art Publishers, 1939), pp. 185–268.

[21] H. G. McCurdy, "A Note on the Dissociation of a Personality," *Character and Personality,* X (1941), pp. 33–41.

[22] M. Prince, *The Unconscious* (2d ed.; New York: The Macmillan Co., 1921), chaps. xv–xvii.

namely, a conflict between a conforming and a guilty non-conforming trend."[23] Many people find it hard to believe that genuinely independent self-systems can be set up within one body. But if we consider the additional selves as no more than greatly extended and elaborated amnesic systems or fugues, built up until they assume the scope of selfhood, it becomes less difficult to accept their genuineness. Multiple selves happen very rarely, but they do seem to happen.

HYSTERIA

Our discussion of hysteria can be relatively brief. Because it was the first neurosis to attract persistent medical attention, our historical introduction (Chapter 1) has already made us familiar with many of its manifestations. Charcot's studies of hysterical symptoms, and Janet's study of the mental state in hysteria, were milestones in modern thinking about neurosis. Freud's first work, in association with Breuer, dealt with a typical if extreme case of hysteria. The case of Pearson Brack (Chapter 2) is technically an example of hysteria, as is the patient described at the end of the last chapter who became blind after a very minor motor accident. Our present task will not be to examine new cases but rather to summarize the general facts about hysteria in so far as they are known today.

Varieties of Hysterical Symptoms. In addition to the amnesias, fugues, and multiple personalities considered in the last section, hysterical symptoms take a wide variety of bodily forms. On the motor side there are the *paralyses* which may include an arm, a leg, both legs, or one whole side of the body. These symptoms can be distinguished from true organic injuries by the fact that normal reflexes are retained in the paralyzed area, and that little or no muscular degeneration occurs. Sometimes the diagnosis is made still easier by the anatomical nonsense that characterizes the symptom: both hands, for instance, may be paralyzed, while the arms retain their motility, a state that could be produced organically only by a highly peculiar nerve injury in both wrists. Other motor symptoms are *mutism* (inability to speak), *aphonia* (inability to speak above a whisper, to "voice" the speech), *tremor,* and *tics* (spasmodic jerking in a small coordinated group of muscles). On the sensory side there are the many varieties of *anaesthesia.* These may accompany the paralyses, but they sometimes occur alone. Within any one sense department the anaesthesia may take a number of forms. In vision, for instance, the possibilities include total blindness, blindness in one eye, contraction of the visual field to a small focal point, blindness in the left half or right

[23] G. Murphy, *Personality: A Biosocial Approach to Origins and Structure* (New York: Harper & Row, 1947), p. 443.

half of both eyes, and many other curious fragmentations of the visual process. Another symptom is the *hysterical fit*, which in some respects resembles an epileptic seizure but can generally be distinguished from it. Finally, there are sometimes *hysterical twilight states* in which the patient is confused and distressed, experience having an unreal and dreamlike quality. The loss of contact with reality is less complete than would be the case in psychosis.

The more bodily forms of hysteria are sometimes given the title *conversion hysteria.* The bodily symptoms, this title implies, represent a converted form of energy. The force contained in impulses, which because of anxiety can be allowed no outward expression, is converted or diverted into sensory-motor channels in such a way as to block the functioning of some organ. This theory of converted energy was introduced by Freud, who regarded it as a highly hypothetical process difficult to understand or to verify. The interference with bodily functions is generally of an inhibitory character, and when this is true it is easy to regard the symptom as the outcome of defensive inhibition. In various degrees, then, hysterical symptoms can be looked upon as expressions of the defensive process and expressions of the anxiety-linked impulse. The mechanism, however, is certainly an obscure one, and it may even be quite different in different cases.

Kretschmer's Study of Hysterical Tremor. A valuable clue to the nature of hysterical symptom formation is given in a monograph by Kretschmer,[24] based on observations during World War I. Strictly speaking, it applies only to one type of symptom—hysterical tremor—originating under the traumatic conditions of combat. It would be hasty to generalize from this finding to all hysterical symptom formation, but the clue remains a useful one.

Tremor is a biologically preformed component of the anxiety reaction. When stress is past, it subsides and disappears. Many men emerged from acute trauma trembling violently all over, but in most cases the tremor gradually subsided. In certain cases, however, the tremor did not subside; it lasted and became a permanent hysterical symptom. A wish to fall ill in order to be withdrawn from danger could readily be presumed in such cases, and Kretschmer worked out the following explanation of how a wish to fall ill, very likely unconscious, could prolong the tremor indefinitely without the patient's becoming aware of his collaboration in the process. It is generally true, Kretschmer pointed out, that reflexes can be reinforced by a voluntary diffuse tensing of the whole motor system.

[24] E. Kretschmer, *Hysteria* (Nervous and Mental Disease Monographs, No. 44 [New York: Nervous and Mental Disease Publishing Co., 1926]).

Thus the knee jerk can be amplified by clenching the hands and slightly tensing all the musculature. Sometimes a weak reflex can be brought above the threshold by this procedure. If one tries to reinforce a reflex directly, the result is a failure. Trying to amplify the knee jerk by direct volition actually interferes with the reflex act and adds an entirely secondary voluntary kick. It is only the gentle diffuse hypertonicity of the muscles that facilitates reflexes.

One additional fact is of great importance. The indirect reinforcement of a reflex in no way changes the character of the reflex and is not in the least sensed as a voluntary act. The tremor patients, therefore, could be conceived as quite involuntarily sustaining their reflex tremor by keeping up a slight hypertonicity of the musculature. The aid they were giving to the tremor would not enter consciousness or stir up guilt feelings. If this unwitting aid were continued for a short while so as to prevent the tremor from subsiding, the symptom would become established as an independent habit system that would continue indefinitely. Kretschmer considered that his hypothesis was to some extent verified by the fact that treatment consisting of prolonged muscular relaxation often stopped the symptom, especially in its early stages. Relaxation counteracted the unwitting trick whereby the patient sustained his tremor.

Placement of the Symptom. The crucial problem of hysterical symptom formation concerns the placement of the symptoms. How is the organ system chosen and how is the form of symptom determined? The possibilities are suggested in the following statements:

1. Kretschmer's hypothesis gives us one possibility. The symptom consists of some natural part of the anxiety reaction, unwittingly reinforced and sustained by the patient until it becomes permanent.

2. A somewhat similar process occurs when the symptom starts with a true organic injury. Unwitting prolongation turns what should be a temporary disability into a permanent thing. There are various reflex responses which tend to immobilize an injured part. The muscles of a wounded leg, for instance, will stiffen to prevent further motion and pain. If these immobilizing reflexes are prolonged by a mechanism akin to Kretschmer's, the wounded leg becomes an hysterically paralyzed leg.

3. The term *somatic compliance* has been coined to suggest that weak organs may be chosen as the site of hysterical symptoms. If a person has always been a little lame, or has had eye trouble or difficulties with his voice, the effect is to heighten the importance of that particular system in his mind. When neurotic breakdown occurs, that system is compliant to the need for symptom formation.

4. Temporary somatic compliance may exist when some organ is in a peculiar condition at a crucial moment of crisis. There was a good ex-

ample of this in the Breuer case:[25] a paralysis of the right arm had its origin in the occasion when the patient, watching beside her father's sick bed. dozed and had a terrifying nightmare while her arm hung in an awkward position, "asleep" over the back of the chair. In neuroses of traumatic onset it sometimes appears that the symptom falls on an organ system that was highly active at the moment of acute crisis. If an explosion catches the soldier in the act of firing his rifle, the symptoms may place themselves in the form of paralyzed hands, bent neck, closed eye, etc.

5. Direct connection between some organ system and the neurotic conflict may serve to choose the location. This is particularly true in what are called *occupational* neuroses—for example, mutism or aphonia in a salesman, paralysis of the fingers in a pianist, writer's cramp in a writer, or, to extend slightly the meaning of "occupation," sexual impotence in a Don Juan. In all such cases there are conflict and anxiety over carrying out the occupation successfully, and the symptom definitely prevents further activity.

6. The placement of a great many hysterical symptoms can be understood only by assuming—in some cases actually discovering—a roundabout associative or symbolic connection between the organ system and the conflict. Our study of phobias showed how extensive such possibilities might be. There is a connection between symptom and conflict, but one can grasp it only by untangling the chains of personal meaning that have been formed in the patient's mind in the course of experience, revery, and dream.

7. Anticipated *secondary gain* seems to play an especially important part in hysterical symptom formation. The gain is not consciously anticipated nor the symptom voluntarily devised, but the symptom shows an unmistakable relation to certain effects on the patient's environment. This is nicely illustrated in one of H. V. Dick's cases.[26] A middle-aged married woman had to nurse her mother-in-law, who was paralyzed in both legs. Her husband forced her to do this, and seemed to become concerned only with his mother, forgetting his wife. One day the wife took a walk, feeling rebellious, but at the same time very anxious as she became dimly aware of angry wishes that the old lady would die. She felt faint and sat down on a park bench. A moment later she tried to rise, only to discover that both her legs were paralyzed and that she now needed as much of her husband's attention as did his mother.

The Changing Picture of Hysteria. It will perhaps not have escaped notice that there is an old-fashioned sound to most of the literature about

[25] See above, pages 27–29.
[26] Dicks, *op. cit.*, p. 93.

hysteria. During the last forty years there has been a widespread impression, especially among American psychiatrists, that cases of hysteria are becoming rare. Gratifying as this is on humanitarian grounds, it has sometimes proved frustrating to medical educators who could not find any patients to demonstrate to students the disorder that occupied such an important place in medical history. In France in the time of Charcot and Janet, in Austria during Freud's early work, in the United States when Prince made his studies, hysterical patients seemed always to be present in great abundance. Has this form of disorder really declined, or has it somehow changed its manifestations?

On the question of frequency we cannot go much beyond a vague impression. It is likely that many cases now classed as psychosomatic disorder would have been called hysteria in earlier years. But the possibility of changes in symptom pictures is a real one in a disorder in which suggestion plays such a prominent part. There has recently been a renewed research interest in conversion hysteria, which has by no means vanished from the clinical scene.[27] Apparently the great increase in popular knowledge of medicine has had a real effect on hysterical symptoms. Patients from backward rural areas may still have crude, anatomically impossible symptoms such as the glove anaesthesia; but such symptoms are no longer available to hysterics who know more about diseases, especially to those who have been trained as physicians, nurses, or medical secretaries. Cases are reported in which there is detailed simulation of a complex disease like multiple sclerosis, but it turns out that the patient has picked up the necessary details in the course of being examined for possible organic disorder. More often among relatively sophisticated patients the hysterical symptom takes the form of pain. The favorite conversion symptom, so to speak, in contemporary hysterias is pain in some part of the body believed by the patient to be organically diseased.[28] The dramatic hysterias so memorably described by Janet are indeed in decline, but hysteria as a variety of neurosis continues to exist in forms more adapted to present cultural expectations.

PROBLEM OF THE CHOICE OF NEUROSIS

An anxiety-defense theory of neurosis such as has been presented in the last three chapters is primarily a theory of the *dynamics* of neurosis. It traces the origins to situations in childhood in which anxiety was gravely aroused and crippling defensive processes set in motion. It explains protective traits and overdriven strivings as techniques slowly

[27] P. Chodoff and H. Lyons, "Hysteria, the Hysterical Personality, and 'Hysterical' Conversion," *American Journal of Psychiatry,* CXIV (1958), pp. 734–40.

[28] F. J. Ziegler, J. B. Imboden, and E. Meyer, "Contemporary Conversion Reactions: A Clinical Study," *American Journal of Psychiatry,* CXVI (1960), pp. 901–10.

developed for maintaining a feeling of security. It understands neurotic breakdown by pointing to increased subjective threats and to changes in the efficacy of protective devices. Finally, it explains symptoms by showing their relation to anxiety and their service in the cause of defense. A dynamic theory deals with forces, particularly the forces generated by danger and the need for security. If correctly conceived it offers an explanation of the forces that produce and maintain neurotic behavior.

Is there anything else about neurosis that needs to be explained? As we have already indicated, a dynamic theory leaves one question untouched: it does not explain the choice of neurosis, the appearance of one symptom syndrome rather than another. How does it come about that the patient develops just this kind of neurotic symptoms rather than some other kind? A fully adequate theory of neurosis has to answer this question. It is not enough to specify the dynamic background, even though this is indispensable; eventually there must be a solution to the problem of the choice of neurosis.

Predisposition to Neurosis. Logically we should start our discussion a step further back and raise the question of a possible predisposition to neurosis in general. The argument has often been advanced that individuals should be conceived as differing widely in their natural susceptibility to fear. This contention is perhaps strengthened by Gantt's studies of experimental neurosis in dogs, in which an identical procedure produced breakdown only in certain cases, and by the findings of Hall, who found it fairly easy to produce through selective breeding two strains of rats one of which was in all situations more timid than the other.[29] Some workers have argued that susceptibility to anxiety is created by very early and primitive stress such as a severe birth trauma or acute situations during the first few weeks of life.[30] Thus far it has proved impossible to obtain satisfactory evidence that crises of this kind are more frequent in the histories of neurotic patients. Slater has made a case for predisposition by examining reports on breakdown in British flying personnel during World War II. He demonstrated a negative relationship between amount of stress during service and amount of predisposition; that is, with greater predisposition less stress was required to produce breakdown.[31] Predisposition, however, had to be estimated

[29] C. S. Hall, "Temperament: A Survey of Animal Studies," *Psychological Bulletin*, XXXVIII (1941), pp. 909–43. Gantt's work is described above, page 195.

[30] Otto Rank's views on the centrality of the birth trauma are discussed and broadened by P. Greenacre, "The Predisposition to Anxiety," *Psychoanalytic Quarterly*, X (1941), pp. 66–94.

[31] E. Slater, "The Neurotic Constitution: A Statistical Study of Two Thousand Neurotic Soldiers," *Journal of Neurology, Neurosurgery, and Psychiatry*, VI (1943), pp. 1–16.

from case records, which somewhat weakens the force of this demonstration.

Findings of this kind suggest that something akin to a predisposition *may* exist, perhaps in the form of a low threshold for the arousal of anxiety, perhaps in the form of a poorer capacity to control and defend against anxiety. None of the evidence, however, is fully satisfactory. None of it excludes the possibility that alleged differences in predisposition are really the consequences of different exposures to emotional stress during childhood. The scientific task of isolating predispositions, woven as they must be into the whole tissue of life experiences, presents formidable obstacles to research. A clearer conception of constitutional variables and more direct ways of measuring them might ultimately show that they played a significant part.[32] In the meantime the question of general predisposition to neurosis remains without an answer.

Choice of Symptom Syndromes. Moving on to the more specific problem of choice of neurotic syndrome, it should be noticed in the first place that observers have long been impressed by differences in the "kinds of people" who fell ill with different disorders. The contrast seems particularly marked between hysterics and obsessional neurotics. The cool affect, the predominant aggression, the complex thought processes of the obsessional patient seem utterly foreign to hysterical neurotics. Dependence, love, and sex are the critical issues in the hysteric's life and in his neurosis. Such patients are given to vividness in behavior and a tendency to dramatize. Their ability to imagine themselves vividly in different roles appears in multiple personalities and in symptoms which copy another person's illness. We would not find it difficult to predict that a cool cerebral friend would become obsessive, a impulsive histrionic one hysterical, if it should be their misfortune to be overtaken by neurotic breakdown.

Observations of this kind suggest that the "choice" of symptom syndrome is by no means a "decision" that is made at the last minute, when neurotic breakdown becomes unavoidable. There is an integral relationship between the symptoms finally produced and certain more general characteristics of the patient's personality which have been present for a long time. Our problem is to find the origin of these general characteristics. Should they be referred to as constitutional differences that shape behavior in certain directions, more or less regardless of emotional crises and the effects of the family constellation? Or should we think of them as consequences of learning and thus as an inherent part of the psychodynamic process? Or, more wisely, should we conceive them to be prod-

32 See the discussion of this problem by H. J. Eysenck, *Dimensions of Personality* (London: Routledge & Kegan Paul, Ltd., 1947), pp. 41–51.

ucts of a constant and subtle interaction between individual constitution and the environmental influences surrounding the course of growth?

Evidence that can truly clarify such a fundamental problem is difficult to obtain and interpret. For the present we must be content to glance briefly at three main approaches to it.

1. *Constitutional Differences.* The individual's innate make-up might predispose him to use certain types of defense, to favor certain kinds of protective organization, and to adopt a certain style of life. Repression and dissociation, for example, might be readily available to one person, whereas intellectualizing and isolating techniques would come most naturally to another. There is a certain amount of experimental evidence which seems to be in harmony with this idea. It has been shown, for example, that Janet's time-honored distinction between hysteria and "psychasthenia"—his word for obsessive and anxiety neuroses—has considerable consistency as a trait difference that runs through the population as a whole.[33] Even well people who incline toward the hysteric or extraverted side are more given to repression in the form of forgetting failures and anxiety-arousing incidents; they are more suggestible, less openly aggressive, and more generally optimistic than people inclined toward the psychasthenic or introverted side.[34] Eysenck has advanced the hypothesis that behind these differences lies a basic difference in the balance of nervous functioning. It is of the same nature as the one postulated by Pavlov to account for individual differences in the behavior of dogs in conditioned reflex experiments; it turns on a presumably innate difference in the relative strengths of excitatory and inhibitory processes. This variable might be important for the child's response to the socialization process, and Eysenck offers experimental evidence to support the idea of its existence in the human nervous system.[35]

2. *Reaction Patterns Reinforced by Family Attitudes.* The most straightforward environmental hypothesis assumes that symptoms are an extreme form of broader reaction tendencies which have been encouraged in the person by the circumstances of his life. This view owes a great deal to Adolf Meyer, who was responsible for the concept of *reaction-types* and for the idea that psychological disorders spring from well-learned reaction patterns that prove to be maladjustive in the long run, though originally they seemed adjustive in the particular environment in which they

[33] H. J. Eysenck, *The Structure of Human Personality* (London: Methuen & Co., Ltd., 1953).

[34] C. W. Eriksen and A. Davids, "The Meaning and Clinical Validity of the Taylor Anxiety Scale and the Hysteria-Psychasthenia Scales from the MMPI," *Journal of Abnormal and Social Psychology,* L (1955), pp. 135–37.

[35] H. J. Eysenck, *The Dynamics of Anxiety and Hysteria* (New York: Frederick A. Praeger, Inc., 1957).

were learned. The clearest and most systematic exposition of this general hypothesis is to be found in the work of Norman Cameron.[36] Disordered reactions, according to Cameron, always represent the "extravagant, restricted, or inappropriate use of techniques which everybody uses in attempting to reduce the tensions of need and anxiety."[37] They spring from the universal repertory of human behavior. Hysterical symptoms are derived from everyday processes familiar to all of us: for instance, the blocking out of impressions that lie outside the focus of interest, the turning over of habituated reactions to automatic and unwitting performance, and the unconscious imitating of role models. Obsessional symptoms, in contrast, are exaggerated forms of normal self-control and self-criticism. There is thus a straight line of evolution from reaction patterns to symptoms.

What favors the development of one or another reaction pattern in the child? Cameron looks for the answer in the personal history, and he attaches especial importance to parental attitudes. If the parents are themselves credulous and suggestible, if they reward the child for showing off and dramatizing himself, or if they fuss unduly over illnesses, they tend to build up the reaction patterns which under future stress might advance into hysterical symptoms. If they make a great point of certainty and correctness, load the child too soon with decisions and responsibilities, or heighten the sense of guilt, they contribute to an obsessive and compulsive reaction pattern. Personality differences are thus attributed quite literally to the patterns of parental reward. The connection is plausible but remains hypothetical until much more is done to study children and their families intensively as they grow up together.

3. *Time and Content of the Nuclear Neurotic Problem.* The third approach comes from the work of Freud and the psychoanalytic school. Although Freud often remarked upon the possibility of constitutional differences, the theory can be described in psychodynamic terms. It is based on the idea of universal stages of development through which everyone passes: oral, anal, phallic. In the course of growth, particularly sharp crises may be experienced at one or another stage, producing a fixation on that stage and on the feelings and behavior appropriate to it. These fixations are responsible for differences in normal character, and they are also responsible for types of disorder, the more so because anxiety begets a regression to the point of strongest fixation and a reanimation of the earlier patterns. Schizophrenia and manic-depressive disorders are based upon fixation at the oral stage, obsessional neurosis at

[36] N. Cameron, *The Psychology of Behavior Disorders* (Boston: Houghton Mifflin Co., 1947); N. Cameron and A. Magaret, *Behavior Pathology* (Boston: Houghton Mifflin Co., 1951).

[37] Cameron and Magaret, *ibid.,* p. 3.

the anal stage, hysteria and anxiety states at the phallic stage with special emphasis on the Oedipus complex. Differences in symptom syndrome are determined at least in part by differences in the mental maturity that is characteristic of these stages. Obsessional symptoms, for example, even when clothed in the garb of adult intellectual maturity, betray primitive ideas of power, hostility, and right and wrong. In the case of Peter Oberman one can detect the notion that thought is omnipotent, that an evil thought can create real harm, that an expiatory thought or a purely symbolic action can undo real harm. These ideas, which are magical for an adult, fit the cognitive development of a child of two or three, who has not yet made firm discriminations between thoughts and real events.

It is to be presumed that different defense mechanisms become available at different points in development. The suggestion has also been made that certain forms of defense are particularly appropriate for dealing with certain kinds of impulse. Anna Freud proposes that repression may be most effective against sexual impulses, the existence of which is all but denied in some parts of our society, whereas aggression lends itself more readily to control by a variety of reaction formations such as excessive scrupulousness or a uniform docility in human relations.[38] If this be the case, regression to the anal stage with its intense problems of aggression would tend to animate the kind of defenses seen in obsessional neurosis; regression to the more sexually colored Oedipal stage would accentuate the repressive tactics so common in the symptoms of hysteria.

Again we are in the realm of hypothesis. It cannot be said that even the painstaking psychoanalytic recovery of childhood memories and fantasies yields decisive proof that this whole theory is correct. Much as we have learned about psychodynamics, the theory of neurosis remains in important respects unfinished. The problem of the choice of neurosis has yet to find its full solution.

SUGGESTIONS FOR FURTHER READING

Descriptions of the different symptom syndromes in neurosis can be found in several places. From the Freudian standpoint a brief account appears in F. Alexander & H. Ross's *Dynamic Psychiatry* (Chicago, University of Chicago Press, 1952), Ch. 5; the subject is covered in scholarly detail by Otto Fenichel in *The Psychoanalytic Theory of Neurosis* (New York, W. W. Norton & Co., Inc., 1945), especially Chs. 11–14. A somewhat independent view is taken by H. V. Dicks in his *Clinical Studies in Psychopathology* (2d ed., London, Edw. Arnold & Co., 1947) who surveys the main syndromes in Chs. 1–5. The outlook of Adolf Meyer inspires the systematic "biosocial interpretation" given by Norman Cameron in *The Psychology of Behavior Disorders* (Boston, Houghton Mifflin Co., 1947), Chs. 8–12.

[38] A. Freud, *The Ego and the Mechanisms of Defence* (London: Hogarth Press, Ltd., 1937), chap. iv.

A reader familiar with French has access to what is probably the most brilliant clinical description of phobias and obsessions: P. Janet's *Les Obsessions et la Psychasthénie* (Paris, Alcan, 1903). The same author's *Major Symptoms of Hysteria* (2d ed., New York, The Macmillan Co., 1920) contains equally classic descriptions of dissociated states and hysterical symptoms.

Morton Prince's *The Dissociation of a Personality* (2d ed., London, Longmans, Green & Co., Ltd., 1913) is fascinating reading, though a little on the dramatic side. It should be followed by his more conservative but more dynamic paper, "Miss Beauchamp: The Psychogenesis of Multiple Personality," reprinted in *Clinical and Experimental Studies in Personality* (2d ed., Cambridge, Sci-Art Publishers, 1939), Ch. 7. In Ch. 8 of the same work and in Chs. 18–20 of *The Unconscious* (2d ed., New York, The Macmillan Co., 1921), Prince gives an account of the B. C. A. case, in many ways more representative of multiple personality. Another case is reported by S. I. Franz, *Persons One and Three* (New York, McGraw-Hill Book Co., Inc., 1933). An excellent discussion of the problems raised by multiple personalities, both for abnormal and general psychology, occurs in Ch. 18 of Gardner Murphy's *Personality—A Biosocial Approach to Origins and Structure* (New York, Harper & Row, 1947).

8

Psychotherapy: Basic Methods and Principles

One can turn to the topic of psychotherapy with a real sense of getting down to brass tacks. Most of what we know about neurosis, and a good deal of what we know about simpler maladjustments, was learned in the course of trying to bring about cure. If one sat down to devise a logical plan for understanding psychogenic disorders, one would probably start with a program for finding out the facts by observation and experiment, after which the knowledge could be applied to the practical art of therapy. Historically, the process moved in the opposite direction. Practical art preceded science and became the means whereby it was possible to accumulate a body of knowledge. What we know about psychogenic disorders has come largely from the observation, the wisdom, and the blunders of people who tried to cure them.

We are thus really getting down to brass tacks—that is, to the source of most of our information—when we reach the topic of psychotherapy. But we are getting there in another sense: we now face the question of *what can be done* to help the people whose misfortunes and distress have occupied us so unceasingly up to this point. Maladjusted individuals are not as happy and effective as they might be. Neurotic individuals fall still further short of taking joy in life and of developing their full potentialities. This is a tragedy both for the individual and for society. We now begin to consider the possibilities for rectifying maladjustments and neuroses. To what extent can people be restored to psychological health?

Our plan for describing psychotherapy is to consider first (in this chapter) the basic methods and processes, then to take up (in the next chapter) a number of variations, technical aids, and adaptations of these processes to special purposes such as work with children and treatment in groups. If the reader hopes to find that psychotherapy is perfectly understood, that everyone agrees on how it should be done, and that its results can be presented with the sharpness of surgical statistics, he must be prepared for disappointment on all three counts. During the last ten or fifteen years there has been an admirable quickening of interest in research on psychotherapy, but the difficulties are formidable and the results thus far small compared to what needs to be known. Meanwhile psychotherapy as an activity flourishes and is in much demand. Variations in method and theory continue to appear, sometimes in the belligerent form of new schools of thought. This burgeoning may well be a token of vitality, but it is not necessarily a sign of clear thinking. But we shall postpone contemporary controversies to the next chapter and try here simply to get acquainted with the basic happenings in psychotherapy as they have come to light since Freud discovered the possibilities in free association.

PRELIMINARY CONSIDERATIONS

The Meaning of Psychotherapy. First let us try to be clear as to the limits of our discussion. Psychotherapy should have a distinct and restricted meaning. It does not mean everything that a psychiatrist does to his patients. It does not mean everything that is done to maladjusted, neurotic, and psychotic individuals. We need to bound it carefully on two sides: first, to mark it off from therapy that is essentially somatic or that consists of practical management; second, to distinguish it from attempts to influence people by educative methods or exhortation.

1. As we saw in our introductory chapters, disordered personal reactions can spring from two classes of events: the psychogenic and the somatogenic. Treatment naturally falls into the same two categories—psychotherapy and somatic therapy. Some patients with fairly severe disorders are benefited by techniques such as shock treatment or brain surgery. With epilepsy and certain other disorders, the control of diet and the application of specific medicines may be indicated. All of these measures are therapy but not psychotherapy. In some cases a great deal can be done in the way of practical management. Placement and care in a hospital is the outstanding example, but such steps as a change of work, removal from an uncongenial family situation, or, in the case of children, the finding of suitable schools, camps, or foster homes may be of substantial importance. Even these steps are not, strictly speaking, psychotherapy. This term should be limited to those methods which depend on a direct interaction between patient and therapist. Psychotherapy operates on the learning process rather than on the body tissues or on the environment. Its benefit lies in the relearning or new learning

that the patient is able to accomplish through talk with the therapist and through the ensuing personal relation.

2. On the other side, psychotherapy must be distinguished from the vast array of activities that go under the headings of education, persuasion, and exhortation. Teachers and ministers, speakers and writers, propagandists and advertising men all operate through psychological channels and attempt to influence the learning process. There is no doubt that such methods are psychological, but there is no point in calling them therapy. When a person acts in the capacity of a therapist, his goal is to bring about a state that has been variously described as good adaptation, adjustment, or psychological health. He undertakes to do this as far as possible without teaching any particular subject matter, advocating any doctrine, or selling any favorite product. His position is thus analogous to that of a physician of the body whose aim is to restore physical health. The analogy is the more strongly felt because modern psychotherapy started within the medical profession and is culturally defined as part of medical practice. Perhaps the analogy is ultimately sound, but at this point in our study it can be seriously misleading. Ordinary ideas about health, and what the doctor does to restore it, do not prepare us well to understand what is involved in psychotherapy.

Forces at Work in Psychotherapy. It is important to realize at the outset that psychotherapy operates with very small forces. Its aim is to bring about a process of growth in the patient, and this process can only be encouraged, not hurried or pushed or performed by the therapist for the patient. Much of our everyday thinking about medicine is colored by the dramatic achievements of modern surgery and of the so-called wonder drugs. In an operation lasting an hour or two, the surgeon can remove a nucleus of infection and put the patient on a rapid road to recovery. In a matter of minutes he can inject a drug that will act within a short time to subdue the infecting organisms. It is evident that no comparable means exist for removing a neurotic nucleus or for undoing the cumulative effects of childhood anxieties on the learning process. What originates as a learning process can be rectified only by a new learning process. Thus the psychotherapist has at his command no means of making the kind of radical intervention that occurs to bodily processes in surgery. His intervention is less radical than the ordinary giving of medicines and drugs. He has to promote a process of relearning, and all he can do is to provide favorable circumstances.

If the forces at his command seem slight in comparison with those often available in the cure of the body, they seem slight also when put alongside the forces that created the disorder and that still may be acting to sustain it. Perhaps for twenty years the parents of the patient created conditions favorable to the development of a neurotic way of life; now the therapist comes in with the assignment of creating conditions to undo all that learning. Perhaps the patient's contemporary situation is full of exasperating frustrations; the hour in which the therapist tries to assist growth has to compete with eight hours during which a tyrannical boss keeps the patient pressed back against his neurotic anxieties. There is certainly nothing remarkable in the fact that psychotherapy often fails and almost always takes a long time. The wonder is that it ever succeeds.

But the psychotherapist has one strong card, and if he plays it skillfully he need not always lose out in competition with these other forces. He is in a position to establish a unique relationship with the patient, one that is unusually favorable for new learning. The patient is unhappy and discouraged. Whatever steps he has taken to help himself have proved of no avail. Everyone is tired of hearing about his problems, tired even of his having problems. The relation with the therapist fills him again with new hope. This time his listener is a medical man or someone similarly trained, uncommitted to any goal save health. He is presumed to be wise in human suffering and experienced in setting it right. He listens to the intimate secrets, the fears and hopes and loves, and without blaming the patient for any shortcomings he indicates that these secrets are really important. They interest him, he takes them seriously, they are the seat of the trouble and also of possible cure. One looks in vain among the other relationships of life for just this combination of qualities. The pastor is too strongly identified with standards of right and wrong. The friend will not listen very long without giving nervous reassurance or talking about his own troubles. The loved one may listen, but cannot be counted upon to give authoritative advice. No one hits the happy combination of interest, detachment, and knowledge that characterizes a skillful psychotherapist. It is this unique atmosphere that supports the patient's growth.

Corrective Emotional Experience. One of the commonest errors in regard to psychotherapy is to think of it as an intellectual process. It is widely conceived as a replacing of what is unconscious by what is conscious, as an increasing of the patient's insight, or in other ways that suggest a quite false supremacy of intellect. This outlook implies that maladjustment and neurosis result from lack of understanding. As soon as the patient perceives the folly of his ways he will voluntarily mend them. Along with this error goes a still more serious one: the belief that insight and understanding can be *given* by the therapist to the patient. Let the therapist make his diagnosis as rapidly as possible, convey his results to the patient, point out the maladjustive behavior, indicate the overdriven strivings, explain the inferred neurotic nucleus, and the patient will go home completely cured—such is the implication.

It is unfortunate that such theories about psychotherapy are not correct. Often the doctor can make a pretty good reconstruction of the patient's difficulties in a fairly short time. Sometimes a single consultation reveals most of the trouble and suggests the whole course of development that led up to it. Much time would be saved if this knowledge, conveyed directly to the patient, were capable of curing the disorder. It is instructive to consider what happens when a therapist, either because he is poorly trained or because he is naturally impatient, unsympathetic, and domineering, puts this theory into practice. The patient leaves the office and does not return. Perhaps he tells his friends that the doctor is a fool, sarcastically quoting some of the ridiculous notions the doctor had about him. Perhaps he retires into a deep state of gloom and guilt because he cannot do away with the foolish behavior that has been revealed to him. But in any event the symptoms and sufferings remain. Mere intellectual insight proves worthless, if not harmful.

Psychotherapy does not take place primarily in the sphere of intellect. Its basic principle is, as Alexander expresses it, "to re-expose the patient, under more favorable circumstances, to emotional situations which he could not handle in the past." The patient must "undergo a corrective emotional experience," and his "intellectual understanding of the genetics has only an accessory significance."[1] Psychotherapy is designed to bring about learning, but it cannot get anywhere by the lecture method. Its sphere of operation is the patient's feelings.

Corrective emotional experience is essential even for the simpler maladjustments. The maladjusted person may perceive his trouble without *knowing how* to act differently. In spite of its conflicts, his familiar way of life has been rewarded and he has not learned to act in other ways. He has to learn, through corrective emotional experiences, that it is possible to behave differently and that such behavior leads to a more rewarding state than he has attained before.

If anxiety plays an important part in the disorder, there is the added difficulty that the patient does not *dare* to alter his behavior. He is afraid to change lest he come into contact with acute danger. Only the outside observer knows that the danger is something long outgrown. To the patient himself it feels real and it blocks change. For the neurotic patient the most important corrective emotional experiences are those that permit a relaxing of defenses. Neurosis takes its start when threat is present and when conditions are just right to freeze some of the defenses. To correct

[1] F. Alexander, T. M. French, *et al.*, *Psychoanalytic Therapy* (New York: The Ronald Press Co., 1946), pp. 66–67.

this situation the defenses must be unfrozen. The patient must gradually feel the anxiety derived from his earlier history, react less defensively, and thus learn to appraise the old dangers at their true current value. When overdriven strivings have invaded the whole personality and a complex protective organization has been built up, it requires a long series of corrective emotional experiences to bring about a return to health. The principle is no different, however, from what takes place when a recent highly traumatic incident is liquidated. The patient resumes contact with the memories of his fright and relaxes his defenses. Strengthened by the presence of the therapist, he dares reappraise the danger and finds that it can be tolerated without resort to the crippling mechanism of repression. The crucial thing in treating a neurosis is to create conditions in which the patient will *dare to reappraise his anxieties and relax the defenses.* This is for him the truly corrective type of emotional experience.

Clearly a process of this kind requires something different from what is implied in the ordinary relation between doctor and patient. It will not be sufficient for the patient to have merely a trustful dependence on the therapist, leaving it to him to do what is needed. The patient is bound to be much more aware of his own participation than he is when he lies in bed and lets bodily reparation take its silent course. The relation can hardly remain a purely formal one of expert and client. The two parties are bound to become more personally involved in the course of their extended conversations. Once we conceive of psychotherapy as a relearning process, we can see that the patient needs strong continuing motivation to work at his problems and that his relation to the therapist is an evolving, integral part of the whole experience.

Isolating the Fundamental Procedures. In their actual practice most psychotherapists are guided by general ideas similar to the ones we have thus far considered. These ideas, however, do not tell us very much about the actual transactions between therapist and patient. Psychotherapy is not accomplished merely by good intentions and the creation of a warm permissive relationship. Knowledge and skill are required to facilitate the corrective emotional experiences that are necessary for the patient's improvement. The interviews are taken up by conversation, but it must be conversation of a quite special type if the consequence is to be the cure of a neurosis or even the setting right of a lesser maladjustment. Psychotherapy can be understood only to the extent that we can isolate the fundamental processes in this most unusual kind of conversation.

Much psychiatric treatment and psychological counseling goes on in an unspecialized fashion. The conversation is adapted to the peculiarities of the individual patient and to the particular problems that arise. It may take the form of questions and answers, reconstruction of past history, or discussion of current difficulties. It may consist of an emotion-laden monologue by the patient, or at the opposite extreme the therapist may have to take the initiative in making the patient speak at all. The therapist may offer encouragement, give information, give advice; these more positive actions on his part still lie within the meaning of psychotherapy. In the hands of an experienced and skillful therapist, this freedom and flexibility is an advantage. The therapist does a little of this and a little of that, depending on the circumstances that arise. Often the patient is bettered, but neither he nor his doctor knows just what it was that produced the change. The advantages are balanced by certain risks. The inexperienced and unskillful therapist may do a little of this and a little of that at the wrong time, and he is apt to discover his blunders only through their bad effect on the patient. The characteristic error of inexperienced therapists is to move too fast for the patient. Interpretations are offered and advice is given before the patient is ready to assimilate them. The therapist is constantly tempted to substitute his own insights and suggestions for a true corrective emotional experience in the patient. The very flexibility of most psychotherapy, an advantage in skillful hands, makes it hard for the young therapist to learn his art except through trial and error at the expense of the patient.

The same flexibility and lack of system makes it hard for the student of psychology to grasp the nature of the therapeutic process. We need to know what are the crucial events that make for corrective emotional experience. A substantial contribution to this end was made by Carl Rogers, who took the lead in securing, analyzing, and publishing stenographic transcriptions and phonographic recordings of therapeutic interviews. The advantages of such records need scarcely be mentioned. For the first time it became possible for the therapist to go back and see what he said, under what circumstances he said it, and what effect it had on the patient. In addition to this technical advance—and largely because of it—Rogers succeeded in isolating what he considers to be the central type of event or crucial process in psychotherapy. He worked out a procedure whereby this crucial process is utilized systematically for all it is worth, without interference by other processes.[2] We shall begin our study of psychotherapeutic techniques with his work.

[2] C. R. Rogers, *Counseling and Psychotherapy* (Boston: Houghton Mifflin Co., 1942). This book contains the verbatim record of a treatment that lasted for eight sessions. Other transcribed case reports are given in W. U. Snyder, *Case Book of Non-Directive Counseling* (Boston: Houghton Mifflin Co., 1947), and in several more recent publications, for example, R. Callis, P. C. Polmantier, and E. C. Roeber, *A Casebook of Counseling* (New York: Appleton-Century-Crofts, Inc., 1955), drawn from counseling with college students.

CLIENT-CENTERED PSYCHOTHERAPY

Rogers first gave his method the title of *non-directive counseling*. Subsequently the name was changed to *client-centered therapy*, but the central procedure has remained very much the same.[3] It will be noticed that Rogers refers to the people who consult him as clients rather than patients. This is appropriate, inasmuch as his counseling technique can be usefully applied to many problems not serious enough to qualify as sickness. More consistently than others he believes that the client should always take the lead in the therapeutic process. The counselor should not intervene by asking questions, by giving information or advice, or even by directing the course of the conversations. His goal is to help the client grow in the client's own directions, and his intervention is limited to removing whatever emotional obstacles lie in the client's path. Even when we speak of "removing obstacles" we use an expression that sounds more active than the behavior which Rogers considers ideal in a counselor. The client removes the obstacles; the counselor merely serves to make this possible. The principle of not directing the client is adhered to with the utmost consistency.

Rogers maintains that when the non-directive principle is faithfully and skillfully followed, events take a fairly regular course. The whole therapy is "an orderly, consistent process, even a predictable process in its major outlines."[4] He maintains further that when the treatment is properly conducted, "the client is likely to be able to handle his own affairs after six to fifteen contacts," although here there will be wide individual variations.[5] We are dealing with a therapeutic process, then, which is held to be regular, predictable, and fairly short; all this in spite of the fact that the client leads the way and that the counselor practices a minimum of intervention. Before we consider the regular course of events, we must understand precisely what the counselor does. In spite of his passive non-intervention he is, after all, an indispensable part of the process.

Recognition of Feelings. The counselor uses one therapeutic tool, and one only. This tool is called the acceptance, recognition, and clarification of feeling. Apart from creating a therapeutic relationship such as we discussed earlier in the chapter, a relationship characterized by a warm and friendly interest and a permissive, non-censorious attitude, the counselor confines himself to a single activity. He simply re-states what the client has just said, but he re-states the feeling side of it rather than the content. This is not as easy as it sounds. All our habits of conversa-

[3] C. R. Rogers, *Client-Centered Therapy* (Boston: Houghton Mifflin Co., 1951).
[4] Rogers, *Counseling and Psychotherapy*, *op. cit.*, p. 44.
[5] *Ibid.*, p. 232.

tion are built on the idea of responding to content. If someone says, "I didn't have a good time at *X*," a very natural social response would be, "Oh, didn't you? I thought it was a fine place when I was there." To borrow one of Rogers' examples, if a student says that his study habits are wrong and that he is not really so stupid as his grades indicate, it is natural to ask him what his grades are. In both cases the response is made to content, not to feeling. The respondent talks about the objective characteristics of *X* or the objective grades on the student's report card. It is quite another matter to respond to the feeling that was expressed: the first person's dislike of *X*, the second person's disappointment at his grades and concern lest they be taken as the true measure of his ability.

The acceptance, recognition, and clarification of feeling is the crux of the counselor's art. It is a real art and a real skill. The counselor must be able to perceive and follow the feelings that are being expressed in each statement, a thing by no means easy in itself and certainly impossible if his own feelings get in the way. Rogers has recently amended his account in order to avoid the elusiveness of the word "feeling." The counselor must learn to perceive things as the client perceives them, to enter as fully as possible into the client's "internal frame of reference," and to "indicate to the client the extent to which he is seeing through the client's eyes."[6] When the counselor is successful in doing this, the client finds himself in a unique situation. The way he feels, the way things look to him, the things that really matter to him, are constantly appreciated and are clearly the things in which the counselor, too, is interested. Successful recognition of the internal frame of reference thus leads to the expression of more and more feelings. The client has probably never before had a listener who paid so much attention to his perceptions and feelings. As a result, it often happens that within a single hour he talks about many things he has never told to anyone else.

The consistent use of just this one therapeutic tool distinguishes non-directive or client-centered counseling from other forms of psychotherapy in which advice, information, interpretation, and practical assistance are intermingled. The Rogers technique deserves its original title of "non-directive" and justifies its claim to be completely "client-centered." The feelings, interests, values, goals of the therapist are hardly mentioned; those of the client dominate the whole procedure. At times the counselor is almost amusingly evasive. He replies to the client's anxious queries by acknowledging that the client feels anxious, or he parries a request for advice by recognizing that the client would like someone to settle the question for him. But he sticks to his non-directive principles and the client soon learns that he himself must take all the initiative.

[6] Rogers, *Client-Centered Therapy, op. cit.*, p. 34.

Course of Treatment. The regular series of events which Rogers claims to be characteristic of client-centered therapy begins with a process called *structuring the counseling relationship.* This consists of explaining to the client that the hour belongs to him, that he can talk about what he pleases, that the counselor has no preconceived answers to his problems, that benefit may result from talking everything over together. This process of structuring may have to be repeated many times, even well along in the series of interviews. It is not really what the client expects or wants. Especially if he is distressed and suffering he wants a greater display of reassurance and sympathy than he is likely to get from the counselor. Rogers shows, however, that very often the giving of reassurance is valueless because the client is not really able to accept it. Above all, every client, at one time or another, tries to get the counselor to give advice and solve his problems for him. Restructuring must be often repeated.

As the counselor succeeds in establishing an outflow of feelings, the client at first uses the opportunity to pour out his *negative feelings.* He gives vent to his doubts, guilts, inferiorities, anxieties, and hostilities. The counselor steadfastly accepts, recognizes, clarifies. When the negative feelings have been fully expressed, there occurs "one of the most certain and predictable aspects of the whole process," the faint and tentative expression of *positive impulses.* Social feelings, love, self-respect, the desire to be mature make their appearance in the client's conversation. When these are duly clarified there begin to be distinct signs of the *achievement of insight.* Having expressed so many feelings on both sides of the ledger, the client begins to see himself in a new light. He begins to talk about possible decisions and courses of action. Before long one witnesses the *initiation of positive actions,* possibly minute but generally significant. The timid high-school boy takes the step of going to a dance; the formerly frantic and resentful mother devises a way of showing affection and respect for her child; the prim and prudish young girl comes to the decision of bobbing her hair as the other girls have done. The first positive actions may be hardly more than symbolic. They may be initiated only after a series of attempts to persuade the counselor to sanction or advise them. But in any event they are important because they represent just the kind of step the client has been unable to take before.

As the client becomes increasingly able to take these positive actions, he begins to experience a decreasing need for the counselor. The relationship undergoes a subtle change. The client shows less strain and more confidence; he feels that he is working with the counselor on a plane of greater equality. He begins to speak occasionally of the approaching end of the relationship. The closing of treatment is a delicate matter that must be correctly timed. At first the client is apt to be a little terrified at the prospect. This feeling reappears when an actual date for the last meeting has been set. Sometimes the client feels worse again at the last meeting, but this may betoken nothing more than a wavering of confidence at the prospect of losing the relationship that has resulted in a definite improvement. Usually the client is allowed to depart with the assurance that he can come back if he needs to do so.

Changes Occurring in the Client. While success is of course not universal, there is no doubt that counseling according to this plan leads to changes in the client. A substantial number of research studies based upon many series of recorded interviews tend to confirm the course of events just described.[7] It has been verified, for instance, that negative feelings give place to positive feelings and that the initiation of positive actions increases during the course of the treatment. Although nothing is done except to recognize feelings and personal perceptions of experience, although no drastic interpretations are given and no attempt made to recover events of importance in the previous history, clients emerge from the experience with a sense of greater self-confidence and greater insight. They have achieved a corrective emotional experience through expressing their feelings and having these feelings made explicit for them by the counselor's constant recognition. The counselor has never told them what was wrong with them. By reflecting back upon them the feeling implications of each thing they have said, he has given them the chance to find out for themselves at least some of the things that are the matter with them. Change occurs, and it occurs in a fairly short time. We must put the question, therefore, whether the change is profound, whether it is enduring, whether the accompanying insights have a lasting effect on future development.

To look first on the bright side, we take one of Rogers' most successful examples, the case of sixteen-year-old Barbara.[8] During her junior year in high school this girl had what was described as a "nervous breakdown," characterized by "fears and sensations of an overwhelming sort which were very troubling." Her case appears to qualify as at least a mild neurosis. The root of her difficulty was discerned to be in an overstrict religious background and in a too strong identification with her scholarly father. Sixteen sessions of non-directive counseling brought about the following changes in her insight, accompanied by appropriate positive actions. (1) She passed from rather fantastic intellectual ambitions and an intense desire for perfection to a more realistic acknowledgment of what any one person, and herself in particular, would be able

[7] *Ibid.*, chap. iv; C. R. Rogers and R. F. Dymond, *Psychotherapy and Personality Change* (Chicago: University of Chicago Press, 1954).

[8] Rogers, *Counseling and Psychotherapy*, op. cit., pp. 185–94, 211–13, 223–28, 250–51.

to achieve. This progress did not end in a sad sense of limitation but rather in a cheerful acceptance of things as they are. (2) She changed from an "ultra-saintly person, afraid of any social instincts, to a person who wanted to get along with and enjoy other young people." Her social interests were very greatly expanded. (3) She had always "hated sweetheart stuff," but as the interviews progressed she was first able to acknowledge a distinctly affectionate interest in a certain boy friend, then later to appreciate the "puppy-love" character of this infatuation, recognizing its shallowness compared to what she really wanted. (4) Starting from the position that she wanted to be a man and greatly disliked children, she gradually came to feel that the role of woman and wife would not be objectionable. Her dislike of children began to evaporate.

These are large and important changes, having the effect of bringing the girl out of a blind alley of serious maladjustment into the main path of healthy development. Considering her youth and her apparent capacity for change, there is little reason to doubt that the benefit would be permanent. Unfortunately the amount of change does not always seem to be so large as it is in this example. When one studies the case of Herbert Bryan, for instance, a neurotic in his late twenties, whose eight interviews are printed verbatim in Rogers' earlier book,[9] there is room for considerable doubt as to whether the improvement was more than transient. Many problems clearly touched upon in the client's conversation were as unsolved at the end as at the beginning, and it is hard to feel confident that the brief spurt of self-assurance shown in the last two interviews would carry him through future difficulties. In contrast to Barbara, the course of whose life appears to have been set right by non-directive counseling, Herbert Bryan, older and with a more stubborn neurosis, sounds as if he left the counseling relationship very much as he came to it.

Evaluation of Client-centered Psychotherapy. The method developed by Rogers has been widely adopted, especially by non-medical counselors. It is appreciated for its clarity, its consistency, and the fact that it is unlikely to do the client any harm. It is all too easy during a therapeutic interview to mix up the principles one is employing and thus to destroy the efficacy of any of them. Thus an inexperienced or careless therapist may proceed for a while non-directively, thus affirming his respect for the client's ego, then be tempted into an interpretation which says in effect that he does not quite trust the client's ego, then hope to go back to the non-directive atmosphere just as if he had not wounded the client's ego. Rogers has shown how this kind of confusion can be avoided. He has shown how to proceed consistently on the basis of respecting the client's ego and letting him take all the initiative. What-

[9] *Ibid.*, pp. 261–437.

ever else it accomplishes, this work should have a profoundly clarifying effect on the training of future therapists, who should hereafter be able to realize much more clearly what they are doing at each moment, even if they decide to use other therapeutic tools besides the recognition of feelings.

But this desirable effect of Rogers' work should not overshadow the real limitations that begin to be apparent in client-centered psychotherapy. Considerable criticism has been evoked by his arrogation of the terms "non-directive" and "client-centered," with its implicit suggestion that all departures from this method must be autocratically directive and centered elsewhere than in the client. Perry and Estes take issue with the idea that counseling ceases to be client-centered the moment the counselor does anything except recognize feelings. "Any counselor-participation," they say, "which is assimilated by the client to a set in which he perceives himself as ultimately responsible for initiative and evaluation is properly described as client-centered."[10] Once the client has adopted this set the counselor will not break it merely by using his knowledge at appropriate places to give advice and make suggestions. Other workers express disapproval of the rigid use of a single therapeutic process regardless of circumstances. Beier, for example, calls attention to the large number of "involuntary clients" many counselors must deal with: delinquents, prisoners, employees, persons referred by the courts. The principles enunciated by Rogers appear to imply that these unmotivated people cannot be helped, yet it often happens that a little preliminary work consisting of advice, information, and persuasion turns them into motivated clients who profit from counseling.[11] Saslow points out that in the psychosomatic disorders the patient is often initially concerned only to be free from his physical symptom. Through proper guidance during the medical study such patients often come to see the need for psychological treatment. In cases of this common kind "a determined refusal to expand the client-centered orientation probably implies refusal to benefit a great many clients."[12]

The sharpest and most systematic criticism of non-directive therapy comes from Thorne, who considers it "definitely not the complete answer to all therapeutic problems, even in mild personality disorders."[13] Thorne

[10] W. G. Perry, Jr., and S. G. Estes, "The Collaboration of Client and Counselor," in O. H. Mowrer (ed.), *Psychotherapy: Theory and Research* (New York: The Ronald Press Co., 1953), p. 105.

[11] E. G. Beier, "Client-Centered Therapy and the Involuntary Client," *Journal of Consulting Psychology,* XIV (1952), pp. 332–37.

[12] G. Saslow, "Psychotherapy," in *Annual Review of Psychology,* V (Stanford: Annual Reviews, Inc., 1954), p. 315.

[13] F. C. Thorne, "A Critique of Non-Directive Methods of Psychotherapy," *Journal of Abnormal and Social Psychology,* XXXIX (1944), pp. 459–70; "Directive and Eclectic Personality Counseling," in J. L. McCary and D. E. Sheer (eds.), *Six Approaches to Psychotherapy* (New York: The Dryden Press, 1955), chap. v.

laments the failure to obtain any kind of history, pointing out that the counselor cannot be sure he has really uncovered the major problems if he does not permit himself to ask questions about the patient's past life. Furthermore, what facts the patient elects to reveal are not checked by corroborative evidence from other sources. As a result it is to be questioned whether a "comprehensive evaluation of the dynamic mechanisms operant in the total personality" has been made. Not enough is done to prevent the treatment from concentrating on one small and secondary portion of the patient's difficulties. Some of the published reports justify Thorne's remark that the patient "browsed along the edges of his problem, coming to grips with it only in terms of a few partial insights." It is the duty of the counselor to prevent this kind of evasion from taking place, unless he judges that greater insight would be seriously disturbing. It is his duty to use whatever methods are appropriate on a given occasion, including reassurance, support, and direct advice. Above all, in Thorne's view, it is the counselor's duty to use his knowledge to formulate in his own mind what is wrong with the client and to develop the best possible plan of treatment.

These criticisms cannot be overlooked. Non-directive counseling works on a client in just one way and neglects the possibility of using other approaches in a wise and timely fashion. What effect would it be likely to have on a fairly serious neurosis such as those we described in the last chapter? There is nothing in the procedure to prevent a patient from avoiding contact with his really important sources of anxiety. He can always change the subject if the conversation touches upon them too closely. Defensive tactics of this kind can be penetrated only by using stronger measures than the recognition of feeling. Such measures need not be highly directive. They are stronger in the sense that they produce more profound corrective emotional experiences. These measures have been most painstakingly worked out in Freudian psychoanalysis, to which we now turn.

STANDARD PSYCHOANALYSIS

It is not strictly correct to speak of any one procedure as standard psychoanalysis. Each worker who uses the method originally devised by Freud adapts it somewhat to his own personality and to the very different problems offered by his patients. Freud once likened psychoanalysis to chess, in which only the opening moves and a few typical concluding situations can be taught. With allowance for all the variation that must necessarily exist, however, we shall still be justified in referring to those forms of psychoanalysis as standard which have these characteristics: (1) the systematic use of free association, interpretation, and transference neurosis, and (2) the goal of uncovering and resolving the major emotional problems of the patient's childhood. By standard psychoanalysis, then, we really refer to the *full-length* variety, much as it was originally set forth by Freud.

In contrast to client-centered counseling, standard psychoanalysis takes a very long time. Treatment is usually scheduled to take place for one hour a day, five days a week. In spite of this rigorous schedule, it is rare for a psychoanalysis to be completed in less than one year, it is common for the treatment to last two or three years, and in some cases improvement is reached only after periods of five or more years. These figures become startling when we realize one of their implications—that a busy psychoanalyst who used only the standard technique would have time in his whole professional career to treat barely more than a hundred cases. When we consider, however, that a neurosis is the end result of a series of developments starting in childhood, it seems less remarkable that treatment should take such a long time. Unlearning and relearning cannot take place overnight. We should remember also that briefer methods of psychoanalysis could scarcely have been discovered without the patient full-length work of Freud and his followers.

Free Association. Psychoanalysis is distinguished from psychological counseling in the first place by its use of the specific technical tool of free association. The use of this tool does not imply disregard for recognition of feelings, which we saw was the special device used in client-centered therapy. Quite the contrary: free association is intended to promote the recognition of feelings by both patient and physician. It may even be considered a radical device for achieving this goal. In so far as the patient is successful in giving free associations, everything he says is governed by an emotional logic rather than a conscious and critical logic.

The early sessions of psychoanalysis are devoted to the taking of a case history. When this is accomplished, the patient is instructed in the technique of free association. Alexander summarized what is communicated to the patient in the following words:[14]

> The patient is requested to report everything that occurs to him in the analytic session. He is asked to verbalize everything that occurs to him in the original sequence and form without any modification or omission. He is asked to assume a passive attitude toward his own trains of thought; in other words, to eliminate all conscious control over his mental processes to which he gives free rein and merely report them.

This technique tends to heighten the activity of feeling, including feeling that is usually suppressed. As Alexander put it, "once the patient abandons the conscious control and direction of his ideas, the train of free

[14] F. Alexander, *The Medical Value of Psychoanalysis* (New York: W. W. Norton & Co., Inc., 1937), pp. 40–41.

spontaneous associations is guided more by the repressed material than by conscious motives."

The most interesting fact about free association is the obstacles it encounters. It was through a study of these obstacles—the silences, blockings, embarrassments, and anxieties of the patient which came to be called resistance—that Freud built up his concept of repression. It is worth while to point out and expressly reject a common misunderstanding about free association, the idea that it opens a highway over which repressed memories and fantasies roll smoothly into consciousness. No such miracle takes place, and the maximum effect that can possibly be attributed to the free association technique is a small reduction in the efficacy of habitual defenses, a weakening of the top layer of conscious control. Small as this change may be when thought of in terms of behavior dynamics, it is just enough to upset the delicate balance of personality organization in favor of hidden feelings. If repressed material starts to ooze upward, there is now an appreciable interval before it is met by the customary defenses, a precious moment during which the physician, if not the patient himself, can catch a glimpse of both parties to the conflict.

An Example of Free Association and Resistance. Free association and the resulting resistances play such a central part in psychoanalysis that we may profitably stop to examine a brief example. The following excerpt gives the opening remarks of a college student during his first hour of free association. After hearing the instructions from the examiner (*E*) the subject (*S*) proceeded as follows:

S: The thing uppermost in my mind at present is the hour exam I just had. Rather easy exam. I wasn't feeling particularly brilliant this morning. I don't know whether I made any mistakes or not. Quite a bit hinges on this exam because I want to get a scholarship for the second semester. If I get it, I will be able to carry through my work to my Master's degree. If I don't, I don't believe I'll be able to make it. It's hard to borrow money these days. I would like to keep on at college though because with the kind of work I get here I will get the kind of job I want. I am particularly interested in research work and this course that I am taking fits me for that.

E: I am afraid you are telling me a story rather than telling me what is coming into your mind. (After the first few sentences S has been giving a reasoned statement of his financial position. This is contrary to instruction and hence constitutes the first manifestation of resistance.)

S: I have an experiment this afternoon and I'm darned if I know what it is about. (This remark may contain a double meaning: S is wondering what the present session is about, as well as the afternoon's experiment. But he has abandoned his first form of resistance, the next topic being a good example of free associations.)

S: I wonder how my Dad is getting along. He is on his last legs, so to speak. Dad and I never got along very well. I remember one time when I was a youngster I was supposed to be watching some cows that were grazing near an orchard. I got so interested in reading that I forgot about the cows and they entered the orchard and ate some of the fruit off the trees. Dad was angry as the devil. He came around the corner and made a bee-line for me and I ran and he, being the old backwoods type, took a healthy swing at me with his foot as I went by and he slipped and nearly broke his arm on the wet grass. (At this point S turned around on the couch to look at *E*.)

E: What did you think when you turned around?

S: The reason I turned around was to look directly at you.

E: Why did you want to look directly at me?

S: If you are trying to put over a point and look directly at the person it is generally better. In sales work, for instance . . . (Again S has departed completely from free association to the idea of making a point and selling an argument. This is another form of resistance, similar to the first. At the same time he has dramatized his feeling toward *E*. Doubtless annoyed because *E* corrected him on account of his first lapse from the fundamental rule, he thinks of an earlier incident in which he lapsed from duty but eluded his father's wrath, and indeed turned the tables by being the cause of his father's hurting himself. This line of thought, however, awakens so much anxiety that he has to turn around to make sure that *E* is not getting angry. At this point *E* again reminds S of the fundamental rule.)

S: (Long pause.) I am to report what comes into my mind and nothing seems to come in. I don't care much for your paintings that you have, or whatever they are.

E: What don't you like about them?

S: I have disagreeable memories of paintings of that type. The framed diploma is a plain-looking thing to have on the wall. Is that yours, by the way?

E: Tell me what comes into your mind about it.

S: I thought it might be yours, but when I look at the inscription, it says "M.D.," so I guess that can't be yours. (For a moment S appears to free associate, but he has chosen another method of resistance, that of describing objects in the room. Almost at once his feelings betray themselves: he criticizes the objects, and leads up to a very neat indirect way of saying to *E*, "You are no doctor.")[15]

The subject, in this case, was not a patient but a participant in a study of personality. He was therefore treated less gently than would be advisable in the first session with a troubled neurotic individual. The excerpt nonetheless illustrates the difficulty of abandoning one's conscious vigilance. It shows the resistances and even anxieties that creep into the free associative process almost as soon as it is instituted.

Interpretation. Free association is the first distinguishing mark of psychoanalysis. The second point that distinguishes it from other methods is the systematic use of interpretation. It is true that interpretation enters to some extent into many therapeutic procedures, although it is scrupulously avoided in client-centered counseling. In psychoanalysis, however, it is the outstanding means used to bring about a corrective emotional

[15] This case is fully described in H. A. Murray, *Explorations in Personality* (Fair Lawn, N. J.: Oxford University Press, 1938), chap. vii. See especially pp. 639–40.

experience. As Hendrick puts it, "The analyst has become essentially a technician in reducing unconscious resistance. The chief implement in his technique is interpretation."[16] Hendrick makes it plain that interpretation is not used to instruct the patient, but rather to bring about a new feeling on his part. "The role of the analyst as interpreter," he continues, "is not to paraphrase what the patient reports, but to indicate at appropriate moments what he is *not* reporting."

These words neatly draw the contrast between psychoanalysis and client-centered therapy. The non-directive counselor does little more than paraphrase, though with a selective emphasis on the feeling aspect of what has been said. The psychoanalyst deliberately tries to point out to the patient that he is using a defense, that he is shifting away from a topic that has occurred to him, or that he is apparently trying to conceal something. This is the specific implement that psychoanalysis uses against the patient's defenses. Free association is designed to heighten the prominence of these defenses; interpretation is designd to show them to the patient and slowly wear them down.

It is obvious that the timing of interpretations is a matter of crucial importance. They must be given precisely at the moment when the patient is able to take them, and no sooner. If the patient cannot take them—if they awaken too much anxiety—he is forced to apply defenses against the interpretations and the analyst, and this delays the progress of treatment, in some cases even causing it to be broken off. An interpretation is rightly timed when the patient is able to perceive his defense, experience the impulse against which it is a defense, realize that he need not be afraid of this particular impulse, and thus achieve a relaxing of the defense. There is a gain of insight in this process, but its chief value lies in the corrective emotional experience. The essential thing is that the patient has stopped being afraid of some impulse in himself. Usually the feeling that results is one of relief and relaxation with a renewed outpouring of free associations.

At first the interpretations are what might be called superficial. They are nowhere near the neurotic nucleus and may have reference to the most trifling defenses such as mannerisms, tricks of speech, or minor acts that pass as conventional. Perhaps it is noticed that the patient repeatedly follows a sequence which consists of making a critical remark but denying that it is his own view of the matter. One day he says that an interior decorator might consider the therapist's wallpaper too dark, though he himself likes it. Another day he observes that a person with sinus trouble would not care for so much tobacco smoke in the consulting room, though he himself is happily free from that trouble. If the analyst calls his atten-

[16] I. Hendrick, *Facts and Theories of Psychoanalysis* (2d ed.; New York: Alfred A. Knopf, Inc., 1939), p. 215.

tion to this sequence, the patient is likely to be surprised; he has never noticed it himself. But if the interpretation has been correctly timed the patient will realize both his defense and the hostile impulse that necessitates the defense. He will be able to feel his own real annoyance and to relax his defense at least to the extent of expressing distaste for dark wallpapers and smoke as his own feelings rather than someone else's. This is typical of those short steps that are the most a patient can at first accomplish toward overcoming his deeper anxieties.

Interpretations may have to be repeated on several occasions before the patient fully and permanently relaxes his defense. Then, before long, the problem is likely to come up in a new guise, and once more a defense must be relaxed. The dangerous impulse has to be perceived and felt in all its manifold forms and connections. This slow process has been called *working through*. It is necessary, because the patient, even with the best will in the world, cannot relinquish all at once his defensive attitudes. The conflict has come to be represented in a great many contexts. Defense that is relaxed at one point crops up again in another context. Each fresh reminder of the pathogenic conflict sets it going again, calling for a new relaxation of defenses. Fortunately each new experience makes the work a little easier.

Rightly timed interpretations have the effect of relaxing defenses at points where the patient, if left to himself, would presumably maintain them. Interpretation is an implement for gently pushing the patient a little bit closer to his anxieties and defenses. Why is he able to relax a defense under these circumstances? Probably for two reasons which operate together. (1) He perceives that the danger is not as real as his defense had implied. The defense is excessive, and it is safe to let it down. We can express this another way by saying that he becomes able to reappraise the danger situation. (2) He is strengthened by the presence of the analyst, who serves as a guarantee of safety, even while he urges renewed contact with the threat. To the extent that the patient is dominated by anxieties he may be likened to a frightened child. Alone he cannot face the threats, but in company with the analyst he dares to peek at them and finally approach them. The patient becomes a little more daring because he is not alone in the enterprise. This increase of daring is the heart of his corrective emotional experience.

Transference Neurosis. In addition to free association and interpretation, standard psychoanalysis makes extensive use of the transference neurosis. We have already looked into Freud's concept of the transference.[17] As treatment proceeds, the patient begins to manifest a variety of personal feelings toward the analyst. These feelings run all the way

[17] See above, pages 34–36.

from admiration and affection to hostility and fear. When the transference is positive, the analytic work proceeds smoothly. The patient produces many associations, accepts interpretations fairly readily, and may begin to feel much better. When the transference is negative, the work goes on slowly, with difficulty, without signs of benefit to the patient.

Transference neurosis refers to an acute development that occurs fairly regularly in full-length psychoanalysis and that is considered essential for a complete cure. The relation to the analyst is intensified to a point where it becomes more important to the patient than does his own recovery. He seems to be engaged in a struggle with the analyst, trying to win various kinds of emotional satisfaction from him. In this stage it becomes abundantly clear that the patient's attitudes have little relation to the actual situation; they are "transferred from earlier ones, especially from childhood conflicts with the parents." Freud referred to this development as a "new edition" of the old neurosis. The following paragraph from Hendrick deserves careful attention.[18]

> Because this occurs with such consistency in every analysis, we can understand that the transference has developed to a point where the transference emotions are more important to the patient than the permanent health he is seeking. This is the point where the major unresolved, unconscious problems of childhood begin to dominate. They are now reproduced in the transference with all their pent-up emotion. The patient is unconsciously striving for what he failed to gain or to do without in actual childhood. Only those who have observed it will appreciate how fully much of the reaction to the analyst at this period is like a child's. Petulance, irritability, defiance, even a childishness in tone of voice are frequent, even in people who are otherwise quite mature.

The transference neurosis is reached only after the more superficial defenses have been relaxed. It signifies that the patient has at last reanimated his nuclear neurotic processes. When he has struggled through this stage with its crucial corrective emotional experiences, his treatment is nearly finished. The steps that remain consist of dissolving the therapeutic relationship and implementing the new freedom from anxiety by appropriate positive actions outside the consulting room. The dissolving of a relationship that has carried so much emotional weight takes a considerable time. When this is successfully accomplished, however, there is no aftermath of dependence, and the patient turns freely to the new life that has become available to him.

The transference neurosis occurs with little direct provocation from the analyst. But it is fair to say that the whole analytic situation encourages this particular development. The psychoanalyst typically makes himself a shadowy figure, a blank screen on which the patient can project whatever fantasies lie close to his heart. The analytic patient lies on a

[18] Hendrik, *op. cit.*, p. 208.

couch, relaxing in the interests of free association. The therapist sits out of sight and does not have much to say. As a matter of policy, most analysts rule out any social contacts with patients outside the office. While always present as a source of reassurance and strength if necessary, the therapist does not become as clearly differentiated a figure as those one meets in daily life. Peck described his role as follows: "He loans himself, as it were, for the subject to react upon in a sort of test experience, and, instead of being drawn into that experience, his part is to reveal to the patient what is going on."[19] By restricting himself to this kind of a part, he makes it easier for the patient to use him as a father, a mother, an authority figure, a rival, or whatever person is needed in working out the neurotic nucleus.

One of the features of client-centered therapy is its unceasing respect for the client's maturity. The counselor always allows him to take the lead in what goes along as an ordinary conversation. The psychoanalyst does not attempt to handle his patient so gently. From the start, when he instructs the patient in free association and when he gives interpretations that necessarily constitute a criticism, he creates a relationship that has a little of the quailty of teacher and pupil if not of parent and child. The non-directive counselor is unfailingly permissive. The analyst is permissive toward all kinds of impulses and fantasies in the patient that would win condemnation in everyday life, but he is not permissive when it comes to using defenses and failing to associate freely.[20] It is appropriate in comparing the two procedures to quote another remark of Peck's to the effect that psychoanalysis is "the major surgery of psychotherapy." "Like major surgery, analysis does not help everything, nor is it usually the first method to be thought of in trouble. It should be reserved for those problems which less radical procedure does not reach."[21]

The working through of the transference neurosis is accomplished by the familiar implements: free association and interpretation. Interpretation operates with its greatest effectiveness at just this point. If a patient has been expressing fury at the analyst for not showing the loving attention of a father, and if he then experiences sharp anxiety lest the father punish or desert him, it becomes peculiarly easy for him to appreciate the archaic character of his feelings. The discrepancy between the actual therapeutic situation and his childlike demands and fears is dramatic and inescapable. The intense but inappropriate emotions that constitute the

[19] M. Peck, *The Meaning of Psychoanalysis* (New York: Alfred A. Knopf, Inc., 1931), p. 188.

[20] For a searching discussion of this contrast, see J. M. Butler, "The Interaction of Client and Therapist," *Journal of Abnormal and Social Psychology,* XLVII (1952), pp. 366–78.

[21] Peck, *op. cit.,* pp. 159–60.

transference neurosis can thus have a peculiarly powerful corrective effect.

Dream Analysis. The analysis of dreams plays a prominent part in standard psychoanalysis. We have not discussed it up to this point because in spite of its prominence it introduces no new therapeutic principles. Dreams may be regarded as spontaneous free associations. They are used in psychoanalytic treatment as a starting point for further free associations, and sometimes as objects for interpretation. They are of service to the extent that they allow feelings and attitudes to leak into awareness faster than might otherwise be the case. What they bring forward, however, is utilized no differently from other material.

When a patient is undergoing psychotherapy his sleep is likely to be disturbed by a great many tensions set up during the treatment and left unresolved at bedtime. Psychotherapy is a disturbing business. It stirs up feelings and problems that one would prefer to avoid. The dreams that occur concurrently with treatment are therefore likely to be numerous and heavily loaded with matters pertaining to the illness. Among other things they often portray with crystal clearness the state of the transference relationship. Direct expression of transference emotions, whether affectionate or hostile, is for most patients not easy. Even free association does not always suffice to bring such material into verbal expression. Here the patient's dreams will often take the lead, expressing this feeling in disguised but dramatic form and thus opening a road for less roundabout expressions.[22] Dreams thus help to keep the treatment in motion and sometimes pull it out of doldrums when everything seems blocked. Occasionally a dream marks a dramatic and significant change, becoming the means of sudden forward progress. We shall describe an example of this kind in the next section.

PSYCHOANALYTICALLY ORIENTED PSYCHOTHERAPY

Thus far we have concentrated on extremes. Client-centered therapy is the shortest, and standard psychoanalysis the longest, method of psychotherapy. The client-centered or non-directive method is criticized chiefly for the fault of being too superficial. Standard psychoanalysis is never criticized on this ground, but constantly has to answer questions as to whether such thoroughness is necessary and whether the process cannot in some way be hastened. Our study of psychoanalysis will have shown that hastening or shortening is no simple matter. One cannot talk

[22] An illuminating analysis of a series of dreams dealing with progressive changes in the transference relationship is given by T. M. French, *The Integration of Behavior, I., Basic Postulates* (Chicago: University of Chicago Press, 1952), especially chaps. xvii, xviii, and xxxiii–xxxv.

sensibly about shortening the process without showing just how and where the shortening is to take place. Is there to be a shortening or elimination of the transference neurosis? Is the process of working through to be curtailed? Are the interpretations to be speeded up, and if so, what is to prevent the patient from leaving the analysis in disgust? Critics of psychoanalysis usually do not sense the full difficulty of speeding up a process that calls for corrective emotional experience and that has to struggle with an affect so powerful as anxiety. It is clear, however, that a procedure as lengthy as standard psychoanalysis cannot go far toward meeting the vast human need for psychotherapeutic services. While we have no way of knowing how much the actual need may have increased, it can be said with certainty that during the last twenty-five years there has been a widespread cultural change in awareness of the need and willingness to seek psychological help. The new demand severely overtaxes existing resources for giving help. There can be no doubt that shorter psychotherapy is urgently needed.

As a consequence of this dilemma there is today a growing use of what has come to be called *psychoanalytically oriented psychotherapy*. This expression implies that the therapist is familiar with psychoanalytic principles; that he acknowledges the importance of unconscious motivation, the defense mechanisms, and Freud's stages of psychosexual development; and that he attempts to use these insights in understanding his patients and planning their treatment. It does not imply that the treatment is carried out according to standard psychoanalytic technique. There may be considerable departures dictated by circumstances and limitations of time, and the goal of resolving all major emotional problems may have to be replaced by an attempt to resolve only those problems that are most acute and most ripe for resolution. If the methods become wholly random and opportunistic, it is hardly accurate to call them psychoanalytically oriented; and some therapists, while still using this designation, have certainly drawn from other sources besides Freud. Strictly speaking, the term should be used only for a *planned reduction* of the standard procedure. How this reduction can be accomplished has been well described in a report by Alexander and French.[23]

The Principle of Flexibility. In the opinion of Alexander and French, it is possible to vary the psychoanalytic technique very widely in accordance with the needs of particular patients. By adapting the method to the patient, they find it possible to shorten the average length of treatment without thereby making the therapy superficial. "As we now practice psychoanalytic therapy," they say, "we seldom use one and the same

[23] Alexander, French, *et al., op. cit.*

method of approach from the first to the last day of treatment."[24] Instead, the guiding principle is the principle of flexibility.

Varying the Details of Procedure. The principle of flexibility can be expressed by saying that every aspect of the technique is varied as much as may be necessary to fit the patient's problems and progress at that particular moment. Sometimes the patient lies on the couch and gives free associations. At other times it is more economical to have him sit in a chair facing the therapist and talk about his problems in the ordinary manner. Interviews may be held every day, but this may encourage the patient to procrastinate and withdraw more deeply than is necessary into early memories and a reconstruction of childhood experiences. On the whole it is preferable to have daily interviews only when the patient is acutely distressed or highly resistant. Otherwise one or two meetings a week makes for more rapid progress, giving each meeting a more important character. Another matter that can be varied is the emotional intensity of the interviews. Patients differ a great deal in the amount of emotion they can endure. The standard free association teachnique is well adapted to those whose tolerance is low, but some patients profit by the kind of insights and emotional experiences that arise out of direct conversation, argument, and challenging interpretations. The pace of interpretation can be increased for those patients who are able to stand it. Often it is advantageous to interrupt treatment for a period of time in order to let the patient work his problems over in his own mind and test his own resources. He does some of his working through by himself. In all these respects, therefore, technique can be varied in the interests of more rapid improvement.

Manipulating the Transference Relationship. Particularly important is flexibility in regard to the transference relationship. Increasing doubt has arisen as to the wisdom of allowing a full transference neurosis to develop in all cases. It is an interesting fact, a valuable addition to scientific knowledge, that the transference neurosis can develop and that it does so spontaneously if given the opportunity. Much has been learned in this way about the childhood origins of neurosis. But as a practical matter the full development of transference neurosis in all its aspects does more than anything else to lengthen the treatment, and Alexander and French hold that it is in most cases unnecessary. The problem is seen in a new light. The transference neurosis must be kept within workable limits and confined to those aspects which reflect the really nuclear problems. In some cases it is not allowed to develop at all. The manipulation of the transference is accomplished by the therapist's attitude and his interpretations. If his interpretations call attention to the

[24] *Ibid.*, p. 25.

infantile character of the patient's behavior, transference neurosis is greatly encouraged. If he directs interpretations only toward the present situation, transference neurosis is discouraged. Thus it is within the therapist's power to control this feature of the relationship in the interests of maximum efficiency.

Encouraging Activity Outside the Analysis. Another aspect of flexibility is seen in the use of experiences outside the therapeutic relationship. Standard psychoanalysis tended to neglect this possible resource in treatment. The value of extratherapeutic experiences is well brought out in the following quotations.

> It is important to keep in mind that the patient will finally have to solve his problems in actual life, in his relationships to his wife and his children, his superiors and his competitors, his friends and his enemies. The experiences in the transference relationship are only preparations, a training for the real battle. The sooner the patient can be led against those real obstacles in life from which he retreated and can be induced to engage in new experimentation, the more quickly can satisfactory therapeutic results be achieved.
>
> There is no more powerful therapeutic factor than the performance of activities which were formerly neurotically impaired or inhibited. No insight, no emotional discharge, no recollection can be as reassuring as accomplishment in the actual life situation in which the individual failed.[25]

In addition to encouraging the patient when he seems prepared to take active steps of some kind, the therapist sometimes makes contact with his spouse, employer, or a friend. A change of attitude by a person of importance in the patient's life may helpfully speed the patient's own progress.

Alexander and French believe that the practice of briefer psychoanalysis requires experience with the full-length standard technique. No matter how greatly the treatment may be abbreviated, it is always a planned reduction of the full-scale analytic process. One cannot say, they contend, that briefer psychoanalysis is simpler psychoanalysis. It requires greater rather than less skill. The matter of timing, for instance, which is crucial enough in standard psychoanalysis, becomes even more crucial and delicate when not only interpretations but also changes in technique, the emotional intensity of the sessions, and the encouragement of outside activities have to be correctly timed. It is necessary for the therapist, moreover, to have a correct and early grasp of the patient's problems in order to plan an economical strategy for the treatment. The therapist's understanding may be revised from week to week and his plan of treatment may have to change. But this makes the process longer; the maximum saving is achieved when the initial diagnosis and plan of

[25] *Ibid.*, pp. 38, 40.

treatment are correct. Great burdens are thus placed on the analyst's skill, wisdom, and experience.

An Illustrative Case. We can accomplish more by describing a case than by further general discussion. The following case was chosen by Alexander and French as an illustration of the principle of flexibility.[26]

A businessman of forty-two years had suffered for a long time from an uncontrollable jerking of his arms. On three occasions he had had brief periods of unconsciousness. Neurological examination failed to disclose any sign of brain injury which might account for these attacks or for the jerking. The patient had a long history of irritability and a domineering attitude which injured his human relationships. At one point his wife divorced him on account of these intolerable traits, but later they were remarried. The immediate occasion for seeking medical help was the fact that his wife was again considering separation. In addition, for a number of weeks he had suffered a complete loss of sexual potency.

The treatment consisted of twenty-six interviews extending over a period of ten weeks. Brief as it was, the results were entirely satisfactory.

The patient's troubles were discerned to have their origins in his relation to his father. The father had been a self-made man with huge self-confidence and a violent temper. He was a tyrant both at home and in his business. He never tired of making the son feel inferior, and though at times there was sharp conflict between them, the son always gave in. Among other things the father had intimidated the patient in the matter of sexual expression. To meet all this pressure and somehow preserve self-respect, the patient had built up his own assertive and domineering attitude. He was ruled by a vast compensatory need to appear important and strong. When the father died, the patient took over the family glassware works and with great energy expanded it well beyond what his father had been able to accomplish. He felt impelled to surpass his father, yet along with all his competition and rebellion there was a great deal of admiring devotion.

From the very start the patient reproduced in the therapeutic situation his combined attitudes toward his father. He wanted rules to be made for him, and scrupulously obeyed one or two that had to be suggested. But his conversation was otherwise designed to impress the analyst with his importance, and whenever the analyst explained anything he quickly began to explain something about which he himself was expert: business or sports. He literally tried to force the doctor to become tyrannical so that he could rebel and compete with him. This attitude was so clear that after two meetings the analyst undertook to create a corrective emotional experience by behaving in just the opposite fashion. He let the

[26] *Ibid.*, pp. 55–65.

patient take the lead, avoided statements that could be thought arbitrary, admitted the limitations of psychiatry, expressed admiration for the patient's good qualities, took an interest in his business and social activities. Under this treatment the patient became distinctly confused. He plainly thrived in the permissive, encouraging atmosphere, but he was unable to check his competitive feelings and still tried to fight battles with the analyst. This offered the perfect opportunity for crucial interpretations. The patient could not help seeing that his aggression was completely out of relation to the analyst's behavior. His chief overdriven striving was exposed and he became able to enter a more genuine relationship with the doctor.

The change in his attitude toward the therapist was soon reflected at home. He became less domineering and was able to assume a more appropriately benevolent and helpful role toward his son. But his need to make a tyrant out of the analyst finally yielded only after a particularly vivid dream and its aftermath. The patient dreamed that he had manufactured some glassware and that the analyst angrily broke it all to pieces. The dream reminded him of an occasion when his father smashed a set of glassware because he did not like the design. During the hour which began with the reporting of this dream, the analyst asked the patient to tell more about his work. The patient eagerly embarked on a condescending lecture. The corrective emotional experience occasioned by thus assuming authority over the therapist was so great that the patient thereafter recovered his sexual potency. His old role of the now-rebelling, now-submitting son could be outgrown as he found it possible to have a relation of friendly give and take with an authoritative person. As he achieved this new learning on the social plane he outgrew his sexual intimidation.

The remaining few hours of treatment were devoted to fuller discussion of the transference relationship. In childhood the patient had often been obliged to accept help from his father, but the father had always made him feel inferior on such occasions. This led him to react with a compensatory striving to prove that he was really the better man. Accepting help from the analyst had thus reanimated from the start the very core of the neurotic problem. The analyst's radical assumption of exactly the opposite role, giving help along with interest, permissiveness, and a complete lack of the father's dogmatic self-confidence, led to an unusually rapid corrective emotional experience. At the end of treatment the patient's arms no longer jerked, which may be taken as presumptive evidence that the jerking originated from the tension of suppressed rage. His emotional and sexual relations with his wife were better than ever before, talk of separation had ended, and his irritable and domineering tendencies had greatly diminished. The patient was at least much improved, if not fully cured.

Analysis of the Therapeutic Process. Let us consider this case as a planned reduction of the standard psychoanalytic technique, at the same time comparing it with the client-centered method. Free association on the couch was not used extensively. Most of the interviews were conducted as ordinary conversations. In this respect the procedure did not differ from counseling. The therapist did more, however, than recognize and clarify the patient's feelings. Guessing at the nature of the central problem from the very start, he deliberately took a more actively conciliatory and participating attitude. He used interpretation freely at critical points. It is questionable whether the patient would have moved ahead so rapidly if the therapist had not taken the initiative in pointing out the inappropriateness of his competitive aggression. The case illustrates particularly well the controlled use of the transference neurosis. If the analyst had remained a passive blank-screen, the patient would probably have stayed for many weeks fighting out his angers and his timid submissions, learning only gradually that they were not appropriate in the therapeutic situation. By taking a clear attitude and being a definite person quite unlike the patient's father, the analyst brought about a much quicker realization and abandonment of these defensive actions. Yet the events that did take place qualify as a limited transference neurosis. "The main factor was that the patient was given an opportunity in his relationship to the analyst, first, to develop the same emotional conflict he had toward his father (the transference neurosis) and, second, to find a new, less neurotic solution for this conflict."[27]

It should be realized that this successful treatment in twenty-six interviews is unusually short. There are elements of luck as well as planning in briefer psychoanalysis. It was a peculiar piece of good fortune that the whole analytic situation so readily aroused the nuclear problem. Had the patient happened to consult a woman physician of about his own age instead of an older man, it would not have been possible to adopt the same procedure. One must recognize in this patient a rather unusual degree of ego potentiality and capacity to endure emotional tension. Success could scarcely have been attained so quickly with someone of less energetic disposition. Nevertheless it is quite apparent that the principle of flexibility did much to hasten the process of treatment.

In the years that have elapsed since the publication of Alexander and French's book there has been a strong trend in the directions they indicated. There has also been sharp controversy. Some workers have taken the position that shortened forms of treatment simply abandon the best

[27] *Ibid.*, p. 62.

features of standard psychoanalysis and therefore stand less chance of producing fundamental changes and a lasting cure in the patient.[28] On the whole, however, the movement is certainly toward flexible alterations in the standard technique with a view to accomplishing the therapeutic goal in a shorter time.[29]

SUMMARY OF BASIC PROCESSES

We are now in a position to try to discern the fundamental processes that are at work in psychotherapy. Nothing that we have studied violates the general principle that the essence of therapy is a corrective emotional experience which opens the way to changes in feeling and behavior. No one today will raise the flag for bare intellectual understanding as a means of treatment. Our search for basic processes therefore resolves itself into an attempt to isolate the measures taken to favor corrective emotional experiences.

It seems possible to name five processes which pretty well cover the action that goes on in psychotherapy.

1. Therapeutic Relationship. First there is the creation of a unique situation and a unique personal relationship. There are four important aspects of the therapeutic situation. (a) The therapist is *expert,* in the sense that he possesses special training, experience, and knowledge about maladjusted and disordered behavior. (b) The therapist is *permissive,* in the sense that he serves only the interests of health and makes no censorious judgments upon the patient's acts or feelings. (c) The therapist is *interested and friendly,* communicating in this way a certain warmth that makes the relationship more personal than is ordinarily the case in a professional consultation. (d) The therapist is a *source of encouragement.* While it is necessary to avoid all false reassurance, the effect of his presence is to increase courage. The patient dares to express feelings and relax defenses because of his strengthening alliance with the therapist. It is within the shelter of this relationship that corrective emotional experience begins to take place.

2. Expression of Feelings. Steps are taken to encourage the patient to express his feelings. This may be done by asking questions, by taking

[28] K. R. Eissler, "The Chicago Institute of Psychoanalysis and the Sixth Period of the Development of Psychoanalytic Technique," *Journal of General Psychology,* XLII (1950), pp. 103–57.

[29] An interesting account of a highly flexible use of Freudian principles is given by N. Reider, "Psychotherapy Based on Psychoanalytic Principles," in *Six Approaches to Psychotherapy* (New York: The Dryden Press, 1955), chap. iv. See also a paper by A. Karush, "Reparative Psychotherapy and Adaptational Theory," illustrated by two case reports, in M. I. Stein (ed.), *Contemporary Psychotherapies* (New York: The Free Press of Glencoe, Inc., 1961), pp. 319–37.

a case history, or by encouraging the patient to give his own story. From non-directive counseling, however, we learned that feelings come to expression more readily when the patient rather than the therapist leads the way in the conversation. In this chapter we have also studied a technical device for increasing the expression of feelings. *Free association* is intended to remove superficial resistances and bring into prominence the emotional patterns that stand in need of correction. In the next chapter we shall examine several additional technical devices having much the same purpose.

3. Pointing Out of Feelings. The action of the therapist upon what the patient expresses consists essentially of pointing out the feelings. In this way the patient becomes more fully aware of his feelings; he develops insight and is thus better able to profit by further experiences in which he is moved by the same feelings. We have examined two forms of the pointing out procedure. (a) *Recognition of feeling,* the process neatly isolated by Rogers, consists of paraphrasing what the patient says in such a way as to emphasize its feeling implications. The therapist sets the focus of interest on feeling and brings about a greater expression of feeling than is usual for the patient. The changes that ensue from this free expression in the presence of the therapist constitute in themselves a corrective emotional experience. (b) *Interpretation,* the cornerstone of psychoanalytic procedure, may be regarded as a more active form of recognition. Instead of recognizing the patient's feelings as they are expressed, the therapist recognizes feelings before they are expressed or when they are still being expressed in disguised ways—at all events, before the patient himself has recognized them. When suitably timed, this procedure also results in corrective emotional experience.

4. Transference. The initial therapeutic relationship can readily become colored by childlike attitudes in the patient. The importance of the treatment is so great, and the emotions involved so strong, that the patient can hardly avoid developing certain feelings that have little to do with the actual situation and much to do with his own past. The transference of childlike feelings into the therapeutic relationship can be either discouraged or encouraged by the therapist. If the patient is allowed to develop the same emotional conflicts in relation to the therapist that he had with parental and other important figures in early life, a situation is created that is peculiarly favorable for interpretation. The *transference neurosis,* as developed in Freudian psychoanalysis, is a state of very real emotion, but the experience becomes corrective only when through interpretation the patient realizes the inappropriate character of his feelings and reappraises the archaic dangers from which they spring.

5. New Behavior. As treatment progresses, the patient begins to behave in new ways outside the therapeutic relationship. He starts to replace his rooted maladjustive patterns with better adjusted forms of behavior. To the extent that these new actions are successful and prove rewarding, they constitute corrective emotional experience. The possibility of dissolving the therapeutic relationship can be gauged from the success and stability of the patient's new behavior. A variety of attitudes can be taken toward what the patient does in his actual life, ranging all the way from simple recognition through encouragement to persuasion and direction. We saw that the client-centered counselor never explicitly urged any line of new conduct upon his client but was quick to recognize it when it occurred, thus strengthening it by implicit subsequent approval. Standard psychoanalysis also steers away from explicit direction, preferring to work out the transference relation thoroughly before the patient tries his wings in new ventures. Psychoanalytically oriented psychotherapy is more apt to be flexible on this matter, but not to the point of bluntly urging the patient to behave differently and change his attitudes.

The reluctance of psychotherapists to exert a direct pressure of this kind should not blind us to the presence of a certain indirect pressure. Jerome Frank argues that in all methods of psychotherapy there is an inescapable element of persuasion.[30] Even if nothing is said about new behavior, something is inevitably implied. The therapist may sedulously avoid comments of a censorious nature and try to keep his own preferences and ideals out of the conversation; but it is clear that in the end he is against the irrational anxieties, defensiveness, and symptoms that make for neurosis, and in favor of a more free and healthful pattern of life. Patient and therapist alike know that change is desirable; the whole point of their relation is to produce it. Thus it is likely that a subtle kind of persuasion plays its part in the process of psychotherapy, but the work we have thus far studied suggests that better results are obtained when this is kept out of the foreground.

CHOICE OF PATIENTS FOR PSYCHOTHERAPY

As a practical matter it has long been recognized that some patients are more suitable than others for psychotherapy. Although corrective emotional experience and subsequent relearning do not seem to imply any special kind of talent, therapists have learned that in any given case of psychogenic disorder it is wise to try to estimate the patient's chances of developing and profiting by such experiences. Obviously the presence

[30] J. D. Frank, *Persuasion and Healing: A Comparative Study of Psychotherapy* (Baltimore: Johns Hopkins Press, 1961).

of important organic difficulties and instabilities makes psychological treatment problematical and suggests that if used at all it should be combined with supportive and somatic measures. The real circumstances surrounding the patient also have to be carefully assessed. He may be burdened by inescapable responsibilities which contribute heavily to his trouble. Ideally the patient should be in a position to change those circumstances in his life that tend to reinforce neurotic patterns of behavior and to oppose new ones. On this account it is generally true that youth is an advantage, though advanced age is not an absolute contra-indication. In private practice there is also the question of ability to pay, and here and in public clinics the patient may find it difficult to set aside the necessary time. All of these considerations, however, lie outside the psychological sphere. Are there any strictly psychological dimensions to the problem of selecting patients?

There seems to be substantial agreement among different workers concerning three such dimensions.

1. First there is the question of motivation or need. As Rogers expresses it, the patient must be "under a degree of tension, arising from incompatible personal desires or from the conflict of social and environmental demands with individual needs."[31] Discomfort and tension must be great enough to overbalance the stress that inevitably arises during treatment. When patients seek help of their own accord, this first condition is usually met, but when they have been sent for treatment the therapist must judge carefully whether their own motives will become enlisted. Psychotherapy is a learning situation, and the factor of motivation cannot be neglected.

2. Intelligence cannot be ruled out, inasmuch as psychotherapy proceeds through the medium of conversation and requires a coherent reporting and synthesizing of one's experience. Feeble-mindedness would bar psychotherapy, and there is considerable doubt about the dull-normal range.

3. An elusive factor variously known as adaptability, ego potentiality, and capacity to cope with life must be weighed as well as possible in estimating the chances for success. Hendrick refers to this factor as "strength of character" or, more precisely, "the capacity to endure an excess of emotional tension, to strive for reasonable goals in spite of inner difficulties which tempt one to accept the decision, 'I am just made that way,' as an excuse for withdrawing from struggle." He adds, "The patient's capacity to fight the neurosis is a great asset, and it varies as greatly among individuals as does the degree of neurosis itself."[32] Obviously it is no mean task to estimate such a capacity beforehand. The

[31] Rogers, *Counseling and Psychotherapy, op. cit.*, p. 76.
[32] Hendrick, *op. cit.*, pp. 240–41.

patient's life history may give substantial evidence, but often the decision cannot be made without a trial of psychotherapy.

Any process of selection opens the way to all kinds of personal preferences and prejudices on the part of the therapist. Even though everyone recognized this possibility, it came as a rude shock to discover that the chances of a patient being selected for treatment were significantly correlated with social class position. Hollingshead and Redlich, in a noteworthy analysis of the prevalence and treatment of disorders in a whole community, were responsible for bringing this disturbing fact to light.[33] Taking only the publicly supported clinics, where the therapists are on salary and the patient's financial arrangements, if any, are made with someone else, they showed that senior psychiatrists prefer to work with patients high on the social ladder, turning over those of lower class to internes and medical students. Class position proves to be very definitely related to both the amount and the expertness of treatment received. These findings were a painful blow to the staff members of the clinics, who did not have the slightest intention of practicing class discrimination. But the authors were able to show that all the psychiatrists in the community belonged to the top social classes, some having arrived there quite recently.

The findings deserve careful scrutiny, for it is not likely that they represent pure snobbishness on the part of the psychotherapists. Two factors seem to be responsible for the pattern of selection: one of intelligence and the other of general outlook. Research on social stratification uses number of years of schooling as one of its criteria for placing people in the class structure. This suggests that the psychotherapists were choosing partly on the basis of effective intelligence as shown in the first interviews; they preferred the better educated, intellectually livelier patients. The research also showed great differencs in outlook between higher- and lower-class positions. Patients with relatively little schooling and poor economic prospects are apt to lead somewhat humdrum lives, read almost nothing beyond the daily papers, and depend for entertainment on television, and they do not have much real belief that their fortunes will be bettered. They tend to think of emotional disorders in the impersonal terms we use for physical disease, as caused by infections or bumps on the head; and they expect to be cured, if at all, by a pill or an injection. The idea of achieving maximal self-realization through insight into one's own behavior—the goal of psychoanalysis—is beyond the comprehension of a great many patients who arrive for treatment, and often the therapist struggles in vain to secure its acceptance even in rudimentary form.

[33] A. B. Hollingshead and F. C. Redlich, *Social Class and Mental Illness: A Community Study* (New York: John Wiley & Sons, Inc., 1958).

Hollingshead and Redlich's report thus serves to remind us that psychotherapy in its modern form has moved rather far toward intellectual sophistication. It is best adapted to patients accustomed to living hopefully, reflectively, and at least with a fair amount of intellectual control. The report also reminds us of the importance of a kind of compatibility between therapist and patient. Summarizing a considerable body of research since this report appeared, Hans Strupp characterizes as follows the attributes of a good patient as seen by therapists.

> Patients considered good prognostic risks are described as young, attractive, well-educated, members of the upper middle class, possessing a high degree of ego-strength, some anxiety which impels them to seek help, no seriously disabling neurotic symptoms, relative absence of deep characterological distortions and strong secondary gains, a willingness to talk about their difficulties, an ability to communicate well, some skill in the social-vocational area, and a value system relatively congruent with that of the therapist. Such patients also tend to remain in therapy, profit from it, and evoke the therapist's best efforts. By superficial criteria, such patients may not appear very "sick"; however, neither our culture nor our psychological tests are very sensitive to unhappiness, silent suffering, and despair.[34]

Strupp makes the further point that "only a relatively restricted band of the population meets these criteria, which, incidentally, are not very different from the ones originally postulated by Freud." When we think back to the crude hypnotic tactics of Mesmer and to the only slightly more sophisticated suggestive methods of Charcot, we are perhaps justified in saying that Freud started psychotherapy on a kind of social ascent, paying little attention to the needs of average clinical patients and turning it into a refined method of self-development with aims far beyond the removal of symptoms and the relief of immediate suffering. It will be helpful to bear this in mind as we examine further methods of treatment in the next chapter, and particularly when we come to the highly controversial topic of the results of psychotherapy.

SUGGESTIONS FOR FURTHER READING

The literature on psychotherapy has become voluminous in the last few years. A fine initial orientation, with historical sweep, can be obtained from Jerome D. Frank's *Persuasion and Healing: A Comparative Study of Psychotherapy* (Baltimore, Johns Hopkins Press, 1961). The therapeutic relation is searchingly examined in Frieda Fromm-Reichmann's *Principles of Intensive Psychotherapy* (Chicago, University of Chicago Press, 1950), Ch. 1.

For client-centered psychotherapy the sources are two books by Carl R. Rogers, *Counseling and Psychotherapy* (1942) and *Client-Centered Therapy* (1951) (both published by Houghton Mifflin Co., Boston). A short presen-

[34] H. H. Strupp, "Psychotherapy," in *Annual Review of Psychology,* XIII (1962), pp. 470–71.

tation of these ideas is given by N. Hobbs in *Six Approaches to Psychotherapy* (J. L. McCary & D. L. Sheer, eds., New York, The Dryden Press, 1955), Ch. 1; in Ch. 5 of the same book will be found criticisms of the Rogers position and a contrasting viewpoint by Thorne.

Freud's *General Introduction to Psychoanalysis* (New York, Liveright Publishing Corp., 1920) gives a good introduction to his views on treatment in Chs. 27–28. I. Hendrick devotes Part III of his *Facts and Theories of Psychoanalysis* (2d ed., New York, Alfred A. Knopf, Inc., 1939) to the same topic. A more detailed and technical account of psychoanalytic technique, departing somewhat from the classical formulations to take account of recent advances in ego psychology, is L. J. Saul's *Technique and Practice of Psychotherapy* (Philadelphia, J. B. Lippincott Co., 1958). A searching study of the effects of interpretation has been given by J. Strachey, "The Nature of the Therapeutic Action of Psychoanalysis," *International Journal of Psychoanalysis,* 1934, Vol. 15, pp. 127–59. The topic of transference is the subject of a detailed discussion by B. Wolstein: *Transference, Its Meaning and Function in Psychoanalytic Therapy* (New York, Grune & Stratton, Inc., 1955).

Our account of briefer psychoanalysis is drawn from *Psychoanalytic Therapy* by F. Alexander, T. M. French, *et al.,* (New York, The Ronald Press Co., 1946). This is the most systematic presentation of a currently common trend. Fromm-Reichmann's book, already mentioned, also stands in this tradition.

The problem of relating psychotherapy to general psychological principles, especially to learning theory, has been carried well forward by J. Dollard and N. E. Miller in *Personality and Psychotherapy: An Analysis in Terms of Learning, Thinking, and Culture* (New York, McGraw-Hill Book Co., Inc., 1950). See also Ch. 5 by E. J. Shoben, Jr., and Ch. 6 by O. H. Mowrer in *Psychotherapy: Theory and Research* (O. H. Mowrer, ed., New York, The Ronald Press Co., 1953).

9

Psychotherapy: Variations and Technical Aids

It would be impossible to consider in a single chapter all the named varieties of psychotherapy that exist today. We are in a period of prolific experimenting with the therapeutic process and of equally prolific writing about it. Of the writing it can be said that as a whole it is a somewhat tangled forest in which one can easily feel lost. The events of psychotherapy do not lend themselves to brief and lucid communication. We shall undertake to guide ourselves in this chapter by frequent reference to the five basic aspects of the therapeutic process which we discerned toward the end of the last chapter. It will be necessary to restrict the account to the more important variations and adaptations of psychotherapy and to the chief technical aids that have been advocated to hasten one or another of the basic processes.

PSYCHOTHERAPY AS ART AND AS SCIENCE

The full range of controversy over how psychotherapy should be done can best be appreciated if we start with extreme points of view. In terms of the five basic processes, some workers concern themselves almost entirely with the first, the human relation between therapist and patient, whereas others put practically all the emphasis on the last, the replacing of maladjusted behavior by new behavior. Exaggerating a bit, we can say that at one extreme the claim is made that if the human relation is really right the rest of the processes—expressing and recognizing feelings, transference, and new behavior—will take care of themselves. At the other extreme we find the claim that the first four processes are subjective and superfluous, and that the real business of treatment is to discover objective techniques for changing behavior. The wide gap between these extremes can be dramatized by noticing their criticisms of Freud. Those who cherish the human relation in its uniqueness accuse him of misplaced scientific impersonality. They see cold detachment in his custom of sitting at the head of the couch, out of the patient's sight; and they find in his interpretations a rigid use of generalized scientific concepts, such as id, ego, and super-ego, which blinded him to individuality. Those who fix their attention on change of behavior picture Freud as a soft-headed romantic who let his patients float interminably in a bath of subjectivity and self-inspection, never properly addressing himself to the job of curing their symptoms. They see him as turning his back on the objective science of behavior, as represented, for instance, in Pavlov's work on conditioning, and as trying to bring about change without any knowledge of its fundamental laws. Parodied in this way, the two views seem to come from different worlds; but let us see what can be learned from each of them.

The Art of Human Interaction. When psychotherapy is conceived largely in terms of human interaction, there is a tendency to emphasize the therapist's state of mind and feeling rather than what he does. There is also a tendency to emphasize the patient's individuality rather than what he has in common with other patients. As an illustration of these tendencies we take a recent paper by Margaret Rioch, who applies to psychotherapy some of Martin Buber's philosophical ideas on the "realm of the interhuman."[1] Buber draws a distinction between *being* and *seeming;* the latter is represented by our concern for how we want to appear to others, what we want our "image" to be, and how we fit ourselves to the expectations involved in a professional role, in contrast to a straightforward expression, in a direct "I-Thou" relation, of how we really feel. *Seeming* rather than *being* characterizes, as we saw in a previous chapter, people under the sway of the "persona" (Jung) or of the "marketing orientation" (Fromm). Does it not tend to characterize the therapist, who occupies a professional role in his dealings with patients? As Rioch expresses it, "The wish to appear to the patient as an understanding, competent expert in the interhuman is natural, especially in the beginning therapist. But inevitably it interferes with his *being* just that."[2] Buber also contrasts the perception of another person as unique with the perception of him in schematic categories. If the psychotherapist becomes too bent on constructing the patient's past in psychodynamic formulas—on "explaining the illness"—he may fail to keep seeing his patient as a unique person in the present. This last point is given central importance in

[1] M. J. Rioch, "The Meaning of Martin Buber's 'Elements of the Interhuman' for the Practice of Psychotherapy," *Psychiatry,* XXIII (1960), pp. 133–40.
[2] *Ibid.,* p. 135.

existential analysis, a method of therapy eclectic as to techniques but insistent that the therapist enter fully into the patient's point of view, trying to understand his world and his problems as he himself sees them.[3]

In a recent paper Carl Rogers puts himself the question: "How can I create a helping relationship?"[4] His answers can perhaps be taken as in part a more detailed specification of *being* as opposed to *seeming.* The therapist must be trustworthy, he writes, "but this does not demand that I be rigidly consistent, but that I be dependably real."[5] To be dependably real means to act as one feels; it means, for instance, showing annoyance with the patient when it is felt, even if this is not in accord with the usual picture of the therapist's role. It means being able to communicate one's feelings, both the negative ones and the positive, such as warmth, liking, and respect. It means responding with understanding to the patient's feelings without losing oneself to the point of being "downcast by his depression, frightened by his fear, or engulfed by his dependency."[6] It means, finally, being able to find in him not only the immature child and the neurotic adult but also the mature self that is struggling for a better way of life. It is this last that must be confirmed by the whole experience of interaction with the therapist.

One can see in these reflections a searching attempt to understand the subtle art of human interaction. The psychotherapist who brushes off this sort of thing may later wonder why he has so many failures. If we imagine, however, a therapist who is capable of creating a perfect interpersonal relation, alike in marriage, family life, friendships, and therapy, we are entitled to ask what distinguishes the therapeutic from the other relations. For psychotherapy is not just a rich "I-Thou" experience; it is a meeting for the explicit purpose of overcoming the patient's difficulties. Without denying that it is something of an art, we must recognize in it also something of a science.

The Science of Changing Behavior. Turning abruptly to the opposite conception, which makes the production of new behavior the central issue, we find vigorous attempts to relate the therapeutic process to elementary behavior theory as represented in Pavlov's conditioning, Watson's behaviorism, and Hull's learning or reinforcement theory. Although these theories are based on experiments at fairly simple levels of behavior, they all deal with learning; we should therefore expect them to bear on the relearning that takes place in successful therapy. One school

[3] R. May, E. Angel, and H. F. Ellenberger (eds.), *Existence* (New York: Basic Books, Inc., 1958).

[4] C. R. Rogers, "The Characteristics of a Helping Relationship," in M. I. Stein (ed.), *Contemporary Psychotherapies* (New York: The Free Press of Glencoe, Inc., 1961), pp. 95–112.

[5] *Ibid.,* p. 104.

[6] *Ibid.,* p. 106.

of thought, headed by H. J. Eysenck in London, favors a systematic reworking of the whole field of abnormal psychology in these terms, abandoning the psychodynamic tradition and attempting to build afresh on the findings of the psychological laboratory.[7] In a similar vein, Bindra believes that the psychodynamic account "has turned out to be a wrong 'lead,'" and that research on treatment "should concentrate on developing techniques of manipulating the conditions that currently control the patient's undesirable responses rather than on unearthing the conditions which initially produced his disorder."[8] Other workers have seen the problem not as one of casting out idols but of detecting in psychodynamic processes the operation of basic principles of learning.[9] Can one see in the therapeutic relationship, in the expression and recognition of feelings, and in transference any parallels to the concepts of conditioning and instrumental learning?

Several parallels of this kind are pointed out in a recent survey by Bandura.[10] It is clear that some of the events of psychotherapy can be brought under the concept of *counter-conditioning.* The original model is provided by the work of Mary Cover Jones in 1924.[11] A child named Peter was afraid of furry things and small animals; the anxiety response had become conditioned to such objects. Counter-conditioning was successfully achieved by introducing the feared objects, first at a distance and gradually closer, while the child was pleasantly engaged in eating a meal. Final triumph came when Peter allowed a white rat to climb upon him as he ate his dinner; the pleasure and security conferred by eating had won out over the anxiety response. In ordinary psychotherapy the patient discusses his anxieties in the unaccustomed secure comfort of a relationship in which he is heard with interest, sympathy, and support. He starts with the superficial anxieties and makes his way at his own pace to those that are more central. Just as Peter's therapist might have spoiled the whole process by moving furry objects too close too soon, evoking and strengthening the anxiety response, so the psychotherapist may wreck things by pushing his interpretations too close to the neurotic nucleus. If sufficient time is allowed, however, the things that

[7] H. J. Eysenck, *The Dynamics of Anxiety and Hysteria: An Experimental Application of Modern Learning Theory to Psychiatry* (New York: Frederick A. Praeger, Inc., 1957), pp. 267–68.

[8] D. Bindra, "Experimental Psychology and the Problem of Behavior Disorders," *Canadian Journal of Psychology,* XIII (1959), pp. 135–50.

[9] O. H. Mowrer, *Learning Theory and Personality Dynamics* (New York: The Ronald Press Co., 1950); J. Dollard and N. E. Miller, *Personality and Psychotherapy* (New York: McGraw-Hill Book Co., Inc., 1950).

[10] A. Bandura, "Psychotherapy as a Learning Process," *Psychological Bulletin,* LVIII (1961), pp. 143–59.

[11] M. C. Jones, "A Laboratory Study of Fear: The Case of Peter," *Journal of Genetic Psychology,* XXXI (1924), pp. 308–15.

formerly caused anxiety can be faced with a feeling of confidence. In this respect it seems legitimate to interpret psychotherapy as counter-conditioning.

Another basic learning process is *extinction,* which occurs when a conditioned response is repeatedly not reinforced by the unconditioned stimulus. If the bell is not followed by food, its value as a signal is eventually extinguished. The therapist's permissiveness can be seen as a use of this principle. The patient confesses wishes, impulses, and behavior which in the past have been associated with anxiety, guilt, or shame. He discovers, often with real surprise, that the therapist does not reinforce these feelings by signs of disapproval; the confessions are received without criticism or censure. The process is shown in an ingenious experiment by Dittes, who recorded the galvanic skin responses of a patient during the course of therapy. Early in treatment the galvanic skin responses were larger whenever the patient alluded to sexual matters, but in the course of time this topic came to be discussed without marked autonomic disturbance.[12] In most cases, extinction of old responses through failure of reinforcement does not have to work alone. The new behavior of taking a fresh look at one's anxieties will be reinforced by *rewards.* The therapist's esteem and interest, his alliance in the treatment, are rewards of no small importance. Several studies have shown that a patient's conversation veers more and more toward topics in which the therapist has evinced signs of interest, even if only by slight sounds of assent such as "Mm-hm." It is legitimate, furthermore, to suppose that processes described as increases of insight can be understood in terms of *discrimination learning.* Overgeneralized emotional responses are changed through conscious recognition and labeling into more discriminating, realistically guided behavior.

The therapist who thinks in psychodynamic terms can thus be seen as working in accord with certain basic principles of relearning. Does this mean that he is muddle-headed and ought to change his vocabulary to one of conditioning and instrumental learning? Here we confront the fact that contemporary learning theory is still expressed very much at the level of elementary processes. It speaks a language of drives like hunger and of problems like running a maze. The psychotherapist must understand highly ramified forms of motivation as revealed in fantasies, dreams, symbolic acts, and free associations. He must deal with highly complex products of learning such as displacements, reaction-formations, neurotic protective organization, and idealized self-pictures. Psychodynamic concepts have been developed in order to have some way of think-

[12] J. E. Dittes, "Extinction During Psychotherapy of GSR Accompanying 'Embarrassing' Statements," *Journal of Abnormal and Social Psychology,* LIV (1957), pp. 187–91.

ing about these complex but humanly important processes. At present the psychotherapist would probably only cripple his thinking and blunt his powers of observation if he hastened to translate everything into the sparse language of learning theory. But there should be no ultimate contradiction between the two levels of description. Psychodynamic theory is, after all, a theory of motivation and learning. Even Rogers' refinements of the helping relation could probably be expressed in these terms. If the "I-Thou" relation is deeply satisfying rather than coolly businesslike, permissiveness will more successfully promote extinction and reward will more effectively reinforce new behavior.

We shall begin our study of variations and technical aids by examining several methods, past and present, in which the common theme is a relatively direct action on the patient's difficulties. The story begins with the older hypnotic techniques, and it will bring us eventually to recent work based on a direct application of learning theory.

METHODS BASED ON SUGGESTION AND PERSUASION

Eighty years ago it seemed likely that hypnotism would become the psychotherapy of the future. Rescued from scientific disrepute by Charcot and put to new uses by Janet and Breuer, it seemed destined to become the method of choice in treating the neuroses. Between 1880 and 1900 hypnotic treatment reached a peak of popularity. Dozens of clinics were opened, thousands of patients were treated, several professional journals were started, and textbooks began to appear giving minute instructions in the hypnotic art. The range of disorders reported cured was astonishingly wide. Only the severe psychoses seemed immune to hypnotic benefit, and some of the reports claimed success with diseases clearly of organic origin. Not only were cures obtained but they were obtained in a short time. Sometimes three or four sessions were enough, sometimes ten or a dozen, rarely more than twenty.

The Older Hypnotic Methods. The method used by most of the hypnotic practitioners was some form of direct suggestion. The patient was placed in a deep hypnotic state and given suggestions that his symptoms would disappear. Sometimes the suggestions were directed not only at the symptoms but also at what were presumed to be the attitudes and problems underlying the symptoms. Looked at from the vantage point of modern dynamic psychology this attempt to reach the underlying factors seems ridiculously crude, but it was a step in the right direction, taken in the interests of rendering the cure more permanent. Both Janet and Freud used hypnosis to explore the patient's buried memories and secure an abreaction of suppressed feelings. This innovation sometimes brought success where direct suggestion had failed. The hypnotic therapist of

1900 seemed destined to succeed with problems that had long baffled the medical profession. With direct suggestion and abreaction at his command he seemed fully equipped to deal with neurotic disorders.

Before long it became clear that hypnotic therapy was not entirely satisfactory. Some patients were barred from its benefits by the fact that they could not develop a sufficiently deep hypnotic state; others could not be hypnotized at all. More important was the growing evidence that hypnotic cures were rarely permanent. Apparently cured when dismissed from treatment, the patients often came back later with new symptoms or a recurrence of the old ones. Sometimes a cure by direct hypnotic suggestion was permanent, but in the majority of cases, the effects were transient and had to be renewed at fairly frequent intervals. The earlier reports of therapeutic success had to be largely discounted. Unless it could be shown that a patient remained well for at least a year after treatment, the statement that he was cured meant nothing. These findings led to a decline in hypnotic therapy. The decline was hastened by the rise of psychoanalysis, so that by 1920 only a small minority of workers used hypnotic methods.

As we look back on this rise and decline of hypnotic therapy it is easy to see what was the matter. The whole thing was conceived too much along the line of a doctor giving medicine to a patient. Mesmer, the founder of hypnotic therapy, believed himself to be employing a physical agent, an invisible fluid which transmitted animal magnetism into the patient's ailing body. When the theory of animal magnetism was abandoned, its place was taken by psychological theories hardly less naïve. The hypnotist gave doses of suggestion, he implanted ideas in the patient's mind, he set certain automatisms in motion. Such concepts are inappropriate, we realize today, for describing the known facts about hypnotism. Hypnotic behavior is produced by the patient, not forced upon him by the hypnotist. Just as a psychoanalytic patient can be cured only by his own corrective emotional experiences, not by the analyst's insights, so the patient in hypnotic therapy must be cured by his own reactions to the hypnotic experience, not by ideas or suggestions implanted by the operator. As modern dynamic psychology made this fact progressively clearer, hypnotism moved into the position of a technical aid in psychotherapy rather than an independent system. Its appropriate sphere is that of a special technique which can be called upon to assist in various ways the carrying out of more comprehensive treatment.

In a survey of the literature on hypnotherapy Brenman and Gill warn us against too hasty a dismissal of the older suggestive methods.[13] Some-

[13] M. Brenman and M. M. Gill, *Hypnotherapy: A Survey of the Literature* (New York: International Universities Press, Inc., 1947), pp. 52–66.

times direct hypnotic suggestion permanently removes a symptom or changes an attitude that is troublesome to the patient. Recurrence of symptoms or the formation of substitute symptoms is not inevitable. Schneck also believes that "relieving a patient of individual symptoms probably has possibilities far greater than is generally conceded," but he makes it a requirement that the therapist have a thorough understanding of the patient. The decision to try merely symptomatic therapy must be based on a judgment that it is suitable to the particular case. The therapist must try to decide on what might be called the depth of the patient's need for the symptom. If it is a relatively superficial maneuver designed to gain certain immediate benefits, or if it appears to be a habit without much ramifying significance, it may yield satisfactorily to hypnotic suggestion.[14] But lack of permanence has always been recognized as a limitation of direct suggestive techniques. The suppression of symptoms without insight, without a corrective emotional experience such as we described in the last chapter, does not touch the deeper sources of illness.

The following case illustrates the difficulties, even the dangers, that can result from purely suggestive hypnotic treatment. The patient was a married man of 41 whose life was characterized by energy, assertiveness, and active participation in things. A successful business man with a territory to cover, he had used air travel without uneasiness for fifteen years. One day he had an uncommonly rough flight and developed a fear so strong that he could not bring himself to fly again. As his locations could be reached by train this was not a fatal handicap, but his colleagues and even his secretary made such fun of his phobia that he finally consulted a hypnotist. Without taking an adequate life history the hypnotist set to work at counter-conditioning; he evoked in the patient vivid hypnotic imagery of being in the airplane and feeling comfortable and secure. After six sessions the patient again made a flight. The next day found him in a diffuse and intense anxiety state, unable to eat, sleep, or decide anything, beset by weird ideas and feelings of panic. He had to be taken to a hospital and given intensive psychotherapy which at length restored him to the relatively benign condition of having only a phobia. His history showed much emotional turmoil behind the outwardly successful active life. He was afraid of aggression, afraid of pain to the point of fainting when given an injection, compulsively worried about money and about decisions, troubled by crudely sadistic sexual fantasies. The treatment did not have the goal of unraveling the origins and connections of all this, but "the airplane phobia was obviously

[14] J. M. Schneck, *Hypnosis in Modern Medicine* (2d ed.; Springfield, Ill.: Charles C Thomas, 1959), p. 145.

related to some more central issue," and the attempt to remove the symptom had only precipitated a breakdown.[15]

Hypnotism as a Technical Aid. Considered as a technical aid in connection with more searching kinds of treatment, the hypnotic state has its chief value in the increased vividness with which situations can be imagined. Past happenings can be recalled with an intensity that amounts to reliving, and present thoughts and feelings can be given a dreamlike clarity. It is this property of the hypnotic state that makes it useful in accomplishing the purposes otherwise left to free association and spontaneous dreaming.

Hypnotic Revery. The hypnotice state is conducive to unusually free and vivid reveries. This fact has been turned to account by Kubie who has worked out a specialized technique for maintaining a drowsy state of revery for long periods of time—several hours if necessary.[16] Kubie reports on one case in which this method stimulated a rapid outpouring of important emotion-charged memories that had failed to appear in more than a year of standard psychoanalysis.

Hypnotic Dreams. The interpretation of dreams forms a valuable part of standard psychoanalysis. With the aid of hypnosis it is possible to stimulate dreaming and thus hasten and enrich the material that is produced from this source. The hypnotic induction of dreams has been particularly developed by Wolberg.[17] Patients may be given the suggestion to dream while hypnotized or to dream when asleep the following night. A certain amount of training is required to make such suggestions effective, but time is saved in the end. Patients can be stimulated to dream about topics which they are still not able to express or experience directly; the interpretation of their dreams then brings the material more rapidly to awareness and to corrective emotional experience. The induced dream is a particularly good medium for bringing out the patient's attitudes toward the therapist.

Hypnotic Recall and Abreaction. Probably the most dramatic achievement of hypnosis is its effect on memory. Its value in stimulating the recall of traumatic memories and the abreaction of suppressed emotions was demonstrated by Janet, Breuer, Freud, and the military psychiatrists of World War I. In psychotherapy it is particularly valuable at points where serious resistance is encountered, where normally the patient might

[15] M. J. Meldman, "Personality Decompensation After Hypnotic Symptom Suppression," *Journal of the American Medical Association,* CLXXIII (1960), pp. 359–61.

[16] L. S. Kubie, "The Use of Induced Hypnagogic Reveries in the Recovery of Repressed Amnesic Data." *Bulletin of the Menninger Clinic,* VII (1943), pp. 172–82.

[17] L. R. Wolberg, *Hypnoanalysis* (New York: Grune & Stratton, Inc., 1945), pp. 182–94.

linger for days and even weeks before being able to produce the anxiety-laden material. Lindner claimed that hypnosis performs its greatest time-saving service at just such points.[18] He used ordinary free association as his basic method, but recommended shifting to the hypnotic state as soon as the associations become blocked. The patient is hypnotized and then reminded of his last few associations and recollections. If the analyst has been able to make a good guess as to the character of the repressed material and the time in the patient's life when the anxiety-laden events occurred, he can use an even more direct method for restoring memory: *hypnotic regression*. The patient is told that he is back at some previous age level and that he feels exactly as he did at that time. It is a nice art to bring about these regressions. Erickson has developed the technique in considerable detail.[19] He begins by disorienting the patient for current time and place relationships, asking him progressively to forget the date, week, month, year, etc., after which the suggestion of an earlier age can be more readily accepted and vividly developed. Good hypnotic subjects are able to behave as if they were three or six or ten years old with remarkable fidelity. The revived memories of the early period are often so vivid as to stir up great emotion and produce abreaction in the hypnotic state.

Hypnosis would serve little therapeutic purpose if it merely stimulated the outpouring of memories and feelings in the hypnotic state. If resistance is to be truly overcome, this material must be dealt with in the waking state and become fully integrated with the self or ego. Whatever is brought forward in hypnosis must sooner or later become the topic of conversation and corrective emotional experience in the waking state. It is for this reason that the technique is sometimes called hypnoanalysis—a true combination of hypnotic and psychoanalytic procedures.

Drug-induced Relaxed States. States of relaxation very similar to the hypnotic state can be produced by drugs. Before World War II some use was made of this fact to increase the productiveness of interviews. The so-called "sodium amytal interview" had as its purpose the revealing of repressed material so that the therapist could be better guided in his handling of the case. Sodium pentothal was presently found preferable; it wore off gradually without producing amnesia, and thus permitted a readier passage of the repressed material into normal waking consciousness. Grinker and Spiegel seized upon this advantage to develop the technique called *narcosynthesis*, which we have already mentioned when

[18] R. M. Lindner, *Rebel Without a Cause: The Hypnoanalysis of a Criminal Psychopath* (New York: Grune & Stratton, Inc., 1944), pp. 15–24.

[19] M. H. Erickson and L. S. Kubie, "The Successful Treatment of a Case of Acute Hysterical Depression by a Return Under Hypnosis to a Critical Phase of Childhood," *Psychoanalytic Quarterly*, X (1941), pp. 583–609.

discussing neuroses of traumatic onset.[20] Like hypnoanalysis, this technique aims to hasten the recall and abreaction of crucial repressed experiences, then to accomplish a synthesis of this material with the patient's waking self. The method proved valuable in dealing with neuroses of traumatic onset during World War II. Its unique service in combat zones has been thoroughly demonstrated. When time is limited it is by far the most practical means for liquidating the defenses against recent trauma. Its value as a technical aid in treating the neuroses of civilian life has proved to be considerably smaller. As a therapeutic adjunct its services are similar to those rendered by hypnosis.

Persuasive Re-education. Many names have been used to describe active methods: explanation, persuasion, re-eduction, direct psychotherapy, education of the will, etc.[21] Some of the techniques, like the persuasive methods of Dubois and Dejerine in Europe and the re-education procedure of Riggs in this country, have grown up entirely outside the influence of psychoanalysis. Other workers, such as Stekel and Adler, began with Freud but presently diverged from his therapeutic principles. Though varying greatly in detail, they all cast the doctor somewhat in the role of a teacher who explains things to the patient and urges him to act upon the explanation. For our present purpose they can be lumped together under the heading of *persuasive re-education.*

Persuasive re-education is undoubtedly capable of bringing about a corrective emotional experience. This is particularly true when it is used with delicacy by workers who are sensitive to the motivational conditions under which relearning can take place. If the doctor points out the patient's evasive defenses before the patient has begun to like and respect the doctor, learning is not likely to take a therapeutic form. The most that the patient will be able to learn is that the doctor is an insulting fool who is to be strictly avoided in the future. It was probably Dejerine who handled this problem with the greatest insight.[22] He believed in the efficacy of pointing things out to the patient, but he did this only after gaining the patient's absolute confidence through sympathetic exploration of his problems. Under these circumstances persuasion is practicable and can be used to hasten the therapeutic process. It is possible

[20] R. R. Grinker and J. P. Spiegel, *Men Under Stress* (Philadelphia: The Blakiston Co., 1945), pp. 170–78, 389–406. Narcosynthesis was used successfully in the case of Pearson Brack (see above, pages 61–68); for its use in neuroses of traumatic onset, see above, page 211.

[21] Several such methods are described by K. E. Appel, "Psychiatric Therapy," in J. McV. Hunt, *Personality and the Behavior Disorders* (New York: The Ronald Press Co., 1944), Vol. II, especially pp. 1110–18, 1125–33.

[22] J. Dejerine and E. Gaukler, *Psychoneurosis and Psychotherapy* (Philadelphia: J. B. Lippincott Co., 1913).

to relax defenses and learn new behavior when you are assured of the warm interest and expert guidance of an impressive therapist.

Alfred Adler was one of the first in Freud's circle to become impatient with the length of psychoanalytic therapy. His own simpler conception of the neuroses, which we have mentioned in earlier chapters,[23] permitted him to believe that a more rapid re-education was possible. Starting from the usual *therapeutic relationship,* Adler secured an *expression of feelings* by directed conversation and dream analysis. His characteristic activity was most apparent in the process of *pointing out feelings.* As the patient little by little unfolded his story, Adler indicated the episodes that revealed strivings for superiority, roundabout ways of dominating people, evasions of the real issues of life, underlying feelings of inferiority, failure to develop true social feelings, and all the rest of the neurotic style of life. While he diverged greatly from Freudian psychoanalysis in the things he elected to point out, it is not incorrect to consider his tactics as a speeding up of the process of interpretation. Standard psychoanalysis points out a great deal to the patient in the course of two or three years. Adler worked faster and did not pay so much attention to the delicate question of timing the interpretations so that the patient could use them to relax his defenses. Such methods are not without success. Clifford Allen, an unsparing critic of Adler in several respects, raises the question whether you can cure neurotic sufferers by this technique, and answers that "you most certainly can." "There is no doubt that a certain type of patient will respond to Adler's methods very well. Moreover, in those cases which do respond, the time taken for treatment will be considerably reduced, although naturally the illness is not attacked at such a fundamental level as it would be by Freudian methods."[24]

Directing New Behavior. In view of the ultimate importance of new behavior, one possible strategy for speeding the therapeutic process is to direct the patient to undertake specific pieces of new behavior. Obviously this cannot work if the proposed behavior awakens too much anxiety and resistance; one cannot direct the patient to be well and to disregard his neurosis. The strategy can succeed only when the proposed task is so nearly within the patient's present capacity that he needs only a little added impetus to carry it out. Like interpretations in psychoanalysis, tasks must be directed at first against superficial aspects of the neurosis and only later reach the deeper problems.

The following example, taken from Herzberg, will help to clarify this active mode of procedure.[25] A wife felt strongly hostile toward her hus-

[23] See above, pages 38–40, 233–36.

[24] C. Allen, *Modern Discoveries in Medical Psychology* (New York: The Macmillan Co., 1937), p. 184.

[25] A. Herzberg, *Active Psychotherapy* (New York: Grune & Stratton, Inc., 1945), pp. 51–52.

band because of his lack of initiative and failure to earn well. At the same time she liked him for his kindness and consideration. For the sake of their children she wanted the marriage to continue, and her own hostility therefore filled her with self-reproach. Her aggressive feelings were thus constantly turned back on herself in the form of blame, and this finally resulted in depression with insomnia and various bodily symptoms. By concentrating fiercely on her symptoms she could now forget her aggression toward her husband. This neurotic solution of the main conflict, however, soon became exploited for secondary gain. By constant complaining about her illness she obtained increased attention from her husband, who took her out every day in order to make her feel better and who allowed her to keep a maid. Before long she was receiving presents and financial aid from her parents. Because of her condition she refused sexual intercourse, thus in effect punishing her husband. How can therapeutic tasks be used in treating this neurosis? Obviously it would be futile to direct them straight at the main emotional problem, telling her to stop hating her husband or punishing herself. Tasks were assigned instead which had the effect of removing the secondary gain. Progressively she was required to stop speaking of her symptoms at home, to discharge her maid and do her own housework, to resume sexual relations and discontinue her daily requests to be taken out, and to refuse all assistance from her parents. As these steps were successfully accomplished it become possible to go on to more nuclear problems.

Direction of new behavior is a highly active procedure. It is not at all what a neurotic patient wants when he takes his problems to a therapist. It is strong medicine, and the doses must be selected with the utmost skill. If the patient fails in the first few assignments, or does them at great cost in anxiety, he is likely to be so badly discouraged that he breaks off treatment. This often happens when active methods are used, and one cannot overlook the possibility that such a consequence leaves the patient in poorer condition, and less disposed toward further therapeutic attempts, than he was in the first place. On the other hand, when everything goes well the patient experiences a rapid growth of confidence. He learns that he can take action and win at least a local victory over his neurosis. It is under these circumstances that the direction of new behavior may serve to shorten the course of treatment.

Limitations of Suggestive and Persuasive Methods. The greatest liability of these methods is that they will slip over from encouraging the *expression* of feelings to encouraging their *suppression*. There is a constant danger that the therapist's activity will outstrip the patient's capacity to grow. As we saw in studying standard psychoanalysis, the patient often requires a long time for the working through of a given interpretation. The anxiety and its defense crop up in a new form; what seemed accomplished yesterday has to be accomplished again today. A young analyst in training once remarked that he got tired of hearing himself give the same interpretation day after day, yet the patient always needed it. Persuasive and suggestive methods tend to build a therapeutic relationship in which the patient greatly admires the doctor and hates to displease him. Under such circumstances he will try to keep up with the doctor and struggle to produce the new behavior which he perceives to be the latter's ultimate desire. When he cannot relax defenses fast enough to achieve this goal, he resorts to suppressing his symptoms and neurotic trends. It is difficult to end the therapeutic relationship without producing a relapse. What has been done to please the therapist requires that he should keep on showing his pleasure.

It is also characteristic of persuasive and suggestive methods that they use transference without analyzing it. The patient's feelings toward the doctor are used to promote progress without being pointed out or interpreted. The therapeutic situation itself is not turned into an opportunity for the patient to practice his growing capacity for mature human relationships. The therapist relies on new behavior outside the office to provide the needed corrective emotional experience. Inside the office he allows the patient to remain in a childlike role, dependent and admiring. If the persuasive therapist undertook to interpret the transference and work out all its emotional implications, his procedure would probably take just as long as standard psychoanalysis.

These are the dangers, but we must take account of the fact that all the methods described in this section have a certain amount of success. Hypnotic suggestion, persuasion, vigorous interpretation, and the assignment of tasks sometimes produce the intended new behavior without provoking fatal resistance or touching off unbearable anxiety. If we assume that patients differ in strength of anxiety, stubbornness of defense, and degree of involvement of the symptom in underlying problems, we can suppose that these successes occur with the milder disorders. So long as the therapist recognizes the patient's feelings correctly and rewards him with solicitous interest, the patient will be able to keep pace with what is proposed and to cut short the laborious process of working through. Growth will be possible without the forcible suppression of important problems. Under these circumstances, furthermore, it may be possible to dispense with interpreting the transference. At first the patient needs constant rewards of approval from the therapist in order to change his behavior. If change is rapid, however, the rewards inherent in better-adjusted living will supersede those obtainable from the therapist. The shy and awkward patient, for instance, at first needs encouragement to undertake new social contacts, but if these are successful they become self-rewarding. If these gains take place rapidly, without the discouraging relapses that are characteristic of the severe neuroses, the transference fades away without leaving harmful traces. The patient has outgrown his childlike dependence on the therapist just as a healthy child outgrows his dependence on the parents.

METHODS BASED ON DIRECT APPLICATION OF LEARNING THEORY

We have seen that all forms of psychotherapy undertake to effect relearning, and that all may be considered to exemplify basic principles of learning. In most instances these principles are not made explicit, and some workers have argued that more could be accomplished by making a direct application of learning theory. If the child Peter could overcome his fear of furry objects by straightforward counter-conditioning, will not other troubles yield to the same kind of direct attack?

An example of success along these lines is to be found in a technique developed by the Mowrers to overcome bedwetting in children.[26] An apparatus was devised whereby the first moisture on a pad placed in the bed set off a bell loud enough to wake up the child. In due course the stimuli preliminary to urination became connected with the response of waking, enabling the child to control himself long enough to reach the bathroom. Success was not universal, but in the majority of cases the child obtained a gratifying sense of mastery while the parents found welcome relief from worry and the nuisance of washing sheets.

The more difficult problem of phobias has been studied in detail by Wolpe, who has developed a systematic technique called "reciprocal inhibition," using essentially the process of counter-conditioning.[27] Wolpe's procedure involves taking a history and deriving from it a list of the things that awaken anxiety; the list is then arranged in a guessed hierarchy of intensity, so that the less disturbing stimuli can be used first in the treatment. The patient is then placed in a state of comfortable relaxation, often with the aid of hypnosis, and in this atmosphere of security is encouraged to imagine the mildly disturbing situations. If the therapist sees that too much anxiety is developing, he quickly changes the subject or returns to stimuli lower in the hierarchy; otherwise he proceeds up the list until the most feared situations can be tolerated. When the counter-conditioning is correctly paced, phobias may disappear in a relatively small number of sessions—for instance, 22 interviews over a period of three months in an interesting case described in detail

[26] O. H. Mowrer and W. M. Mowrer, "Enuresis: A Method for Its Study and Treatment," *American Journal of Orthopsychiatry*, VIII (1938), pp. 436–59.

[27] J. Wolpe, "Psychotherapy Based on the Principle of Reciprocal Inhibition," in A. Burton (ed.), *Case Studies in Counseling and Psychotherapy* (Englewood Cliffs, N. J.: Prentice-Hall, Inc., 1959).

by Rachman[28] Wolpe has reported a 90 per cent rate of recovery in a series of 122 patients treated according to his method.[29] A few of the cases involved complex neuroses such as the obsessive and hysterical, but nearly two thirds of the patients were suffering from anxiety states and phobias. The method seems most applicable when anxiety is the main symptom.

Sometimes the chief symptom is an approach response rather than an avoidant one. This is true of some of the disorders we shall discuss in the next chapter: perverse sexual activity, delinquent behavior, and the excessive use of alcohol. Learning theory suggests that such behavior can be stopped by a procedure of counter-conditioning which connects it with an extremely noxious stimulus such as electric shock. In point of fact, one of the methods sometimes used with chronic alcoholics follows this very principle. Alcohol is administered together with antabuse, a drug that produces violent nausea. Reports in terms of going on and staying on the wagon run as high as 60 per cent of the patients treated.[30]

The use of reward to reinforce desired new patterns of behavior is advocated by Skinner and has been tried particularly with socially unresponsive patients.[31] In a study by Peters and Jenkins, hospitalized schizophrenic patients, so withdrawn that they could not be touched by social rewards, were given objective tasks for the doing of which they were reinforced by the primitive stimulus of food. In the course of time the patients began to respond to the investigators who gave the reward, and the tasks were made to include interaction with others. This slow procedure of reinforcement produced a beneficial effect on the patients' adaptation to hospital life and responsiveness to those around them.[32]

These are but a few samples of recent efforts to apply learning theory directly to therapeutic procedures. It will be noticed that they all work on symptoms, defining the task of psychotherapy as removal of symptoms. No attempt is made to give the patient a better understanding of himself or to unearth the origins of the difficulty. Some workers consider this to be a virtue. Eysenck takes the extreme position that psychotherapy *ought*

[28] S. Rachman, "The Treatment of Anxiety and Phobic Reactions by Systematic Desensitization Psychotherapy," *Journal of Abnormal and Social Psychology*, LVIII (1959), pp. 259–63.

[29] J. Wolpe, *Psychotherapy by Reciprocal Inhibition* (Stanford, Calif.: Stanford University Press, 1958).

[30] Bandura, *op. cit.*, p. 150.

[31] B. F. Skinner, *Science and Human Behavior* (New York: The Macmillan Co., 1953), chap. xxiv; O. R. Lindsley, "Operant Conditioning Methods Applied to Research in Chronic Schizophrenia," *Psychiatric Research Reports*, V (1956), pp. 118–38.

[32] H. N. Peters and R. L. Jenkins, "Improvement of Chronic Schizophrenic Patients with Guided Problem-Solving Motivated by Hunger," *Psychiatric Quarterly Supplement*, XXVIII (1954), pp. 84–101.

to be symptomatic, having no other business than to remove the symptoms about which the patient complains.[33] Such a view seems justified by every case in which hypnotic suggestion, persuasion, direction, or the just described relearning methods produce removal of the symptom without untoward side effects or early relapse—and we have seen that there are many such cases. It is put in question, however, by every case in which symptom removal is followed by the appearance of other symptoms, by prompt reappearance of the same symptom at the end of treatment, or by generalized breakdown of the kind we described in the patient who had a phobia of airplane travel. We must accept the long-accumulating evidence that symptomatic treatment can be successful, but we must not overlook the equally long-accumulating evidence that symptoms are in many cases the surface phenomena of more complex emotional difficulties.

The difference can be illustrated by recalling Freud's case of the five-year-old boy Hans, who had a phobia of horses.[34] The history showed certain frights associated with horses, but Freud became convinced that these were insufficient to account for the symptom. He saw the fear of horses as a somewhat distant displacement of a much more serious and inescapable dread of the father, developed out of the conflicts of the Oedipal situation. If the phobia had actually originated in frights connected with horses, it could presumably have been removed by direct counter-conditioning procedures. If it was a displacement, such procedures would not have affected the central cause of anxiety; removal of the phobia would have left this problem unsolved, and a fresh defense against anxiety would presumably have been needed. Thinking about it in this way, Freud advocated treatment that developed the boy's insight into his feelings about his father. Treatment was thus directed at the nuclear fear rather than at the symptom.

It is worth noticing, moreover, that most workers who make a direct application of learning theory do not approach treatment with the coolness of a technician taking a blood sample. The reports already mentioned by Wolpe and Rachman, for instance, show concern for establishing a therapeutic relation and for giving the patient a sense of comfort and security. The therapist communicates confidence in his methods. His history-taking conveys his interest in the patient's problems, and his techniques for producing relaxation tend to strengthen a sense of trustful alliance. There has been a tendency among learning theorists to describe what happens in purely mechanical terms, but this does not mean that in actual practice the therapist behaves like a computer. If he did so, his

[33] Eysenck, *op. cit.*, pp. 267–68.
[34] See above, page 256.

power to bring about counter-conditioning, to produce extinction, and to reward new behavior would be greatly reduced.

PSYCHOTHERAPY WITH CHILDREN

Psychotherapy with children is not fundamentally different from psychotherapy with adults. The same principles operate, but their emphasis and application have to be adjusted to the fact that the patient is immature and dependent. The child does not come for treatment of his own consent. As a rule he does not even perceive himself as sick or in need of treatment. The therapist therefore has to proceed somewhat differently in creating the *therapeutic situation.* He has to prove to the child that he is a helpful kindly companion and that he can become an interesting part of the child's world. Sometimes this can be accomplished in the first interview, but often it takes a longer time for the therapist to sell himself to the young patient. Anna Freud describes an example in which a ten-year-old boy, whose symptoms included phobias, deceptions, and thefts, was convinced only after many meetings that it was worth while to bother with the therapist. "I had to inveigle myself," she says, "into a confidence which would not be won directly, and to force myself upon a person who was of the opinion that he could get along very well without me."[35] She accomplished this by adapting herself to the child's whims, making herself an interesting participant in his play, proving herself useful when he was in trouble, and allying herself with him by returning things he had stolen and protecting him from punishment. When a patient comes for treatment from any other motive than his own need for help, the therapist has to exert himself to create a workable therapeutic situation.

The *expression of feelings* must also be accomplished in a different fashion. For younger children, at any rate, conversation is a poor medium for this purpose, and the principle of free association cannot be grasped. Fortunately a good substitute is available. If left to himself a child will play, and the therapist can do no better than encourage him to play. Play is a spontaneous and unguarded activity. It is the child's natural mode of expressing his feelings, developing his interests, and working on his problems. When play was first suggested as a substitute for conversation and free association, it was conceived largely as a means of diagnosis. Soon it became apparent, however, that play was itself to a certain extent therapeutic. The child uses it not only to express his anxieties but also to reduce them by putting himself in the position of

[35] A. Freud, *Introduction to the Technic of Child Analysis* (New York: Nervous and Mental Disease Publishing Co., 1928), p. 8. This essay is included in A. Freud, *The Psycho-Analytic Treatment of Children* (New York: International Universities Press, Inc., 1959).

actively mastering the dangers. By introducing the young patient into a small world of toys—dolls and animals, houses and furniture, cars and trucks, water, sand, and building blocks—the therapist at one stroke accomplishes two things. He opens an easy path for creating the initial friendship, and he links himself to the child's own preferred means of expressing feelings and achieving corrective emotional experience.

Another process that is considerably altered in work with children is the *transference*. The child develops various feelings, sometimes quite violent ones, toward the therapist, but these may constitute a new relationship rather than a transferred repetition of older attitudes toward parents. As Anna Freud neatly expresses it, "the child is not ready to undertake a new edition of its love relationships because the old edition is not yet out of print. Its original objects, the parents, are actually in existence as love objects, not in fantasy."[36] Often it happens that a child who is well loved at home mistrusts the therapist, whereas a rejected child at once strikes up a warmly affectionate relationship. At other times, to be sure, genuine transference does occur: the child repeats in relation to the therapist the emotions that he feels toward one of his parents. But the value of a *transference neurosis* is by no means as great as it is in adult psychoanalysis. Little gain could be expected from working out at the office a new edition of parental relationships if upon going home the child was simply plunged back into the old edition. Psychotherapy makes a patient less afraid of dangers that are no longer real. Its efforts are undone if the danger proves to be still real.

On the question of *new behavior* there is a corresponding difference when psychotherapy is applied to children. New behavior can serve as corrective emotional experience only when it is met with a new and more favorable reception. The child is in a poor position to make his environment treat him differently, even when his own behavior has greatly changed. He is still dependent and relatively helpless, he still occupies his accustomed positions in the family and among his playmates. The therapist must therefore place considerable reliance on changing the environment so that it will treat the child differently and allow his new behavior to become corrective emotional experience. Sometimes progress is possible only by putting the patient in a new environment: a new school, a camp, or even a foster family. Many workers feel that it is futile to practice psychotherapy with children under fourteen unless the parents can be influenced at the same time. Simultaneous treatment for mother and child is strongly recommended at most guidance clinics.

Levy's Release Therapy. We begin with a method that is applicable only in certain situations but that has the virtue of great simplicity.

[36] *Ibid.*, p. 38.

David Levy has given this method the name of *release therapy.*[37] Its distinguishing mark is its dependence on the child's acting out his problems and anxieties in play. This acting out in play, together with the permissive and sympathetic attitude of the therapist, constitutes the whole therapeutic process. No attempts are made to point out to the child the feelings he has expressed, to develop a transference relationship, or to promote any kind of new behavior. The method thus uses only two of the five basic processes: the therapeutic situation and the expression of feelings. Nevertheless it is highly successful for certain types of problems with children in the age range from two to ten. It is clearly capable of creating a corrective emotional experience.

The probable cause of anxiety in each case is judged from the history as given by the parents. The therapist then prepares a suitable arrangement of toys which gives the child the opportunity to play actively with the situations that caused him fear. The therapist may even take the lead in playing with the chosen toys and encourage the child to join him. As an example we may take the case of a boy of seven who had been having severe nightmares, awaking in sobs to recount dreams in which he was bound and tortured. The precipitating incident proved to be a story read at school in which two knights nailed an innkeeper by the hands to the door of his own inn. A few months earlier there had been a real incident when some boys bound him to a tree in the park and pretended to torture him. Both the story and the real incident contained grave threat because of their similarity to two harrowing experiences a few years earlier when he had been bound in blankets for puncture of the eardrums without anaesthesia. This boy was cured of his nightmares by four sessions of play. Toys were chosen to represent knights and an inn, boys, ropes, and a tree, blankets and a doctor. The patient played actively with this equipment and thus immunized himself to his fears.

Not all cases can be so quickly cured. For the series of 35 patients given in Levy's paper the average number of sessions was about 15. Not all the young patients have such clearly focalized sources of danger. In another case, for example, fear seemed to rest on all manifestations of messiness and aggression. The cause was presumed to lie in too early and too severe discipline, but no specific terrifying incidents were given in the history. Throughout the 19 sessions of treatment the little girl, once she overcame her initial anxiety, spent her time throwing clay and stepping on it, splashing water and sitting in it, cutting things to pieces and hurling them around the room. While this went on at the office, notes from the mother reported a constant increase of relaxation, contentment, and outgoing affection at home. The child began to blossom when the

[37] D. M. Levy, "Release Therapy," *American Journal of Orthopsychiatry,* IX (1939), pp. 713–36.

burden of guilt was lifted from her destructive and hostile tendencies by the therapist's permissive attitude. Yet in this case, as in the majority of Levy's cases, there was not a word of interpretation. The younger children—those under six—were apparently cured without knowing why they had been sent to the clinic to play and without perceiving any relation between their play and their behavior at home. This is corrective emotional experience reduced to its lowest terms.

One of the virtues of Levy's report is its clear statement of the conditions under which release therapy can be successfully applied. He offers the following criteria for selecting patients: (1) The problem should consist of a definite symptom syndrome precipitated by a relatively specific event: a fright, birth of a younger sibling, divorce of the parents, or something of the sort. (2) The fear should not have been in existence too long, so that it has had time to ramify throughout the personality and affect many aspects of behavior. Release therapy is thus not indicated for children over ten. (3) On the other hand the problem must center on something that happened in the past rather than on a chronic continuing situation. A background of satisfactory family relationships must be assumed. Release therapy is not indicated for chronic parental rejection, maternal overprotection, or similar enduring difficulties in the home situation. Only the effects of past experiences can be "released."

There is a certain resemblance between release therapy with young children and emotional abreaction as applied to adult neuroses of traumatic onset. Levy's criteria make it plain that release therapy is chiefly of value for children's neuroses of traumatic onset. It is not a sufficient treatment for those childhood neuroses that creep into a tangled existence out of chronic parent-child friction. Apparently the child in playing out his traumatic situations achieves much the same corrective emotional experience that occurs when the soldier under sodium pentothal rehearses his frightful scenes of combat. In play the child resumes contact with the threat and reappraises it. This time he achieves active mastery—he nails the innkeeper to the door, or ties the doll to the tree and has it break its bonds asunder. Probably the greater success with younger children comes partly from the fact that play and reality are less strictly differentiated. For a small child, doing something in play is almost the same as doing it in reality.

Simultaneous Treatment of Mother and Child. Unfortunately Levy's criteria exclude the majority of neurotic and maladjusted children. It is not often that the existing family situation plays a negligible part in the difficulty. When the problem arises out of parent-child relationships, it is futile to try to solve it purely by changing the child, who is the least strong and mature party to the relationship. Under these circumstances it is becoming a common practice to draw the mother into a simultaneous therapeutic relationship. Ideally the father should also be drawn in, but he can usually escape on the plea that he has to earn money to pay for the treatment. The mother has to bring the child to the office; she is generally upset over his condition, and it is not difficult to ease her gently into a therapeutic relationship.

Simultaneous treatment of child and mother has become standard procedure with most child guidance clinics. While the child is in the psychiatrist's office, the mother gives her version of things to the social worker and is progressively encouraged to express her feelings. Work with the mother is quite likely to follow the pattern of non-directive counseling described in the last chapter, except when a more openly supportive and reassuring attitude is required. When children show disordered behavior the mother is usually deeply entangled in it. The mere separation of mother and child at the clinic provides a good setting for the work of untangling. The child at once experiences the novelty of being able to behave without maternal supervision, encouragement, criticism, or whatever has characterized the relation. By slow degrees he makes his own relation with the therapist and assumes responsibility for his own actions. Children often try to make the doctor assume responsibility; they want him to treat them the way their mothers do. The significant step of doing things because they want to, rather than to please the doctor or resist him, comes later and with difficulty. The mothers meanwhile change in much the same direction. Frequently the mother has been as much enslaved to the child as the child has been to the mother. Both parties need to be disentangled so that they can become individuals in their own right.

The procedure is illustrated in the case of Solomon, a ten-year-old boy suffering from tics and general nervousness.[38] Whatever their origin, the symptoms served the purpose of enslaving an already devoted mother who fussed anxiously over Solomon's difficulties. The child soon discovered that the therapist was not going to fuss anxiously over his symptoms, and these were rarely manifested at the office. At the third interview Solomon stated that his mother thought he was better. At almost the same moment the mother was telling the social worker that the symptoms were very much worse; then she suddenly blurted out, "What will I have left when the children are grown?" Her own difficulty in letting Solomon, her youngest child, grow up was clearly a contributing cause of his illness. Solomon, meanwhile, began to learn the satisfactions of growing up, though he resisted them stoutly for a time. There were several scenes in which he debated whether he should bravely go to bed alone rather

[38] F. H. Allen, *Psychotherapy with Children* (New York: W. W. Norton & Co., Inc., 1942), chap. vi.

than having his mother take him upstairs at night. He tried to cajole the therapist into ordering this new behavior, and his feelings were hurt when the therapist said that the act should not be done simply to please him. Finally, however, Solomon began to do things on his own initiative. He expressed an interest in growing up and being like his older brothers. The change in both child and mother was neatly symbolized at the close of the last interview. For the first time Solomon struggled uncomplainingly to put on his heavy coat with its awkward collar, working until he succeeded, and for the first time his mother did not offer to help him.

It seems likely in this case that work with Solomon alone would have gone to waste. He readily gave up his symptoms at the office, but would he ever have been able to discontinue them at home if his mother solicitously fussed over him and thus rewarded the symptoms? Treatment of the mother alone would also have gone rather slowly. Would insights gained at the office survive the primitive appeal of her child's tearful trembling at the prospect of going to bed alone? Each party could make rapid and substantial progress only when the other party also changed. This problem of changing a relationship rather than merely changing a patient is often the central one in child guidance.

Family Psychotherapy. The bold step of trying to influence the whole family is certainly in accord with present theories about the origins of disordered behavior. In practice, however, it is no small feat to secure the cooperation of all the members of a family. Ackerman favors doing so whenever possible, arguing that the treatment of one member of a close group necessarily entails changes for all the others.[39] He adopts the procedure of interviewing the whole family at once. Much can be deduced from the way the members enter the room, offer greetings, and distribute themselves among the available chairs. Conflict, confusion, the dominance hierarchy, and preferred modes of acting as a family may reveal themselves sharply in the problem of seating. Significant family alignments, alliances, exclusions, and scapegoating may come to light early in the proceedings. The therapist meanwhile tries to create an atmosphere of rapport that will favor a reduction of concealments and defenses. To achieve a therapeutic result "he must permit himself to be drawn into the center of the family disturbance," but he must also preserve objectivity and freedom so that he can serve as umpire and even as controlling authority if things threaten to get out of hand.[40] Family psychotherapy is obviously no job for a novice. To improvise appropriate action in what can easily become a whirlpool of passions

[39] N. W. Ackerman, *The Psychodynamics of Family Life* (New York: Basic Books, Inc., 1958).

[40] N. W. Ackerman, "Further Comments on Family Psychotherapy," in Stein, *op. cit.*, pp. 245–55.

requires rare gifts of alertness and a seasoned skill in grasping the emotional meaning of behavior.

Child Psychoanalysis. A group of workers once headed by Melanie Klein in England may be said to practice standard psychoanalysis with children. Klein substituted play for free association, but otherwise she followed closely the Freudian pattern of adult analysis. Systematic use is made of interpretation, the transference neurosis is fully developed, and no unusual attempts are made to influence the child's environment.[41] In general, however, psychoanalysis with children is not sharply set off from other methods of treatment. The principle of flexibility, at last fully recognized in briefer psychoanalysis, has from the start been inescapable in work with children.

It would perhaps be fair to say that therapy with children could be classed as psychoanalysis when substantial use is made of interpretation. Yet there are a good many child analysts who argue for a sparing use of interpretation. Lippmann, for instance, really reduces interpretation to the recognition of feelings when he says: "Interpretations are made only when the child has so worked through the material that the meaning is quite clear to him."[42] For our purposes it is not important to draw a sharp line between what is child psychoanalysis and what is some other kind of therapy. It is important, however, to learn everything we can about interpretation and to see how it fits into the therapeutic process when the patient is a child.

A discerning account of this problem has been given by Erikson.[43] He calls attention to the phenomenon of *play disruption,* defined as "the sudden and complete or diffused and slowly spreading inability to play."[44] Playfulness implies a certain freedom and relaxation, a peaceful state of mind. When the child's play leads him to dangerous topics and anxiety-laden ideas, this freedom is lost and his play either comes to a standstill or assumes a compulsively repetitive character. Play disruption is thus the equivalent of the resistances that arise in the course of adult free associations. If the child can play out his problems and bring them to a more successful conclusion, as happens in release therapy, interpretation is unnecessary. Corrective emotional experience can take place without it. But when his play terminates in disruption—when he becomes unable to

[41] M. Klein, *The Psychoanalysis of Children* (London: Hogarth Press, Ltd., 1932), especially chaps. i and ii.

[42] H. S. Lippmann, "Child Analysis," *American Journal of Orthopsychiatry,* IX (1939), pp. 707–12.

[43] E. H. Erikson, "Studies in the Interpretation of Play: I. Clinical Observations of Play Disruption in Young Children," *Genetic Psychology Monographs,* XX (1940), pp. 557–671.

[44] *Ibid.,* p. 563.

cope with the anxieties to which his play intentions have led him—then release is impossible without help from the therapist.

> Those children who transfer not the solution but the insolvability of their problems into the play situation and onto the person of the observer need to be induced by *systematic interpretation* to reconsider, on a more verbal level, the constellations which have overwhelmed them in the past and are apt to overwhelm them when reoccurring. Where *this* goal is given, child psychoanalysis begins.
>
> Child analysis proper seeks to provide the child with an opportunity for catharsis only in the frame of an intimate therapeutic contact in which *repeated interpretation* furthers the *verbal communication* of inner dangers and the establishment of a *supremacy of conscious judgment* over unmanageable or incompletely repressed tendencies."[45]

Interpretation is not a single act; it must be repeated as often as is necessary to permit the child a ready and relaxed verbal expression of his troubles. When such expression becomes possible, when the young patient can verbalize his tendencies with comfort and even with humor, he not only feels a vast immediate relief but he is also protected against future eruptions of the same crippling feelings.

The things that need interpreting are the child's fears, guilts, aggressions, and sexual tendencies. The therapist points them out before the child has verbalized them, but if possible not before the child is able to verbalize them. When interpretations are rightly timed they produce an immediate corrective emotional experience. This happens because the therapist's verbalization, occurring as it does within the permissive and friendly therapeutic relationship, says in effect that it is natural to have aggressive or sexual tendencies and that one need not feel afraid or guilty on their account. The child can reappraise the dangers when he finds that the therapist appraises them calmly rather than embodying them. A certain amount of sheer instruction goes along with the interpretation. The child's conception of the sex act and the reproductive process is likely to be highly distorted, and in the end it is better for him to know the true state of affairs.

It is probably impossible to dislodge the more severe neuroses of childhood without taking active steps of interpretation.

Aids to the Expression of Feeling. The crowded children's psychiatric ward of Bellevue Hospital in New York has been the scene of several valuable therapeutic experiments. Forced by necessity to shorten treatment as much as possible, workers under the direction of Lauretta Bender have tried various methods for hastening the expression of feeling. We shall select for brief description one of these methods, which

[45] *Ibid.*, pp. 563–64.

uses puppet shows to secure a loosening of feelings in several children at the same time.

The use of puppet shows is reported by Bender and Woltmann to be particularly effective in the age range from six to twelve.[46] The shows are devised to represent the common emotional problems of childhood and to provide ready identification figures. The hero, Caspar, is "active, curious, sociable, and uninhibited; he is immune to any real harm and in the end he finds a solution to his problems." There is a mischievous monkey, a dreadful alligator, witches, cannibals, giants, and kind parents. Caspar gets into various scrapes and the monkey is constantly in trouble, but in the realm of puppets the forces of evil can always be overcome. The shows are conducted in such a way as to invite active participation by the audience. At crucial moments the children are asked to tell the puppeteers what happens next. Led on in this fashion they soon begin to give advice, shout warnings to Caspar that the alligator is creeping up behind him, denounce the witches and giants, urge clemency for the monkey, sometimes even get into brawls amongst themselves.

Bender and Woltmann call attention to three therapeutic benefits that result from this procedure. (1) Although the children rarely develop real anxiety as they watch the shows, they participate emotionally in Caspar's adventures. They share his daring and his aggression against the figures of authority and punishment that threaten him; they share also in the happy outcome which leaves these threatening forces defeated and harmless. Thus they gain some of the benefit that comes from spontaneous play. (2) "It is undoubtedly one of the greatest therapeutic factors that the child learns that other children about him are experiencing the same feelings that he is, and he is aided and abetted in the expression of his aggressive tendencies by the fact that others about him are loudly proclaiming his own feelings." In a show that deals with sibling rivalry, for example, the children shoutingly urge Caspar to throw the baby into the garbage can or drop him down the toilet, thoughts that would come to expression much more slowly without group support. (3) Subsequent individual therapy gets off to a good start by having the child retell the puppet story. Just as the feelings experienced in hypnosis make their way more readily into waking free association, so here the feelings stirred up while the child is in the puppet audience become easily available for discussion in the therapeutic interview.

Puppet shows serve as a time-saving technical aid in securing an expression of feelings, but they are simply an adjunct to individual psychotherapy. At the same time they introduce an element of group activity.

[46] L. Bender and A. G. Woltmann, "The Use of Puppet Shows as a Psychotherapeutic Method for Behavior Problems in Children," *American Journal of Orthopsychiatry,* VI (1936), pp. 341–54.

They thus lead us naturally to one of the newest and most interesting developments in psychotherapy: working with patients in groups.

GROUP PSYCHOTHERAPY

The original impetus to group psychotherapy was a purely practical one. Psychiatrists in mental hospitals and large clinics, confronted by an impossible amount of work, could help a substantial number of their patients only if they invented some radical device for saving time. Here and there, starting about fifty years ago, workers began to experiment with the possibility of treating patients in groups. In the beginning these groups were considered to be classes; the group leader served as a teacher and sometimes even as a sort of preacher who used persuasive and inspirational methods. As the technique developed, it became customary for the leader to open each meeting with a talk about some psychological topic, such as defense mechanisms or emotions and their bodily accompaniments. Simple diagrams or drawings on the blackboard were used whenever possible, not only to clarify what was being said but also to serve as an anchorage point for subsequent discussion. Sooner or later the group members would be doing most of the talking, and it often happened that they were able to bring up personal problems, discuss the problems of others, and free themselves from considerable burdens of guilt and anxiety. It was helpful and reassuring for patients to learn in this vivid way that disordered behavior was understandable and that their own guilty secrets and contemptible weaknesses were not unlike those of other people.

As experience with group psychotherapy increased, the didactic methods of the earlier classes gave place to an atmosphere more truly psychotherapeutic. Especially when the work was extended to neurotic patients it became apparent that meetings might be conducted without prepared topics, in a client-centered fashion, the course of conversation being determined by the spontaneous offerings of group members. The part played by the group leader became more and more like that of the individual therapist who uses only such tools as the recognition of feelings and the interpretation of behavior. Today one can see much the same range of opinions about group psychotherapy that exists with respect to individual treatment. Some workers advocate a strictly "group-centered" procedure that copies the permissiveness and non-directiveness of Rogers' client-centered psychotherapy.[47] Some adhere as closely as possible to Freudian psychoanalysis and concentrate on interpreting the

[47] N. Hobbs, in C. R. Rogers, *Client-Centered Therapy* (Boston: Houghton Mifflin Co., 1951), chap. vii.

transference reactions that occur during the meetings.[48] Others favor a principle of flexibility, using different degrees and kinds of activity according to the nature and circumstances of the group.[49] Still others, chiefly those working with more seriously disturbed patients, find it advisable to use tactics of a more directive character.[50] Similarly, there is a range of opinion about the length of time required to secure good results. Twenty to forty weekly sessions represent an average duration in many clinics and outpatient services, but one worker, George Bach, who argues strongly that group therapy should be intensive, considers a group still new when it has met only fifty times and states that "intensive group psychotherapy certainly does not represent a short-cut in terms of therapy hours, although it is economically easier for most patients."[51]

The Course of Group Therapy. It will be clear from the variations just described that we cannot give a standard account of the course of group therapy. Yet in order to convey some idea of what happens we must select certain features, even if they are not universal. In work with neurotic patients the group is likely to number about eight. Meetings are held once or twice a week, with leader and group members sitting informally around a table. At first the members direct all their remarks toward the leader, and it is evident that they expect him to answer questions, give advice, and generally function in an authoritative manner. The leader meets this by a method described by Foulkes as "leadership by default"; he simply says, "Let me hear what *you* think about this question."[52] As in individual therapy, patients at first find this non-directiveness quite frustrating, but the leader's "defaulting" eventually forces them out of their initial attitude of dependence. It can now be observed that patients begin to talk to each other rather than to the therapist; they may even begin to favor each other with therapeutic suggestions. From this point on, the leader serves chiefly as an alert interpreter, though occasionally he will have to steer things more actively to protect a member from being overwhelmed by advice or diagnosis on the part of other members. Presently the leader begins to raise questions about the motives behind what is being said. He wonders what prompted A to give the

[48] H. Ezriel, "A Psychoanalytic Approach to Group Treatment," *British Journal of Medical Psychology,* XXIII (1950), pp. 59–74; J. D. Sutherland, "Notes on Psychoanalytic Group Therapy: I. Therapy and Training," *Psychiatry,* XV (1952), pp. 111–17.

[49] S. R. Slavson, "Group Psychotherapies," in J. L. McCary and D. E. Sheer, *Six Approaches to Psychotherapy* (New York: The Dryden Press, 1955), chap. iii.

[50] J. W. Klapman, *Group Psychotherapy: Theory and Practice* (New York: Grune & Stratton, Inc., 1946).

[51] G. R. Bach, *Intensive Group Psychotherapy* (New York: The Ronald Press Co., 1954), p. 213.

[52] S. H. Foulkes, "Concerning Leadership in Group-Analytic Psychotherapy," *International Journal of Group Psychotherapy,* I (1951), p. 319.

advice he just gave to B. This examining of motives is gradually taken up by the group members, who start to become aware of their own motives and the consistent kind of impact they have on others. C discovers, for example, that his remarks are always directed toward the less assertive patients, and he thus learns that he tends to be fearful of reprisal. D discovers that he always intervenes when there is tension between two other patients, and he thus realizes the force of his own fear of hostility. Much of this discovery is made spontaneously or with the help of other group members. The leader is no longer the only source of interpretations.

What is talked about in these meetings? The patients discuss their symptoms and other things that are troubling them. They air the exasperations of their current life. They talk about the process of therapy and speculate on what is involved in getting well. A good deal of time may be spent in narrating important episodes in their past lives. As time goes on, the conversation turns more and more to what is happening in the group: how the patients feel about the leader, how they are affected by the behavior of other members of the group, how they themselves seem to affect others. This bringing to expression of feelings and counterfeelings, so different from what happens in ordinary social life, constitutes a unique experience in human relations and may well prove to be the central advantage of group psychotherapy over individual treatment.[53]

A technique that adheres more literally to psychoanalytic principles has been developed by a group of workers, notably Bion, Ezriel, and Sutherland, at the Tavistock Clinic in London. The distinguishing feature of their method is the early and consistent use of interpretation. Although the interpretations include behavior of patients toward one another, there is a major emphasis on the relationship with the therapist. If a patient displays a certain attitude in the therapist's presence, it may be that he thereby conceals an attitude toward the therapist which is laden with anxiety. Thus, as Nevitt Sanford expresses it, "interpretations regularly take the form: you express this relationship, e.g., solicitude for other members of the group, because you must avoid this relationship, e.g., hostile jealousy of their supposed better standing with the therapist, because you fear this calamitous result, e.g., total and irrevocable rejection."[54] These interpretations are believed to have much the same effect as transference interpretations in individual psychoanalysis. The clear discrepancy between the patient's unconscious fear, for instance of rejec-

[53] Samples of recorded sessions are given in Bach, *op. cit.;* they are listed in a table of contents, p. xi. See especially the discussion on the subject of mothers, pp. 83–88.

[54] N. Sanford, "Clinical Methods: Psychotherapy," in *Annual Review of Psychology,* IV (Stanford: Annual Reviews, Inc., 1953), p. 318.

tion, and the actual attitudes of the therapist serves to dramatize for the patient the irrational element in his own behavior and provides him with an opportunity to reappraise the ancient childhood danger.

Curative Processes. Group psychotherapy embodies all of the basic processes discussed at the end of the last chapter. The *therapeutic relationship* is set up on the basis of permissiveness and an interest that is both friendly and expert. *Expression of feelings* is obtained by free conversation, occasionally supplemented by more active methods. The *pointing out of feelings* is accomplished either by recognition or by more systematic and strenuous interpretation. *Transference* occurs and may be encouraged up to a point, although the concept of transference neurosis seems rather too strong for what usually happens in group therapy. Lastly, *new behavior* takes place directly in the therapeutic sessions as well as in outside life. Reduction of defenses, reappraisal of old dangers, and a resumption of blocked learning processes characterize equally well the curative events of individual and of group therapy.

There are, however, distinctive properties of group psychotherapy, and these may be conceived either as helps or as hindrances. The outstanding property is, of course, the presence of other patients in the therapeutic sessions and the possibility of interaction with them. In individual treatment the patient's social adjustment is largely left to the patient. New behavior may be explicitly encouraged, but it is not observed by the therapist and can be interpreted only in whatever form it is reported by the patient. Group psychotherapy brings this important step directly into the clinic. The therapist is in a position to interpret what is really happening in the patient's social relationships. Furthermore, the responses of other group members, growing more and more candid as the sessions progress, provide the patient with an insistent schooling in observing not only his own feelings but the effect he has upon others. He becomes fully alerted to the relation between his own behavior and the responses of others. The patient emerges from the work with a new and generally constructive social experience behind him. This bridges the gap that is often present in individual treatment between the patient's progress in his relationship with the therapist and his progress with the relationships of everyday life. In this respect group therapy is a more real experience than individual therapy.

On the other hand the criticism is often made that group treatment does not make fully adequate provision for liquidating deeper defenses and anxieties. Encouraging as the group may be, it cannot provide quite the security of the individual session, nor can it permit the long-continued probing and struggle that may be necessary to arrive at nuclear neurotic problems. The majority of workers seems inclined to favor a combination of group and individual therapy. To the individual sessions are assigned the resolving of problems that can not be dealt with adequately in the group and the working through of resistances that are deeply attached to childhood anxieties. In spite of its great value, group psychotherapy does not yet seem destined to displace individual work.

Application to Children: Activity Groups. An interesting adaptation of group therapy to children has been worked out by Slavson and tested on a rather large scale under the Jewish Board of Guardians in New York City.[55] Small groups or "clubs" were formed for children in the age range from eight to thirteen, providing them with the opportunity to meet, play, practice handicrafts, and occasionally take trips under the guidance of a carefully trained leader. Outwardly resembling the numerous clubs already in existence in most communities, these activity groups actually had a psychotherapeutic purpose. Children were chosen who needed practice in social adjustment, either because they were shy, submissive, and isolated, or because they were aggressive, self-willed, and unaccustomed to sharing. They were chosen, one might say, from a middle zone of social ineptitude: on the one hand, not too badly maladjusted to preclude participation in a group; on the other hand, not capable of going directly into an ordinary group organized without therapeutic intent. Slavson's activity groups are analogous to group psychotherapy as practiced with adults, except that no attempt is made to instruct or to point out feelings. The corrective emotional experience comes from simply being in the group under the conditions about to be described. If the child is in need of more radical treatment, this is accomplished by simultaneous individual therapy carried out by someone other than the group leader.

The therapeutic character of the groups is maintained by the behavior and attitude of the leader. His behavior is designed to create maximally favorable conditions for social learning. At the outset his attitude is almost completely permissive. He busies himself with handicrafts, takes little notice of aggressive and destructive behavior, allows the group to blow off steam and then bring itself to some kind of order. He is friendly and gentle but not too personal; he carefully avoids establishing relations that will lead to feelings of favoritism and "sibling rivalry" within the group. Keeping to this half-impersonal role, he nevertheless makes it a business to give recognition and praise whenever a child does something well. This sets a fashion which eventually is copied by the children. Group recognition as well as the leader's recognition becomes available for all good performances.

[55] S. R. Slavson, *An Introduction to Group Therapy* (New York: Commonwealth Fund, 1943).

Under these circumstances social development takes place with gratifying speed. The group is given the chance to try mischief, rough-house, disorganized fooling around, and to discover for itself the greater satisfactions of orderly cooperative behavior. These satisfactions are strengthened by the leader's reward in the form of recognition, but the leader does not take the initiative in producing the orderly behavior. Spontaneously a sense of responsibility develops in the group, so that the chores connected with having the meetings and serving refreshments are more and more taken over by the children. At the end of six or eight months of weekly meetings most of the children have progressed sufficiently with their social adjustments and social skills so that they can transfer to ordinary clubs and neighborhood groups.

Moreno's Psychodrama. A variant form of group psychotherapy is the psychodrama originated by J. L. Moreno.[56] The essential principle of psychodrama is to stimulate the expression of feelings through unrehearsed, spontaneous play-acting. Other patients take part in the action, and still other patients and observers make up the audience. Moreno himself has surrounded the procedure with an array of grandiose concepts, but the central ideas seem to be quite simple. Drama stands as a midway point between fantasy and reality. It is real in the sense that there is a stage with lights, a group of spectators, and other actors toward whom one is behaving. It is unreal in the sense that the whole thing is only a play. Unrehearsed drama has a certain similarity to free association. Giving free associations is real in the sense that a therapist is listening and that relief from a neurosis is being sought. It is unreal in the sense that what one says is illogical and fantastic, quite unsuitable for communication in everyday life. Proponents of psychodrama maintain that it is better than free association as a means of securing expression. Although at first it may be hard for patients to act with freedom, they can be slowly induced into an atmosphere in which they learn to express themselves with great spontaneity and often with great enjoyment.

The following case report by Sarbin will make the procedure clearer.[57] A seventeen-year-old high-school boy seemed quite incapable of social relationships. Listless and shy, he stayed by himself most of the time, but from interviews and tests it was clear that he fantasied himself as a popular high-school boy. He was first asked to participate as a spectator while other patients acted their psychodramas. Then he was asked to prepare a short scene of his own for a subsequent session. He chose the role of a radio commentator and gave a simple scene that required no

[56] J. L. Moreno, *Psychodrama* (Beacon, N. Y.: Beacon House, Inc., 1946), especially Sections 1, 2, and 6.

[57] T. R. Sarbin, "The Concept of Role-Taking," *Sociometry, VI* (1943), pp. 273–85.

supporting characters—altogether a safe and undemanding performance. At the next meeting he was requested to serve as a minor character in a drama being enacted by other patients. He was the buddy of a soldier who received abusive treatment from a tough sergeant. He was able to imitate freely the actions of his buddy and even develop them in his own way. For his next assignment he prepared an original scene calling for several supporting characters. For the first time he was able to act without self-consciousness, genuinely absorbed in the drama. Next he took the part of father in another young patient's drama. This role proved highly congenial; he "stole the show" as he acted out what were unmistakably his own father's attitudes toward him. Only after this success was he requested to enact what corresponded to his own most cherished fantasy. He was asked to depict a day in the life of a high-school boy. Choosing various characters to represent his parents and his fellow students, he put on a spontaneous drama remarkable for its animation and conversational freedom as well as its revelation of his emotional difficulties at home.

There were various other sessions, but what concerns us more is the patient's off-stage progress. Instead of sitting alone he began to come into the center of the group. Instead of retiring between scenes he began to use these intervals for conversation with others. Listless shyness gave place to more alert participation. The parents were surprised at the rapid increase of interest in people and events and at his spontaneous seeking for companionship. The patient even gained weight while these improvements were going on. In the realm of psychodrama he had become able to behave in a way that corresponded to his ego-ideal and that gave him self-esteem. The change carried over into new behavior in everyday life.

As is the case with group psychotherapy generally, it is still too early to tell what will prove to be the most effective uses of psychodrama and what kinds of patients will respond to it most favorably. It would seem to be an ideal technique for patients with a certain degree of generalized inhibition. It supplies just the right lift and social support for overcoming inhibitions that are not too deeply rooted. Moreno has used it for marriage problems and even for matrimonial triangles.[58] Here psychodrama is sometimes successful in liberating the deeper feelings that discolor and clog the relationships. A scene can be started from whatever clues the parties offer in their preliminary interviews. Although these clues may have to do with superficial or side issues, "it is a reliable psychodramatic experience," according to Moreno, "that, once the subjects are working on the therapeutic stage, they are carried by the momentum of

[58] *Ibid.*, pp. 233–45, 328–49.

psychodramatic dynamics from the surface to the deeper level of their relationship."[59]

Considered in relation to the five basic therapeutic processes outlined at the end of the last chapter, psychodrama bears particularly on the *expression of feelings* and on *new behavior*. Spontaneous drama serves as a medium for securing a free and often intense expression of feelings. This expression goes directly over into new behavior on the psychodramatic stage. In these respects, therefore, psychodrama does not basically differ from other forms of group psychotherapy which utilize group discussion for the release of feelings and for new social interactions. Moreno's description of his work leaves doubt as to whether much use is made of pointing out or interpreting feelings, whether much permanent insight is gained, and whether sufficient attention is paid to what the patient accomplishes in everyday life. These faults, however, are not inherent in the psychodramatic technique. They can readily be avoided by combining psychodrama with individual therapy. Used in this way, psychodrama will probably take its place as another of the technical aids or adjuncts that in suitable cases hasten the process of psychotherapy.

RESULTS OF PSYCHOTHERAPY

It might be supposed that the results of psychotherapy would long ago have been measured and put on an objective basis. This expectation dissolves as soon as one starts to think about the problem of measurement. Only on rare occasions can there be an objective criterion of improvement such as resuming work, return to military duty, or the disappearance of a focal symptom like phobia which is clearly either present or absent. The larger, more subjective, and perhaps more lasting changes at which psychotherapy generally aims could be estimated with accuracy only through a massive research effort using many judges, extended follow-up studies, and psychological tests better than those now available. If research has moved slowly, it is not because of failure to recognize the importance of knowing the results of psychotherapy. It is because of the almost insurmountable difficulty of making the necessary measurements.[60]

Reported Results. Estimates of results have usually been derived from therapists' judgments of improvement in the patients they have treated. Comparable reports of this type, recently surveyed by Eysenck, number

[59] *Ibid.*, p. 329.

[60] The problems are well described by M. Zax and A. Klein, "Measurement of Personality and Behavior Changes Following Psychotherapy," *Psychological Bulletin*, LVII (1960), pp. 435–48.

over 50 and include more than 15,000 patients.[61] Results are generally expressed in terms of several degrees of improvement; but if we gather into one group such headings as "cured," "much improved," and "improved," calling these successful outcomes, and interpret "slightly improved" and "not improved" as unsuccessful outcomes, the findings show a reassuring consistency. With adult patients the proportion of successes hovers around two thirds. With children, results at termination of treatment show almost exactly this same proportion of successes, while results estimated from later follow-up studies carry the figure above 70 per cent. Taking these figures at face value, and bearing in mind the small forces with which psychotherapy must operate, we can see that being able to help two thirds of one's patients would be ground for considerable satisfaction.

It is noteworthy in the figures for adults that standard psychoanalysis did not show better results than briefer forms of treatment; if anything, the outcomes were a little poorer. This finding is not easy to interpret. Aiming to liquidate the original anxieties and to change all aspects of personality distorted thereby, the psychoanalysts may have set themselves exceedingly high standards of improvement. The claim that these far-reaching changes fortify the patient against future breakdown could not be adequately tested. On the other hand, the results could be taken to mean that standard psychoanalysis is an inefficient method of treatment. Its virtue as a tool of exploration might detract from its effective bearing on change, which may not require such a thorough uncovering of the past as Freud originally supposed. The successes claimed for shorter forms of treatment, whether or not psychoanalytically oriented, tend to support the interpretation that the thoroughness of the standard method is not generally necessary.

There is, of course, a logical flaw in all these reports of improvement. Success in two cases out of three can be attributed wholly to psychotherapy only on the assumption that untreated neurotic patients do not improve. As we shall see, there is no reason to make this assumption; and we need to know more about recovery from neurosis without therapeutic intervention. For a strict statistical demonstration of the effects of psychotherapy, there should be a control group of similarly disordered people who receive no treatment and whose change over an equivalent period of time can be satisfactorily measured. Attempts to use this design have thus far been badly hampered by inadequate methods of measurement, but independent studies of untreated neurotic patients provide evidence for a surprisingly high rate of spontaneous remission. This is

[61] H. J. Eysenck, *Handbook of Abnormal Psychology: An Experimental Approach* (New York: Basic Books, Inc., 1961), pp. 712–15.

illustrated in the following study by Denker.[62] A survey was made of a series of five hundred patients who were receiving disability payments from an insurance company because of neurotic disturbances severe enough to keep them from work. These patients were treated by their own physicians, general practitioners untrained in psychotherapy, who undoubtedly used a good deal of suggestion, reassurance, and persuasion along with sedatives and tonics but who cannot be considered to have employed planned psychotherapeutic procedures. Despite the amateur standing of these physicians, the rate of improvement by the patients was high and the disabling symptoms generally did not recur. A two-year follow-up showed that 72 per cent of the patients had been able to resume work and had not felt a need to seek help again. This proportion of improvements was actually higher than the average of two thirds reported by psychotherapists, but the criterion of returning to work and asking no further help is hardly the same as what a therapist means by improved. The evidence, however, speaks strongly for spontaneous remission, which we must now examine.

Spontaneous Remission. The supposition that untreated neuroses do not improve has no basis whatever in psychodynamic theory. We know that in the case of physical diseases spontaneous recovery is not at all uncommon. With the neuroses there is still less reason to associate recovery exclusively with planned intervention. Neurotics have typically been well for a long time before the breakdown that sends them to the doctor. Our study of the neurotic personality, with its overdriven strivings and restricting protective organization, leads us to have certain reservations about this state of health; but poor as it may be as a way of life it is certainly not illness in the ordinary meaning of the word. Whatever his limitations, the person passes for well, has a job, takes care of the family, and functions with at least minimal adequacy. If after a breakdown he struggles back only to this same level, he will be counted as restored to health.

In our discussion of neurotic breakdown we assumed that circumstances conspired to increase the patient's chronic strain until an unmistakable illness appeared. Neurotic breakdown is precipitated by situations that heighten the reminders of early childhood dangers, that obstruct the use of defensive measures, or that call out defenses so strong that they disrupt behavior. The patient may stick at this low point, or he may get worse, but the chances are loaded that he will get better. If circumstances change again, the swing is likely to be in the opposite direction. Changes in the situation may weaken the reminders of child-

[62] P. G. Denker, "Results of Treatment of Psychoneurosis by the General Practitioner: A Follow-up Study of 500 Cases," *New York State Journal of Medicine*, XLVI (1946), pp. 2164–66.

hood anxiety or strengthen defenses without making them too burdensome. A person who experienced childhood panic about rejection, for instance, may come into a congenial group which gives constant evidences of acceptance, or a person who has all but crippled his endeavors by excessive caution and meticulous attention to detail enters an occupation where these qualities are of great importance and are hailed as rare excellencies. Furthermore, an untreated neurosis may eventually build up so much desperation that the person, feeling that he cannot go on like this any longer, will at last take active steps to lead a more rewarding life and will tolerate the increased anxiety which this at first entails. If the symptoms have made it impossible for the patient to keep his job—the universal plight in Denker's study of insurance cases—he may presently experience the distress of having nothing to do, a distress which we know from studies of unemployment and retirement can be for many people very real. Neurotic breakdown and symptom formation may provide a "solution" at a given point for inner problems of anxiety and defense, but living permanently with this "solution" may prove to be quite another matter. If neurosis sometimes yields secondary gains that reinforce it, sometimes it yields what we might call "secondary pains" that work in the opposite direction. The neurotic "solution," in short, is likely to be a poor one which eventually produces a new balance of forces tending toward remission.

The trouble with using spontaneous recovery as a base line against which to measure the effectiveness of psychotherapy is that the two processes of improvement are probably not at all the same. Denker's study and some others to the same effect have been interpreted to mean that psychotherapy accomplishes no more than would occur anyway through spontaneous remission. This ignores all that we know about the process of psychological treatment as it is experienced by the patient and observed by the therapist. Perhaps it is true that brief methods such as suggestion, persuasion, or direct applications of learning theory, when they are used without trying to increase the patient's understanding of himself, work by processes only slightly different from those of spontaneous remission. When the technique aims to remove or suppress symptoms, it assists the very process that is probably central in spontaneous recovery. The best present guess about unaided remission is that it represents a return to the condition that existed before breakdown. The person with a neurosis reverts to being merely a neurotic personality with all his previous tensions and limitations, which now, however, seem preferable to the outright neurosis.

The object of all psychotherapy that tries to increase the patient's insight is to produce a more radical change. This change may be, as in client-centered counseling, a new awareness of one's feelings and their effects on one's behavior, together with a new sense of the possibility of warmth and free communication in human relations. It may be a new familiarity with one's defensive maneuvers and with impulses that lurk just outside the everyday zone of consciousness. It may involve a long process of uncovering past situations of anxiety and submitting them to corrective emotional experience. All these changes are intended to enrich the patient's life, freeing him not only from symptoms but also from at least some of the handicaps of neurotic personality organization. Patients whose insight has increased generally regard this as a boon, giving them a more alert awareness of themselves and the people around them. Gaining a new appreciation of their own feelings, at the same time they feel better able to guide their behavior in a rational manner. The task of future research is to illuminate the full nature of these changes, compare them with those that occur in spontaneous recoveries, and test the hypothesis that they offer greater protection against future disorders.

In surveying different methods of psychotherapy one seems to hear a babel of conflicting voices, but by closer listening we have been able to realize that they all spoke dialects of a single basic tongue. As Ziskind has pointed out, the different kinds of psychotherapy are *non-specific;* "recoveries occur from all approaches despite differences in theory and technique."[63] Only a small number of techniques—and most of these are merely technical aids—can be considered to possess known *specific* uses. Narcosynthesis is particularly adapted to the prompt recovery of traumatic memories and is therefore an excellent tool for the military psychiatrist in a combat zone. Levy's release therapy is specifically limited to a certain type of childhood problem. Activity groups are to be recommended only for children having moderately severe, but not too severe, problems in social adjustment. This is virtually all that we can say about specific indications. As we saw at the end of the last chapter, all methods have certain processes in common, and it is through these rather than through their individual peculiarities that they achieve the main part of their results. The fundamental principles of psychotherapy are not hopelessly complex. They all have to do with removing blocks in the learning process and promoting new growth. The processes are partly understood and wholly understandable.

SUGGESTIONS FOR FURTHER READING

A collection of case studies representing a large variety of therapeutic methods has been assembled and edited by A. Burton, *Case Studies in Counseling and Psychotherapy* (Englewood Cliffs, N. J., Prentice-Hall, Inc., 1959).

[63] E. Ziskind, "How Specific Is Psychotherapy?" *American Journal of Psychiatry,* CVI (1949), pp. 285–91.

A good introduction to hypnotherapy in general will be found in M. Brenman & M. M. Gill's *Hypnotherapy—A Survey of the Literature* (New York, International Universities Press, Inc., 1947). A detailed presentation of hypnoanalysis is given by L. Wolberg, *Hypnoanalysis* (New York, Grune & Stratton, Inc., 1945). Part One of this book describes at length the treatment of a single case; Part Two is devoted to general principles. The uses of hypnotherapy in military settings are vividly described by J. G. Watkins in *Hypnotherapy of War Neuroses* (New York, The Ronald Press Co., 1949). For the similar use of narcosynthesis the best reference is R. R. Grinker & J. P. Spiegel, *Men Under Stress* (Philadelphia, The Blakiston Co., 1945), Chs. 7 and 17.

A description of active techniques is included in F. C. Thorne's *Principles of Personality Counseling* (Brandon, Vermont, Journal of Clinical Psychology, 1950). For a shorter account of his general position see Thorne's chapter, "Directive and Eclectic Personality Counseling," in J. L. McCary and D. E. Sheer, eds., *Six Approaches to Psychotherapy* (New York, The Dryden Press, 1955), Ch. 5.

Anna Freud's small book, *The Psycho-analytic Treatment of Children* (New York: International Universities Press, Inc., 1946) is still the classic introduction to the special problems of psychotherapy with children. F. H. Allen's *Psychotherapy with Children* (New York, W. W. Norton & Co., Inc., 1942) is particularly successful in describing the problem of separating mother and child from a too-entangling relation. A book by Virginia M. Axline, *Play Therapy* (Boston, Houghton Mifflin Co., 1947) gives in semipopular style and with excellent pictures an account of play therapy conducted according to strictly non-directive principles. D. M. Levy's paper on release therapy is reprinted in S. S. Tomkins, *Contemporary Psychopathology* (Cambridge, Harvard University Press, 1943), Ch. 6. Individual case reports by different authors are included in the collection edited by G. E. Gardner, *Case Studies in Childhood Emotional Disabilities*, 2 vols. (New York, American Orthopsychiatric Association, 1953, 1956). A valuable new contribution on a topic of great present interest is I. D. Harris's *Emotional Blocks to Learning* (New York, The Free Press of Glencoe, 1961), which is a study of the psychological reasons for failure at school.

An excellent and detailed book on group psychotherapy is George R. Bach's *Intensive Group Psychotherapy* (New York, The Ronald Press Co., 1954). A shorter account which is also more explicitly psychoanalytical is given by S. H. Foulkes in *Introduction to Group-Analytic Psycho-Therapy* (London, Wm. Heinemann Medical Books, Ltd., 1948). S. R. Slavson's work on activity groups is reported in his interesting monograph, *An Introduction to Group Therapy* (New York, Commonwealth Fund, 1943). In *Six Approaches to Psychotherapy*, mentioned above, Slavson gives a bird's-eye view of the whole field of group therapy (Ch. 3). To be recommended also is *Group Psychotherapy: Theory and Practice* by H. Mullan and M. Rosenbaum (New York, The Free Press of Glencoe, 1962).

10

Conduct Disorders

The psychological origins of disordered personal behavior were discovered in the course of treating neurotic patients. The neuroses and psychotherapy, to which we have devoted the last five chapters, can thus be regarded as the classical themes in modern dynamic psychology. Upon their study was founded the *psychogenic hypothesis,* in accordance with which we have learned to look for causes of disordered behavior in such realms as attitudes learned in the family circle, critical problems in childhood emotional development, the personal meaning of events, and above all the effects of anxiety and the defensive operations used to hold it in check. The illumination provided by the psychogenic hypothesis is not confined to the neuroses and lesser maladjustments. In this chapter and the next we shall extend our survey to several more varieties of disordered behavior in which psychogenic factors play a significant part.

The disorders to be examined here do not have a great deal in common. If convenience did not call for a brief chapter heading we would simply list the contents: delinquency and criminal behavior, psychopathic personality, deviant sexual behavior, addiction to alcohol. In choosing *conduct disorders* as a title for the chapter we select a term that has no very precise technical meaning but which does at least suggest one general way in which these disorders differ from the neuroses. The neurotic patient typically conforms in outward ways to social expectations, taking out his inner conflicts and frustrations upon himself in the form of symptoms, suffering, fatigue, and chronic dissatisfaction. In contrast, the people to be studied here can be described as *acting out* some part of their problems at the expense of others, as taking out their troubles on the world by violating codes and conventions or by leading an irresponsible and useless life. The opposition to the demands of society may be widely generalized, so that the person is always against law, order, and social expectation. It may be highly focalized: the person offends only in respect to sexual behavior or the chronic use of alcohol and drugs, other tendencies being managed by mechanisms essentially neurotic. The super-ego in neurotics is strong and all too effective in suppressing unsocialized impulses. It is for this reason that psychotherapy puts such emphasis on securing an expression of imprisoned feelings. In this chapter we shall be dealing with people in whom the super-ego is either feeble or so formed that it permits leakage of antisocial conduct at certain points.

DELINQUENCY AND CRIMINAL BEHAVIOR

Delinquency and criminal behavior are defined by society and the law rather than by psychology and medicine. A young person is designated delinquent, an older person criminal, when his behavior violates the rules and standards of society. The child who runs away from home, the truant from school, the gang member who breaks windows and steals from fruit stands, the professional thief, the racketeer, and the first-degree murderer all qualify for membership in the social outgroup with which we shall first be concerned in this chapter. It is obvious that we are not dealing here with a single type of disorder. We can assume in advance that among the people classed as delinquent or criminal there will be many varieties of personality and many kinds of contributing cause. Our problem is to consider the numerous ways in which a person comes into opposition to the standards of society. Delinquent and criminal behavior bear a significant relation to surrounding social and economic conditions. The whole problem forms a chapter in social pathology as well as a chapter in abnormal psychology.

Cultural Deviance. Behavior that is called delinquent sometimes results from an entirely normal process of psychological development. If a boy is brought up in a clan of pirates, he will develop a super-ego that tells him never to work for something when it is possible to steal it. Identifying with his father, he will build an ego-ideal of bigger and better piracy. In such a case the process of socialization is accepted. The person is called a criminal by the major society, but within the minor society of pirates he is simply growing up to be a solid and respected citizen. Before concluding that a given case of delinquency represents a failure to accept prescribed standards of conduct, it is necessary to ascertain what standards of conduct prevail in the family and in the immediate neighborhood. Merrill reports the case of the three Maguire brothers who during late childhood and early adolescence ran up a collective total of twenty-four court appearances.[1] The mother was always in court

[1] M. A. Merrill, *Problems of Child Delinquency* (Boston: Houghton Mifflin Co., 1947), pp. 284–89.

to defend them, and the father saw no objection to their eking out the slender family income derived from his business as a peddler. The Maguires were a well-knit, affectionate family, free from conflicts and emotional disorders, handicapped only by somewhat limited intelligence which made it difficult to earn a living. Every social agency knows cases of this kind in which the whole family pattern is one of delinquency.

In cases of this kind the individual is not delinquent from that segment of society which is closest to him. He is better described as a *cultural deviant:* "a product of a particular subculture which sanctions activities that are considered antisocial or inadequate by the larger society."[2] He may be a loyal and conforming member of his subculture, identified with others, capable of feeling guilt if he violates their standards, free from guilt when he acts in sanctioned opposition to the alien larger society. The situation can be dramatized by an item from a case history: a mother expected her children to provide food for the family by stealing it from neighboring vegetable gardens and roadside stands, and the children were punished if they returned from their missions empty-handed. There may be nothing capricious about the discipline or vague about the standards in a deviant subculture. It is only to the larger society that the cultural deviant presents a problem.

Delinquency Areas. Shaw and his associates have made a detailed study of juvenile delinquency in Chicago and several other American cities.[3] The incidence of juvenile delinquency varies greatly in different parts of a city. The rate is highest in slum sections inhabited by low-paid workers mostly of foreign origin. It is lowest in outlying residential sections having a native-born business and professional population. In the intervening areas the rates vary in proportion to the distance away from slum areas. By careful analysis Shaw was able to rule out a number of factors which at first glance might appear to bear on these differences. While it is true that intelligence level tends to be lowest in the slum areas and highest in the outlying residential areas, this fact does not serve to explain the rates of juvenile delinquency. Within any given area the delinquent population is not mentally inferior to the non-delinquent population. The ethnic origin of the populations similarly fails to explain the obtained differences. When the figures are broken down into Irish, Scandinavian, Italian, Slavic, Negro, and other national and racial groupings, there are slight differences in the average rate of juvenile delin-

[2] S. K. Weinberg, *Society and Personality Disorders* (Englewood Cliffs, N. J.: Prentice-Hall, Inc., 1952), p. 288.

[3] C. R. Shaw and H. D. McKay, *Report on the Causes of Crime* (National Commission of Law Observance and Enforcement, 1931). A summary of this work is given by R. E. L. Faris in J. McV. Hunt (ed.), *Personality and the Behavior Disorders* (New York: The Ronald Press Co., 1944), Vol. II, pp. 741–46.

quency, but these are by no means so large as the differences between areas. All national and racial groups have high rates if they inhabit slum areas. All have lower rates if they have moved out toward the stable residential districts.

It turns out that the most important determinant of the rate of juvenile delinquency is the degree of social organization prevailing in the area. The slum areas included in these studies were socially disorganized. This means that the population is constantly on the move. The neighbor of today is gone tomorrow, and his place is very likely taken by a family of different national origin and different language. Diverse cultural standards flourish side by side with little interaction and little community solidarity. Under these circumstances it is difficult for parents to maintain control over their children, even though the majority try to do so. The parents have to work single-handed without reinforcement from the neighbors. In a stable community each family is known and each child is known in the neighborhood. Reputations have to be maintained, and behavior is governed by neighbors and acquaintances as well as by members of the family. It is this extended reinforcement of standards that is lacking in a disorganized area. In its place are the street corner gangs and the opportunity to become an apprentice in an adult criminal group. Social disorganization is an important factor in the rate of juvenile delinquency.

The Individual Delinquent. Thus far we have examined two factors which tend to produce delinquent behavior: deviant subcultures, where a super-ego is formed that includes opposition to the larger society, and disorganized areas, where parental standards receive no systematic reinforcement outside the home. These ideas are important, but they are only a first step in explaining delinquent and criminal behavior. Not every child brought up in a deviant subculture or in a socially disorganized area takes the pathway that leads to the juvenile court. Failure to absorb the standards of the larger society must also be approached as a problem in individual development. Modern criminology now includes the study of the individual. This development was initiated about 1909 by William Healy when he became associated with the juvenile court in Chicago. Healy's first major book, *The Individual Delinquent,* was built upon detailed case studies of young offenders.[4] He studied the immediate environment, the family situation, and the mental and emotional life of each delinquent in order to build the equivalent of a psychiatric case history. Nothing short of this can illuminate the inner nature of delinquency.

[4] W. Healy, *The Individual Delinquent* (Boston: Little, Brown & Co., 1915).

The immediate result of this kind of study is to show that a great variety of personal meanings can become attached to delinquency. Healy and Bronner mention the following general possibilities.[5] (1) Delinquent behavior may mean to the child an escape or flight from a tense and unpleasant situation. Truancy and running away usually have this significance. (2) The escape is made more effective by the thrill that accompanies delinquent adventure. Unhappiness and bitterness can perhaps be drowned only by intense excitement and the running of risks. (3) If delinquent acts are performed with a group, the achievement of recognition and status in the group may constitute the most important meaning. (4) To act the part of a criminal is a fairly easy way to prove oneself courageous, masculine, and a "regular guy." This is especially true in America where the gangster has been dramatized in the light of an almost heroic figure. Delinquency is thus well suited to serve as a denial of dependence, inferiority, and femininity. For girls a corresponding meaning attaches to sexual delinquency. Feelings of inferiority and rejection can be both drowned and denied in sexual promiscuity. (5) Delinquency can have the meaning of revenge against the parents. Their life is made difficult and they are disgraced by the actions of their child. (6) Finally, there is the paradoxical motive of seeking punishment in order to alleviate an unconscious sense of guilt. This motive played an unmistakable part in the case of Bert Whipley and is found every so often in other cases. Strictly speaking, it is a neurotic mechanism: the presence of guilt feelings implies that part of the parental standards has been fully introjected. A mixture of neurotic and delinquent mechanisms is not impossible, as we learned from Bert Whipley.[6]

Children Who Hate. The meaning behind certain kinds of delinquent and disorganized behavior has been searchingly analyzed by Redl and Wineman in the course of intensive work with a small group of highly aggressive boys.[7] These boys, ranging in age from 8 to 11, were selected for treatment at Pioneer House, a residential center established for the purpose in Detroit. They showed all the signs that are usually taken to signify a lack of ego strength. Small frustrations, such as a momentarily stuck door or having to wait for a traffic light, threw them into violent temper tantrums. Opportunities to steal or to use objects for wild play could seldom be resisted. A large phonograph, for instance, was at first

[5] W. Healy and A. F. Bronner, *New Light on Delinquency and Its Treatment* (New Haven: Yale University Press, 1936), chaps. iv–vii, also pp. 133–34.

[6] For an interesting case study of this particular problem, see D. J. Levinson, "Criminality from a Sense of Guilt: A Case Study and Some Research Hypotheses," *Journal of Personality*, XX (1952), pp. 402–29.

[7] F. Redl and D. Wineman, *Children Who Hate: The Disorganization and Breakdown of Behavior Controls* (New York: The Free Press of Glencoe, Inc., 1951).

used mainly for climbing and jumping down, the records meanwhile sailing through the air at the walls or at other children. Personal possessions, even those that seemed to be treasured, were almost immediately lost or broken. Signs of guilt feeling were rare, and when confronted with their misdeeds the boys seemed unable to recognize their own contribution to the events, blaming everyone else for what had happened. The staff members at Pioneer House received torrents of curses and abuse when they tried to enforce rules. Quiet could be obtained at meals and at bedtime only if the staff outnumbered the boys and could swiftly isolate those who became centers of excitement.

The picture of impulsivity and destructiveness could hardly be more complete, yet when viewed from another angle the children's behavior showed effective organization. It becomes possible to see this when we take into account what the boys were trying to do. They were not simply *showing* impulse gratification; they were bent on *defending* it at all costs. "Far from being helpless, the ego of these children is suddenly a rather shrewd appraiser of that part of reality which might be dangerous to their impulsive exploits"; in the interest of protecting delinquent fun it even becomes "an efficient manipulator of the world around them."[8] With amazing deftness the boys found excuses for their misconduct: somebody else started it, the other fellow had it coming to him, I had a right to it anyway. With great intuitive skill they picked out the companions who would fit in with their plans and support their escapades. Equally sharp was their appraisal of staff members, who obviously constituted a threat to their delinquent ways. Sensing the "battle-relevant areas," they soon learned "what type of argument would appease or divert or fool us most readily, what cajoling or affection-seeking behavior on their side would throw us off the scent most effectively."[9] In defending their right to be impulsive and aggressive the boys displayed many evidences of ego strength.

Careful observation of these cases showed that the super-ego was heavily submerged but not absent. Every so often there would emerge some piece of considerate behavior, some act of kindness, that represented a "value island" retained from the past. Tough as the boys had learned to be, they showed traces of dependent love and of identification with non-delinquent values. Their histories were full of neglect, rejection, broken homes, disorganized neighborhoods, and a lack of stable identification figures. Yet it seemed to Redl and Wineman that "even neglected children rescue some one or other 'relationship memory' out of the debris of their infancy, and that occasional 'identification loop-

[8] *Ibid.*, p. 144.
[9] *Ibid.*, p. 175.

holes' pierce the seemingly impenetrable wall of human coldness and disinterest."[10] The boys were not total strangers to supporting love, but we must assume that they had been badly disappointed in it. As a consequence they had taken the pathway of gratifying their own impulses by their own efforts and hating the adult world that tried to stop them. One of their defensive measures was to keep out of affectionate relationships lest they be tempted and again disappointed. The foreswearing of love and repression of guilt lent added compulsive force to their defense of waywardness.

Membership in Delinquent Groups. In an earlier chapter we studied the importance of group memberships in the development of personality.[11] We saw that in early adolescence group membership rose to a peak of importance in the individual's life, taking over to a considerable extent the functions of emotional support hitherto concentrated in the family. Many delinquents are unhappy at home. Long before puberty they welcome and need whatever support and recognition can be obtained from group memberships. The group may early become the boy or girl's only home in an emotional sense. Groups outside the home generally mean more in the lives of delinquents than they do in the lives of other children.[12]

Of itself, however, this fact does not explain the superior attraction of delinquent groups over those that stay out of conflict with law and order. Even in an area that suffers from maximum social disorganization there is a choice of groups. The peculiar attraction of the delinquent group arises from the exciting and lawless character of its activities. Delinquent groups are often in a state of crisis. The excitement is highly advantageous to one who wants to drown the memory of a distressing home life. Even more important is the lawlessness. The individual who needs support in his rebellion against parental standards finds this support in good measure in a group that rebels against all of society's standards. Bert Whipley's career as a joy rider in stolen cars clearly illustrates these advantages. Bert was quite aware that he had chosen delinquent companions when others were available. To him joy riding was more fun than anything the non-delinquent children were doing. He found welcome esteem from older boys when he successfully stole some number plates for them. He greatly enjoyed the thrill of riding at high speed while a rain of police bullets spattered around the tires. Particularly important was the chance to defy, insult, and outwit the police.

[10] *Ibid.*, p. 203.

[11] See above, pages 162–70.

[12] A. K. Cohen, *Delinquent Boys: The Culture of the Gang* (New York: The Free Press of Glencoe, Inc., 1955).

Joy riding in stolen cars is easier than might appear. Bert completed something like fifty such missions without being caught or hurt. It was a perfect means of demonstrating the powerlessness of all that his father espoused.

The significance of delinquency areas becomes clearer in the light of this analysis. The average child, relatively contented at home and at school, is but mildly attracted by delinquent acts and is prevented from joining in them by fear and guilt. For the child who is in rebellion against parental standards, however, delinquency is peculiarly attractive and satisfying. But a bent in this direction may never lead to overt behavior unless it is encouraged by others. In socially disorganized areas there is a strong invitation to delinquency arising from the presence of numerous street corner gangs. One might express it by saying that in such areas no one who would like to be delinquent need lack the opportunity. Bert Whipley found the organized sport of joy riding already in existence when his family moved into a slum area. He did not have to create his own opportunities for the behavior that proved so satisfying.

Failure To Introject Parental Standards. Socialization can be regarded as the outcome of a bargain that is struck between parents and child. The child's part of the bargain is to give up the privileges and unrestraint of a small child in favor of the responsibilities of a larger one. The parents' part of the bargain is to set models of considerate and socialized behavior and to make it worth the child's while, in the coin of affection and praise, to undertake the required sacrifices. The parents, who are in the position to manage the bargain, must steer a middle course and maintain a workable balance. The demands they make must be neither too small nor too great in proportion to the rewards they give. Conversely, the rewards they give must be neither too small nor too great in proportion to the demands they make. We have already examined the relation of these facts to maladjustment and neurosis. Our present concern is to work out some of the patterns that result in a failure by the child to introject and be guided by parental standards.

One of these patterns consists of making no demands and setting no standards. The child is simply "spoiled," allowed to do everything he pleases with no loss of rewards. This gives him no motive to take the uphill road toward socialization. He expects everything to come easily, as his just due, and it is easy for him to slip over into the attitude that he might as well take what he wants. This kind of training produces indifference, perhaps mild contempt, toward the restraints and ideals of society. Often enough, however, the result is merely a passive, dependent, irresponsible attitude rather than a career of crime. In Levy's study of maternal overprotection there was only one case of a subsequent criminal way of life.[13] Indulgent overprotection may, but certainly does not regularly, predispose to enduring delinquency.

A contrasting pattern is that in which demands are made but rewards of love are more or less completely withheld. The parents are severe and unloving; they require that socialization shall take place, but they give the child no praise or affection when he succeeds, only punishments when he fails. The child's sacrifices are thus made unpleasant, and nothing is offered to cancel the aggression that he feels in submitting to such a bargain. As a result he submits to it less and less until he becomes an avowed rebel against the constraints of society. He is not only indifferent to social standards; he is actively hostile toward them.

These general formulations have been the subject of considerable detailed investigation. One valuable source of information is the Cambridge-Somerville Youth Study, a project launched in the 1930's to test the possibility of reducing juvenile delinquency through the resources of psychotherapy and social work. Boys were selected for the study who had not yet shown serious delinquency, but who were believed to be possible candidates for it in the future. Extensive material, including the family background, was gathered on more than 500 cases. Examining this material years later, when it was known which boys had actually become delinquent, the McCords and Zola compared the family backgrounds of the delinquent and non-delinquent groups.[14] One of the most important influences proved to be the cohesiveness of the family and the consistency of discipline. Much higher rates of subsequent delinquency were associated with families described as quarrelsome, neglectful, and lax in discipline. Particularly conducive to a criminal career was a regime of punitive but erratic discipline; whereas consistent discipline, even when severe, led to better socialization. With respect to parental behavior the investigators found that love on the part of the mothers, even when they were anxiously overprotective, and warmth and a relative passivity on the part of the fathers were associated with fewer delinquent outcomes. When fathers were cruel, neglectful, or absent, and when mothers were cruel, neglectful, or passively helpless, the rates of ultimate delinquency were high.

In a study of aggressive adolescent boys by Bandura and Walters, the findings are related more closely to theory.[15] Serious delinquency turns not only on failure to absorb parental standards but on an active, hostile

[13] D. M. Levy, *Maternal Overprotection* (New York: Columbia University Press, 1943), pp. 220–26.

[14] W. McCord, J. McCord, and I. K. Zola, *Origins of Crime* (New York: Columbia University Press, 1959).

[15] A. Bandura and R. H. Walters, *Adolescent Aggression* (New York: The Ronald Press Co., 1959).

opposition to them. This opposition depends upon the possibility of hating the parents, at least the one most closely associated with standards. If the child clings to a hope of getting love from the parents, his hostility will be repressed and he will be in a fair way to start a nuclear neurotic process. Bandura and Walters therefore attach importance to the vicissitudes of dependence and to the hostility growing out of shortages and deprivations of love. Once the scales are tipped toward hostility, the boy embarks on a course characterized by active aggression and self-sufficiency. When established, this course tends to be self-perpetuating: dependence is feared, signs of love and esteem are mistrusted, and friendly relations are thwarted by a quick display of aggression. One of the findings made by Bandura and Walters was that aggressive adolescents fared less well with everyone, even with their contemporaries, than did the control group. The investigation also showed the importance of relations between fathers and sons. "The fathers of the aggressive boys were typically hostile to, and rejecting of, their sons, expressed little warmth for them, and had spent little time in affectionate interaction with them during the boys' childhood."[16] Antisocial aggression was especially likely to be the outcome when the mothers, rather than mitigating this state of affairs, added to it by discouraging dependence and perhaps subtly rewarding the steps toward self-sufficiency.

It is clear that the causes of delinquency are numerous and that their influence is often reciprocal. A secure relation with the mother can counterbalance a hostile one with the father, but if the security is insufficient the two relations may become a joint influence toward delinquency. Erratic punitive discipline and a disorganized neighborhood may combine to produce a result that neither would often produce by itself. Intensive studies by the Gluecks of 500 delinquent boys and 500 controls have shown that the boys' own characteristics make their contribution to the matrix of causative influences. Delinquency occurs with somewhat greater frequency in boys with strongly mesomorphic physique.[17] This is not surprising when we remember the large elements of activity, excitement, and rebellion in delinquency, and when we recall that mesomorphy is the strong, sturdy, athletic aspect of physique.[18] Here again we are dealing with a contributing cause, not one that works by itself. The path of rebellion, when other things make it attractive, is chosen a little more readily by those with a natural leaning toward vigorous activity.

[16] *Ibid.*, p. 354.

[17] S. Glueck and E. Glueck, *Unraveling Juvenile Delinquency* (Cambridge: Harvard University Press, 1950); *Physique and Delinquency* (New York: Harper & Row, 1956).

[18] See above, pages 154–56.

Treatment of Juvenile Delinquency. As we have seen, juvenile delinquency is not a single syndrome. It is a way of behaving that is adopted by many different kinds of children for many different reasons. The prevention of juvenile delinquency is thus an operation on many fronts. The obstacles presented by deviant subcultures and delinquency areas do not belong strictly in the psychologist's province, yet it may be that little can be done to change the family atmospheres that contribute to delinquency until these central economic and social problems are brought nearer to solution. In the meantime, the attempt to bring favorable influences to bear on young people through social service and recreational agencies may show little outward result. Such is the conclusion of the ten year Cambridge-Somerville Youth Study, which found little difference in the incidence of delinquency between a group of boys given abundant services of this kind and a group given no special services.[19] The forces disposing toward delinquency seem to outweigh those that can be mustered in later childhood by social agencies. Not often are the results as good as those reported by Healy and Bronner for a group of cases treated under highly advantageous conditions.[20] With these cases intensive treatment was directed at both the delinquent child and his parents. School authorities and social agencies worked together with psychiatrists and social workers to produce a maximum therapeutic and educative influence. Under the influence of this "total push," just over 50 per cent of the cases were benefited to the extent that delinquency ceased. From follow-up studies covering four to seven years it appeared that 72 cases were non-delinquent, 15 were much improved though with occasional mild delinquency, and 51 continued to be as delinquent as before.[21]

The alternative to prevention is treatment, and our interest here is in the possibility of using psychotherapy. In any attempt at treatment the therapist starts at a serious disadvantage. To the delinquent he is an enemy; he represents law and order and is presumed to be trying to convert his patient to the hated cause. Few delinquents come willingly to psychotherapy. The therapist has to convince them that it is worth their while. Discussing this problem, Eissler describes a beginning phase in which patients reveal a curious latent belief in the omnipotence of the authorities they spend so much time attacking. Again and again they create outside situations which seem designed to test the therapist's

[19] E. Powers and H. L. Witmer, *Experiments in the Prevention of Delinquency: The Cambridge-Somerville Youth Study* (New York: Columbia University Press, 1951).

[20] Healy and Bronner, *op. cit.*, pp. 141–57.

[21] A more detailed discussion of treatment by a psychoanalytically oriented psychiatrist will be found in K. Friedlander, *The Psychoanalytic Approach to Juvenile Delinquency* (New York: International Universities Press, Inc., 1947), pp. 191–287.

permissive forgiveness and his power to rescue them from trouble. Only after repeated experience can they convince themselves that a psychotherapist, who seems to be on the side of society, will really maintain a benign and helpful attitude.[22]

In an ingenious departure from the conventions of psychotherapy, Slack has shown that chronic delinquent boys who are unreachable because of their contempt for professional help can be brought into a kind of treatment by the expedient of hiring them for pay.[23] They are engaged to assist the experimenter by telling their life stories to him and his tape recorder, and by taking a number of his psychological tests. The subject need not perceive for some time that any personal benefit is intended. During this time he has a chance to contemplate his own life, to establish confidence in the therapist, and to find out what psychotherapy would be like. Confidence will be felt more readily if the boy finds in the therapist someone who can see things from his point of view and convey a sense of alliance, yet not be taken in by the bluff and big talk that is part of his usual stock in trade. Slack's highly unconventional method has shown promise of success where nothing else is likely to succeed.

Aichhorn worked out a method of treating delinquents that may be said to consist of establishing a new parental relationship and giving the delinquent a second and more favorable chance to achieve socialization.[24] With boys in training institutions Aichhorn tried to make himself a substitute father, loved but respected, who maintained an acceptable balance between demands and rewards. Standards and restraints were presented in a more favorable light, and group life in the institution led to a readier understanding of the need for ordered and controlled behavior. Aichhorn used this method successfully even with extremely aggressive boys in violent revolt against authority. Harsh discipline would only have strengthened their antagonism, so the opposite was put into effect. The task was first to compensate the boys for the lack of love experienced at home, then cautiously and gradually to make demands upon them. One group responded to the permissiveness by smashing its living quarters beyond repair, but by long patience Aichhorn was able to turn even this group into a reasonably well-behaved social unit.

Similar in spirit to Aichhorn's method was the work done at Pioneer House in Detroit by Redl and Wineman.[25] These workers emphasize the

[22] K. R. Eissler, "Ego-Psychological Implications of the Psychoanalytic Treatment of Delinquents," *Psychoanalytic Study of the Child,* V (1952), pp. 97–121.

[23] C. W. Slack, "Experimenter-Subject Psychotherapy: A New Method of Introducing Intensive Office Treatment for Unreachable Cases," *Mental Hygiene,* XLIV (1960), pp. 238–56.

[24] A. Aichhorn, *Wayward Youth* (New York: The Viking Press, Inc., 1935), chap. vi.

[25] F. Redl and D. Wineman, *Controls from Within: Techniques for the Treatment of the Aggressive Child* (New York: The Free Press of Glencoe, Inc., 1952).

necessity of creating a therapeutic milieu which will subtly affect the child throughout his waking hours. The highly aggressive children treated at Pioneer House represent a group that can neither be reached by the usual psychiatric interview nor reformed by the unsympathetic application of restraints. They must live in a therapeutic environment characterized by affection, good care, much tolerance and permissiveness yet also a firm insistence on really essential rules and standards. They must be provided with programs of activities that will stimulate constructive interests and thus encourage controlled behavior. They do not need scheduled interviews, but the alert worker must exploit whatever opportunities are provided by events and spontaneous crises to have impromptu interviews, striking while the iron is hot. Under this regime it is possible to salvage children who otherwise seem destined for permanent antisocial careers. Unfortunately the method calls for such a large and well-trained staff that it usually requires a greater financial outlay than society is willing to make for its delinquent members. Pioneer House itself was run as an experiment for less than two years, then closed for lack of community support. The problem of resources, human and financial, looms even more darkly here than in the treatment of the neuroses.

PSYCHOPATHIC PERSONALITY

We turn now from the broader consideration of delinquency and criminal behavior to a problem more strictly psychiatric. It is evident that delinquents and criminals cannot be characterized in any simple way and that their difficulties with society have important roots in disordered social and economic conditions. The possibility remains, however, that *some* delinquent and criminal individuals suffer from a true psychological disorder which interferes with the process of socialization. Can we detect a syndrome or entity that will help us to understand those cases of persistent antisocial and disorganized living that otherwise seem to defy explanation?

A Problem in Psychiatric Classification. For a long time there has existed a diagnostic category variously called *psychopathic personality* and *constitutional psychopathic inferiority*. Theoretically these titles refer to a specific class of mental disorders, but in actual practice they are used as a sort of wastebasket to contain disorders that do not belong anywhere else. The concept originated with an English psychiatrist, Prichard, who in 1835 described a "form of mental derangement" in which intellect seemed unimpaired but in which the "power of self-government" was lost or lacking, so that the individual was incapable of "conducting himself with decency and propriety in the business of life."[26] Prichard

[26] J. C. Prichard, *Treatise on Insanity* (London: Gilbert & Piper, 1835).

called such patients "morally insane" or "morally imbecile," terms which still persist in British psychiatry. Toward the end of the century the hypothesis was advanced that people who answered the description given by Prichard probably suffered from some hereditary weakness of the nervous system; hence the term *constitutional psychopathic inferiority.* This was only an hypothesis—an inference from the way the patient behaved—but it fitted the prevailing scientific fashion and thus preserved for another fifty years Prichard's notion of a specific mental derangement.

These two ideas—a defect in the realm of socialized behavior and an innate weakness lying behind it—have continued to dominate most thinking about psychopathic personality. It has proved impossible, however, to reach general agreement as to what should be included under this heading. Kraepelin distinguished seven subtypes: the Excitable, the Unstable, the Impulsive, the Eccentric, Liars and Swindlers, the Antisocial, and the Quarrelsome. Some current textbooks add sexual deviations to the list, and others include addiction to alcohol and drugs. Such liberality tends to defeat the purposes of psychological understanding. Preu makes it clear that the whole concept of psychopathic personality has become scientifically unsound.[27] It is not a diagnostic entity in the ordinary sense, with its own specific pattern of symptoms. The diagnosis is established by a process of exclusion; it is applied to long-standing social maladjustments which do *not* belong under the headings of defective intelligence, psychosis, or neurosis. Obviously this is no way to isolate a specific form of mental derangement. Psychopathic personality has become a true wastebasket category designed to receive, as Partridge neatly expressed it, "the unclassified remainder of mental disorders."[28]

The problem can be clarified by restating the nature of the alleged disorder in developmental terms. The people now diagnosed as psychopaths have this in common: they have developed in such a way that parental and social standards have never been introjected. They have failed to respond adequately to the process of socialization. When the problem is viewed in this light it becomes possible to limit the category rather than treating it as a scrap heap. A thoroughgoing attempt of this kind has been made by Cleckley.[29] He rules out those cases in which social standards are rejected only in respect to some one particular kind of behavior: for example, alcoholism or deviant sexual behavior in a person otherwise adapted to social demands. He also rules out those cases in which delinquency and crime have been adopted as a positive

[27] P. W. Preu, "The Concept of Psychopathic Personality," in Hunt, *op. cit.*, Vol. II, chap. xxx.

[28] G. E. Partridge, "Current Conceptions of Psychopathic Personality," *American Journal of Psychiatry,* X (1930), pp. 53–99.

[29] H. Cleckley, *The Mask of Sanity* (2d ed.; St. Louis: The C. V. Mosby Co., (1950).

way of life—in which the person is an enemy of society but is capable of being a loyal and stable member of a delinquent gang. There remains a group characterized by a diffuse and chronic incapacity for persistent, ordered living of any kind. These are, in Cleckley's view, the true psychopathic personalities. They need not be diagnosed negatively, by exclusion of other possibilities. They constitute a true clinical entity with a characteristic pattern of symptoms.

Questions of psychiatric classification need not long detain us in this book. But Cleckley has succeeded in isolating a relatively homogeneous group of disordered personalities, and these we should endeavor to understand.

A Sample Psychopath. One of Cleckley's cases serves as a particularly good example because the neighborhood and family influences were outwardly of the very best.[30] The patient was studied during his several visits to a mental hospital. These occurred when he was in his thirties and early forties. He was the only child of parents who were active church members and much respected members of the community. As a child he was well-adjusted and popular, but in high school his adjustment underwent steady deterioration. At home he began to be petulant and dishonest, at school arrogant and irritable so that he drifted out of all group memberships. At sixteen he began to run away from home. The second time this occurred his father sent him money and helped him to find a job. He soon began to drift from job to job, each move being occasioned by a quarrel with his employers. He loafed a good deal, preferred to live in a dreary section, and found transient companionships with prostitutes and with the street corner gangs. He exhibited downward social mobility, but as he descended the social ladder he more and more took to boasting about a mythical great past. Alcohol proved irresistibly attractive. He sometimes lay out in a field all night, at other times staggered home uproariously, waking the neighborhood.

The father meanwhile played what looked like a helpful part, getting his son out of trouble, finding him jobs, never publicly referring to his disgraceful behavior. When at last the father saw no course but hospitalization, the son submitted, but to the psychiatrist he denied ever having used alcohol and expressed resentment at his father's meddling. In all he visited the hospital three times, leaving each time with protestations of reform. Between these visits his behavior became more and more erratic, his drinking sprees more serious, his antagonism toward his parents more open. To get money he would call on quiet old ladies, friends of the family, even rousing them from bed to provide him with needed cash. On one occasion he moved into the temporarily closed house

[30] *Ibid.*, pp. 80–94.

of family friends, taking a prostitute with him. When the friends returned they found the house in the greatest disorder, filthy and rather badly damaged.

Central Pattern of Traits. After studying a great many cases of this kind, Cleckley finds it possible to draw up a "clinical profile" of the characteristics they have in common. In interviews the patient makes an unusually pleasing impression: alert, well-informed, able to talk well. Intelligence is good and does not deteriorate. One soon finds out that there is marked absence of sense of responsibility in matters both great and small; this includes an inability to tell the truth. The patient does not accept blame for any of his conduct nor feel shame about it. He readily gives a plausible excuse for everything that has occurred. While he is able to reason satisfactorily, in some cases even brilliantly, he shows the most execrable judgment about attaining his ends, whatever these may be. He gets into the same trouble over and over again, so much so that Cleckley describes him as regularly failing to learn from experience. No life plan is followed consistently unless it be a plan to make life a failure. On the side of affect there are grave difficulties. The psychopath seems incapable of real love and real attachment. Strong, deep, and lasting feelings do not seem to exist. Although the patient talks a great deal about feelings, he gives the impression of merely using words without insight into the nature of real feeling.

A very similar picture is sketched by Henderson, with emphasis on the immature character of the behavior.[31]

> From every point of view, it is clear that the psychopath, irrespective of his particular type, is a person who cannot accept things as they are; he is unable to fit into the life of the herd, but tends to lead an independent, individualistic type of existence with no thought or feeling for his family, his friends, or his country. He is as blunted emotionally as many a schizophrenic, he shows a "belle indifference" equal to that of the hysteric, an absence of judgment and reason as great as that of a wayward spoiled child. With all his faults, for a time he may prove very charming, but as his attraction fades, bewilderment, pity and alarm arise when it becomes evident that maturity is exerting no mellowing influence. For some inscrutable reason he fails to grow up, he remains at the level of a primitive savage with a distinct distaste for reasoning and an "impermeability to experience" which allows him to live, think, feel, and act in a manner foreign to his more civilized neighbors.

It is clear that we are dealing with a fairly serious disorder. There are grave disturbances in the patient's affective life as well as in foresight and the control and organization of behavior. Cleckley considers the condition serious enough to be classed as a psychosis. Although the

31 D. K. Henderson, *Psychopathic States* (New York: W. W. Norton & Co., Inc., 1939), pp. 128–29.

patient outwardly presents a "convincing mask of sanity" and "a mimicry of human life," he has lost contact with the deeper emotional accompaniments of experience and with its purposiveness. To this extent he may be said to have an incomplete contact with reality, and it is certainly very hard to approach him and influence him therapeutically.[32]

Psychogenic Aspects of the Disorder. The most important clue to a possible psychogenic factor would appear to lie in the weakness of feeling toward other people. The emotional blunting, the lack of affectional ties, the mimicry of love without evidence of real feeling all point to a possible disturbance in the child's early human relations. Parental rejection immediately comes to mind; but, as we have seen, this can also produce neurotic and delinquent outcomes. The neurotic craves human relations, the delinquent fights them, but the psychopath seems to be merely indifferent. We can make the hypothesis of a very early injury to affectionate relations, a serious deficit of gratifying love and care perhaps even in the first year. Lacking a strong initial attachment to the mother, the child as he grows up may learn to adapt shrewdly enough to the realities around him and may become socialized to the extent of presenting a pleasant front; but the real meaning of his life is still the direct gratification of impulse, and this childlike value is not importantly tempered by close affectional ties or by a feeling of involvement in the human community.

The concept of parental rejection does not fully suggest the childhood situation just described. A child can be psychologically rejected yet remain in continual contact with his parents, identify with them, and cherish the hope of at least some morsels of affection. In an attempt to specify the critical situation more precisely, Goldfarb speaks of *psychological privation* and considers that it is best illustrated by infancies spent in foundling institutions or by childhoods in which there were frequent shifts of parent figures.[33] Goldfarb made a comparative study of two groups of adolescents; one had spent the first three years of life in impersonal institutions, the other in the more homelike conditions provided by foster families. Despite the intervening years, the two groups showed marked differences in behavior, and the traits of the former institutional children had much in common with fully developed psychopathic personalities. From this and similar studies there is a good deal of justification for a psychodynamic hypothesis in the form we have described.[34]

[32] Cleckley, *op. cit.*, chap. xxiii.

[33] W. Goldfarb, "Psychological Privation in Infancy and Subsequent Adjustment," *American Journal of Orthopsychiatry*, XV (1945), pp. 244–57.

[34] A valuable discussion will be found in a symposium edited by B. Karpman, "Psychopathic Behavior in Infants and Children," *American Journal of Orthopsychiatry*, XXI (1951), pp. 223–72.

Somatogenic Aspects of the Disorder. During the second half of the nineteenth century there were repeated attempts to show that criminals were constitutionally inferior. This conception of the problem was a natural consequence of the somatogenic hypothesis which for a time completely dominated psychiatric thinking. The criminal behaved differently from other people, therefore something must be different about his constitution or his nervous system. The results of these investigations are not particularly impressive. Although voices are still raised for constitutional inferiority, there is no compelling evidence that requires a somatogenic hypothesis in this sweeping form.

Less easy to dismiss is the much more specific hypothesis that the particular disorder we are discussing here—psychopathic personality—is related to brain injury or brain inadequacy. Sometimes following a severe head injury, and sometimes following an attack of encephalitis (which is known to injure brain tissue), the behavior of a previously well-adjusted child will change in what might be called a delinquent direction. The child becomes overactive and aggressive; he has outbursts of emotion and irritation, and he is unable to concentrate or to accept the restraints of the schoolroom. He seems to have lost some of the regulating control that previously characterized his behavior. Under such circumstances it is harder for him to accept the restraints of socialization. The control of impulse and temper, the postponement of immediate satisfactions, the mere restraint of sitting still at table or at school become suddenly more difficult than they were before. In view of these facts it is at least a legitimate hypothesis that some subtle inadequacy of cerebral tissue might underlie the psychopath's inability to be governed by the standards and restraints of society.

The recently developed technique of the *electroencephalogram* (EEG) opens a new path for investigating this question. The EEG is a graphic recording of the electrical activity of the cortex. When electrodes are attached to the scalp and connected with an amplifier it is possible to record fluctuations in voltage, popularly known as "brain waves," which appear to arise from activity in cerebral tissue. Under basal conditions—that is, with the subject awake but resting quietly with closed eyes—the normal adult record shows a predominance of slow waves, *alpha rhythms,* averaging about 10 cycles per second. Superimposed on these waves are the faster *beta rhythms* with a frequency anywhere up to 40 cycles per second. Waves of less than 8 per second, sometimes called *delta waves,* are rare in the records of normal adults. They are typical of infants in the first year of life, and their frequency of occurrence decreases with age. An abnormal EEG is one that includes a distinctly greater frequency of very slow waves (less than 8 per second) than is characteristic for that particular age level. Thus an EEG may be abnormal for a child of eight although the same record would be normal for a child of four.[35]

Abnormal EEG's are obtained with considerable regularity from patients with known brain disorders such as tumors, inflammations, and gross degenerative changes. They are also obtained following the administration of certain drugs. They are likely to appear following a severe blow on the head or an attack of encephalitis, especially when these result in the behavior disturbances already described. Sometimes abnormal EEG's are obtained when there is no known history of injury or brain disease. In such cases one might be tempted to assume that a subtle disorder exists, but it should first be noted that abnormal EEG's are obtained in something like 20 to 30 per cent of normal people and of patients whose behavior bears no resemblance to that of psychopathic personalities. The EEG is still a somewhat crude diagnostic tool.[36]

Several different investigators have reported a much higher incidence of abnormal EEG's in persons classed as psychopaths. The findings range from 50 to 80 per cent, and the association appears to be strongest with psychopaths who are markedly impulsive and aggressive.[37] Evidence of this kind suggests that brain abnormalities contribute in some way to the psychopath's behavior. These abnormalities might be acquired during childhood through infection or head injury; they might result from birth damage or injury during the fetal period; or they might be the product of hereditary influences.[38]

Perhaps a judicious conclusion about the part played by brain abnormalities can be reached by examining a particular study. Jenkins and Pacella investigated the EEG's of delinquent boys in a training school.[39] On the basis of behavior the boys could be divided into two subgroups. The first group showed assaultive tendencies, irritability, poor control, restless distractibility, and great trouble in adjusting to routine and

[35] For a detailed review of electroencephalography, consult H. Strauss, *Diagnostic Electroencephalography* (New York: Grune & Stratton, Inc., 1952).

[36] R. J. Ellingson, "The Incidence of EEG Abnormality Among Patients with Mental Disorders of Apparently Nonorganic Origin: A Critical Review," *American Journal of Psychiatry*, CXI (1954), pp. 263–75.

[37] D. Hill and D. Watterson, "Electroencephalographic Studies of Psychopathic Personalities," *Journal of Neurology and Psychiatry*, V (1942), pp. 47–65; D. J. Simons and O. Diethelm, "Electroencephalographic Studies of Psychopathic Personalities," *Archives of Neurology and Psychiatry*, LV (1946), pp. 619–26; J. S. Gottlieb, M. C. Ashby, and J. R. Knott, "Primary Behavior Disorders and Psychopathic Personality," *Archives of Neurology and Psychiatry*, LVI (1946), p. 381; S. K. Ehrlich and R. P. Keogh, "The Psychopath in a Mental Institution," *Archives of Neurology and Psychiatry*, LXXVI (1956), pp. 286–95.

[38] J. M. Nielsen and G. N. Thompson, *The Engrammes of Psychiatry* (Springfield, Ill.: Charles C. Thomas, 1947), pp. 168–76.

[39] R. L. Jenkins and B. L. Pacella, "Electroencephalographic Studies of Delinquent Boys," *American Journal of Orthopsychiatry*, XIII (1943), pp. 107–20.

restriction. The second group, much the larger of the two, had histories of stealing, especially group stealing and similar offenses in company with street corner gangs. A considerable number of the boys in the first group had had either head injuries or encephalitis, and the EEG was abnormal in 73 per cent of the cases. In the second group abnormal EEG's were obtained from only 30 per cent, which is not significantly out of line with results obtained from normal subjects. For the second and larger group, therefore, there is no justification for assuming that abnormal brain conditions contributed significantly to the delinquency. These boys, of course, with their predominant offense of stealing, are precisely the ones whose conduct is well explained by psychogenesis and socially disorganized delinquency areas. For the first and smaller group, however, cerebral injury of some kind, reducing the efficiency of cortical action and showing itself in the abnormal EEG, probably played an important part in the delinquency. These boys are the ones who seem well on their way to becoming psychopathic personalities.

The concept of psychopathic personality is, as we said, much narrower than that of delinquency or crime. It can be considered a specific entity or syndrome of disorder, having certain characteristics that are common to all cases despite numerous outward differences. There is evidence that it can be produced by severe privation of affectionate support in early childhood, which leaves the child without adequate motive to identify himself with adult models and to introject restraints and social standards. There is also evidence that it can be produced by generalized brain injury which weakens the capacity for inhibition and control. Neither type of evidence is as yet by any means secure, and both kinds of explanation may ultimately be needed to understand the problem of psychopathic personality.[40]

In the meantime, the treatment of the psychopath is anything but an inviting task. He brings no motivation to psychotherapy, which is therefore very hard to initiate. Under present laws governing commitment to mental hospitals, he cannot be kept long at an institution because he is not mentally deranged in the sense of intellectual confusion or disorientation. For the most part psychopaths move in and out of the portals of institutions as readily as they move in and out of jobs, spending a good part of their time at liberty where they are costly to society. Nevertheless there is considerable promise in some recent therapeutic ventures, particularly the one undertaken by Maxwell Jones in England.[41] The

[40] W. McCord and J. McCord, *Psychopathy and Delinquency* (New York: Grune & Stratton, Inc., 1956).

[41] M. Jones *et al., The Therapeutic Community: A New Treatment Method in Psychiatry* (New York: Basic Books, Inc., 1953); "Society and the Sociopath," *American Journal of Psychiatry,* CXIX (1962), pp. 410–14.

patients, not all psychopaths but including a good many of these, are brought together in a hospital which is designed to become a therapeutic community rather than a treatment center in the usual sense. The patients work in the hospital shops for four hours each day, receiving vocational training if necessary. They also have opportunities for group psychotherapy, and a good deal of emphasis is put upon programs of social activity for which the patients themselves become increasingly responsible. Although supervision is fairly close and regulations are enforced, the staff members are trained to perform their duties in a benevolent and uncensorious spirit. It is interesting to notice the similarity between this large-scale therapeutic milieu for adults and the smaller communities created by Aichhorn and by Redl and Wineman to deal with conduct disorders in children. Patients who are at war with the larger society are best moved in the direction of peace by temporary membership in a smaller society particularly designed to draw out whatever potentialities they still may have for living harmoniously with others.

DEVIANT SEXUAL BEHAVIOR

Next to be considered is a group of disordered reactions that are focalized on sex. Delinquents and psychopaths often include deviant sexual behavior in their repertory of rebellion against social standards, but their disorder centers upon the rebellion rather than upon sexual satisfaction. The cases to be considered here are those in which deviant sexual behavior constitutes the chief departure from social standards. In some cases it is even the sole departure in a person who in all other respects introjects the standards of his society.

Deviation as a Developmental Abnormality. In an earlier chapter we took up the normal course of sexual development and the various points at which maladjustment might arise.[42] Sexual excitability and sexual interests exist in early childhood. They take the form of masturbation, curiosity about the genitals, self-display, mutual investigation with other children, and crushes and affectionate relationships sometimes accompanied by possessiveness and jealousy. For the most part the sexual tendencies of children are such as would be called perverted if they persisted into adult life. An extensive process of relearning goes on at puberty, with the result that childish object choices and childish modes of satisfaction are put aside in favor of the normal, adult, socially expected pattern.

In most parts of our society the child's sexual interests typically undergo a stormy struggle with parental and cultural disapproval. In certain social classes and in some primitive societies the cultural pressure

[42] See above, pages 116–22.

is much lighter. Malinowski's studies in the Trobriand Islands showed that when growing boys and girls are allowed more or less complete freedom in regard to sexual interests and sexual experimentation, the result is a minimum of deviant sexual behavior.[43] If the sex urge is left to itself it seems to flow easily into normal adult channels. In other primitive societies there is often an attitude more repressive than our own. Seward points out that in the Manus our mistakes in this respect are exaggerated to the point of caricature.[44] Roughly speaking, there seems to be a positive correlation between the frequency of sexual deviations and the severity with which the culture suppresses sex.

It was Freud who first offered the theory that deviant sexual behavior represented a repetition of childhood sexual tendencies. The diffuse "partial impulses" that constitute the child's sexuality are normally gathered into a new pattern at puberty. The excitability of the genitals becomes the primary factor, and the act of orgasm the central goal. Freud classified sexual aberrations under two headings: deviation in respect to sexual *object* and deviation in respect to sexual *aim*.[45] The chief deviation in respect to object is homosexuality, the choice of an object of the same sex. This, as we have seen, is a natural object choice in later childhood, when boys associate mainly with boys and girls with girls. Deviations in respect to aim include such phenomena as *exhibitionism* and *voyeurism*. In the former, displaying the genitals or the naked body becomes an essential element in obtaining a satisfactory sexual experience. In the latter, observing the bodies and sexual acts of others plays the same indispensable part. These can be regarded as exaggerated perpetuations of childish display and curiosity. *Sadism* and *masochism* have similar counterparts in childhood when the relation between sexual and aggressive feelings is often misunderstood and confused. The sadistic deviation makes violence and the giving of pain an indispensable condition for sexual satisfaction. The masochistic deviation similarly associates sex and the receiving of pain.

Deviant sexual behavior is thus conceived as a developmental abnormality. The relearning required at puberty is not accomplished, or is so feebly accomplished that regression to childhood sexual orientations remains easy. When this happens, the full force of genital sexuality becomes channeled into some childhood pattern of sexual behavior. The urge is as great as it is in normal people, but the problems it creates are obviously far more difficult. Sex becomes firmly associated with the for-

[43] B. Malinowski, *Sex and Repression in Savage Society* (New York: Harcourt, Brace & World, Inc., 1927).

[44] G. H. Seward, *Sex and the Social Order* (New York: McGraw-Hill Book Co., Inc., 1946), chap. viii.

[45] S. Freud, *Three Contributions to the Theory of Sex,* trans. A. A. Brill (New York: Nervous & Mental Disease Publishing Co., 1930), chap. i.

bidden, the dangerous, the disgraceful. It loses its chance to enrich and strengthen a marital relationship and to serve as a constructive force in the individual's life.

Comparison with Neurosis and Delinquency. Traces of childhood sexual tendencies are doubtless present in everyone. Normal sexual development does not imply that these traces have gone out of existence. It implies merely that their attraction is too small to compete with adult sexual interests. Many healthy people remember the sexual inclinations and episodes of their childhood, remember them even with a certain pleasurable interest. They are not bothered by such feelings because they do not find them uncontrollable or of an attraction comparable to that of adult sexuality. Deviant inclinations do not constitute a problem unless they tend to crowd out a normal sexual adjustment. There is a world of difference between the young fellow who merely as a pastime trains his field glasses on the windows of the women's dormitory and the Peeping Tom who, indifferent to normal sexuality, knows a genuine erotic thrill only when climbing on fire escapes. We can speak of sexual perversion only when the deviated inclination is stronger than the normal one and prevents normal sexual activity from yielding satisfaction.

Neurosis disturbs most human relationships, including sexual ones. In many neurotics the traces of childhood sexuality are strongly activated. This activation does not, however, result in overt deviant behavior. It results rather in an equally strong activation of the childhood conscience —the super-ego—and the perverse inclinations are repressed. In the neuroses, deviant sexual tendencies are associated with great anxiety. They simply cannot be tolerated in consciousness. If they give rise to symptoms, these are disguised and are experienced as ego-alien. In sharp contrast stands the psychopath and the habitual delinquent, who is often fully aware of such tendencies and may practice them without any sense of guilt. The simpler sexual deviant stands midway between these two extremes. His perverse inclinations do not have the status of neurotic symptoms. They are not experienced as ego-alien or forced upon him; he recognizes them as *his* inclinations which if expressed give him genuine sexual satisfaction. In short, his deviant urges are not inhibited by childhood anxiety. On the other hand he cannot practice them with complete comfort. They entail real dangers in the form of social disgrace if not legal action, and they conflict with his mature conscience and his ego-ideal. There are other cases in which the deviant urges are experienced as compulsive and uncontrollable, but they are neither fully repressed nor fully projected.

Deviant sexual behavior is thus not usually understandable as a form of delinquency or as an aspect of psychopathic personality. It is not immediately understandable as a symptom of neurosis, although there may be similarities of underlying process. In sexual deviation there seems to be a selective exemption of certain socially unacceptable impulses from constraints that are effective elsewhere in the personality. The scientific problem is to explain this exemption within a personality that in other respects has not proved averse to adjustment.

Homosexuality. It will be more profitable for us to concentrate on one kind of deviant sexual behavior than to describe superficially the many varieties that exist. The most common and well-known variety is homosexuality. Until the advent of psychoanalysis this deviant form of object choice was believed to be a biological abnormality. In the writings of Havelock Ellis, for example, great importance was attached to the fact that many homosexuals reported having preferred members of their own sex as far back in childhood as they could remember.[46] In view of what has since been learned about early childhood sexuality and about repression, this kind of evidence is clearly of no value. Following Freud, emphasis shifted to the psychogenic side of the problem. Homosexuality was perceived as a developmental rather than a biological abnormality.

The evidence for biological abnormality has been reviewed by Seward.[47] It is not particularly impressive. The most important finding has to do with the androgen-estrogen balance in male homosexuals. Androgen (the male sex hormone) and estrogen (the female sex hormone) are both present in the human body, the former predominating in males and the latter in females. Several studies have shown that in a majority of male homosexuals the balance is somewhat shifted in the direction of estrogen. Some investigators further claim to have shown a certain association between homosexuality and feminine body characteristics in men. Taken together, these findings suggest that men of a somewhat feminine biological make-up are a little more likely than others to have homosexual inclinations. But the relation is a slight one and does not go far toward explaining the homosexual object choice. Many men with somewhat feminine bodily physique are quite free from homosexual interests, and some male homosexuals are of distinctly rugged and powerful physique.

The problem is further complicated by the fact that the concept of homosexuality includes two rather different kinds of deviation. The disorder may be strictly limited to the choice of object. In so-called active male homosexuality and passive female homosexuality the person takes a role entirely appropriate to his or her sex, stipulating only that

[46] H. Ellis, *Studies in the Psychology of Sex* (3d ed.; Philadelphia: F. A. Davis Co., 1928), Vol. II, chap. iii.

[47] Seward, *op. cit.*, pp. 176–79.

the partner shall be of the same sex. The situation is different with passive male homosexuals ("fairies") and active female homosexuals ("Lesbians"). Here the role appropriate to the opposite sex is desired. It would be only in the latter cases that one would expect the contribution of biological factors to be significant.

The simplest psychogenic explanation of homosexuality would be that the person became fixated upon this object choice because of gratifications happening in childhood or early adolescence. The Kinsey reports and other evidence make it plain, however, that even quite extensive homosexual experiences in childhood and adolescence often do not interfere with later normal adjustment. It becomes necessary to assume, therefore, that the preference for objects of the same sex is really based on a distaste for objects of the opposite sex. Some emotional obstacle prevents the person from feeling a sexual interest in members of the opposite sex. In cases of enduring homosexuality there is a strong connection of some kind between heterosexual interest and anxiety. To this extent the basic process resembles the nucleus of a neurosis. Childhood punishments or experiences of a terrifying character elicit the defense of repression; thereafter the person is unable to become aware of heterosexual feelings, and may even fortify his defense by experiencing disgust at such inclinations. Under these circumstances an interest in the same sex becomes the most available substitute for the repressed inclinations.

This way of explaining homosexuality is not complete unless it is possible to show how the deviant object choice escapes the repression that has descended upon heterosexual interest. In some way the repression acts selectively, blocking heterosexual interests and exempting homosexual ones. One might say that it is the super-ego rather than the sexual urge which exhibits perversity. Yet in early childhood a misunderstanding of this kind could easily happen. The reasons for punishment are not always clear to a young child, especially when the parents make no attempt to explain. Thus when punished for erotic play a child may understand that what is bad is doing it with someone of the opposite sex; the punishment is not perceived as covering erotic play with one's own sex. It can be hypothesized that in cases of enduring homosexuality there was a particularly heavy attachment of anxiety to heterosexual expressions, and that homosexual interests were not apprehended as entailing anything like the same dangers.

Psychoanalytic study of homosexual patients shows that the repression of heterosexual interest often goes back to anxiety over the anatomical differences between the sexes. The little boy may be led to fear that his penis will be cut off as a punishment for sexual play. If this preoccupation is active at the time he discovers anatomical differences, his fear may be abruptly increased. He may assume that girls and women have already been punished in this way, and that the danger is really acute. Women's genitals become phobic objects because they remind him too strongly of the danger of castration. Thus the possibility of being interested in them, curious about them, even of seeing them, becomes firmly repressed. In the case of girls the motives entering this neurotic nucleus are somewhat different. The lack of a prominent genital organ may be sensed as an inferiority and a cause of envy. If anxiety on this subject is strong, it may override and repress any erotic interest in the opposite sex. In both cases fear causes sexual interest to be deflected from heterosexual objects. Homosexual objects become the only safe ones, and the assertion of homosexual inclinations serves as a protective denial of the dangerous heterosexual ones.[48]

Sexual Perversions Leading to Crimes of Violence. Every so often one reads in the newspaper that a murder has been committed by a "sex fiend." In those cases where sex is really involved, there is found to be a deep confusion between sexuality and aggression. The aggressive act does not occur in response to immediate irritation or even as a consequence of long-stored resentment. It is pushed by far less rational motives, generally not in the least understood by the person himself, but having the persistent compulsive force that characterizes the sex urge. These are cases of deep sexual perversion in which the force of sexuality becomes channeled almost exclusively into fantasies and acts of violence.

Healy has shown that certain cases of juvenile stealing result from an association between this delinquent act and sexual excitation.[49] Such association occurs most readily before puberty, when sexual excitation is still diffuse and none too clearly understood. Healy's cases include many like the following: A girl of eight went around with older girls who taught her to steal in shops and who also aroused her interest by free talk about sex. Presently this girl began compulsive stealing accompanied by unmistakable sexual excitement. A boy of eleven often went to the beach with other boys who would steal from shops along the way and later, when undressed, practice mutual masturbation. Before long the boy felt an irresistible impulse to steal whenever he heard talk about sex. These examples are not too serious cases, but they shed a certain light on those which become more serious. There is a plastic quality to the sexual urge, especially in childhood. Under a peculiar combination of circumstances, presumably involving serious anxieties and repressions, it can be drawn into channels very remote from normal sexuality.

[48] O. Fenichel, *The Psychoanalytic Theory of Neurosis* (New York: W. W. Norton & Co., Inc., 1945), pp. 328–41.

[49] W. Healy, *Mental Conflicts and Misconduct* (Boston: Little, Brown & Co., 1917), chap. xiv.

The strange complications in such cases can be illustrated by the following example. A seventeen-year-old student was found guilty of three brutal murders and a large number of burglaries.[50] On the wall of one apartment, in which he killed a young woman, was found written with lipstick, "For heaven's sake catch me before I kill more; I cannot control myself." Sexually deviant behavior began in his case at the age of nine and took the form of fetishism. He repeatedly stole women's underclothing, took it to his room, and dressed himself in it with great sexual excitement. At thirteen he began securing the desired objects by going into houses through windows. Sexual excitement gradually became concentrated on this act. He often struggled to prevent himself from leaving home at night, but sometimes desire would break down his resolutions. At the sight of an open window at a place that might be burglarized, he experienced sexual excitement with erection. Usually as he passed through the window he experienced orgasm. If so, he generally left without taking anything. The impulse to kill came only if he was startled in the act of burglary. On one occasion, however, he experienced orgasm when he hit a woman who interrupted him, and he left at once without hitting her again.

Reports on this case do not disclose the sequence of events and fantasies that led the sexual need into such peculiar channels. They do show, however, that there were severe blocks on normal channels. At first he indignantly denied that he had ever practiced masturbation, but he later admitted having tried it twice without being able to secure any sexual excitement. With equal reluctance he admitted occasional petting with girls, but reported the experience to be so upsetting and repulsive that he usually burst into tears. The pattern of guilt feeling could hardly be stranger. He was much less upset in speaking of his brutal murders than he was when questioned about normal sexual behavior.

Treatment of Deviant Sexual Behavior. Psychotherapy with sexual deviants involves no new principles beyond those already discussed. An initial difficulty lies in the patient's motivation. Even when he is distinctly uncomfortable over his deviant fantasies or greatly embarrassed by his overt behavior he is apt to have decidedly mixed feelings about changing. His fantasies and behavior have at least been sexually satisfying, whatever their practical consequences. Thus the patient is sometimes not scared enough and not badly enough handicapped by his disorder to endure the emotional hardships of treatment. Nevertheless the results of treatment are often satisfactory, though the results are not quite as good as those reported for neuroses. In his analysis of the results of psycho-

[50] F. Kennedy, H. R. Hoffman, and W. H. Haines, "A Study of William Heirens," *American Journal of Psychiatry*, CIV (1947), pp. 113–21; Lucy Freeman, *"Before I Kill More": The William Heirens Story* (New York: Crown Publishers, 1955).

analytic therapy Knight shows that sexual disorders distribute themselves as follows: apparently cured or much improved, 48.5 per cent; slightly improved or unchanged, 51.5 per cent. The corresponding figures for neurosis in his report are 68 per cent and 38 per cent.[51] Similar differences are reported when other techniques are used.

The chances of overcoming a sexual deviation depend a great deal upon the patient's age and upon another factor which might be described as the magnitude of the deviation. Homosexuality is a deviation of small magnitude: the object is another person, the feeling is affectionate and tender, the goal is sexual contact of some kind, and the only peculiar feature is the insistence on an object of the same sex. Perversions that lead to crimes of violence are deviations of much greater magnitude. Sexual excitement is completely divorced from love and linked up with feelings that are antagonistic to affectionate human relationships. For the most part these criminal cases are placed in penal rather than medical institutions, and this in itself adds to the difficulty of reclaiming them for socialized living. But in any event their treatment would be extremely difficult. Even when they are young, the nature of their deviation injures the constructive forces, especially the capacity for human relationships, on which successful therapy depends.

CHRONIC ALCOHOLISM

On the face of it, the excessive use of alcohol is not a separate variety of disordered behavior. Alcohol can be woven into the texture of almost any kind of disorder. It can be used as a way of evading or temporarily easing a variety of distresses. This makes it difficult to conceive of chronic alcoholism as an entity based either on a particular developmental disorder or on a physiological pecularity. We must keep in mind the possibility, however, that some people might be especially vulnerable to alcohol through physical constitution or a particular constellation of psychological problems.

The Effects of Alcohol. Although we often speak of its stimulating effects, alcohol is actually a narcotic. This is clear enough when a person is quite drunk, with failing locomotion and incoherent speech. The initial stimulating effect results from the fact that alcohol acts selectively on neural mechanisms. Its narcotic action first touches the most recently evolved areas of the cerebral cortex, which have a predominantly inhibitory function. Disinhibition produces a sense of well-being and relaxation, freedom of thought and pleasantness of affect. It is conducive to conversation, hence the wide use of alcohol as a social lubricant.

[51] R. P. Knight, "Evaluation of the Results of Psychoanalytic Therapy," *American Journal of Psychiatry* XCVIII (1941), pp. 434–46.

As intoxication increases, events take a fairly regular course. There is a difference of opinion about this course, depending upon whether or not the observer participates. To a slightly narcotized judgment it will be apparent that everyone is talking with great zest, wit, and wisdom. The world is full of glowing possibilities; the heart is full of warm, friendly, and expansive feelings. But an observer who enters the field at this point in a state of zero narcosis wll be apt to see the picture a little differently. He will agree on the zest and expansive feelings, but he will be likely to detect the effects of narcosis on matters of judgment and intellectual keenness. It will occur to him to question whether the gentleman who is informing the company how to construct outdoor fireplaces is really an authority on that subject, and he will doubt whether the great plans for world reform that are being loudly developed in another part of the room will prove practicable in the cold light of morning reality. If he stays around long enough, he will observe further signs of deterioration as narcosis progresses to other parts of the nervous system. Speech, hand coordination, locomotion become increasingly impaired until finally a state of stupor is reached.[52]

Normal and Abnormal Drinking. There are many people who use alcohol frequently but never to excess. In some circles moderate drinking is part of the routine of life, though immoderate drinking is regarded as reprehensible. These facts make it possible to speak of *normal drinking* and to look for some kind of a line beyond which drinking can be called *abnormal.* Such a line might be drawn according to external signs: drinking in the morning, being unable to face any important situation unless "fortified," being unable to drink socially without getting drunk, etc. All of these external criteria, however, get their meaning from the strength of motivation toward alcohol. The crucial question is how urgently and for what the alcohol is needed. The mild disinhibition that is obtained from one or two drinks, with its relaxation, sense of well-being, freedom from restraint, and easy flow of conversation, is a temporary benefit that most people can appreciate. A person who needs alcohol for this benefit and for nothing more is a normal drinker and is likely to remain so. He is under no serious temptation to drink beyond the point where this benefit is obtained, and it is not worth it to him to wake up next morning with a hang-over. Furthermore, he is not so dependent on this benefit that he cannot forego it when circumstances so require. The normal drinker, in short, has no strong further motive for using alcohol beyond the enjoyment of its mild disinhibitory effects.

[52] Studies of the effects of alcohol on behavior are summarized in H. J. Eysenck (ed.), *Handbook of Abnormal Psychology: An Experimental Approach* (New York: Basic Books, Inc., 1961), pp. 664–70.

Alcohol has further potentialities, however, and these constitute its appeal for the person who becomes an abnormal drinker. As intoxication increases, as restraint and judgment become increasingly narcotized, impulses may come to expression which are in no way satisfied in everyday life. Take the case of a college student whose outward personality was marked by a tendency toward derogatory verbal criticism and a certain aloofness from all but his closest friends. Under the influence of sufficient alcohol he became extremely belligerent, picking quarrels and coming to blows with men in bars. His friends often had to rescue him because, although he fought like a demon, his slight physique was really unequal to these encounters. At mixed parties he regularly passed through the belligerent stage to expressions of a different character. He would lay his head on a girl's lap and weep piteously for her loving care, describing himself as a lonely outcast. The following day he would dimly remember his aggressive adventures but his extreme show of dependence would be safely wrapped in complete amnesia.

This is the sort of case that is likely to progress from normal to abnormal drinking. There is a *repressed* but still active craving for loving maternal care. There is also a very strong aggressive need, *suppressed* by circumstances to the extent that it comes to expression only in verbal form. Alcohol does a lot for these two needs. It permits the young man to act as aggressively as he really feels, without forcing him to assume full responsibility for his actions. It permits him to gratify his dependent cravings without forcing his sober consciousness to become aware of them. Alcohol thus allows him to satisfy strong needs without disturbing the neurotic protective organization that ordinarily keeps them in check. One can easily see the fatal attraction of alcohol for a personality organized on these lines.

Abnormal drinking sets in when alcohol fits into personal problems in some such way as the one described. When it temporarily alleviates conflict by allowing expression to otherwise blocked needs, especially when its amnesic properties are utilized to prevent realization of the needs that have been expressed, alcohol is likely to become irresistibly attractive. In such a case the charm of mild disinhibition is but a minor part of the motive for drinking. The major goal is relief from conflict and the expression of cravings that cannot be satisfied in real life.

Predisposing Factors. Recurrent in the literature on chronic alcoholism is the suspicion that some people have an unusual physical vulnerability.[53] Alcohol, it is argued, produces a more drastic effect on such people because of their biochemical constitution. In circles where social drinking

[53] O. Diethelm (ed.), *Etiology of Chronic Alcoholism* (Springfield, Ill.: Charles C. Thomas, 1955).

is encouraged, it is quite easy to observe individual differences in responsiveness and enjoyment. Sheldon in his studies of physique and temperament reached the conclusion that men of ectomorphic (fragile slender) physique generally found alcohol unpleasant, responding to it less with exhilaration than with a sort of depression.[54] It is hard to pin down the physiological conditions that might make for vulnerability; but biochemistry is a rapidly moving, optimistic branch of science and the possibility of definitive discoveries along this line should not be excluded from one's thinking.

On the psychological side the suspicion has been that drinking would have roots in problems of the oral stage, and that a current craving to escape from the strain of action and responsibility would make a person particularly vulnerable. Support for this view is provided by the McCords in a further analysis of the Cambridge-Somerville Youth Study, where a certain number of the well-studied boys of the 1930's have since become chronic alcoholics.[55] Among these men there appeared with significant frequency a psychological pattern consisting of strong continuing dependent needs suppressed by an urge toward self-sufficiency and full acceptance of an exaggerated masculine role. Other evidence supports the idea that heavy drinking has its onset when acceptable outlets for dependence have been progressively closed.

Treatment of Alcoholism. The treatment of alcoholism offers at least one peculiar difficulty. The patient's main symptom is so available and so attractive that he often cannot resist it. At any point where treatment proves emotionally costly, he is under a terrific temptation to escape into drunkenness. Alcohol constantly offers him an easy solution to the problems both of life and of treatment. Most patients stubbornly cling to the idea that after being cured they will become normal drinkers. Most therapists, on the other hand, believe that only total abstinence will work in a person who has been alcoholic. Once the patient has been in love with the easy solutions offered by intoxication, he can rarely be so fortified against them that he learns to stop after the second drink. Records of treatment are full of relapses which begin when the patient decides that his improved condition has made him capable of normal drinking.

Special methods therefore have to be employed to block a relapse into drinking. Hope has been entertained that certain drugs would reduce the craving for alcohol. Benzedrine, atropine, strychnine, and caffeine have been tried with some success. Particularly valuable for reducing acute alcoholic states, they reportedly serve also as a means of lowering

[54] W. H. Sheldon, *The Varieties of Temperament* (New York: Harper & Row, 1942), pp. 91–2.

[55] W. McCord and J. McCord, *Origins of Alcoholism* (Stanford, Calif.: Stanford University Press, 1960).

the chronic craving for alcohol. Marked success has been claimed for a rigorous method of treatment which consists of establishing a conditioned avoidance response: as mentioned earlier, the patient is given alcohol together with a strong emetic that causes prolonged nausea and vomiting.[56] These methods, like hospitalization itself, should be regarded as technical aids to treatment. The real work has to be done on the problems of maladjustment that have made the patient an abnormal drinker in the first place.

Strecker and Chambers describe a representative method which combines psychotherapy with certain supportive measures designed to prevent relapses.[57] The purely psychotherapeutic part of the program runs to somewhere around 100 hours of interview and does not involve principles beyond those already studied in this book. The patient is called upon, however, to adhere to certain rules. He is required to abstain from alcohol during the period of treatment. He is also required to be entirely frank and honest with the therapist, notifying him as soon as possible in case of a relapse. In addition, steps are taken to assure an optimal physical condition. Nutrition and metabolism are carefully watched, exercise and diversion are called for, and the patient is particularly cautioned against fatigue. Finally, a re-educational program is laid out in some detail. This includes reading on psychological problems, adherence to a schedule of daily activities, attention to the development of hobbies, and vocational guidance.

One of the most successful methods of dealing with alcoholism is the movement known as *Alcoholics Anonymous.* This movement was originated by a group of cured alcoholics. It is now represented in a great many American cities. The nucleus is a sort of social club. The meetings are given over partly to entertainment and partly to discussions of the common problem, usually with testimonials from members who have been cured. There are no specific religious affiliations, although the members are expected to believe in some higher power beyond themselves. When a new member is added, very likely still deeply alcoholic but genuinely desirous of changing, he is at once given some office or responsible task in the society so that he will more readily become identified with the group. In short, every attempt is made to provide an immediate sense of fellowship and group support as a counterpoise to the member's old haunts and drinking companions. The new life must be more attractive than the old. Another feature of the program consists of providing strong individual support when a member is in the grip of his old temptation.

[56] These techniques are described, with references, in Hunt, *op. cit.,* Vol. II, pp. 1145–47.

[57] E. A. Strecker and F. T. Chambers, *Alcohol: One Man's Meat*—(New York: The Macmillan Co., 1938), pp. 133–230.

Other members will spend considerable time with him, perhaps even staying with him for days on end, to keep him from relapsing into drink. The success of such maneuvers naturally depends on the fact that every member has had his own troubles with alcohol. When a patient is really struggling to overcome his addiction, he welcomes the help of someone who has been through it all himself. In certain respects a fellow-sufferer can be a better therapist than a trained person who has never been alcoholic. The success of *Alcoholics Anonymous* gives testimony to the healing power of both group membership and sympathetic insight.

SUGGESTIONS FOR FURTHER READING

A good initial survey of delinquent and criminal personalities, with abundant references, can be obtained from Kimball Young's *Personality and Problems of Adjustment* (2d ed., New York, Appleton-Century-Crofts, Inc., 1952), Ch. 22. Two books can be strongly recommended for their insight into psychological dynamics: *Roots of Crime: Psychoanalytic Studies,* by F. Alexander & W. Healy (New York, Alfred A. Knopf, Inc., 1935), and *Children Who Hate,* by F. Redl and D. Wineman (New York, The Free Press of Glencoe, Inc., 1951). The latter book contains one of the most detailed descriptions of ego functions that has yet appeared. A systematic study of the influence of child-training practices and family relations in delinquency is made by A. Bandura and R. H. Walters in *Adolescent Aggression* (New York, The Ronald Press Co., 1959). A short but illuminating work on social backgrounds is *Delinquent Behavior: Culture and the Individual,* edited by W. C. Kvaraceus and W. B. Miller (Washington: National Education Association of the United States, 1959). For a vivid account of the lives and thoughts of members of youth gangs, see L. Yablonsky, *The Violent Gang* (New York, The Macmillan Co., 1962).

As an introduction to psychopathic personalities S. K. Weinberg's *Society and Personality Disorders,* Ch. 12, is suggested (Englewood Cliffs, N. J., Prentice-Hall, Inc., 1952). A thorough study of this disorder, liberally illustrated with interesting histories, is H. Cleckley's *The Mask of Sanity: An Attempt to Reinterpret the So-Called Psychopathic Personality* (2d ed., St. Louis, The C. V. Mosby Co., 1950). The whole subject is well reviewed, with a new study on treatment, by W. and J. McCord, *Psychopathy and Delinquency* (New York: Grune & Stratton, Inc., 1956). An enlightened venture in treatment is described by Maxwell Jones and others in *The Therapeutic Community: A New Treatment Method in Psychiatry* (New York, Basic Books, Inc., 1953).

Freud's monograph, *Three Contributions to the Theory of Sex* (New York, Nervous & Mental Disease Publishing Co., 1930), represents the first attempt to understand deviant sexual behavior as a developmental disorder. The psychoanalytic theory of these disorders is given by O. Fenichel, *The Psychoanalytic Theory of Neurosis* (New York, W. W. Norton & Co., Inc., 1945), Ch. 16. A searching study of the emotional background of male homosexuality is to be found in I. Bieber and others, *Homosexuality: A Psychoanalytic Study of Male Homosexuality* (New York, Basic Books, Inc., 1962).

A good introduction to alcoholism, its problems, and its treatment, will be found in *Alcohol: One Man's Meat—,* by E. A. Strecker & F. T. Chambers, Jr. (New York, The Macmillan Co., 1938). *Alcoholics Anonymous* (New York,

Works Publishing Co., 1939) tells the story of a most interesting experiment in treatment. A more thorough account of alcoholism is made by H. Haggard and E. M. Jellinek in *Alcohol Explored* (Garden City, N. Y., Doubleday & Co., Inc., 1942). An unusually illuminating case history of a chronic alcoholic who was later cured by Alcoholics Anonymous has been written by Eugenia Hanfmann, "The Life History of an Ex-Alcoholic," *Quarterly Journal of Studies on Alcohol,* 1951, Vol. 12, pp. 405–43. A new study of social and family backgrounds is given by W. and J. McCord in *Origins of Alcoholism* (Stanford, Calif., Stanford University Press, 1960).

11

Psychosomatic Disorders

Up to this point we have been concerned almost entirely with the psychological side of abnormal behavior. Maladjustment and neurosis are problems in psychological development, or, to put it another way, problems of motivation, learning, anxiety, and defense. The same can be said of psychotherapy, which is always an attempt to remove the inner obstacles that interfere with psychological development. In the last chapter we strayed a little from the psychological theme. It proved necessary to consider the social conditions that contribute to delinquent and criminal careers. We also could not overlook the possibility that brain disorders play a part in chronic maladjustment to social requirements. Nevertheless we were dealing primarily with developmental disorders rather than diseases or purely external conditions. Apart from concepts like constitution, temperament, and somatic compliance, our study has proceeded with little reference to the body and the nervous system. This is not because of an inclination to regard people as disembodied spirits. It is because we know absolutely nothing about the neural changes that accompany learning. Thus far we have studied disorders in learning, and neurology offers nothing to assist us.

Our attention must now be turned to a group of disorders in which the somatic complications are fully as important as the psychological. Disorders of adjustment are linked up with bodily processes in such a way as to produce real organic illness. The patient complains of stomach trouble or heart trouble; perhaps it is asthmatic attacks or skin diseases or excessive fatigue that bring him to the physician's office. His ailments are not in the least imaginary. Examination discloses serious malfunctioning in the organs about which he complains, sometimes even tissue changes such as ulcers in the stomach or eruptions on the skin. The somatic disorders require treatment in their own right. Ulcers must be dealt with by rest and diet or by surgical means; acute asthma attacks must be checked with adrenalin. But there is a growing body of evidence that disorders of this kind do not always result from organic weakness or from purely local tissue changes. Sometimes the bodily disorder is the end-product of emotional maladjustment. Medication can temporarily relieve it, but recurrence is almost certain unless the emotional maladjustment can be set right.

Disturbances in which emotional maladjustment leads to chronic dysfunction in some organ system are nowadays referred to as *psychosomatic disorders*. As so often happens, the title is not particularly suitable. The term appears to include every disorder in which psychological and somatic factors both play a part, but in practice no one intends to give it such a sweeping meaning. It is best to limit it to those disorders in which chronic maladjustment is the primary process and somatic dysfunction the result or by-product. One might keep in mind the opposite term, *somatopsychic disorders*—though it is not widely used—for those cases in which bodily disorder is primary and psychological changes secondary. Such a term could be applied to head injury or encephalitis, for example, in which dysfunction of the cerebral cortex produces the result of impulsiveness and poor control so that the person has difficulty in accepting social restraints.

In practice, the term *psychosomatic disorders* is further limited to cases in which the somatic dysfunction is in organs controlled by the autonomic nervous system. This serves to exclude hysteria, which otherwise qualifies perfectly as psychosomatic but which long custom classifies as a neurosis. The bodily symptoms of hysteria—the sensory and motor symptoms such as paralysis and anaesthesia—occur in organs innervated by the cerebrospinal portion of the nervous system. Psychosomatic disorders occur in such regions as the gastro-intestinal tract or the circulatory and respiratory systems, which are under the control of the autonomic division.

Currently there is a tremendous increase in the frequency of psychosomatic disorders. Figures on neuropsychiatric breakdowns during military service show a relatively smaller incidence of hysteria and anxiety neurosis in World War II than in World War I, but a much greater frequency of psychosomatic disturbances. The same trend is clearly shown in statistics based on civilian populations.[1] To some extent, changes of this sort result from fashion in diagnosis. Some disorders are now called psychosomatic which would have been classed as hysteria a generation ago. To a certain extent, moreover, increase in the frequency of a given disease may reflect the advances of medicine in treating other diseases. The greater frequency of cardiac disorders, for instance, may partly

[1] J. L. Halliday, *Psychosocial Medicine: A Study of the Sick Society* (New York: W. W. Norton Co., Inc., 1948), chap. iii.

reflect the hard pace of modern life, but it also arises from the fact that a larger proportion of the population now survives into the middle and later decades when cardiac disorders are in any event more common. Neither of these considerations, however, seems sufficient to account for the reported increase of psychosomatic disorders. Halliday offers some interesting speculations on the causes of the relative decline of hysteria and rise of psychosomatic disturbances, pointing out that the atmosphere and conditions of child training changed significantly between the late nineteenth and early twentieth centuries.[2] One cannot yet be sure of the answer, but in the meantime psychosomatic disorders constitute an active focus of contemporary research, and we must set ourselves to understand them.

EMOTION AND BODILY CHANGES

Emotion is obviously related to certain bodily states. There are many common phrases in which this is recognized. The heart is said to ache or to be broken; in its more turbulent moments it can be in one's mouth or go down to one's boots. The color of the face can change over a wide range from white as a sheet to purple or even black with rage. We say that we have no stomach for a job or that we haven't the guts to do it. In China it is appropriate for a man to say to his lady love that his intestines tie themselves in knots while she is away. Language would hardly have become so replete with psychosomatic phrases without some kind of factual basis.

Everyday Observations. Turning from metaphor to observed fact, we still need not set up an experimental situation in order to find examples of psychosomatic relationships. Everyday observation teaches us quite a few lessons on this subject. As a first example we can take the nervousness that many people feel when they have to make a speech or appear in some other capacity before an audience. Stage fright carries with it a number of well-known bodily reactions. For the last meal preceding the public appearance there is poor appetite, possibly even a complete inability to eat. As the great moment approaches, the heart beats rapidly, the mouth becomes dry, the hands tremble and grow cold, and there is a strong desire to urinate and move the bowels. The upset state of mind is reflected in an upset state of body. A contrasting example is offered by the emotion of joy. This will show itself not only in erect posture, springy step, bright eyes, and smiling face, but also in systems under autonomic control. The joyous person usually shows a good color, has a strong deep pulse, breathes deeply, has a good appetite, enjoys his food, and digests and eliminates well. His viscera share in his mental well-

[2] *Ibid.*, chap. vi.

being. For a third example we can take grief, which is usually accompanied by marked somatic distress.[3] There is apt to be an aching tightness in the throat, sometimes a choking sensation, shortness of breath, and a frequent need for sighing, all of these being related to a feeling of wanting to cry. Another element is a feeling of weakness and easy exhaustion, so that the bereaved person can scarcely summon energy to climb the stairs or walk for any distance. Disturbances of eating are highly characteristic: appetite is extremely poor and there are complaints such as that all food tastes like sand. Grief ramifies throughout the body, affecting a large number of functions controlled by the autonomic nervous system. We have no reason to doubt that other feelings and emotions besides nervousness, joy, and grief have a widespread influence on the whole bodily economy.

Hypnotic Experiments on Psychosomatic Processes. Hypnosis offers a means of extending the study of psychosomatic reactions. By suggesting various emotional states rather than waiting for them to arise in the course of life it is possible to observe the somatic reactions under well-controlled conditions.

An experiment by Wolberg illustrates this kind of study and at the same time affords an interesting comparison between neurotic and psychosomatic mechanisms.[4] In hypnotically susceptible subjects it is possible to create a state of post-hypnotic conflict. This is done by giving contradictory suggestions which are to be executed post-hypnotically with amnesia for the fact that suggestions were given. Wolberg's instructions to the hypnotized subject were as follows:

> When you awaken you will find next to you a bar of chocolate. You will have a desire to eat the chocolate that will be so intense that it will be impossible to resist the craving. At the same time you will feel that the chocolate does not belong to you and that to eat it would be very wrong and very bad. You will have no memory of these suggestions when you awaken, but you will, nevertheless, react to them.

Wolberg reports the results with three different subjects. One was a patient under treatment for conversion hysteria, and the reaction was a characteristic hysterical symptom: a psychogenic blindness. Although he saw everything else, the patient simply could not see the bar of chocolate that lay beside him. Even when the investigator picked it up and tossed it down, the patient asserted that he saw no chocolate bar. Conflict was avoided by not perceiving the stimulus that would have set it off. The patient maintained his negative hallucination for twenty minutes; there-

[3] E. Lindemann, "Symptomatology and Management of Acute Grief," *American Journal of Psychiatry,* CI (1942), pp. 141–48.

[4] L. R. Wolberg, "Hypnotic Experiments in Psychosomatic Medicine," *Psychosomatic Medicine,* IX (1947), pp. 337–42.

after, he saw the candy but refused to eat it. Another subject reacted to the post-hypnotic conflict with symptoms of anxiety and neurocirculatory collapse. Though he tried to avoid looking at the chocolate bar, this defense was insufficient. He complained of dizziness and faintness, proved unable to walk, became pale and cold, then broke out in violent tremor. When his pulse was taken it was found to be rapid and thin. So distressing was his anxiety attack that it became necessary to rehypnotize him and remove the conflict. Very different was the reaction of the third subject, who maintained complete outward composure but showed the effects of conflict by a psychosomatic symptom. At first he talked loquaciously about food and eating, remarked that visitors were expected to accept food when it was offered, and started to eat the chocolate with gusto. Before he finished, his face showed sudden surprise and he remarked that the chocolate tasted bitter. A moment later he complained of stomach pains and nausea, then went to the bathroom and vomited. In this last case one of the conflicting impulses utilized psychosomatic channels. The impulse to eat was not resisted, but the feeling that this act was "very wrong and very bad" came to expression through reversed gastric peristalsis.

The effects of hypnotic suggestion on the digestive system have been considerably investigated. It has been shown, for example, that gastric peristalsis is increased by suggestions that a meal is being relished, decreased by suggestions that the food is poor or disgusting. In similar fashion, the acid secretion of the stomach can be increased by suggestions of relish or decreased from normal by suggestions of disgust. Even when no meal is eaten, the digestive apparatus responds appropriately to suggestion. If a hungry person is made to hallucinate the eating of food, the contractions of his stomach ("hunger pangs") may cease entirely. Furthermore, the secretions of the digestive tract apparently vary according to the composition of the hallucinated meal, just as they do according to the composition of a real meal. The suggested drinking of clear soup produces a thin yellow secretion appropriate for digesting soup, while suggested eating of butter produces a dark viscous secretion.[5]

Experiments of this kind are often classed with the wonders of hypnotism. It is more accurate to class them with the wonders of psychosomatic processes. The contribution of hypnotism is not uniquely important—it

[5] The experiments up to 1933 are reviewed by C. H. Hull, *Hypnosis and Suggestibility: An Experimental Approach* (New York: Appleton-Century-Crofts, Inc., 1933), pp. 274–84. See also R. E. Scantlebury and T. L. Patterson, "Hunger Motility in a Hypnotized Subject," *Quarterly Journal of Experimental Physiology*, XXX (1940), p. 347; and J. H. Lewis and T. R. Sarbin, "The Influence of Hypnotic Stimulation on Gastric Hunger Contractions," *Psychosomatic Medicine*, V (1943), pp. 125–31. A more recent review will be found in A. M. Weitzenhofer, *Hypnotism: An Objective Study of Suggestibility* (New York: John Wiley & Sons, Inc., 1953), pp. 130–45.

consists merely in heightening the imaginative processes so that the somatic reactions are evoked more strongly than would otherwise be possible. Similar effects can be obtained by imagination without hypnosis. Digestive secretions can be provoked merely by talking about thick juicy steaks or other relished foods. For our present purposes the important thing is the close relation between psychic and somatic processes. States of conflict, feelings of relish or disgust, thoughts and fantasies about eating are all closely linked to bodily processes governed by the autonomic nervous system. This is the basic fact that lies behind psychosomatic disorders.

Hypnotic experiments have not been confined to digestive processes. One of the most interesting lines of investigation is the production of blisters by hypnotic suggestion. The technique consists of touching the hypnotized person on the forearm with a pencil which is declared to be burning hot; as a control, a like spot on the other arm can be touched with the same pencil now stated to be cool. It has frequently been claimed that under these circumstances a true blister will presently be found on the spot supposedly burned. Some years ago Pattie reviewed all the reported experiments on blisters, numbering more than a dozen.[6] Some of the experiments were not sufficiently controlled and some gave negative results, but there remained a few in which true blisters were raised at or near the stimulated spot. The production of blisters in response to real burns is mediated in part by local circulatory changes. Apparently the hypnotized person can imagine the burn so vividly as to bring about the local changes appropriate for healing a burned area.

The Autonomic Nervous System. The autonomic nervous system, sometimes called the "involuntary" or the "vegetative" nervous system, is a system of motor nerves governing what Cannon has called "the domestic affairs of the interior of the organism." It is intimately connected with the cerebrospinal system, having centers in the medulla, midbrain, hypothalamus, and cerebral cortex, yet it is to some extent set apart both anatomically and functionally. In general, the axons of autonomic neurons do not proceed from the central nervous system directly to muscles or glands; instead, they pass to outlying ganglia which serve as relay stations on the way to the final goal. In contrast to the cerebrospinal system which innervates the striated muscles responsible for movement and posture, the autonomic system acts upon the glands and smooth muscles of the viscera and blood vessels.

The autonomic is divided into two subsystems which have somewhat antagonistic effects. The *sympathetic* system is mainly concerned with

[6] F. A. Pattie, Jr., "The Production of Blisters by Hypnotic Suggestion: A Review," *Journal of Abnormal and Social Psychology*, XXXVI (1941), pp. 62–72.

mobilizing the resources of the body for use in work or in emergencies. Anatomically it is well designed to act more or less as a whole: the sympathetic ganglia lie in an interconnected chain so that excitation at any one level is likely to spread upward and downward to reach all the organs affected by the system. The *parasympathetic* division is mainly concerned with conserving and storing the bodily resources. Its action is less unified, the ganglia not being interconnected, but some of its nerves branch in such a way as to reach several organs. The vagus nerve, for example, reaches the heart, the bronchi, the stomach, and the intestine. Thus both divisions of the autonomic act with less precision and more diffuseness than the cerebrospinal system.

It is easy to exaggerate the antagonism between the two divisions. As we saw in an earlier chapter, Cannon originally conceived that all strong emotions such as anger and fear activated the sympathetic, suppressed the effects of the parasympathetic, and thus put the organism on an emergency footing. The studies of Gellhorn and others have shown that this conception of an emergency reaction is somewhat too simple. If the organism is to react effectively in a crisis, a rise in parasympathetic activity must closely follow the initial burst of sympathetic discharge. The interaction between the two divisions proves to be quite complex; reciprocal action is necessary to maintain an effective bodily state either in emergencies or in quieter times. For our present purposes it is probably better to emphasize not the two parts but the action of the autonomic system as a whole in managing the domestic economy of viscera, blood vessels, and glands.

Normally the autonomic nervous system maintains an effective equilibrium. Strong emotion is accompanied by overactivity in some part of the system, but strong emotion is usually transient. Anger subsides, and heart rate and blood pressure go back to normal levels. Acute grief passes, and appetite returns to its customary state. The healthy digestive tract, heart, circulation, and respiratory system are equal to quite a large amount of overactivity if occasion demands. Naturally there are limits, beyond which prolonged overactivity tends to create serious dysfunction and even permanent injury. Psychosomatic disorders occur when some autonomic pattern remains persistently overactive. The bodily accompaniments of an emotional reaction do not subside, although the person himself is unaware of emotional disturbance. Perhaps the blood pressure remains consistently high, causing unpleasant symptoms and danger of possible heart injury. Perhaps organic injury actually develops as is the case with gastric ulcers. In order to explain psychosomatic disorders it is necessary to show why certain patterns of autonomic discharge remain persistently active in the absence of what appears to be suitable circumstances.

As a first step toward answering this question we need to consider an important difference between the dangers that threaten animals and those that threaten man. Emergencies in the lives of animals are apt to be of relatively short duration. The protective reactions governed by the autonomic nervous system seem to have been planned, so to speak, with this is mind. The general fact is well expressed in Selye's formulation: the adaptive reaction to stress occurs in three stages, an *alarm reaction* that quickly mobilizes the body's defensive forces, a *stage of resistance* in which many further reactions occur in order to sustain the continued meeting of stress, and, if stress continues too long, a *stage of exhaustion* in which the protective reactions fail and the animal succumbs.[7] The animal's fate depends on time. A tough and healthy creature can sustain a long hard fight or flight, but there is a time limit to the internal protective reactions, and if pressed close to this limit they begin to produce destructive tissue change in the organs that are involved. This we can consider to be the biological basis of psychosomatic disorders in man.

Emergencies in the lives of men are quite commonly not of short duration. One of the great assets of the richly developed human brain is that it permits extensive imagining of future events and planning to cope with them effectively. Animals respond mainly to situations immediately present and do not, as far as we know, worry about the future. They may have hot wars but they do not have cold wars. In man it often becomes necessary to use the autonomic reaction patterns designed for hot wars in those more extended emergencies that are analogous to cold wars. Future events may be the subject of worry long before they happen; past deeds may be regretted long afterwards; resentments may simmer for a long period of time. Despite the adages, we have a marked tendency to cross bridges before we come to them and to cry over spilled milk. As Wolff expresses it, "man, feeling threatened, may use for long-term purposes devices designed for short-term needs."[8] And if the term lasts too long, destructive tissue changes may happen in the organs that participate in the physiological protective reaction.

Wolff points out another way in which the human use of autonomic protective reactions may lead to psychosomatic disorders.[9] The protective reactions may be used not only for too long a time but also in a way that is not appropriate to the actual situation. Thus the body may be mobilized to fight—to engage in strenuous muscular activity—when the real provocation to anger has been of a social or symbolic kind. Perhaps the

[7] H. Selye, "General Adaptation Syndrome and Diseases of Adaptation," *Journal of Clinical Endocrinology*, VI (1946), pp. 117–28.

[8] H. G. Wolff, quoted by S. Cobb, in *Emotions and Clinical Medicine* (New York: W. W. Norton & Co., Inc., 1950), p. 138.

[9] H. G. Wolff, *Stress and Disease* (Springfield, Ill.: Charles C. Thomas, 1953).

source of annoyance is a child's misbehavior which must be dealt with by verbal punishment; perhaps it is a slur cast by an acquaintance which must be countered by repartee or an intelligent argument. When the mobilized bodily resources are not used in the ensuing behavior, the products are not dissipated and the restoration of an internal balance may be long delayed. Wolff illustrates this thesis by citing observations made by Graham.[10] If the forearm is struck a smart blow with a ferule, capillary changes immediately occur which make the area red and produce a swelling or wheal. The same result can then be produced by a sham blow. In both cases there is rapid recovery. In a certain patient who suffered from frequent attacks of hives, the very same result—the appearance of redness and wheals on the arms—was produced by talking about a painful family situation in which the patient reacted to "the things they did to me" with a feeling as though he were being struck. "It is to be noted that the bodily pattern which protected against a blow from a ferule in the first instance could here afford little protection against symbolic blows."[11]

These general views about the autonomic nervous system and its protective activities furnish us with a groundwork for understanding the psychosomatic disorders. Further hypotheses are needed, however, to account for the production of specific symptoms. What principles govern the selection of the organ system that finally breaks down? How does it happen that sometimes the gastrointestinal system, sometimes the cardiovascular system, sometimes the respiratory tract becomes the seat of illness? How does it come about that prolonged autonomic reactions produce results so different as rheumatoid arthritis, skin disease, migraine headaches, back pains, and diabetes?

Hypotheses Concerning the Location of Disorder. The simplest hypothesis would be that each person breaks down at his weakest point. Serious disturbance occurs first in the organ that happens to be weakest or most vulnerable. The person with a sensitive digestive tract has gastritis or ulcers, the one with a sensitive skin has eczema or some other inflammation, the one with inherent breathing difficulty has asthma. If this hypothesis is used alone, as an attempt at complete explanation, it makes no use of the possibility that different emotions are associated with different autonomic patterns. It can be founded upon the idea of innate differences in the sensitivity of organs, or it can be widened a little by the assumption that the afflicted organ has been weakened by

[10] D. T. Graham, "The Pathogenesis of Hives: Experimental Study of Life Situations, Emotions, and Cutaneous Vascular Reactions," *Research Publications of the Association for Research on Nervous and Mental Diseases*, XXIX (1950), pp. 987–1009.

[11] Wolff, *op. cit.*, p. 7.

illness or injury. The argument for constitution has a persuasive advocate in George Draper, who for many years, starting before the current interest in psychosomatic medicine, followed the tradition established by Hippocrates in pointing out associations between disease and physical type. These associations cannot be overlooked, although they are rarely so close and inevitable as to support a purely constitutional theory.[12]

At the opposite extreme is the so-called "specificity hypothesis," which makes a maximum use of the idea that different emotional states have different patterns of autonomic discharge. Radically stated, the hypothesis would run as follows: Each variety of psychosomatic disorder results from a specific emotional constellation. As Franz Alexander expressed it in an early statement: "Just as the nature of the chronic unrelieved emotional state varies, so also will the corresponding vegetative disturbance vary."[13] In order to justify the hypothesis of specificity it is necessary to demonstrate a close correlation between type of somatic disorder and type of emotional maladjustment. The argument becomes much stronger if it is possible to go further and show a rationale for the correlation, a credible chain of processes leading from the unrelieved emotional state to the end result of organic dysfunction. Occasionally it has seemed that both points could be carried as regards some particular disorder, but Alexander himself finally concluded that the specificity hypothesis would not stand alone.[14] As so often happens, a simple hypothesis that seemed adequate in an early stage of research became discredited when the problems were more intensively studied.

A theory that is sufficient to encompass what we know today about psychosomatic disorders must be more complex than either the constitutional or the specificity hypothesis. These two, however, can guide us for the time being, and we shall be in a better position to improve our formulations when we have looked more closely at some of the disorders. We shall concentrate on a small number of psychosomatic disorders rather than try to survey all varieties. It is more important to understand a few disorders thoroughly, to see how they probably work and what problems arise in their study, than to take a rapid and confusing tour of what is now a very active field of research. We shall give disproportionate attention, therefore, to one class of psychosomatic disturbances, those located in the gastro-intestinal system, and within this group we shall somewhat concentrate on peptic ulcer. Most of the problems of psychosomatic medicine can be demonstrated in connection with this

[12] G. Draper, C. W. Dupertuis, and J. L. Caughey, *Human Constitution in Clinical Medicine* (New York: Paul B. Hoeber, Inc., 1944).

[13] F. Alexander, "Fundamental Concepts of Psychosomatic Research: Psychogenesis, Conversion, Specificity," *Psychosomatic Medicine,* V (1943), pp. 205–10.

[14] F. Alexander, *Psychosomatic Medicine: Its Principles and Applications* (New York: W. W. Norton & Co., Inc., 1950).

one disorder. Not all, however; we shall therefore save space for chronic high blood pressure and bronchial asthma.

GASTRO-INTESTINAL DISTURBANCES

Digestive and eliminative processes are subject to many kinds of disorder. There are disorders of appetite and eating: at one extreme stands *bulimia,* marked by inordinate appetite and excessive eating; at the other extreme *anorexia nervosa,* a loss of appetite so severe that it sometimes threatens life. Next to be mentioned is *gastritis,* sometimes called "nervous stomach," marked by gastric distress and pain, occasionally with vomiting. In gastritis there is irritation of the walls of the stomach but no sharply localized injury. *Peptic ulcer,* on the other hand, is a focal lesion of the mucous lining of stomach or duodenum, an inflamed crater that may even cause an internal loss of blood. At the eliminative end of the tract the two possibilities are *chronic constipation* and *chronic diarrhea.* The latter is usually called *colitis* (inflammation of the colon); it may be associated with chronic spasm of the smooth muscle of the colon or it may involve ulceration of the inner walls. None of these disorders is necessarily psychogenic. Infections, metabolic disorders, glandular malfunctioning, structural defects, long-continued faulty diet, and many other conditions can throw the gastro-intestinal system off balance. There is reason to believe, however, that each of these disorders is sometimes truly psychosomatic. They are sometimes cured by psychotherapy.

Mechanisms of Peptic Ulcer Formation. We first turn our attention to peptic ulcer, one of the most intensively studied of the psychosomatic disorders. The formation of ulcers usually comes after a prolonged period of chronic gastric distress. The discomfort is felt about two hours after eating and can be alleviated by taking food. During the day the patient can keep fairly comfortable by frequent snacks, but at night his distress is likely to increase. Ulcer formation results from chronic overactivity and oversecretion by the stomach. Under normal circumstances the stomach becomes active when a meal is to be digested. With the accomplishment of this task and the passing of the meal into the intestines, the stomach comes to rest and its acid secretion stops. In ulcer patients the stomach continues to be active just as if more food were on the way. The acid secretions are poured forth, but as there is no food to absorb them they only irritate and inflame the mucous lining of the stomach. They similarly irritate the upper part of the small intestine (duodenum). If this goes on long enough, ulcer craters are formed, and the continuing hyperacidity makes it difficult for them to heal.

Various experiments have been performed with animals to show that prolonged acid secretion in the stomach eventually produces ulceration. These results are sufficiently conclusive, but hardly as dramatic as those obtained with a human patient by Wolf and Wolff.[15] The patient at the age of nine had drunk some scalding soup which seriously burned his esophagus so that it became closed with scar tissue. In order to feed him, a surgical opening (gastric fistula) was made directly into the stomach through the abdominal wall. At the age of fifty-six the man was in excellent health and rarely suffered digestive difficulties. The fistula was in regular use; it was sufficiently large to permit observation of the stomach walls, and, to make matters perfect for science, a collar of gastric mucosa had grown out to surround the fistula, thus exposing to direct view a small amount of tissue essentially similar to that which lines the stomach. We shall have more to say about this man in a moment. What is important here is the experimental demonstration that gastric juice produces ulceration. A small erosion occurring on the exposed gastric mucosa, where the supply of mucus was poor, was artificially kept moist with gastric juice for four days. The erosion increased in size, resembled in every way a chronic ulcer, and was painful when touched. When a dressing was placed so as to protect the ulcer from gastric juice, the area healed completely in three days, leaving no trace of a scar.

What is the cause of the increased motility and acid secretion on the part of the stomach? Why do the digestive processes go on night and day instead of rising and falling in response to the taking of food? Digestive peristalsis and secretion are stimulated by the parasympathetic division of the autonomic nervous system, acting through the vagus nerve. Various experiments have shown that chronic vagal stimulation, resulting either from injuries in the midbrain or from appropriate drugs, produces gastric ulceration. This carries our inquiry back into the brain. Why does the parasympathetic keep the digestive processes going twenty-four hours a day? As there is no reason to assume local brain injury in all peptic ulcer patients, especially those that are cured, we reach the point where a psychosomatic hypothesis is in order.

Dependence in Cases of Peptic Ulcer. Peptic ulcer occurs much more frequently in men than in women. It often appears in men with strongly ambitious, hard-driving tendences. It has sometimes been called a disease of business executives and others in important and responsible positions, and it once had the nickname of "Wall Street stomach." Alexander psychoanalyzed several such patients and found that a very different emotional constellation existed beneath the surface.[16] Desires for rest and

[15] S. Wolf and H. G. Wolff, "Evidence on the Genesis of Peptic Ulcer in Man," *Journal of the American Medical Association*, CXX (1942), No. 9. Reprinted in S. S. Tomkins (ed), *Contemporary Psychopathology* (Cambridge: Harvard University Press, 1943), chap. x.

[16] F. Alexander, "The Influence of Psychological Factors upon Gastro-Intestinal Disturbances," *Psychoanalytic Quarterly*, III (1934), pp. 501–39. Reprinted in Tomkins, *op. cit.*, chap. viii.

comfort, cravings for support and loving care proved to be active in the lives of these otherwise assertive, competitive men. There were very strong dependent tendencies against which the outward assertiveness and responsibility constituted a reaction formation. It was clear that the patients felt ashamed of their dependence. They wanted to fit the American masculine pattern. Sometimes they even assumed more responsibilities than were required of them. But these strenuous efforts did not prove sufficient to drive their dependence out of existence. Longings for rest, care, and affection came out in their fantasies and dreams. Could it be that the same longings came out in chronic parasympathetic stimulation of the digestive processes?

The last question is the crux of the psychosomatic problem. The conflict between active assertion and dependent longings is readily understandable, especially in a competitive business society which places a high value on the former trend. The crucial point that requires explanation is the relationship between dependent longings and the process of digestion. On this point Alexander offered the following hypothesis. When dependent longings are severely suppressed either by reaction formation or by the pressure of external circumstances they receive no gratification and hence remain in a more or less chronic state of tension. This tension activates the digestive processes because of a long-standing associative link between the receiving of loving care and the receiving of food. In infancy these benefits are received all at once: the baby is taken up, cuddled, stimulated, fed, loved, then put down again to go to sleep. Being fed is the predominant element in this complex of affectionate care, and a conditioned response is formed which links anticipatory digestive activity with all the rest of the complex. Very likely, Alexander admitted, this linkage exists in everyone. Most people, however, either sufficiently outgrow their dependent longings so that no great tension accumulates on that score, or at least do not react violently against them, allowing them sufficient indulgence to reduce the tension. It requires a quite special situation to evoke chronic stimulation of digestive processes. The situation must be such that dependent longings are strong but denied any overt satisfaction. As an added support for his thesis Alexander pointed out that ulcer patients sometimes recover without medication when they go to bed or go to the hospital. Recovery could not occur unless parasympathetic stimulation ceased, relieving the digestive tract of its acid excess. The fact of his illness removes the patient from strenuous activity. He can now legitimately relax and accept the attentive ministrations of nurses or members of the family. At last his dependent longings are satisfied and do not have to expend themselves in chronic stimulation of the digestive process.

The medical measures used to cure peptic ulcers include rest, a bland diet to minimize irritation of the stomach and duodenum, and frequent feeding in order to utilize the acid excess. If the ulcers do not heal under this regimen it becomes necessary to remove them surgically. Occasionally the vagus nerves are severed at the stomach in order to prevent further hypermotility and hypersecretion, but this is an operation of last resort. With the exception of the last operation, these measures would not be expected, according to Alexander's hypothesis, to prevent a recurrence of the disorder. When a strenuous reaction formation plays an important part in the genesis of ulcers, the only permanent cure is psychotherapy. The aim of this therapy is to relax the patient's defenses against his dependent longings. When he is able to admit them and ease his overdriving reaction formation, he alters the crucial situation that kept his digestive tract ceaselessly active. He learns to permit himself a certain amount of passive gratification without shame, and he avoids the extremes of activity that only serve to build up dependent longings. In short, he learns to conform to an emotional regimen that suits his personal pattern of motives and that likewise suits his autonomic nervous system. In many cases this opens the way to a further outgrowing of dependent longings.

Alexander and his co-workers at the Chicago Institute for Psychoanalysis have successfully treated a number of peptic ulcer patients whose response to other medication was only temporary. This constitutes favorable though not conclusive evidence that the emotional constellation just described is the crucial factor in some cases. Other studies have confirmed the importance of passivity and dependence, but at least three different investigations have shown that repression and reaction formation are not essential aspects of the picture. A substantial number of ulcer patients appear to accept their passivity and dependence and live their lives accordingly.[17] The assumption can be made, and was included in Alexander's original statement, that external pressure as well as internal guilt or inferiority feelings might suppress the dependent longings. This, however, makes the emotional constellation much less specific by eliminating the defense mechanisms of repression and reaction formation.

Aggression in Cases of Peptic Ulcer. Other investigators believe that resentment and hostility play a central part in the genesis of peptic ulcer. Mittelmann and Wolff, for example, induced emotional states in ulcer

[17] S. Rubin and K. M. Bowman, "Electroencephalographic and Personality Correlates in Peptic Ulcer," *Psychosomatic Medicine*, IV (1942), pp. 309–18; F. T. Kapp, M. Rosenbaum, and J. Romano, "Psychological Factors in Men with Peptic Ulcers," *American Journal of Psychiatry*, CIII (1947), pp. 700–704; J. Ruesch, *Duodenal Ulcer* (Berkeley: University of California Press, 1948).

patients and in normal subjects by discussing with them various emotionally charged situations in their lives.[18] When these discussions gave rise to anxiety, hostility, and resentment, there was increased motility and acidity in the stomachs of all ulcer patients and of some normal subjects. Acidity and motility could be reduced by inducing feelings of contentment and well-being. The man with the gastric fistula reported by Wolf and Wolff behaved in a similar fashion. Gastric changes suitable for ulcer formation—increased motility and acidity—came at moments in his life when he was dominated by feelings of anger and resentment. They were particularly acute when he was discharged from a small outside job on grounds of inefficiency, and when a man who lent him money tried to meddle in his affairs. When he experienced fear or sadness, on the contrary, the gastric mucosa became pale and motility and acidity dropped. Margolin has carried this type of investigation still further in work with another person having a gastric fistula. This patient was in psychoanalytic treatment, and Margolin was able to show that the emotional state of anger produced several different gastric patterns depending on the origin, aim, and object of the anger. Fantasied physical violence was accompanied by the kind of gastric overactivity that might produce ulcers, whereas fantasies of an oral sadistic character gave rise to milder and more random responses.[19]

Facts of this kind have been discussed in a paper by Szasz and coworkers.[20] Their discussion brings out the full difficulty of reaching valid conclusions in regard to psychosomatic mechanisms. Where Alexander postulates an association in infancy between feeding and the reception of love, Szasz postulates an association between feeding and anger. The infant responds to frustration by angry crying. When his frustration takes the form of hunger, he cries with mounting fury until he is fed. The emotion of anger is thus followed directly by feeding, and this temporal connection is sufficient to establish a conditioned response. Presumably the connection is gradually weakened in the course of life, the sequence being one that ceases to occur as the child grows older. Nevertheless the traces are not lost and the connection can be reanimated, a process termed by Szasz "regressive innervation," under special circumstances such as prolonged suppressed anger.

The disagreement between two groups of workers as to the specific emotional constellation associated with peptic ulcer serves to underline

[18] B. Mittelmann, H. G. Wolff, and M. Scharf, "Emotions and Gastroduodenal Functions," *Psychosomatic Medicine,* IV (1942), pp. 5–61.

[19] S. G. Margolin, "The Behavior of the Stomach During Psychoanalysis," *Psychoanalytic Quarterly,* XX (1951), pp. 349–73.

[20] T. S. Szasz, E. Levin, J. B. Kirsner, and W. L. Palmer, "The Role of Hostility in the Pathogenesis of Peptic Ulcer: Theoretical Considerations with the Report of a Case," *Psychosomatic Medicine,* IX (1947), pp. 331–36.

the inherent difficulties in psychosomatic research. Where it is necessary to posit a *learned connection* between a somatic process and emotional states there is room for a wide variety of different learnings. The situation is different when the connection is more or less innate. The association between rage and high blood pressure appears to be universal for man and the higher animals. It is therefore probable on the face of it that psychogenic high blood pressure will be associated with a specific emotional constellation involving rage. But the moment learning comes into play, especially infantile learning and unconscious learning, the hope of demonstrating specificity begins to dwindle. One is then moving over into the sphere of *personal meanings,* a realm always marked by great diversity.

Constitution in Cases of Peptic Ulcer. The foregoing discussion seems to conjure up baffling difficulties in psychosomatic research, but we have not yet exhausted the problem. What does the body contribute, and what part is played by constitutional predisposition in cases of peptic ulcer? We introduced the concept of somatic compliance when studying the formation of hysterical symptoms. Obviously it cannot be neglected in the psychosomatic disorders.

It has long been noticed that ulcer patients tend to the linear, lanky type of physique. In the terms introduced by Sheldon, they incline away from the soft, round, endomorphic component and toward the slender, fragile, ectomorphic component, generally with a certain secondary strength in the sturdy, muscular, mesomorphic component. On the basis of anthropometric measurements, Draper describes male ulcer patients as follows.[21] They are generally of slender build, a little above average in height but below average in weight. Head and face tend to be narrow, features small, the chest particularly narrow and of small circumference. The male physique tends to be of somewhat feminine character, though not as markedly as is the case in certain other disease groups. Draper points out that not all ulcer patients conform to this physical description. Yet their tendency in this direction is so marked that one cannot consider it a chance phenomenon. A certain type of physical constitution is more liable than others to develop peptic ulcer. Not all the cases studied by Draper are necessarily psychogenic, but even the most enthusiastic supporters of psychogenesis remark on the frequency of the linear physique among their ulcer patients.

In his studies Draper works out with great care the history of the patient's attacks of gastric pain and ulceration. Many times an acute attack is precipitated by conflict with a mother figure in which the patient feels

[21] G. Draper, C. W. Dupertuis, and J. L. Caughey, *Human Constitution in Clinical Medicine* (New York: Paul B. Hoeber, Inc., 1944), p. 117.

rejected. Quite frequently the wife's pregnancy and the withdrawal of her interest from the patient to a newborn child provoke gastric difficulties. Often the patient has an extreme sense of guilt over sexual relations, but his guilt revolves chiefly around pleasing or not pleasing his partner. On the other hand an event that creates a sense of failure can be the precipitating cause. In addition, it happens not infrequently that anger and aggression are the outstanding emotions just prior to an attack. These findings argue against a specific emotional constellation as the cause of the gastric conditions that lead to ulceration. The cases vary; in some, dependent longings and their frustration appear to be uppermost, while in others the linkage would seem to be with hostility and resentment. In nearly all cases, however, a certain passivity and dependence forms some part of the total constellation.

Draper's studies of the "ulcer type" suggest that constitution has something to do with the tendency to break down in this particular way. A more direct approach to the problem has been made by Mirsky and his associates, who have found that ulcer patients have significantly high levels of pepsinogen in the blood, a sign of the capacity of the gastric mucosa to secrete it abundantly, and who propose that "high pepsinogen secretors represent that segment of the population with a maximum secretory capacity which is most likely to develop duodenal ulcer when exposed to precipitating circumstances."[22] Another disorder, pernicious anemia, occurs in people with naturally low pepsinogen secretion. Mirsky suggests testing the pepsinogen level of large numbers of people and then following them in later life to see whether or not the incidence of ulcers and pernicious anemia follows predictions made from the original measures. A positive result would greatly favor the idea of constitutional predisposition.

Anorexia Nervosa. We turn next to a disorder that is characterized by a highly negative attitude toward food. Appetite and eating are suppressed, the thought of food being positively unpleasant to the patient. In some cases the symptom is so stubborn that much weight is lost, and in a few cases it has been impossible to prevent death by starvation. It is hard to believe that so damaging a disorder could occur unless eating were associated with severe anxiety. The probable mechanism of this association has been worked out in a good many cases, but the results show little uniformity. The one uniform finding is that eating has come to mean something to the patient that awakens severe anxiety and guilt. The particular personal meaning varies from case to case. In a paper on eating disturbances in childhood, Rose makes the point that

[22] I. A. Mirsky, "The Psychosomatic Approach to the Etiology of Clinical Disorders," *Psychosomatic Medicine,* XIX (1957), pp. 424–30.

eating may be associated with growing up and with advancing to more difficult levels of adjustment.[23] Eating is the focus of certain early and crucial developmental steps—the advance from nursing to drinking from a cup, the advance from being fed to feeding oneself, etc. Refusal to eat is an easy way for the child to resist these steps when he is given no love or help in making the required adjustments. Many mothers concentrate on getting their children to eat, show frustration when eating is resisted, and thus provide their children with a perfect weapon for showing hostility and resisting unwelcome change. Not to eat can thus acquire the personal connotations, doubtless unconsciously, of not growing up or of not giving in.

More specific personal meanings have been disclosed in detailed studies of anorexia. The disorder is much more common in women than in men, and occurs with more than accidental frequency in connection with such steps in growth as puberty, sexual relationships, and marriage. Sometimes the motivation seems to turn on the desire to remain thin, flat-breasted, and sexually unattractive; there is anxiety connected with becoming sexually mature. In other cases the anxiety arises from an unconscious fear of oral impregnation, the association between food and impregnation being based on a childhood misconception as to the nature of the latter process.[24] In still other cases anorexia has the significance of an aggressive resistance to parental demands, together with a self-punishment for guilt-laden dependent or grasping tendencies. The diversity of personal meanings tells against the hypothesis of specific psychosomatic relationships. One has to be satisfied with the following limited specificity. There is an effective association between eating and some anxiety-laden or guilt-laden step in development. So close is the association that inhibition against taking the required step carries with it an inhibition against eating.[25]

Disorders of Elimination. Alexander and his associates at Chicago have advanced several hypotheses in regard to the disorders of elimination.[26] Chronic constipation and chronic diarrhea (colitis) have to be under-

[23] J. A. Rose, "Eating Inhibitions in Children in Relation to Anorexia Nervosa," *Psychosomatic Medicine,* V (1943), pp. 117–24.

[24] J. Waller, M. Kaufman, and F. Deutsch, "Anorexia Nervosa: A Psychosomatic Entity," *Psychosomatic Medicine,* II (1940), pp. 1–16.

[25] For a discussion of this disorder, with case illustrations, see S. Cobb, *Emotions and Clinical Medicine* (New York: W. W. Norton & Co., Inc., 1950), chap. ix. For a recent analysis of the emotional roots, see B. C. Meyer and L. A. Weinroth, "Observations on Psychological Aspects of Anorexia Nervosa," *Psychosomatic Medicine,* XIX (1957), pp. 389–98; and on treatment, J. A. Wall, "Diagnosis, Treatment, and Results in Anorexia Nervosa," *American Journal of Psychiatry,* CXV (1959), pp. 997–1001.

[26] Alexander, "The Influence of Psychological Factors upon Gastro-Intestinal Disturbances," *op. cit.*

stood, these workers claim, with reference to the child's early experiences with elimination. Moving his bowels at the required time and place is one of his first experiences of giving something when it is expected. Moving them at the wrong time and place, on the other hand, constitutes one of his early aggressive gestures. The function of elimination is therefore mixed up with problems of giving or retaining and with problems of conforming or rebelling. Just as the desire for affection and support retains in later life the power to activate the digestive process, so the desire to express angry contempt, for instance, keeps its power to activate untimely and spasmodic movement of the bowels. Similarly the wish to be autonomous and free from the demands of others retains the power to affect the colon so that feces are not passed. Alexander's early views were an extension of his theories in regard to peptic ulcer. When a tendency is suppressed by circumstance or repressed because of anxiety, it may activate some autonomic pathway with which it was connected earlier in life.

As was the case with peptic ulcer, however, many workers are unwilling to assign so much weight to the symbolic meaning of the symptoms. A less speculative approach is represented in the work of White, Cobb, and Jones, who studied sixty patients suffering from mucous colitis.[27] This particular form of eliminative disturbance usually begins with chronic constipation which later passes over into diarrhea, generally of a painful character and accompanied by excessive secretion of mucous in the colon. The condition seems to be provoked by chronic overaction of the parasympathetic pathways which govern the colon. It has not proved possible to produce colitis by direct stimulation of parasympathetic fibers, but there is strong indirect evidence for their overactivity. The authors showed that mucous colitis patients had little in common in the way of physique but were alike in exhibiting marked emotional tension. "The three emotions, anxiety, guilt, and resentment are those most commonly associated with tension in patients with mucous colitis."[28] The patients were generally overconscientious, dependent on the opinion of others, easily thrown into a state of guilt. Acts of injustice to themselves or others filled them with resentment which brought guilt in its train. Of particular importance was the tendency toward rigid, obsessive thinking which led to long periods of brooding preoccupation. This constant preoccupation was presumed to be responsible for the prolonged tension and hence for the action of the parasympathetic system on the colon.

[27] B. V. White, S. Cobb, and C. M. Jones, "Mucous Colitis: A Psychological Medical Study of Sixty Cases," *Psychosomatic Medicine Monographs*, I (1939).
[28] *Ibid.*, p. 95.

ESSENTIAL HYPERTENSION

It was stated earlier that not all the problems of psychosomatic research could be examined in connection with gastro-intestinal disturbances. In the remainder of this chapter we shall briefly describe two forms of psychosomatic disorder, both of which bring up important new points.

Nature of the Disorder. The term "hypertension" does not refer to general tenseness but rather to the specific symptom of high blood pressure. Chronic elevation of blood pressure can result from various organic conditions, especially diseases of the blood vessels and of the kidneys. Hypertension is called "essential" only in those cases which prove to be free from organic disease. In such cases there is a presumption that the hypertension is being maintained by continuing action of those sympathetic nerves which have the function of accelerating the heart and constricting the blood vessels. Hypertension can create unpleasant symptoms such as headache and dizziness; if prolonged, it may lead to fatal vascular accidents or cardiac failure. These dangers can be averted by radical surgery in which the sympathetic fibers to the heart are cut. This operation allows the patient to lead a fairly normal life, but he has to observe certain restrictions in regard to effort; his heart rate can no longer be much increased to meet extra demands.

There is no apparent organic cause for essential hypertension. The sole pathological feature is the chronic overactivity of the sympathetic nerves that control blood pressure. This opens the way for a psychosomatic hypothesis. Constant vasoconstriction and acceleration of the heart might result from an enduring state of emotional tension. The emotion of anger immediately seems implicated, inasmuch as rage produces precisely this effect on the circulatory system. If something were wrong in the patient's management of aggression, this might tend to produce a state of chronic hypertension.

Evidence for a Specific Emotional Constellation. A psychoanalytic study of cases of essential hypertension was reported by Saul.[29] Based on seven cases, it must be accepted as a strictly preliminary study, but it revealed certain psychological patterns that were common to all the patients. In all cases there was at least one parent who took a very dominating attitude. The patient responded with submissiveness and even with considerable dependence. This submissiveness became characteristic of all his important relationships, but was always a cause of annoyance to him. A state of constant hostile but unsuccessful rebellion was the result. Occasionally there would be outbursts of overt rebellion, but

[29] L. J. Saul, "Hostility in Cases of Essential Hypertension," *Psychosomatic Medicine,* I (1939), pp. 153–61. Reprinted in Tomkins, *op. cit.,* chap. xiv.

these were difficult to sustain because of the guilt feelings they engendered. As Saul puts it, "These patients were neither passive and dependent nor hostile and aggressive. They could give in to neither trend. During periods when they could and did, their blood pressures were markedly lower."

As an example we may take the case of Miss D., a woman in her early twenties, who was the breadwinner for her widowed mother and younger sisters. Of quiet and gentle manner, she sacrificed her own life and pleasure to care for the rest of the family and put her sisters through college. When she was at home her relation to her mother was highly dependent. The mother fed her and cared for her, yet her longing exceeded the supply and her dreams harped on the theme of being fed by her mother. At the same time she was aware of a bitter resentment against her submission to the mother and had to be careful to control her hostile feelings. Even harder to conceal were her violent feelings of anger against her boss. Several times a day at the office she was likely to boil with rage at his inconsiderate behavior and arbitrary ways. Her blood pressure was constantly elevated.

Another of Saul's cases, Mr. B., in early middle age was a model citizen and a compliant subordinate in business. Both parents had been domineering, creating in him a dependent and submissive attitude. Mr. B. was aware of a furious desire to defy his boss and rebel against his own submissiveness, but he never dared express even a hint of this lest he lose the esteem of his boss and business associates. Mr. B. found an occasional outlet in solitary drinking followed by a search for promiscuous sexual relationships. These attacks of rebellion always followed some situation in which he submitted when he wanted to show defiance. His escapades gave him no real satisfaction and did not serve to lower his chronic high blood pressure.

The problem of hypertension has been studied with a larger number of cases by Binger and co-workers.[30] The findings are not necessarily inconsistent with those obtained by Saul, although the authors offer their results in a considerably more tentative spirit. In general their hypertensive patients exhibited a group of characteristics that might be gathered under the headings of social maladjustment and timidity. Their social activities were restricted, their sexual interests were poorly developed, and they tended to be uncomfortable and submissive in the presence of others. They were somewhat reserved and detached, somewhat fearful, inclined to feel weak and defenseless. This pattern of char-

[30] C. A. Binger, N. W. Ackerman, A. E. Cohn, H. A. Schroeder, and J. M. Steele, "Personality in Arterial Hypertension," *Psychosomatic Medicine Monographs,* VIII (1945).

acteristics could easily lend itself to conflict between resentful feelings and fear of expressing them.

Status of the Hostile Impulses. Saul has advanced an interesting hypothesis concerning hostility in his hypertensive patients. In spite of their generally gentle outward manner, his patients suffered from intense and chronic anger. Inside, they boiled with rage. Their anger was strongly inhibited, but it was in no sense repressed. All the patients were well aware of their rebellious hostility, recognizing it clearly even though they controlled it. This was a unique feature of the psychological impasse in which the patients found themselves. They seemed unable to reach a solution either by expressing the hostility more openly or suppressing it more firmly in favor of dependent tendencies. Saul raises the question whether this curious midway position of the hostile impulses, neither expressed nor repressed, might be the specific feature that produces essential hypertension. In itself there is nothing unique about a conflict between dependent submission and hostility. The conflict can be solved in various ways, such as avoiding situations that evoke submissive behavior, expressing the rebellion more openly, or repressing the hostility more deeply so that it manifests itself, if at all, in neurotic symptoms rather than a psychosomatic disorder. It is only this particular constellation that is found associated with essential hypertension: a double blocking in which the patient submits but is never reconciled to submitting, feels furious but never discharges his fury.

These studies suggest a new aspect of psychosomatic relationships. Perhaps the type of hypothesis advanced to explain essential hypertension will be found to have a more general significance. It may be that in looking for a specific emotional constellation to go with each form of disorder one should not rest content with describing the impulses and defenses that are involved; one should rather pay particular attention to the status of the impulses. Are some of them trapped in a midway position between being expressed and being repressed? Is it specifically this status of an impulse that allows it to activate autonomic pathways and spill its trapped energies into the viscera? If this way of looking at the problem were extended to Alexander's theory in regard to peptic ulcer, one would have to examine carefully the status of the dependent longings. Do they activate the digestive processes when they are suppressed but not deeply repressed? There are at present no factual answers to these questions, and it is of course a difficult matter to define and determine the status of an impulse. We raise the questions here not because they can as yet be answered but because they clearly deserve consideration in the theory of psychosomatic disorders.

BRONCHIAL ASTHMA

The suggestion that asthma may sometimes be a psychosomatic disorder is often met with immediate opposition. Asthma is one of the fields in which medicine has in recent years scored a triumph. Many chronic asthmatics have been given allergy tests, found allergic to certain common substances, and cured by regular inoculation with these substances. When there is chronic asthma without discoverable allergic sensitivity, it is at least as reasonable to suggest that an undiscovered allergen is provoking the attacks as it is to assume emotional factors. It is sometimes observed, moreover, that a tendency to asthma runs in families, suggesting an inherent structural weakness or innate sensitivity of the breathing apparatus. In the face of these facts one should not assume that asthma can be psychogenic unless the claim can be supported by very strong evidence.

There is certainly no ground for assuming psychogenesis in all or even in a majority of asthma cases. Evidence exists, however, that in certain cases the breathing difficulty has become curiously linked to emotional problems. The central piece of evidence is that asthmatic attacks occur in these cases in a specific type of emotional situation. Otherwise there is no regularity and no lawfulness in the occurrence of the attacks. When the attacks are thus regularly associated with a certain emotional situation and not regularly associated with anything else, one is justified in assuming that the disorder is psychosomatic.

Emotional Precipitation of Asthma Attacks. The results of psychoanalysis with twenty-four patients who suffered from bronchial asthma were reported by French.[31] In all of these cases allergy played a part. Outwardly the patients presented a wide variety of personality patterns, and many of them were seeking treatment for problems other than asthma. The first method of approach was therefore to notice with great care the situations that preceded those asthmatic attacks which occurred during the period when treatment was going on. There proved to be considerable regularity in these incidents. Even dreams from which the patients awakened wheezing dealt with similar situations. "In each case," French states, "the patient is exposed to a temptation which would estrange him from a parental figure, usually the mother." Further study showed that the temptation was generally of a sexual character. In the male patients it was typical to find that the mother had been overprotective, binding the child in a dependent relation, yet sternly thwarting any behavior that had a remotely erotic character. In the female

[31] T. M. French, "Psychogenic Factors in Asthma," *American Journal of Psychiatry*, XCVI (1939), pp. 87–101. Reprinted in Tomkins, *op. cit.*, chap. xiii.

patients there were recollections of childlike sexual interest in the father which seemed to have been permitted by him but vigorously suppressed by the mother. Thus sex became closely linked with losing the mother's love. It was the cardinal sin; it meant maternal rejection.

Detailed study of the patients led French to conclude that the problem of separation from the mother played an important part in all their lives. "The common feature," he writes, "in the otherwise divergent personalities of our asthma patients is the fact that the personality of these patients is built up in large part around the task of mastering by one means or another the patient's fear of being separated from the mother." When this dread event threatens, there is a sharp mobilization of anxiety. It is also true of these patients that they show a strong urge to maintain the maternal bond by promptly confessing their evil thoughts and thus asking forgiveness. A male patient, for instance, was seduced by a girl, but before the situation reached its logical climax he rushed home to his mother to confess the episode. With most patients, however, situations of this kind lead to a severe block. Sexual temptation is felt to endanger the mother's love, yet just because it is sexual it cannot be confessed. To control his anxiety the patient wants to confess, cry, and obtain forgiveness, but this impulse is balanced by equal anxiety lest the mother become angry and reject the patient anyway.

French believes this to be the specific situation that precipitates an attack of asthma. The urge to confess and cry, itself driven by anxiety, is blocked by an equal anxiety lest the confession be rejected. The asthmatic wheezing can be interpreted as a blocked cry. Instances were observed in which an asthma attack turned into crying, at which point the asthmatic manifestations ceased. It seems likely that a blocked cry can set off an asthmatic reaction only with the help of previous allergic sensitivity. The reaction must be first prepared, so to speak, on an allergic basis if it is to be available as a substitute for inhibited crying. The exact mechanism still remains to be worked out. French reports, however, that "in a number of patients" the attacks were "greatly relieved" by analytic therapy. They gave place to a willingness to cry, and this was followed by a lessening of the fear connected with sexual temptation.

Emotional Constellation and Choice of Symptom. The personality pattern in asthma patients has been investigated in a different way by Rubin and Moses.[32] These workers studied the life histories and behavior of fifty-four male cases of bronchial asthma. They also studied the electroencephalographs of the same patients. Previous work with the latter technique has shown considerable individual differences in the propor-

[32] S. Rubin and L. Moses, "Electroencephalographic Studies in Asthma with Some Personality Correlates," *Psychosomatic Medicine,* VI (1944), pp. 31–39.

tion of alpha waves (10 per second) to faster waves. A dominant alpha record, one in which the slower waves are extremely prominent, is associated with a passive and dependent personality structure. Rubin and Moses found three times as many dominant alpha records in their group of asthmatics as would be obtained from a normal control group. The personality data were entirely harmonious with this finding. The asthmatics displayed a "single fairly definite personality constellation" marked by passive dependence and a history of maternal overprotection and dominance. The patients "have not cared for, striven for, or gained any marked degree of independence in life and continue to seek care and protection from the environment."

These findings fit well with French's hypothesis, but one notices that much the same description would fit the majority of peptic ulcer patients. Draper's constitutional studies represent the ulcer patient to be very similar to this account of the asthma patient. Those ulcer patients, of course, who develop a vigorous reaction formation against dependence behave in a different fashion. But dominant alpha records are obtained in about three quarters of ulcer patients.[33] Many ulcer patients are passive dependent individuals like many asthma patients, yet they do not have the same psychosomatic disorder. One way to meet this dilemma is to follow French in specifying the emotional constellation in great detail. The relationship with the mother that is contained in French's hypothesis is not merely one of passive dependence. It has little to do with being cared for or fed. The central need is to enjoy the mother's confidence and companionship; the central danger is that she will be angry, distant, and unaffectionate, as if her feelings were hurt because the child turned to enterprises of his own. The theme is sin and forgiveness, not deprivation and feeding. By this kind of refined analysis it might be possible to specify a theme for each kind of psychosomatic disorder. This very specificity, however, seems to be the point on which research workers find it difficult to agree. Miller and Baruch, for example, while confirming French in some respects, change the theme significantly by emphasizing the asthmatic child's hostility toward a rejecting mother.[34] Long and others change it by emphasizing the child's wish for closeness and "the mother's wish to maintain the child in an infantile dependent state," an emotional problem that can hardly be distinguished from the one which prevails in school phobias.[35] Knapp and Nemetz strike a final blow at specificity by reporting that while personality dis-

[33] Rubin and Bowman, *op. cit.*

[34] H. Miller and D. W. Baruch, "A Study of Hostility in Allergic Children," *American Journal of Orthopsychiatry,* XX (1950), pp. 506–19.

[35] R. T. Long *et al.*, "A Psychosomatic Study of Allergic and Emotional Factors in Children with Asthma," *American Journal of Psychiatry,* CXIV (1958), pp. 890–99.

turbances of some kind are the rule, there is no single type of disturbance that is characteristic of all their asthmatic patients.[36]

PROBLEM OF SYMPTOM PLACEMENT

Having examined several varieties of psychosomatic disorder, we are in a position to reconsider the difficult and critical problem of symptom placement. In a way the problem is similar to that of the choice of neurosis, but in psychosomatic disorders the chain of events is longer, extending into the domain of the autonomic nervous system and of bodily physiology. Early in this chapter we set up as guide posts two relatively simple hypotheses concerning the placement of psychosomatic dysfunctions. One of these hypotheses invoked constitutional differences and stated in effect that a disorder would make its appearance in the weakest or most vulnerable organ system. The other, the specificity hypothesis, stated that each variety of psychosomatic disorder resulted from a specific emotional constellation which affected the autonomic system in a particular way. The facts we have examined make it clear that neither hypothesis can stand in simple and sovereign form. The easy models that appeal to our need for simplification do not seem to fit this particular segment of reality.

Take first the specificity hypothesis. Certain connections of a quite general nature have been confirmed by several different researches, but the attempt to correlate highly specific emotional constellations with particular disorders has led to little agreement. There is much support for the view that suppressed hostility is the leading emotional problem in essential hypertension, that thwarted passive dependent feelings are prominent in peptic ulcer, and that dependence also obtrudes itself in patients with bronchial asthma. These general associations, however, do not carry us far toward explaining the location of symptoms. As we include more kinds of disorder we begin to run out of broad emotional constellations to distinguish them. Dependence, passivity, guilt, and aggression recur with monotonous frequency, so much so that one worker has proposed to simplify the whole problem by means of the formula that all psychosomatic patients are immature, inadequate people who have failed to achieve independence and an adult channeling of aggression.[37] The explanatory power of these general associations is further weakened by complications such as the evidence obtained by Szasz and by Margolin that hostile feelings as well as dependent ones can activate the kind of digestive processes that lead to ulcers.

[36] P. H. Knapp and S. J. Nemetz, "Personality Variations in Bronchial Asthmatics," *Psychosomatic Medicine,* XIX (1957), pp. 443–65.

[37] J. Ruesch, "The Infantile Personality—the Core Problem of Psychosomatic Medicine," *Psychosomatic Medicine,* X (1948), pp. 134–44.

The specificity hypothesis would be much stronger if regular connections could be demonstrated between psychosomatic symptoms and emotional constellations of a highly differentiated kind. We have examined three such attempts: Alexander's relating of peptic ulcer to repressed dependence and outward self-sufficiency, Saul's relating of hypertension to a drawn battle between hostility and submissiveness, and French's equating of the asthmatic attack with a suppressed cry for the mother's love when some impulse in the patient threatens to sever this bond. French's and Saul's hypotheses have won some assent, but Alexander's explanation has proved too specific to cover all cases, and we must also bear in mind the great variety of constellations found in patients with anorexia nervosa, a situation that is typical for several other kinds of disorder. Whatever the fate of these highly specific proposals, one point is of great importance: the present constellation and its autonomic associations are decidedly childlike and must have originated quite early in life.

Take next the constitutional hypothesis. The work of Draper indicates some association between physical type and disease type. French doubted that an emotional constellation could be responsible for asthmatic attacks without the help of allergic sensitization. Alexander came to believe that the peptic ulcer syndrome occurred only when psychological and constitutional factors joined their forces. Various experimental studies bear on the question of individual differences in the patterns of autonomic response. Of particular relevance is a report by Lacey and Van Lehn, who studied a group of normal children at the Fels Institute.[38] Each child was given the cold pressor test, in which a lively autonomic response is evoked by immersing the hand for one minute in painfully cold water. Autonomic activity was measured in several ways, including blood pressure, heart rate, and perspiration. It was found that the children exhibited characteristic individual profiles of autonomic reaction, and that these profiles could be reproduced through a later administration of the test. There seems to be, in other words, a hierarchy of autonomic responses which is stably characteristic of each individual so that it can be referred to as his "autonomic constitution." With one child the response to stress may be most conspicuous in heart rate, with another in peripheral blood pressure, with another in perspiration, and so on.[39] Research with psychosomatic patients does not supply such tell-

[38] J. I. Lacey and R. Van Lehn, "Differential Emphasis in Somatic Response to Stress," *Psychosomatic Medicine,* XIV (1952), pp. 71–81.

[39] E. L. Lipton, A. Steinschneider, and J. B. Richmond, "Autonomic Function in the Neonate. II. Physiological Effects of Motor Restraint," *Psychosomatic Medicine,* XXII (1960), pp. 57–65; A. Thomas, S. Chess, H. Birch, and M. E. Hertzig, "A Longitudinal Study of Primary Reaction Patterns in Children," *Comprehensive Psychiatry,* I (1960), pp. 103–12.

ing evidence of early individual differences, but it yields results of the same kind. Cardiovascular patients, for example, respond to laboratory stress situations with predominant cardiovascular changes and little change in muscular tension, whereas patients complaining of head and neck pains react to the very same stress with marked muscular tension and little change in the cardiovascular system.[40]

There is no reason to doubt the existence of individual differences in the pattern of autonomic responses under stress, and there is no reason why we should hesitate to believe that some of them are innately determined. Constitution, however, does not operate in a vacuum. Almost at once it manifests itself in the child's behavior and affects the responses of others to him. This point has been worked out by Mirsky in connection with differences in the general level of gastric activity.[41] If an infant has very intense oral needs, his feeding demands may seem exorbitant even to a normally nurturing mother, especially if she has had other less greedy babies, and a relationship may be set up in which oral satisfaction is never complete. Constitution, in short, exerts much of its effect on the transactions that take place between the child and his early human environment.

It will be observed that both lines of our inquiry have arrived at the same point. On the one hand, we have been forced back from adult emotional constellations to the early childhood conditioning of autonomic patterns; on the other hand, we have been forced forward from innate differences to the effect these differences may have on the conditioning of autonomic patterns in the child's early environment. The spotlight turns to the first year or two of life, and this is exactly where we should look, according to Grinker, if we hope to unravel the secrets of psychosomatic disorders.[42]

Grinker's exposition of this theme starts from the observation that the newborn child shows very little differentiation of responses to stress. The frustrated infant "functions with everything it has available": crying, salivating, regurgitating, defecating, thrashing, becoming red in the face. The first protective response is a mass response. Differentiation of autonomic patterns soon starts, however, and may have advanced a long way before the child emerges from his preverbal life of feeling into more

[40] R. B. Malmo, C. Shagass, and F. H. Davis, in *Life Stress and Bodily Disease* (Baltimore: The Williams & Wilkins Co., 1950), pp. 231–62. J. Schachter, "Pain, Fear and Anger in Hypertensives and Normatensives," *Psychosomatic Medicine*, XIX (1957), pp. 17–29.

[41] I. A. Mirsky, S. Kaplan, and R. Bro-Kahn, "Pepsinogen Excretion (Uropepsin) as Index of Influence of Various Life Situations on Gastric Secretions," *Proceedings of the Association for Research in Nervous and Mental Disease,* XXIX (1950), pp. 628–46.

[42] R. R. Grinker, *Psychosomatic Research* (New York: W. W. Norton & Co., Inc., 1953), especially chaps. v–vii.

organized psychological patterns. Sometimes early infections or enzyme deficiencies begin the process of accentuating some and suppressing other parts of the autonomic repertory. This process is in any event strongly influenced by the atmosphere of the nursery, the circumstances of feeding, the manner in which training is carried out, the use of diets, laxatives, enemas, and special medications, in fact by anything that tends to subdue some functions and overload others. The result of all this early conditioning can be observed in many ways, but the adult anxiety response furnishes a particularly good example. Each individual has his own particular way of feeling anxious, no matter what the nature of the threat. With some people there are sinking abdominal sensations, with others shortness of breath, with others diarrhea, with others vomiting, with others palpitations, and so on through hundreds of variations. The general protective reaction has become individualized through conditioning in early childhood.

On this basis it becomes possible to explain the wide variety of organ systems that becomes involved in psychosomatic disorders. As a consequence, illness finally occurs in those elements of the bodily reaction that have been most accentuated in the course of early childhood conditioning. This explanation differs from the hypothesis of specific emotional constellations in attaching less psychological weight to the current symptom. Today's asthmatic attack does not mean that the patient is in conflict precisely over the issue of acting on an impulse or confessing it to his mother. It means that this was once a vital issue, that bronchial constriction became an accented part of the reaction to stress, and that now any prolonged reaction to stress is likely to culminate in asthmatic symptoms. Specific emotional constellations may have existed in childhood at the time when autonomic patterns were being differentiated and conditioned. Present problems *may be* very similar to the original ones, but they *do not have to be* in order to produce the symptom. All that is needed is prolonged stress. The historically conditioned autonomic patterns will do the rest.

It is not surprising, in view of this, that rather modest therapeutic results have been reported when standard psychoanalysis was used. The alteration of childhood autonomic patterns cannot really be expected. They are something with which the patient must learn to live. Marked benefit can result from freeing blocked impulses like the hypertensive's simmering anger or the asthmatic's desire to cry; furthermore, the patient can learn to perceive threats in a more conscious, discriminating way that makes them less threatening. It is probably through such changes that the reported cures by psychotherapy actually come about. This does not require a deep, "uncovering" technique, but it does call for a skilled and sensitive use of more superficial measures. In a program of this kind the boon of relief from symptoms can be expected for about two patients out of three.[43]

IMPLICATIONS FOR GENERAL MEDICINE

Psychosomatic research raises far-reaching problems and carries radical implications as regards the general practice of medicine. How many of the supposedly bodily ailments that bring patients to the office of the general practitioner are really based on emotional maladjustment? There is no telling, but many conservative observers are putting their estimates as high as fifty per cent. A new meaning is being given to the old ideal of a sound mind in a sound body. Two generations ago the implication of this phrase was that you could not have a sound mind unless you had a sound body. Today we begin to wonder whether it is possible to have a sound body unless you have a sound mind—or, as we would be more likely to say, unless you have a sound emotional adjustment. For the general practitioner and family physician this is a startling change. Possibly half the time he is dealing with emotional maladjustments that have come to some kind of bodily focus.

It is foolish to exaggerate the psychogenic point of view. A doctor would be stupid to diagnose a case of high blood pressure as psychogenic without making thorough tests for kidney, vascular, and other possible organic disorders. Equally foolish would be a recommendation of psychotherapy for asthma without making skin tests or taking a history of seasonal and geographical variations in the attacks. When we speak of psychosomatic disorders we do not mean that the somatic part of the disturbance has ceased to be important. The phrase implies only that the psychological aspect may also be important.

The general pracitioner is at present neither well trained nor well situated to practice psychotherapy. Patients do not currently expect their physician to advise in other than strictly bodily matters and might well resent it if he seemed to be meddling in their "private affairs." These expectations will change slowly, and the doctor must always respect them. Furthermore, the training of physicians does not generally include a sufficient background in psychology to warrant their meddling in the realm of emotional adjustment. More harm than good is done by the doctor who, having excelled in chemistry and learned to regard a patient as a complex piece of machinery, leans back in his chair and tells the piece of machinery how to lead its life. Psychotherapy is a difficult art that calls for practiced skill. Some psychiatrists believe, however, that it is both possible and necessary to train the general physician along this line. In any event it is important that he recognize the patient's emotional

[43] Cobb. *op. cit.*, pp. 145–47.

maladjustments and show the patient that bodily changes can be closely related to emotions. He must not, as so often happens now, encourage the psychosomatic patient to sink into a routine of invalidism and medication if there is a chance that his emotional adjustment can improve. The physician must be capable of psychosomatic diagnosis. He must know when and how to refer a patient for psychotherapy, just as he knows when to send him for any other kind of specialized treatment. He should be able to understand not only his patient's bodily economy but also his economy of happiness.

Psychosomatic medicine opens up the area where mind and body overlap, where it is no longer possible to distinguish between them. The physician of the future, whether he be general practitioner, specialist, or research worker, must be a psychosomatic physician. He must be able to describe with equal precision the tissue changes in organs, the neural pathways, and the emotional constellations that may have sent traffic over the neural pathways. The physician will be forced more and more to take account of man's emotional nature.

SUGGESTIONS FOR FURTHER READING

A critical and stimulating appraisal of current psychosomatic concepts will be found in *Psychosomatic Research* by Roy R. Grinker (New York, W. W. Norton & Co., Inc., 1953). An emphasis on experimentally observed effects of stress and an exposition of the concept of protective reaction patterns marks the essay by Harold G. Wolff entitled *Stress and Disease* (Springfield, Ill., Charles C. Thomas, 1953). Stanley Cobb's *Emotions and Clinical Medicine* (New York, W. W. Norton & Co., Inc., 1950) is particularly strong on the anatomy and physiology of emotions. Six excellent journal articles are reprinted in S. S. Tompkins' *Contemporary Psychopathology* (Cambridge, Harvard University Press, 1943), Chs. 8–11, 13–14. Most of these papers have been referred to in the text of this chapter. A systematic survey of psychosomatic disorders is to be found in *Psychosomatic Medicine* by E. Weiss and O. S. English (2d ed., Philadelphia, W. B. Saunders Co., 1949). An interesting array of cases has been brought together by H. H. W. Miles, S. Cobb, and H. C. Shands in *Case Histories in Psychosomatic Medicine* (New York, W. W. Norton & Co., Inc., 1952). Therese Benedek's *Studies in Psychosomatic Medicine—Psychosexual Functions in Women* (New York, The Ronald Press Co., 1952) describes important studies concerning the relation of hormonal changes to emotional and sexual response in women.

12

Effects of Injuries and Abnormal Conditions in the Brain

In our clinical introduction we made the acquaintance of a patient with a severe brain disorder. The case of Martha Ottenby formed a sharp contrast with those patients whose disorders arose from personal problems. She was the victim of a disease, an impersonal affliction that struck her without the slightest relation to her emotional adjustments or her economy of happiness. In studying psychosomatic disorders we saw that it is possible for a bodily dysfunction to come as the result of chronic emotional maladjustment. We now turn our attention to disorders in which the situation is chronologically reversed. Disordered behavior, disordered emotions, disordered mental processes come as the result of bodily dysfunction that directly affects the nervous system. The trouble starts in neural tissue; the psychological changes are secondary. The cause lies in certain states of the body, and the cure, if any exists, must be effected by somatic rather than psychological therapy.

The disorders to be discussed in this chapter depend directly upon somatic dysfunction, but they nevertheless bring us to some new and fascinating aspects of mental activity. Maladjusted and neurotic people are disordered as regards their feelings and human relationships, but they do not differ from the normal in their manner of perception or mode of thought. Anxiety and defense may serve to distort in certain ways the neurotic's conception of the world and of his fellow men, but this is the result of a persistent selection of experience rather than an alteration in the mechanics of understanding. Thus far in our study we have concentrated chiefly on *psychodynamics.* We have been concerned with abnormalities in that part of the learning process whereby the individual attempts to adjust his needs and his security to the demands of socialized living. Abnormal psychology does not end with the study of abnormal psychodynamics. It includes the *mental and behavioral changes* that result from injuries or other abnormal conditions in the nervous system. These changes have to be described and measured, which is in itself no small undertaking. Then they have to be related insofar as possible to changes, either general or local, in the central nervous system.

VARIETIES OF PATHOLOGICAL PROCESS

What mishaps can befall the central nervous system, especially the brain? Encased within bony walls, the brain, like the spinal cord, is protected against certain obvious hazards. But it is by no means immune to injury or to internal conditions that impair its proper functioning. By way of initial orientation we shall quickly survey the pathological processes that affect brain activity.

Survey of Pathological Processes. The first possibility is an inadequate development of brain tissue, technically called *aplasia.* Occasionally a child is born with almost no development of the cerebral cortex, a truly rudimentary brain. In cases of less severe defect the brain may be completely formed but of smaller than average size and with less well-marked convolutions, suggesting a primitiveness of structure. One variety of severe mental defect, microcephaly, is characterized by a greatly diminished size of the upper skull; within this constricted space the brain is small and poorly developed. In mongoloid deficiency the abnormality in the shape of the head is less marked, though still distinctive, and the brain shows few obvious structural defects, but mental performance is sluggish and rarely rises above the imbecile level. These severe shortcomings in development can be regarded as sporadic accidents caused by faulty growth of the embryo. They do not seem to run in families. In contrast, there is a strong familial tendency in the higher grades of feeblemindedness lying in the I.Q. range from 50 to 80. In these cases the brain shows no structural defect, but either a structural or a biochemical abnormality must be assumed in order to explain the inheritable character of the condition.

Next on the list of cerebral mishaps is *trauma,* some direct physical injury to brain tissue. The head and the underlying cerebral tissue may be traumatized at the time of birth if the labor is extremely prolonged and difficult, so that the head is exposed to severe pressure. Any severe blow on the head may produce swelling and injury of brain tissue. Most children, of course, fall on their heads from time to time without damage, but occasionally one of these accidents produces temporary and even permanent brain injury. If the skull is fractured, and especially if brain tissue is penetrated as is the case in bullet or shrapnel wounds, a marked change in mental performance may result. Even when the wounds heal there may be atrophy and scar formation in the brain which impairs its normal functioning. Another form of direct injury is caused by *cerebral tumors.* As a tumor grows, it crowds and distorts the surrounding brain tissue. Up to a certain point, especially if the growth is slow, the brain tissue can adapt itself to the change without functional impairment, but eventually the crowding prevents normal metabolism in the nerve cells.

The nervous system may become the seat of *infection* by micro-organisms. Certain not very common forms of illness such as encephalitis lethargica (epidemic "sleeping sickness") represent an inflammation of cerebral tissue resulting from infection. In the first chapter of this book we used another infectious disease, general paresis, as an example of the somatogenic disorders. Although resistant to most varieties of infection, brain tissue has certain susceptibilities that may lead to serious damage.

The functioning of the brain can be disturbed by unfavorable alterations in its internal environment. The maintenance of an internal condition that is optimal for cerebral functioning is part of the general process of homeostasis. *Metabolic disorders* may throw out the balance in one way or another so that optimal functioning is impaired. Certain endocrine disorders, for instance, especially those affecting the thyroid gland, bear a direct relation to mood, initiative, and intelligence. Furthermore, recent research has shown that vitamin deficiency plays a part in certain kinds of mental disorder. The internal environment can also be altered by the action of *toxins* or poisons. The toxic effects of excessive alcohol come under most frequent observation, but analogous changes result from opium and its derivatives, certain metals like lead, and certain gases like carbon monoxide. *Shortage of oxygen* has a marked effect on mental activity and may permanently injure the nervous system. *High fever* produces a gross though temporary interference with normal brain activity that is reflected in the mental state of delirium.

Finally, the central nervous system is subject to *degenerative changes.* Usually these are associated with old age, but sometimes, as in Pick's disease (from which Martha Ottenby suffered) and the rather similar Alzheimer's disease, changes of an apparently degenerative character begin in middle life. Sometimes a thickening and hardening of the arterial walls is at fault (cerebral arteriosclerosis), so that the supply of blood to the brain cells becomes progressively less adequate. A nutritional deficiency in brain tissue can probably be assumed even when the arteries are not radically hardened. Much remains to be learned about the cerebral changes that go with old age, but there is little doubt that these changes play the predominant part in the mental disorders of later life.

Classification of Pathological Processes. The foregoing survey shows that the brain is exposed to numerous and diverse ailments. The concept of somatogenesis begins to need further refinement. Cobb has proposed that somatogenesis be broken down into three parts according to the character of the bodily disorder.[1] These subdivisions are called *genogenic, histogenic,* and *chemogenic.* The psychogenic factor remains as a fourth category.

1. *Genogenic disorders* have their source in the genes. The less severe forms of mental retardation have already been mentioned as showing familial trends, and the same seems to be true of epilepsy. There is considerable evidence for some kind of genogenic contribution in the manic-depressive and schizophrenic psychoses. The evidence for genogenic influences has to be sought, for the most part, in statistical studies bearing on familial trends. Recently, however, there has been remarkable progress in the microscopic study of genes, making it possible to detect abnormalities in the number and arrangement of genes in certain forms of disordered behavior.

2. *Histogenic disorders* are those in which the predominant part is played by nonhereditary lesions of the nervous system. Here belong the disorders that result from trauma, from cerebral tumor, from infection with resulting inflammation, and from degenerative changes. In these disorders the abnormality in the nervous tissues is sufficiently great to be either grossly or at least microscopically visible. The term *histogenic* is derived from histology, the branch of biological science that deals with the structure of tissues.

3. *Chemogenic disorders* have their origin in the effects of chemical agents on the nervous system. Too much or too little of some substance upsets the chemical balance of nervous tissue. In this category belong the metabolic disorders and the disorders that result from toxins or poisons. The classification is admittedly arbitrary. Some toxins and metabolic disorders produce visible lesions of nervous tissue, while some inflammations are believed to create chemical products that progressively injure neighboring tissues. But this difficulty can be settled by considering primacy—when the chemical action comes first the resulting disorders may be classed as chemogenic.

Overlap in classifications is to be expected. Cobb's three headings are not intended to represent exclusive categories. They should rather be conceived as component factors in the total somatogenic process. No

[1] S. Cobb, *Borderlands of Psychiatry* (Cambridge: Harvard University Press, 1943), pp. 20–21.

disorder, strictly speaking, can be assigned to a single category; it can be *weighted* with respect to all three, and also, of course, with respect to psychogenic factors. Future research will very likely improve and refine this classification. In the meantime it is convenient.

Plan of the Next Two Chapters. If this book were a textbook in psychiatry, intended to train medical students to meet their manifest professional obligations, it would be necessary at this point to embark upon a detailed description of the organic psychoses. There are many varieties, subvarieties, and cross-varieties of these disorders. Most of them occur infrequently, but the psychiatrist must be in a position to recognize them and establish a differential diagnosis. The student of abnormal psychology is in a more fortunate position. It is his privilege to select those disorders which are most instructive, which have the most to teach him as regards mental processes and their cerebral correlates. Not yet in professional training, he can afford to concentrate on topics that will most effectively contribute to his understanding of disordered personal reactions, thus ultimately to his understanding of human nature.

This privilege is reflected in the plan of this chapter and the next. We shall first examine rather briefly some examples of chemogenic disorder. This section will illustrate the general notion of the internal environment and its effect on brain activity. Then we shall consider in much greater detail the effects of brain injury. Although brain injuries are not particularly common, they have recently been investigated by ingenious new methods, and the use of brain surgery in the treatment of certain forms of mental disorder has yielded further important information. In the following chapter we shall take up some common symptom syndromes of cerebral disorder: mental retardation, epilepsy, general paresis, and the disorders that come with old age.

SOME EXAMPLES OF CHEMOGENIC DISORDER

Effects of Anoxia. Nervous tissue is highly dependent upon oxygen. Complete deprivation of oxygen, even for a few seconds, causes irreparable damage to nerve cells, especially to those in the brain. Partial deprivation produces less drastic effects which are nevertheless of great practical importance to mountain climbers and airmen who operate at altitudes where the supply of oxygen is markedly reduced. Experiments on the effects of anoxia have been conducted at high altitudes and, more conveniently, in specially built chambers in which the concentration of oxygen can be controlled. As the oxygen content of inspired air is diminished, a fairly regular sequence of changes takes place. According to

McFarland and his associates, these are as follows.[2] First comes a loss of self-criticism and judgment. Sometimes this is accompanied by feelings of exhilaration similar to those produced by mild alcoholic intoxication. Attention and concentration then begin to show impairment, and the speed and accuracy of mental work decline; scores on mental tests fall off. Motor and sensory performances resist somewhat longer, but as the anoxia increases there is a loss in such skilled acts as handwriting and an impairment of visual and auditory perception. Ultimately there is loss of consciousness.

The effects of long-continued low-grade anoxia are less clearly established. People who live for a long time at high altitudes usually become acclimatized, but there are individual differences in this compensation. Certain individuals become irritable, get along badly with their companions, suffer mild feelings of depression, and experience difficulty in concentrating on mental tasks.[3] With a return to lower altitude the symptoms disappear. There has been considerable discussion as to whether or not the cumulative effects of slight anoxia cause a loss of efficiency in airplane pilots after years of service. Opinions differ, but it appears unlikely that mild anoxia leaves permanent effects. Severe deprivation of oxygen, however, undoubtedly injures brain tissue. Destruction of brain tissue has been revealed at autopsy in cases of fatal poisoning by carbon monoxide.[4]

These observations on the effects of anoxia show the close dependence of the brain on its internal environment. The energy needed to keep brain cells going is obtained from the oxidation of glucose, with the help of enzymes which act as catalytic agents. This metabolic process is of crucial importance: it is estimated by Himwich that fully 25 per cent of body metabolism goes on in the brain. Any shortage of either oxygen or glucose causes a drop in the rate of brain metabolism. If the rate drops to 60 per cent of normal there will be marked behavioral impairments and some loss of contact with the environment. A slightly greater drop produces unconsciousness, and a fall to 25 per cent of normal will probably prove fatal. Himwich reports that significantly low rates of brain metabolism are found in mongolian idiocy, cretinism, general paresis, and cerebral arteriosclerosis, but it has not been demonstrated in any other disorder.[5]

[2] R. C. McFarland, "The Psychophysiological Effects of Reduced Oxygen Pressure," *Research Publications of the Association for Research in Nervous and Mental Diseases*, XIX (1939), pp. 112–43.

[3] R. C. McFarland, "Psychophysiological Studies at High Altitudes in the Andes," *Journal of Comparative Psychology*, XXIII (1937), pp. 191–258, and XXIV, pp. 147–220.

[4] This and other evidence on the effects of anoxia are reviewed by N. W. Shock in J. McV. Hunt (ed.), *Personality and the Behavior Disorders* (New York: The Ronald Press Co., 1944), Vol. I, chap. xix.

[5] H. E. Himwich, *Brain Metabolism and Cerebral Disorders* (Baltimore: The Williams & Wilkins Co., 1951).

By the use of suitable drugs it is possible to alter slightly the flow of blood to the brain. Altschule capitalized on this fact to make a study of the relationship between cerebral blood flow and vividness of imagery. In normal subjects decrease had the effect of heightening the vividness of visual imagery for past events. In schizophrenic patients an increase in cerebral blood flow reduced the force and frequency of visual hallucinations. It appears that imagery is favored by a slight drop in cerebral efficiency, a conclusion that fits well with the fact that dream imagery attains such astonishing vividness.[6]

Effects of Acute Intoxication. In everyday speech we use the word "intoxication" chiefly to refer to the effects of alcohol, but it has a less restricted medical meaning. There are many *toxins* or poisons that have a deleterious effect on the nervous system; intoxication can be produced by bromides, barbiturates, opium, marihuana, illuminating gas, lead, and other agents besides alcohol. An intoxicated person is one in whom the functions of the nervous system are seriously, though in most cases temporarily, disturbed. The introspective reports of the intoxicated are anything but lucid, yet a study of their plight can supply important information about normal brain activity and its derangement.

If intoxication is severe, the patient is in a state of *delirium.* The characteristics of this state have been carefully analyzed by Cameron and Magaret, who point out that there are many common features in delirious behavior no matter what its cause.[7] A delirious person is typically restless, confused, and disoriented. He misidentifies people and things, shows marked defects of recent memory, and appears to be at the mercy of dreamlike and often terrifying images. It is difficult to catch and hold his attention, and sometimes even a simple question is answered in groping, rambling speech that quickly drifts away from the point. Cameron and Magaret summarize the characteristics of this behavior under four heads. It shows (1) *incoordination,* best illustrated in the staggering gait, fumbling manipulation, and slurred speech; (2) *interpenetration,* when one sequential act invades another, as in the case of a man who starts to change his clothes for dinner and ends up in pajamas; (3) *fragmentation,* when actions and even sentences are broken off before they are completed; and (4) *overinclusion,* shown in the failure to keep one's behavior from being constantly influenced by momentary impulses and surrounding impressions. All of these defects come from a disturbance of "attitude organization." "The delirious patient is deprived of his ability to maintain

[6] M. D. Altschule, "Effects of Factors That Modify Cerebral Blood Flow on Hallucinations in Schizophrenia," *Journal of Clinical and Experimental Psychopathology,* XII (1951), pp. 123–29.

[7] N. Cameron and A. Magaret, *Behavior Pathology* (Boston: Houghton Mifflin Co., 1951), pp. 452–77.

habitual anticipant and supporting attitudes in the presence of competing and discordant stimulation."[8]

This analysis should give us a new respect for what the normal intact brain accomplishes even in the ordinary affairs of life. A tremendous task of ordering, selecting, and excluding goes on throughout our waking hours. The necessary control and direction is provided by certain attitudes, the nature of which can be made clear by an illustration. When a physician interviews a patient he gives selective attention to the story of the illness, the symptoms, the probable cause and probable remedy, excluding all stimuli which are not relevant to this purpose. The guiding principle is provided by an anticipant attitude—to try to understand this particular case—behind which lies a general set of supporting attitudes—to fulfill the role of physician, to be of service, etc. What the delirious brain seems unable to accomplish is the maintaining of these directive attitudes. Without them, behavior simply falls to pieces and loses its organized plan. Memory depends upon organization, and it is therefore easy to understand how little a person can recall of the events of delirium.

Excessive use of alcohol sometimes culminates in a serious condition, *delirium tremens,* generally known as "the D.T.'s," which usually occurs as the result of a prolonged binge during which little food or rest has been taken. There is marked muscular tremor, particularly of the small musculature of hands, face, and tongue. The mental symptoms can be summarized as an acute hallucinatory confusion. The hallucinations are predominantly visual and often have a content of animals in active motion. One patient while still at home reached for his bottle, only to discover a bull terrier glowering at him from the neck of the bottle. The patient is continually excited, disgusted, terrified; he frantically picks revolting creatures from his person and bed or tries to escape from the murderous assaults of great beasts and human enemies. Sometimes the patient is more calm, feeling interest and even amusement at the hallucinations. Anything that happens, any slight stimulus, is swept into the fast-moving stream of delirium. Personal problems may creep in. A paranoid theme may develop: the patient is thrown into terror and despair by audible accusations of homosexuality or visible threats of vengeance. But these psychogenic phenomena are not the direct cause of the delirium. Typically, the attack goes on for about three days and ends in recovery after a long sleep.

In some cases an attack of delirium tremens gives place after a few days to a characteristic symptom-complex known as *Korsakow's syndrome.* This is associated with a diffuse inflammation throughout the nervous system, even in the peripheral nerves. Occasionally it follows

[8] *Ibid.,* p. 474.

poisoning by some agent other than alcohol. There are two distinctive mental symptoms: a defect in memory and a covering of this defect by fabrication. The memory defect is most severe for current happenings. It sometimes extends into the past, but the events of early life and long-distant occurrences are not affected. Although the failure to record and recollect current happenings causes the patient to be disoriented in time and space, his bearing is calm and he converses with superficial lucidity. He is always ready with a detailed confabulation to cover gaps in his memory. For example, a patient who had been confined to bed for several days was asked what he did the day before. He promptly told of having gone to the horse races, giving conversations he had with people there and telling which horses had won. It is possible to regard the confabulation as an attempt to restore order, but as such it is badly hampered by the lack of valid material conserved in recent memory.

Effects of Endocrine Disturbances. We conclude our small sampling of chemogenic disorders by mentioning disturbances in the activity of the endocrine glands. These glands secrete directly into the blood stream and thus affect the nutrition of all nerve cells. Their influence is very great but also very complicated; the secretions of one gland affect several other glands, making it difficult to isolate the functions of any one part of the system. This difficulty is least great in the case of the thyroid, and it will suffice for our present purpose to limit ourselves to the effects of thyroid disturbance.

Thyroid deficiency from birth results in an atrophy of development known as *cretinism.* In mature years an untreated cretin is short, fat, coarse, and severely retarded. Bone development is arrested and mental development remains at the idiot or imbecile levels. Nowadays a child born with thyroid deficiency receives immediate treatment in the form of thyroid extracts to compensate for the lack in his own system. The results are not always successful, but in many cases the treatment makes possible a relatively normal development.

Gesell reports on a case followed from the age of six months to thirteen years.[9] At six months the little girl showed a picture of behavior that would be normal for the age of one month. Thyroid therapy was initiated, and within three weeks the child's behavior had risen to the three-month level. The change in alertness and responsiveness was incredibly rapid. By the end of a year of thyroid treatment the child's general development reached the lower borderline of normality. Apparently this represented her maximum potentiality; in subsequent examinations, up to the age of thirteen, her performance remained consistently at the dull-normal bor-

[9] A. Gesell, C. S. Amatruda, B. M. Castner, and H. Thompson, *Biographies of Child Development* (New York: Paul B. Hoeber, Inc., 1939), pp. 86–91.

derline. Special interest attaches to this case because of an unintentional experiment performed when the girl was nine years old. A druggist misread the prescription, and for one month the child was given thymus instead of thyroid extract. Even this short space of time was sufficient to bring out many signs of cretinism, including a dulling of mental activity. These symptoms retreated as soon as thyroid medication was restored.

This case illustrates with unusual clearness the dependence of the nervous system on the state of its internal environment. A brain capable of borderline performance, doubtless structurally intact, lay dormant in the infant until it was "sparked" by sufficient thyroxin. It was then capable of developing normally, or just subnormally, from year to year, but relapsed quickly to a sluggish level of activity when the supply of thyroxin was lowered.

When thyroid deficiency begins in later life the disorder is called *myxedema*. The patient becomes dull and listless, losing interest in his environment. He feels tired, moves as little as possible, speaks in a slow and monotonous voice. Thought processes are retarded. There is a rapid gain in weight which along with other changes causes the patient to look dull and stupid. The symptoms of thyroid overactivity, *exophthalmic goiter*, are roughly the opposite. The patient becomes active and irritable; his emotions are easily aroused and he finds it impossible to relax or to sleep soundly. The ceaseless activity causes a loss of weight. The eyes protrude in a startled expression, and the patient often experiences typical states of anxiety. Thought is speeded but becomes somewhat disorganized in the process. Overactivity of the thyroid is less easy to treat than underactivity. Surgical removal of part of the gland, thus reducing its functional capacity, is sometimes successful.

EFFECTS OF LOCALIZED BRAIN INJURY

In war and in civilian accidents the brain is sometimes the site of direct physical injury. This injury is chiefly to the cerebral cortex, which lies directly beneath the skull, although it may reach the thalamus and lower brain centers as well. Occasionally the cortex is the site of disease such as brain tumor or a degenerative process, so that parts of the tissue have to be surgically removed. These accidents and interventions are the source of such information as we have about the functions of the human brain. From the point of view of scientific research, the situation is far from ideal. The scientist can seize such opportunities as are offered him by the heartless course of events, but he cannot create the experimental conditions that might help him to answer crucial questions. Our knowledge of the brain, in spite of a large amount of research, is still very limited; and the interpretation of what goes on remains quite speculative.

One possible idea about the cerebral cortex would be that each bit of it governed some particular process or activity. We know that in the spinal cord there is clear localization of this kind, and that in lower brain structures such as medulla, cerebellum, and thalamus it has been possible to find centers for fairly specific functions. In 1861 the French surgeon Broca made a discovery that suggested precise localization in the cortex itself. He had the opportunity to examine carefully and later to do an autopsy on a patient who for many years had been unable to speak. There were no defects in the muscles involved in speech, and the patient could communicate by signs in a way that indicated unimpaired intelligence. The autopsy showed a small circumscribed lesion, apparently of long standing, in the left cerebral hemisphere. This led Broca to conclude that he had located the center for speech. His discovery inspired subsequent investigators to try to map the functions of the rest of the cortex. Most of the research was done with animals, but there were occasional opportunities to make parallel observations with human subjects. On the whole the results have not been what Broca would have expected. Some areas, to be sure, have a certain specificity. It can be predicted, for instance, that injury to the occipital poles, at the very back of the head, will cause an interference with visual functions but not affect auditory or motor processes; similarly, that injury to the temporal lobes, in the temples, is likely to affect auditory functions but leave vision undisturbed. The largest part of the cortex, however, seems to have very little specificity of function; and its injury has often produced fewer identifiable consequences than might have been expected.

Findings of this kind have led some workers to believe that the functions of the cerebral cortex are of a highly general nature. In the most radical form of this theory, it is claimed that the various parts are largely equipotential: defects will be in proportion to the amount of tissue that is damaged, more or less regardless of its location. In effect this assigns to the cortex a generalized organizing power, leaving to lower centers the specifics of what is to be organized. Comparing the two views, the student will recognize one of those situations where the truth is more likely to lie somewhere in the middle than at either extreme. There is certainly some localization in the cortex, but it is equally certain that we would miss important information if we were not alert to the general consequences of abnormal conditions in the brain.

We shall consider first the effects that seem to be closely connected with location. The cortex has been mapped by Brodmann into forty-six areas distinguished by the architecture of the cell layers. Part of this scheme is represented by the numbers on the accompanying figure (Figure 1) which shows the left cerebral hemisphere as it would be seen from the left side. These structurally different areas, however, correspond

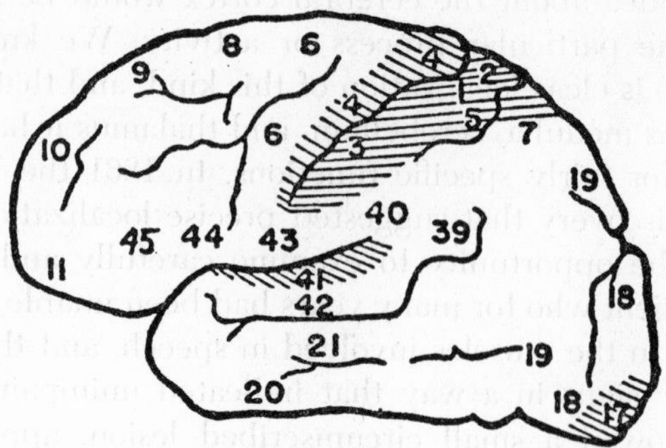

Figure 1

Schematic drawing of the left lateral aspect of the human cortex. The numbers are those assigned by Brodmann on the basis of cellular architecture. The shaded areas are those having fairly definite functions, as described in the text. Areas 9, 10, 11, and 45 together constitute the prefrontal area. The parietotemporal area is represented by the numbers 39, 40, 42, 43, and 44 (From S. Cobb, *Foundations of Neuropsychiatry* [Baltimore: Williams & Wilkins Co., 1941], p. 72.)

in only a few cases to areas having known specific functions. The diversity of architecture is not matched by diversity of functions.

The main sensory receiving stations in the cortex occupy a relatively small space. Area 17 is the center for vision, area 41 for hearing, areas 1, 2, 3, and 5 for touch and pressure from skin and deep end organs. The areas immediately surrounding these centers probably have a somewhat restricted function; area 18, for instance, is believed to be limited to the perceptual elaboration of visual impressions. Area 4 is the motor area which when stimulated gives rise to specific muscular movements, and area 6 seems closely related to the motor sphere. This is about as far as one can go with specific localizations. Of the remaining parts of the cortex, two large zones are of particular interest. One of these is the *frontal* area, represented by the numbers 9, 10, 11, and possibly 45. It is the elaborate development of the frontal cortex that gives man his high forehead and intelligent appearance in comparison with chimpanzees and monkeys, so that in popular thought the frontal areas are associated with the distinctively human attainments. The other area, the *parietotemporal,* represented on the diagram by the numbers 39, 40, 42, 43, and 44, turns out in fact to bear a special relation to the distinctively human attainments of language and the meaning of symbols. Curiously enough, this complex array of skills is dependent only on the leading or dominant hemisphere, the left in right-handed and the right in left-handed people. Injury to the parietotemporal area in the dominant hemisphere is a disaster. Injury to the corresponding area in the other hemisphere has somewhat less serious consequences, having no effect, for instance, on language. To this extent there is localization of function between the two hemispheres. Research on penetrating head wounds indicates that the areas in the left hemisphere governing the right hand do not exactly correspond to the areas in the right hemisphere controlling the left hand, which suggests that the whole organization of the two sides of the brain may be different.[10]

Many difficulties beset the investigator of localized injuries. Even when lesions can be fairly precisely located, account must be taken of the character of the injury. It has been shown that focal and diffuse lesions on the same site produce detectably different effects; that static and progressive lesions have different results; and even that it is possible to discern different consequences of lesions due to tumor, vascular disease, inflammation, and degenerative disorders.[11] Furthermore, the same kind of lesion in the same place will produce effects that differ from one person to another. As Cobb points out, no two human brains are alike. "Lesions destroying exactly the same areas in two different brains would not cause exactly similar symptoms. This is because the life experience of each person has conditioned and changed the brain so that it is unique."[12] The effect of an injury is also influenced by the time of life at which the lesion occurs. The example of encephalitis lethargica (epidemic sleeping sickness) is instructive in this respect. The virus of this disease strikes both adults and children, and the resulting neural lesions appear from autopsy studies to be just about the same. But the effects are considerably different. When a young nervous system is affected, there are grave deficiencies, as we shall presently see, in the realms of both intellect and emotion. When an adult contracts the disease, he may be left with tremor and other somewhat disabling motor symptoms, but there is rarely any emotional disorder or intellectual deficit.[13] Organized behavior seems less vulnerable to brain injury when it is well established and habituated than when it is still in process of being learned.

Injury in the Parietotemporal Area. Injury to the parietotemporal area in the dominant hemisphere produces an effect chiefly on language. This area lies between the centers for vision, the centers for hearing, and the motor centers. The use of language involves vision (apprehending the written word), hearing (apprehending the spoken word), and the motor acts of speaking and writing. It is not surprising, therefore, that

[10] J. Semmes, S. Weinstein, L. Ghent, and H. L. Teuber, *Somatosensory Changes After Penetrating Brain Wounds in Man* (Cambridge: Harvard University Press, 1960).

[11] R. M. Reitan, "Psychological Deficit," in *Annual Review of Psychology*, XIII (Stanford: Annual Reviews, Inc., 1962), p. 421.

[12] S. Cobb, "Personality as Affected by Lesions of the Brain," in Hunt, Vol. I, chap. xviii, p. 553.

[13] *Ibid.*, p. 561.

injury to the parietotemporal cortex disturbs the language function in one way or another. The resulting conditions are known by the general name of *aphasia.*

The results of injury are extremely complex. At first sight the disorders seem highly selective and highly restricted. Thus one patient may display only an inability to read, his understanding of spoken language and his speech and writing being uninjured. Another may have a specific inability to find words, especially nouns, to express the thoughts he has in mind. Such a patient may show by gestures and fragments of speech that he remembers perfectly the details of a walk he has just taken, but he is unable to bring out the proper words to describe the objects he has seen along the way. A patient described by Hollingworth used almost no substantives, but inserted the automatisms "seriat" and "feriat" in their place.[14] When asked where he lived, he said, "I come from seriat." When asked his occupation, he said, "I am a feriat." He drew a picture of an anvil, which he called a "seriat," and remarked that he worked at it. When the examiner called it an anvil he brightened and said, "That's it, you said it, it's a seriat." When he tried to read aloud he pronounced practically every word "seriat." Sometimes the disorder is even more narrowly selective. A foreign language is lost but the native tongue is unaffected. The extreme is represented in the case of a patient formerly able to read music who after his injury could read music in the key of C, with some difficulty in the key of G, and not at all in other keys. In all these cases it is apparent that general understanding is not greatly injured. The patient seems to grasp much more than his injured language function is able to represent.

The high specificity of some of these losses has tempted many workers to think that the different aspects of language are localized in small specific parts of the cortex. Injury at one spot causes word blindness, at another spot word deafness, at a third spot the comprehension of sentences, at a fourth spot the speaking of nouns, etc. The parietotemporal cortex has even been compared to a typewriter keyboard, to a complex piece of electrical wiring, and more recently to a computing machine.[15] There may be something to these analogies, though at present they seem a little too metallic to explain the workings of an organ made up of living cells. The work of Penfield and his associates at Montreal certainly indicates that there is some specialization among the cortical areas that subserve language. These workers have investigated the cortex very carefully in the course of brain surgery conducted with local anaesthesia of the scalp. The patients were comfortable and fully conscious,

[14] H. L. Hollingworth, *Abnormal Psychology* (New York: The Ronald Press Co., 1930), p. 455.

[15] N. Wiener, *Cybernetics* (New York: John Wiley & Sons, Inc., 1948).

hence able to report upon their experiences. Electrical stimulation somewhere in the region of areas 43 and 44 produced an arrest of speech: the patient knew what he wanted to say but could not say it. A little further back the effect of stimulation was to prevent the finding of names and nouns as in the case mentioned above.[16] Such findings leave no doubt that there is an appreciable division of labor within the area responsible for language.

Two points are of especial importance here for the understanding of aphasic disorders. In the first place, the effect of electrical stimulation in the parietotemporal area appears to be inhibitory rather than excitatory. It does not, like stimulation in the motor area, produce involuntary overt movement. It does not cause the patient to speak aphasically or to make incorrect writing movements. The patient must be engaged in conversation and must speak on his own initiative in order to reveal the consequences of the stimulation. These consequences can be understood only as a suppression of accustomed behavior patterns. In the second place, what is suppressed can best be conceived not as specific elements of speech but as larger linguistic functions such as the finding of words appropriate to express one's thoughts and the placing of words in grammatical arrangement. Penfield's experimental findings on speech are therefore consistent with the ideas of Hughlings Jackson, who in the nineteenth century conceived the aphasias to be disturbances of "propositional thinking," and of Henry Head, who after much experience with brain injuries in World War I reached the conclusion that the central disorder was of "symbolic formulation and expression." It is not parts of speech that are lost through injury; it is rather some part of the organizing activity that goes on in the understanding and use of language.

These reflections make it possible to grasp more clearly the process of recovery from aphasia. Good results are often obtained by a process of retraining. Sometimes a portion of language behavior is gone beyond repair, so that it is necessary to teach the patient some roundabout method of overcoming the defect. This is illustrated in a case reported by Gelb and Goldstein, in which the patient had become unable to recognize any objects through visual experience.[17] It was impossible to retrain his visual recognition, but he learned to read again by a combination of eye movements and finger movements. He traced the letters with his fingers and followed them with his eyes, providing himself in this way with the cues necessary for recognition. More typically, however,

[16] W. Penfield and T. Rasmussen, *The Cerebral Cortex of Man* (New York: The Macmillan Co., 1950).

[17] The case is described briefly in K. Goldstein, *Aftereffects of Brain Injuries in War* (New York: Grune & Stratton, Inc., 1942), pp. 149–52, and in more detail in W. D. Ellis, *A Source Book of Gestalt Psychology* (New York: Harcourt, Brace & World, Inc., 1938), pp. 315–25.

retraining does not involve new learning; it involves the reappearance of old learning which had been suppressed by the injury.[18] It may take a long time to bring about some use of the suppressed function, but once it has begun to operate again it may soon be restored as a whole. If our aphasic ironworker, for example, could be brought to use a few appropriate nouns instead of "seriat" and "feriat," he might presently recover the complete use of substantives. That a resurgence of old learning is taking place, rather than new learning, is shown in the following incident. A Southerner with total aphasia was trained for a year by a New England teacher. The training was successful, and it was noteworthy that the patient resumed talking without any impairment of his southern accent.[19]

Injury to the Frontal Areas. It was long supposed that the frontal lobes were the seat of the highest intellectual functions. Studies soon began to show, however, that the effects of injury were not large in the intellectual sphere. In fact, the trend of recent thought has been in the opposite direction, emphasizing the smallness of deficit in intellectual functions. One of the best older studies was made by Rylander, of Stockholm, who reported on 32 cases in which the frontal area was surgically removed on one side.[20] In the majority of the cases there was deficit in respect to memory, concentration, and speed of thought. But there was also an exaggerated sense of well-being (euphoria) in 20 cases, restlessness in 14, loss of initiative in 12, depression in 8, these changes being distinctly of a non-intellectual character. By and large, unilateral excision of the frontal area does not produce extensive changes. Cobb remarks, "On the whole I believe a man can lose one frontal pole with insignificant disability."[21]

More radical consequences might be expected to follow extirpations involving both frontal lobes. Reviewing the literature in 1945, however, Hebb found little evidence of intellectual impairment and no satisfactory demonstration of localization of specific functions.[22] Fifteen years later, after a great deal more research, the evidence still tells in the same direction. Meyer reaches the conclusion that "frontal lobe lesions, compared with lesions elsewhere, are not more disruptive of complex intellectual

[18] J. M. Wepman, *Recovery from Aphasia* (New York: The Ronald Press Co., 1951).

[19] H-L. Teuber, review of Wepman's *Recovery from Aphasia,* in *Journal of Abnormal and Social Psychology,* XLVII (1951), pp. 610–11.

[20] G. Rylander, *Personality Changes After Operation on the Frontal Lobes* (Fair Lawn, N. J.: Oxford University Press, 1939).

[21] Cobb, "Personality as Affected by Lesions of the Brain," *op. cit.,* p. 569.

[22] D. O. Hebb, "Man's Frontal Lobes: A Critical Review," *Archives of Neurology and Psychiatry* (Chicago), LIV (1945), pp. 10–24.

performance," and that "the research so far available has not conclusively established the dependence of any function on this area."[23]

This does not imply that the frontal lobes are a mere luxury without functions. It means that the functions are general, hard to measure, and perhaps not mainly intellectual in character. A clue to their possible nature is suggested in a case studied with great care and reported in a book by Brickner.[24] The patient, a successful broker, was operated for cerebral tumor in 1930. The growth was extensive so that it proved necessary to remove from the left side most of area 8 and all of areas 9, 10, 11, and 45; from the right side a slightly larger area was excised. At the time of operation the patient was forty years old. Prior to his illness he had been an energetic, intelligent businessman, but in other respects a rather mild and submissive individual. As a child he was quiet and shy, dependent on his mother. When he married, following a courtship in which the girl took the active part, he expressed the desire to continue living in his parents' home. He rarely displayed aggression except in the form of facetious and somewhat boastful stories. Such was the man upon whom the operation was performed. The effect of removing the frontal lobes was sufficiently great so that the patient was never able to go back to work. Initiative was impaired, memory was imperfect, distractibility was increased, and the patient showed a clear deficit in judgment and logical reason. More striking, however, was the change in his self-criticism and self-restraint. After the operation he experienced considerable euphoria and appeared to lose all restraint over his previous mild boastfulness. He proclaimed himself the best of all businessmen, the man whom nobody could fool, and he told stories of youthful sexual exploits and of playground fights in which he knocked down all comers. Along with boastfulness and aggression his dependent tendencies were also exaggerated. He allowed others to bathe and dress him and care for all his wants. The constructive organization of personality was more markedly injured than the intellectual processes.

GENERAL EFFECTS OF BRAIN INJURY

The facts we have examined do not support the idea of extensive localization of functions in the cerebral cortex. The best evidence on aphasia drove us away from the conception of precisely localized part-functions of language, suggesting instead injury to a higher "propositional" or organizational activity. Evidence on the frontal lobes, indicat-

[23] V. Meyer, "Psychological Effects of Brain Damage," in H. J. Eysenck (ed.), *Handbook of Abnormal Psychology: An Experimental Approach* (New York: Basic Books, Inc., 1961), p. 542.

[24] R. M. Brickner, *The Intellectual Functions of the Frontal Lobes* (New York: The Macmillan Co., 1936).

ing a weakening of the hierarchical ordering of motives and purposes, was likewise more consistent with an organizational deficit. We must now try to form a clearer conception of these more general functions of the cortex, partly to satisfy curiosity as to how things work, partly to forward our understanding of patients who have suffered the misfortune of damage to the brain.

Symptoms Arising Directly from Defect. Although the brain-injured patient is inclined to be apathetic rather than excited, it is possible to detect certain similarities between his general impairments and those seen in delirious patients. *Overinclusion*, for instance, is highly characteristic of the brain-injured, who are readily distracted by external impressions, and a *fragmentation* of behavior is often the consequence. Probably we can assume that there is a similar difficulty in maintaining directive attitudes, but the wild disorder of delirious behavior is counterbalanced in the brain-injured by a tendency toward rigid perseveration. Attention sometimes becomes riveted on some object of interest, and if the patient manages to solve some difficult problem he keeps trying to repeat this solution on new tasks.

Many workers attach considerable importance to another consequence of cerebral injury. This is described as a blurring of the boundaries between figure and ground. It is very obvious in normal perception, especially visual perception, that a certain portion of what is perceived constitutes a clearly defined figure, the remainder being a less clearly defined ground. In certain ambiguously drawn pictures it is possible to make figure and ground reverse themselves in rapid succession, but ordinarily the two can be clearly discriminated. This characteristic of perception applies also to any complex process in the nervous system. An action such as raising the arm constitutes figure, but is accompanied by a ground of readjustments in other muscles which keep the body in equilibrium. In brain injury, then, especially in injury to the cortex, the relation of figure and ground is disturbed and leveled.

This phenomenon can be illustrated by performance on a test devised especially for brain-injured children by Werner and Strauss.[25] The examiner takes an ordinary marble board having 100 holes arranged in 10 rows. He places marbles in some of the holes, making some kind of a figure, for example two overlapping hollow squares. He then gives the child an empty board and marbles and asks him to copy the arrangement. It may be noticed in passing that this is a type of test which permits the examiner to observe the whole course of the patient's performance, with all its pauses, errors, and false starts. Tests in which the subject merely

[25] Cf. A. A. Strauss and L. E. Lehtinen, *Psychopathology and Education of the Brain-Injured Child* (New York: Grune & Stratton, Inc., 1947), pp. 31–49.

gives answers, without revealing how he got them, are all but valueless in the study of brain injuries. The marble board experiment proves particularly difficult for brain-injured children. Inspection of their performance shows the source of the difficulty. Unlike normal children, and unlike mentally retarded children without brain injury, these children are unable to separate figure from ground—the figure made by the marbles from the ground made by all the rest of the holes. They place their marbles in a random, disorganized fashion, and even if they get the placements approximately right they show no sign of realizing that the stimulus consisted of figures such as the two squares. Brain injury makes it difficult for figure to achieve salience over ground.

Loss of the Abstract Attitude. Goldstein has attempted to conceptualize the most important general consequence of brain injury as a loss of the abstract attitude. With this notion we are already somewhat familiar because it was well illustrated in the case of Martha Ottenby. In describing how she got lost when returning from the hospital workroom, how she determined whether it was winter or summer, and how she ran into the street to talk with her brother who was actually dead, we reached the conclusion that her behavior was bound by immediate and concrete impressions.[26] She was unable to detach herself from these impressions or to think about her behavior in abstract terms. Even in test performances she was blocked by the simplest abstraction, although she could perform quite well with concrete problems.

Goldstein conceives the abstract attitude broadly. It is not an acquired mental set or even a specific aptitude. It is rather "a capacity level of the total personality."[27] In contrast to the concrete attitude, which is realistic, immediate, and unreflective, the abstract attitude includes in its scope more than the immediately given situation. The real stimulus is transcended and dealt with in a conceptual fashion. Objects before us are seen as members of a class or category, or they are apprehended in a framework of wider implications. To take a very simple example: a patient shows great skill in throwing balls into boxes that are located at different distances from him, but he is unable to say which box is farthest away or how he manages to aim differently. He is able to function concretely but not to manage the abstract idea of distance, and he can give no account of throwing harder or less hard. Another patient can count numbers on his fingers and in other roundabout ways, coming out with results that look like good arithmetic, but he cannot state whether 7 is more or less than 4. The importance of loss of the abstract attitude becomes even clearer when we consider the following limitations:

[26] See above, pages 84–91.

[27] K. Goldstein and M. Scheerer, "Abstract and Concrete Behavior: An Experimental Study with Special Tests," *Psychological Monographs,* LIII (1941), pp. 1–31.

the patient cannot keep in mind several aspects of a situation at one time, cannot readily grasp the essentials of a given whole, cannot plan his actions ahead in ideational fashion.

Shortcomings in the capacity for abstraction make themselves apparent in tests which involve sorting. Strauss and Werner have used the technique of confronting children with fifty or more small objects, the instructions being to put those things together "which go together, which fit together."[28] The objects can be classified by function (key with padlock, light bulb with electric socket) or they can be grouped on the basis of important common features such as form (candle and crayon) or color (red poker chip and red button). Brain-injured children run to more far-fetched and peculiar principles of combination. They group on the basis of unessential details, for example putting sandpaper and match cover together because there is a little piece of sandpaper on the match cover. Again, they find far-fetched relations, such as placing a metal cover and knife together because the knife can be used to take off covers. Sometimes a merely imagined connection suffices to make a grouping: a round piece of wood and a knife go together because the wood is a loaf of bread to be sliced.

These examples give a decided impression of loose connection and poor capacity for organization, but an even clearer notion can be obtained from the picture-object test used by Strauss and Werner. Two pictures are put up, one showing a house on fire, the other a boy struggling in water. The child is then asked to put in front of each picture those toy objects lying on the table which go with the picture. A brain-injured boy of twelve put some appropriate objects, such as a fire engine, in front of the house on fire, but also added some very peculiar items. Wrench and pliers were supplied to repair the car in case it was burned; a "slow" sign was set up to keep people from running into the fire; a black train was introduced to match the black suits of people watching the fire; a fork was added because one of the witnesses thought he saw food in the burning building; an envelope was put in place so that the firemen could read the address and find their way to the fire. To a mind that finds these groupings appropriate, it is evident that the world might become at times a little confusing.

Not all workers agree with Goldstein that the described changes are best interpreted in terms of concreteness and abstractness. There is little doubt, however, that we are dealing with a loss of organization, a kind of flattening of mental activity which makes it hard to exclude the irrelevant, subordinate associative processes to consecutive thought, and govern behavior in the direction of steadily imagined future goals.

[28] Cf. Strauss and Lehtinen, *op. cit.*, pp. 54–74.

Symptoms Expressing the Struggle with Defect. Whatever the merits of the concept of abstract attitude, we owe to Goldstein an illuminating recognition that the brain-damaged patient is a person who is trying to adapt himself to the limitations imposed by injury. The symptoms of brain injury are not entirely a direct result of damaged tissue. We shall begin with those symptoms which constitute an indirect or secondary result, which express, as Kurt Goldstein puts it, "the struggle of the changed organism to cope with the defect and to meet the demands of a milieu with which it is no longer equipped to deal."[29] In part, these symptoms show the struggle to meet demands; in part, they reveal the patient's attempt to avoid situations with which he cannot cope. The latter symptoms are analogous to defense mechanisms.

Brain-injured patients often show a very strong reaction to failure on some item of a test. Goldstein describes this reaction as follows.[30]

> Here is a man with a lesion of the frontal lobe, to whom we present a problem in simple arithmetic. He is unable to solve it. But simply noting and recording the fact that he is unable to perform a simple multiplication would be an exceedingly inadequate account of the patient's reaction. Just looking at him, we can see a great deal more than this arithmetical failure. He looks dazed, changes color, becomes agitated, anxious, starts to fumble, his pulse becomes irregular; a moment before amiable, he is now sullen, evasive, exhibits temper, or even becomes aggressive. It takes some time before it is possible to continue the examination. Because the patient is so disturbed in his whole behavior, we call situations of this kind *catastrophic situations.*

Because this reaction occurs simultaneously with the attempt to solve the problem, rather than after the failure, and because the patient often does not have the slightest idea why he was upset, Goldstein concludes that the patient's behavior is not simply an expression of humiliation on account of failure. The reaction is more primitive and immediate. To be unable to meet an environmental demand is highly threatening to the patient. Failure in a test item, unimportant in itself, raises for the brain-injured patient the whole threat of incompetence and helplessness, a threat that he experiences repeatedly because of his actual defect in meeting environmental demands. For him, simple failure has a catastrophic meaning.

Many curious traits of brain-injured patients become explicable as attempts to avoid this type of catastrophic situation. In various ways the patient tries to find an environment or make an environment in which demands that are beyond his reduced resources will not occur. Brain injury makes it difficult to deal with anything that is unexpected. It is frequently observed that the patients start violently when they are

[29] Goldstein, *op. cit.*, p. 69.
[30] *Ibid.*, p. 71.

addressed. One means of protection against sudden irritations of this kind is to be constantly busy. "Concentration upon a particular activity makes him relatively impervious to the undesired and dreaded stimulation from outside."[31] The activity may not be important in itself, but the patient cherishes it because of its protective character. Another frequent trait is excessive orderliness. All the patient's belongings are kept in the most meticulous arrangement, and he is upset and confused if something happens which disturbs this arrangement. The function of orderliness is similar to that of constant activity: it protects the patient from the unexpected. Everything can be found and used with a minimum of mental exertion, and the possibility of surprise is excluded. In these and other ways the patient tries to establish an environment to which he will always be equal.

Studies of Brain-injured Children. The subject of brain-injured children was touched upon in an earlier chapter in connection with delinquency. We saw that children with a history of head trauma or encephalitis often showed, along with an abnormal electroencephalogram, marked restlessness, emotional instability, and difficulty in accepting the restraints of socialized living. From the studies of Werner and Strauss we have just learned that brain-injured children display several distinct peculiarities, notably a ready distractibility, a blurring of figure-ground organization, and an incapacity for the abstract attitude. The behavioral peculiarities of these children are closely related to their mental peculiarities. It has often been noted, for example, that they tend to be inconsiderate of the rights and feelings of others. On what does consideration for others depend? As we saw when we studied the development of moral insight, it depends to a large extent on being able to see things from another person's point of view.[32] It calls for multiple perspectives. One of the traits used explicitly by Goldstein to define the abstract attitude is the ability to hold simultaneously in mind various aspects of a situation. If brain injury renders a child incapable of taking the abstract attitude, it also makes him virtually incapable of being considerate of others. Such a child cannot transcend moral realism. His failure to become a socialized member of groups comes partly from an intellectual inability to grasp what it means to be a considerate group member.

The difficulties experienced by brain-injured children can be illustrated from one of the case reports given by Strauss and Lehtinen.[33] The boy in question had a birth injury that evidently affected the brain tissues. His I.Q., tested on various occasions, averaged somewhere in the

[31] *Ibid.*, p. 74.
[32] See above, pages 175–77.
[33] *Psychopathology and Education of the Brain-Injured Child*, *op. cit.*, pp. 35–38.

60's, and his performance on the marble board test was extremely disjointed, indicating severe blurring of figure and ground. When given tests he showed the typical distractibility; "at times, despite repetition of questions, it was difficult to know whether or not he had actually heard because his attention wandered and his interest span was so short." Constant restlessness was also prominent in test situations. "He moved around continually, leaning back in the chair or yawning or handling material on the desk." When admitted to the training school at the age of ten he had to be constantly reminded of routine requirements, partly because his distractibility prevented him from remembering them, partly because he defiantly disregarded them. He "liked to fuss around with odd jobs to keep busy." Perhaps this was an outlet for his restlessness, but it may also have been an attempt to avoid catastrophic situations by constant activity. Though often "friendly and good-humored," he was "insistent about his likes and dislikes," and "made himself very unpopular with the group because of his continued interference in the business of others." On one occasion he tore down decorations for a party as fast as they were put up. On another he decided that the furniture should be moved around, shouted to the other boys to move desks and chairs, and himself seized a large table, knocking down other furniture in his path. He was frequently in fights, apparently over trifles. His best adjustment was to work in the shop, where in spite of his "enthusiastic and 'slam-bang' abandon" he was capable of functioning as a good worker. Returned to his family at sixteen, the boy made a good adjustment, handling merchandise on a shipping dock of a large hotel. He took pride in his responsibilities and in his ability to earn an independent living.

This boy was living under a grave handicap. It was very hard for him to keep still or to resist whatever impulses or emotions presented themselves. Thus, without having particularly hostile intentions, he was constantly at odds with the group. The reader should imagine himself in the position of having to discipline this boy, either at school or at home. Even with the best intentions in the world it would be almost impossible not to get furious with him. Ideas of awaiting his turn, sharing with others, remembering obligations, taking pains and doing things slowly would have little effect on a person so restless, impulsive, concrete, and disorganized. Small wonder that friction almost always exists between such a child and his mentors. Yet the outcome shows that it is sometimes possible to train brain-injured children so that within certain limits they lead a useful and contented life.

Training has to be adapted to the limitations imposed by injury. Strauss and Lehtinen describe some of the measures used to improve the child's performance, especially in schoolwork.[34] Everything must be done to minimize distraction. The schoolroom must be undecorated, bare, removed from outdoor noises, its windows painted so that the children cannot see out. Desks should be far apart, perhaps even facing the walls, so that the children will not distract each other. Gloomy as this sounds, it is often welcomed with great appreciation by the children themselves, who suddenly find themselves able to keep their minds on their tasks. Restlessness and hypermotility must be met by a program which includes many activities, and by devices which link learning with motor action. To overcome the leveling of figure and ground it is often necessary to prepare the teaching materials with a sharp outlining of the essential figures in color. All of these devices are used only to get the children started on a better educational performance; as rapidly as possible they are trained to participate in a more traditional school routine.

Training for social adjustment and for the responsibilities of adult life are clearly more complicated problems. It is hard to find general principles. In the case of the boy just described, a fortunate combination of circumstances made him feel secure, useful, and competent when he returned to his home environment, and this allowed him to reach his optimum of socialized behavior. Brain-injured children are injured children, however, and one should not expect their optimal social and vocational adjustment to be too high. Many of them require permanently simplified and limited environments.

PREFRONTAL LOBOTOMY

As we have seen, injury to the frontal cortex in adult patients affects mainly the organization of motives and purposes and does not produce large intellectual defects. It was this lead which prompted the Portuguese surgeon Moniz to make the bold experiment of trying to relieve certain serious mental symptoms by deliberate surgical injury of the frontal lobes. He reasoned that patients who showed a tremendous excess of control, with constant tension, anxiety, and anguish, might be relieved and placed in a more relaxed frame of mind by such an operation. His first series of cases showed encouraging gains, and "psychosurgery" quickly spread to research hospitals all over the world. We shall examine prefrontal lobotomy with the twofold purpose of considering its value as a method of treatment and seeking more information about the frontal lobes.

Although prefrontal lobotomy has been in use for only twenty-five years, there are already several different techniques for performing it.

[34] *Ibid.*, chap. ix; A. A. Strauss and N. C. Kephart, *Psychopathology and Education of the Brain-Injured Child* (New York: Grune & Stratton, Inc., 1955), Vol. II, chap. viii.

Most of the dangers that beset the earlier work have been overcome, and certain unfavorable consequences can now be regularly avoided. Admittedly the first attempts were "highly empirical"—a medically polite way of referring to surgery in which you don't know what you are doing but just go ahead anyway on a hunch. Improved techniques have made it possible to work with considerable precision and to specify fairly accurately the area that is affected. The operation does not involve the removal of nervous tissue, and the cerebral cortex is touched only to the extent that may be required for introducing the instrument. The purpose of prefrontal lobotomy is to sever some of the neural connections between the frontal lobes and other parts of the brain, particularly the thalamus and hypothalamus. It might be described as an attempt to reduce the action of the frontal lobes upon the rest of the system, and it actually effects a partial isolation of the prefrontal cortex—areas 9, 10, 11, and 45.[35] Although surgery of any kind is naturally frightening, the operation itself is not unusually difficult for the patient. It can be carried out under local anaesthesia with the patient fully conscious and able to talk.

Effects of the Operation. Patients recover quickly from the slightly stuperous and confused condition that prevails immediately after the operation. Within a few days, or at most within a few weeks, their minds appear to function about as well as before. Alertness and an interest in the environment return and may even surpass the preoperative state. On ordinary tests of intelligence the patients are often able to make as good a showing as they did before, sometimes a little better. Some authorities are inclined to say that lobotomy produces no intellectual impairment worth mentioning.[36] Others find significant though not necessarily very large deficits. There is some evidence, not fully confirmed, that lobotomized patients show a deficit in the Porteus Mazes, a test in which success depends upon planning several moves ahead.[37] Less in doubt is their deficiency in generalizing, which suggests a possible weakening of the abstract attitude, and in such things as accuracy and profiting from past mistakes.[38] In short, there seems to be evidence for certain kinds of impairment, but the deficits are neither great nor widespread, and the

[35] It is redundant to say "prefrontal" instead of "frontal," but the term is in common use to indicate that only areas 9, 10, 11, and 45 are affected, not areas 8, 6, 4, and 44. Many workers prefer the expression "leucotomy" to "lobotomy," and there are several terms, such as "topectomy," that refer to different ways of performing the operation.

[36] J. Zubin, "Abnormalities of Behavior," in *Annual Review of Psychology*, III (Stanford: Annual Reviews, Inc., 1952), pp. 261-82.

[37] S. D. Porteus and H. N. Peters, "Maze Test Validation and Psychosurgery," *Genetic Psychology Monographs*, XXXVI (1947), pp. 3–86.

[38] A. Petrie, *Personality and the Frontal Lobes* (Philadelphia: The Blakiston Co., 1952).

findings as a whole are consistent with beliefs previously held that the functions of the frontal lobes are not primarily intellectual.

In the majority of cases there are, however, clear changes in the patients' behavior. These changes are not at all on the scale of those described in Brickner's patient, whose prefrontal cortex was almost entirely removed, but they are perhaps a little in the same direction. Petrie calls attention to a weakening in the niceties of social restraint and to a less adequate sense of responsibility as shown in such matters, for instance, as keeping promises.[39] Greenblatt and Solomon, however, are perhaps showing the brighter side of much the same coin when they report that in the hospital ward the patients interact more freely with other patients and show more friendliness and positive affect.[40] Jenkins and associates have compared the responses of chronic schizophrenics on a sentence completion test before and after lobotomy. The following samples are completions of the sentence fragment, "The best thing about old age is . . ." One patient before operation completed the sentence with the gloomy thought "that one doesn't have long to live;" afterwards, the completion was "social security." Another patient changed from "a person is more tolerant and mellow" to "rich cake Grandma used to bake." Still another changed from "more knowledge" to "comfort." Such changes support the authors' conclusion that "lobotomy simplifies the world for the patient," leading him to think of "the more tangible, even sensual enjoyments of social security benefits, rich cake, and ease."[41]

One of the most interesting changes was first pointed out by Freeman and Watts, who introduced prefrontal lobotomy in America. They gave it the name of "affective bleaching."[42] Ideas which formerly troubled the patient to the point of ruining his life simply lose their emotional pressure without being eliminated from his mind. A paranoid woman, for example, believed herself constantly persecuted by enemies who sprayed gas into her room and flew over her house in planes dropping poison. After prefrontal lobotomy she continued to describe these persecutions, but her attitude toward them had changed. Fear gave place to amusement, and amusement eventually gave place to insight and the abandonment of the

[39] *Ibid.*, pp. 111–13.

[40] M. Greenblatt and H. C. Solomon, *Frontal Lobes and Schizophrenia: Second Lobotomy Project of Boston Psychopathic Hospital* (New York: Springer Publishing Co., 1953).

[41] R. L. Jenkins, J. Q. Holsopple, and M. Lorr, "Effects of Prefrontal Lobotomy on Patients with Severe Chronic Schizophrenia," *American Journal of Psychiatry*, CXI (1954), pp. 84–90.

[42] W. Freeman and J. W. Watts, *Psychosurgery* (Springfield, Ill.: Charles C Thomas, 1942). See also a paper by the same authors, "The Frontal Lobes and Consciousness of the Self," *Psychosomatic Medicine*, III (1941), pp. 111–20; this is available also in Tomkins (ed.), *Contemporary Psychopathology* (Cambridge: Harvard University Press, 1943), chap. xxi.

ideas. The compulsive and frightening character of the ideas seemed to be weakened by severing the connections between frontal cortex and thalamus. The phenomenon of affective bleaching has been confirmed by Cattell, who used intensive psychotherapy with patients before and after psychosurgery and reported that major conflicts were altered only in the sense of seeming less urgent and threatening.[43]

Attempts to give a theoretical account of these changes are hampered by the difficulty of describing complex psychological events. If one thinks particularly of the change in affect, there is a good deal of virtue in the formula that the operation brings about a reduction of anguish. If one considers the change toward a relaxed, impulsive, less responsible attitude, it is not inappropriate to say that the super-ego or that conscience has been weakened. The most persistent attempt at theoretical explanation has been made by Freeman, who starts with the hypothesis that the frontal lobes are concerned with what might be described as foresight. Broadly speaking, this means the person's projection of himself into the future: his planning of what he desires to accomplish, his recognition of the means to be employed, his awareness of the extent to which he reaches this goal. Of course, the patient can still make plans, perceive means to ends, and make judgments about himself, but somehow these processes no longer come together into an effectively functioning whole. Robinson and Freeman have shown by means of special tests that lobotomized patients have a reduced feeling of self-continuity and of concern about the self.[44] Similarly they are less concerned about the attitudes of others toward them. The patients become a little obtuse to the impression they are making on others, and they are less restrained by images of making themselves ridiculous. For patients who are highly overconcerned and self-conscious this can be regarded as a shift in the direction of health. In Freeman's words, "the problem in surgery is therefore to reduce the function of self-regard and of sensitivity to limits that can be tolerated by sick persons, without sending them too far in the other direction."[45]

Therapeutic Value. Many voices have been raised against psychosurgery. Relatives are often reluctant to give permission for so drastic an operation. To some extent the objections are based on an exaggerated idea of the changes produced, which may be pictured as reducing the patient to a vegetative existence, turning him into an irresponsible delin-

[43] J. P. Cattell, "Some Observations on the Selection of Patients for Psychosurgery and Psychotherapy After Operation," *American Journal of Psychotherapy,* VII (1953), pp. 484–91.

[44] M. F. Robinson and W. Freeman, *Psychosurgery and the Self* (New York: Grune & Stratton, Inc., 1954).

[45] W. Freeman, "Psychosurgery," *American Journal of Psychiatry,* CXI (1955), pp. 518–20.

quent, or permanently ruining his most precious faculties. Lobotomy has been criticized as cruel and without moral justification. Most physicians, on the other hand, emphasize the similarity between this and other kinds of surgery as a result of which the patient may have to accept some limitations for the sake of relief from great misery. If the patient's tension and anguish are very high, they argue, and if every other means of relief has been tried without avail, he should be given the chance of a calmer and happier life even if it be at something below an ideal level. Prefrontal lobotomy is an operation of last resort, to be recommended only for certain types of disorder and only when all other methods have failed.

Within the last decade there has been a marked decline in the use of psychosurgery. The introduction of tranquilizing drugs has put into the hands of hospital psychiatrists an easier and safer method of working toward the same end. To the extent that the drugs do not produce the desired results, there may still be room for the operation of last resort; but the peak of its popularity has undoubtedly passed. In the meantime we can take advantage of the fact that for a while it was widely used in order to gauge its effectiveness as a therapeutic measure.

Clinical reports indicate that the best results are obtained with neurotic conditions characterized by states of intense anxiety and high tension, and with persisting agitated depressions. In these forms of disorder the awareness of self is peculiarly exaggerated. The patient is constantly preoccupied and constantly worried about himself, his thoughts, his guilt, his future, so that his interest is largely withdrawn from the environment. The condition of these patients is one of desperate unhappiness, and the successful cases experience great relief after operation. Favorable results are reported with severe chronic schizophrenia, but with patients who are already disorganized, impulsive, irresponsible, and not much concerned about their condition the operation is distinctly not indicated. In such cases one could wish for a way to make the frontal cortex more active rather than less active. Recently it has been shown that lobotomy can be used to relieve intractable pain. Patients suffering continual pain from inoperable cancer, for example, can be spared much agony for whatever period of time they still have to live.

Reports on the use of the operation from many hospitals in many lands indicate that between a quarter and a third of the patients treated are sufficiently improved to be ready for discharge from the hospital. About a quarter remained unchanged by the operation. The remaining 40 or 50 per cent are improved, though not sufficiently to warrant their return to the community. One should not regard the improvement of this latter group as a matter of minor importance. Considering their deplorable and nearly hopeless initial condition, their gain represents a tremendous benefit to themselves as people, to the feelings of their relatives, and to the hospital staff which is responsible for their care. The foregoing figures should of course be checked against the rate of spontaneous recovery for similar untreated patients, though this rate is very low in conditions of such severity. One study compared matched groups of lobotomized and untreated chronic schizophrenics and found more than twice as much definite improvement in the former group.[46] Another study, comparing 228 operated patients with 202 for whom operation was recommended but permission refused by the relatives, showed that a year later 85 of the operated patients, but only 5 of the others, were well enough to be at home.[47] A British Ministry of Health Report based on 10,365 patients operated upon during the period from 1942 to 1954 shows that 46 per cent were discharged, some of them only a considerable time after the operation.[48] Perhaps the proper way to read this report is to say that more than half of the patients were not improved enough to go home even after several years, and we should not overlook the fact of unfavorable changes in a little more than 4 per cent of the whole group. No doubt there would have been some spontaneous remissions and some deteriorations if the patients had not received the operation; the British figures must be interpreted as signifying at most a modest rate of success. Prefrontal lobotomy, however, will probably continue to be used as a specialized therapeutic tool for the treatment of certain severe and otherwise intractable forms of disordered behavior.

SUGGESTIONS FOR FURTHER READING

For the student who wants to review the anatomy and functions of the nervous system, the concise but clear book by Stanley Cobb is recommended: *Foundations of Neuropsychiatry* (5th ed. Baltimore, The Williams & Wilkins Co., 1952). A compact older review of the effects of physiological factors on behavior is given by N. Shock in J. McV. Hunt's *Personality and the Behavior Disorders* (New York, The Ronald Press Co., 1944), Vol. I, Ch. 19. Cobb's Ch. 18 in the latter work is a good introduction to the subject of brain lesions. An excellent introduction to the endocrine glands is R. G. Hoskins' *Endocrinology: The Glands and Their Function* (New York, W. W. Norton & Co., Inc., 1941).

The student with a serious interest in the functioning of the brain should familiarize himself with D. O. Hebb's book, *The Organization of Behavior* (New York, John Wiley & Sons, Inc., 1949) which constructs a working hypothesis based on the type of facts discussed in this chapter.

Goldstein's important contributions to the study of brain injury can be gleaned from his *Aftereffects of Brain Injuries in War* (New York, Grune &

[46] Jenkins *et al., op. cit.*, pp. 84–90.

[47] W. Freeman *et al., Journal of the American Medical Association,* CLVI (1954), pp. 939–42.

[48] G. C. Tooth and M. A. Newton, "Leucotomy in England and Wales, 1942–54," *Ministry of Health Reports on Public Health and Medical Subjects* (London: H. M. Stationery Office, 1961), No. 104.

Stratton, Inc., 1942). Available in S. S. Tomkins, *Contemporary Psychopathology* (Cambridge, Harvard University Press, 1943), are two papers which are helpful in grasping Goldstein's notion of the abstract attitude. The first of these is a paper by Goldstein himself (Ch. 22), and the second is a superb clinical description by Eugenia Hanfmann (Ch. 23). The fact that both papers are about schizophrenia rather than brain injury does not lower their value as explications of the abstract attitude. A recent book by A. A. Strauss and L. E. Lehtinen, *Psychopathology and Education of the Brain-Injured Child* (New York, Grune & Stratton, Inc., 1947), has already provided material for this chapter; it contains a summary of the researches performed by Heinz Werner and Strauss, and also goes into the question of training.

Probably the best introduction to aphasia is J. M. Wepman's *Recovery from Aphasia* (New York, The Ronald Press Co., 1951). Goldstein's important views on the retraining of aphasics will be found in the second part of his *Aftereffects,* mentioned above. Anyone who wants to pursue further the fascinating problem of localization in the brain should consult *The Cerebral Cortex of Man* by Wilder Penfield and Theodore Rasmussen (New York, The Macmillan Co., 1950).

The history of lobotomy and a large number of relevant studies with animals are described in brief compass by J. F. Fulton in *Frontal Lobotomy and Affective Behavior* (New York, W. W. Norton & Co., Inc., 1950). A valuable monograph is *Personality and the Frontal Lobes* by Asenath Petrie (Philadelphia, The Blakiston Co., 1952), which reports upon changes found, favorable and unfavorable, when lobotomy was used with severely neurotic patients. Conservative medical opinion is reflected in P. H. Hoch and L. B. Kalinowsky's *Shock Treatments, Psychosurgery, and Other Somatic Treatments in Psychiatry* (2d ed., New York, Grune & Stratton, Inc., 1952).

13

Common Symptom Syndromes of Cerebral Disorder

The subject matter of the preceding chapter was organized around known conditions of abnormality in the brain. We pursued the theme of cerebral injury and cerebral abnormality wherever it might lead. Under chemogenic disorders we noticed some of the effects of changes in the internal environment. Under brain injuries we progressed much farther toward an understanding of the functions of higher centers. Several patterns of disordered behavior, such as alcoholic psychosis and the aphasias, were mentioned along the way, but we made no effort to survey the common manifestations of cerebral abnormality as they are seen in guidance centers, clinics, and hospitals.

In this chapter we shall describe several common symptom syndromes of cerebral disorder. Our series is arranged in chronological order according to the time in the life cycle at which abnormality in the brain begins or assumes serious proportions. The first topic is mental deficiency, in which the cerebral peculiarity is either determined by the genes or acquired before birth through an abnormal growth of the foetus. The next syndrome, epilepsy, has somewhat diverse origins in which genogenic factors and birth injuries may play a contributing part, but the great majority of patients who come for treatment are children and young people. General paresis, our next consideration, almost always has its onset between the ages of 30 and 50. To complete the life cycle we shall finally turn our attention to the mental changes and disorders of old age, a topic which is attracting much interest today because of the marked increase in the average life span. Although the central theme is set by brain disorder, our previous study of developmental psychology and psychodynamic processes should not be put away in a drawer. People with abnormal brain conditions are still people, with personalities and problems of adjustment, and it is often possible to benefit their lives greatly even when nothing can be done about their cerebral condition. If this seems too obvious to mention, it is worth while to remember that medical progress in the past has often been seriously delayed by failure to distinguish between symptoms strictly traceable to cerebral disorder and symptoms having more to do with problems of personal adjustment.

MENTAL DEFICIENCY

A milestone in the history of psychology was established early in this century when Binet devised his first test for the measurement of intelligence. The practical request which prompted this venture was to find some way of sorting out beforehand those school children who could not keep up with their classes. The unprecedented success of Binet's scales led to a close association between intelligence tests and the whole concept of mental deficiency. In some places mental deficiency was even legally defined as a Binet intelligence quotient of less than 75, and the criterion of the I.Q. was considered sufficient for placement in special classes or in state schools for the feeble minded. The same basis was used in making the now customary division of mental deficiency into three grades: mild subnormality (*moron*) with I.Q. from 69 to 50 and adult mentality on the level of children of 8 to 12 years; moderate subnormality (*imbecile*) with I.Q. from 49 to 20 and mental age of 3 to 7 years; and severe subnormality (*idiot*) with I.Q. of 19 or less and mental age no higher than 2 years.

Eventually the flood tide of enthusiasm for the I.Q. began to recede, making possible a more balanced and realistic conception of intelligence. The tests were too much like school tasks and placed too much emphasis on verbal and intellectual skills. They were not always successful in predicting the adequacy of behavior in the practical concerns of everyday life. It was in order to meet this difficulty that Edgar Doll worked for many years to perfect the Vineland Social Maturity Scale.[1] This is a scale to be filled out by observers of the child's daily behavior, and it includes motor performances and social adjustments as well as linguistic development. The criterion of social incapacity can thus be added to the results of tests, and mental deficiency comes to have the more reasonable meaning of a lack of "common sense" or of general adaptability.

[1] E. A. Doll, *Measurement of Social Competence* (Vineland, N. J.: Educational Publishers, 1953), especially chaps. i–iii.

By far the largest part of the feeble minded belong in the category of *moron.* We shall follow Sarason in referring to this level as "garden-variety" mental deficiency.[2] Inasmuch as it is the brain that subserves intelligent behavior, we are justified in assuming in such cases that the brain is not working very well, but there is no evidence for any gross structural defect. The majority of cases do not have an abnormal electro-encephalogram (EEG) and do not, if they come to autopsy, show distinctive peculiarities in cerebral tissues. When asked to copy designs in the marble board experiment they may simplify the more difficult designs, but they are not troubled by the confusion of figure and ground that is characteristic of brain-injured patients.[3] On the other hand they characteristically come from families in which other members also display mental deficiency. These facts suggest that garden-variety mental deficiency represents the lower end of the curve of distribution for innate intellectual endowment. The deficiency is genogenic: these people are genetically the least gifted members of the population with respect to intelligence.

Of course one can never reach such a conclusion with a feeling of absolute certainty. Garden-variety mental deficiency occurs most frequently in run-down neighborhoods where the families are poor if not destitute, where the outlook is discouraging, and where mental stimulation is at a minimum. Several studies have shown that higher average I.Q.'s are found in more stimulating environments, and Skeels and Dye have measured substantial rises in the I.Q.'s of children after transfer from a dull orphanage to an institution where they became the objects of much affection and encouragement.[4] Like any other potentiality, intelligence has to be brought out by reasonably favorable circumstances, and these are often sparse in the histories of morons. We must therefore qualify the genogenic theory enough to make room for depressing environmental conditions, but it seems unlikely that these will ever tell the whole story of garden-variety mental deficiency. Even the most enlightened attempts at training produce large results only in the exceptional case.

With the more extreme mental defects, at the levels of imbecility and idiocy, there are almost always clear evidences of gross developmental abnormality. Structural defects are apparent both in the nervous system and in other organs. For most of these disorders there is strong evidence against simple inheritance; they typically occur in families of average

[2] S. B. Sarason, *Psychological Problems in Mental Deficiency* (New York: Harper & Row, 1949), chap. v.

[3] H. Werner and A. A. Strauss, "Causal Factors in Low Performance," *American Journal of Mental Deficiency,* XLV (1941), pp. 213–18.

[4] H. M. Skeels and H. B. Dye, "A Study of the Effects of Differential Stimulation on Mentally Retarded Children," *Proceedings of the American Association on Mental Deficiency,* XLIV (1939), pp. 114–36.

intelligence and sometimes in the offspring of highly gifted parents. There are several recognized varieties of severe mental deficiency, but most of them occur quite rarely.[5] In this chapter we shall describe only mongolism, the most common form, which will suffice to draw the contrast between the less severe and more severe levels of defect.

Garden-Variety Mental Deficiency. The overtones of the word "moron" are not attractive, especially to people who prize intelligence and make their living by it. A typical moron might indeed give offense in certain quarters by evidences of lower class status, and he would certainly prove to be something less than a lively and witty companion, but otherwise the impression he makes is not particularly odd. Possibilities for useful employment are restricted only by his mental limitations. Capacity to lead a contented life is blocked only by his own poor judgment in matters affecting his welfare and by the tendency of other people to expect too much of him, to regard him with contempt, perhaps even to exploit him. Quaint pictures of the "happy moron" are not true to life, but garden-variety mental deficiency is not a deviation of such magnitude that we need think of the patient as existing in a foreign world.

Very often the signs of limitation are first detected at school. Lessons are apt to present a problem from the start. Mental deficiency is not, however, a specialized disability, and close observation will usually reveal evidences of incapacity in many aspects of behavior. The difficulties can be illustrated from a case history prepared by Bice.[6] A girl of 13, inmate of a training school, was given trial placements as a household helper in nearby homes. Although she had been trained in household duties at the school, she could not carry out independently any long series of actions. She could not, for example, carry out the general order to clean a room; she had to be told to sweep here and sweep there, dust this shelf and dust that table, wash this panel and then wash that door. There seemed to be no unwillingness, simply an incapacity to judge what needed to be done and to arrange the steps in sequence. Similarly, this girl performed creditably in caring for younger inmates of the school when a supervisor was always on hand, but she could not care for children when no one was present to guide her. It proved impossible to employ her even in the simplest work as a household helper. Supervision had to be so constant that her presence was of no real help.

This case quite properly conveys the sense of limitation that is felt so often by those who work with mentally deficient children. No matter how patiently and lovingly one tries to teach them, a weighty ceiling seems to rest on their powers of judgment and adaptability. This is

[5] For descriptions, see Sarason, *op. cit.*, chap. viii.

[6] H. V. Bice, in A. Burton and R. E. Harris (eds.), *Case Histories in Clinical and Abnormal Psychology* (New York: Harper & Row, 1947), pp. 383–97.

probably the typical situation, but Sarason has reviewed several follow-up studies which show that a number of individuals diagnosed as morons go on to make a successful occupational and family adjustment.[7] Perhaps this means that the original diagnosis depended too heavily on intelligence tests and underestimated the person's capacity in practical affairs. Perhaps it means that the person found employment of a routine, monotonous kind, working at a machine or with a crew under constant direction. There are quite a few occupations for which no more than moronic intelligence is required. Perhaps the person found a spouse who made home life easy by taking all the initiative. These cases who seem to push through the expected ceiling emphasize the urgency of developing more accurate methods for diagnosis and prediction. One does not want to discourage the aspirations of any child who, though now judged to be deficient, can profit from training so as to take an independent place in the community. On the other hand it is cruel to expose children to competition with the better endowed if there is no hope that they can ever succeed. The true garden-variety mentally deficient person should ideally have an easier, protected environment with a great deal of supervision. In such an atmosphere he can flourish.

Recently there has been a good deal of interest in exploring the possibility that certain cases of apparent mental defect might be psychogenic. Sarason points out that conditions variously described as early childhood schizophrenia, autism, or disturbance of affective contact, all characterized by a marked lack of responsiveness, are sometimes mistaken for mental deficiency when in fact they signify not a defect but an inhibition of mental activity.[8] Early emotional trauma, it can be argued, may strike with such force and with such connotations that a protective inhibition comes to rest on some vital aspect of mental functioning. Of interest in this connection are the conclusions of a team of workers who use psychoanalytic therapy in certain cases of severe learning difficulty. These workers believe that early hostile and destructive fantasies linked with severe anxiety may sometimes be responsible for the inability to learn. The taking in of knowledge may become associated with danger and death, or the expression of curious interest may be equated to an aggressive search for forbidden information.[9] Therapeutic success with a substantial rise in learning capacity has been obtained in some cases, but treatment is always slow and sometimes ineffective. Even if the theory is correct, it is by no means certain that the early damage can

[7] Sarason, *op. cit.*, pp. 107–14.

[8] *Ibid.*, pp. 215–21.

[9] B. M. Sperry, N. Staver, and H. E. Mann, "Destructive Fantasies in Certain Learning Difficulties," *American Journal of Orthopsychiatry*, XXII (1952), pp. 356–65.

always be undone. In general, there is sufficient evidence to support the idea that some difficulties with learning are psychogenic.[10] There is certainly no reason, however, for believing that inhibition is responsible for more than a tiny minority of cases of mental deficiency.

Mongolism. Nearly a century ago a British physician gave the name of mongolism to a form of mental deficiency in which it struck him that the child had the facial characteristics of the Mongolian races. The alleged resemblance is actually found only in the eyes, which especially during the first few years are almond shaped and slope upward toward their outer corners. Mongolism is a severe form of mental deficiency in which the imbecile level is rarely surpassed. But it is more than a mental deficiency; in view of the many associated physical symptoms, it must be considered a form of general developmental arrest. The whole head is peculiarly shaped, quite flat on the back and with depression of the nasal bridge. The tongue is large and coarsely fissured; in many patients it protrudes from the mouth a good deal of the time. The hands and feet are stubby and square, and there is often a wide separation between the big toe and the other toes. Stature is small for age, the musculature tends to be hypotonic or rubbery, and gait is awkward and shambling. The appearance of mongoloid children is decidedly odd and becomes only more so if they grow to adulthood. Their adjustment to society would be no easy matter even if intelligence were normal.

On post-mortem study, mongoloid brains are found to be clearly abnormal, showing signs of widespread interference with the growth of brain cells. These structural deficiencies are, according to Benda, "the result of a chronic deficiency of oxygenation or sugar metabolism," two things upon which cerebral tissues are closely and constantly dependent.[11] It appears that a metabolic deficiency has prevented the brain cells, as well as other tissues, from making a normal growth.

There is a considerable diversity of opinion about the causes of mongolism, but a certain number of facts are well established. One of these is a positive correlation between the frequency of mongolian births and maternal age. A young mother can have a mongoloid baby, but the incidence increases sharply during the years when reproductive capacity is nearing its end. Another fact, already mentioned, is that the parents and siblings of mongoloid children shown no signs of mental deficiency and may be superior, thus ruling out any hereditary tendency in the usual sense. Some workers have pointed out that the diverse physical symptoms of mongolism make a certain sense when one considers them

[10] G. H. J. Pearson, in *The Psychoanalytic Study of the Child* (New York: International Universities Press, Inc., 1952), Vol. VII, pp. 322–86.

[11] C. E. Benda, *Mongolism and Cretinism* (New York: Grune & Stratton, Inc., 1946), p. 97.

as lying in those organs which undergo crucial differentiation during the second and third months of embryonic life. The foetus that is destined for mongolism shows during this period a deceleration of normal development which is not compensated in the later months before birth. It is noteworthy that at precisely this period there is a fairly radical readjustment in the maternal hormone pattern in order to sustain the further development of the foetus.

Recent advances in genetics have added an important factor to the explanation. It turns out that mongoloid children have an extra chromosome, the result of unusual divisions and combinations of chromosomes at the time of fertilization. Pointing out that chromosomes are the biochemical representatives of genetic inheritance, the organizers and enzyme systems that determine the course of growth, Benda remarks that "the extra chromatin material may indicate the presence of some unknown enzyme systems which interfere with the cellular metabolism and the synchronism of organ development."[12] The tendency toward chromosome abnormality is attributed to the mother rather than the father because of the correlation with maternal age; it has been shown that there is no correlation between paternal age and the frequency of mongolism. The abnormality in the mother is not of such a nature as to have influenced her own development in any way; and it breaks through, so to speak, most readily only when her reproductive capacities have begun to decline. But the evidence now strongly suggests that the foetus is abnormal from the very start.[13]

Mongoloid children are not destined for substantial improvements in intelligence. Thyroid and other medications produce no more than a slight improvement in general alertness. For a while great hopes were entertained for glutamic acid, which seemed to produce an immediate rise in the I.Q.'s of mongoloid and other severely deficient children. Some workers believe that these gains are genuine and lasting, though others are quite skeptical; in any event the gains are simply not large enough to make any real change in the patients' prospects.[14] With or without medication, a few mongoloid children will advance to the point of mastering very simple speech and doing simple chores. More typically, speech is absent or confined to a few hoarsely spoken sounds, and activi-

[12] C. E. Benda, "Mongolism: Clinical Manifestations, Pathology and Etiology," in *Mental Retardation* (Proceedings of the First International Conference on Mental Retardation), P. W. Bowman and H. V. Mautner, eds. (New York: Grune & Stratton, Inc., 1960), pp. 340–63.

[13] L. Eisenberg, "Child Psychiatry; Mental Deficiency," *American Journal of Psychiatry,* CXVIII (1962), pp. 600–604.

[14] F. T. Zimmerman and B. B. Burgemeister, "Permanency of Glutamic Acid Treatment," *Archives of Neurology and Psychiatry,* LXV (1951), pp. 291–98; A. W. Astin and S. Ross, "Glutamic Acid and Human Intelligence," *Psychological Bulletin,* LVII (1960), pp. 429–34.

ties consist of rather repetitive play. Despite their limited equipment, mongoloid children are not necessarily sluggish or unhappy. Institutional workers find them more friendly, happy, and affectionate than other severely handicapped children. Their physical health, complicated by glandular dysfunction, is not rugged, and few mongoloids live very far into adulthood.

Attitudes Toward Mental Deficiency. Not so long ago the public attitude toward mental deficiency was one of looking away and forgetting. Institutions were poorly financed, research was weakly backed, special training opportunities were provided on a most inadequate scale. Even the parents of severely retarded children sometimes fell in with this attitude, placing the child in an institution and pretending that he did not exist. The problem for parents, however, was always much complicated by the inadequacies of institutions. Most state training schools do not admit children under five years, and most have a long waiting list which delays admittance two or three years longer. Furthermore, financial and emotional considerations often conspired to favor attempting to bring up the deficient child at home. Many severely deficient children live at home, though usually against professional advice and often at considerable cost to the happiness and adjustment of normal siblings.

Today there are signs of a decided change in the public attitude. For this change the parents of deficient children are largely responsible. There is now a National Association for Retarded Children with active branches in many cities and towns. The local associations work for the improvement of state institutions and for more and better special classes in the public schools. As parents sharing a common plight, the members give each other a sense of support and understanding, and morale is strengthened by the discovery that something can be done through joint effort. Similar developments have occurred with respect to cerebral palsy and epilepsy. In the long run it may prove to be not the least of the services rendered by these movements that they awakened interest in research and stimulated financial support for it. We are clearly in no position as yet to deal, for instance, with the problem of preventing mental deficiency. Any hope of reaching this goal depends upon a great advance in knowledge.

EPILEPSY

Epilepsy is based on a disordered condition of the brain which leads to periodic seizures. The most distinctive feature is a temporary loss of consciousness, but this may be accompanied by varying degrees of motor and autonomic perturbation. It occurs in something like one half of one per cent of the general population. This figure seems small, but it means that about 650,000 persons in the United States are afflicted with epilepsy. Although the disorder is not continuous, and the person is in a perfectly normal state between attacks, it constitutes even in its milder forms a serious handicap to adjustment.

Varieties of Epileptic Attack. There are three main types of epileptic seizure or fit. Most dramatic and most frequent of occurrence are the *grand mal* attacks, which correspond to the idea most people have of an epileptic fit. The second variety, *petit mal,* is not badly described as a smaller fit limited to a brief loss of consciousness with few motor accompaniments. The third variety, the least common of the three, has not yet been stably christened. It is variously known as *psychic seizures, psychic equivalents, psychic variants,* or *psychomotor seizures.* The reader will easily deduce from this fumbling with names that the third class of epileptic phenomena is still but little understood. The condition is an interesting one, however, and it may prove to be of considerable importance.

Grand Mal. Grand mal attacks are often preceded by warning symptoms generally called the *aura.* These may consist of dizziness, tingling, numbness, peculiar sensations in the head, discomfort in the abdomen. They last for but a few seconds and often do not give the patient time enough to prepare for the fit. The seizure itself is introduced by sudden muscular rigidity. Respiration is suspended so that the face turns dark, and if not supported the patient falls heavily to the ground. Almost at once the tonic phase (with muscular rigidity) gives place to the clonic phase of the seizure, characterized by rapid jerking movements of the muscles. The jaws are included in the jerking movements so that the tongue is often bitten and frothy saliva gathers on the lips. Autonomic disorganization is shown in involuntary urination and sometimes defecation. Within a few minutes the clonic phase gives place to coma. Consciousness may be regained almost at once or only after a matter of hours. Some patients have grand mal attacks very infrequently, perhaps once or twice a year. Usually the attacks occur more frequently, and in severe cases there may be several convulsions a day.

Petit Mal. The petit mal attack is of shorter duration and is limited to loss of consciousness, perhaps with a few small twitchings of the eye and face muscles. No mental confusion attends these attacks; there is simply a "mental black-out," starting and stopping suddenly and lasting from a few seconds to a minute or two. The effect may be so transient that other people set it down to a mere moment of absent-mindedness. Petit mal attacks may occur with great frequency, many times a day. While not as disturbing either to the patient or to those around him, they may constitute almost as severe a handicap as the grand mal attacks.

Psychomotor Attack. The third variety of seizure is characterized by at least a partial loss of consciousness without suspension of organized motor activity. There may be slight signs of tonic rigidity for a moment, but thereafter the patient continues to perform purposeful acts. But he is completely out of touch with his environment, pays no attention to what is said to him, and presently returns to normal consciousness with no recollection of the attack. Psychomotor seizures may last for as much as an hour or even longer. Conceivably a person might commit acts of a violent and criminal nature during the course of an extended psychomotor epileptic attack. This possibility has to be considered when there is genuine confusion and amnesia for the period during which the offense was committed.

About one half of the victims of epilepsy have only one type of seizure. The other half have two and even three types, sometimes mixed in the same fit. The three varieties of attack are thus not three different kinds of disease. They can be assumed to spring from very similar conditions in the brain.

The Electroencephalogram in Epileptics. At no point has electroencephalography proved of greater value than in the study of epilepsy. Whatever the nature of the underlying neural disturbance, it reflects itself with extraordinary clearness in the electrical activity of the cortex. The outstanding finding is that during seizures the EEG becomes radically abnormal, and that the pattern of abnormality is different for each of the three varieties of attack. The accompanying diagram (Figure 2) shows four tracings which are typical for grand mal, petit mal, a variant form of petit mal, and the psychomotor seizure. Each tracing begins with a section of normal record, affording a sharp contrast with the record during seizure. The tonic phase of grand mal is accompanied by very fast waves of high voltage. These give place in the clonic phase to waves still of high voltage having a characteristically erratic form. In petit mal attacks there is a typical association of slow waves with spikes, each pair coming at the rate of three a second. Sometimes the rate is even slower: at two a second it is called petit mal variant and is not usually associated with an overt seizure. The waves are shaped quite differently in psychomotor attacks. Voltage is abnormally high, and the waves frequently have square tops. They occur at the rate of between four and eight a second.

These findings were originally made by Gibbs, Davis, and Lennox.[15] The same workers were also able to show that 85 per cent of epileptic patients showed abnormal EEG's between seizures. These abnormalities consisted of short bursts of waves having higher than normal voltage

[15] F. A. Gibbs, H. Davis, and W. G. Lennox, "The Electroencephalogram in Epilepsy and in Conditions of Impaired Consciousness," *Archives of Neurology and Psychiatry,* XXXIV (1935), pp. 1133–48.

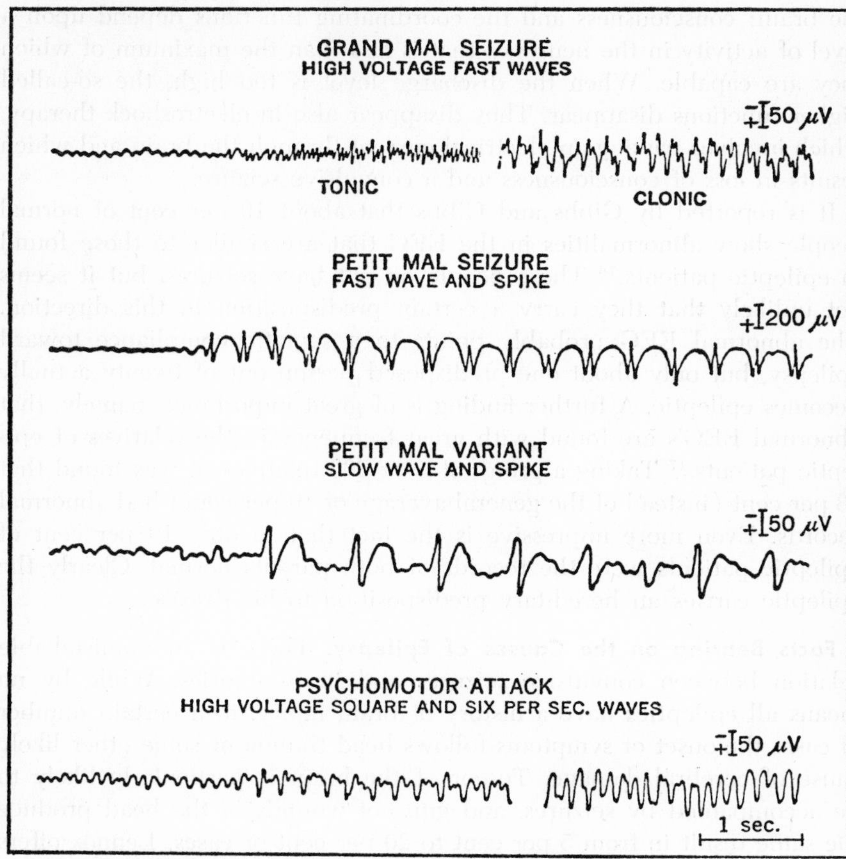

Figure 2

Representative electroencephalograms of four patients to show records taken before, and during, four different types of seizures: grand mal, two forms of petit mal, and a psychomotor attack. At the right is the perpendicular deflection made by a 50-millionth or 200-millionth volt potential, and at the bottom the time marked by one second. The left of each tracing is a portion of the person's normal record. The rest of the tracing was made during a seizure. The uppermost record is the tonic, and then, after an interval, the clonic phase of a grand mal convulsion. The second tracing is the three-a-second alternate wave and spike of petit mal. The third tracing is of the relatively rare two-a-second wave and spike called petit mal variant. The fourth tracing was taken during two phases of a psychomotor seizure. The tracings are about one-third their natural size. (From F. A. Gibbs, E. L. Gibbs, and W. G. Lennox, *Archives of Neurology and Psychiatry,* XXXVIII [1939], p. 1112.)

and taking a form similar to those recorded during seizures. The evidence suggests that what is going on during the attacks is an abnormal discharge of energy by the neurones of the brain, and that the patient's brain has a tendency toward excessive discharge even between attacks. If this conclusion is correct we learn a new and interesting fact about the brain: consciousness and the coordinating functions depend upon a level of activity in the neurones that is less than the maximum of which they are capable. When the discharge level is too high, the so-called higher functions disappear. They disappear also in electroshock therapy, which involves passing an electrical current through the brain and which results in loss of consciousness and a convulsive seizure.

It is reported by Gibbs and Gibbs that about 10 per cent of normal people show abnormalities in the EEG that are similar to those found in epileptic patients.[16] These people do not have seizures, but it seems not unlikely that they carry a certain predisposition in this direction. The abnormal EEG probably points to a somatic compliance toward epilepsy, but only about one predisposed person out of twenty actually becomes epileptic. A further finding is of great importance, namely, that abnormal EEG's are found with great frequency in the relatives of epileptic patients.[17] Taking a group of over 200 relatives, it was found that 53 per cent (instead of the general average of 10 per cent) had abnormal records. Even more impressive is the fact that in only 10 per cent of epileptic patients were the records of both parents normal. Clearly the epileptic carries an hereditary predisposition to his disease.

Facts Bearing on the Causes of Epilepsy. There is an unmistakable relation between convulsive seizures and brain injuries. While by no means all epileptics have a history of brain injury, in a certain number of cases the onset of symptoms follows head trauma or some other likely cause of cerebral damage. Tumor of the brain is particularly likely to be accompanied by seizures, and gunshot wounds in the head produce the same result in from 5 per cent to 20 per cent of cases. Lennox offers the following generalization: "Given a predisposition to seizures, almost any abnormality of the brain seems to be a precipitating factor."[18]

The way in which brain injuries lead to convulsions has been the object of special study by Penfield and Erickson.[19] In certain cases of epilepsy it can be shown that the attacks always begin with excessive neuronal discharge in a particular region of the brain, spreading from there to involve the cerebrum as a whole. This form of the disorder is called "focal epilepsy" in contrast to the many cases in which no local point of origin can be detected. Focal epilepsy sometimes permits surgical inter-

[16] F. A. Gibbs and E. L. Gibbs, *Atlas of Electroencephalography* (Boston: F. A. Gibbs, Boston City Hospital, 1941).

[17] W. G. Lennox, E. L. Gibbs, and F. A. Gibbs, "Inheritance of Cerebral Dysrhythmia and Epilepsy," *Archives of Neurology and Psychiatry*, XLIV (1940), pp. 1155–83.

[18] W. G. Lennox, "Seizure States," in J. McV. Hunt (ed.), *Personality and the Behavior Disorders* (New York: The Ronald Press Co., 1944), Vol. II, p. 964.

[19] W. Penfield and T. C. Erickson, *Epilepsy and Cerebral Localization* (Springfield, Ill.: Charles C Thomas, 1941).

vention with removal of the offending tissues, an operation for which Penfield and his associates became famous. The first step in locating the focal point is to make a careful study of the aura, which is actually a part of the attack even though it precedes the loss of consciousness. If the aura always contains certain sensations or motor actions, this constitutes presumptive evidence for a focus in the corresponding sensory or motor area of the cortex. If there are repetitive dream-like images in the aura the temporal lobes are likely to be involved. The second step in the search is to refine the location by means of the EEG. The electrodes are placed on different parts of the head until the spot is found that most regularly yields an abnormal record. If these steps point to a fairly circumscribed area—which is by no means always the case—a direct investigation of the cortex is made. Under local anaesthesia a flap of bone and skin is cut and turned back, exposing the suspected area. It is then possible to explore by means of electrical stimulation until the precise spot is found that produces an aura, if not actually a convulsion, and the pathological tissues can be examined and removed.

In these focal cases there is pretty certain to be evidence of an old injury, very likely the consequence of some internal mishap such as a hemorrhage rather than a trauma from outside. In the area of injury part of the tissues will be dead, but dead tissues are not responsible for fits. Penfield and Erickson often found that the crucial tissues were those on the edge of a dead area, alive but insufficiently supplied with blood to permit normal functioning. They proposed the hypothesis that these nerve cells suffered from anemia "due to periodic impairment of blood flow through one or other of the small local blood vessels," and that a certain degree of anemia is "irritative in the sense that greater activity occurs in local neurones."[20] Perhaps there is an analogy here to the frantic struggle of a drowning man or of a person partly asphyxiated; the deprived cells, struggling to stay alive, fire with everything they have. However this may be, the hypothesis has virtue in explaining the facts discovered about epilepsies with a highly focalized point of origin in the cortex. Excessive discharge in one area can eventually overload the whole system and provoke the generalized overdischarge that constitutes the seizure. What we do not know, of course, is whether this hypothesis can be extended to encompass the commoner cases in which no local starting point for the convulsive seizures can be detected. Recent evidence suggests that in such cases there might be a local point of origin in subcortical structures rather than in the cortex, but more research will be needed to evaluate these findings.[21]

[20] *Ibid.*, pp. 198–99.

[21] W. T. Liberson, "Emotional and Psychological Factors in Epilepsy: Physiological Background," *American Journal of Psychiatry*, CXII (1955), pp. 91–106.

The influence of psychogenic factors seems to be distinctly secondary in epilepsy. It is true that the individual attack is often precipitated by a situation involving emotional stress. It does not follow from this, however, that emotional factors play a significant part in causing the patient to have epilepsy in the first place. There is one variety of psychogenic disorder, however, which closely resembles the grand mal attack and is sometimes mistakenly diagnosed as epilepsy. This is the *hysterical fit* that played such a large part in Mesmer's hypnotic cures. These convulsions can usually be distinguished from grand mal attacks by certain signs which indicate that the neural disturbance is less profound. In hysterical fits the patient does not bite his tongue, void his bladder, or hurt himself when falling. Otherwise the convulsion may look a good deal like a grand mal attack. One can speculate that such a symptom may be available only to the hysteric who also has a certain predisposition to cerebral dysrhythmia. In such cases one looks for a neurotic character structure and for possible cure by psychotherapy. Most convulsive seizures, however, are not psychogenic problems.

Effects of Epilepsy on Personality. It might be supposed that severe and lasting epilepsy would produce marked mental deterioration. When tests of intelligence are chosen as the means of measurement, this deterioration appears but is not very great.[22] Mental ability as such remains unimpaired in a certain number of cases.

Concerning the effect of epilepsy on the personality as a whole, the evidence is rather more complicated. There has been much controversy over the existence of a distinct epileptic personality structure. Among those who believe that epileptics have a good many traits in common, there is further controversy as to whether the typical pattern precedes the illness or comes as a result of it.[23] L. P. Clark took the stand that it was possible to describe a typical epileptic personality, and that the traits composing this personality were present long before the illness began. He emphasized four traits in particular: eccentricity, supersensitiveness, emotional poverty, and rigidity. In the childhood histories he found a good deal of irritability, distractibility, and insistence on having one's own way. School records were impaired by inattention and restlessness. He found evidence also for quarrelsome, stubborn, selfish tendencies with a marked resistance to discipline. A shallow emotional life, along with frequent emotional outbursts, completed Clark's picture of the

[22] A. L. Collins, "Psychometric Records of Institutionalized Epileptics," *Journal of Psychology*, XI (1941), pp. 359–70; A. L. Collins, C. R. Atwell, and M. Moore, "Stanford-Binet Response Patterns of Epileptics," *American Journal of Orthopsychiatry*, VIII (1938), pp. 51–63.

[23] This material is summarized by Lennox, in Hunt, *op. cit.*, pp. 953–63; extensive references are given.

epileptic personality. Other workers who have studied epileptics have confirmed a number of Clark's observations as to current traits, but have not been convinced that a typical personality structure existed before the onset of epilepsy.[24]

The discoveries made by means of the EEG, taken together with the facts we have studied about brain-injured children, lead to a far better understanding of this whole problem. It is possible to group the so-called epileptic traits into two classes: (1) those about which we can make the guess that they go with abnormal conditions in the brain, and (2) those about which we can make the guess that they result from the fact of being an ill person in a society of well people. The first group of traits may well be present before overt symptoms of epilepsy develop; they may in fact be characteristic of all people who have sharply abnormal EEG's. We saw that brain-injured children tended to be overactive, distractible, poorly controlled, inconsiderate of others, insistent on their own wants, resistant to discipline and restraint. Apparently an injured and inadequately functioning brain produces this group of traits that is so inimical to ordered and socialized living. It is not far-fetched to assume that a brain with a tendency toward dysrhythmia would produce some of the same characteristics. On the other hand the fact of illness, especially when the affliction is so overwhelming and so meaningless, makes it necessarily hard for the patient to take life in a calm and joyous spirit. Especially if he has grand mal attacks, he knows that every so often he is likely to pass into a state of unconsciousness which is terrifying to others, which makes people want to avoid him, which precludes the holding of most jobs and such activities as driving a car—in short, which handicaps him severely in leading a satisfactory life. That a person should become morose and oversensitive under such circumstances, that he should appear self-centered, emotionally shallow, a little antagonistic toward others, is a most natural outcome of his psychological situation. The epileptic personality can thus be readily conceived as the combined result of an abnormal brain condition and a social handicap.

Treatment of Epilepsy. Although the surgical procedures used by Penfield and others are often successful when there is a highly focalized cortical lesion, it is obvious that they cannot be used with the majority of epileptic patients. Early efforts at less radical treatment were based on the observed effects of physiological changes on the frequency of seizures. Acidosis has been found to diminish the frequency, while the opposite condition of alkalosis increases it. Seizures are increased by

[24] The problem has recently been reviewed by B. Tizard, "The Personality of Epileptics: A Discussion of the Evidence," *Psychological Bulletin*, LIX (1962), pp. 196–210.

flooding the body with water and decreased by dehydration. Increased oxygen concentration of the blood is another condition that reduces the attacks. It is possible to control seizures to some extent simply by diet and a well-planned health regime. Still more effective, however, is the use of certain drugs such as phenobarbital and dilantin sodium. In these days of burgeoning experimentation with new drugs, epileptics have been among the beneficiaries; and we can hope for steady progress toward finding the best preparations. Very great improvement can often be obtained by means of these drugs, although the doses sometimes have to be held down because of other unfavorable effects on the body. This line of research holds the greatest promise for sufferers from epilepsy. In many cases seizures can be suppressed entirely, in others brought to a degree of control that greatly reduces the interference with normal living. Proper medication can give to a substantial proportion of epileptics, probably 75 per cent, the chance to lead satisfactory lives, with no marked intellectual handicaps at school or occupational impairments in adulthood.

Psychotherapy can be an important adjunct, though obviously not with the goal of curing the brain condition. In the first place, it can be helpful in reducing conflicts and tensions in general, and this in itself is sometimes found to diminish the frequency and severity of seizures. In the second place, it can help the patient to work out the worst of his anxiety and resentment over the fact of being handicapped, enabling him to meet his frustrations with something closer to equanimity. In the third place, it can help him to overcome the warping that may have occurred in his development through the bewilderment and anxiety of his parents. Cobb cites the case of a young man of 17 who had suffered from convulsive seizures since infancy. His father, disgusted with him, was morosely uncompanionable, and his mother was so oversolicitous that she became practically his jailer. Social experience and a feeling of independence were simply absent, and it became the task of therapy to encourage and watch over these developments as they belatedly occurred. Medically the patient progressed to the point of having no more than occasional petit mal attacks; "socially he became a changed human being."[25]

GENERAL PARESIS

In the historical introduction to this book we described the series of steps by which general paresis was isolated from other disorders and correlated with a specific condition in the brain. The typical symptom-

[25] S. Cobb, *Borderlands of Psychiatry* (Cambridge: Harvard University Press, 1943), pp. 112–13.

complex included delusions of grandeur, mental deterioration, and progressive paralysis. The brain condition, first known from autopsy studies to consist of a widespread destruction of nervous tissue, was later found to be produced by the infectious agent, *treponema pallidum,* that is responsible for syphilis. In certain cases of syphilis, though by no means the majority, the infection makes its way into nervous tissue and eventually produces a destructive effect. It may be many years before this effect is great enough to be noticeable in behavior. One of the tragic features of general paresis is that the early deterioration of behavior generally passes for a reprehensible weakening of the patient's moral fiber. Only later is it realized that he is the victim of a serious cerebral disease.

General Course of the Disease. In its earliest stages the disorder takes the form of a subtle deterioration both in character and in mental and physical stamina. The patient finds it harder to keep his mind on his work, to remember appointments and the details of business, to maintain the organization of his daily life. Presently it may appear that his judgment is failing. He is planning unwise ventures and perhaps lending and borrowing money freely without keeping adequate accounts. Here and there on his clothing an undone button or an unaccustomed amount of dirt shows that he is becoming inattentive in the matter of personal neatness. Thoughtfulness and courtesy give place to cantankerous irritability. Sustained interest and affectionate relationships deteriorate into displays of exaggerated emotion followed by periods of indifference. Possibly the patient becomes excessive in the use of alcohol and in the search for promiscuous sexual pleasure. Possibly he merely begins to steal golf balls or draw foolish pictures in the margins of business memoranda. The early stages show changes that are more or less characteristic for all kinds of brain damage: irritability, restlessness, distractibility, weakened memory for recent events, shaky judgment, and poor emotional control.

If the disease progresses, the paralytic phenomena become increasingly prominent. General paresis affects all parts of the cortex and extends to lower centers. Its effects are therefore seen in writing and speech, in locomotion, in all finely coordinated activity, and even in reflexes such as the knee jerk and pupillary reflex to light. Speech is a particularly sensitive sign. The earliest symptoms of defect may consist of nothing more than an occasional hesitation, slurring, or mispronunciation. In the course of time the patient's speech may cease to be intelligible, words or syllables being omitted or run together or jumbled into a disintegrated, stuttering series of sounds. A similar disorganization can be traced in handwriting. Tremor disturbs the whole script, besides which there are omissions, elisions, a running together of words, and great variations in pressure. The spotty, erratic appearance of the handwriting is curiously similar to the spotty, "moth-eaten" appearance of the brain at autopsy. Walking is unsteady, with frequent stumbling and occasional falls. The patient is easily fatigued and may have an acute sense of his loss of strength.

With further progress of the disease, both the paralysis and the dementia become increasingly severe. The patient is likely to have seizures which resemble apoplexy or epileptic attacks. As his speech, handwriting and locomotion reach low levels, his memory correspondingly fails, and he becomes incapable of the simplest mental operations. He is disoriented even within the hospital, sometimes being unable to find his room, and his contacts with the outside world, even with his closest relatives, are completely severed. In the days when methods of treatment were still unknown, the end point of this deterioration was early death.

Individual Variations in the Pattern of Symptoms. Thus far we have described the course of the disease as if it consisted of two elements: paralysis (motor deterioration) and dementia (mental deterioration). The original or classic pattern included a third element: delusions of grandeur. Increasing skill in diagnosing general paresis has shown that this third element is by no means invariable. For a time it was customary to distinguish three forms of paresis: (1) the *exalted* or *expansive* type having grandiose delusions, (2) the *depressed* type having characteristic symptoms of melancholia, and (3) the *demented* type showing progressive deterioration without marked emotional upsets or delusional ideas. Even this classification, however, is too simple and arbitrary to fit the clinical facts. Some paretics alternate between excitement and depression. Some develop elaborate delusions of persecution. In some cases there is extreme agitation with constant restlessness, insomnia, progressive emaciation, and death from exhaustion, while other patients with the same infection merely become feeble, discouraged, and stupid. Even on the physical side there are pronounced differences in the onset and course of the disorder. In a certain number of cases the first detected symptom is a convulsive attack or short period of unconsciousness.

These wide individual variations make the picture of general paresis more complicated, but they need not render it confusing. General paresis is a physical disease of the brain. Why it strikes some syphilitic patients and not others we do not know; the question of differential susceptibility remains for future research to solve. But at all events the disease strikes very different people who have lived very different lives. It attacks people with different physical constitutions, different abilities, different predispositions. It strikes brains in which different personal histories have been recorded and by which different emotional attitudes have been learned. Like any other disease, general paresis does not attack a schematic organism and produce a standard effect. It attacks a living organism and injures a brain which, having lived part of a life, has become the seat of innumerable personal attitudes. Similar reasoning can be applied to all mental diseases. This outlook helps to simplify the problem of so-called "mixed forms" and sometimes amusing mixed diagnoses such as "schizophrenia with manic-depressive features and senile complications." Every case of general paresis is a case of general paresis plus features of the individual personality complicated by predispositions to other forms of disorder.

In view of this discussion, and recalling what we learned in the last section about cerebral dysrhythmia and epilepsy, it becomes easy to guess why certain cases of paresis show convulsions as the initial symptom. If we were right in assuming that cerebral dysrhythmia indicates a predisposition toward convulsive attacks, then the brain injury produced by *treponema pallidum* might well set off these attacks before creating any other visible symptoms. Similarly, if paresis attacks a person predisposed to mania, or depression, or manic-depressive cycles, the resulting disorder will be colored by the predisposition as well as by the injury to neural tissue. Again, if a person has restrained with difficulty his aggression, his sexuality, or his desire for personal glory, the lowered control occasioned by brain disease will release these strivings into vigorous and fantastic expression. But if he has always longed for peace and rest, he will become a rather quiet paretic; if he has always struggled to suppress anxiety, he will become an agitated one; if he has carried a heavy load of guilt, his general paresis will take the form of melancholy self-accusations. It is always necessary to consider both the disease and the person who has the disease.

The curious ideas expressed by paretic patients reflect both their strivings and their dementia. This is best revealed in the delusions of grandeur. They can be understood as wish-fulfillments, but their absurd and extravagant character clearly reflects the decreased control and judgment that betoken mental deterioration. The patients fancy that they have the strength of prize fighters, that they can lift colossal weights, that they are destined for championships at the next Olympic games. Fabulous wealth is in their possession, marvelous inventions are springing from their brains. One morning in a hospital ward a patient began inviting everyone to his country estate for the following week end. Each staff member and each patient in the ward was asked to set down his name on a piece of paper to signify his acceptance of the invitation. The attractions were specified in great detail: the rolling acres, the vast house, the riding horses and tennis courts and golf course, the beautiful women who would grace the occasion. In a confidential whisper each guest was advised that these beautiful women would be available for whatever purposes might come to mind. The patient thoroughly enjoyed his plans for the week end and showed not the slightest sense that they were incongruous with his present situation. In the meantime he was quite willing to humor the staff by submitting to examinations and routine procedures. By the time the week end arrived he was deep in an entirely different chapter of fantasy.

When the patient is depressed the content of his thought is equally unrestrained. He stands accused of the gravest faults; the hopelessness of his condition beggars description. Ideas of persecution are also on a large scale and rarely show the stable elaboration and struggle after logic that characterized the delusional system of L. Percy King. A paretic patient is incapable of organizing a stable and continuing world of fantasy that persists from day to day. Just as his memory is weak for the real events that occur, so it is weak for the events of yesterday's fantasy.

Treatment of General Paresis. In the last century general paresis was regarded as a fatal ailment. At least 80 per cent of the patients died within a few years of the onset. Today the situation is so changed that only a very small number of paretic cases come to a fatal end. Therapeutic successes were first obtained by means of the same drugs that were used to cure syphilis. For a while high hopes were entertained for salvarsan and tryparsamide, but arrest of the symptoms proved to be obtainable in only a small proportion of cases treated with these preparations. The next step was the use of fever therapy. Patients were inoculated with tertian malaria which produces bouts of high fever reaching 104 degrees, sometimes even more. The infection could be terminated with quinine if the fever proved too taxing to the patient. The technique was presently improved by using artificial fever produced by placing the patient in an air-conditioned warmed chamber. The high body temperature was apparently fatal to the *treponema* so that further destruction of nervous tissue was prevented. Fever therapy arrested the disease in at least 60 to 80 per cent of cases. Still more recently, equal if not greater success has been obtained by using penicillin, which has now become the therapy of choice in treating general paresis.

Destroyed or injured nervous tissue cannot be replaced. Technically speaking, general paresis can only be arrested, not cured. Most patients do not regain the mental level at which they functioned before illness. Nevertheless in many cases there is an improvement following therapy. This must be attributed largely to reduction of the inflammation prevailing in injured tissue, and the restoration of an optimal chemical environment for the tissue that has escaped injury.

The treatment and control of syphilis are being reflected in a decreased incidence of general paresis. In countries where the medical campaign against syphilis is vigorously prosecuted, it seems likely that general paresis will become a rather rare disease.

MENTAL CHANGES AND DISORDERS OF OLD AGE

One person out of five entering a mental hospital suffers from a disorder associated with old age. The frequency of such disorders is steadily increasing. This is an indirect consequence of the general advance of medical science. As fewer people die of such diseases as tuberculosis, diphtheria, and pneumonia, more survive into the sixties and seventies when senile changes begin to take place. It is to be expected that this trend will continue. If medicine succeeds in conquering such enemies as cancer and heart disease, an even greater part of the population will live into the seventies. In 1850 only 2.6 per cent of the population lived beyond 65; in 1950, 7.6 per cent exceeded that age. Whether this will mean a steadily increasing incidence of senile mental disorders depends upon our ability to understand and alleviate these afflictions of later life. The senile psychoses can be looked upon as exaggerated forms of the changes that are inseparable from aging. Some of these changes are bodily, others are psychological. We shall first consider the normal course of change with advancing years, thus establishing a background for the understanding of senile disorders.

The Decline of Abilities. As age advances, there is a marked decline of physical energy. One after another the more vigorous forms of physical exertion have to be avoided. Even for a person who takes his physical limitations good-naturedly, it is hard to avoid a feeling of growing helplessness. The decrease in motor capacity is matched by a weakening of sensory acuity. Less sharpness both in vision and hearing is characteristic of the older years. There is also a decline in the speed of response. Studies of reaction time show a steady decrease, beginning in the second or third decades of life, and proceeding at a faster rate in the later decades. There are wide individual differences, but the general trend is clear. An older person registers his environment less keenly, responds to it less quickly, and is able to respond in less varied and energetic ways.

A similar decline is observed in those functions that are measured by intelligence tests. This is partly but not wholly a function of speed. In tests where speed is not important the decrease is less marked but still present. Not all types of performance are equally affected. Tests of vocabulary and tests of general information show the smallest losses with advancing years, whereas tests requiring ingenuity in new performances are particularly vulnerable. The effects of age may be markedly resisted in the case of knowledge and skills that continue in active use. Thus an elderly scholar who keeps steadily at work may show a minimum of impairment in his special field of expertness, remembering details in a way that startles younger people who do not share his interest in the field. Nevertheless, intellectual competence as a whole undergoes a definite decline comparable to the falling off of sensory and physical prowess.

Failing memory is one of the most obvious symptoms of aging. The inability to remember names is often extremely frustrating to the person himself. Although tests of rote memory do not show much impairment until after the age of eighty, the assimilation of memories and the power to act upon them appear to decline somewhat earlier. It is a generally observed fact that the memory loss of older people is greatest in respect to recent events. They may remember current happenings so poorly as to seem almost disoriented, yet remain completely clear about the earlier events of their lives, even of their childhood. There is no fully satisfactory explanation for this fact, which is also found in cases of brain deterioration caused by general paresis and chronic alcoholism. It is possible that attention and initial registration are more at fault than recall. In any event the net result is a weakening of memory, especially for recent and current happenings.[26]

The decline of abilities can be measured at even more basic levels than those just discussed. Behind the weakening physical and mental capacity it is possible to conceive a more generalized impairment which affects the cells of all tissues, including those in the central nervous system. This general idea is developed by Shock, who points out that normal cellular metabolism becomes increasingly difficult with age.[27] In old tissues there is an increase of inert material, chiefly fibrin and collagen. This inert material surrounds many cells and simply by mechanical blocking impairs the delivery of oxygen and nutrient materials to the still active or metabolizing cells. There is, furthermore, a diminution of the number of functioning cells in older tissues. In addition, the flow of blood may be less adequate and regular, especially if the artery walls have hardened and thickened. The result of these changes is to interfere with normal cellular metabolism. If temporary anoxia occurs here and there, a vicious circle is set in motion. Anoxic cells produce more fibrin, which in turn further obstructs the delivery of oxygen even when the blood flow is restored. Vitamin deficiencies may further injure the processes of cellular metabolism. All these changes are of particular im-

[26] J. G. Gilbert, *Understanding Old Age* (New York: The Ronald Press Co., 1952), chap. iv.

[27] N. W. Shock, "Physiological Aspects of Mental Disorders in Later Life," in O. Kaplan (ed.), *Mental Disorders in Later Life* (Stanford: Stanford University Press, 1945), chap. iii.

portance for the cells of the central nervous system, but Shock suggests that similar impairment may affect all the cells of the body.

The effect of this general lowering of cellular efficiency is an increasing difficulty in maintaining homeostasis. The body becomes less capable of maintaining the constancy of its internal environment and has to work harder to achieve this goal. Reserve capacities and emergency reactions must be drawn upon more freely, leaving less surplus energy for other activities. Stress continues to occur, and a greater proportion of available energy has to be devoted to restoring equilibrium. If we consider the maintaining of homeostasis as the first demand on any organism, it becomes clear that a general restriction will necessarily be felt in all activities not directly concerned with that central demand.

Psychological Situation of the Aged. Various traits are ascribed to older people. Perhaps the most general pattern can be suggested by the three words: conservative, opinionated, selfish. Traits of this kind clearly do not result from the mere fact of declining capacities and lowering energy. They result from the interaction between these factors and the psychological situation of the aged.

When the family unit is large, as is still the case in some primitive societies, and to some extent in rural areas generally, the older people are expected to remain in the family circle. As a matter of course the household includes grandparents, parents, and children, often with a few other relatives thrown in. The grandparents continue to play an essential though reduced part in the life of the family, and they need not fear for their support. The situation is different in the small urban family unit which at least in the United States is rapidly becoming the standard pattern. The family unit typically consists of but one pair of parents and their children, and a grandparent living in the home is quite generally felt to be a burdensome intrusion. Many older people face the alternative of being an unwelcome visitor in the household of one of their children or of living by themselves in restricted and lonely circumstances. In either case they are likely to feel themselves useless and superfluous. Whereas in simpler times grandfather might putter around the farm with relatively useful results, he is now more likely to be distinctly retired and out of a job. If grandmother wants to help in the kitchen or with the children, she is likely to be told that her ideas on psychology are old-fashioned and that she must be careful not to break the kitchen machinery. The fact that our times are rapidly changing has the effect of decreasing the utility of older people. The wisdom of the aged is less wise in a time of rapid change.

If we are to understand the psychological situation of the aged, we must realize that changing times have taken from older people one of their best ways of maintaining self-respect. To be consulted because of one's accumulated wisdom means to be an active participant in life. Through the asset of long experience one continues to exert some influence upon today's and tomorrow's events. For a long time, and especially in recent years, American culture has been strongly centered upon youth. The young do not want to look middle-aged, but the middle-aged want to look young, and they spend millions of dollars every year trying to create this illusion. In this cultural climate the old tend to be pushed aside much as used to be the case with mentally defective children. For reasons both technological and cultural, old people have thus dropped out of a position of significance in their society. They are likely to be treated with condescension, even by youthful psychologists and social workers bent on helping them to adjust. Small wonder that senior citizens, when asked what they want, say that they would like a voice in their own retirement and that they want somehow to remain an active part of the community, doing some kind of purposeful and productive work. They do not want to be put away on a shelf.[28]

Under present circumstances, therefore, old age means for many people a readjustment almost as great as that which is required at adolescence. Often it is necessary to move to a new home in a new neighborhood, producing a sense of isolation from friends and old associations. If the older person remains in the same home, the situation is only relatively better. He is likely to experience a constant loss of friends by death, and he is not in a very good position to make new ones. Thus in any event he tends to become socially isolated and to lose the benefit of group membership. At the same time he may become to some extent financially dependent, very likely on the same people whose diapers he used to change and whose naughtiness he used to chastise, although this particular hardship is being reduced by extensions of social security benefits. Just as in adolescence it is necessary to establish independence, self-sufficiency, group memberships, vocation, and channels for an increased sex drive, so in old age it is necessary to adapt oneself to dependence on others, dwindling group memberships, life without a vocation, and a reduced vitality and sexual interest.

What resources are available to accomplish this readjustment? Less energy, less plasticity, less buoyancy of interest than was present at adolescence, but above all less real motive for change. The adolescent's time perspective is highly favorable. Most of life is before him. The person that he is to become is still unformulated, and many splendid achievements are within the range of possibility. The old person's life is

[28] J. E. W. Wallin, "The Psychological, Educational, and Social Problems of the Aging as Viewed by a Mid-Octogenarian," *Journal of Genetic Psychology*, C (1962), pp. 41–46.

mostly behind him. What he has achieved and what he has become as a person are both matters of history. If an old person keeps his life rich and full to the last, it is just for the sake of keeping it rich and full. He is not helped by images of a better future for himself on earth.

These considerations are important in understanding certain traits that younger people find irritating. A young person has little interest in hearing how things used to be before he was born, especially if he must hear about them with the implication that things have been going to the dogs ever since. He wants to talk about the present and future rather than the past. Very likely the old person cannot talk about the present because his memory for current happenings is becoming poor, but in any event he is not strongly motivated to contemplate the future. The conflicting viewpoints of youth and age can be clarified by an illustration. Suppose the old person has been a successful architect in his day, designing many important public and private buildings. Trained around 1910, he will have given to his early work a massive dignity, even his private homes having weighty columns, large entrance halls, and spacious rooms with high ceilings. His rise to eminence will have occurred during the period of Coolidge prosperity, when his big designs were in perfect harmony with the expansive spirit of the times. Today he expresses himself caustically about flimsy ranch houses, box-like colonials, homes no bigger than hen coops, churches that look like factories, city halls that cannot be told from mere office buildings. It is hard for a young listener to accept all these judgments or to understand why the old man is oblivious to changed economic conditions and new kinds of building materials. But the old person cannot budge from his opinions. To do so would be equivalent to admitting that his whole professional career was a failure. What appears to be the obstinate conservatism of old people is often a determined effort to preserve self-respect.

The psychological situation of the aged is not easy. It is the more remarkable, therefore, that so many people succeed in growing old gracefully, usefully, and happily. In a study of men and women over 65 in a midwestern community it was found that 75 per cent considered themselves happy, 79 per cent considered themselves healthy, only 6 per cent were homebound, and many were continuing to lead a fairly active life.[29] Old age nevertheless contains a great variety of serious threats. It involves progressive limitations and a shrinking of personal significance. The desire to be loved and valued does not decline with age, but the very limitations of the elderly make them irritating to younger people. The difference in tempo alone is responsible for much impatience. To wait for slow movements, slow speech, slow comprehension can be extremely

[29] R. J. Havighurst and R. Albrecht, *Older People* (London: Longmans, Green & Co., Ltd., 1953).

frustrating. Such surface irritations obstruct the expression of affection and esteem. In view of these major problems and major threats in old age, it is not surprising that neurotic reactions not infrequently occur. The most common pattern is hypochondriasis, an anxious concern over the bodily functions and their ailments. Another common pattern is chronic fatigue or neurasthenia. A certain somatic compliance doubtless helps to increase the frequency of these two syndromes. The other two most common forms of neurotic reaction are anxiety states and reactive depressions. It is not difficult to discern their relation to the psychological situations of old age.

Senile Psychoses. When a chronic mental disorder occurs in an elderly person and is accompanied by signs of mental deterioration, it is called either senile psychosis or senile dementia. Both terms are in a way correct. These conditions are really a combination of senile deterioration with special reactions that still further increase the loss of contact with reality. Depressed states, agitated states, delirious and confused states, or paranoid reactions may add themselves to the general picture of impairment. The onset is gradual, sometimes almost imperceptible. The patient becomes a little more egocentric and conservative, inefficient and forgetful, sad, disturbed, or suspicious, until it seems to everyone that he can no longer take care of himself outside the hospital. Perhaps forgetfulness crosses the line into confusion: he goes for a walk and cannot find his way home. Perhaps querulous complaints about his food and digestion slip over into delusions that his daughter-in-law is trying to poison him. Sometimes a physical illness or some situational stress marks the boundary a little more sharply. Perhaps the family home has to be sold and the old person moved to new surroundings. Sickness or ailments of a lasting sort may suddenly restrict the range of available activities. In all such cases the person is called upon rather suddenly to make a whole series of readjustments, and he proves unequal to the strain. But deterioration has been in progress and the onset is never really sudden.

Senile patients are apt to be restless and sleepless. Often they wander in the night and at such times are likely to be particularly confused. Irritation is frequent, judgment is poor, attention is erratic, and the registration of impressions decidedly irregular. On top of this general picture of impairment go the depressed, agitated, or paranoid reactions. As the disorder advances, intellectual deficit increasingly dominates the picture. Speech becomes rambling and incoherent, and failing memory may be pieced out with fabrications. The patient may fail to recognize his relatives. In the course of time, episodes of confusion, occasionally with hallucinations, occur with greater frequency. Social amenities and courtesy are preserved almost to the last, but the end point is a state of helplessness and vegetation in which the patient becomes oblivious to his surroundings. It is obvious that not much can be done for senile patients except to make them comfortable, keep them in physical health, provide occupations that are within their powers, and protect them from unnecessary difficulties.

The changes in the brain that underlie senile psychoses are best conceived as consequences of inadequate blood supply. It has been shown, for instance, that in such cases there is a significant reduction in the uptake of oxygen by cerebral tissues, this in turn being probably due to increased vascular resistance which reduces blood flow through the brain.[30] At autopsy it is found that there are marked changes in nervous tissue, especially in the cerebral cortex. On the whole the frontal areas are most seriously altered. There is a general shrinkage of the brain tissue as a whole, a reduction in the number of nerve cells, and a thickening or change of some kind in the intercellular tissues. All the changes are diffuse; they are not concentrated in any one spot sufficiently to alter the cortical architecture. The changes are not peculiar to senile psychoses, being found with lesser severity in normal older people and with greater severity in Alzheimer's and Pick's diseases. They are congruent with Shock's theory of injury to nerve cells through impaired diffusion of oxygen and nutrient materials.[31]

Psychoses with Cerebral Arteriosclerosis. When there is a considerable degree of arteriosclerosis, the changes in the brain are of a more devastating character. Hardening and thickening of the walls of the blood vessels, including not only the large arteries but also the small arterioles and capillaries, reduces the supply of blood to all tissues. The effect of this reduction is especially serious in the brain, where the tissues are peculiarly dependent on an adequate supply of oxygen and nutrient materials. The brains of arteriosclerotic patients at autopsy show a variety of severe focal lesions in which the cerebral structure is completely destroyed, although surrounding nervous tissue may be in a state of good preservation. Softened and disintegrated tissue is found at the points of lesion. The temporal and occipital areas seem to be particularly vulnerable. While the cause of these focal softenings is not definitely known, the best hypothesis seems to be that they occur as a result of restricted blood supply, just as in the more gradual senile psychoses.

[30] F. A. Freyhan, R. B. Woodford, and S. S. Kety, "Cerebral Blood Flow and Metabolism in Psychoses of Senility," *Journal of Nervous and Mental Disease,* CXIII (1951), pp. 449–56.

[31] This account of neural changes follows D. Rothschild, in Kaplan, *op. cit.,* pp. 237–46. It may not do justice to intrinsic aging processes in nerve cells, as pointed out by J. E. Birren, "Psychological Aspects of Aging," *Annual Review of Psychology,* XI (Stanford: Annual Reviews, Inc., 1960), pp. 161–98.

There are usually various premonitory symptoms prior to the development of full psychosis. Physical and mental letdown may be noticed, along with headaches and dizziness. In more than half the cases the onset of the acute psychosis is sudden, differing in this respect from senile psychoses. It takes the form of an attack of confusion with clouding of consciousness, incoherence, great restlessness, and complete loss of contact with the environment. The confused state may last for weeks or months. In about half the cases it subsides, leaving the patient with considerable senile impairment but in a much less confused condition. Later attacks are the rule, however, and cure is not to be expected.

The condition of the brain caused by cerebral arteriosclerosis is fairly similar to the condition found in general paresis. The mental changes are of a somewhat similar order. It is therefore interesting to notice certain differences in the content of the symptoms and the psychological processes which they imply. Occasionally there are delusions of grandeur and persecution in psychoses with cerebral arteriosclerosis, but these are far less characteristic and less extravagantly developed than is the case in general paresis. This difference seems to be attributable to the age of the patients or, more directly, to the general level of vitality at which they are living. An old person, already physically handicapped and living within shrunken horizons having no perspective toward the future, typically becomes confused, perhaps with a touch of depression or agitation, when his brain reaches a point of damage that is no longer consistent with integrated action. A person in middle life, still relatively vigorous, ambitious, with considerable strength of drive, reacts to brain damage with symptoms of a more compensatory kind. His thoughts may be delusions, but they are delusions that place him in satisfying and glorious situations or that use the mechanism of projection to free him from any sense of personal shortcoming. Thus even in the study of brain diseases it is impossible to overlook psychological factors, even though these are not responsible for initiating the disorder. The disease happens to the man, and the man puts his stamp on the standard symptoms that result from the disease.

SUGGESTIONS FOR FURTHER READING

The classical handbook in the field of mental deficiency is A. F. Tredgold's *A Text-Book of Mental Deficiency,* first published in 1908 and now in its seventh edition (Baltimore, The Williams & Wilkins Co., 1947). Excellent particularly for its discussions of concepts and research problems is S. B. Sarason's *Psychological Problems in Mental Deficiency* (New York, Harper & Row, 1949). Problems of training set the theme in *Educating the Retarded Child* by S. A. Kirk and G. O. Johnson (Boston, Houghton Mifflin Co., 1951). Highly recommended both for the parents of retarded children and for those who are interested in work with the retarded is the book by Edw. L. French and J. Clifford Scott, *Child in the Shadows* (Philadelphia, J. B. Lippincott Co., 1960).

There are two excellent books on epilepsy: *Science and Seizures* (New York, Harper & Row, 1941) by W. G. Lennox, and *Convulsive Seizures* (Philadelphia, J. B. Lippincott Co., 1943) by T. J. Putnam. Lennox gives a summary of the subject in J. McV. Hunt, *Personality and the Behavior Disorders* (New York, The Ronald Press Co., 1944), Vol. II, Ch. 31. Penfield's work and reflections appear in a large work entitled *Epilepsy and the Functional Anatomy of the Human Brain* (W. Penfield and H. Jasper, Boston, Little, Brown & Co., 1954).

A general survey of the problems of old age is given by Jeanne G. Gilbert, *Understanding Old Age* (New York, The Ronald Press Co., 1952). An informative collection which includes a number of case studies is *Aging in Western Societies*, edited by E. W. Burgess (Chicago, University of Chicago Press, 1960).

14

Depressive and Manic Disorders

In any given year the admissions to mental hospitals are distributed roughly as follows: schizophrenia, 20 per cent; depressive and manic conditions, 14 per cent; disorders with cerebral arteriosclerosis, 12 per cent; senile psychoses, 9 per cent; alcoholic conditions, 10 per cent; general paresis, 6 per cent; and the remainder scattered in various categories.[1] Of the disorders named, we have now studied all but the first two, but these two account for a third of the hospital admissions. These two, moreover, have long been designated the "major psychoses," and until the recent rise of disorders connected with old age they certainly constituted the major problems faced by mental hospitals. Depressive and manic disorders, to be taken up in this chapter, and schizophrenia, which will occupy us in the next, have been extensively studied for many years, yet in both cases there is still a great deal of uncertainty about the real roots of the disorder.

Joy and sorrow are obvious and important features of human life, and their exaggerated forms, mania and melancholia, were among the earliest mental symptoms to be recognized by medical men. In some respects they seem to be opposites, but long before modern times it was observed that in certain patients mania and melancholia succeeded each other. On the whole the opinion prevailed that these were cases in which one disease transformed itself into another. Toward the middle of the last century, however, there were frequent suggestions that mania and melancholia belonged together in a single disease process, both being exaggerations

[1] U. S. Department of Commerce, *Patients in Mental Institutions, 1942* (Washington, D.C.: U.S. Government Printing Office, 1945).

in the sphere of mood. Designations such as "cyclical insanity" were from time to time proposed. Finally, in 1899, Kraepelin introduced the term *manic-depressive insanity,* including under this heading not only the alternating forms but the simple manias and melancholias as well. "In the course of years," he wrote, "I have been more and more convinced that all of these pictures are but forms of a single disease process. Certain fundamental features recur in these morbid states notwithstanding manifold external differences."[2] Thus the concept of *manic-depressive psychosis* became firmly established in psychiatric thought.

There is no question that these two disorders of mood frequently occur in the same person. In some cases, however, depression occurs without any tendency toward subsequent mania, and in other cases mania occurs as the sole symptom. Furthermore, there are certain varieties of depression, such as *involutional melancholia* and *neurotic depression,* which have never been included in the concept of manic-depressive psychosis, although it would tax any clinician severely to distinguish some of the cases on the basis of symptoms alone from the depressions that later give place to mania. We have seen throughout this book that psychiatric classification is full of pitfalls. Certainly the classification of the affective disorders is far from satisfactory, and the relation between manias and depressions is anything but clear.

Further trouble arises over the use of the term *psychosis.* The distinguishing mark of psychosis is a serious loss of contact with reality. Roughly speaking, a disorder is called a psychosis if the patient's condition meets the legal criteria of *insanity:* the patient is either unable to take care of himself, or is dangerous to others, or both. These criteria are met in severe depressed states and highly manic states, for both of which it is essential that the patient be hospitalized. On the other hand, patients are constantly seen at clinics or in private practice who show marked mood changes, generally along with other symptoms, yet who are not in the least disoriented, "out of their heads," or in need of hospital care.[3] There is substantial disagreement among psychiatrists as to whether these cases should be labeled mild psychosis or placed in some other category such as neurosis or even psychosomatic disorder. It may be that depressions, especially, are not all made out of the same stuff, in which case this chapter will not be dealing altogether with psychosis.

These initial remarks about classification can hardly be said to start us on a nicely charted course. It is all the more important, therefore, to begin our account at a descriptive level, considering depressed states and

[2] Quoted by S. Jelliffe, "Some Historical Phases of the Manic-Depressive Synthesis," *Journal of Nervous and Mental Diseases,* LXXIII (1931), pp. 353–74, 499–521.

[3] J. D. Campbell, *Manic-Depressive Disease* (Philadelphia: J. B. Lippincott Co., 1953), pp. 2–5.

manic states in their own right. If we can lay a reasonably solid factual foundation we may be able to straighten out some of the confusion which seems to prevail in the study of depressed and manic disorders.

DEPRESSED STATES

Retarded Depressions. The typical symptoms of retarded depression can be grouped under the headings of underactivity and a dejected mood. In their mildest form they shade imperceptibly into a normal state of discouragement. The underactivity shows itself in slowness of movement and speech. Exertion is experienced as difficult; the patients prefer to sit in one place with folded hands, and cannot summon the energy to perform the simplest errands. If questioned they speak slowly, in a low tone, with great economy of words, and they prefer not to speak at all. There is a similar retardation in the sphere of thought. Ideas do not come to mind and a great inertia seems to block the solving of problems. As one patient described it, "At these times my brain feels paralyzed; I have not the strength or ambition to do anything. . . . I have the impulse to act, but it seems as if something shuts down and prohibits action."[4] Illustrative of the retardation in thought is the patient's reaction to reading. What is read seems to call up no associations; it is not assimilated, and the whole business of keeping up continuous attention is felt as painfully exhausting.

The dejected mood may take the form simply of unrelieved sadness. The patient cannot be cheered; everything looks gloomy to him. If he talks about his troubles, he paints a picture of utter hopelessness. Some patients concentrate their woes on bodily complaints, feeling sure that they have an incurable disease or that their internal organs are rotting away. More characteristic, however, is a conviction of sinfulness and worthlessness. The patient believes he has committed unforgivable sins and is responsible for all the misery he perceives around him. He is full of self-accusations, and the one theme on which he has strength enough to converse is that of his wickedness and the dire punishments that must be in store. The mechanism of projection seems to be generally unavailable to depressed patients. Their minds are full of self-blaming, and they do not lift this burden by transferring the blame to outside persecutors. In severe cases the hopelessness is so profound that the possibilities of suicide cannot be discounted.

It is convenient in the description and diagnosis of these patients to mark off three degrees of depression. The first level is generally called by such names as mild or subacute depression or simple retardation.

[4] W. A. White, *Outlines of Psychiatry* (13th ed.; New York: Nervous and Mental Disease Publishing Co., 1932), p. 161.

The second level is called acute depression or acute melancholia. The third level, characterized by immobility and speechlessness, is generally referred to as depressive stupor. These levels cannot be sharply separated. Each degree represents a little more underactivity and a little more dejection than the previous one.

Example of Depression. In our historical chapter we mentioned the autobiography of Clifford W. Beers, a book which did a great deal to establish the mental hygiene movement. Beers was in a psychotic condition with ups and downs for three years. The seriousness of his condition first became fully apparent when he tried to commit suicide by throwing himself out the window of his bedroom. For the next two years he was in a depressed state, complicated in various ways by hallucinations and other less usual features. At the end of this time he changed rather quickly to a manic condition. His account of his experiences will provide us with illustrations for both conditions.[5]

Because of injuries sustained in his jump from the window, Beers was first taken to a general hospital in his home city. He conceived that he was under a criminal charge for attempted suicide, and that his crime must be known to everyone in the city. "The public believed me the most despicable member of my race. The papers were filled with accounts of my misdeeds." The hospital was located on the street that led to the university athletic field, and a crowd of students and graduates went by on their way to a class-day game. Beers was sure that every one of these people loathed him for having disgraced his alma mater. "When they approached the hospital on their way to the athletic field, I concluded that it was their intention to take me from my bed, drag me to the lawn, and there tear me limb from limb." Some time later he was taken to a sanatorium in another community. "The day was hot, and, as we drove to the railway station, the blinds on most of the houses in the streets through which we passed were seen to be closed. I thought I saw an unbroken line of deserted houses, and I imagined that their desertion had been deliberately planned as a sign of displeasure on the part of their former occupants. I supposed them bitterly ashamed of such a despicable townsman as myself."

Nearly two years later Beers was still convinced that he was to go on trial. His brother, who visited him often, was apt to comment favorably on his health and to add, "We shall straighten you out yet." To Beers this was an ambiguous phrase "which might refer to the end of the hangman's rope, or to a fatal electric shock." He interpreted his

[5] C. W. Beers, *A Mind That Found Itself* (Garden City, N. Y.: Doubleday & Co., Inc., 1931). The depressed phase of the illness is described on pp. 11–87, the manic phase on pp. 87–189.

improving physical health as a sign that the doctors were fattening him for the slaughter after his trial which, of course, could have but one outcome. Suicide seemed a preferable fate, and for many weeks he devised a series of schemes to bring about this result. Everything that happened only served to remind him of his misery. He could take no pleasure in his daily walks with his attendant, for example, because he was sure that everyone knew his black record and impending punishment. "I wondered why passers-by did not revile and stone me. It was not surprising that a piece of rope, old and frayed, which someone had carelessly thrown on a hedge by a cemetery that I sometimes passed, had for me great significance."

These examples show the pervasive effect of the dejected mood. Even quite incidental impressions receive a distorted meaning which fits them into the patient's depressed state of mind. His sense of sin and worthlessness is so dominating that he can no longer interpret experience in any other terms. This exaggeration of the self and its problems is characteristic of other psychotic conditions besides depression. We shall see presently that it is true of mania, and we have learned already from the experience of L. Percy King that it occurs in paranoid schizophrenia. King had the same tendency as Beers to twist the meaning of commonplace events so that they bore on his all-consuming problem. He could not see a sign in a window without thinking that its words accused him, or threatened him, or represented a trap set by his pursuers. King, however, had enlisted the service of projection which spared him the burden of self-blame. He felt himself the victim of a purely malicious persecution, whereas Beers believed himself utterly contemptible and worthless.

Agitated Depressions. There is another clinical syndrome that includes depression without retardation of action or thought. There is the same mental content of hopelessness, worthlessness, and self-accusation that appears in the retarded depressions. Thoughts of death are prominent and suicide is a real danger. But instead of sitting silently in an attitude of despair, the patient is extremely active and talkative. He cannot keep still, he cannot sleep, he can only pace up and down with moans and sighs and wringing of the hands. The existence of this variant form of depression makes it clear that dejected mood and underactivity do not necessarily go together. As a matter of fact patients are sometimes found who combine mood and activity in the reverse pattern: action and thought are seriously retarded, but the mood is one of exultation. In the case of agitated depressions the patient's behavior reflects a combination of depressed mood and anxious tension.[6]

[6] A detailed clinical study of different patterns of depressive illness is reported by R. R. Grinker, J. Miller, M. Sabshin, R. Nunn, and J. C. Nunnally, *The Phenomena of Depressions* (New York: Paul B. Hoeber, Inc., 1961).

The following is given by Strecker and Ebaugh as a fairly typical case.[7] A fifty-three-year-old woman of apparently healthy ancestry and good educational background was admitted to the hospital in a highly agitated and deeply depressed condition. As a young woman she had been quiet, conscientious, and self-sacrificing, but distinctly sociable, well-liked by her friends, and a capable manager of the house. At twenty-five she married a man who proved to be a hopeless alcoholic and drug addict. This was the beginning of a life that grew more and more difficult. The patient was constantly worried about her husband, her children, and the family finances. When the husband's deterioration made further home life impossible, she separated from him and took to running a rooming house in order to support herself and the children. For five years before her illness she had been unable to secure help and was constantly exhausted by the work of the house. As a result she had severe attacks of grippe every winter and was in a badly run down condition. The psychosis came on suddenly. She began to moan, pace up and down, and wring her hands. She felt herself a wicked sinner for having left her husband; she ought never to have been born because she brought such trouble on the whole world.

In this condition she arrived at the hospital. She was in a state of almost ceaseless activity, squirming in her chair, walking rapidly about, pulling at her hair, pinching her cheeks, biting her fingers. Her deeply lined face bore an expression of unutterable woe. At times she was frankly terrified; at other times she shrank from the nurse's hand because she felt herself unworthy to be touched. She believed that all her family had been killed because of her wrongdoing. "Oh, what have I done!" she would exclaim. "Can't I be saved? What is in store for me?" Then she would get started on her poverty: "Not a cent left, not a cent." She made one unsuccessful attempt at suicide. In spite of her miserable state and violent self-accusations, she was not disoriented or hallucinated nor were there any discernible gaps in her memory. At the end of a year she was well on the way to recovery, with the beginnings of insight into the distorted nature of her previous ideas.

MANIC STATES

Characteristics of Mania. In its mildest stages, often called hypomania or subacute mania, a manic state is difficult to distinguish from a normal state of good spirits and high efficiency. There is a certain amount of overactivity, expressing itself both in motor channels and in a free flow of ideas and speech. There is also a show of confidence and enterprise

[7] E. A. Strecker and F. G. Ebaugh, *Practical Clinical Psychiatry* (5th ed.; Philadelphia: The Blakiston Co., 1940), pp. 356–60.

that may drift over into boastful self-assertion. Ordinary people are apt to envy a patient in this stage, and business offices consider him ready for promotion. The signs that all is not well do not show themselves in single actions but rather in the continuity of one action or idea with another. It will be apparent that the patient flies from one idea to a different one, makes a plan one moment only to cancel it the next, and is unduly irritated if the least frustration lies in his path. Cameron compares subacute mania to mild alcoholic intoxication. The patient is gay, witty, and jolly, free in speech and high in self-confidence. He is full of plans and not bothered by the thought of difficulties or risks in carrying them out. Just as in alcoholic intoxication, his efficiency is lowered but his illusion of efficiency is raised.[8] He may be having a wonderful time and see not the slightest reason why anyone should be concerned about him.

It is customary to recognize three degrees of mania: subacute or hypomania (as just described), acute mania, and hyperacute or delirious mania. The subacute form shades down into a state of normal elation, the delirious form shades off into violent and disorganized behavior that cannot be distinguished from any other form of wild excitement. The true hallmarks of the disorder can best be perceived in the middle stage called acute mania.

Outstanding is the stream of talk, which seems never to abate. The rapid flow is full of puns and play on words. Taken in short units it is perfectly coherent, but change from topic to topic is constantly taking place. These changes reveal the patient's distractibility. Whatever he sees or hears may divert his attention completely, and may cause him to make personal remarks that take visitors aback: "My, how gray your hair is," or "Your trousers certainly need to be pressed." In the motor sphere there is constant restlessness. The patient is always busy, never tired. He sleeps little at night and is eager for action long before sunrise. If he cannot find enough ways to use up his energy, he may burst into shouts and song, smash furniture, or do setting-up exercises. The need for action amounts to an irresistible pressure. Continued over many days and through sleepless nights it presently begins to tell on the patient's health. Continuous hot baths or sedatives may be necessary to keep him quiet for a little while.

The prevailing mood is one of joyous elation. The patient is full of confidence and is quite willing to carry his enterprises to the White House, to Wall Street, to Hollywood, or wherever he believes they will be most rapidly dispatched to their splendid conclusions. The confident

[8] N. Cameron, "The Functional Psychoses," in J. McV. Hunt (ed.), *Personality and the Behavior Disorders* (New York: The Ronald Press Co., 1944), Vol. II, chap. xxix.

mood easily rises to domineering arrogance, especially toward those in authority. Very inconsiderate of those around him, the patient is easily aroused to anger and fury if his activities are in any way curbed. If his thoughts take a sexual turn, he will show a similar lack of restraint. All impulses come to immediate expression in words and in acts in so far as these are permitted. Any kind of restraint is extremely uncomfortable because of the pressure to activity.

Disturbances of thought and loss of contact with reality are incidental results of the overactivity and overconfidence. The patient is too distractible to perceive the environment with accuracy, too changeable to turn his flight of ideas into consecutive thinking, too elated to take account of facts that run counter to his mood. Delusions of great wealth or accomplishment readily develop, but the distortion of reality rarely extends to hallucination. In a way a manic patient does not strike an observer as being as crazy as a schizophrenic or general paretic. The effect is rather of a person abnormally speeded up and thus seriously disorganized, but not unintelligible or queer. The patient is highly incompetent to carry on his own affairs and needs to be hospitalized for his own good and for the sake of his health. But he does not seem as far away from the normal as is the case with other psychotics.

Example of Manic Behavior. We turn to the third year of Clifford Beers' psychosis for a concrete example of the manic state. While there were many preliminary signs that Beers' depression was lifting, the decisive change of mood came quite suddenly. The sensation was like the lifting of a cloud, and at once his mind began to be flooded with ideas for a vast program of humanitarian reform. The following day he attended a church service. Instead of discovering gloomy forebodings and veiled threats in the service, he now heard every word as if it were a personal message from God. Phrases from the psalms clearly referred to the great projects that were coursing through his mind, and to his own role as the instrument chosen to carry them out. "My heart is inditing a good matter," he heard, "my tongue is the pen of a ready writer." This surely referred to his heart and his tongue, so he began writing letters about everything that had happened to him. Soon exhausting his supply of stationery, he arranged to secure large quantities of wrapping paper which he cut in strips a foot wide and pasted together into vast rolls. "More than once, letters twenty or thirty feet long were written, and on one occasion the accumulation of two or three days of excessive productivity, when spread upon the floor, reached from one end of the corridor to the other—a distance of about one hundred feet. My hourly output was something like twelve feet. . . . Under the pressure of elation one takes pride in doing everything in record time. Despite my speed my letters were not incoherent. They were simply digressive, which was to be expected, as elation befogs one's 'goal idea.'"

The writing of colossal letters soon proved an insufficient means of using up his energy. "I proceeded to assume entire charge of that portion of the hospital in which I happened at the moment to be confined. What I eventually issued as imperative orders were often presented at first as polite suggestions. But, if my suggestions were not accorded a respectful hearing, and my demands acted upon at once, I invariably supplemented them with vituperative ultimatums." Beers soon determined to conduct a complete investigation of the hospital. This proved very trying to the staff and resulted in serious friction. It led to his being placed in a small cell in the violent ward where for want of paper he proceeded to write all over the walls. Angered at his treatment, he rigged up a fake scene of suicide to frighten the attendants—a striking contrast to his serious and persistent attempts to take his life when depressed. Before long his mind turned to inventions. Characteristically, these were not of a minor order; he decided "to overcome no less a force than gravity itself." Tearing a carpet into strips, he managed to suspend his bed with himself in it between the window and a transom over the door. "So epoch-making did this discovery appear to me that I noted the exact position of the bed so that a wondering posterity might ever afterward view and revere the exact spot on the earth's surface whence one of man's greatest thoughts had winged its way to immortality."

The successful overcoming of gravity seemed to open endless possibilities. Great wealth would soon be in his hands. And with this he planned to transform his home city into a veritable garden spot and center of learning. Scores of parks would be dotted with cathedrals, libraries, art galleries, theaters, and great mansions, the whole scene to be crowned by the most magnificent and efficient university in the world. But his mind was presently recalled from these splendid prospects by the more immediate problem of correcting the abuses in state hospitals. With great ingenuity he smuggled a long letter to the governor, who was sufficiently impressed by the tales of violent treatment to interrogate the staff of the institution.

It is interesting to observe the continuity between Beers' intentions at this time and his career following recovery. So lasting was the impression made upon him by his treatment in mental hospitals that he dedicated his life to what presently became the mental hygiene movement. He became instrumental in bringing about reforms that were much needed and highly constructive. His scientific experiments were discontinued and his plans for improving his home city fell by the wayside, but one at least of the goals conceived at the height of his illness was capable of realistic fulfillment. Again one is impressed with the fact that the manic patient is less basically confused than other psychotics. He is overdriven, speeded up, and expansive, and this results in a distorted relation to reality, but the radical change of tempo takes place in a fundamentally sound mind. When normal tempo and normal mood are restored, mental function shows not the slightest trace of impairment.

PSYCHOLOGICAL MEANING OF DEPRESSED AND MANIC STATES

The facts thus far examined have led many observers to believe that depressed and manic states are analogous to drugged and intoxicated conditions. Some peculiarity of metabolic regulation, it is argued, makes the patient's mood shoot down or up as if he had taken a strong drug or a strong drink. This is essentially the theory proposed by Kraepelin and favored by those who prefer a somatogenic explanation for depressed and manic conditions. We shall see presently that the evidence for something of this kind is considerable, but this does not exempt us from searching for the psychological meaning of the two states. Even if we suppose that depressions and elations come from purely autonomous fluctuations in the metabolic system, we must examine all the available evidence, including what the patient experiences and how he behaves, for clues as to the nature of this fluctuation. Furthermore, we can hardly be satisfied with the idea that depressed and manic states are *analogous* to drugged or intoxicated conditions. We must weigh the closeness of the analogy and consider the possibility that the resemblance may not be great enough to support much parallel reasoning. Finally, there is always the psychogenic hypothesis: we must ask whether the metabolic fluctuations are really autonomous happenings or whether they should be conceived as stress responses set off by distinctive psychological problems that put the patient in a state of acute tension. It is possible that we have to deal here with a very close, subtle, and continuous interaction between psychodynamics and somatic events.

Depressions Following Combat Stress. The responses to combat stress in an active war theater include neurotic breakdowns, psychosomatic disorders, and schizophrenic reactions. They also include depressions, and the nature of depressive breakdown is sometimes more transparent here than it is apt to be in civilian life. The circumstances that are most prominent in these cases, that flood the patients' minds with pain and guilt, include separation from the other members of the unit, failure to perform the expected duties, and the loss of comrades, either older ones on whom there has been dependence or contemporary and younger ones with whom there has been close friendship. These are fairly common circumstances in combat zones, but they are felt in a particular way by men who react with depression. Outstanding in the response is a feeling of being deserted, of losing an indispensable source of supporting love and esteem. Separation from the unit means separation from the strong power of group support, which leaves the patient feeling alone, unloved, inadequate. Loss of respected officers or companions who were a source of strength has a similar emotional meaning. Failure to complete one's duties, even when others express no blame, recreates an inner feeling of desertion, as if one had behaved like a bad child and incurred rejection by one's conscience and parents. There is often, however, another element in the response which comes out most clearly when the patient is preoccupied by the loss of a close comrade of whom he was fond. The patient may constantly blame himself for the comrade's death, even when he seems to have been not in the least negligent. In such cases it seems as if the patient made himself the victim of his own hostility, belaboring himself ceaselessly for misdeeds he never performed.[9]

The reason for this second element, an extreme form of self-punishing or *intropunitive* behavior, comes out when it is possible to probe somewhat deeply into the meaning of the comrade's death. In one case, for example, much was heard at first about the dead friend's virtues, his generosity, his wonderful qualities of companionship. Only later did it come out that there was another side to the relationship, less clearly conscious: the two men were also keen rivals in matters of prowess and had been competing intensely for the position of flight leader. On the mission which proved fatal to the friend, the patient had been designated flight leader. Near the target the friend had drawn his plane out of formation and tried to take the leader's position, but the patient refused to yield. It was at this point that the friend's plane had been struck by ground fire and gone down in flames. The patient's childhood history had left him with strong competitive feelings, behind which there is always a good deal of hostility toward rivals. His anger must have been unbounded when his friend on a dangerous mission refused to play fair and stay in formation. The outcome must have seemed a perfect piece of justice, but for a person in whom jealous hostility is repressed it is a terrific threat to have a death wish come true. The case of Bert Whipley has taught us how shattering this can be in early childhood. In the present case the patient berated himself for his friend's death and for many other incidents in which his conduct had actually been blameless. He experienced the overwhelming guilt of a child whose aggressive naughtiness has had serious and irreparable consequences.[10]

Neurotic Depression. It is for cases of this kind that the concept of neurotic depression has been introduced. The patient feels deserted and

[9] This analysis follows the one given by R. R. Grinker and J. P. Spiegel, *Men Under Stress* (Philadelphia: The Blakiston Co., 1945), chap. xii.

[10] *Ibid.*, pp. 281–88.

despairing, sinful and worthless, unlovable and deserving of the utmost punishment. Yet these symptoms, which we might call signs of an overactive and relentless superego, seem to be direct consequences of psychodynamic conflict. There is no particular tendency for the disorder to become recurrent or to develop a cyclical pattern with contrasting manic states. Neurotic depression seems to be based on an exaggerated response to bereavement, loss, or misfortune. The exaggeration is determined by personal history, which has given situations of this kind a heavy loading of threat. The patient is peculiarly sensitive to desertion or loss either as happenings over which he has no control or as consequences of his own hostility. When real situations of this kind occur, or when his human relationships take a turn which he can interpret as loss or desertion, he begins to manifest the symptoms of depression. Many workers today favor this kind of explanation for some cases, at least, of depression, and it is not uncommon to find depression listed as one of the symptom syndromes of neurosis. Like other forms of neurosis the disorder can be understood in psychodynamic terms without invoking a sudden metabolic change. With such cases psychotherapy achieves results comparable to those obtained with other varieties of neurosis.

Psychological Content of Manic States. By concentrating first on cases in which manic symptoms play no part we have achieved a forward step in psychological understanding. But if we become unduly elated over this advance we would be imitating manic-depressive patients rather than studying them. The sobering thought should now be introduced that a great many patients have elated moods as well as depressed ones, and that these moods may succeed each other quite rapidly, as in the case of Clifford Beers. Is it possible to make sense out of manic states and to discern any intelligible relationship between them and states of depression?

The first thing to notice is that the two states are at opposite poles with respect to self-esteem. This is true even of the mood fluctuations of normal people. In a study of college women who recorded their mood levels every day on a self-rating scale, it was found that self-esteem, measured by an independent test, was higher on the good days than on the bad.[11] In depression there is an utter collapse of self-esteem. The patient can hardly find words strong enough to express the depth of his degradation and worthlessness. In manic states, on the other hand, self-esteem is joyfully boundless. All things seem possible, and the patient's feeling of competence extends in every direction. There is often a sensation of being flooded by plans for today, tomorrow, and the distant

[11] A. E. Wessman, D. F. Ricks, and M. M. Tyl, "Characteristics and Concomitants of Mood Fluctuation in College Women," *Journal of Abnormal and Social Psychology*, LX (1960), pp. 117–26.

future, yet the patient is not bothered by the thought that time and resources may prove to be limited. To an observer who does not share the manic mood there is something false about this high level of self-esteem. It is different from the expansive planning of a person whose self-confidence is founded on a record of real achievement. It is maintained by two devices: speed and change of direction. Like a good broken-field runner in football, the patient's mind races forward at top speed and dodges sharply whenever it is in danger of being tackled by a hard fact. Records of manic conversation show that there is tremendous distractibility, but the distractions are not entirely at random. They achieve the purpose of avoiding thoughts that would be detrimental to security and self-esteem.

It seems reasonable to deduce that the manic patient is making heavy use of the mechanism of *denial.*[12] He denies the existence of every fact and every thought that might make him feel depressed. His overactive behavior can also be considered to constitute a *reaction formation* against the possibility of being depressed. It is the heavy use of these two mechanisms that gives to the patient's buoyancy its element of falseness. A similar pattern of behavior is sometimes seen in response to sudden tragedy. To a particularly tragic bereavement, for instance, the person may respond by immersing himself at once in work, business plans, activities, even amusements, his whole behavior constituting a daily assertion that he is not deserted, grief-stricken, or helpless. Occasionally it happens that a true manic attack develops as the first response to a situation that involves loss and a threat to self-esteem. It seems likely that manic denial operates not only on the facts and thoughts that threaten self-esteem but also on those that signify being deserted and unloved and on those that carry reminders of one's evil hostile impulses. If such be the case, manic states are full psychological opposites of depressed states and can be viewed as attempts to control depression and recover from it.

The Adjustive Attempt in Depressed States. Our examination of manic states thus shows them to have an adjustive purpose. By an effective use of denial and reaction formation the patient manages to affirm that all is well and that grounds for depression do not exist. Our study of depressions did not disclose a similar adjustive attempt. These states seemed rather to represent breakdown and collapse with little sign of a struggle to rectify the situation. While it is true that certain extreme disorders—for example, the disorganization that goes with total panic—represent pure breakdown, we must always be on the watch for signs of attempted

[12] B. D. Lewin, *The Psychoanalysis of Elation* (New York: W. W. Norton & Co., Inc., 1950), chap. iii.

repair and restoration. Can we detect a purpose in depressed behavior, a struggle to accomplish something that will improve the patient's situation and reduce the force of his distress?

An affirmative answer to this question is given by Rado, who has devoted many years to the psychoanalytic study of depressed patients.[13] In agreement with the views already described in connection with neurotic depressions, Rado interprets the depressed spell as a reaction to loss. Perhaps a loved person dies or deserts the patient. Perhaps the patient loses the moral support of a congenial group, as when a soldier is separated from his unit. Perhaps the loss is of a more subtle and symbolic nature, as when the patient senses a cooling of interest on the part of his spouse or a reduction of applause on the part of audiences formerly enthusiastic. Whatever the current nature of the loss, Rado believes that its extraordinary significance for the patient lies in the fact that it reanimates terrible childhood experiences of loss of the mother's affection. Some part of a depressed person's behavior can be understood as a cry for love: a display of helplessness and a direct appeal for the affection and security that have been lost. But the whole reaction is greatly complicated by the presence of angry hostility toward the deserting person and by guilty fear that this hostility has actually caused the desertion. Early in a depressed spell there may be signs that the patient is trying to vent aggression directly and force some return of affection. The verbal equivalent for this behavior—"you are wicked to desert me, you must now love me"—reveals at once the tactical weakness of this move, especially when we imagine it as taking place in the relationship of a small child to its mother. As a consequence, repentance soon gains the upper hand and the rage becomes directed against the self. The patient's unending self-criticism is intended as an act of expiation. He fully accepts the blame for his anger, confesses his unworthiness, and attempts thereby to deserve again and win back the lost affection. Rado points out elsewhere that these tactics, too, are likely to miscarry. The pain of self-punishment and the despair caused by the constant downgrading of self-esteem may become unbearable, even driving the patient to suicide, before the attempted expiation brings any sense of restored love.[14] But there is still a method in the madness, and the depressive spell can be conceived as an attempt, however misguided, to repair the situation created by serious loss of supporting love.

[13] S. Rado, "Psychodynamics of Depression from the Etiological Point of View," *Psychosomatic Medicine,* XIII (1951), pp. 51–55.

[14] S. Rado, "Hedonic Control, Action-Self, and the Depressive Spell," in P. H. Hoch and J. Zubin (eds.), *Depression* (New York: Grune & Stratton, Inc., 1954), chap. xi.

Certain further facts that have been observed about people liable to depressions and elations fit rather well with this general line of thought. It has long been noticed that in their periods of remission, and reportedly also before the first onset of their disorder, manic-depressive patients show a characteristic pattern of traits. This pattern, known technically as the *cyclothymic* pattern, is not one that suggests weakness or maladjustment; on the contrary, it contains many elements that are generally associated with psychological health. Cyclothymic people are apt to be energetic, lively, and full of interests. They are warmly responsive to others and are often esteemed as delightful companions. In their closer relationships they are affectionate, loyal, and strongly attached. When in good health they function very well, often leading rich and highly satisfying lives. Yet there is a vulnerable point in the organization of their personalities. Beneath the surface they are acutely dependent upon their principal love-objects and cannot tolerate frustration or disappointment from this source. As Edith Jacobson expresses it, "what they require is a constant supply of love and moral support from a highly valued love-object." This love-object is usually a person, "but it may be represented by a powerful symbol, a religious, political, or scientific cause, or an organization of which they feel a part."[15] The weak spot in these otherwise healthy personalities is this dependence on a high income of supporting love. One might liken them to flourishing plants which, however, have no capacity to endure drought. They wilt and droop when other plants seem still able to draw nourishment from the dry ground. They require lavish support from Mother Earth.

There is a natural tendency for strong dependence to create a weak spot in a person's feeling of competence. He may be effective in all other respects, but when it is a question of securing his central supply of supporting love he faces a problem that cannot be handled by direct, assertive measures. Love cannot be commanded; it has to be won. But this is an issue on which the cyclothymic individual cannot afford to lose, or even to be moderately frustrated. A recent intensive study of manic-depressive patients brings to light one of the adjustive techniques whereby they try to compensate for the weak spot. This technique is described as gratifying one's dependency by a skillful manipulation of others, maneuvering them into positions where they either want or feel obliged to express devotion and give emotional support.[16] Along such

[15] E. Jacobson, "Contribution to the Metapsychology of Cyclothymic Depression," in P. Greenacre (ed.), *Affective Disorders: Psychoanalytic Contribution to Their Study* (New York: International Universities Press, Inc., 1953), p. 67.

[16] Mabel B. Cohen *et al.*, "An Intensive Study of Twelve Cases of Manic-Depressive Psychosis," *Psychiatry*, XVII (1954), pp. 103–39; R. W. Gibson, Mabel B. Cohen, and R. A. Cohen, "On the Dynamics of the Manic-Depressive Personality," *American Journal of Psychiatry*, CXV (1959), pp. 1101–7.

lines the patient may feel some competence, but this kind of maneuvering is at best an uncertain business. If the patient fails in one of his vital manipulations there is nothing else he can do, and his self-esteem falls precipitously. The importance of this drop in self-esteem has been emphasized by Bibring, who believes that depression occurs when the patient is swept by "a feeling of powerlessness and helplessness with regard to his loneliness, isolation, weakness, inferiority, evilness or guilt."[17]

Hypotheses Concerning Infantile Origins. Psychodynamic explanations of depressed and manic disorders are often met by the criticisms that they do not account for the depth and intensity of the patient's disorder. All of us at times experience loss of affection, feel despairing, and blame ourselves for mistakes and aggressions that have offended others. All of us at times become elated and overlook the obstacles to our optimistic plans. What is it that makes manic-depressive patients plunge to such depths or vault to such heights that they lose their grasp on reality and have to be taken to the hospital? It is here that we shall presently find it useful to consider the part played by genogenic and chemogenic factors, but the intensity and irrationality of depressed and manic states do not necessarily lie outside the province of psychodynamics. In our study of the neuroses we saw that the nuclear anxieties were intense and highly irrational, though their effect on behavior was not such as to disorient the patient and cause him to be judged crazy. It is the fact of having originated in early childhood that gives neurotic anxieties their damaging force. It is when present frustrations reactivate certain never-outgrown dangers of childhood that neurotic breakdown typically occurs. In manic-depressive and schizophrenic disorders the influence of childhood may be even stronger. According to the theories developed by Freud and Abraham, the psychoses involve a deeper regression than the neuroses; that is, the reactivated dangers lie even earlier in infancy, and the ways of perceiving them and mechanisms for dealing with them have the earmarks of a very early stage in mental development.[18] In this view, then, the intensity and irrationality of the depressive attack come from the fact that the patient's present difficulties have reactivated the sense of loss and the helpless rage of an infant in the first year of life.

Two kinds of observations can be cited on behalf of this interpretation. In the first place, it has been observed for some time that depressed patients lose appetite, eat little, and are apt to lose considerable weight. This happens even when they are retarded and quiet. The mental content that parallels this change usually takes the form of fears of impover-

[17] E. Bibring, "The Mechanism of Depression," in Greenacre, *op. cit.*, p. 42.

[18] S. Freud, "Mourning and Melancholia," in *Collected Papers* (London: Hogarth Press, Ltd., 1925), Vol. II; see also O. Fenichel, *The Psychoanalytic Theory of Neurosis* (New York: W. W. Norton & Co., Inc., 1945), chap. xvii.

ishment, and these are always direful regardless of the actual state of the patient's bank account. Sometimes the manic state is ushered in by an abrupt recovery of appetite, and quite typically the elated patient is sure that he has much money to spend—again, regardless of the actual state of his bank account. This optimism about money is one of the ways in which a manic patient gets himself into serious trouble. He may sign agreements to purchase expensive cars and even houses that are beyond his means. Money is something that is easily counted, and the patient's utter failure to test reality on this point, whether he is depressed or elated, strongly suggests that money is substituting for something else. It is serving as a symbol, and many workers are of the opinion that what it symbolizes is revealed in the attitudes toward food. When depressed, the patient acts as if he feared starvation; when elated, he acts as if food were abundantly available.[19] The depressed patient's concern about starvation bears no more relation to present reality than his concern about having no money. But starvation can be a very real fear, indeed one of the central fears, in the experience of an infant who feels himself deserted by his mother.

The second kind of observation that bears on infantile origins is more direct. As mentioned earlier in this book, Spitz has described actual depressive reactions in infants during the second half of the first year of life.[20] The occasion for these reactions is a loss or diminution of the "emotional supplies" provided by the mother or her substitute. When the child is shifted from a mothering to an impersonal environment, he soon begins to show signs of withdrawal, anxiety when approached, loss of appetite, and loss of weight. In the course of time the picture is further complicated by loss of motility, difficulty in sleeping, and a general slowing down of mental development. When one thinks of the adult depressive patient's losses of appetite and weight, insomnia, and motor and mental retardation, it seems likely that Spitz's observations point to the kind of experiences in infancy that can set the stage for later depressive reactions. Many features of the depressive state seem to be borrowed directly from the infantile reaction to a loss of "emotional supplies."

Our study of the psychological meaning of depressed and manic states may seem to have led us far away from the theories of Kraepelin and others who favor a somatogenic hypothesis. By following the regressive course of these disorders back to infancy, however, we have actually veered from a purely psychological to a psychosomatic way of thinking

[19] Rado, in Hoch and Zubin, *op cit.*, pp. 166–69.

[20] R. Spitz, "Anaclitic Depression: An Inquiry into the Genesis of Psychiatric Conditions in Early Childhood, II," *The Psychoanalytic Study of the Child*, II (1946), pp. 313–42; "Infantile Depression and the General Adaptation Syndrome," in Hoch and Zubin, *op. cit.*, pp. 93–108.

about them. The possibility of a truly psychosomatic theory will be weighed after we have reviewed what is known about the somatic side of the problem.

NATURE OF MANIC-DEPRESSIVE DISORDER

Mania and depression succeed each other in the same patient too often to be regarded as unrelatd disorders. Even if we had detected no psychological relationship between them we would still have to explain their statistical relationship. Kraepelin dealt with the question by making the following hypotheses: (a) Mania and depression are opposite conditions, exhibiting a sharp polarity, which are nevertheless (b) based on a single disease process, (c) consisting of some kind of metabolic instability that causes fluctuation from one extreme to the other. These hypotheses provide a model for thinking about the somatogenic side of the disorder, even though the facts may lead us finally to express them in somewhat different language.

The need for a somatic explanation is most striking in those cases in which depressed and manic episodes are regularly recurrent. Every so often, sometimes almost on a predictable schedule, the patient is overtaken by a depression, followed perhaps by a contrasting manic period. Typically there is spontaneous recovery, but after a period of good health the patient again becomes depressed and the cycle repeats itself. In such cases there is no discernible relationship between onset and stress in the patient's personal life, nor can one detect any psychological reason for the recovery. Emotional stress can be a subtle thing, and for any one attack we might suppose that we were simply failing to perceive it, but the psychogenic hypothesis is strained to the breaking point if we have to believe that emotional stress creeps up on the patient regularly every four months, let us say, for a period of several years. It is to be observed also that the patient's experience of the onset is different in the more cyclical cases. This is especially true when the first phase is a retarded depression. The patient experiences the slowing up as a kind of mental and physical fatigue that comes on like a bodily illness. It is felt as originating in the body, as something foreign to the self, indeed as something the self can observe for a while with a certain detachment. This is very different from the experience of depression that follows the building up of intense emotional disturbance.

The Genogenic Factor. Disorders of the manic-depressive type have a marked familial incidence. While figures reported by different investigators do not perfectly agree, they regularly show a higher incidence of mental disorder in the parents of manic-depressives than is the case with any other major form of psychosis. For about 20 to 25 per cent of manic-depressive patients the history shows that one parent or the other had a mental illness, generally manic-depressive illness. The evidence has been reviewed by Kallman, who adds to it some studies by himself and others on the incidence in siblings and twins.[21] The incidence in siblings and dizygotic (two-egg or non-identical) twins is 20 to 25 per cent, approximately the same as in parents, and much greater than in the population at large, where the incidence of manic-depressive psychosis is under one-half of one per cent. In monozygotic (identical) twins it is much higher, running in different studies from 66 to over 90 per cent. These figures are necessarily based on hospitalized patients and may therefore give a stronger picture than would be drawn if milder cases could be included. They are sufficient, however, to show that a genogenic factor exists, presumably some kind of predisposition to break down in this particular fashion. Obviously, predisposition is not a sufficient explanation of any given case, but it may well function as a contributing cause of disorder.

Another line of evidence is based on the study of physique. Kretschmer point out a marked association between manic-depressive psychosis and the so-called *pyknic* component of physique.[22] Further research has in general confirmed this relationship, though the correlation is far from perfect. The pyknic constitution can best be described according to Sheldon's components of physique.[23] It has its major strength in the first or endomorphic component, so that the body form is softly rounded with relatively massive trunk and viscera. There is secondary strength in the second or mesomorphic component, imparting more strength and energy than would be the case with a more "pure" example of the first component. Both Kretschmer and Sheldon have reported associations between this general physical type and a pattern of personality traits that corresponds to the cyclothymic pattern described in the previous section of this chapter.[24] These observations were not made under ideally controlled conditions, but they suggest some degree of genetic relationship among three separately observable aspects of the human being; pyknic physical constitution, cyclothymic personality pattern, and incidence of manic-depressive psychosis.

Chemogenic Factors. We come now more directly to Kraepelin's idea of a metabolic instability. Both the activity and the sense of well-being

[21] F. J. Kallman, "Genetic Principles in Manic-Depressive Psychosis," in Hoch and Zubin, *op. cit.*, pp. 1–24.

[22] E. Kretschmer, *Physique and Character*, trans. W. J. H. Sprott (London: Routledge & Kegan Paul, Ltd., 1925), chap. ii.

[23] See above, pages 154–55.

[24] W. H. Sheldon and S. S. Stevens, *The Varieties of Temperament* (New York: Harper & Row, 1942).

shown by manic patients suggest a high rate of speed in vital processes, whereas the depressed mood and general retardation seem to imply that the whole bodily system has slowed down. It was doubtless this contrast which led Kraepelin to frame his hypothesis around the idea of metabolism—the rate of vital activity in the tissues as a whole. Better methods of examination have since shown, however, that Kraepelin's formulation requires certain changes. It has been shown that mania and depression are not polar opposites as regards bodily functions. After reviewing the literature, Cameron concludes that there is no evidence for biological opposition between the two states.[25] If one takes measures such as basal metabolism, blood pressure, blood sugar level, rate of blood flow, etc., there are no important differences between manic and depressed patients. Wherever significant differences have been found, they have proved to be related to activity level rather than mood. At the biological level, therefore, agitated depressions and manic states are very much alike, both differing significantly from retarded depressions. "It is the general activity of the person," says Cameron, "rather than his particular mood that seems to correlate with whatever metabolic changes are found."

These findings serve to shift the focus of inquiry from mood to activity level. Cyclical changes in activity level can sometimes be observed in forms of mental disorder other than the manic-depressive. Perhaps the extreme example, reported by Richter, is that of a patient who for several years was well and happy one day, miserable and complaining the next, happy again the next, and so on with the utmost regularity.[26] Longer cycles are naturally more typical, but in any event it seems that even in the regularized environment of a hospital there is a tendency on the part of certain patients to experience recurring changes in activity level and general sense of health. Observations of this kind led Richter to attempt to produce similar cycles experimentally in animals. Regular cycles appeared in rats as a consequence of interference with the endocrine system. Surgical injury to the thyroid gland or disturbance of its function by drugs produced cyclical ups and downs of activity which could still be observed after 500 days—a long time in a rat's life. In female rats sexual functions were suppressed during the phases of low activity. Feeding of thyroid substance put an end to the cycles. Similar results were obtained by injury to the pituitary gland, and further research suggests that lesions in the hypothalamus, the sub-cortical brain center that is most directly involved in regulating the endocrine system

[25] N. Cameron, "The Place of Mania Among the Depressions from a Biological Standpoint," *Journal of Psychology,* XIV (1942), pp. 181–95.

[26] C. P. Richter, "Behavior and Metabolic Cycles in Man and Their Experimental Production in Animals," in P. H. Hoch and J. Zubin (eds.), *Experimental Psychopathology* (New York: Grune & Stratton, Inc., 1956).

and governing emotional responses, also tend to set up cycles of behavior. Of particular interest is the discovery that spontaneous cycles can be initiated by severe stress which brings the animals to the brink of physical exhaustion. Rats are good swimmers, but if made to swim for 40 hours, which is just about their limit, they sometimes showed thereafter a marked fluctuation of activity level on about a 40-day cycle. Presumably the endocrine system is driven to the utmost to prevent exhaustion and collapse, and this makes it unable for a long time afterwards to perform its regulating functions in a balanced manner.

Much evidence can be assembled to show that in depressive and manic disorders there is a general disturbance of autonomic regulation. Mention has already been made of the highly characteristic loss of appetite, weight loss, and insomnia that occur in depressed states; improved sleep and relish for food are sometimes the first definite symptoms of recovery. With female patients menstruation often stops during depressions. Other signs of autonomic disturbance are legion, though less constant from one case to another. Campbell, in a chapter summarizing this topic, mentions "woozy" feelings and headache, disturbances of heart rate and circulation, gastro-intestinal disorders, skin difficulties, and many other items which sometimes appear alone as psychosomatic disorders but sometimes occur in close connection with depressive and manic states.[27] Other workers have found evidence for a close association between depressed states and the physiological pattern that goes with an excess of epinephrine.[28] This would signify that the medulla of the adrenal gland was being lavish in the performance of one of its emergency functions and that the normal balancing control of this function had broken down. All in all, a strong case can be built for the hypothesis that the autonomic nervous system, and the endocrine system to which it is so closely related, are operating in a deranged manner in depressive and manic disorders.

Further light can be shed on this irregularity by considering a form of disorder that has long been known as *involutional melancholia*. The title means that the outstanding symptom is depression and that the time of onset is the involutional period—in women between the ages of 40 and 55, in men between 50 and 65. It seems likely that the physiological changes that accompany the decline of sexual functions play a significant part in the onset of these depressions. These changes are earlier and more drastic in women, and involutional depressions occur with decidedly greater frequency in women. Even when the menopause is not accompanied by mental disorder it is apt to be a period of strain. Restlessness

[27] Campbell, *op. cit.*, chap. iii.

[28] D. H. Funkenstein, M. Greenblatt, and H. C. Solomon, "An Autonomic Nervous System Test of Prognostic Significance in Relation to Electro-Shock Treatment," *Psychosomatic Medicine*, XIV (1952), pp. 347–62.

and fatigue, feelings of discomfort, autonomic instability, sudden crying spells give testimony to the difficult biochemical readjustments that are in progress. These symptoms are sometimes lowered by the giving of estrogen, replacing the hormone that is being inadequately produced by the sex glands and thus allowing the whole hormonal readjustment to proceed at a slower rate. Unquestionably the middle years of a woman's life offer psychological as well as physiological difficulties, but we should notice here the special relationship between depression and a spontaneous change in hormonal balance. This is a case where we know something, at least, about the temporary glandular imbalance, and it is not without significance that the commonest associated mental symptom should be depression.

Our study of chemogenic factors points strongly to irregularity of function in the autonomic and endocrine systems. When the endocrine system is thrown out of balance by injury, exhaustion, or the aging process, difficulty seems to ensue in maintaining the complicated system of controls and adjustments that is required for normal operation. It is possible to conceive that the chemogenic contribution to depressed and manic states consists of a regulatory weakness or failure that allows certain responses, such as the secretion of epinephrine, to go on too long without being compensated. These biochemical excesses may affect mood, though our most direct evidence is that they affect activity level and such functions as appetite and menstruation. Some workers believe that the trouble should be traced to the regulatory nerve centers in the hypothalamus, but our most direct evidence points to a more peripheral cause, such as weakness in some gland that is essential for balanced operation. These statements, indefinite as they are, represent a considerable advance over the original hypothesis proposed by Kraepelin. It may be that they bring us a step nearer to a truly psychosomatic hypothesis.

THE PROBLEM OF PSYCHOSOMATIC INTERACTION

In the last two sections we have considered depressive and manic disorders first from the psychogenic and then from the somatogenic point of view. It is obvious that the story is far from complete on either side. In this situation we might be well advised to await the results of further research before attempting any theoretical reconciliation between the two outlooks. To do this, however, would be to leave the impression that there are two unrelated systems of thought which do not have anything in common. Furthermore, research does not usually prove more than it is planned to prove, and if the planning never includes a serious attempt to examine psychosomatic interactions they will probably never be observed. We shall therefore try a bit of speculation, but with an important prefatory note: this is probably not the way things really work, but it represents the kind of guessing that we must keep doing if we are ever to understand the depressive and manic disorders.

According to the somatogenic account, the predisposition to break down in this way has a genetic foundation. Manic and depressive conditions tend to run in families and are to some degree associated with the pyknic bodily constitution and cyclothymic type of personality. The psychogenic story points rather to anxiety-laden traumatic experiences in infancy, special importance being attached to deprivation of maternal "emotional supplies." From the behavior of the adult patient it can be inferred that the predisposing situation involves a strongly felt loss of feeding gratifications, perhaps even a fear of starvation. It also seems to involve an angry, demanding effort on the part of the child and some dim preverbal awareness that the anger increases the loss. This tends to place the crucial episodes at the period of infancy at which anaclitic depressions, as Spitz calls them, have actually been observed to take place following the loss of mothering.

The somatogenic and psychogenic accounts are certainly different, but there is at least one point of possible relationship between them. The pyknic constitution has also been called the "visceral type" because of its relatively strong development of the digestive viscera. Its healthy adult representatives tend to be great enjoyers of food. The pyknic body is also quite energetic and the cyclothymic personality pattern includes a tendency to express strong feelings. We can postulate that the healthy hungry baby who eats well and gets great gratification from feeding is the very one who can be most severely frustrated and made most angry by deprivations in this cherished sphere. Babies with poor appetites, digestive upsets, colic, and other things that make eating a chore are less vulnerable to this particular kind of frustration. The *psychological* predisposition to depressive and manic disorders is more apt to be laid down in infants who are *constitutionally* good eaters.

The physiological responses observed by Spitz in infantile depressions have a certain resemblance to those of adult depressions. There is, for instance, the same loss of appetite and ultimate weight loss. We must assume that in the infant this represents an upset in autonomic balance occasioned by the frustration, anger, and resulting tension. Perhaps the infant with a strong pyknic constitutional endowment is already predisposed toward certain poorly balanced autonomic patterns. When we studied the psychosomatic disorders in a previous chapter we noticed that there seemed to be certain stable individual differences in "autonomic constitution." We also noticed that infancy is a time when specific autonomic patterns are being differentiated from the initially diffuse emergency reaction. It seems plausible that the infantile situations we are here considering have the effect of organizing, or at least strengthening, a particular autonomic pattern. This pattern might include a strong emergency production of epinephrine and an inhibition of digestive processes—as if the child were too angry to eat. Such a pattern is then ready to be elicited by any future emergency which at all resembles the original ones. We have seen that the adult patient is sensitive to frustrations of dependent love and responds to them as if they were infantile deprivations involving loss of feeding gratification. This means, on the bodily side, a reactivation of the infantile autonomic pattern and the sensations that go with it. In a sense there is physiological as well as psychological regression.

This way of describing the psychosomatic relationship permits us to understand those cases of depression in which somatic disorder seems to play the leading part. Illness, injury, exhausting effort, or menopausal changes place stress on the autonomic and endocrine systems, which then tend to react with the well-laid infantile deprivation pattern. The patient feels as if the deprivation were happening again, and although he may have suffered no actual losses in human relationships he quickly evolves a mental content appropriate to such loss. In the case described earlier, of the agitated and depressed woman who ran a rooming house, we might say that the actual situation warranted discouragement, but there was certainly no reason for her conviction of sin, for her taking the blame in regard to the failure of her marriage, or for her feelings that she had brought all her relatives to their deaths. These elaborations represented attempts to explain the dreadfulness of her feelings, in other words to deal with the autonomic pattern, set off by her recent menopause and illness, which all too forcibly reminded her of infantile deprivation.

Conceivably there may be cases of purely psychogenic and purely somatogenic depressive and manic disorders. Neurotic depressions following combat stress come nearest to the former, while mood changes that keep a fixed temporal schedule approximate the latter. But there is equal propriety in the assumption that battle stress, which produces a huge variety of disorders, never produces depression unless the patient has become predisposed to react in that way; and that cycles, which can show themselves in ways other than mood swings, never produce depressed and manic states unless the patient is similarly predisposed. The predisposition itself, as we have described it, is both somatic and psychological, and everything that follows it can probably best be conceived in psychosomatic terms.

METHODS OF TREATMENT

Depressive and manic disorders do not usually manifest themselves early in life, although a few cases of their occurrence in childhood are on record.[29] The most frequent period of onset is the decade of the thirties. The disorders are somewhat more common in women than in men. On the whole, spontaneous recovery is the rule. From a half to two-thirds of hospitalized patients with manic and depressive states are discharged in good health and do not have a later recurrence of illness important enough to require a return to the hospital. In some cases, however, the attacks recur and repeated hospitalization is necessary, and in a very small proportion of cases recovery is not sufficient to warrant discharge from the hospital. The expectation of at least temporary spontaneous recovery is so high that it is difficult to evaluate the effects of therapeutic measures. Most of the patients get well anyway, regardless of what is done. Therapeutic goals can not be set up in terms simply of recovery, but must include considerations such as shortening the period of illness, reducing the recurrence, and freeing the patient's life from unnecessary psychological burdens.

Psychotherapy. Until recently there has been no very persistent attempt to use the more elaborate methods of psychotherapy. Psychoanalysis was originally conceived as a method of treating neurosis, and Freudians for some time entertained little hope of using it effectively with psychotic patients. When depression and mania are severe it is clearly impossible to do more than keep the patient safe and as comfortable as possible. Milder states, however, permit the use of certain therapeutic procedures, and formal psychotherapy is possible between attacks. The treatment of mildly depressed patients involves a considerable amount of support and direction and a fairly sparing use of interpretation. In the last few years psychoanalytically oriented workers have shown increased interest in developing variations of technique that are suitable for depressed and manic conditions.[30] It is too early to evaluate the results of this effort.

Electroshock. First introduced only twenty-five years ago, electroshock quickly came into common use in treating depressive and manic disorders. The full title, *electroconvulsive therapy* (ECT), describes exactly the essence of the procedure: electrical currents are passed through the brain from electrodes attached to the head, and the patient responds with a convulsion that is very much like a grand mal seizure. Conscious-

[29] Campbell, *op. cit.*, chaps. ix and x.

[30] See especially G. Bychowski, *Psychotherapy of Psychosis* (New York: Grune & Stratton, Inc., 1952), chaps. xxi–xxx; M. B. Cohen *et al.*, "An Intensive Study of Twelve Cases of Manic-Depressive Psychosis," *Psychiatry*, XVII (1954), pp. 103–39.

ness is lost immediately when the current is applied; the patient is unaware of the convulsion and awakens quietly some time afterwards, usually feeling no worse than a little cloudy and stiff. There is some loss of memory at first, but this typically disappears within an hour or two. Among the more remote and lasting effects is often a restoration of normal mood. Manic patients are returned to a calm and balanced mood, and depressed patients are raised to a more cheerful outlook. The technique has been refined and varied in several ways, for instance by the use of drugs to reduce the violence of the motor reactions, but the central principle remains the same.[31] A typical short course of ECT consists of five treatments given every other day. Longer series are used if this does not bring about a favorable change.

The wide use of electroshock has made it possible to accumulate a good deal of information about results. There is diversity in the reported figures, but complete remission seems to be obtained in from 40 to 80 per cent of patients in depressed states, somewhat less in patients having manic attacks. The involutional depressions generally show the highest rate of improvement. Of course the rate of spontaneous remission is high in the affective disorders, but ECT serves to hasten the remission and spare the patient many unpleasant and expensive weeks of hospitalization. On the question of recurrence the reports strike a less cheerful note. Shock-treated patients in the manic-depressive category are a little more likely to reappear in the hospital, and to reappear sooner, than patients who regained their health without shock.

The results can be pictured more clearly by considering a specific study from the Pennsylvania Hospital in Philadelphia.[32] Comparisons are made between 567 depressed or manic patients in the years 1925–1934, before ECT was available, and 563 patients in the years 1940–1946, when ECT was regularly available and used in the majority of cases. In recovery rate the second group shows a definite though not very large advantage, 72 per cent as against 59 per cent. With patients where a 5-year follow-up study could be completed the difference largely disappeared, the lasting recovery figures being 66 per cent and 64.5 per cent respectively, but the figures for the ECT group are based on a much reduced sample of the original 563. Most striking is the difference found for average length of stay in the hospital: 4.5 months in the earlier period, 2.3 months in the years after the introduction of ECT. Recurrence of disorder occurred more often in the shock-treated cases. At the end of one year, 16 per cent of the earlier cases had broken down again, 28 per

[31] For a brief review, see E. H. Parsons *et al.*, "Modern Methods of Electroshock Therapy," *American Journal of Psychiatry*, CXII (1955), pp. 18–22.

[32] E. D. Bond, "Results of Treatment in Psychoses—with a Control Series," *American Journal of Psychiatry*, CX (1954), pp. 881–87.

cent of the later group, and this difference seemed to be sustained through several more years.

It is clear from these figures that ECT performs its greatest service in reducing the length of attacks. Particularly with depressions, where its benefit is largest, it can spare the patient many days of despair and acute suffering. On the other hand it clearly cannot rank as fundamental therapy in the sense that it reduces the likelihood of future attacks, and the evidence seems to show that it immunizes the patient even less than a spontaneous recovery. There have always been misgivings about its use. Patients dislike it and often become anxious about it. The very efficiency of the treatment has led to indiscriminate use and an attitude on the part of the physician that has suggested the phrase, "push-button psychiatry." The idea that ECT produces brain damage and mental impairment receives no clear support from research thus far performed, but we can never be wholly confident that present tests are adequate to detect all kinds of impairment. It is troublesome to many workers that no acceptable hypothesis has emerged concerning the mode of action of ECT. Even psychiatrists who warmly advocate its use admit that its action is "shrouded in mystery."[33]

In view of all these circumstances it is not surprising that ECT has been extensively supplanted, though by no means eliminated, by treatment through newly developed drugs.

Drugs. The use of ataractic drugs, commonly known as tranquilizers, can be viewed as the major breakthrough of the past decade in the treatment of severe disorders. Medical history follows a twisting course, marked like anything else by swings of enthusiasm and fashion. Before the introduction of shock methods it was supposed that gentleness and sympathy held the key to succesful work with psychotic patients. Then came a period when the field was suddenly swept by efficient and impersonal methods which subjected patients to a violent physical reaction. Another swing of the pendulum finds everyone hoping for therapeutic triumphs through chemically induced tranquility. That the pendulum has moved so vigorously must be attributed to the earnest desire of physicians to find some effective way of helping patients so impervious to the ordinary channels of influence. We have already remarked that the use of tranquilizing drugs has for the first time turned the tide with respect to hospitalized patients, making possible a substantially increased rate of discharge. As therapy, drugs are probably no more fundamental than ECT; but in a far easier way they serve to shorten and dampen the distresses of mental illness.

[33] L. B. Kalinowsky and P. H. Hoch, *Shock Treatments, Psychosurgery, and Other Somatic Treatments in Psychiatry* (2d ed.; New York: Grune & Stratton, Inc., 1952).

With respect to depressive and manic disorders it is clearly the latter that stand in need of tranquility. Drugs such as chlorpromazine and reserpine, with their numerous variants and successors under dozens of trade-names, have proved somewhat effective with manic states. They seem most effective, however, with agitated and anxious depressions; their special service seems to be that of reducing anxiety and tension. For retarded depressed states the need is almost the opposite: the patient requires an elevation of spirits and an increase of activity. Progress with antidepressant drugs has not been as rapid as with the tranquilizers. Several preparations are now available, but in many cases the patients develop a tolerance that rather soon reduces the effectiveness of the drugs. It is partly because of this slower progress with chemical antidepressants that ECT is still often needed to alleviate depressions.[34]

Having in mind the dramatic victories of penicillin over infectious diseases, it is easy to think of the tranquilizing and antidepressant preparations as "wonder drugs" destined for like triumphs. The evidence does not support this optimism. The reported results are always, to coin a medical-sounding term, sub-miraculous: the effects are somewhat irregular, and only part of the patients are substantially benefitted. Furthermore, all drugs that are powerful enough to lower anxiety and tension or to relieve depression are likely to have other effects, some of which may be harmful and dangerous. Public attention was caught in 1962 by the shocking example of thalidomide, a seemingly innocent tranquilizer which, when taken during pregnancy, produced the side-effect of gross abnormality in the developing foetus. The usual side-effects are not of this disastrous order. Some preparations, however, produce drowsiness and dizziness; some interfere with motor coordination; and some tend to have too great an effect on heart rate and liver function. These consequences set limits to the dosage and especially to the continued use of drugs on a maintenance basis.[35] The perfect drugs for long-term treatment, if they exist, have certainly not been found; and even for initial treatment the matching or drug, dosage, and patient is still very much a matter of trial and error. These limitations should be borne in mind even while we recognize the progress that has been made in lightening the burdens of depressive and manic disorders.

SUGGESTIONS FOR FURTHER READING

It is difficult to find books on depressed and manic conditions which do not show intense partisanship for either the somatogenic or the psychogenic point

[34] W. Sargent, "The Physical Treatments of Depression: Their Indications and Proper Use," *Journal of Neuropsychiatry,* II (1961), Supplement No. 1, pp. 1–10; N. S. Kline, "Comprehensive Therapy of Depressions," *ibid.,* pp. 15–26.

[35] J. Wortis, "Physiological Treatment," *American Journal of Psychiatry,* CXVIII (1962), pp. 595–99.

of view. One exception is the review by Leopold Bellak, *Manic-Depressive Psychosis and Allied Conditions* (New York, Grune & Stratton, Inc., 1952), which takes a strictly psychosomatic position. This is a very thorough review of the recent literature and will serve as an invaluable guide to the student who wants to pursue the topic intensively. The somatogenic position is warmly espoused in J. D. Campbell's *Manic-Depressive Disease* (Philadelphia, J. B. Lippincott Co., 1953) which otherwise surveys the disorder quite fully. Excellent for its clinical descriptions is E. Kraepelin's *Manic-Depressive Insanity and Paranoia* (trans. by R. M. Barclay, Edinburgh, Livingstone, 1921). The psychoanalytic contribution is summarized by O. Fenichel in *The Psychoanalytic Theory of Neurosis* (New York, W. W. Norton & Co., Inc., 1945), Ch. 17; more recent contributions are contained in *Affective Disorders,* a series of papers edited by P. Greenacre (New York, International Universities Press, Inc., 1953). For a conservative account of psychotherapy with depressed and manic patients, see G. Bychowski's *Psychotherapy of Psychosis* (New York, Grune & Stratton, Inc., 1952), Chs. 21–30.

In addition to C. W. Beers' *A Mind That Found Itself* (Garden City, N. Y., Doubleday & Co., Inc., 1931) which is used in the text to provide illustrations of depressed and manic states, there are other interesting inside accounts of manic-depressive psychosis: for instance, *Reluctantly Told* by J. Hillyer (New York, The Macmillan Co., 1927), and *A Mind Restored* by E. Krauch (New York, G. P. Putnam's Sons, Inc., 1937). Some cases of this kind are contained in a collection edited by B. Kaplan, *The Inner World of Mental Illness* (New York, Harper & Row, 1963).

15

Schizophrenia

Schizophrenia is the most common form of psychosis. One person out of five admitted for the first time to a mental hospital is given this diagnosis. Starting early in life, often during adolescence and still more often in the decade of the twenties, it can wreck the person's whole adult career and prevent him from making any useful contribution to society. If spontaneous recovery does not occur, or if treatment is not successful, the patient may become a public charge for forty or fifty years. Because the disorder has a chance to last so long, schizophrenics accumulate in mental hospitals and constitute something like 50 per cent of the inmates at any given time. The disorder must be considered highly costly, whether we reckon the cost in dollars spent or in the more important coin of human lives gone wrong.

Although schizophrenia has been the object in recent years of a massive effort of research, its puzzles have by no means been solved. The fundamental nature of the disorder cannot yet be set down in a wholly satisfactory statement. Because the different subvarieties exhibit a tremendous diversity of symptoms, some workers have challenged Kraepelin's historic step of classifying these divergent pictures under a single heading. The majority of workers, however, agree with Kraepelin that the different varieties of schizophrenia have enough in common to warrant giving them a common name, but the basic nature of the disorder is not thereby established. Most of the cases have obvious psychodynamic features, the psychosis coming as the culmination of a history of unsuccessful adjustments. On the other hand, certain of the phenomena are so bizarre and so extravagant that it has seemed impossible to explain them without resort to chemogenic and histogenic hypotheses. In the study of schizophrenia there is no room for rivalry and antagonism between the psychogenic and somatogenic points of view. The disorder can be understood only when constitution, physiology, the nervous system, mental changes, emotional changes, adjustment and defense, and the character of the social environment are all spread upon the canvas. Only workers who can grasp subtleties in all of these fields can solve the problems of schizophrenia.

The term *schizophrenia* was introduced by Bleuler in 1911. It now largely, though not wholly, supersedes Kraepelin's name *dementia praecox.* The older title reflected the belief that dementia, starting early and running a slow progressive course, was characteristic of all cases. As the disorder does not always start early, and as the presence of true dementia has been widely challenged, neither part of Kraepelin's title is in the least appropriate. Bleuler's term, which means a splitting of the personality, is more satisfactory provided it does not suggest such gross "splits" as occur in hysterical dissociations and multiple selves. Bleuler had in mind a general loosening of associative connections and of the organization of thought and behavior. He considered this fragmentation of integrated behavior to be the truly central disorder in schizophrenia.

VARIETIES OF SCHIZOPHRENIA

In widespread use is a classification of schizophrenia into four subgroups. Like most such groupings, these four are by no means mutually exclusive. There is much overlap, and sometimes the predominant symptoms change markedly in the course of the illness, crossing the line to another subgroup. Nevertheless the classification forms a convenient starting point for describing the disorder.

The Simple Form. The simple form, sometimes called *schizophrenia simplex,* has as its positive symptoms a gradual loss of interest, a failure of early promise, and an increasing ineffectiveness in meeting social demands. Instead of expanding his social horizons and increasing his participations as he passes through adolescence and early adulthood, the patient drifts into a simple and rather solitary way of life. He is satisfied with an outwardly routine existence and shows no ambition for personal advancement in the world of his contemporaries. In some cases apathy and irresponsibility go a little further so that the patient becomes an idler and ne'er-do-well. No type of patient is more colorless and more unlike the popular idea of a lunatic. On the whole, schizophrenics of the simple type are quiet and contented. Their most violent manifestations are an occasional irritability and a grouchy refusal to accept pressure or suggestions from outside. After a while it may become apparent that thinking and attention are not particularly good, but memory is usually little impaired and any loss of mental capacity seems secondary to the general slumping of interest. The patient's affective life is outwardly shallow and uneventful. He does not seem to want or to need strong feeling. A simple and restricted life appears to suit him.

Close study of patients with the simple form of schizophrenia shows that they are not in any general sense out of contact with reality. What seems to be most characteristic of them is a lack of assertiveness. This is so great that it prevents them from making a good sexual adjustment, from expressing anger, from standing up for their rights, and even from making friendly overtures toward the people around them. It is often quite clear that patients of this type would like to make better contact with others, but even this small amount of assertiveness is difficult for them.[1]

In part, the diagnosis is established negatively, that is, by the absence of the more severe symptoms that characterize the other three subgroups. The more carefully the history is taken, the less great are the chances that the case will be classified under the simple form. This is because the patient may have experienced delusions and hallucinations and may have engaged in queer behavior when by himself without revealing these facts to anyone. There is certainly a difference, however, between typical cases of schizophrenia simplex and the more colorful cases that belong under the other headings.

The Paranoid Form. Next to be mentioned is the paranoid form, with which we are already familiar through the example of L. Percy King. The outstanding feature is the rich development of delusions. King's case is atypical to the extent that his delusional system was better organized and more stable than is usually the case. Schizophrenic delusions are typically changeable, numerous, fantastic, and accompanied by hallucinations. The patient does not rest content with thinking that people are persecuting him; he hears them murmuring against him, sees them lurking at the windows, feels the electric ticklings they are directing at his skin, tastes the poison that they have slipped into his food. He does not stop with the mere belief that he is Christ or Napoleon or Hitler or George Washington; he hears voices announcing his fame and bringing him important messages of state. In the early stages of the illness it is generally possible to see a connection between the patient's misinterpretations of reality and his personal wishes, needs, and fears. As time goes on, however, the delusions tend to spread out in a disorganized fashion. Magical forces and mystical powers come into the picture, and strange influencing machines are supposed to exist which the patient may draw in great detail. The whole universe created in the patient's mind becomes increasingly bizarre.

[1] O. Kant, "Clinical Investigation of Simple Schizophrenia," *Psychiatric Quarterly*, XXII (1948), pp. 141–51.

There is a form of psychosis, *paranoia*, in which the symptoms are confined to the development of a delusional system. This psychosis is generally assigned independent status outside of schizophrenia. The clearest distinguishing feature is the absence of hallucinations. Falsification of reality is restricted to misinterpreting events; what happens is correctly perceived, but peculiar inferences are drawn from it. Except for the delusional system, the patient is perfectly oriented and perfectly normal in his conduct. The personality does not become disorganized, and interest in the environment is substantially preserved. One might say that paranoia is a restricted psychosis, sufficiently circumscribed so that it does not invade and disintegrate the personality as a whole. We shall consider presently the nature and origins of paranoiac thinking. The disorder is mentioned here because of its similarity to the paranoid form of schizophrenia. Both show an extensive use of the mechanism of *projection*. In paranoid schizophrenia, however, there is a more far-reaching loss of interest, loss of contact with reality, and general disintegration of personality.

In studying the case of L. Percy King we became familiar with the psychological service performed by the mechanism of projection. The person spares himself intolerable anxiety by attributing certain of his tendencies not to himself but to other people. He transforms his wishes and fears into external facts for which he himself is not in the least responsible. When a patient claims that God has chosen him to lead mankind to its salvation, he is expressing an extremely grandiose wish but he is assuming no responsibility for it. When he claims that pursuers and unseen forces are preventing him from achieving great things, he is expressing both a grandiose wish and a fear of his incompetence to fulfill it, but he is again avoiding responsibility for this conflict. When he finds himself the victim of sexual advances, he is neatly disclaiming the presence of any such inclinations in himself. The delusional and hallucinatory aspects of paranoid schizophrenia are thus intelligible in terms of desire, anxiety, and defense. Further principles of explanation, however, are needed to understand the more strictly schizophrenic aspects of the disorder: the loss of interests, the growing confusion, the gradual deterioration of thought and conduct.

The Catatonic Form. In the catatonic variety of schizophrenia the focus of the disorder is on motility. There are peculiar postures and gestures, curious grimaces, and stereotyped actions that are repeated endlessly. More dramatic are the phases, sometimes alternating, of catatonic stupor and catatonic excitement. The excited episodes are usually of short duration, but while they last they are often extremely violent with real danger of both homicide and suicide. Sometimes the frenzy is accompanied by delusions, hallucinations, and feelings of great power; at other times it looks more like a wild, disorganized outbreak of energy. Much of the activity, however, has symbolic significance that can be related to the patient's personal problems and fantasies. The stupors are of longer duration, going on sometimes for weeks and months. The patient sits in one position and does not speak. His immobility may extend to the point that urine and feces are not passed until they move involuntarily and that saliva is not swallowed so that it accumulates and falls from the mouth. The patient has to be dressed and undressed, moved in bed, and fed through a tube. This state of exaggerated immobility may start suddenly and may disappear in an instant. Older theories which posited degenerative changes in the nervous system were discredited by these abrupt onsets and remissions.

Careful study of catatonic stuporous states has shown that they are less passive than they appear. It is usually more accurate to say that the patient is in a state of active immobility. If anyone attempts to change his position, there will be strong muscular resistance. The patient is not in a limp state, and he is also not in a state of mental stupor. He refuses to react, but his mind is alertly observant of what is going on. Often a patient can afterward report in great detail the things that happened and were said around him while he was in apparent stupor. He is in a state of acute negativism, so acute that it invades the whole motor system, but his vigilance is not suspended. It can be inferred that rumination and fantasy go forward during the stuporous periods. Sometimes the stupor ends in response to an hallucinated command, evidently the climax of a silent inner drama.

The Hebephrenic Form. The hebephrenic form of schizophrenia is the least clearly defined of the four. To some extent it serves as a wastebasket category which is used for patients more severely disordered than in the simple form, yet without predominant delusional formations or disturbances of motility. There are certain more positive phenomena, however, the chief of which are silliness, inappropriate smiling and laughter, bizarre disorganized ideas, and an incoherent stream of talk studded with words made up by the patient (neologisms). There are scattered delusions and hallucinations which have little continuity and no organization. Deterioration takes a fairly rapid course so that before long the patient is found eating with the fingers, neglecting dress and toilet habits, smearing feces, and otherwise dropping the restraints of socialized living.

The disorganization and fleeting strange ideas are well illustrated in the following piece of ward conversation.[2] The doctor addresses the

[2] W. A. White, *Outlines of Psychiatry* (New York: Nervous and Mental Disease Publishing Co., 1932), p. 228.

patient, a Negro, with a standard question to which he receives a surprising answer.

"How old are you?"

"Why, I am centuries old, sir."

"How long have you been here?"

"I have been now on this property on and off for a long time. I cannot say the exact time because we are absorbed by the air at night, and they bring back people. They kill up everything; they can make you lie; they can talk through your throat."

"Who is this?"

"Why, the air."

"What is the name of this place?"

"This place is called a star."

"Who is the doctor in charge of your ward?"

"A body just like yours, sir. They can make you black and white. I say good morning, but he just comes through there. At first it was a colony. They said it was heaven. These buildings were not solid at the time, and I am positive this is the same place. They have others just like it. People die, and all the microbes talk over there, and prestigitis you know is sending you from here to another world. . . . I was sent by the government to the United States to Washington to some star, and they had a pretty nice country there. Now you have a body like a young man who says he is of the prestigitis."

"Who was this prestigitis?"

"Why, you are yourself. You can be a prestigitis. They make you say bad things; they can read you; they bring back Negroes from the dead."

If this conversation is compared with the letters of L. Percy King, the difference between hebephrenic and paranoid schizophrenia becomes clear. For all the strangeness in King's productions, he at least proceeds logically, with coherent sequence, and under the guidance of a theme. The hebephrenic, in contrast, jumps from image to image and merely returns now and then to a theme. In the hebephrenic disorder everything is jumbled. Even the feelings seem jumbled and pulled out of coherent relation to events. The patient laughs foolishly when describing his best friend's death or weeps when explaining how well he feels.

A combination of paranoid and hebephrenic characteristics appears in the following excerpt from an essay written by a patient. The attempt at system is typical of the paranoid form. The use of language, however, is a nice example of what a French writer has called "word salad," a phenomenon that is particularly well developed in the hebephrenic form. The essay is entitled "Mother of Man" and begins with this paragraph.

This creation in which we live began with a Dominant Nature as an Identification Body of a completed evolutionary Strong Material creation in a Major Body Resistance Force. And is fulfilling the Nature Identification in a like Weaker Material Identification creation in which Two Major Bodies have already fulfilled radio body balances, and embodying a Third Material Identification Embodiment of both; which is now in the evolutionary process of fulfillment but fulfills without the Two Parents' Identification Resistances, therefore shall draw the resistances and perpetuate the motion interchanging of the whole interrelationship; thus completing this Creation in an interchanging Four in Three Bodies in One functioning self contained, self-controlled and self-restrained comprising the Dominant Moral Nature and consummating a ratio balanced Major Body of maximum resistance, in a separated second like Weaker Material Major Body Functioning Counter Resistance Force to the Strong Material Major Body Resistance Force, the beginning of this creation; and the Dual Force Resistances then as a Major Body and Major Body Functioning completes a Universe in material balance functioning the preservation of all things.

The reader may experience difficulty in grasping the patient's thought, but to the patient herself it was full of significance. She had gone over her typescript with great care, correcting the punctuation and inserting words or phrases to clarify any possible obscurity in her meaning. Her paragraph is not without a theme. One can infer that she is writing about the creation of new life by the union of two bodies, though she is careful to keep her subject at a metaphysical plane. But the language gets completely out of hand. Words are strung together in incongruous chains, happily liberated from their usual task of conveying precise ideas. Whatever the patient had in mind, one cannot say that she achieved successful communication. To communicate with others, either through speech or writing, is a social act, and it is in the sphere of social acts that the schizophrenic disorder is most apparent.

Is Schizophrenia a Unity? What common features are to be found which justify the placing of these diverse symptom pictures under a common heading? One thing that can be said about all of them is that they show a disturbance of relationship with people. Even in the simple form there is failure to interact effectively with others, and this failure is much greater in the other three forms, where sometimes the attempt to communicate seems to be altogether abandoned. It is often said that the schizophrenic withdraws from social participation and retires into himself, living more and more in the world of his thoughts and fantasies. It seems clear, however, that this process of withdrawal does not explain all the strangeness of schizophrenic behavior. Just as we cannot explain depression as the uncomplicated result of discouragement or loss, so we cannot understand the bizarre character of schizophrenia as a direct outcome of social withdrawal. In all but the simple form there is a degree of disorganization that goes beyond anything we might reasonably ascribe to lack of human contact. The patient's contact with his inanimate surroundings also becomes seriously impaired. Jenkins has expressed the view that although "schizoid withdrawal is a typical precursor of schizophrenia" it is not the essential psychotic process. Jenkins reminds us that "withdrawal from emphatic contact with the human environment is a stable long-term characteristic of many personalities who never show schizophrenic disorganization." What turns withdrawal into a disorder is a "progressive personality disorganization," a breakdown of integrated thinking and integrated adaptive behavior.[3] It is perhaps here that one can make the strongest case for the unity of the several forms of schizophrenia.

This was the central point of Bleuler's theory of schizophrenia, advanced in 1911 and now regarded as a historical milestone.[4] Bleuler believed that disorganization reflected the root disorder. It appeared with fewest complications in schizophrenia simplex, where it consisted of "a particular type of alteration in thinking, feeling, and relation to the external world." The more dramatic symptoms—the delusional systems, the word salads, the catatonic excitements—were to be regarded as secondary developments. Bleuler believed that the central disorder could exist in various degrees of severity and that it could run a variety of courses. With some patients there would be steady deterioration, with others, intermittent attacks; the disease might take a chronic downward course, but it might be subject to arrests and remissions. Because of these variations in onset, course, and prospects, he often referred to the "group of schizophrenias." On the basis of 515 cases admitted to the Swiss hospital where he worked, he reported that 22 per cent advanced to severe deterioration and that 60 per cent recovered sufficiently to be capable of earning a living. He did not regard the recovered patients as completely well, and some of them eventually relapsed, but others apparently remained free from incapacitating illness.

How far have we been able to advance beyond Bleuler's view of schizophrenia? Hardly at all, it may be, with regard to therapeutic results. Using recent statistics from the Delaware State Hospital, Freyhan shows that the proportion of recoveries and deteriorations continues to be strictly in accord with Bleuler's expectations. Despite improved methods of care and treatment, despite even the tranquilizing drugs, we have failed to halt the inexorable 22 per cent of patients destined for severe deterioration; and the number of satisfactory, though perhaps not permanent or complete, recoveries still hovers around 60 per cent.[5] Such evidence seems to indicate a disorder of a fundamental character that is still beyond the reach of current knowledge of psychodynamics, neurophysiology, and biochemistry. This impression is further strengthened by evidence of an entirely different sort. Cross-cultural studies show that

[3] R. L. Jenkins, "The Schizophrenic Sequence: Withdrawal, Disorganization, Psychotic Reorganization," *American Journal of Orthopsychiatry,* XX (1952), pp. 738–48.

[4] E. Bleuler, *Dementia Praecox or the Group of Schizophrenias,* 1911, trans. J. Zinkin (New York: International Universities Press, Inc., 1950).

[5] F. A. Freyhan, "Eugen Bleuler's Concept of the Group of Schizophrenias at Mid-Century," *American Journal of Psychiatry,* CXIV (1958), pp. 769–79.

in all parts of the world and in all varieties of culture, it is possible to recognize certain individuals whose behavior has the typical earmarks of schizophrenia. Within the American culture it has been shown, for example, that Irish and Italian schizophrenics reflect their subcultural backgrounds: the Italian patients are more overtly aggressive and more given to motor expression, whereas the Irish are more compliant, restrained, and imaginative. Yet both alike are schizophrenic.[6]

VARIETIES OF ONSET AND COURSE

The division of schizophrenia into simple, paranoid, catatonic, and hebephrenic forms is a classification based largely on symptoms. For descriptive purposes it is convenient, but it suggests little by way of explanation. Recent workers have inclined toward the view that Bleuler's ideas on onset and course can be the basis for a more fundamental distinction. Some cases of schizophrenia develop slowly over months and years with gradually increasing withdrawal and signs of disorganization. Eventually the illness can no longer pass unrecognized and the patient is sent for help. In other cases a full-blown psychosis develops almost overnight—sometimes literally overnight, when the patient awakens to a changed world and seems to others to have gone suddenly out of his head. Ausubel proposed that these forms receive separate names, "evolutionary" and "reactive."[7] The first form is now generally known as "process" schizophrenia, and it is assumed to depend on an insidiously developing process; in contrast, the "reactive" form is assumed to occur under conditions of acute stress. There is some tendency for the simple and hebephrenic varieties to go in the process category, the paranoid and catatonic in the reactive, but this division is not sharp. The process-reactive classification has found considerable favor with research workers, who have tried to develop a systematic account of the differences.[8]

Process vs. Reactive Patterns. It has long been a common clinical observation that the prognosis is better in cases with relatively abrupt onset. These are also the cases in which anxiety is acute and in which the patient seems to be struggling actively with his problems. It is usually possible to relate the onset to a sharp emotional crisis caused by an impasse in the patient's development. Comparing these reactive patients with those having a gradual onset, it is much harder to find in the latter any unusual emotional situation which might have precipitated the

[6] M. K. Opler, "Cultural Perspective in Research on Schizophrenics: A History with Examples," *Psychiatric Quarterly,* XXXIII (1959), pp. 506–24.

[7] D. P. Ausubel, *Ego Development and the Personality Disorders* (New York: Grune & Stratton, Inc., 1952).

[8] W. G. Herron, "The Process-Reactive Classification of Schizophrenia," *Psychological Bulletin,* LIX (1962), pp. 329–43.

breakdown. Research has disclosed differences also in the earlier histories: the reactive patients have generally shown a higher level of social competence and less evidence of difficulty in relation to parents, often differing but little in these respects from healthy people.[9] Psychological tests indicate in process schizophrenics a greater impairment of abstract thinking, and physiological measures give results that suggest a greater deficit in physiological responsiveness.[10] All these differences point to more severe illness in cases with gradual onset, although admittedly the acute cases seem just about as seriously disorganized during their worst periods. It should be noted that none of the findings require a division into two distinct types of illness; they are consistent with Bleuler's idea of a single basic disorder that differs in severity, temporal course, and degree of relatedness to situations of personal stress. We shall examine instances that lie somewhat toward the extremes of the process-reactive continuum.

Acute Schizophrenic Episodes with Recovery. The outbreak of unmistakable schizophrenic behavior sometimes occurs under circumstances that illuminate the nature of the patient's inner turmoil. Strecker and Ebaugh illustrate this with two cases in which the sexual phenomena of puberty precipitated serious symptoms.[11] A girl of fourteen became rather suddenly withdrawn, preoccupied, full of ideas of reference. She believed that the teachers were against her and that the other girls were constantly talking about her. It turned out that she was horrified by her first menstrual period, believing that it signified a serious abnormality and that she might bleed to death. A boy of seventeen dropped from the head of the class to total school failure and was reported increasingly silly, peculiar, and disinterested. He proved to be excessively worried about masturbation, which he believed caused insanity, and he felt sure that his schoolmates were chatting disdainfully about his evil and dangerous habit. Both of these young patients were helped by correct sexual information, together with encouragement along lines of increased social and athletic participation. It is to be noticed in each of these cases that because of misinformation the sexual phenomena were interpreted as great personal shortcomings and abnormalities. The immediate cause of

[9] E. Zigler and L. Phillips, "Social Competence and the Process-Reactive Distinction in Psychopathology," *Journal of Abnormal and Social Psychology*, LXV (1962), pp. 215–22; N. Garmezy and E. H. Rodnick, "Premorbid Adjustment and Performance in Schizophrenia: Implications for Interpreting Heterogeneity in Schizophrenia," *Journal of Nervous and Mental Disease*, CXXIX (1959), pp. 450–66.

[10] A. Meadow, M. Greenblatt, D. H. Funkenstein, and H. C. Solomon, "The Relationship Between the Capacity for Abstraction in Schizophrenia and the Physiologic Response to Autonomic Drugs," *Journal of Nervous and Mental Disease*, CXVIII (1953), pp. 332–38; see also Herron, *op. cit.*, pp. 332–34.

[11] E. A. Strecker and F. G. Ebaugh, *Practical Clinical Psychiatry* (5th ed.; Philadelphia: The Blakiston Co., 1940), pp. 423–24.

breakdown was a sharp blow to self-esteem that may well have been already precarious. Both patients, moreover, had the delusion that people were talking about them. They exhibited not only a withdrawal but also a true disorganization of behavior.

French and Kasanin have published a detailed analysis of two cases of recovery from schizophrenia.[12] They make two points: (1) that an acute psychosis can sometimes be regarded as a temporary episode that marks the transition from an old to a new adjustment, and (2) that in his delusions the patient may foreshadow the means he is going to employ in achieving the new adjustment. In the first patient, a woman of twenty-four, the critical breakdown occurred soon after she left home to make an independent life for herself and soon after she accepted for the first time sexual attentions from a man. Both steps were radical ones, especially the second, which was sharply at variance with the severe moral standards of her parents. Apparently these steps were at first too much for her. A typical schizophrenic psychosis developed with many strange and incoherent delusions. The theme of most of these delusions was punishment and suffering for what she had done. She felt that she was dead and that she was being transformed into a snake which was loathsome to everyone. In this delusion she probably expressed in a symbolic way her inability to take the steps toward sexual expression. Another set of delusions made no sense at first, but afterwards appeared to foretell the mechanism of her recovery. She was being kidnapped and transported to Italy, this being the land of her ancestral home, and in addition she had become a Catholic, this being her ancestral faith but not the faith of her parents. As time went on her delusion of having become a Catholic increasingly took the form of a desire to confess her sins and receive absolution. This desire eventually brought her back into contact with the hospital staff and especially with the psychiatrist, who could function in a role not unlike that of a priest. It would seem an unwarrantable piece of interpretation to say out of hand that the patient's delusion about Italy and the church meant that she wanted to resume her growth, but needed the guidance and support of someone whose attitude would be kindly and forgiving. Yet this was precisely the means by which the patient recovered. At first leaning heavily on the psychiatrist for advice at every step, then with steadily increasing independence, she gradually achieved the new learning that brought her to vocational and sexual adulthood. Follow-up over several years showed distinctly superior adjustment in marriage.

[12] T. M. French and J. Kasanin, "A Psychodynamic Study of the Recovery of Two Schizophrenic Cases," *Psychoanalytic Quarterly*, X (1941), pp. 1–22. Reprinted in S. S. Tomkins (ed.), *Contemporary Psychopathology* (Cambridge: Harvard University Press, 1943), chap. xxvii.

The second patient reported by French and Kasanin, a nineteen-year-old boy, was blocked in much the same developmental problem. He was unable to accept masturbation as his sole sexual outlet, yet girls he regarded as far too pure and remote to be fitting objects for a physical interest. During his schizophrenic episode he performed acts and developed delusions that expressed his desire to give up and renounce the whole attempt at new adjustment. He also busied himself, however, with metaphysical theories and finally reached a formula which appeared to give him the key to the universe. His formula dealt with the achievement of perfect unity, and it included the proposition that one means of achieving this perfect unity was through the sexual union of man and woman. Apparently the solution of his problem in the abstract was a necessary and constructive step toward solving it in reality. He had to conceive of sexual union as part of the harmonious working of the universe before he could accept it as personal behavior. The solution proposed in his psychotic philosophizing was the one adopted by him in his subsequent good adjustment.

These transient schizophrenias can be described as retreats from reality. When viewed in the light of their later outcome, however, they can better be characterized as tactical retreats having the function of a delaying action until the patient can gather himself together for a fresh attack on the problem of new adjustment.

Gradual Onset with Progressive Disorganization. In cases where the onset is more gradual it is sometimes possible to detect warning signs that something more than withdrawal is taking place. In a study of adolescent patients Hinsie was able to reconstruct the typical sequence of events as follows.[13] During childhood the patients give evidence of "clinging to the mother's apron strings" and avoiding rough, competitive play. Very often there is early success with school work and a continuing interest in studies. Thus far the pattern cannot be called morbid, though it may lack something of assertiveness. Before long, however, it becomes possible to observe something more serious: a general retraction of interests. Outside observers may sense that the youngster's interests are becoming less intense and less numerous. The individual himself may feel that he is growing more passive in his attitude and that outside events are losing their meaning for him. He ceases to make new friends, even older or younger friends, and his interest in schoolwork declines into dreamy inattentiveness. This change for the worse is likely to occur at puberty. So long as interest is maintained in some form of constructive activity—art or writing, for example—there may be a chance that the

[13] L. E. Hinsie, *The Treatment of Schizophrenia* (Baltimore: The Williams & Wilkins Co., 1930).

person will find his way back, along the lines of his specialty, to social acceptance and participation. But if interests are retracted to the point of listlessness and apathy, so that fantasy reigns without further correction by real experience, then the condition must be regarded as ominous.

Hinsie also found that ideas of reference tend to creep gradually into the picture without at first assuming the status of delusions. The incipient patient is keenly aware of outside stimulation even though he does not overtly respond to it. For a long time he recognizes that the source of his difficulties is in himself. Nevertheless he cannot help feeling that the world is a little hostile, or at least inconsiderate, and that other people take a derogatory attitude toward him. Highly aware of his own fantasies, he wonders what other people would think if they knew what was going on in his head. It is a short step to occasional fleeting delusions. The patient half believes that people are actually saying derogatory things and behaving in a hostile fashion. In this borderland of half belief he may remain for some time, only gradually slipping over to the point where insight is lost. It is when he is already in this borderland, we may suppose, that any downward slipping of self-esteem is likely to precipitate overt psychosis.

The general retraction of interests can be considered a first sign of impending disorganization. It is not a logical consequence or natural extension of defensive withdrawal from people. The patient now seems to be giving up the attempt to move forward even along unsocial lines. Sometimes the retraction of interest finds expression in ideas that the world has changed and that everything is dying. The affective change in the patient is perceived as a physical change in the world.

The following case illustrates both the gradual appearance of disorganization and the way in which events can progressively deepen a schizophrenic reaction. A boy in high school was considered by his friends to be sensitive, solitary, and a little eccentric. They knew that he was an orphan and lived with an elderly, somewhat peculiar foster mother. The boy was good in his studies, especially in history and literature. His English teacher, who constantly read his literary productions, noted distinct talent but many eccentricities of content. Themes of death and decay, images of dilapidated castles and gardens gone to seed, scenes of an ancient glory now crumbling to dust—these and similar gloomy ideas dominated his beautifully written verses. Although the boy spent a good deal of time alone, he had several friends among the students who were preparing for college. At graduation he was separated from his chums, he himself being unable to go to college. Occasionally he visited them, but it was clear that he resented his inferior position and the interruption of his own education. His friends now began to suspect that he was building up fictions about himself. He showed them an application blank that he had received from an art school. They believed that he had prepared it on his own typewriter. He also discoursed at length on his distinguished French ancestry, a theme which he was able to fill out convincingly from his knowledge of history. He repeatedly mentioned that his real mother, a countess, was now living in the city, and that he was in frequent communication with her. The friends began to feel that he was a liar, and they laid plans to expose him. One day they confronted him with numerous fatal inconsistencies in his stories and accused him of fabrication. He thereupon admitted that his stories were not true, but explained that he had been forced to disguise himself in this way in order to elude a hostile power known as the Third Element. He now claimed that he and his mother, the countess, had collaborated in preparing a set of disguising fictions to keep the Third Element off their trail. He told his accusers that the situation was growing increasingly serious. Most of his friends had turned against him, and only three remained on his side.

It is clear that this boy's history showed signs of schizophrenic disorganization before he graduated from high school. That event, with separation from his circle of friends, gave his adjustment a downward jolt and sharply increased his symptoms. He now began to lose track of the line between fantasy and fact, speaking of his fantasies of noble lineage is if they were true. The motive behind these fabrications was pathetically clear: if he could not go to college, he would at least have some form of distinction to keep him on a footing with his friends, and while he was at it he provided himself with a mother. Unfortunately his attempts at compensation only irritated his friends, and their unsympathetic action constituted a second, more direct, and more personal rejection. This event threw him into deeper psychosis. His delusions about hostile friends and a hostile Third Element reflected the real feeling of hostility that he sensed in his accusers. Unfortunately the delusions now began to assume a generalized form which made him more and more inaccessible to friendly advances from others.

In general it can be said that sharp downward steps on the path to schizophrenia occur in connection with events that lower the patient's already feeble self-esteem or challenge in some way his adequacy. Anything that makes him feel more different from others, or less competent than he already thinks himself to be, has a devastating effect upon his contact with reality. The sexual changes of puberty, and such major challenges as engagement, marriage, childbirth, or heavy vocational responsibilities, often serve as precipitating events. Each step toward fuller independence and maturity stands like a threat and may deepen the schizophrenic reaction.

DISORGANIZATION IN SCHIZOPHRENIC THINKING

From the descriptions already given it will be clear that the problem of schizophrenia can be approached from several directions. As in the neuroses, emotional problems crop out at every turn: difficulties with sex and aggression, with love and hate, with competence and self-esteem are everywhere apparent in the case histories. This leads our thoughts toward the family circle and the interaction of parents and child during the early years. We notice also a weakening of social interest and a progressive failure of communication with others, suggesting unusual difficulties in the process of social adaptation. Thus far we might be dealing with another variety of neurosis; but then we are confronted everywhere by signs of disorganization, a seeming breakdown in the very structure of thinking that has no counterpart in the neuroses and is somewhat like what we studied in connection with brain injuries. Can such fundamental disorganization be understood in psychodynamic terms? If so, we must not be satisfied with general concepts like rejection, domination, or overprotection; it is necessary to find specific connections between emotional situations and the disorganization of behavior. Can the fundamental changes be understood as consequences of biochemical conditions in the brain? If so, we must not be satisfied with vague hypotheses; it is necessary to find specific connections between disorganization and demonstrable biochemical states. Psychodynamic and somatogenic hypotheses alike converge on disorganization, and we shall do well to try to strengthen our understanding of this central fact.

It is extraordinarily difficult to follow the thought processes of a schizophrenic patient. With other types of patient the observer can usually establish empathy and follow the course of thought even though it appears somewhat strange. It is not difficult, for instance, to comprehend the deluded paretic who offers us a pleasant week end at his country estate, or to understand a manic patient when he lays vast plans for humanitarian reform. These patients are crazy, but somehow the schizophrenics seem crazier. Their thinking falls to pieces, it defies logic, it contains weird constructions like prestigitis, the Third Element, and the Strong Material Major Body Resistance Force. Nevertheless it is not always impossible to understand what is going on in schizophrenic thought. What we have to realize is that the thought processes are autistic, like dreams and daydreams; more than that, they are full of conceptions that seem to be infantile in nature. The patient may use adult forms of speech, but he is trying to communicate what Sullivan called "types of processes that most of us ceased to have within clear awareness by the time we were two-and-a-half."[14]

[14] H. S. Sullivan, *The Interpersonal Theory of Psychiatry* (New York: W. W. Norton & Co., Inc., 1953), p. 327.

The Development of Paranoid Thinking. The study of schizophrenic thought is most easily begun at the point where it is least abnormal. We shall therefore begin by considering delusions. A delusion is essentially a misinterpretation of experience. It does not, like an hallucination, entail a distorted registering of experience or a false perception of what is going on. An hallucinated patient hears voices in the ventilating system that loudly discuss his faults and denounce his sins. A merely deluded patient proceeds with more respect for reality. He correctly perceives a number of people talking, and although he does not overhear them he infers that they are discussing his faults and denouncing his sins. In delusions the disorder is localized at the point where inference or the interpretation of experience begins. Otherwise the contact with reality is correctly maintained.

In a paper on delusional thinking Cameron develops the thesis that one is dealing mainly with a disorder of communication.[15] As we have seen, children learn to react to themselves by noticing how others react to them.[16] Their criticism of their own behavior contains a distillation of the criticisms they have received from others. Gradually the child learns to see himself in different perspectives. He learns to judge his conduct as his mother judges it, as his brother judges it, as his teacher judges it, as his chum and as his rival judge it. He becomes able to shift his perspectives and thus to take different attitudes toward his behavior. Cameron describes the capacity to do this as "skill in role-taking, *i.e.*, in taking the attitudes of others and thus having their perspectives in one's own behavior." Skill in role-taking is an acquired skill, and there are great individual differences in the extent to which it is acquired. "The adult who is especially vulnerable to paranoid developments is one in whom this process of socialization has been seriously defective."[17] Like everyone else he draws inferences from what he observes, but unlike others he remains an amateur in realizing how these inferences might appear to someone else.

Now suppose that a person whose lack of social experience has caused him to retain a rigidity of perspective and a one-track outlook becomes involved in emotional difficulties. More specifically, suppose that his internal economy of aggression, sense of competence, and self-esteem suffers a downward jolt. The effect of this is to sensitize him to any impressions that have to do with his standing in relation to others. Cameron illustrates the matter of special sensitivity by mentioning the

[15] N. Cameron, "The Development of Paranoic Thinking," *Psychological Review,* L (1943), pp. 219–33.

[16] See above, page 148.

[17] N. Cameron, "The Paranoid Pseudo-Community Revisited," *American Journal of Sociology,* LXV (1959), pp. 52–58.

woman who goes out for the first time with a new hat. She is set to respond to any hint of surprise or criticism. A man smiling over a joke he has just recollected, a woman frowning to remember her shopping list, are perceived as reacting unfavorably to her new hat. Thus she selects fragments of behavior of other people and weaves them together into a fictitious audience reaction. The problem is the same, though much more serious, for the person whose self-esteem has been blasted. Everything that happens seems related to this consuming problem. He selects fragments of the behavior of others and interprets them into a consistent picture of judgments about himself. These judgments are fictitious because they do not correspond to what others are thinking. They correspond only to what the person is thinking about himself.

The critical point in the development of delusions, however, is the *failure of correction.* Weak in habits of role-taking, accustomed to puzzle and brood alone, the person becomes trapped in his own single perspective and shares his misgivings with no one. The result is cumulative misinterpretations; "the lone individual lacks the usual checking over with other persons which might modify and correct them." Before long he has built up what Cameron calls a "pseudo-community." He ascribes imaginary attitudes and functions to the real people in his environment. They are detectives, they are gangsters, they are pursuers who mean harm. The more he organizes this pseudo-community, the more it becomes necessary for him to take action in it. Eventually he does something in the way of protective or aggressive behavior. He takes action in the real social field, and is judged by the other persons in that field to be insane.

In a further discussion of the paranoid pseudo-community, Cameron points out that in spite of distortion of reality there is an attempt on the patient's part to regain contact with other people.[18] Social withdrawal has occurred, but the paranoid patient does not stop there; he attempts restitution of his human environment and a new basis for social behavior. It is important to bear this general principle in mind in our study of schizophrenia. On many occasions psychosis involves not only disorganization but also a peculiar or psychotic reorganization of experience.

We can learn something more about this by examining an instance of abrupt break with reality.

The Changed World in Schizophrenia. A case of catatonic schizophrenia reported by Angyal is of unusual service at this point because the initial break with reality was clearly recalled by the patient after his recovery.[19]

[18] *Ibid.*

[19] Andras Angyal, "The Psychodynamic Process of Illness and Recovery in a Case of Catatonic Schizophrenia," *Psychiatry,* XIII (1950), pp. 149–65.

The characters in the story are the patient, B, a 22-year-old electrician; the girl, D, to whom he was engaged; and a music teacher, K, a man twice B.'s age who was very much attached to him. B lived at home in a stormy relation with his incompetent widowed father, for whom he had no respect. His engagement to D, a girl from a lower middle class background like his own, was the culmination of a typical history of normal interest in girls. The unsatisfactory character of his life at home lent special significance to his friendship with K, who gave him free singing lessons, guided his reading, took him to the theater, and opened the door upon a world of culture and refinement to which he had always been attracted. K became a good father to him and a man in whom he could confide. One would assume a homosexual interest on K's part, but this was never openly manifested; however, it is not without significance that K, who wished to monopolize B, was jealous of D and declared that she was too crude and unrefined for B. A situation thus developed in which D and K became conflicting goals: D meant heterosexuality, marriage, and an independent but unrefined life; K meant music, culture, emotional support, but a dependent relationship and unconsciously a threat of homosexuality. This problem was completely unsolved when B was inducted into the Army. Some seven weeks later, without warning or preliminary signs of illness, he awakened one morning to a new world.

Outwardly B's new world looked like the old one, and he behaved the same way in it, but everything had assumed a new meaning. B knew for a certainty that he was selected to serve as an FBI agent in the camp, that K was the person in charge who had selected him, and that he was being tested as to his fitness for a special secret assignment. He was very proud and happy. He realized that everything happening around him had a significance for his new position. If the coffee tasted bad, it was doped with a narcotic as a test of his ability to keep a secret even though drugged. When people spoke, an assignment was being conveyed to him surreptitiously; by carefully piecing together a word here and a phrase there he could decode his orders. After several preliminary assignments which got him into no trouble he received the final order: he was to take a new name and report home to K for the next phase of his career. The attempt to carry out this order was viewed with disfavor by his officers, and when they found him insisting upon a new name they referred him to the station hospital.

This example of the sudden onset of a delusional system can best be understood by means of the concepts introduced by Jung and further developed by Sullivan. Jung in 1906 made the first serious attempt to understand the content of schizophrenic thinking. Studying schizophrenic productions and associations in much the same way that Freud had studied the associations of neurotic patients, Jung reached the conclusion that emotional conflicts played the decisive part. The patient was completely absorbed in his "complexes" and had no energy left over for adjustment to reality. "The separation of the schizophrenic patient from reality," Jung wrote, "the loss of interest in objective happenings, is not difficult to explain when we consider that he persistently stands under the ban of an invincible complex. He whose whole interest is chained by a complex must be like one dead to all surroundings. He dreams with open eyes and psychologically no longer adapts himself to his surroundings."[20]

Sullivan carried the matter further by pointing out the historical connection between a "complex" and infantile ways of thinking. Grave anxieties in early childhood lead to the formation of *dissociated systems of motives*—Sullivan's equivalent for Jung's "complex" and the Freudian concept of repression. A dissociated system is thereafter kept out of the self system; the motives it represents are felt as abhorrent and foreign to the self. These motives, therefore, can find expression only in autistic, dream-like ways and are never channeled into adult logic and realistic thinking. When circumstances stimulate a dissociated system to the point where it begins to control behavior, autistic thinking also takes control and has a disintegrating effect on the regular forces of government. The intruding system commands only autistic and infantile processes, with which equipment it undertakes to operate the personality when it finally prevails over the reigning self. The revolution, of course, is never complete. As Sullivan put it, "a dissociated system which has broken cover in this way can only very briefly continue to be free from complication by what remains of the self system."[21] It is the struggle between rationality and intruding primitive logic that makes schizophrenic thought so confusing to the observer.

Sullivan's account is well illustrated in the case of B. Through some drama of inner forces B was tempted to solve his problems by going over completely to K. In realistic terms this would have meant allowing K to be his mentor and direct his life, and it would further have meant turning his back on D and independent adulthood. Behind this solution, however, one can infer a dissociated system of motives compounded of dependence and passive homosexual desires, and it was this system which brought forward the primitive ideas of omnipotence, mysterious communication, and magical practices like changing oneself into a different person.

Sullivan's somewhat pictorial conception fits these facts, but they can also be viewed a little differently. In a recent contribution Arieti has

[20] C. G. Jung, *The Psychology of Dementia Praecox*, trans. A. A. Brill (New York: Nervous & Mental Disease Publishing Co., 1936), p. 89.

[21] Sullivan, *op. cit.*, p. 327.

proposed that the regression to primitive levels of thinking occurs as a means of achieving a purpose, as a security measure when anxiety is severe. He favors *"the principle of teleologic regression: regression* because less advanced levels of mental integration are used; *teleologic* because this regression seems to have a purpose, namely, to avoid anxiety by bringing about the wanted results."[22] Applying this idea to B, we can see that his craving to be the recipient of K's affectionate support and guidance was at odds with reality, as well as with other needs in himself. If he really abandoned D and tried to live as K's favorite son, people would certainly assume that the relationship was a homosexual one and he would suffer a kind of social rejection that would jeopardize any future progress toward independent adulthood. Clearly B's inclinations toward K would release great anxiety, and they could exist in awareness only when disguised in regressed fantasies.

Nature of the Intellectual Disorder. It is natural to suppose that the disorganization in schizophrenic thinking will be accompanied by a drop in level of intelligence. In point of fact the deficit on intelligence tests is smaller than might be expected. This is shown in a study by Kendig and Richmond, who used the Stanford-Binet test of intelligence with 500 schizophrenic patients and several other groups serving for purposes of comparison.[23] On the whole the patients tested were below normal. Close inspection of their performances, however, revealed that the weakness was regularly in tasks demanding sustained attention and sustained effort. Apart from this weakness there were no particular mental functions that showed impairment, and there was no evidence for general deterioration. The patients were re-tested after a considerable interval of time and showed no loss in the second performance.

The weakness in sustained effort and attention is sufficient to produce peculiar results in schizophrenic thinking. In another experiment Cameron has undertaken a direct comparison between the performance of schizophrenics and that of senile patients in whom cerebral deterioration could be legitimately inferred.[24] The comparison was made by means of two tests: a sentence completion test that involved supplying a causal relationship, and a block sorting test. Both the deteriorated seniles and the schizophrenics made poor over-all performances, but the reasons for their failures were not the same. The senile patients were able to stick to the assigned task, performing monotonously and persistently in ways

[22] S. Arieti, *Interpretation of Schizophrenia* (New York: Robert Brunner, 1955), p. 192.

[23] I. Kendig and W. Richmond, *Psychological Studies in Dementia Praecox* (Ann Arbor: Edwards Publisher, Inc., 1940).

[24] N. Cameron, "Deterioration and Regression in Schizophrenic Thinking," *Journal of Abnormal and Social Psychology*, XXXIV (1939), pp. 265–70.

that were too simple and too restricted to reach the correct results. Their tendency to rapid forgetting prevented an effective organization in time. In contrast, the schizophrenics could not stay within the boundaries of the task. They borrowed impressions from all over the room and freely threw in their own personal preoccupations. Whereas a senile subject might get stuck in a wrong solution and go on endlessly sorting blocks by colors, a schizophrenic would mix things up by trying to include the examiner's yellow pencil with the yellow blocks, or his arms with the red blocks because they contained red blood. The schizophrenic tendency toward loose clustering was not at all characteristic of the senile patients. Schizophrenic thought is disorganized in its own peculiar way. It is different from the thinking of people with brain injuries and cerebral deterioration.

One way to understand schizophrenic thought is to suppose that infantile, preverbal conceptions are pushing their way forcibly into the fabric of adult logic and rationality. Resemblances between schizophrenic thought processes and those of children have been pointed out in detail by Werner, and have recently been summarized in a paper by Goldman.[25] It is certainly true that schizophrenic thinking is structurally much like that of young children. It shows similar characteristics of simplicity and concreteness; it tends to be stimulus-bound, overgeneralized, distractible, weakly governed by sets and principles of relevance. This similarity, however, does not lead us to an easy explanation. The psychoanalytic concept of regression seems badly stretched if it must include a literal return to childhood forms of thought, and often enough patients alternate rapidly between adult thought patterns and primitive ones. Regression would seem to apply metaphorically rather than literally.

More significant is the clue provided by the weakness of sustained effort and attention. It is almost as if the patient could not regularly summon the mental energy necessary for the organization of thought of which he is still capable. Frankl has called attention to a very general characteristic of schizophrenic experience which he calls the "passivizing of the psychic functions."[26] The patient feels helpless, observed, photographed, influenced, the passive object of things happening around him; we are reminded of L. Percy King with his pursuers and their influencing devices. Patients complain that the world has become shifting and kaleidoscopic; this perhaps betokens a kind of perceptual passivity in which all stimuli have a claim on attention and nothing can be excluded.

[25] H. Werner, *Comparative Psychology of Mental Development* (New York: International Universities Press, Inc., 1948); A. E. Goldman, "A Comparative-Developmental Approach to Schizophrenia," *Psychological Bulletin*, LIX (1962), pp. 57–69.

[26] V. E. Frankl, *The Doctor and the Soul* (New York: Alfred A. Knopf, Inc., 1955), pp. 247–57.

They perform poorly on complex learning tasks with many alternatives because they cannot maintain the learner's active role of selecting the relevant and excluding the irrelevant. They fail in sustained abstract thinking because they do not muster the necessary degree of active control over intellectual processes. The passivizing of thought may be the most telling description of the change that characterizes schizophrenic mental operations. It is this that a biochemical or a psychodynamic hypothesis must explain.

SCHIZOPHRENIA IN CHILDHOOD

Of late years there has been a great deal of interest in childhood schizophrenia; and a great deal of research has been conducted, mostly through the medium of attempts at psychotherapy. Considering the substantial difficulties of diagnosis, the many varieties of clinical picture, and the different ages of the children studied, it is not surprising that some rather different formulations have appeared in print. What is overwhelmingly clear, however, is that serious disorders having a resemblance to adult schizophrenias make their appearance early in life.

Early Infantile Autism. One fairly clear category, *early infantile autism*, was established by Kanner in 1943 and seems to have passed the test of time at least up to the present.[27] This disturbance is seen as early as the first two years of life. It is readily distinguished from feeble-mindedness by the facts that the infant's face has an "intelligent and pensive" expression and that he shows normal if not superior skill in dealing with his inanimate environment. The difficulty shows itself in a serious lack of contact with people, a backwardness in the use of language for communication, and "an obsessive desire for the preservation of sameness."[28] This last trait conveys the impression that the child cannot tolerate anything new; his sense of security depends upon keeping the environment constant and free from surprises. If we imagine these traits as remaining throughout the course of development it is clear that the end result would correspond in many respects to the unassertive adult schizophrenic who faces hesitantly each new stage of growth, communicates poorly with his fellow men, and has no strong affective contact with anyone around him. By calling this condition *early infantile autism* Kanner hoped to avoid a premature assumption that such children supplied recruits for later schizophrenia, but most workers are inclined to view it as the start of at least a strong trend in that direction.

[27] L. Kanner, "Autistic Disturbances of Affective Contact," *The Nervous Child*, II (1943), pp. 217–50.

[28] L. Kanner, "The Conception of Wholes and Parts in Early Infantile Autism," *American Journal of Psychiatry*, CVIII (1951), pp. 23–26.

Early infantile autism is a relatively specific symptom syndrome which should not be confused with childhood schizophrenia as a whole. The distinguishing marks are early appearance and the central symptom of unresponsiveness to the human environment. Clinical reports sometimes indicate that the baby seemed unresponsive from the very beginning even when attempts were made to mother, cuddle, and play with him. Observational studies confirm the child's insulation: he cannot be coaxed into interactive play such as pat-a-cake or rolling a ball back and forth.[29] It is difficult to be sure, but the evidence suggests not just a lack of response but an active resistance to the human environment. The child looks past or through his adult would-be playmate, turns his back, occupies himself with something else; there is perhaps some similarity to the resistiveness that is apparent in catatonic stupor. The autistic child's impairment is less marked when he is dealing with the inanimate environment. Here he seems able to establish some of the sense of competence he is unable to feel with people.

In Kanner's description of autistic children the mothers are described as cold, distant, obsessive, and mechanical in their handling of their babies. Among them are many educated and successful women, which lends plausibility to the idea that they reject the maternal role, suppress the associated feelings, and experience the care of their children as a routine, unrewarding duty. A study of the fathers seems to put them in a male version of the same attitude: they pay no attention to babies and evince no desire to give them a place in their lives.[30] The family picture is thus one of intellectual, controlled, preoccupied parents whose particular form of adjustment is disturbed and threatened by the child's presence.[31] One might put it that the autistic child responds in kind to the treatment he receives. But these unflattering descriptions of the parents have been challenged by other workers who point out, thinking in more interactive terms, that an initial unresponsiveness on the infant's part would make the mother's role unrewarding and at the same time fill her with anxiety. Furthermore, as we have already seen so many times, the disorganization of the child's behavior has to be understood; and it is not altogether easy to derive it from the parental relation. Although we have no evidence of gross brain disorder in autistic children, their

[29] S. Ritvo and S. Provence, "Form Perception and Imitation in Some Autistic Children: Diagnostic Findings and Their Contextual Interpretation," *The Psychoanalytic Study of the Child* (New York: International Universities Press, Inc., 1953), Vol. VIII, pp. 155–61.

[30] L. Eisenberg, "The Fathers of Autistic Children," *American Journal of Orthopsychiatry,* XXVII (1957), pp. 715–24.

[31] I. Kaufman, E. Rosenblum, L. Heims, and L. Willer, "Childhood Schizophrenia: Treatment of Children and Parents," *American Journal of Orthopsychiatry,* XXVII (1957), pp. 683–90.

behavior has a good deal in common with certain rare cases in which autopsy revealed an early degenerative brain disease.[32] In a recent monograph Rimland collects evidence for the idea that autistic children have a specific impairment "in a function basic to all cognition: the ability to link new stimuli with remembered experience. . . . The child is thus virtually divested of the means for deriving meaning from his experience."[33] He cannot form a comprehensive perception of the world, which tends to remain kaleidoscopic for him; boundaries between himself and others cannot be made firm; hence relationships are vague and unmanageable. He is thus destined for affective isolation.

Childhood Schizophrenia. It is usual to reserve the term *childhood schizophrenia* for disorders that make their appearance after the first four or five years. There are various symptom pictures, but on the whole they cannot be interpreted simply as autism of later onset. This is most sharply shown in a pattern described by Margaret Mahler as *symbiotic psychosis.*[34] In contrast to autism, where the child displays no attachment to the mother or anyone else, in this group of cases there is a tremendously strong relationship between mother and child. The term *symbiosis,* which is in general use in biology, refers to close mutual dependence between two organisms, each requiring the other for its continued existence, as bees require flowers for honey and flowers require bees for fertilization. The symbiotic psychosis may be said to exist when the mother-child relationship has been so close that the infant fails to differentiate his mother from himself and thus stumbles over the whole process of distinguishing himself and his thoughts from external realities. Any threat of separation throws the child into disorganized panic, which is the central aspect of his numerous more acute symptoms. Mahler's description is built on direct study of young child patients, but it is possible to imagine this kind of thing lying latent in a person whose development has otherwise proceeded toward adulthood. In someone thus predisposed, later stress in the form of separation from home or from supporting groups might readily activate the infantile state in which reality testing was not attempted and subjective and objective events were confused.

[32] C. E. Benda, "Childhood Schizophrenia, Autism and Heller's Disease," in P. W. Bowman and H. V. Mautner (eds.), *Mental Retardation,* Proceedings of the First International Congress on Mental Retardation (New York: Grune & Stratton, Inc., 1960), pp. 469–92.

[33] B. Rimland, *Kanner's Syndrome of Apparent Autism* (New York: Appleton-Century-Crofts, Inc., 1963).

[34] M. Mahler, "On Child Psychosis and Schizophrenia," *The Psychoanalytic Study of the Child* (New York: International Universities Press, Inc., 1952), Vol. VII, pp. 286–305.

At somewhat older ages, in the juvenile era and later childhood, the diagnosis of schizophrenia can usually be made on the strength of behavior which is more openly and obviously bizarre. A six-year-old boy described by Ross, for example, rummaged through women's purses whenever he got a chance, entered rest rooms to examine the pipes under bathroom fixtures, got on his hands and knees to look at women's legs, hit other children on the head, was deeply preoccupied with the daily mail delivery, crawled under parked trucks to examine fender aprons, frequently swung his arms around in purposeless movements, was acutely anxious in games with other children, and tried to keep his mother at his side as much as possible.[35] If we reduce these eccentricities to the formula of aggression, anxiety, dependence, and curiosity about anatomy, they are not different in kind from the interests of normal younger children and from continuing unconscious trends in older ones, but we do not expect them to be expressed so openly, controlled so poorly, or pursued with such repetitive intensity that no energy is left over for general enjoyment or constructive growth. It is in fact this "lack of nuance and proportion" that strikes one observer, Annemarie Weil, as a central characteristic in many cases: "these children hardly ever hit the middle line; they react in extremes."[36] Their attacks of anxiety illustrate these extremes, reminding one of "states of anxiety in very young children, before the ego emerges and consolidates." On the whole it seems appropriate to say that there is in these cases a retardation of ego development. Instead of flexible control and a wholesome respect for reality there is impulsiveness, explosive behavior, over-intense pursuit of certain goals, and also passivity and fear. Weil points out that the diagnosis of schizophrenia in middle and late childhood is best made not on the strength of any one pathological feature but with reference to a generally "inadequate progression" toward a level of development appropriate to the child's age.

One cannot help having the highest respect for professional workers who have addressed themselves to the task of treating autistic and schizophrenic children. Their work is slow and discouraging; it requires infinite patience and persistence, and it must often go unrewarded by responsiveness and improvement on the child's part. Comparing such results as have been reported with Bleuler's expectations for adult schizophrenics, success would appear to be considerably less. Substantial recovery is claimed for only 20 to 25 per cent of child patients; and those who remain

[35] A. B. Ross, "A Schizophrenic Child and His Mother," *Journal of Abnormal and Social Psychology*, LI (1955), pp. 133–39.

[36] A. P. Weil, "Clinical Data and Dynamic Considerations in Certain Cases of Childhood Schizophrenia," *American Journal of Orthopsychiatry*, XXIII (1953), pp. 518–29.

unchanged or deteriorate run from 23 to 33 per cent, as against Bleuler's 22 per cent for adults.[37] Schizophrenias that are already crippling in childhood can be presumed to be unusually serious, so perhaps the thing we should emphasize in the figures is that something like a quarter of these severely disordered children can be rescued.

PSYCHODYNAMIC ASPECTS OF THE DISORDER

With these facts before us we can turn directly to a consideration of causes. In this section we shall look at things from the psychodynamic point of view, emphasizing the child's experience in the family circle. It should ke kept in mind that a fully adequate theory must account not only for emotional problems but also for schizophrenic disorganization.

Parent-Child Interactions. It is already clear that parents, especially mothers, play a vital part in those events of infancy which are assumed to be the starting point for schizophrenic developments. Recently the mothers of schizophrenics have begun to receive a pitiless barrage of psychological scrutiny and speculation. They have been dubbed "schizophrenogenic mothers," an expression which sounds like a proper ingredient for a word salad and which has been called by Hill "a bit of name-calling without proof and without much serious effort to prove it."[38] Indeed the descriptions of these mothers are so astonishingly unfavorable as to suggest that some of the observers may have slipped from scientific inquiry into a search for scapegoats. Perhaps, as Hill suggests, this flaw in the observer is a natural consequence of his excellence as a therapist. Successful work with schizophrenics requires a strong empathic understanding of their regressed feelings and thoughts. It must be hard not to share in some degree the hostility toward the mother which comes up so constantly when a schizophrenic patient begins to emerge from his difficulties.

Making due allowance for all this, it seems clear that the mother plays a vital and predominating part in the life of the child who is schizophrenic or who will later become so. It seems equally clear, however, that this part is not uniform in every case. Kanner's description of the mothers of autistic children would seem to be almost the opposite of the pattern which prevails in the symbiotic form of childhood schizo-

[37] L. Eisenberg, "The Course of Childhood Schizophrenia," *A. M. A. Archives of Neurology and Psychiatry*, LXXVIII (1957), pp. 69–83; P. Errera, "A Sixteen-Year Follow-Up of Schizophrenic Patients Seen in an Outpatient Clinic," *A. M. A. Archives of Neurology and Psychiatry*, LXXVIII (1957), pp. 84–88; M. J. Boatman and S. A. Szurek, "A Clinical Study of Childhood Schizophrenia," in D. D. Jackson (ed.), *The Etiology of Schizophrenia* (New York: Basic Books, Inc., 1960), chap. xiv.

[38] L. B. Hill, *Psychotherapeutic Intervention in Schizophrenia* (Chicago: University of Chicago Press, 1955), p. 104.

phrenia, where mother and child are closely bound together. Here the mother's behavior is likely to be overprotective to the point of grave interference. She has a tremendous need for the child, feels empty and incomplete without him, and is actually dependent upon the child for the emotional rewards and meaning of her life.[39] In this situation the infant forms an all too strong relationship with the mother and may even be supposed to develop a precocious responsiveness to her wishes and anxieties, conscious or unconscious.[40] The developmental difficulty then lies in emerging from the relationship to a sense of independent selfhood. Studies of withdrawn children in later childhood sometimes show that the central problem is to protect oneself from a demanding, interfering, overwhelming mother.[41]

The origin of this type of relation has been worked out as follows by Hill, who considers these mothers to be themselves disordered personalities.[42] They are not just overprotective or interfering or mechanical or rejecting; rather, they tend to be several of these things at once, or in alternation. If they were consistently any one thing, the child would perhaps learn somehow to deal with it, but what he cannot learn to deal with adequately is the combined pressures and changes of pressure that characterize his first human environment. Hill attaches particular importance to the mother's pervasive anxiety and guilt, her "suspicion of others," her "avoidance of immediate intimacy," and especially her "pattern of denial of unpleasant reality."[43] These qualities isolate her from others and cause her to attach herself hungrily to the baby. But her tensions and anxieties are communicated to the baby, whose uneasiness is communicated back to the mother, thus starting a cycle of mounting tension from which the only escape for the child is to go out of contact and become somnolent.[44] Hill writes as follows:

> To be secure, fed, and comforted is an inborn drive, but it can be conditioned so that to please, secure, or quiet the mother becomes what the child experiences as drive. Eventually hunger comes to evoke action to secure the mother's ability to feed the child. . . . This train of experience is one of un-

[39] R. W. Lidz and T. Lidz, "Therapeutic Considerations Arising from the Intense Symbiotic Needs of Schizophrenic Patients," in E. B. Brody and F. C. Redlich (eds.), *Psychotherapy with Schizophrenics* (New York: International Universities Press, Inc., 1952), pp. 168–78.

[40] M. Sperling, "Reactive Schizophrenia in Children," *American Journal of Orthopsychiatry*, XXIV (1954), pp. 506–12.

[41] L. Nagelburg, H. Spotnitz, and Y. Feldman, "The Attempt at Healthy Insulation in the Withdrawn Child," *American Journal of Orthopsychiatry*, XXIII (1953), pp. 238–52.

[42] Hill, *op. cit.*, chaps. vi and vii.

[43] *Ibid.*, p. 137.

[44] H. S. Sullivan, *The Interpersonal Theory of Psychiatry* (New York: W. W. Norton & Co., Inc., 1953), pp. 55–61.

certainty and discouragement. It contributes to a sense of futility in that the child does not have expectation of regular success in the simple business of being nourished and staying alive. . . .

The low self-esteem that is conspicuous in all schizophrenic patients may well be a subjective evaluation which the child makes of itself because of this lack of goodness from the mother—lack of built-in, incorporated goodness which it can call its own. The great danger which the child senses in the precarious instability of the mother interdicts anger against her. The child literally believes that anger could destroy the symbiosis and amount, thereby, to suicide. Not only is the anger turned in and made a problem of inner economy both somatic and psychic, but the processes are not established and the techniques are not organized whereby anger and aggression can be directed outward. The child may dream but must not act upon hostile impulse.[45]

Attempts have been made to support these clinical insights through questionnaire studies. In one such study twenty psychiatrists were asked to sort statements about parent-child relations, each doctor being requested to make his choices on the basis of his own experience with schizophrenic patients.[46] There was little consistency in the replies. The qualities ascribed to mothers included protectiveness and anxious control, a seeking of power in devious Machiavellian ways, and the helpless uncertainty of a person who wants only to be guided. Fathers could be coolly autocratic, but they were pictured also as awkwardly ineffective and even anxiously compliant. Certainly no single impression of parental characteristics emerged from this investigation, and the same can be said about studies in which questionnaires on traits and attitudes have been given to the parents of schizophrenics.[47] If some of the questionnaire results have favored the image of an anxiously protecting and interfering mother, their meaning has been thrown in doubt by a study by Klebanoff in which exactly the same pattern was found to prevail in the mothers of mentally retarded children.[48] Here the natural inference would be that the mothers' behavior was not a cause but a consequence of dealing constantly with a slow, unresponsive child whom one wanted to nudge into greater activity. Direct observations of mothers when in the company of their adult schizophrenic sons show clearly in some cases the continuing tightly bound relation that is so characteristic of the

[45] Reprinted from *Psychotherapeutic Intervention in Schizophrenia*, pp. 141–43, by L. B. Hill, by permission of the University of Chicago Press. Copyright, 1955.

[46] D. D. Jackson, J. Block, Jeanne Block, and V. Patterson, "Psychiatrists' Conceptions of the Schizophrenogenic Parent," *A. M. A. Archives of Neurology and Psychiatry*, LXXIX (1958), pp. 449–59.

[47] V. D. Sanua, "Sociocultural Factors in Families of Schizophrenics," *Psychiatry*, XXIV (1961), pp. 246–65.

[48] L. B. Klebanoff, "Parental Attitudes of Mothers of Schizophrenic, Brain-Injured and Retarded, and Normal Children," *American Journal of Orthopsychiatry*, XXIX (1959), pp. 445–54.

symbiotic psychoses of childhood.[49] Here again we cannot be certain that the mothers originally imposed this relation on normally behaving children.

Family Irrationality. Nowhere than here is it more important to replace the cause-effect idea of parent-child relations by an interactive conception. The tendency in recent work on schizophrenia is to study the whole family, including particularly the relation between the parents and the character this gives to the family as an environment for growth. On the basis of intensive studies of patients and their families, Lidz and his colleagues have reached the conclusion that "schizophrenic patients virtually always emerge from homes marked by serious parental strife or eccentricity."[50] It is not the characteristics of either parent taken singly that create an unfavorable climate. In a group of fourteen families Lidz described no less than five types of fathers, and his research group has shown that individual parental patterns in the families of male patients are very different from those in the families of female patients.[51] The crucial thing, the constant factor in patients' families, is disorganization created by basic discord between the parents and irrational ways of handling it. Many of the marriages were "torn by schismatic conflict between the parents," either overt or covert; furthermore, in several cases at least one of the parents "suffered from serious and crippling pathology." The parents' attempts to deny and smooth over their difficulties "created a strange emotional environment that was perplexing to the child."[52] One consequence was an imperviousness to feelings which still further confused the child in his attempts to interact with his human environment. The future patient is thus seen as growing up in a situation filled with irrationality, emotional distortion, and faulty reality testing, all of which tend to hinder the growth of a strong ego.

It will be noticed that this account of "schizophrenogenic" families includes a bridge from psychodynamics to the disorganization of thought. The patient's weak hold on rationality is attributed to the irrationality amidst which he is brought up. This connection has been worked out in

[49] J. Dworin and O. Wyant, "Authoritarian Patterns in the Mothers of Schizophrenics," *Journal of Clinical Psychology,* XIII (1957), pp. 332–38; M. Bowen, "A Family Concept of Schizophrenia," in D. D. Jackson (ed.), *The Etiology of Schizophrenia* (New York: Basic Books, Inc., 1960), chap. xii.

[50] T. Lidz and S. Fleck, "Schizophrenia, Human Integration, and the Role of the Family," in Jackson, *op. cit.,* chap. xi.

[51] T. Lidz, A. R. Cornelison, D. Terry, and S. Fleck, "The Intrafamilial Environment of the Schizophrenic Patient. I. The Father," *Psychiatry,* XX (1957), pp. 329–42; S. Fleck, T. Lidz, and A. R. Cornelison, "Comparison of Parent-Child Relationships of Male and Female Schizophrenic Patients," *A. M. A. Archives of General Psychiatry,* VIII (1963), pp. 1–7.

[52] Lidz and Fleck, *op. cit.,* pp. 332–33.

more detail in the theory of the "double-bind," proposed originally by Bateson and others.[53] This theory directs attention to the kind of communication that goes on between parents and child. In a recent exposition, Weakland describes the process as follows.[54] The child keeps receiving communications that involve at least two conflicting messages. An everyday example is the popular bit of evasiveness represented in the question, "Wouldn't you like to open the window?"—at once an order and a denial that the speaker is giving an order. We met another example in connection with school phobias: the mother requires the child to go to school but at the same time communicates her anxiety over the separation. Weakland and Frye have made a special study of letters written by mothers to their schizophrenic offspring.[55] "Almost no statement is allowed to stand, clearly and unambiguously," they report. "Rather, another message disqualifying it, in any of a variety of ways, occurs." Thus criticisms are canceled by assertions of love, and praise is drained of its virtue by belittlement or blame right at its heels. The "double-bind" situation is one in which double or confused comunications of this kind constantly reach the child from his parents and protectors. Dependent as he is upon them, he has to try to make adequate responses; and he is not allowed to question the messages or show that he perceives their inconsistencies. In the end he learns to make responses that are perhaps equally confused and that generate a split between overt content and covert affect. Obviously the "double-bind" tends to be compounded when the messages are coming from two parents deeply involved in unadmitted hostilities of the sort described by Lidz.

Limits of Psychodynamic Explanation. These analyses of emotional conflicts in the family, and of the subtle communication of irrationality to the child, represent a great advance over earlier studies of the "schizophrenogenic" mother. They are impressive, but they have by no means stilled the voices of controversy. It is prudent to remember that psychodynamic explanations of the neuroses and of delinquent behavior generally imply no small amount of emotional stress in the family, leading, however, to quite different outcomes in the child. When one tries to isolate what might be peculiar to the family of the schizophrenic—the irrational methods of dealing with conflict and the "double-bind" type of communication—one can hardly avoid misgivings about the specificity. It has certainly not been demonstrated that parental behavior is less

[53] G. Bateson, D. D. Jackson, J. Haley, and J. H. Weakland, "Toward a Theory of Schizophrenia," *Behavioral Science,* I (1956), pp. 251–64.

[54] J. H. Weakland, "The 'Double-Bind' Hypothesis of Schizophrenia and Three-Party Interaction," in Jackson, *op. cit.,* chap. xiii.

[55] J. H. Weakland and W. F. Frye, "Letters of Mothers of Schizophrenics," *American Journal of Orthopsychiatry,* XXXII (1962), pp. 604–23.

pathological and communication less irrational in the families of neurotics and delinquents. We may even suspect, listening to the average level of communication in the fast-moving daily events of family life, that a goodly portion of irrationality and "double-bind" is universal in childhood. It is important not to contrast the "schizophrenogenic" family with a wholly fanciful image of normal rationality. In addition it must be kept in mind that not every child in a family is likely to be schizophrenic. There is no reason to doubt that each child will be treated a little differently, but if we want the psychogenic hypothesis to be completely adequate we must be prepared to show how the well children escaped the fate of the sick one.

Psychodynamic studies thus continue to leave open the possibility that there is something unusual about the child who, earlier or later, succumbs to the schizophrenic disorder. We must now consider what progress has been made toward detecting a somatogenic component.

SOMATOGENIC ASPECTS OF THE DISORDER

It seems clear that one cannot conceive of schizophrenia as a somatic disease that is analogous to general paresis. It does not take a course or have a character that is consistent with gross cerebral pathology. The schizophrenic disorder is entirely consistent, however, with such possibilities as a generalized weakness, an oversensitive disposition, or even a subtle chemical deviation. It is possible that psychodynamic processes of the kind we have discussed serve as necessary causes but not as sufficient causes of schizophrenia. The disorder cannot occur without them, but it does not occur simply as their consequence. Something else must be added, some element of somatic compliance, which might plausibly take the form of an innate temperamental peculiarity or of a physiological deviation that would have an insidious but cumulative effect. What weight of evidence can be adduced for hypotheses of this kind?

Evidence for Genogenesis. In spite of the many difficulties that arise when hospital records are used as the basis for statistical investigations, there is considerable evidence that schizophrenia appears with abnormal frequency in certain family trees. The most vehement proponent of genogenesis is Kallmann, who studied the blood kin of all schizophrenics admitted to a Berlin mental hospital between 1893 and 1902, the records being followed to 1929.[56] The original group of patients numbered over a thousand. Kallmann's most important findings are the following. Schizophrenia occurs in approximately 0.85 per cent of the general popu-

[56] F. J. Kallmann, *The Genetics of Schizophrenia* (New York: Augustine, 1938). A condensed summary is given by M. Garrison, "The Genetics of Schizophrenia," *Journal of Abnormal and Social Psychology,* XLII (1947), pp. 122–24.

lation. If one parent is schizophrenic, however, the same disorder develops in 16.4 per cent of the children, and if both parents are schizophrenic it occurs in 68.1 per cent of their offspring. The same tendency can be shown by considering the siblings of patients. Schizophrenia was found in 85.8 per cent of cases where the sibling was an identical twin of the patient, in 14.7 per cent of fraternal twins, in 14.3 per cent of full siblings, and in 7.0 per cent of half-siblings. The incidence is greater for closer relatives of patients than it is for more distant relatives. The figures obtained by Kallmann are in general higher than those found by other investigators, but the trends are in the same direction.[57]

These figures probably exaggerate the importance of the genogenic factor. It is difficult to control the non-genetic factors in studies of this kind. A schizophrenic parent is not a good mentor in realistic adjustment, and the atmosphere of a home in which there is psychosis is anything but advantageous for sound dvelopment. Even those who are skeptical about the size of the reported figures, however, are likely to concede that a hereditary trend prevails in schizophrenia.[58] The findings mean that a schizophrenic psychosis is at least more likely to develop in individuals who carry a certain inherited predisposition.

The nature of this predisposition can be conceived in different ways. Some workers place the emphasis on an innate passivity and unresponsiveness. There is no doubt that infants differ consistently in activity level. Fries has described the more passive ones as being inclined to somnolence, so that they may have to be awakened for nursing and may drop into a doze before the feeding is completed.[59] Erikson observes that in some cases of infantile schizophrenia "the primary deficiency in 'sending power' was in the child," who might "very early and subtly fail to return the mother's glance, smile, and touch."[60] When one considers the autistic children described by Kanner, or the adult cases of simple schizophrenia with their general lack of energy and assertiveness, it seems entirely legitimate to postulate that their behavior has been influenced by a constitutional trait of passivity. It is also legitimate to speculate that a child of this kind would call forth in certain mothers no little anxiety and guilt. The resulting need to stimulate the child to a normal level of activity and responsiveness might produce in the end a constant interference in his life.

[57] C. Landis and J. D. Page, *Modern Society and Mental Disease* (New York: Farrar & Rinehart, 1938), pp. 81–85; B. Malzburg, *Social and Biological Aspects of Mental Disease* (Utica: State Hospitals Press, 1940).

[58] Jackson, *op. cit.*, pp. 80–81.

[59] See above, page 138.

[60] E. H. Erikson, *Childhood and Society* (New York: W. W. Norton & Co., Inc., 1950), p. 181.

On the other hand the schizophrenic predisposition can be conceived in a way that seems almost the opposite of passivity. The child is considered to be alert, highly responsive, but extremely sensitive to discomfort, pain, and fear. There might be a "very lively readiness to be anxious," as Hill expresses it, which in turn would lead to premature, overgeneralized habits of avoidance.[61] This would mean, on the one hand, a tendency to avoid tense and unpleasant situations by somnolent withdrawal; on the other hand, a tendency to form large dissociated systems of impulses split off from the self. Kretschmer, in his studies of physique and mental disease, reported a marked association between schizophrenia and the slender, fragile build which he called *asthenic* or *leptosome*.[62] He also studied healthy people having this type of physique and found them to be on the whole shy, sensitive, unrobust and socially awkward—findings which have since been verified under different conditions.[63] In Sheldon's scheme the physique in question is described as *ectomorphic* and the corresponding temperament as *cerebrotonic*.[64] Sheldon's conception of cerebrotonic children includes several traits that might lend themselves to a schizophrenic pattern if sufficiently encouraged by the environment. Such children are restrained in action but "intent, nervous, inquisitive, and jumpy." Reactions are relatively fast, so much so as to constitute a social handicap. "The individual tends to become flustered and tangled up in his own reactions." His attention is so strained that he is easily confused in a social situation; he acts like a "man trying to attend to several conversations simultaneously." He is oversensitive to pain, to loud sounds, to any form of strong stimulation, including the rough and tumble of the playground. "Strained, distressed, and uncomfortable in the face of any social relationship," he "retreats from company as from physical pain." A child endowed in the manner here described would hardly be a good candidate to deal with a difficult family situation or to outgrow his early troubles by building a strong social adjustment.

Findings of the sort made by Kretschmer and Sheldon are more suitable for understanding schizoid withdrawal than for explaining schizophrenic disorganization. The most thoroughgoing attempt to delineate a genetic basis for childhood schizophrenia has been made by Lauretta Bender, who believes that the initial trouble is a general lag and irregu-

61 Hill, *op. cit.*, p. 136.

62 E. Kretschmer, *Physique and Character*, trans. W. J. H. Sprott (London: Routledge & Kegan Paul, Ltd., 1925), chap. ii.

63 C. C. Seltzer, F. L. Wells, and E. B. McTerman, "A Relationship Between Sheldonian Somatotype and Psychotype," *Journal of Personality*, XVI (1948), pp. 431–36.

64 W. H. Sheldon and S. S. Stevens, *The Varieties of Temperament* (New York: Harper & Row, 1942), pp. 69–94.

larity of maturation starting during the embryonic period.[65] As summarized by Freedman, one of her co-workers, the maturation pattern shows marked disturbance, with precocity in some areas and retardation in others.[66] Balance in the vegetative system is poorly maintained, regular sleep patterns are established belatedly, muscular patterns are not well integrated. "Because of this physiologic immaturity, such children from the first day respond with an overwhelming and at times catastrophic anxiety that cannot be assuaged." They experience special difficulties in constructing images of their own bodies and in conceiving their relationships with others. Behavior and feeling are marked by rapid alterations and an interplay of opposites; thus, "a child may be alternately symbiotic and autistic, or actually both at the same time—withdrawing yet clinging." The maturational irregularity prevents the orderly organization of early experience, and a predisposition is thus laid down for later disorganization under stress. It is claimed by Bender's group that much help can be given the schizophrenic child by training that is designed to promote a more even and regular maturation of functions.

Evidence for Chemogenesis. Kraepelin advanced a chemogenic theory of schizophrenia. He believed that the root of the difficulty lay in disordered secretions of the sex gland. This produced a chemical state in the body (autointoxication) that in some way disturbed the proper functioning of the nervous system. When the importance of the endocrine glands was first appreciated, it looked as if Kraepelin's view might receive support. Research by Hoskins, however, pretty much discredited the sex glands as the focus of disorder, and the complexity that was found characteristic of endocrine functions soon discouraged the attempt to specify a single process.[67]

It was one of Kraepelin's hopes that the nature of the chemical alteration would one day be run to earth by experiments on the effects of drugs. If a drug could be found which produced temporarily the symptoms of schizophrenia in normal people, analysis of its properties would point the way to the chemical secret of the disorder. Recently it has been found that two rather different chemicals, mescaline and lysergic acid, come fairly close to having this effect. Typical results with lysergic acid (LSD), concordant with mescaline studies elsewhere, have been

[65] L. Bender, "Childhood Schizophrenia," *Psychiatric Quarterly*, XXVII (1953), pp. 663–81. A similar view is expressed by Sibylle Escalona, "Some Considerations Regarding Psychotherapy with Psychotic Children," *Bulletin of the Menninger Clinic*, XII (1948), pp. 127–34.

[66] A. M. Freedman, "Maturation and Its Relation to the Dynamics of Childhood Schizophrenia," *American Journal of Orthopsychiatry*, XXIV (1954), pp. 487–91.

[67] R. G. Hoskins, *The Biology of Schizophrenia* (New York: W. W. Norton & Co., Inc., 1946).

published by Rinkel and others.[68] The effect on normal subjects is startling alike to themselves and to the observers. It is in many respects closely analogous to a moderately acute psychotic episode with considerable turmoil and confusion. In all cases there are marked disturbances of thinking, perceiving, and feeling. Some of the subjects show catatonic reactions, others hallucinations, others paranoid suspiciousness and delusions. Several subjects reported losing their sense of personal identity and experiencing their bodies in peculiar ways, such as the legs walking of their own volition. People around them look different, sometimes hostile and sinister, sometimes changed in size, sometimes as if transparent or behind a glass partition. The subjects suffer a loss in sociability; more of their behavior than usual is avoidant, hostile, or dependent. In tests of intellectual processes they show an impairment in concentration and consecutive thinking. Attention wanders and is often caught by minute features of the physical environment. Needless to say, the psychotic-like episode lasts for only a few hours, and normal subjects are usually none the worse for their brief visit to insanity. After all, they were no crazier than we all are in our night dreams.

At almost the same time a somewhat different version of chemogenesis began to be reported by Heath and his associates at Tulane University.[69] They discovered a protein substance, taraxein, which can be extracted from the serum of schizophrenic patients but not from normal people. This substance was injected into non-psychotic subjects, prison volunteers being used for the purpose. All the subjects who received taraxein developed primary schizophrenic symptoms consisting of thought blocking, autism, depersonalization, a blank look and dull facial expression. Secondary symptoms which appeared in one or more of the subjects included catatonic stupor and excitement, hebephrenia, delusions of persecution, grandiosity, and auditory hallucinations. The visual symptoms characteristic of mescaline intoxication and the autonomic reactions produced by LSD did not appear. Heath and his associates argued that the effects of taraxein were closer to schizophrenic symptoms than those reported for LSD, which were more like those of the delirious states found in toxic psychoses. Be that as it may, other workers have failed to reproduce Heath's results, and the biochemical analysis on which they were based seems now to be open to a good deal of question.[70] But the

[68] M. Rinkel, R. W. Hyde, H. C. Solomon, and H. Hoagland, "Experimental Psychiatry II: Clinical and Physio-Chemical Observations in Experimental Psychosis," *American Journal of Psychiatry*, CXI (1955), pp. 881–95.

[69] R. G. Heath, S. Martens, B. E. Leach, M. Cohen, and C. Angel, "Effect on Behavior in Humans with the Administration of Taraxein," *American Journal of Psychiatry*, CXIV (1957), pp. 14–24.

[70] H. Hoagland, "Biochemical Aspects of Schizophrenia," *Journal of Nervous and Mental Disease*, CXXVI (1958), pp. 211–20; S. S. Kety, "Recent Biochemical Theories of Schizophrenia," in Jackson, *op. cit.*, chap. iv.

work on LSD and mescaline has likewise produced no adequate biochemical hypothesis, and a simple theory is precluded by the fact that these two substances are not chemically alike.

Similar uncertainty surrounds yet a third biochemical hypothesis based on the action of serotonin on the brain. The first clue to the importance of serotonin came from the discovery that LSD blocked its usual effects on smooth muscle. Generalizing from this, it was hypothesized that drugs whose effects mimicked those of mental disorders produced this result by inhibiting the action of serotonin. Pursuit of this hypothesis has turned up a number of contradictory and puzzling findings, leaving investigators with the feeling that although serotinin is almost certainly important for normal functioning, they have not yet fathomed the manner of its disturbance.[71]

On the whole it is fair to say that the biochemical investigations involving LSD, taraxein, and serotonin have thus far failed to effect a real breakthrough with respect to schizophrenia. We must remember, however, that the biochemical secrets of the brain are well guarded and that research in this complex domain is bound to proceed through many trials and many errors. Difficulties of proof beset the somatogenic hypothesis as they do the psychogenic. Assuredly the facts are not yet all at hand. In the meantime it is an important discovery that such large clusters of symptoms can sometimes be produced by a controlled chemical change. The hypothesis must be kept open that the disorganization and primitiveness of schizophrenic thinking may come from an abnormal biochemical state.

Limits of Somatogenic Explanation. We must be careful to keep within legitimate bounds our ideas about the role of biochemical agents. Wonder-drug reasoning has suggested to some enthusiasts that once we find the magic substance, schizophrenia will be eliminated by the simple process of injection. Unfortunately, this is a little like supposing that a drug can blast a man out of his lifelong habits and convictions. Let us say that the patient's nervous system has operated under a biochemical handicap; nevertheless, it has operated, and the resulting pattern of life cannot be undone in a moment. Whatever else it may be, schizophrenia is certainly a cumulative disorder, based on the habits and attitudes built up through a long individual history. It is not a temporary poisoning that clears up and leaves the patient in perfect health.

To illustrate the point let us imagine that L. Percy King has been given a drug that cures schizophrenia. The medication could not greatly clarify his thinking processes, which are already quite normal except on the subject of his pursuers. It could not remove his lifelong anxious feel-

[71] Kety, *op. cit.*, pp. 134–37.

ings of inferiority, and it would therefore have little effect on his compensatory fantasies devised with the help of the mechanism of projection. King, however, is an older patient whose disorder has become consolidated. If we take an example of incipient psychosis in a younger person whose life is still in the making, we can suppose that the imaginary drug would be more helpful, though still not omnipotent. The electrician B, for instance, whose psychotic episode began so suddenly, might have been restored to greater immediate clarity of thought, although the emotional crisis that precipitated his breakdown would not be dissolved by the drug. The young man who became involved with the Third Element might have been brought to a sharper sense of reality, although he could not really be cured without help of a different sort to make reality seem less frustrating to his yearnings. One must earnestly hope that biochemical mysteries will soon be solved, but this happy event would not eliminate the need for skilled personal treatment of schizophrenia.

TREATMENT OF SCHIZOPHRENIA

Until fairly recent years schizophrenic patients received only the most minimal treatment. For the most part they were committed to mental hospitals which, already overcrowded and chronically understaffed, attempted nothing more than to keep them in good physical health and comfort. Gradually, as some superintendent invented a way to manage things better, or as some hospital was miraculously pulled out of a hand-to-mouth financial position, serious attempts were made to provide an environment that would have a beneficial effect on schizophrenic patients. Therapeutic interviews were included, conducted in whatever fashion and toward whatever goals seemed best suited to the particular case. Eventually standard psychoanalysis was tried in a small number of cases. Its success was dubious, and it has been modified in various ways to meet the special problems of schizophrenia. These modifications afford valuable insight into the nature of the disorder.

The Problem of Creating a Therapeutic Relationship. The earlier attempts to use psychoanalysis encountered what seemed to be an insuperable obstacle. Try as he might, the analyst could almost never break through the wall of the patient's reserve and establish a trustful working relationship. Alexander described as follows the difference between schizophrenic and neurotic patients: "The neurotic must learn to accept repressed *psychological* facts, while the psychotic must learn to accept rejected *external* facts.[72] This difference is vitally important when it

[72] F. Alexander, *The Medical Value of Psychoanalysis* (New York: W. W. Norton & Co., Inc., 1932), p. 151.

comes to establishing the initial therapeutic relationship. The physician can be the ally of the patient whose task it is to accept repressed psychological facts. He cannot occupy this role at once with the psychotic patient because he himself is among the rejected external facts. The schizophrenic patient is often remarkably aware of his inner life. It is of no great value to have him learn more about it. In fact it may even do harm, deepening his preoccupation and increasing his disturbance. The therapeutic task is rather to help him discover that reality can be bearable and even rewarding. This fact must first be discovered in his relation to the therapist.

The crux of the matter is to create a stable and workable therapeutic relationship. An important battle is won when the patient can achieve a relationship with even one member of his social environment, the physician. This topic was discussed in a paper by Fromm-Reichmann.[73] She pointed out that the patient has entered his withdrawn state as a means of protecting himself from the frustrations of reality with its constant reminders of his inadequacy. Suspicious and distrustful of everyone, he is particularly upset by a person "who approaches him with the intention of intruding into his isolated world and personal life." Yet it was her belief that "every schizophrenic has some dim notion of the unreality and loneliness of his substitute delusionary world." A part of him still longs for contact and understanding, and once he has managed to accept the therapist his dependence becomes unbelievably strong. He is so sensitive that almost anything that happens wounds his self-esteem. "One patient," said Fromm-Reichmann, "responded twice with catatonic stupor when I had to change the hour of my appointment with her; both times it was immediately dispelled when I came to see her and explained the reasons for the change." Another patient became furiously angry when the therapist, having granted him several special privileges, announced that she would have to consult the superintendent before giving him permission to visit his relatives. He could not tolerate having another person admitted to the one fragile relationship he had been able to make.

For our purposes the most important feature of Fromm-Reichmann's paper is her convincing demonstration that "the schizophrenic is capable of developing strong relationships of love and hatred towards his analyst." Once a relationship is established, it is of vast importance to the patient and it is charged with strong emotions. Nothing could show more clearly the nature of the schizophrenic disorder. The patient has been many times injured, and he has learned the art of protective withdrawal, but the flame of feeling proves to be not extinguished.

[73] F. Fromm-Reichmann, "Transference Problems in Schizophrenics," *Psychoanalytic Quarterly,* VIII (1939), pp. 412–27.

Direct Methods of Establishing Contact. In some cases it is possible to establish the necessary contact by daily conversation, expressions of consistent interest, and a tactful policy of waiting for the patient to build up confidence in his therapist. The patient is treated as an adult, though a very sensitive one. This process, however, often takes a long time, and it may be quite impossible if the patient is much disturbed or if his regression to infantile patterns is more or less complete. Reports from various sources have lately been coming in which describe more direct and vehement methods of establishing contact. Gertrude Schwing in Vienna achieved remarkable results in a quite uncalculated and intuitive way by being a loving mother to the patients. Sometimes she would sit quietly with a patient for many hours, attending to physical comfort and conveying a sense of assured devotion. Sometimes she would give presents of fruit and candy. According to her own philosophy she gave the patients instinctively the motherliness that had been lacking or unreliably present in their own childhood.[74] In this unexpectedly warm atmosphere it often happened that highly disturbed patients became quiet and accessible, deeply withdrawn ones alert and responsive. Another worker, Sechehaye, achieved success with a schizophrenic girl only after responding to the patient's unfulfilled infantile needs and doing so in the symbolic ways in which the patient was currently feeling them. The patient refused nearly all kinds of food until the therapist offered each food as a present, thus symbolically gratifying the frustrated needs of the nursing period.[75]

Two elements are apparent in these methods of establishing contact. One is the gratification of infantile needs. The other consists of entering into the patient's regressed world, using the kind of language and symbols that dominate his own disorganized thought processes. Both elements are utilized in John Rosen's "direct analysis," which has sometimes been successful in restoring contact with patients in extremely severe schizophrenic states.[76] Rosen's method includes mothering the patients, sitting with them for hours, feeding them, helping them, expressing affection for them. It also involves grasping the meaning of their behavior, gestures, silences, and streams of incoherent conversation, all of which are taking place at a regressed, infantile level. When meaning is perceived it is at once interpreted to the patient. These interpretations,

[74] G. Schwing, *A Way to the Soul of the Mentally Ill*, trans. R. Ekstein and B. H. Hall (New York: International Universities Press, Inc., 1954). (First published in German in 1940.)

[75] M. A. Sechehaye, *Symbolic Realization: A New Method of Psychotherapy Applied to a Case of Schizophrenia* (New York: International Universities Press, Inc., 1951).

[76] J. Rosen, *Direct Analysis: Selected Papers* (New York: Grune & Stratton, Inc., 1953).

with their blunt references to bodily functions, suckling needs, sexual perversions, and primitive hostilities, are often quite shocking to outside observers, but they achieve a very direct kind of communication. The patient at last feels that somebody understands him. Somebody realizes that he is in a panic because his mother's milk is poisoning him or a monster father is going to cut him up. If the doctor understands this, then it is possible to trust the doctor and believe him when he says he will protect the patient from this harm. Rosen's method requires rare skill in grasping the meaning of highly confused productions, and a power of becoming dramatically involved in the patient's plight.

These methods of establishing contact are not complete methods of treatment. They serve to bring the patient out of acute psychosis and thus restore sufficient organization so that a more rational psychotherapy becomes possible. They all show the rescuing power of love, sympathy, and understanding, but the patient must eventually become able to lead his life without depending upon such a bounty of maternal devotion.

Borderline States. Very different is the initial procedure with patients who are not badly disorganized. If the patient is first seen in what is often called a "borderline state," with ego functions relatively little impaired and still in good contact with reality, everything must be done to prevent further disintegration. In a paper on "borderline cases" Knight advocates indefinite postponement of free association and deep interpretation. "Ego rebuilding and strengthening," he says, "should receive prior consideration over exploration until the therapist is sure of his ground with respect to the patient's ego strengths."[77] The patient's threatened inner controls should be given help by outer controls in the form of a regulated life with few confusing choices. This can be most readily provided in a hospital, but it can be approximated with patients seen in office practice. The therapeutic relationship should be similarly patterned to strengthen the patient's hold on reality. The doctor's availability should be limited to the fixed therapeutic hour, and the patient should receive no special privileges. This is quite different from mothering and from the extreme permissiveness that sometimes works wonders with acute cases. Its goal is to define the adult world sharply so that the patient will less easily lose his grasp on it.

The Further Course of Psychotherapy. Some workers now take the view that most psychotherapy with schizophrenics should be conducted in this spirit. Except when it is necessary to rescue the patient from a disorganized state, psychotherapy should be directed toward the adult rather

[77] R. P. Knight, "Management and Psychotherapy of the Borderline Schizophrenic Patient," in R. P. Knight (ed.), *Psychoanalytic Psychiatry and Psychology* (New York: International Universities Press, Inc., 1954), pp. 110–22.

than the infantile aspects of his personality. Fromm-Reichmann in a second paper noted a change in her own opinion about this question. Aware as she was of the patient's sensitivity and the ease with which his self-esteem can be injured, she nevertheless believed that psychotherapy should not "address itself too much to the rejected child in the schizophrenic and too little to the grown up person before regressing."[78] The patient, she continued, "senses at least dimly that his disaster cannot be solved by one person's offering him a type of acceptance otherwise not mutually obtainable in adult society." In spite of this, schizophrenic patients are particularly likely to become dependent on their therapists and even to set up a symbiotic relationship that will defeat all attempts to promote growth.[79] The therapist, much as he may like to be treated as omnipotent and omniscient, is under obligation to promote the patient's sense of his own identity and enhance the patient's self-esteem. Where the neurotic has to learn about his suppressed needs and buried feelings, the schizophrenic has to find out about his evasive adjustive patterns, his retreats in the face of difficulty, and his inclination to let others make his decisions and solve his problems. It is against seeing these things that he shows his strongest resistance.

Fromm-Reichmann's second paper raises an interesting point about the goals of treatment. Conventional goals of social adjustment and extraversion are never likely to be congenial to former schizophrenics, and the attempt to reach such goals may well constitute a hazard for future health. It is necessary, rather, for the patients to "find for themselves their own sources of satisfaction and security, irrespective of the approval of their neighbors, of their families, and of public opinion." Toward this end the therapist can probably be more helpful if he himself is a champion of individuality rather than conventionality.

Insulin Shock. The earliest modern form of shock treatment was the insulin coma method discovered in 1932 by Manfred Sakel. The course of a single treatment runs somewhat as follows. First the patient is given an intramuscular injection of insulin. For an hour or so he shows the symptoms of hypoglycemia, consisting of weakness, excessive perspiration, hunger, and deepening drowsiness. Presently he becomes unconscious and passes into shock, usually with twitchings, tremor, loud breathing, and snorting sounds. Deep coma with complete unresponsiveness is reached only after three or four hours and is allowed to continue for a

[78] F. Fromm-Reichmann, "Notes on the Development of Treatment of Schizophrenics by Psychoanalytic Psychotherapy," *Psychiatry*, XI (1946), pp. 263–73.

[79] R. W. Lidz and T. Lidz, "Therapeutic Considerations Arising from the Intense Symbiotic Needs of Schizophrenic Patients," in E. B. Brody and F. C. Redlich (eds.), *Psychotherapy with Schizophrenics* (New York: International Universities Press, Inc., 1952), pp. 168–78.

period not greater than an hour, usually less. Awakening is accomplished by administering glucose which produces a rapid rise in blood sugar. The depth and type of shock and the time of awakening can be controlled and adapted to the individual patient. Insulin shock treatments are given frequently, usually daily, and the course may continue up to two or three months.

The clearing of the patient's mental state is generally first observed in the periods of hypoglycemia preceding and following the coma. At first the improvement is fleeting, but with repeated treatments it extends further into the post-shock period. The state of improved lucidity and accessibility allows the psychiatrist to establish rapport and initiate psychotherapy. Sakel was insistent that the temporary gains achieved by insulin shock needed to be consolidated by appropriate psychotherapy, but he cautioned against too hasty a use of the newly won rapport. If the patients were too quickly reminded of their symptoms and difficulties they might be thrown back again into the depths of psychosis. The insistence on concomitant psychotherapy has not been so clear in some of the later work with insulin shock. Perhaps this accounts for the less dramatic results. In any event the relation between shock and psychotherapy needs clearer understanding than it has yet received.

It is hard to detect any uniformity in either the physiological or the psychological changes that accompany insulin shock. At the autonomic level there are rapid shiftings of tone between the parasympathetic and sympathetic divisions, generally correlated with emotional changes. Some patients are predominantly calm and drowsy during the hypoglycemic periods before and after coma. Others manifest fear, excitement, and occasionally convulsions. It seems to be characteristic of the hypoglycemic periods that responsiveness is more impaired than comprehension. The patients say nothing in response to questions, but afterwards can recall the questions clearly. There is a certain amount of amnesia, however, for the experiences occurring during these periods, and sometimes the amnesia extends backward to include the more recent psychotic behavior. This more extensive amnesia is as a rule only temporary.

Despite the severity of its effects, insulin shock treatment can be safely applied to the majority of schizophrenic patients. Only a small group having heart weakness or certain other disorders are unable to tolerate the physical stress that is involved. There is great variation among reports of its success in alleviating the psychosis. Sakel's original claim of obtaining 70 per cent full remissions and an additional 18 per cent partial remissions has not been matched in subsequent investigations. Malzburg studied more than a thousand cases of schizophrenia treated with insulin shock and found only 13 per cent fully recovered, with 54 per cent, however, rated as improved. These figures compared favorably with a matched group of untreated cases in which 3.5 per cent were fully recovered and 19 per cent rated as improved.[80] Current favorable reports, which are numerous, approximate Malzburg's figures rather than Sakel's. In their standard reference work on the subject, Kalinowsky and Hoch state that a remission rate of 40 to 50 per cent is the best that can be expected from insulin coma treatment even under ideal conditions, and most reports show a lower rate.[81] There are in fact a certain number of reports which claim that insulin treatment is of no value. They offer statistics showing that insulin-treated and untreated patients have the same rate of recovery. Other reports show that the effects of insulin coma therapy must be regarded as mainly temporary. Shock-treated patients are considerably more likely to return later to the hospital than patients who were dismissed as cured without shock treatment. A finding by Salzman is typical: of forty-four schizophrenics cured by shock, seventeen were back in the hospital within a year, while of forty-five cured without resorting to shock, only six had returned at the end of twelve months.[82]

Tranquilizing Drugs. Discovery of the value of the ataractic drugs has greatly curtailed the use of insulin shock. The oral administration of chlorpromazine, reserpine, and the large number of variants which they have spawned is obviously preferable to the time-consuming process of insulin shock provided it produces something like the same results. In point of fact the results have not always been described in precisely the same way, yet their consequences for the patient seem to be generally similar. The effects of insulin coma are usually expressed in terms of a clearing of confusion, as if the shock experience with its physiological accompaniments acted directly to dispel the disorganization of thought. Tranquilizing drugs are generally supposed to lower tension and anxiety, which might be regarded as a step preliminary to the clearing of thought. Some workers have postulated that schizophrenia is based on a chronic state of tension and anxiety; indeed, one appealing chemogenic hypothesis, which unfortunately has not been well sustained thus far by biochemical research, is that intellectual disorganization comes from a toxic excess of epinephrine, which is secreted as part of the anxiety reaction.[83] It is difficult to suppose that apathetic patients are in a constant state of tension and anxiety, so it may be that tranquilizers have

80 B. Malzburg, "Outcome of Insulin Treatment of One Thousand Patients with Dementia Praecox," *Psychiatric Quarterly*, XII (1938), pp. 528–53.

81 L. B. Kalinowsky and P. H. Hoch, *Shock Treatments, Psychosurgery, and Other Somatic Treatments in Psychiatry* (2d ed.; New York: Grune & Stratton, Inc., 1952).

82 L. Salzman, "An Evaluation of Shock Therapy," *American Journal of Psychiatry*, CIII (1947), pp. 669–79.

83 A. Hoffer, "Epinephrine Derivatives as Potential Schizophrenic Factors," *Journal of Clinical and Experimental Psychopathology*, XVIII (1957), p. 27; Kety, *op. cit.*, pp. 127–29.

other effects besides the ones that have made them popular in the world at large. Their physiological action is still as obscure as that of insulin shock—or, for that matter, of electroshock, which is sometimes used with schizophrenics. We know only that the tranquilizing drugs have produced measurable improvements in patients' behavior in the hospital and an increased rate of discharge.

There are a number of significant similarities between the results of insulin shock and those of tranquilizing drugs. Both forms of treatment are most successful with cases having a recent onset of relatively abrupt character. Both have a smaller effect on patients who have been ill for several years. The likelihood of success seems to be correlated with the acuteness of conflict and anxiety. Results are poorer with patients who have made their peace, so to speak, with a psychotic condition. Both methods produce results that are mainly temporary. Patients improved by drugs will often relapse if treatment is discontinued. Here, however, the drugs have a practical advantage: patients can be kept on maintenance doses even after they have been discharged. The only objection to this is the possible side-effects of these still rather new preparations when used over a long period of time, a point that is under close scrutiny in pharmacological research.

It would be highly satisfactory if we could bring this section to a close by comparing the success of physiological methods with the results obtained by psychotherapy. Unfortunately the use of intensive psychotherapy with schizophrenics is such a recent venture that one cannot yet hope to assess its results objectively. Certainly the older belief that intensive psychotherapy would do no good has been overthrown, but workers agree that the process is long, slow, and by no means always successful. Physicians who use psychotherapy advance the claim that they can produce more cures and much more lasting cures than are obtained by insulin coma and drugs. Especially as regards the permanence of cure this claim would appear to be justified, but one must not overlook the vast difference in the matter of time. Whatever they accomplish, physiological methods work muoh faster; many more patients can be treated by many less doctors. It may seem lamentable that the question of man hours should intrude itself into a discussion of what is best for the patient, but the care of the sick is, after all, a social undertaking that draws heavily on the human and financial resources of society, and it cannot always be done in the best possible way.

The Hospital as Therapeutic Milieu. A dramatic change is taking place in the atmosphere that prevails in mental hospitals. The older conception of an asylum, where the mentally sick could be removed from society and kept out of harm's way—symbolized by building mental hospitals on remote hillsides far from the crossroads of life—is steadily giving place to the idea of the hospital as a therapeutic milieu in which everything is arranged to be conducive to recovery. An early step in this direction was the introduction of occupational therapy, through which in the reassuring setting of work with inanimate objects the patients might recover their interest in the environment, perhaps even in the social part of it. Another step was the self-service cafeteria, offering the patients the opportunity, whether they took it or not, to make mealtime social contacts of their own choosing. Exercises, games, dances, and other recreations followed in all hospitals that tried to keep abreast of the times. Lately this whole movement has been rapidly accelerating. The goal is to make the whole experience in the mental hospital a therapeutic one. A large literature has appeared in the last decade on the theme that the hospital, conceived as an elaborate social system, can be so organized that all patients have a chance to benefit from their membership in it.[84]

To make the change is not as easy as it seems. Quite apart from possible administrative and financial difficulties, the shift from custodial to therapeutic practices involves a profound change in the attitudes of the hospital staff. This means a change in the outlook not only of doctors but also of nurses, attendants, and other workers who are in contact with the patients most of the time. One is reminded of the old joke about librarians who consider it their duty to keep books clean and intact rather than to have them read; if the job is perceived and valued in this way, it is quite a wrench to change to a less orderly but more educational conception. In like fashion, the nurse who has prided herself on keeping the patients in her ward clean and tidy or the attendant who has measured his success in terms of keeping the ward quiet and controlling aggressive outbursts cannot easily sacrifice their established virtues as custodians for the unknown possibilities of a therapeutic role.[85] Nor should we suppose that the new view is always easy for doctors, who have to manage the hospital community and who are aware that there is, after all, a custodial element in the whole operation, failure in which will bring down the wrath of relatives and civic authorities.

The transformation of custodial wards into therapeutic ones has been well described by von Mering and King.[86] They point out the great force

[84] For instance, Maxwell Jones, *The Therapeutic Community* (New York: Basic Books, Inc., 1953); A. H. Stanton and M. S. Schwartz, *The Mental Hospital* (New York: Basic Books, Inc., 1954); M. Greenblatt, D. J. Levinson, and R. H. Williams (eds.), *The Patient and the Mental Hospital* (New York: The Free Press of Glencoe, Inc., 1957).

[85] D. C. Gilbert and D. J. Levinson, "'Custodialism' and 'Humanism' in Staff Ideology," in Greenblatt *et al.*, *op. cit.*, chap. iii.

[86] O. von Mering and S. H. King, *Remotivating the Mental Patient* (New York: Russell Sage Foundation, 1957).

of what they call the "legend of chronicity," the assumption that the patients are there to stay and cannot be expected to get better. The unfortunate thing about this legend is that it guarantees exactly what it predicts: the attitudes of those who believe it create an atmosphere in which the patients will indeed not get better. The staff acts to get the day's work done with the least fuss, and the patients are allowed to sink ever more deeply into their own preoccupations. Quite different is the situation when someone becomes convinced that the ward can be run on a therapeutic basis. When the patients are given generous attention with the implication that things can be better, even severely regressed schizophrenics, who no longer keep clothes on and are incontinent, can recover their lost habits, respond a little to the staff, show an interest in the activities of the ward, and even make a few awkward steps toward helping one another. Less disorganized patients can accomplish much more: they may take over many of the routine jobs, working in groups as dormitory or linen closet helpers; they may arrange birthday parties and other festivities; and they may work out a program of improving and redecorating the ward. Such projects generate pride in the living quarters and reawaken pleasure in social interaction.

While sitting around the tables making things to improve the appearance of their ward, the women began to talk to each other as they had never done before. It was as if a group of apartment dwellers, who formerly had only nodded to each other in passing, were suddenly thrown together in close association, and for the first time began to find out what their neighbors were like.[87]

Yet all of this is accomplished with a minimum of prodding by the staff. It represents the salutary influence of a warm interest that also implies confidence and respect.

Administrative resistance to experiments of this kind is often overcome by the discovery that the financial cost of a "remotivated" ward is less than it was before. The human profit is decidedly encouraging. Some patients advance to making home visits and perhaps to ultimate discharge, while those who remain as permanent residents have the benefit of more alert and rewarding lives. When the "legend of chronicity" is replaced by a "legend of recovery" the results are, to be sure, submiraculous; but there is a distinct change, and it is almost always in the direction of better lives for everyone concerned.

When we say it is better for everyone concerned, we include the staff along with the patients. As Greenblatt has pointed out, there are in American mental hospitals about twenty attendants or aides to every nurse and every doctor, a large corps of people in constant contact with

[87] *Ibid.*, p. 123.

patients but untrained to be more than watchdogs. Often these workers have no feeling of participation in the therapeutic process.[88] One of the most promising moves away from the custodial concept is the training of attendants to realize their importance to the patients, to treat them with friendly respect, and thus to exert a true therapeutic influence. In some places it has been possible to put attendants in charge of group therapy sessions.

Another plan that has proved successful in some places is to establish a form of patient government. Reporting on an experiment of this kind at the Massachusetts Mental Health Center, Greenblatt says:

> Since its formation, patient government has been one of the most stimulating and progressive developments of the hospital. Their activities have expanded to include major responsibility for recreational and social life, the raising of money for purchasing of supplies and equipment (several large TV sets were bought with their funds), supervision of housekeeping and serving of food, conducting tours of the hospital for visitors and students, helping to orient new patients to hospital life, as well as keeping track of countless details of maintenance and needs for improvement which would normally escape notice. Not the least of the beneficial effects to patients comes from holding office, being elected and serving on responsible committees, as well as the group experience of democratic action. Their participation with management in running the hospital makes the hospital distinctly their concern.[89]

Only a beginning has been made with turning the mental hospital into a therapeutic community. Enough has been done, however, to show that betterment is possible in the lives of even severely ill schizophrenic patients. The deteriorated hospital patient was partly a product of crude custodial treatment, representing retreat from a social environment that offered no inducement to stay in contact. Although we cannot suppose that all schizophrenics will be able to resume a normal life, the new conception of treatment can give to many what we might call a normal hospital life and can lead others back to the outside world which for a time they found too difficult.

SUGGESTIONS FOR FURTHER READING

Probably the first thing that should be undertaken by a student who wants to read further about schizophrenia is to get a better idea of how things look to the patient. Ideal for this purpose is the collection edited by B. Kaplan, *The Inner World of Mental Illness* (New York, Harper & Row, 1963). A shorter work with the same intent has been published by V. W. Grant, *This Is Mental Illness* (Boston, Beacon Press, Inc., 1963).

For an up-to-date survey of research on schizophrenia and theories about its origin, *The Etiology of Schizophrenia,* edited by Don D. Jackson (New

[88] M. Greenblatt, in *The Patient and the Mental Hospital, op. cit.,* chap. xxxvi.
[89] *Ibid.,* p. 617.

York, Basic Books, Inc., 1960) is to be recommended. A valuable and provocative selection of research papers is reprinted in C. F. Reed, I. E. Alexander, and S. S. Tomkins' *Psychopathology: A Source Book* (Cambridge, Harvard University Press, 1958), Chs. 22–30, 36–37. For more detailed consideration of the problems of schizophrenic thinking, see E. Hanfmann and J. Kasanin, *Conceptual Thinking in Schizophrenia* (New York, Nervous and Mental Disease Publishing Co., 1942), and S. Arieti, *Interpretation of Schizophrenia* (New York, Robert Brunner, 1955), Chs. 10–13.

The important ideas of Harry Stack Sullivan can be gleaned from his posthumously published lectures, *Schizophrenia as a Human Process* (New York, W. W. Norton & Co., Inc., 1962). An unusually fine introduction to the topic of psychotherapy is Lewis B. Hill's *Psychotherapeutic Intervention in Schizophrenia* (Chicago, University of Chicago Press, 1955), which also has much to say on childhood origins and the general nature of the disorder. As a further step along the same line there is the symposium edited by E. B. Brody and F. C. Redlich, *Psychotherapy with Schizophrenics* (New York, International Universities Press, Inc., 1952), which contains papers by several workers, comments on the papers, and good introductory chapters by the editors.

The best window upon the transformation of mental hospitals from places of custody to therapeutic milieux is provided by O. von Mering and S. H. King in *Remotivating the Mental Patient* (New York, Russell Sage Foundation, 1957). The book edited by M. Greenblatt, D. J. Levinson and R. H. Williams, *The Patient and the Mental Hospital* (New York, The Free Press of Glencoe, Inc., 1957) contains a large number of reports given at an important conference on this theme. A valuable new work on the whole subject by J. and E. Cumming is entitled *Ego and Milieu: Theory and Practice of Environmental Therapy* (New York, Atherton Press, 1962).

16

The Problem for Society

The problem of disordered personal reactions is one that cannot be solved without reference to the society in which they occur. The act of going to a psychiatrist and receiving advice on a personal problem sounds like a private transaction between two individuals. But in reality such an act is deeply embedded in the whole cultural and social structure. The mere fact that the troubled individual thinks of laying his problems before a psychiatrist reflects his membership in a culture. In some cultures personal problems are laid only before a priest, in some they are considered a matter for private moral striving, in still others they are regarded as too disgraceful to be aired before anyone outside the immediate family. Within our own contemporary culture there are still many subcultures in which a serious mental disorder must be hushed up and the afflicted person sent as far away as possible for treatment. The family need not apologize if it has a weakness for pneumonia or cancer or heart disease, but if it is "tainted with insanity" or has a member who is "mentally not just right" it is forever in a state of disgrace. There are still many subcultures, moreover, that take an attitude of contempt toward the less severe disorders—the maladjustments and neuroses. A person is condemned as a weakling or laughed at as a fool if he cannot "snap out of it" and "stop thinking about himself." Thus our hypothetical individual who believes that something is wrong either with his mind or with his emotions, and who thereupon openly seeks the advice of a psychiatrist, is acting very much as a member of a particular subculture, one that has accepted mental and emotional disorders as medical problems to be handled in a scientific fashion.

Will he find a psychiatrist to consult? The existing social structure has a great deal to do with the answer. The training of a psychiatrist is a long and expensive process, depending not only on the selection of talented people who will be good at the job but also on a complex organization of medical schools, hospitals, and clinics to provide the opportunities for training. Medical schools, hospitals, and clinics are losing propositions in a financial sense, so that constant support from the community or state is necessary for their continued existence. Today in the United States the number of psychiatrists is completely inadequate to meet the existing demand for their services. Our troubled seeker after help will be lucky if he finds a psychiatrist, extremely lucky if he gets enough appointments within a reasonable time to meet his needs.

In order to continue our study of his social embeddedness, let us suppose that our sufferer finds a psychiatrist who begins to explore his problems with him. Again we are thrust back upon the social organism of which he is a part. In the family circle a not impossible series of circumstances might be that he has to support aged parents, that his wife has painful arthritis which makes her irritable with him and the children, that he cannot secure a maid and therefore has to take over part of the housework, that sexual relations have had to be discontinued, that one of the children in consequence of encephalitis is a constant behavior problem. Our patient simply has not enough money to deal with all these difficulties, nor can he necessarily find the facilities even if he could pay for them. There may be no comfortable home for the old people, no maids or helpers available in the community, no special classes or schools for the brain-injured child. If the psychiatrist explores the reason for the man's low income, he is at once involved with the whole social order, with inflation and depression, with labor supply in particular industries, perhaps with unfair employment practices and discriminations of one kind or another. It may be that the patient still further reveals himself as a member of his culture when he relates his early ambition for economic and social success and his feeling of shame that he has never been able to move his family to a socially more pretentious neighborhood. In the end the psychiatrist may decide that the patient's condition is sufficently serious to warrant hospitalization, with at least temporary removal from his surrounding sea of troubles. Then it appears that, because the legislature at its last sitting refused to vote the appropriation for a much needed enlargement, there are no beds available at the state hospital and none can be promised for several months.

This tale has been told to illustrate a single point, a point that is at once obvious and easily forgotten. The problem of treating and caring for people whose personal reactions are disordered, still more the problem of preventing their reactions from becoming disordered in the first place, can be solved only by social effort and social organization. In the preceding chapters of this book we have discussed the diverse problems of abnormal psychology as if they were simply problems in scientific understanding. We have tried to find out how disordered behavior comes about and how it can be treated. It is now time to give up this artificially narrowed focus and let the picture expand to its full dimensions. In this chapter we shall first take up the magnitude of the problem that is offered society by abnormal and maladjusted people. Then we shall consider what has to be done in order to deal adequately with the problem. The question of what has to be done brings up the further question of who is to do it. This can be answered only by examining the several professions which minister to abnormal people and weighing both their scope and their training. But inasmuch as the problem cannot be solved by professional workers alone, we shall also consider the contributions that can be made by anyone who cares to make his behavior as a parent and a citizen count in this direction.

SIZE OF THE PROBLEM

In 1955 the Congress of the United States authorized the creation of a Joint Commission on Mental Illness and Health which was to report on the size of the nation's problem and to suggest ways of dealing with it. The final report of the Joint Commission, presented six years later, contains the best figures and estimates we have with regard to mental health.[1]

The Problem of Numbers. The most general estimate is that 17 million people in the United States suffer at one time or another from relatively serious mental disorder. At any given moment the number of sufferers will be around 700,000. Half the hospital beds in the nation, the report further points out, are occupied by mental patients—a vivid reminder of the relative size of this medical problem.[2] The same facts have been expressed a little differently by saying that at any given time 1 out of every 250 people will be resident in a mental hospital.[3] It has also been estimated that mental illness in a form serious enough to require hospital care "strikes about 1 in 5 families and about 1 in 13 people in the course of a lifetime."[4] These last estimates sound so gloomy that they should not stand without a reminder that patients leave mental hospitals as well as enter them. In 1950 some 340,000 patients were discharged, not all fully recovered but at least in a considerably improved condition. Furthermore, since 1956 the rate of discharge has crept ahead of the rate of admission. The Joint Commission's report shows that between 1956

[1] *Action for Mental Health* (New York: Science Editions, Inc., 1961).

[2] *Ibid.*, p. 4.

[3] D. Blain, K. E. Appel, A. E. Scheflen, and R. L. Robinson, "The Current Picture of Mental Health and Psychiatry in the U. S.: Pertinent Statistics," *American Journal of Psychiatry*, CXII (1955), pp. 53–54.

[4] S. K. Weinberg, *Society and Personality Disorders* (Englewood Cliffs, N. J.: Prentice-Hall, Inc., 1952), p. 361.

and 1960 there was a decline of 3 per cent in mental hospital populations.[5]

The estimate of 17 million is intended to cover all kinds of disorder. It is supported most accurately in the case of hospitalized patients, mainly psychotic, who can easily be counted. The element of guesswork becomes greater with respect to people who are treated in outpatient services, in private practice, and by general practitioners; still more so for those whose disorders may not be treated at all. Specialists in a particular disorder have sometimes tried their hands at estimating the number of persons affected. Lennox in 1944 put the incidence of epilepsy at fairly close to 650,000.[6] Cobb gave approximately the same figure for patients suffering from brain injuries and other neurological disorders not classified as psychoses.[7] Sherman estimated the number of the mentally retarded at 2,500,000, of whom about 100,000 lived in institutions.[8] Haggard and Jellinek set a figure of 1,600,000 for chronic alcoholics.[9] It is clear that there can be no reliable figures about delinquents and psychopathic personalities. As a group these people neither seek medical help nor fall into the clutches of the police regularly enough to be counted. Neurotics can be estimated only through intensive community surveys, and the figure sometimes offered of 2,500,000 is very much a piece of guesswork. But it is clear that the frequency of disordered behavior of all kinds is very great. Even if the over-all figure of 17 million should be much too high, the student of abnormal psychology can feel sure that he is not spending his time on a trifling social problem.

Community surveys have begun to throw light on the distribution of different disorders in different sections of the population. The New Haven study brings out the fact that the neuroses tend to be concentrated in the middle and upper social classes, whereas psychoses have a sharply disproportionate frequency of occurrence at the lowest class level.[10] The figure for neuroses may be affected by the circumstance that in a community with a fairly enlightened attitude toward mental health and a relative abundance of psychiatric services, the count at the upper levels will be complete—people who can afford it will be accustomed to seeking help for their neurotic troubles—whereas at lower

[5] *Action for Mental Health, op. cit.*, p. 7.

[6] W. G. Lennox, in J. McV. Hunt (ed.), *Personality and the Behavior Disorders* (New York: The Ronald Press Co., 1944), Vol. II, p. 939.

[7] S. Cobb, *Borderlands of Psychiatry* (Cambridge: Harvard University Press, 1943), p. xiii.

[8] M. Sherman, *Intelligence and Its Deviations* (New York: The Ronald Press Co., 1945), p. 126.

[9] H. Haggard and E. M. Jellinek, *Alcohol Explored* (Garden City, N. Y.: Doubleday & Co., Inc., 1942), pp. 16–27.

[10] A. B. Hollingshead and F. C. Redlich, *Social Class and Mental Illness: A Community Study* (New York: John Wiley & Sons, Inc., 1958).

levels of education and knowledge these distresses may not be recognized as different from the general hardships of life. The New Haven studies show that members of the lowest class tend to lead isolated lives with little participation in organized endeavors of any kind, even in the labor unions that stand for their interests. They see the world as hostile and uncontrollable, and they tend to think of mental and emotional disorders as afflictions of external origin. The same point is made in the Stirling County studies in Nova Scotia, where the people of the "depressed areas" are found to have little sense that they can influence the decisions and policies of those who have power in the community. This suggests the possibility that being always on the receiving end and having no control over your destiny may encourage the use of psychotic mechanisms such as projection. At all events it is in the "depressed areas" that psychosis occurs with greatest frequency.[11]

The Financial Problem. In its report the Joint Commission estimates the direct cost of mental and emotional disorders at one billion dollars a year and the indirect cost at two billion more.[12] It is hard to make figures in billions convey more than a vague sense of vast magnitude. The point of importance here is that mental disorder is by all odds the most costly of the nation's health problems. Even if we said nothing about the loss of happiness and effectiveness, the financial drain would be a problem in its own right.

Financial support for mental health has gone up dramatically during the last twenty years. Before World War II mental illness was a shunned topic, and it was almost impossible to find voluntary sources of money to stimulate better care and research. In 1959 the annual campaign for voluntary contributions to mental health raised 5.5 million dollars, and in 1961 the federal appropriation for the National Institute of Mental Health arrived at 100 million.[13] These are striking figures, representing vast increases over what was done in 1950; but it is necessary to point out that mental health still commands a very small share of what is invested in health as a whole. Consider, for example, the other voluntary health campaigns in 1959: 31.3 million was raised for poliomyelitis, 31.0 for cancer, 26.0 for tuberculosis, 24.0 for heart, 10.3 for crippled children, and 9.5 and 4.6 respectively for cerebral palsy and muscular dystrophy, both of which are vastly less common than mental disorders.[14] The generosity of the public with respect to physical ailments is certainly not to be criticized, but it is fair to say that what needs to be done about

[11] C. C. Hughes, M.-A. Tremblay, R. N. Rapoport, and A. H. Leighton, *People of Cove and Woodlot* (New York: Basic Books, Inc., 1960).

[12] *Action for Mental Health, op. cit.*, p. 4.

[13] *Ibid.*, pp. 7, 15.

[14] *Ibid.*, p. 15.

mental health cannot possibly be done on its present share of the health dollar. Within a single generation things have changed for the better, but not enough to meet the need.

This need can be viewed in several ways. To many people it strikes home hardest when they look for psychiatric help only to find that they must go on a waiting list for six months or a year. To parents the problem may present itself starkly when one of their children needs help and the nearest clinic proves to be not very near and decidedly overloaded. One of the recommendations of the Joint Commission is that there should be a full-time mental health clinic for every 50,000 people, as a main line of defense against mental disorder. This would mean 3,600 clinics; the fact is that there are 1,450, not all of them full-time.[15] To those engaged in research the need strikes home when contemplating the large number of problems still to be investigated, even though funds for research in mental health are much more available than they used to be. But perhaps the most telling expression of the unmet need is found in a report by the American Psychiatric Association in which standards are formulated for the adequate staffing of mental hospitals and clinics. The report shows a trend toward improvement in staffing; but it shows also that in 1958 these institutions had only 57 per cent of the physicians needed for adequate functioning, 75 per cent of the psychologists, 40 per cent of the social workers, and 23 per cent of the registered nurses.[16] The Joint Commission report contains the guess that "more than half of the patients in most state hospitals receive no treatment of any kind designed to improve their mental condition."[17]

The Manpower Problem. A closer look at the unmet need in mental health shows that the difficulty is not wholly financial. There is also a serious manpower shortage in the related professions. In a survey of state and county mental hospitals, for instance, it was found that 25 per cent of the positions budgeted for psychiatrists and psychologists, and 20 per cent of those budgeted for social workers and nurses, remained unfilled because nobody could be found to take them.[18] This shortage contributes to a most unequal distribution of mental health work throughout the nation. With most workers having choices of jobs, there is a high concentration in large cities of the North, East Coast, and West Coast; and the problem of staffing the services in smaller communities and rural areas is everywhere quite severe.

[15] W. E. Barton and W. T. St. John, "Family Care and Outpatient Psychiatry," *American Journal of Psychiatry*, CXVIII (1962), pp. 633–36.

[16] *Action for Mental Health, op. cit.*, p. 8.

[17] *Ibid.*, p. 22.

[18] G. W. Albee, *Mental Health Manpower Trends* (New York: Basic Books, Inc., 1959).

The shortage does not mean that the mental health professions are not growing. The number of psychiatric social workers, for instance, reached 4,000 in 1960 and 4,400 in 1961; in the former year there were no less than 1,000 social work students, at different levels of advancement, who were receiving training in psychiatric facilities.[19] The number of psychiatrists in the United States in 1950 was 5,534; by 1960 it had reached 11,787.[20] Unfortunately these figures cannot be taken to mean that the manpower problem will soon be solved. Albee has shown that at their present rates of production the mental health professions are not gaining at all relative to the rise in the population as a whole. Unless the rates of professional training can be increased, the level of adequacy specified by the American Psychiatric Association will never be reached.[21]

Sometimes it is recommended that the shortage be met by a crash program in professional education. Even if we imagine unlimited financial backing, this is anything but a practical suggestion. A crash program would require not only more students but more people to teach them, more facilities open for training, and more workers in these facilities to supervise the training: in other words, a new toll on staffs that are already shorthanded. Professional education is not the kind of thing that can be stepped up sharply without serious loss of quality, if not in the students at least in the amount of teaching and supervised experience that can be given them. The need for more service must always be weighed against the risk of watering its quality through inadequate training. The safest pattern of growth would seem to be a gradual one.

The complexity of the manpower problem is particularly clear in the case of psychiatry. The medical profession as a whole seems to have lost the enormous popularity it had for young men and women shortly after World War II. In 1960 it was reported that the number of applications for medical school had fallen off for the third successive year.[22] Whatever is true for psychiatry is true also for the rest of medicine. The hastening of psychiatrists into urban private practice, leaving hospital patients with insufficient care, is matched by the crowding of doctors into specialization, leaving grave shortages in the ranks of general practitioners. Medical schools are now producing 7,000 physicians a year; this must rise to 10,000 by 1975 if we are to avert a grave shortage of doctors.[23] But we are all familiar with complaints of grievous shortages in mathematics,

[19] D. E. O'Keefe, "Psychiatric Social Work," *American Journal of Psychiatry*, CXVII (1961), pp. 639–40; J. Wax, "Psychiatric Social Work," *ibid.*, CXVIII (1962), pp. 627–29.

[20] *Action for Mental Health, op. cit.*, p. 9.

[21] *Ibid.*, p. 140.

[22] F. G. Ebaugh and R. H. Barnes, "Psychiatric Education," *American Journal of Psychiatry*, CXVII (1961), pp. 653–54.

[23] *Action for Mental Health, op. cit.*, p. 143.

physics, chemistry, and the social sciences, even though graduate study in these fields costs less than medical training and has been made financially more attractive through generous scholarship policies. The professional manpower shortage is not peculiar to the mental health sciences or to medicine. It is a general problem of a society that is growing so fast, in numbers and in technological complexity, that it is outrunning its own educational systems.

INSTITUTIONS DEALING WITH DISORDERED PEOPLE

A comprehensive program for dealing with the problem of disordered personal reactions covers a great deal of ground. Here we shall undertake to point out only the high spots in such a program. Our first concern will be with institutional resources, especially those institutions that are designed to help in the detection and treatment of disorders and to care for patients while they are ill.

Mental Hospitals and Other Special Institutions. For the mentally retarded, special training schools, removed from the ordinary stream of life, offer the best possibility for happiness and usefulness. In such an environment, handicapped children can be protected from constant competition with the normally endowed and trained in whatever ways and at whatever rates their abilities permit. Certain other forms of disorder are believed to be most easily cared for in separate isolated institutions: for example, colonies for epileptics and farm schools for chronic delinquents and psychopaths. Most institutions of this kind must be maintained at public expense. Adequate provision is all too often blocked by political and economic obstacles. Even in states with good public institutions it is typical to find long waiting lists for admission to schools for the feeble-minded. Sometimes two or three years go by before a prospective patient can be accommodated.

The most important institution, however, is the mental hospital. For most forms of incurable mental disorder, the hospital is capable of providing reasonable comfort and contentment. For the disorders that offer hope of improvement, it is capable of offering, in addition, the best facilities in the way of treatment. When funds are sufficient, a mental hospital is capable of becoming a major force not only in serving its patients but also as a place for professional education and for the advancement of knowledge through research. Future professional workers can learn their trade under the guidance of the hospital's senior staff, simultaneously practising their skills and serving the needs of the institution. Research workers have at their disposal not only the abundant free time of patients, who are often glad enough to take tests and participate in experiments, but also the detailed histories and the facilities for follow-up that form an essential part of modern hospital organization. A first-rate mental hospital is almost like a small university in its special field of mental disorders. It receives and trains students, gives courses and seminars, maintains its library, invites visiting scholars to lecture, supports research projects, yet at the same time cares for its patients with faithful attention. It is a great economy to have care, treatment, research, and teaching all going on in the same institution. There is active cross-fertilization of ideas, a maximum of stimulating discussion, yet no loss of touch with the practical goal of service to unfortunate members of the community. The leading mental hospitals have played an outstanding role in the advancement of knowledge and in the training of professional workers.

During the last few years there has been a rapid growth of research into the social organization of mental hospitals. Much more goes on in a hospital besides care and treatment of patients by the professional staff. Even when there are many scheduled activities the patients have a great deal of time and opportunity to interact among themselves. One study of this interaction used the technique of participant observation: the observer assumed the role of a patient and lived for two months on the ward, his true status being known only by two senior staff members.[24] It was clear that an informal but definite social organization prevailed among the patients, who as a group tried to meet many of the problems of hospital life "by developing a shared set of values and beliefs translated into action through a system of social roles and cliques." Included in the interactions were many examples of help and support, as when one patient sat up all night with another who was experiencing anxiety. A more extensive study has been published by Stanton and Schwartz, who describe with striking detail some of the relationships between staff administrative policies and the social and emotional climate of a ward for disturbed patients.[25] Disagreement among staff members, even when it is not brought to open expression, can communicate itself to patients and cause no small amount of disturbance in the ward. It is profitable, for reasons both practical and theoretical, to study the hospital as a system of hierarchical positions, to grasp the inherent conflicts of different roles in this system, and to give thought to the problem of communication among the different parts of the system. Just as we had to analyze what is communicated in parent-child interactions, so we have to understand what is communicated from doctors to nurses, from doctors to pa-

[24] W. Caudill, F. C. Redlich, H. R. Gilmore, and E. B. Brody, "Social Structure and Interaction Processes on a Psychiatric Ward," *American Journal of Orthopsychiatry*, XXII (1952), pp. 314–34.

[25] A. H. Stanton and M. S. Schwartz, *The Mental Hospital: A Study of Institutional Participation in Psychiatric Illness and Treatment* (New York: Basic Books, Inc., 1954).

tients, and from nurses to patients. In a social system as large as a hospital one can hardly expect that communications reaching the patients will be entirely consistent.

Particularly important for the future is the increased development of outpatient services. The first offering of such a service by a mental hospital occurred as recently as 1912, and the need for outpatient clinics is still far from being met. Neuroses and other less crippling disorders are best treated in an outpatient clinic. One of the complaints of medical students as regards their training in psychiatry is that they do not have the chance to see psychiatric outpatients, the very sort of maladjusted persons they will meet most frequently in their later practice of medicine. For patients, too, such clinics will be the answer to a great need. The United States Public Health Service for several years undertook to establish demonstration mental health clinics at different points throughout the country. Meanwhile some of the states have tried their best to inaugurate services of this kind within their own boundaries. Federal aid for the building of community mental health centers would appear to be a likely next step in making this vital medical service more widely available. It seems possible that intervention at an earlier stage of illness, long before there is any thought of hospitalization, might eventually reduce the number of people who have to be hospitalized. In some places "walk-in" clinics have been opened, analagous to the emergency services of general hospitals and similar in spirit to suicide prevention centers. At any time of the day or night a trained person is on hand to help sufferers when they are in the midst of crisis.[26]

The Patient's Return to the Community. When a patient is discharged from a mental hospital, he does not return to an unchanged situation at home. The behavior that led up to hospitalization may have been disturbingly noticeable in the community and at his place of work. It is certain to have been seriously upsetting to the members of his family. The family has probably been under great strain during the course of the breakdown and has felt no small sense of relief when responsibility could be turned over to doctors and nurses. In many ways the homecoming may be joyful, but we cannot be surprised that everyone has certain misgivings about the returning patient. Will he be able to resume his former place and take up his usual activities? Must he be treated in a special way? Will he break down again?

It is increasingly recognized that cure does not end at the hospital and that the patient's chances of continued improvement depend to some extent on his reception in the community. To a degree the community

[26] Barton and St. John, *op. cit.*, pp. 633–36. An example is the "trouble-shooting" clinic opened by Dr. Leopold Bellak at New York City Hospital at Elmhurst, Long Island.

has lost confidence in him, just as he may have lost confidence in himself. To a degree it may be advisable for him to lead a less strenuous life than before, to be given more care and more privileges. Thus the return to the community is bound to require adjustments, and the former patient can be either much helped or much hindered by the attitudes of those around him. Strictly speaking, mental patients cannot be sent home well. The best that can be done is to send them home in a condition sufficiently improved to justify the hope that they can re-establish themselves satisfactorily in their families and in the community.

Realizing this, progressive workers in the hospitals have tried to reverse the common older attitude that patients' relatives are a nuisance to be kept away. Visits by relatives are encouraged, including talks with the patient's doctor; and the patient is likely to be sent home for short trial visits before final discharge. In some cases doctor, patient, and relatives together work out decisions as to the time of discharge and the immediate plans for the patient's life.[27] Attempts may be made to talk with former or future employers concerning the patient's chances of success. Measures of this kind not only help the former patient to find understanding but also serve to modify some of the anxious attitudes toward mental disorder that prevail in the community. Recent studies suggest that these attitudes are slowly undergoing favorable modification.[28]

Sometimes the situation is more difficult. After a long and severe illness, for instance, the patient's confidence in his ability to live again in the community may be deeply shaken, his contact with other people still painfully fragile. Former patients thus burdened may profit greatly if they can live for a while in an environment purposely made easy for them. This is sometimes accomplished by foster family care. Another method is the so-called "halfway house," a boarding house the occupants of which ideally include patients, a certain number of understanding people who are not patients, and a trained person in charge or at least supervising the operation. In such a setting the former patient can go out to his work every day but return to the house either to mingle with the others or not, as he pleases; and the step of adapting again to his family is postponed to a later time. Another scheme to ease the return is the establishment of community centers or clubs for former patients. With the help of initiative by the staff, these can become scenes of great activity, with regular meetings, amateur shows, dances, concerts, outings, even a weekly newsletter, all of which implies planning, organiza-

[27] O. G. Simmons, J. A. Davis, and K. Spencer, "Interpersonal Strains in Release from a Mental Hospital," *Social Problems,* IV (1956), pp. 21–28.

[28] H. E. Freeman and O. G. Simmons, *The Mental Patient Comes Home* (New York: John Wiley & Sons, Inc., 1963); S. Olshansky, S. Grob, and I. Malamud, "Employers' Attitudes and Practices in the Hiring of Ex-Mental Patients," *Mental Hygiene,* XLII (1958), pp. 391–401.

tion, and committee work which in the end is mostly accomplished by the former patients.[29] The fact that all the members are familiar with mental illness creates a feeling of unusual comradeship and understanding.

There is an even more radical way of assisting the patient's return to the community, and that is not to take him completely out of it in the first place. It is with this in mind that experiments are being carried on with day hospitals.[30] The principle is simple: the patient spends every day at the hospital but goes home at night. This cannot be done, of course, with patients who are highly disturbed or too apathetic to follow the routine; but it is entirely practicable with those whose condition is less severe. At the Massachusetts Mental Health Center in Boston, where the experiment has been under way for some years, 50 per cent of the patients are on day care; and many of these are admitted directly to it, without any period of full-time residence in the hospital.[31] The saving in beds, space, and night care commends the experiment on financial grounds; but the strongest arguments in its favor are psychological. The patient is not taken wholly out of his community, the relatives are not wholly relieved of their responsibility for him, the role of the sick person is not sharply established, and the regressive attractions of bed care are not added to the patient's other difficulties in facing the conditions of his life. When the time comes to end daily visits to the hospital, the transition does not have the character of an abrupt shock.

Child Guidance Clinics. A little more on the preventive side are the child guidance clinics, ministering to the needs of children and young people before their complaints evolve into more serious disorders. The child guidance clinic has its point of historic origin in the psychological clinic opened by Witmer at the University of Pennsylvania in 1896. Witmer was particularly interested in school problems, which he endeavored to solve by careful testing and observation of the child's mental performance. The movement was obscured for a while, especially when the first wave of indiscriminate enthusiasm for intelligence testing swept the country, but it reappeared during the twenties when the National Committee for Mental Hygiene—originally the handiwork of Clifford M. Beers—began to put financial support behind child guidance facilities. In the meantime, however, a second influence had begun to operate, and it soon flowed into the same channels. This was the work set in motion by William Healy when in 1909 he launched in Chicago a five-year study of juvenile offenders. Before long this study evolved

29 An example is Center House Foundation in Boston, directed by Dr. Samuel Grob.

30 B. M. Kramer, *Day Hospital: A Study of Partial Hospitalization in Psychiatry* (New York: Grune & Stratton, Inc., 1962).

31 *Ibid.*, p. vi.

into what was essentially a child guidance clinic attached to a juvenile court and specializing in young delinquents. The first demonstration clinics set up by the National Committee were strongly affected by both lines of work, the guidance of children and the guidance of juvenile delinquents. They were also affected by the influential voice of Adolf Meyer, who for years had maintained that psychiatry should work for prevention as well as cure.[32]

The staff of a child guidance clinic ordinarily consists of a psychiatrist, a clinical psychologist, and one or more psychiatric social workers. Patients are referred by the various social agencies in the community, by schools, sometimes by juvenile courts, by churches and synagogues, and eventually by the parents themselves as the service comes to be known and accepted. Generally speaking, the psychiatrist examines the child physically and mentally, and carries out or at least directs the treatment. The clinical psychologist assists in the diagnosis by various testing procedures and appraises the child's capacities. The social worker secures the parents' version of the history, examines the home and neighborhood, and carries out such measures as advising the parents and changing the child's activities. A child guidance clinic is equipped for psychotherapy, but very often its functions consist of changing the child's environment, getting him to new schools or camps, possibly removing him to a foster home. Another part of its function is to influence the parents so that the home environment will become psychologically more propitious. One can see from this brief description that a child guidance center must be closely integrated with its community. It acts in constant cooperation with other social agencies, schools, courts, and recreational facilities. Half of its influence is lost if this cooperation cannot be maintained. Many communities have undertaken to establish child guidance services on a part-time basis. A visiting staff, however, cannot do the job with half the effectiveness of a permanent staff. In spite of much improvement in recent years, provision of these services still falls far short of meeting the need.

Psychological Services in Schools. Even more a dream of the future, as far as organization is concerned, are psychological services in schools. Some school systems have made a small beginning by appointing a psychologist whose duty is chiefly to test the pupils' mental capacity and appraise their progress in school subjects. This is a valuable beginning because it leads to the early detection of mental retardation and of special difficulties with certain school subjects. For retarded pupils it is advantageous to arrange special classes under a teacher who has been

[32] For a fuller account of the history of child guidance clinics, see H. L. Witmer, *Psychiatric Clinics for Children* (New York: The Commonwealth Fund, 1940), chaps. i–iii.

trained for that particular type of work. When a child is found to be blocked in a certain subject, he can often be trained to surmount this obstacle. Perhaps he got started with wrong basic habits which have to be changed. Great skill has been developed in recent years in the remedial teaching of reading. Often the removal of an apparent educational handicap has a profoundly beneficial effect on a child's emotional adjustment.

Sometimes, however, an educational handicap is itself the result of emotional maladjustment. It is possible for a properly trained psychologist to go considerably further in his activities. When children first come into school they are still very much in process of being moulded by their environment. If the psychologist can be in a position to study each child as early as possible during the first year, not waiting for difficulties to arise but trying to anticipate them and prevent them from arising, he can avert many of the psychological mishaps that might later take months and years to correct. In schools where this plan has been tried for several years there is a reduced frequency of even such seemingly educational disturbances as difficulty with reading. It is possible, moreover, for difficulties having their origin in the family circle to be favorably influenced at this time. How their child is doing at school is one of the topics through which parents can be most easily coaxed to reconsider their own relationship with the child. Psychological services in schools are often classed by taxpayers as unnecessary frills, but in capable hands they can render important service in detecting and averting disordered personal behavior.

With personnel in short supply and with taxpayers dubious, less complete but still useful aid can be given through a consultation service for teachers. A psychiatrist, social worker, or psychologist holds regular conference hours each week at which teachers can discuss problems they may be having with particular children. Under this arrangement the mental health worker does not see the child "patient"; but he can often assist the teacher by pointing out the possible significance of some of the behavior and suggesting how the teacher, without herself trying to play psychiatrist, can best adapt her behavior to that of the trouble-giving child.

PROFESSIONS DEALING WITH DISORDERED PEOPLE

The four professions chiefly concerned with abnormal people are psychiatry, psychiatric social work, clinical psychology, and psychiatric nursing. Each of these represents a specialization within a much larger professional group: medicine, social work, psychology, and nursing. In a very real sense, therefore, four different professions with different traditions and ideals of training meet in the care of mentally and emotionally disordered people. Actually there are several other professions that join in this enterprise. One that is rapidly assuming prominence and developing its methods of training is simply called *counseling*, with various specializations according to the type of client and problem: personal counseling, marriage counseling, educational counseling, vocational guidance, counseling in industry. The line between counseling and psychotherapy is often not a sharp one, and it can be argued that any counseling, if it is properly done, produces at least on a small scale a corrective emotional experience. Then there is *occupational therapy*, which plays an indispensable part in making life in a hospital or institution an interesting and constructive experience. Members of the *ministry* have lately been showing an interest in the problems of abnormal psychology and are undertaking to train themselves for the giving of better guidance. Several other professions, such as *law*, *teaching*, and *group work*, make vital contributions though not specializing on the problems of the abnormal. In the following sections, however, we shall concentrate on the training and functions of three professional groups: the psychiatrist, the psychiatric social worker, and the clinical psychologist.

The Psychiatrist. A psychiatrist is first of all a physician. He has gone through medical school, taken whatever training in psychiatry is offered during the four-year course, received his M.D. degree, and specialized in psychiatry in his subsequent internships. It is incorrect to call anyone a psychiatrist who is not the holder of the M.D. degree. Psychiatry is a medical specialty.

Because of his complete medical training, the psychiatrist is competent to examine patients both physically and mentally. As a specialist he does not undertake to deal personally with other than the simpler physical ills, but he is qualified to recognized them and estimate their weight in the total picture of the patient's condition. This is important in dealing with practically all forms of disorder. Psychotic conditions may be greatly complicated by intercurrent physical disorders. With new patients a correct diagnosis is not always possible unless one can assess the evidence for diffuse infections, endocrine disorders, dietary deficiencies, cerebral damage, and many other somatic disturbances. Even in treating the neuroses it may be necessary to decide whether the patient has produced a new hysterical symptom or whether a true organic disorder has developed. Particularly when dealing with psychosomatic disorders it is essential to be able to observe the subtle interaction between bodily and emotional states.

To the psychiatrist falls the task of taking the patient's history and of making a behavioral examination. Perhaps this does not even sound easy, but it is much less easy than it sounds. Expertness in interviewing is indispensable. Patients are only moderately adept at giving an accurate history of their lives, still less at reporting their feelings, and it is the task of the skillful interviewer to make this material flow forth. While he is conversing with the patient, the psychiatrist must also be silently conducting his behavioral examination, noting appearance, mannerisms, character of speech, mood, evidences of memory defect and general impairment, degree of insight into own condition, underlying attitudes toward self and interviewer.[33] If the patient is confused or stuporous, the doctor's task is obviously difficult. It is an illuminating experience for the student of interviewing to record one of his attempts and play it back to himself several times. The chances are that he will hear himself blocking the patient's confidences, cutting off what afterwards look like the most important leads, hurting the patient's feelings, and unwittingly generating an interpersonal situation that is quite different from the one intended. Skillful interviewing can be accomplished only after long practice.

The psychiatrist is responsible for making the diagnosis and deciding what shall be done about the patient. If what is to be done belongs in the category of therapy, he probably does it himself or at least closely supervises its execution. Prefrontal lobotomy calls for the neurosurgeon, and some forms of treatment draw in other specialists, but the psychiatrist is responsible for shock therapies, drug treatments, and all forms of psychotherapy. He must determine, in other words, the therapeutic program and decide at what point the patient is well enough to be trusted to his own resources. His duties in this respect are entirely analogous to those of any other medical specialist. Once a patient has come into his hands, he is responsible for the diagnosis, care, and treatment. It is of course not usually the case that any one psychiatrist is trained to use all the techniques of psychotherapy described in our earlier chapters. There is specialization within specialization; one man may use only standard psychoanalysis, another may work only with children. But this circumstance does not substantially change the picture for psychiatry as a whole.

Training for Psychotherapy. The training of psychiatrists to perform psychotherapy is still not as well organized as might be the case. Beginning as an observer during interviews and ward rounds, the candidate gradually slips over into conducting interviews and handling simple cases himself. He reports his activities to his superiors and is advised on what to do next. The scope of his therapeutic work gradually increases. Staff conferences and seminars provide a means of exchanging experiences with fellow-students and teachers. All this is extremely valuable; it has often

[33] Cf. P. W. Preu, *Outline of Psychiatric Case Study* (2d ed.; New York: Paul B. Hoeber, Inc., 1943).

turned out great psychiatrists. But there is a certain inherent difficulty in giving the kind of direct supervision that makes for efficiency in training. The surgical intern practices his skill directly under the eye of his superior who can anticipate some of his mistakes, point out others as soon as they happen, and immediately intervene to rectify their consequences for the patient. This superb teaching situation cannot be matched in psychotherapy. The teacher cannot sit in the room criticizing the intern when he says the wrong thing to the patient. The best he can do is to listen silently and criticize afterwards. This may be sufficient, but there is a certain inevitable truth in the statement that psychiatrists are more self-taught than taught. The systematic recording of interviews seems to offer a means of getting around this educational difficulty. Objections to recording are sometimes raised, but the advantages would appear to be very great.

The most systematic training procedure has been developed by the psychoanalysts. Many people are confused as to the distinction between a psychiatrist and a psychoanalyst. The confusion arises from the fact that psychoanalysis grew up somewhat apart from medical schools. Its professional organization in this country still consists of local psychoanalytic societies most of which are bound together in the American Psychoanalytic Association. These societies established their own training standards and offered training in psychoanalysis as a postgraduate specialty quite apart from, or but slightly linked to, medical schools. Most of the applicants were physicians, but some workers were admitted from other professions. It is now the policy of the American Psychoanalytic Association to accept candidates for training only if they are already physicians. According to this policy a psychoanalyst is defined as a psychiatrist who has received additional special training in using the standard psychoanalytic technique or its briefer variations. This is simple enough, but one further fact confuses the picture. The policy has been in force only since 1938, and it is binding only on societies which are members of the national association. There are thus a certain number of workers who have been trained for psychoanalysis without having previously studied medicine. These workers have to be designated psychoanalysts but not psychiatrists. No less a person than Anna Freud belongs in this category, and her father, although a physician himself, took the stand that people who showed unusual gifts for psychoanalytic work should be trained, notwithstanding a lack of previous medical education. The majority of American psychoanalysts have dissented from this weighty precedent; it is increasingly true that psychoanalysts in this country are also psychiatrists.

There are two important features in the training program for psychoanalysts. The first is the candidate's own psychoanalysis, sometimes called a "didactic analysis." This is designed partly to familiarize the candidate with analytic technique and with the outcroppings and workings of unconscious tendencies as exemplified in himself. The second important feature is the "supervised" or "controlled" analysis: the candidate himself conducts several therapeutic analyses, reporting each week to a supervising analyst on the course of his work. In this way his mistakes are to some extent pointed out to him and he learns to perfect his technique. When the analytic sessions can be recorded, a splendid opportunity is provided to examine discrepancies between the dialogues remembered by the student therapist and the ones that actually took place.[34]

There has been some controversy of late over the nature and functions of the didactic analysis. It was intended primarily to familiarize the candidate with the ways in which his judgment is likely to be distorted when he begins to work with patients. Through learning about himself he learns not to overvalue in others those problems which are also his own. If he does not realize how much of his own development has hinged upon overcoming dependence, for instance, he will tend to interpret each patient as a problem in dependence, overlooking the troubles that may have arisen in connection with aggression and sex. Again, through learning about himself he learns not to make another common mistake, that of attributing to patients certain undesirable traits that he himself has repressed. If he does not realize that he has overcome by repression a strong tendency toward aggression, for instance, he may err by constantly attributing aggressive strivings to patients in whom this is really a secondary problem.[35] These are very important things to learn, but question has been raised about the necessity of a protracted standard psychoanalysis as the way of learning them. Candidates learn a great deal about themselves while conducting analyses under supervision; perhaps this is where the most important learning takes place. The didactic analysis, moreover, can never be the equivalent of a therapeutic one: the training analyst has altogether too much power over the candidate's future career to make the situation really free. It is easier, as every student knows, to confide one's problems to someone unconnected with school administration than to confide them to a dean.

The Psychiatric Social Worker. A psychiatric social worker is a social worker who meets two additional criteria: "first, specialized training involving field work in a psychiatric or mental hygiene clinic or a mental hospital; second, experience in an agency combining psychiatric and

[34] L. S. Kubie, "Research into the Process of Supervision in Psychoanalysis," *Psychoanalytic Quarterly*, XXVII (1958), pp. 226–36.

[35] I. Hendrick, *Facts and Theories of Psychoanalysis* (2d ed.; New York: Alfred A. Knopf, Inc., 1939), p. 321.

social work."[36] She is a social worker who by special training is equipped to operate in a team with psychiatrists.

Psychiatric social work came into existence as a result of the frustration of psychiatrists at seeing so much of their work go wrong. Patients were cured in the clinic only to relapse again as soon as they went home. Other patients told tales about their families which could not be verified without an actual visit to the home. Occasionally a psychiatrist, baffled by this situation, tried to investigate the home and neighborhood in person, but the experiment generally showed that he lacked both experience and aptitude for the work. Thus it was found expedient to begin training social workers so that they might serve as extensions, so to speak, of the psychiatrist. Early in the work with a case they secure a social history from the relatives; later they visit the patient in his home to see that recommendations are being carried out and that the patient is not being overwhelmed by circumstances. The psychiatrist functions in the team as an expert on individual behavior; the social worker is the expert on social problems. She tries to help patients with the family entanglements, neighborhood entanglements, job entanglements, and all other social entanglements that are detrimental to their mental health.

Training for psychiatric social work is a two-year course, graduation from college being generally required for admission. The academic side of the training consists of courses in psychiatry and psychology, child development, community organization, and social statistics. Great emphasis is placed upon supervised field training, which occupies at least half of the two-year program. The students are placed at clinics or hospitals where they participate increasingly in the work that is going on, thus learning their trade at first hand under careful supervision. Thus equipped, the worker is prepared to serve as the social arm of a mental hospital, outpatient clinic, or child guidance clinic. She may also become involved in the psychological services offered by school systems. Sometimes a psychiatric social worker is appointed as a visiting teacher to keep a watchful eye upon adjustment problems inside and outside the classroom. Recently the emphasis in training has shifted to include more first-hand experience with research. Increasingly the social worker takes part in institutional research programs, and she needs familiarity with the impersonal rigors of research method.[37]

Role of the Social Worker in Psychotherapy. Once the position of the social worker as an adjunct in the practice of psychiatry was recognized, it became apparent that she would inevitably be drawn into therapeutic

[36] L. M. French, *Psychiatric Social Work* (New York: The Commonwealth Fund, 1940), p. 76.

[37] J. Wax, "Psychiatric Social Work," *American Journal of Psychiatry*, CXVIII (1962), pp. 627–29.

activities of her own. Maladjustments occur in a social setting. More than one person is usually involved, and sometimes one wonders whether the person who happens to come for treatment is really the sickest member of the circle. Perhaps the husband enters the hospital in an acutely alcoholic condition, but then the wife turns out to be nervous and jumpy or sad and depressed, the mother-in-law is slightly delusional, and before long it is revealed that the actual patient is only one member of a disordered social orbit. The psychiatric social worker cannot enter that orbit without finding herself at least in semi-therapeutic relation with some of its members. Whatever her desires in the matter, she begins to practice psychotherapy.

It was among psychiatric social workers that the concepts of "relationship therapy" and "attitude therapy" were first worked out. Beginning about 1930, workers began to pay increasing attention to the personal interaction that occurred between themselves and their clients. They made the discovery, since embodied in Rogers' exposition of non-directive counseling, that by letting the client take the lead, and merely encouraging the expression of feelings, they could secure a very desirable change of attitude. Thus instead of limiting themselves to solving the social and neighborhood problems that contributed to the patient's illness, they began to influence the attitudes of those in his immediate environment. The success of this venture was at length recognized explicitly in child guidance clinics which began to practice the simultaneous treatment of mother and child. Thus the psychiatric social worker became a member of a therapeutic team, not just an adjunct of the psychiatrist's therapeutic endeavors. Included in her expanded role is greater participation in group work and group therapy at the institution and in mental health education in the community.[38]

The relationship between psychiatrist and social worker has always been clearly defined. It is not a relationship of equal status. The social worker is not supposed to assume independent responsibility for diagnosis or therapy. Sometimes she is assigned to undertake a specific therapeutic task with a patient, or she finds herself embarked irresistably in a therapeutic relationship with a relative of the patient. In either case it is understood that she will report her activities fully to the psychiatrist, and that if unexpected complications arise she will turn her case over to him.

The Clinical Psychologist. The third member of the clinical team is the psychologist. In the last twenty years the profession of clinical psychology has been undergoing a rapid evolution. In order to understand the present position of this specialty, and to gain insight into a certain amount of

[38] *Ibid.*

controversy that surrounds it, we need to see it in the framework of recent history.

In the early years of the present century it began to be apparent that the rapidly growing science of psychology could make a helpful contribution to the study of abnormal people. The psychologist, trained in experimental methods and in measurement, was in a particularly good position to assist in the appraisal of capacity. The advent of intelligence tests and their widespread use in schools soon produced a group of workers who were skilled in mental measurement. Hospitals and clinics soon realized the value of this skill and began to employ psychologists as regular members of the staff. Extensive training did not at first seem necessary in order to perform the duties in a satisfactory manner. At the beginning of World War II it was still the common practice to require only the bachelor's degree plus a year of supervised experience at a hospital. With that amount of training the worker was qualified as an expert in mental measurement.

These workers were referred to as psychologists. This was confusing because it drew no distinction between the highly trained experimental psychologist with a Ph.D. degree and the hospital psychologist with a bachelor's degree. The more precise term *psychometrist* was presently introduced; it remains the appropriate designation for a worker whose training is restricted to the use and interpretation of tests. But a certain number of fully trained psychologists holding the Ph.D. degree found their interests leading them into work with abnormal people. Eventually the title of *clinical psychologist* crystallized as the most appropriate way of distinguishing this profession on the one hand from the but slightly trained *psychometrist* and on the other from the academic *psychologist*, equally trained but along somewhat different lines.

Meanwhile the scope of psychological work with abnormal people was undergoing a tremendous expansion. The whole concept of testing burst its earlier bounds. With the introduction of projective methods the business of interpreting test results sprang from a more or less routine matter to a refined psychological art. The clinical psychologist became responsible for appraising not only the patient's intelligence but his capacities and personality as a whole. Even when a psychologist gives a single brief test of intelligence he can treat it as a behavioral examination, a sampling of the whole person in action. A trained observer will not miss such signs as hesitation, anxiety, overeagerness, apologies, excuses, boasting, and disruption by failure. He will notice the precise pattern of tasks on which the subject succeeds and fails, and he will have an eye to the psychological meaning behind this pattern. Does the patient show impairment of the abstract attitude, for example? This cannot be judged simply from test scores or from the mere fact of success or failure on a given task. It has to be inferred from the way the patient goes at the task and from close observation of the precise point of failure. The psychologist observes test performances just as keenly as the psychiatrist observes behavior when he is interviewing a patient.

For the most part, however, psychological testing has advanced far beyond the giving of single tests. The clinical psychologist typically administers a battery of tests so planned as to yield a full and well-rounded appraisal of the individual client. The method is well exemplified in a paper by Shakow, Rodnick, and Lebeaux in which a test battery is described, and the results obtained with a schizophrenic patient are reported in detail.[39] The tests include a standard intelligence test, the Rorschach ink blot test, the Thematic Apperception test, an association test, and several performances in which the person can be placed under stress. The writers emphasize the desirability of testing a patient's performances at different levels, by different examiners, and under conditions of stress as well as relaxed conditions. Several of the tests, for example, measure cognitive ability, and two of these are presented in such a way as to reveal the amount and character of cognitive impairment under stress. It is also shown that content as well as performance is useful for analysis. The content of the associations and Thematic Apperception stories is an invaluable aid in sizing up the patient's emotional attitudes, defenses, and problems of chief concern. The interpretation of the results obtained by such a battery of tests is a highly skilled operation. When properly done it yields a fairly complete and fairly unified psychological portrait.

A portrait of this kind is very useful in the work of diagnosis. A patient is examined by the psychiatrist, his history and social circumstances are worked up by the psychiatric social worker, his physiological, biochemical, and endocrine status is reported from medical examination and laboratory studies. The portrait contributed by the clinical psychologist is often of crucial importance for integrating these diverse findings. "On the one hand, its more controlled and objective nature makes it adaptable for correlation with physiological and biochemical material and, on the other, its behavioral and higher-level functional nature makes it directly comparable with the psychiatric and social data."[40] The psychological findings are often of special value in estimating capacities and suggesting favorable lines of adaptation in the community. Obviously such data are of great value not only for the understanding of the single case but also

[39] D. Shakow, E. H. Rodnick, and T. Lebeaux, "A Psychological Study of a Schizophrenic: Exemplification of a Method," *Journal of Abnormal and Social Psychology*, XL (1945), pp. 154–74.

[40] *Ibid.*, p. 154.

for research on personality in general.[41] We saw that in order to understand schizophrenia it was necessary to study alterations in the thought processes. The skills of the clinical psychologist are much needed in attacking problems of this kind.[42]

Role of the Psychologist in Psychotherapy. During the acute psychiatric emergency created by World War II psychologists often functioned in a therapeutic capacity, and their efforts were not without success. At the close of the war the need for therapeutic services continued to be greatly in excess of the supply of trained workers, as it has continued to this day. Clinical psychologists thus found themselves being drawn irresistably into therapeutic activities. Many of them did not welcome this turn of events. Having chosen their profession with the idea of doing scientific research on personality, they were anything but eager to fill their time with a case load. To others, however, the diagnosis of patients by tests seemed to lead over quite naturally into treatment. Their growing skill in understanding troubled people gave them an urge to do something about the trouble. When patients were asking for help and it was clear that no one else had time to meet their need, psychotherapy by clinical psychologists became inevitable.

Although the situation was inevitable, it raised disquieting questions in regard to professional organization. Many psychiatrists reacted strongly against what they feared might become an invasion of their province by non-medical workers. Steps were even proposed here and there to strengthen state medical practice laws so that non-medical psychotherapy would be explicitly illegal. The ensuing controversy had unbecoming elements of a struggle for professional prestige, but even the most uninvolved observers, thinking only of the public interest, could see that there was a difficult underlying problem. It is clearly in the public interest that skilled psychotherapeutic services should become more widely available as soon as possible. The training of clinical psychologists is at present an indispensable way of meeting that need. It is not in the public interest, however, that psychological testing and research should be substantially weakened or that the profession of clinical psychology should be too sharply dislocated in the direction of therapy. The emergence of a new profession of psychotherapists, standing in any sense apart from medicine, would only create confusion in the public mind. It is for these

[41] For a fuller account, see S. Rosenzweig, *Psychodiagnosis* (New York: Grune & Stratton, Inc., 1949).

[42] D. Rapaport, "The Theoretical Implications of Diagnostic Test Procedures," in R. P. Knight and C. R. Friedman (eds.), *Psychoanalytic Psychiatry and Psychology: Clinical and Theoretical Papers* (New York: International Universities Press, Inc., 1954), pp. 173–95.

reasons that progressive clinical psychologists place so much emphasis on the threefold nature of their profession.

The Task of Research. In addition to diagnostic testing and help with therapy, the clinical psychologist has the duty of conducting research. In the long run this may well turn out to be the sphere of his most important contribution. No one doubts that he is far better trained in research than is the psychiatrist or social worker. His is the only training program that includes the study of scientific method, supervised practice in research undertakings, and the writing of a thesis based on an independent piece of research. It has been clear throughout this book that one of the greatest obstacles to effective work with abnormal people is our ignorance about them. Every hospital and every clinic teems with unsolved problems and offers unparalleled opportunities for solving them. All that is necessary is to find methods and to have time and ingenuity to work them out.

THE PREVENTION OF DISORDERED BEHAVIOR

During the last twenty-five years there has been a marked expansion of facilities for the care of disordered people. There have likewise been great advances in methods of treatment, so that the prospects of regaining health and emotional balance are substantially better than they used to be. These gains, however, come nowhere near to meeting the existing need. When we consider the shortage of professional workers and the difficulty and expense of increasing their number rapidly, it becomes apparent that this need is not likely to be met in the near future. Will it be met in the more distant future, or must we conclude that it puts too great a strain on society's human and financial resources? Drawing upon what we know at present, it is hardly possible to give this question an optimistic answer. Some of the latest developments in treatment, such as intensive psychotherapy with schizophrenic patients and residential treatment for aggressive and disturbed children, require a tremendous outlay of time. A full-scale attack on just these two problems would need pretty nearly all the time of all the psychiatrists, psychiatric social workers, and clinical psychologists in the United States. Obviously there can never be enough workers in these professions to bring intensive treatment to all who need it, as we now understand the need. Attempts to shorten psychotherapy do not usually shorten it enough to solve the problem. We are faced with a situation in which there can be no hope of a full pound of cure. This makes it urgent to consider how near we can come to finding an ounce of prevention.

Preventing Somatogenic Disorder. In view of the finding that manic-depressive psychosis, schizophrenia, epilepsy, some types of feeble-mindedness, and certain neurological disorders have a definite genogenic element, it is sometimes proposed that they be prevented by a program of sterilization. The advocates of such a plan argue that the transmission of "tainted" germ plasm should be blocked for the good of the race. The argument is logically sound, but it breaks down factually in view of our present ignorance about "tainted" germ plasm and its transmission. The evidence is summarized by Klein, who bases his discussion chiefly on a very careful investigation sponsored by the American Neurological Association.[43] The genogenic factor is never more than a contributing or predisposing cause. The number of people coming from supposedly "tainted" stock who themselves develop disorders is greater than chance but still not very great. Thus a wholesale program of eugenical sterilization would prevent the birth of a great many people who would never become disordered and who for all we know might be capable of highly superior contributions. "Many valuable members of society, worth more to it than the cost of maintenance of all state institutions put together, would have been lost if sterilization laws had been enacted on a compulsory basis a few centuries ago."[44] Serious abnormalities are known to have existed in the family lines of Beethoven, Goethe, Newton, and Michelangelo. Newton himself became psychotic after his fiftieth year. It is an interesting thought that eugenical sterilization, foresightedly applied to Newton's ancestors, would have prevented society from being burdened by his psychosis. We can safely conclude that in the present state of our knowledge the proposal to employ sterilization for the prevention of mental abnormality is decidedly premature.

Some of the problems of mental disorder are essentially problems in public health and sanitation. The most important success thus far achieved along this line is the reduction of general paresis through public health measures designed to stamp out syphilis. Certain other countries have been more successful than the United States in this respect. The complete elimination of general paresis is theoretically possible. Prophylactic measures exist which greatly reduce syphilitic infection. But these measures cannot be used without the cooperation of the person exposed to infection, who must realize exactly the dangers that are involved. Thus the campaign against syphilis currently resolves itself into an educational problem rather than a medical one. Another sphere for public health measures is the control of epidemic encephalitis, a problem that has not yet been solved. Even the nutritionist comes into the sphere of mental hygiene. The demonstrated relation between pellagra and vitamin defi-

[43] D. B. Klein, *Mental Hygiene* (New York: Holt, Rinehart & Winston, Inc., 1944), pp. 102–10; A. Myerson, J. B. Ayer, T. J. Putnam, C. E. Keeler, and L. Alexander, *Eugenical Sterilization* (New York: The Macmillan Co., 1936).

[44] Myerson *et al.*, *ibid.*, p. 172

ciency lays at least one group of mental symptoms at the door of faulty diet.

The various medical specialties contribute in several ways to the treatment and prevention of serious abnormality. Neurology and neurosurgery are constantly occupied with troubles which have an important mental aspect. The timely surgical removal of a brain tumor prevents what is almost certain to become a mental disorder. Improved skill in obstetrics means a smaller incidence of brain injuries associated with birth. Correction of endocrine disorders likewise presses the attack on such partially mental disturbances as myxedema and exophthalmic goiter. Frequently a serious physical disease which leaves the person in a weak and discouraged condition serves to precipitate an otherwise latent mental disorder. Thus the maintenance of general bodily well-being has a favorable effect on mental health.

These examples will serve to illustrate the overlap that is characteristically found among the different branches of medicine. The task of alleviating and preventing disordered personal behavior cannot be assigned to a compartment of human effort. Some disorders are wholly, others partly, problems for the healer of bodily ills. The great majority, however, require the special ministrations that belong to psychiatry.

Preventing Psychogenic Disorder. The prevention of somatogenic disorder takes place through methods already familiar in medicine and public health. The bulk of the work is done by the trained expert. Much of the task consists of educating the public, but the information that must be conveyed is relatively simple and factual. The situation is quite different when we turn to the prevention of psychogenic disorder. Our study of psychological development has shown us the importance of the early years of life and of the family which constitutes the social environment of these years. In connection with the neuroses we found that the nuclear processes were probably laid down during the first five years. The emotional deprivations that lie behind delinquency begin at least as early, and our attempt to unravel psychosomatic disorders, depressive and manic reactions, and schizophrenia led us constantly into the first two years, before the establishment of effective verbal habits. The concepts of anxiety and defense were of particular service in understanding these origins, and the behavior and attitudes of parents always seemed to be implicated in the genesis of pathological reactions. From this it would appear that the crucial information for preventing psychogenic disorder has to do with the effects of parental attitudes on early emotional development. This has emerged as the chief message that needs to be conveyed to the general public.

Only to a small extent is the educative task analogous to the usual public health program. Certain ideas about child rearing, such as feeding practices and the best times for weaning and cleanliness training, qualify as factual information which can be directly communicated, but these form a small part of the message. When it comes to parental attitudes of a more general kind one must recognize that the teaching situation is of an entirely different nature. In the first place, the expert who possesses the specialized knowledge cannot do any part of the job of applying it. It is the parents who must put it into practice, who must use the information to become in some sense experts themselves. In the second place, what has to be taught is a whole way of feeling and behaving, a general attitude toward children which will quietly but consistently steer the parents' behavior through all the vicissitudes of daily contact.

Two disquieting questions are raised by this view of the matter. (1) How sound is the information that the psychological professions are currently prepared to convey? (2) What educational methods are suitable for conveying information of this kind?

Limitations of Knowledge. Our knowledge of the effects of parental attitudes on children's development is largely limited to the effects that have been harmful. We have developed a long list of parental evils: emotional deprivation, overt rejection, covert rejection, cold mechanical handling, overprotection and absorption of the child's life, capricious punishments, severe and crushing discipline. The experts are voluble in telling parents what not to do. On the positive side the message has been thin and perhaps a touch sentimental: the atmosphere of the home must be one of unconditional love, acceptance, permissiveness, democracy; the climate must always be warm. One may well feel surprised that so much of this advice, supposedly based on scientific predictability, is expressed in metaphors of the weather. Yet the vagueness can hardly be avoided in view of the essentially negative character of what we know. No doubt there is a certain inherent difficulty in working out the positive side. As we saw in our study of development, maladjustment can often result from either too much or too little of something; for example, too much discipline or too little discipline. Middle grounds and golden means are always more difficult to describe than pathological extremes. Still it is true that our knowledge is gravely incomplete and takes a form where the "do's" are badly snowed under by the "don't's."[45] The

[45] P. V. Lemkau, B. Pasamanick, and M. Cooper, "The Implications of the Psychogenetic Hypothesis for Mental Hygiene," *American Journal of Psychiatry*, CX (1953), pp. 436–42.

main difficulty is that studies of disordered people have not been well balanced by studies of people whose development came out well.[46]

As a consequence of this situation we do not really know how much weight to attach to parental attitudes as causes of unhealthy development. Occasional studies suggest that normal growth can occur in a family circle that seems full of psychological evils. If further work should substantiate this impression, mental health education would have to become more discriminating in its account of what produces disordered behavior. Another thing we do not know much about is the effect of later experience—during the juvenile period, late childhood, adolescence, and even adulthood—in counter-balancing the early influence of the family circle. When breakdown occurs there is regression, and one gets the impression that early childhood influences are all-powerful. What of the children with equally troubled infancies whose later development takes a healthy turn so that they never break down? Such children never show up in clinics or hospitals, so we simply do not know whether they exist, or, if they do, what factors were important in salvaging their development. Lack of all this essential information means that the mental health message of today is communicated to parents in an extremely alarming form. Children can be ruined by their parents in the first few years of life; they can be ruined by behavior and attitudes of which the parent is not fully conscious; and they can then never be saved from emotional disorder except by expensive psychotherapy. This is all that many parents can make of what the experts are telling them.

Difficulties in Communication. Further trouble is encountered in finding the right manner of conveying information. The educative task was naturally assumed by psychiatrists, social workers, and psychologists, who seem to have approached it at first without much foresight as to all that might be involved. Through books, lectures, and magazine articles parents were told what not to do and warned of the dreadful things that would happen if they did not follow the advice. Even today a great deal of parent education is conducted in a spirit that hardly qualifies as warm, accepting, and democratic. Undoubtedly a factor in this difficulty is the tendency of professional workers to side with patients against parents and to perceive parents, either in the present or through their past influence, as the chief obstacles to therapeutic success. It is small wonder that parents sometimes feel they are being berated rather than helped.

Many workers have begun to recognize the unfortunate consequences of what has been done thus far. These consequences are searchingly

[46] R. W. White, *Lives in Progress: A Study of the Natural Growth of Personality* (New York: Holt, Rinehart & Winston, Inc., 1952), pp. 21–25, 356–60.

examined in a paper by Bruch, who is the author of a book significantly entitled *Don't Be Afraid of Your Child.*[47] Bruch points out that "the enumeration of all the possible acts and attitudes that might injure a child creates an atmosphere of uncertainty and apprehension." Instead of being helpfully informed, parents and future parents are in too many cases simply intimidated. Clearly the production of anxiety in parents will defeat the purpose of reducing it in their children. Teaching which makes parents hesitant, self-conscious, and fearful of doing the wrong thing cannot be expected to bring children a feeling of security. Bruch points out another undertone in parent education which might be considered even more sinister. The parents are given an illusion of omnipotence, a supposedly scientific reason for believing that their influence upon the child is paramount, so that they can set "the goal of manipulating him into becoming a perfect adult." This opens the way for the parent to feel not only guilt and anxiety over the child's faults but also a most unbecoming vainglory over his excellencies. Sometimes when a child does something particularly well one hears his parents receiving congratulations for having done a fine job of bringing him up. Can we be surprised that the product of this fine job shows resentment when he senses "that he is supposed," as Bruch puts it, "to prove something about the parents, and not about himself?" Thus far there has been little in mental health teaching that would encourage a parent to respect his child or to take surprised pleasure in the child's competence.

Newer Trends in Parent Education. Thoughtful leaders in the field of mental health are beginning to change their whole approach to the prevention of psychogenic disorder. Parents do not select their attitudes voluntarily, nor do they assume them simply out of ignorance. Attitudes toward children are deeply embedded in the personalities of parents and may be complexly involved with the parents' own problems. The only way to have a beneficial effect on unfortunate attitudes is to make it possible for the parents to have corrective emotional experiences such as are the goal of psychotherapy. They must themselves be motivated to change, they must go at their own pace, they must not be made resistant by untimely interpretations, they must feel that the atmosphere is one of understanding and respect. If these conditions prevail, parents can reach real working insights into how they interact with their young, while at the same time not losing their sense of the child's part in the interaction. They can become better parents without sacrificing the naturalness and individuality of their behavior at home.

[47] Hilde Bruch, "Parent Education or the Illusion of Omnipotence," *American Journal of Orthopsychiatry*, XXIV (1954), pp. 723–32; *Don't Be Afraid of Your Child: A Guide for Perplexed Parents* (New York: Farrar, Straus & Co., Inc., 1952).

This goal can best be accomplished not by the lecture method but by group discussion. Success seems to be greatest when the discussion is conducted with a minimum of direction, so that the topics introduced come straight from the concrete problems of individual parents. Discussion of this sort is sometimes hard to start. There are quite a number of excellent films on child development and mental health which can be used to provide the vivid impressions that are likely to encourage comment. There is a certain advantage in keeping the experts out of sight. The community program of mental health education in St. Louis, for example, accepts volunteers from the community and gives them brief training in mental health concepts and in methods of conducting group discussion. These lay workers then serve as leaders of parent groups throughout the community.[48]

The results obtained by such methods have been examined with great care by Brim.[49] Although adequate measurement is extremely difficult, it appears that there are usually small gains in the right direction, showing most in matters of parental knowledge and least in matters of behavior. Further study of results is clearly needed, but small results should not be interpreted as worthless ones. We cannot expect large corrective emotional experiences to occur under what is a rather light and brief influence, and even small bits of insight may set things moving in a more satisfactory way between parent and child.

Education is always most successful when the learner feels a strong need for what is offered. Parents of nursery school children, uneasy about the early separation and the child's capacity to flourish in the new environment, are often unusually receptive to counsel. In an experiment on community mental health Caplan has sought opportunities to intervene at significant points in people's lives, such as pregnancy, bereavement, adaptation to a defective child, or adjustment to an incurable illness in a family member.[50] These are moments, he maintains, when ounces of prevention will have their traditionally large effects: moments when stress is high and the need for help may be strong.

THE CITIZEN'S CONTRIBUTION

Up to this point we have considered chiefly the work that can be accomplished by trained experts: the psychiatrist, the neurologist, the physiologist, the public health official, the psychiatric social worker, and

[48] E. L. Brashear, E. T. Kenney, A. D. Buchmueller, and M. C.-L. Gildea, "A Community Program of Mental Health Education Using Group Discussion Methods," *American Journal of Orthopsychiatry*, XXIV (1954), pp. 554–62.

[49] O. G. Brim, Jr., *Education for Child Rearing* (New York: Russell Sage Foundation, 1959).

[50] G. Caplan, *An Approach to Community Mental Health* (New York: Grune & Stratton, Inc., 1961).

the clinical psychologist. Many readers of this book, however, will not be planning a professional career in which knowledge of abnormal psychology is generally deemed essential. Their relation to public health, mental hospitals, psychiatry, and child guidance will be no closer than that of an intelligent citizen. They will properly ask themselves what part the citizen can play in alleviating the burden of disordered personal reactions. They will want to know whether abnormal psychology, in addition to its special professional uses, adds anything to the leaven of thought by which the world is changed for the better. The subject is, to be sure, a relatively specialized field of knowledge. In one respect, nevertheless, the knowledge and insight that can be most readily gained by studying it reaches out beyond the bounds of a specialty and becomes significant for anyone who wants to play an enlightened part in human betterment. For the task of preventing disordered personal reactions is not simply one of spreading certain facilities; doctors, social workers and psychologists can by no means do the whole of the work. The task of prevention penetrates deeply into public and private life.

The most direct form of service consists of volunteering for what we might call civilian duty in a mental hospital, school for retarded children, or some other institution that ministers to disordered people. For some time volunteers have been of great service in general hospitals; it is doubtful that the day's work could be done without them. Civilian volunteers cannot be introduced quite so easily into a mental hospital, yet it is possible for them to play somewhat the same useful part. Experiments have been tried recently on the use of college students as mental hospital volunteers.[51] In hospitals that are short of staff and unable to give much attention to chronic patients, visits by college students may do a great deal to brighten the patients' lives and to increase their alertness and interest. Although there is a danger of setting one's hopes too high, most students report the experience to be valuable and instructive. One group of students who had been volunteers later managed to start a halfway house to assist patients back into life in the community.

Another direction for volunteer efforts is the establishment and maintenance of mental health facilities and educational programs in the community where one resides. It is no easy matter to launch an enterprise of this kind. People with an interest in the subject must get together, make plans, arouse the interest of others, patiently establish contact with existing community groups, slowly sell the idea, reduce the doubts and suspicions that may be felt toward it, and, finally, raise the money. It make take five years or even ten to open the doors of a functioning

[51] C. C. Umbarger, J. S. Dalsimer, A. P. Morrison, and P. R. Breggin, *College Students in a Mental Hospital* (New York: Grune & Stratton, Inc., 1962).

service. This sort of thing is indeed a challenge to those who like to take part in community affairs.

The citizen's contribution can be of a much less direct but hardly less important kind. In his personal life he interacts with many other people, and his effect upon them may or may not be conducive to mutual adjustment. We are all familiar with people who have a gift for stirring up trouble. They cannot enter the most harmonious group without throwing it into violent discord, and they seem adept at making the anxious people more anxious, the guilty more guilty, the angry more angry. Other people seem generally to have the opposite effect; things go better when they are around. This desirable effect is not achieved simply by being a peacemaker. There may be strong partisanship and a vehement espousal of ideas, but the person is able to do this without rancor, without implying that every other viewpoint is stupid, without resentment when others disagree or even outvote him. This is one aspect of the many-sided quality which we call emotional maturity. A person can often improve his own maturity when he becomes interested in reflecting on his feelings and noticing his interactions with others. He is not likely to change overnight, but it is part of the citizen's contribution to do what he can in the direction of personal maturity.

It need hardly be mentioned that the citizen in his role of parent can contribute importantly toward mental health. The fallacy of parental omnipotence should be avoided, but the parent is still a significant item in the child's environment. Interest plays an important part in the success of parent-child relationships. When parents are interested in their children and can take them in a spirit that combines affection with a humorous sense of perspective, many excellencies follow as a matter of course. Interest guarantees that they will at least not ride roughshod over the child's strivings and preoccupations. Then there is the matter of respect. While realizing the child's inexperience and immaturity, parents should recognize accomplishments as they appear and let the child know that they appreciate his initiative and growing competence.

One of the obstacles that prevent parents from guiding their children to a healthful development is the social order in which they are compelled to operate. Individual parents are usually wiser and better than the society in which they live. They have outgrown, let us say, any personal inclination to keep up with the Joneses, but they cannot resist the pressure when somebody ridicules their children for not keeping up with the Joneses' children. Perhaps they do not want their children to be prudes, but they cannot resist the prudish atmosphere of the neighborhood. Again, they may hope that their children will not be snobs, but they cannot prevent them from absorbing this social poison if it is in the air. Thus even the best parents are the victims of the culture and social organization in which they live.

Our society has evolved in such a way as to present many startling contradictions. Its standards of socially desirable behavior are both conflicting and confusing. We believe in being gentle, considerate, kindly, and forgiving, but we also believe in competitive success. A child who listens to the voice of the culture will hardly know whether to share his toys with other children or to hoard them and prevent their value from being depreciated. He will scarcely be able to decide whether to turn the other cheek on the playground or to hit first before the other fellow gets his guard up. A certain number of soldiers went to pieces during the war because they could not stand expressing the amount of aggression that came in the line of duty. So well had they absorbed the cultural prohibitions on aggression that they could not readjust when society suddenly placed exactly the opposite demands upon them. Some of our ideals necessarily entail disappointment for all but a few. The glittering life of the advertising pages and the screen is within the reach of but a tiny number of people; all the rest are given a good chance to feel inferior because they cannot attain it. We sing the praises of individual freedom, but actually the great majority is seriously hemmed in by circumstance. The cooperative and kindly ideals of Christianity, the individualism of the frontier, the materialistic values of competitive business, the aggression that is inherent in nationalism, the equality of the Declaration of Independence, the class and caste distinctions that go with great differences in wealth, all mix with the utmost confusion in our stew of values. Diversity of ideals in a free society is to be admired, but flat contradictions make the adjustive task of the child hopelessly difficult. There is a lot of straightening out to be done.

Adjustment is a process of learning, and learning cannot take place advantageously when the cognitive field is not clear. Many intelligent adults would be hard put to it to state the kind of world in which they want their children to grow up. This being the case, it is very hard for them to present a clear cognitive field to their children. Victims of the confused ideals which pervade our culture, they cannot put before their children a series of consistent guides or signposts pointing toward social adjustment. Anything which clarifies the nature and purposes of our society is likely to have a beneficial effect on psychological health. A parent or future parent who seriously tries to think out his system of values, deciding what he really wants to stand for, may be making an important contribution to the emotional health of himself, his children, and the people around him.

It is clear that the task of preventing abnormal behavior is one in which every citizen can participate. To the extent that such behavior arises out of the process of socialization, everyone can be of some help in its prevention. As parent and as teacher, everyone can learn to guide more wisely the steps by which children adapt themselves to the requirements of living together. As voter and citizen, everyone can throw his influence in favor of a social and moral order intelligently fashioned to encourage the best possibilities in human nature.

SUGGESTIONS FOR FURTHER READING

The problem for society receives a general discussion in S. Kirson Weinberg's book, *Society and Personality Disorders* (Englewood Cliffs, N. J., Prentice-Hall, Inc., 1952), which "views the disordered person as an emergent of his social relations within the cultural setting." One of the first books to take this point of view was James S. Plant's *Personality and the Cultural Pattern* (New York, The Commonwealth Fund, 1937), based on studies of personality disorder in relation to disorder in the immediate social environment. The theme is pursued further in James L. Halliday's *Psychosocial Medicine: A Study of the Sick Society* (New York, W. W. Norton & Co., Inc., 1947).

The current situation in the whole field of mental health, including finances, facilities, programs, and manpower, is well covered by the Final Report of the Joint Commission on Mental Health and Illness, *Action for Mental Health* (New York, Science Editions, Inc., 1961). An interesting attempt to invest mental health with positive meaning, rather than the negative one of absence of disease, is made by Marie Jahoda, *Current Concepts of Positive Mental Health* (New York, Basic Books, Inc., 1958). The history and status of mental hospitals in America are described by A. Deutsch, *The Mentally Ill in America* (New York, Columbia University Press, 2d ed., 1948). For an acute and searching study of the mental hospital as a social system, consult *The Mental Hospital: A Study of Institutional Participation in Psychiatric Illness and Treatment,* by A. H. Stanton and M. S. Schwartz (New York, Basic Books, Inc., 1954). B. M. Kramer's *Day Hospital: A Study of Partial Hospitalization in Psychiatry* (New York, Grune & Stratton, Inc., 1962) tells briefly of an exciting experiment in the care of mental patients.

Psychiatric education was the subject of a discussion at the 1952 meeting of the American Psychiatric Association; the main paper by J. C. Whitehorn, "The Meaning of Medical Education in Our Society," and the prepared discussions by Erich Lindemann and Norman Cameron, are printed in *American Journal of Psychiatry,* 1952, Vol. 109, pp. 81–95. The profession of psychiatric social work is fully described in Lois M. French's book, *Psychiatric Social Work* (New York, The Commonwealth Fund, 1940). The scope of clinical psychology can be ascertained in *An Introduction to Clinical Psychology,* edited by L. A. Pennington and I. A. Berg (New York, The Ronald Press Co., 2d ed., 1954).

Mental Hygiene in Modern Living by B. Katz and G. F. J. Lehner (New York, The Ronald Press Co., 1953) will be found "a practical book" which aims "to give suggestions for the kind of behavior that reflects good mental health." Hilde Bruch's *Don't Be Afraid of Your Child: A Guide to Perplexed Parents* (New York, Farrar, Straus & Co., Inc., 1952) is one of the most discerning approaches to child rearing. A little book by Ruth W. Washburn, *Children Have Their Reasons* (New York, William Morrow & Co., Inc., 1941) is rich in the ingredient most often lacking in discussions of child training: respect for children's wisdom and their attempts to solve their own problems. A valuable and straightforward guide toward helping former patients back into the family is the book by K. R. Beutner and N. G. Hale, Jr., *Emotional Illness: How Families Can Help* (New York, G. P. Putnam's Sons, Inc., 1957). In B. Bettelheim's *Dialogues with Mothers* (New York, The Free Press of Glencoe, Inc., 1962) will be found recorded excerpts of conversations between worried mothers and a seasoned expert in giving illuminating advice.

Name Index

Subject Index